CALIFORNIA REAL ESTATE PRINCIPLES

Fourth Edition

CALIFORNIA REAL ESTATE PRINCIPLES

Fourth Edition

Arthur G. Bowman

Attorney at Law

Robert J. Bond

Certified Financial Planner

Scott, Foresman and Company
Glenview, Illinois   London

"Farmland Loss May Bring Crisis" from *Yakima Herald-Republic*, January 17, 1981. Copyright © 1981 by KNT News Wire. Reprinted by permission. "Circular Flow of the National Economy" from *California Real Estate Finance*, third edition, by Robert J. Bond, Alfred Gavello and Dennis J. McKenzie. Copyright © 1984 by John Wiley & Sons, Inc. Reprinted by permission. "Prime Meridian (0°)" and "Greenwich, England" (postage stamps) reproduced by permission of the National Postal Museum. "Interests in Real Property" from *Real Estate Law in California*, third edition, by Arthur G. Bowman. Copyright © 1970 by Prentice-Hall, Inc., Englewood Cliffs, New Jersey. Reprinted by permission. California Association of Realtors® Code of Practice, "Exclusive Authorization and Right to Sell," "Contract of Employment Between Broker and Owner to Exchange, Sell, Lease or Option," "Real Estate Purchase Contract and Receipt for Deposit," "Competitive Market Analysis," and "Standard Residential Lease Form" reprinted by permission of the California Association of Realtors®. "Escrow Instructions" reprinted by permission of Celebrity Escrow Corporation. "Policy of Title Insurance" and "Trustee's Deed Upon Sale" reprinted by permission of Ticor Title Insurance. "Deed of Trust and Assignment of Rents" reprinted by permission of Safeco Title Insurance Company. "Security

(Installment) Land Contract with Power of Sale and Grant to Trustee" and "All-Inclusive Purchase Money Promissory Note Secured by All-Inclusive Purchase Money Deed of Trust" reprinted by permission of Continental Land Title Company. "Senior Citizens Property Tax Relief" reprinted by permission of the State of California Franchise Tax Board. "Real Estate Investing (Get Rich Quick?)" reprinted by permission of Grebb, Johnson, Reed & Wachsmith. State of California Department of Real Estate Code of Ethics and Professional Conduct reprinted by permission of the State of California Department of Real Estate. Code of Ethics of the NATIONAL ASSOCIATION OF REALTORS® published with the consent of the NATIONAL ASSOCIATION OF REALTORS®, author of and owner of all rights in the Code of Ethics of the NATIONAL ASSOCIATION OF REALTORS®. Copyright © 1974 by the NATIONAL ASSOCIATION OF REALTORS®. All Rights Reserved. Code of Ethics of the National Association of Real Estate Brokers, Incorporated, reprinted by permission of the National Association of Real Estate Brokers. California Escrow Association Code of Ethics reprinted by permission of the California Escrow Association. Society of Real Estate Appraisers Standards of Professional Practice and Conduct. Reprinted by permission.

Library of Congress Cataloging-in-Publication Data

Bowman, Arthur G.
    California real estate principles.

    Rev. ed. of: California real estate principles /
Robert J. Bond, Arthur G. Bowman. 3rd ed. c1982.
    Includes index.
    1. Real estate business—California. I. Bond,
Robert J.,   II. Bond, Robert J.,
California real estate principles. III. Title.
HD266.C2B68 1987   333.33'09794   86-25985
ISBN 0-673-16667-8

PREFACE

California Real Estate Principles, Fourth Edition, is an introduction to the study of real estate in California. It presents basic information about the ownership, use, and enjoyment of land and about the economic significance of land in our modern society. It serves as in introduction to the many fields of real estate activity and furnishes the proper foundation—including the language of real estate transactions—for anyone interested in a real estate career. Finally, this text also serves as an initial introduction and reference tool for anyone who is planning to purchase or sell a home or other real estate, or who is beginning an investment program. Many colleges and universities offering business courses recommend or require the study of real estate principles as part of the curriculum. Appropriately, it is now a required course for applicants for a real estate license.

Land has traditionally been considered a unique commodity. Many special rules apply to land transactions, particularly in California with its history of Spanish, Mexican, and American laws and traditions. And today the entire real estate industry is becoming increasingly complex. There are now numerous areas of specialized interest, including real estate practice, finance, appraisal, management, taxation, planning, development, investment, and consultation.

Basic to an understanding of real estate is a course in real estate principles. The many fields of real estate and an indication of the numerous step-by-step phases in the development of one's knowledge is illustrated by the "Real Estate Tree" (Figure P.1), with principles, law, and economics embedded in its roots, and further courses of study indicated in the trunk and branches. Each one of these subjects can be separated into a whole volume of information.

Because of the importance and significance of real estate principles, it is essential that the material be accurate, comprehensible, and relevant to the student's need. This has been our objective, together with a regard for structure and organization of the material. Also, a course of instruction needs to be at the appropriate level of information, whether basic, intermediate or advanced. One book cannot furnish all the information needed to answer all questions that might arise in the real estate field, but a basic book should furnish the information needed to pass an examination for a real estate license and more.

The *Real Estate Reference Book* published by the California Department of Real Estate contains a wealth of information relating to real estate practice, licensing, and examinations, and it is highly recommended that it be used as a reference work in a course on real estate principles.

As indicated above, students who learn the material in this book should be well prepared for the real estate salesperson's examination. However, this text goes far beyond simply supplying enough information to equip a student to pass an examination. We see a college course covering the

Figure P.1
Real Estate Tree

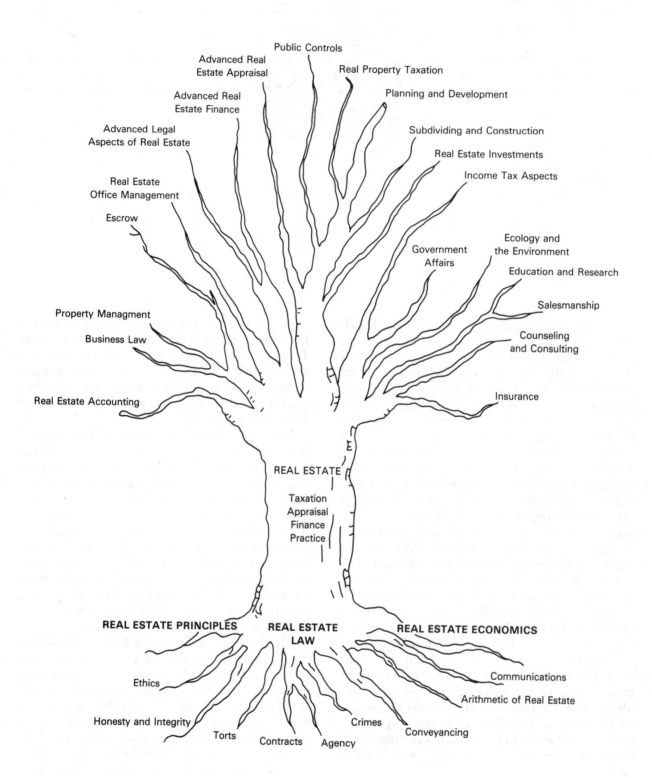

principles set forth here as the launching pad for a successful career in the profession. Such a course will furnish the student with the basic information needed to enter any phase of real estate, and will also make the more advanced courses, some of which are now required by law for a real estate broker's license, more meaningful and profitable.

Integrated in the text are copies and explanations of the many standard forms used in real estate transactions. Understanding these forms is basic to a career in real estate. Charts and other illustrations are both plentiful and pertinent. These will add interest as well as being an aid in the better understanding of the subject.

The chapters in this book in general are arranged to conform with the study guides previously adopted by the California Department of Real Estate. The format is the product of considerable discussion and testing to determine the most desirable way to present a course in real estate principles. However, it is unlikely that a 100 percent consensus on the order of presentation can be obtained. In any event, content should take precedence over form. Although some sections of this text presume a knowledge of terms and concepts presented in earlier chapters, there is still a degree of flexibility in the order in which the chapters may be presented to the students.

Because it is important for the student of real estate to understand the specialized vocabulary of the profession, the glossary in this book is especially comprehensive. A comprehensive review of chapter content is provided by a set of questions at the end of each chapter. The questions are drawn not only from the individual chapters but also from the glossary, and may be used as the basis of class quizzes and midterm and final examinations.

A word of caution: In the words of the Realtor's Creed, "Under all is the land." And because we live in a highly organized society, it can also be said that "Over all is the law." The law is present, in some way, in practically all human activity in modern society. Not only is law a guideline to proper and acceptable conduct, but it is also a rescue line for victims of another person's wrongdoing, as well as a noose line for the wrongdoer. Much of the source of real estate principles is contained in the law. A strong thread of law winds through every real estate transaction.

In the study of real estate principles, we will acquire a considerable amount of legal information about land and its use and about our rights in land. We learn about many rules based on *common law* as well as on *statutory law*. However, the knowledge gained from our studies should not be used as a substitute for an attorney's advice about the application of the law to a particular case. We must always observe the law's requirement that only persons duly licensed to practice law are permitted to do so.

California is a treasure that must be preserved for future generations. The value of the land is therefore immeasurable. An ancient Hawaiian motto states, "The life of the land is preserved in righteousness." To this we might add "and in right use." It is essential that we obtain an appropriate understanding of the nature, value, and use of real estate in California. The objective of this book is to provide a basis for such an understanding.

Arthur G. Bowman/Robert J. Bond

ACKNOWLEDGMENTS

My appreciation to the following for their contributions: Toni Peterson, Evelyn Sutter, and Janet Dugan, Valley Secretarial Service in Ellensburg, Washington; Bryan Schultz, geography major at Central Washington University; and the CPA firm of Grebb, Johnson, Reed and Wachsmith in Ellensburg, Washington.

Arthur G. Bowman

My special gratitude to Nanci Oliva for her help with the development and preparation of the manuscript.

To my three sons, David, Mark, Paul: may your lives be enriched as you journey through these pages.

Robert J. Bond, CFP

The authors are very grateful to the following reviewers for their helpful suggestions in previous editions: Ken Giss, Vincent D. Jantz, and John G. Jurivich. The manuscript for this edition was reviewed by Cecilia A. Hopkins, San Mateo, and we are appreciative of her insightful comments.

AGB RJB

CONTENTS

LIST OF ILLUSTRATIONS

1
INTRODUCTION TO THE STUDY OF REAL ESTATE

cussed, together with real estate and the economy. The importance of real estate finance will be considered. We will trace California's real estate background and California's place in the world. The sources of the many rules and principles we will be encountering in this book will be explained. We will include a brief description of the court system and the application of legal aspects, without, however, intruding unduly into the large and complex subject of real estate law. The chapter will conclude with a brief discussion of the important role of the California Department of Real Estate, particularly as it relates to licensing. (Further consideration of licensing will be included in Chapter 5.)

TYPES OF PROPERTY

Property can be briefly defined as anything which may be the subject of ownership. *Ownership* is the right of a person to use and dispose of property to the exclusion of others. Property is of two types: real property and personal property. A basic distinction between real and personal property is that real property is *immovable property*, whereas personal property is *movable property*. In this context, movable and immovable do not necessarily relate to actual physical movements of land, such as mudslides and earthquakes, but relate to

In this chapter we will briefly consider the types of property and the nature of ownership rights in property, often referred to as a *bundle of rights*, and will then show how land is classified according to its use. We will learn that the word *land* is often used in referring to real property. We will introduce the terms *real estate* and *real property*, terms that in certain contexts have a technical distinction, but which are often used interchangeably, as will be done in this book. The physical and economical characteristics of land will be dis-

the legal concepts of *movable* and *immovable*, to be explained later.

Personal property can be described in the negative: it is anything that is *not* real property. Real property commonly means the land itself, things attached or affixed to land, and things incident or appurtenant to land. In the next chapter we will consider the many ingredients of real property and become more fully aware of what the word *land*, or real property, means and what real property actually consists of.

OWNERSHIP OF PROPERTY— THE BUNDLE OF RIGHTS

Part of our heritage from England is the common law, which has given us the foundations of our modern law of real property. Actually, the idea of what property is, and the way it can be held and transferred, has come down to us from medieval times with comparatively little change. In a sense the word *property* does not refer to the *thing* owned, but rather to the *rights* or interests which the owner has in the thing he owns. The principal rights an owner has in property are the right to possess, use, and enjoy it; the right to dispose of it; and the right to exclude others from using it. These rights are often referred to as a "bundle of rights," and are known as "property rights." These rights can be fragmented if the owner so desires. For instance, the right of possession can be given up, which occurs when an owner leases or rents his or her property to a tenant.

Perhaps a better understanding of the bundle of rights can be gained by viewing the concept as a series of concentric circles, each ring containing a separate and distinct right of the property owner. (See Figure 1.1.)

CLASSIFICATION OF LAND ACCORDING TO USE

Land that is in its natural condition is referred to as *unimproved* land or raw land. Once land has buildings or other structures placed upon it, it becomes known as *improved* property. Basically, land has a wide variety of uses. It is categorized in accordance with its use (or intended use) as residential, commercial, industrial, agricultural, recreational, or mixed (hybrid) property. A large portion of recreational property is located in wilderness areas owned by the federal government or by the State of California. There is a con-

Figure 1.1
Bundle of Rights

tinuing concern for preserving these wilderness areas for man's enjoyment and for ecological reasons. (This subject will be discussed in greater detail in Chapter 12.)

Some land is used for mineral and timber production, or for governmental and military purposes, and such land is classified accordingly. Another classification which has increased in recent years is the use of land for retirement communities.

PHYSICAL CHARACTERISTICS OF LAND

Land has certain physical characteristics that distinguish it from other types of property. These characteristics are *immobility*, *indestructibility*, and *nonhomogeneity*.

Although improvements on land can be moved, the land itself is *immobile* and its geographical location is fixed and ascertainable. Because of its fixed location and the fact that the owner can't hide it, real property is a primary source of taxation. (The impact of real property taxation will be discussed in detail in Chapter 10.)

Another physical characteristic of land is its *indestructibility*. It is considered to be a durable and relatively stable type of investment. Money, goods, stocks and bonds, and other types of personal property may come and go, but land in its basic form will always be here. This does not mean that its value will always be the same, since erosion, strip mining, earth movements, etc., may reduce the value or usability of the land for certain purposes. But the land itself remains, and in most parts of the world the land has had the same use for thousands of years.

The third physical characteristic of land is the fact that it is *nonhomogeneous*. This means that land is unique, and no two parcels of land are the same; what distinguishes one parcel of land from another, although they may appear to be identical, is its exact location on the face of the earth. The word *homogeneity* means the state or quality of having like characteristics or uniformity of nature, composition, or structure. Personal property can have the characteristic of homogeneity or sameness, but parcels of real property will always be different because of their location on the earth's surface.

ECONOMIC CHARACTERISTICS OF LAND

In addition to physical characteristics, land also has several economic characteristics, including scarcity, location, the fixed nature of the investment, and modification or improvements. The dividing line between physical and economic characteristics is not always clear cut, since the physical aspects of land will influence the economic impact of a particular piece of real property.

As population expands in a particular area, the demand for land increases to a point where *scarcity* results in an increase in value. This is particularly true where a certain type of property, such as ocean-front or lake-front, is in limited supply. To paraphrase Will Rogers, "Buy real property—they aren't making it anymore."

Although there is a large amount of land in California, land in a particularly desirable location will eventually become scarce. Land for specific uses in specific locations frequently becomes insufficient to meet demand. This has been true particularly with regard to land for residential and commercial uses. As the population increases, a scarcity of agricultural land could result, and food-producing land might then be much sought after. This is illustrated by the article on farmland loss, which, though published in 1981, is still relevant today.

Location, or situs, of the property is another economic characteristic of land. It has been said that the three most important factors influencing the value of real property are location, location, and location. Two pieces of land can be similar in other respects, but show a great difference in value because of location. A choice location usually results in a continuing increase in value.

A significant aspect of location is the preference shown by people for a given area. This can be dependent upon a number of factors, including natural factors such as weather, quality of the air, scenic beauty, etc.; and human need factors such as convenience to work, transportation, shopping, schools, etc. These factors are not always constant. For instance, with the expansion of the freeway system in California after World War II, the preference for suburban areas for residential purposes dramatically increased. This resulted in declining values in downtown areas. Then, in the 1970s, with the advent of the energy crisis, the trend reversed with a renewed preference for living closer to inner-city activities.

The *fixed nature* of the investment is another economic characteristic of land. The land itself is in a fixed location. When the land is improved, the buildings and related facilities become part of the real property. They are normally designed to last for a substantial period of time, and afford a measure of investment permanence. Real estate investment and land use normally involve a long-range view. Consequently, consideration must be given not only to how the land and improvements will be utilized immediately, but also, to how they will be utilized twenty to thirty years or more in the future. This characteristic of land means that its value is affected by any economic changes in a particular location. Thus, the value of the land and its improvements is intimately connected with its location.

The fourth economic characteristic of land is its ability to be affected in value by *modifications or improvements*, not only to the land itself, but also to surrounding or adjoining land. A good example of this occurs when a large parcel of land is acquired by the state for college or university purposes. The value of the college land itself will increase materially with the installation of facilities. Nearby land that may have been used previously for agricultural purposes suddenly becomes useful for commercial and housing purposes.

REAL ESTATE AND THE ECONOMY

As stated in the California Department of Real Estate's *Real Estate Reference Book* (1984–85 ed., p. 226), the economic system in the United States

---

FARMLAND LOSS MAY BRING CRISIS

WASHINGTON—With prime crop land disappearing under urban sprawl at a rate of 1 million acres a year, a shortage of land to meet soaring demands for food could occur in 20 years, a government report said Friday.

"We're paving paradise and passing the costs—higher food prices and destruction of our rural landscape and heritage—to our children," said Gus Speth, chairman of the President's Council of Environmental Quality.

Speth and Agriculture Secretary Bob Bergland released the National Agricultural Lands Study, which indicates the nation is moving toward a "land crisis" that could rival the energy shortages of recent years.

While such a crisis remains years away and could be averted by a variety of factors, officials said the present trends signal "unprecedented pressure on the nation's best agricultural lands."

Farmers now plant crops on about 413 million acres, but that land is disappearing at a rate of about 1 million acres a year, the study said.

An additional 127 million acres, also disappearing in unknown quantities, could be brought into production but the study predicted that rising food demands could require up to 143 million acres of new crop land by the year 2000.

The study was conducted by the Agriculture Department and the Council on Environmental Quality at a cost of $2.2 million. To avert a land shortage, the study said, the federal government must overhaul its own programs that have helped pay for the streets and sewers that turn farms into housing projects.

Most of the land disappears in small pieces, usually on the fringe of metropolitan areas in growing states such as Florida, Texas and California, as farmers find they can earn more and be hassled less by selling out to developers, the study said.

Source: "Farmland Loss May Bring Crisis", *Yakima Herald-Republic*, January 17, 1981. Copyright © 1981 by KNT News Wire. Reprinted by permission.

---

is referred to as a *mixed capitalistic system*:

> This means that although individuals have the right to own, control and dispose of property and make the majority of decisions about the overall economy, the government is permitted to intervene in the complexities of our markets to influence the general economic trend and assure reasonable competition with stability among various economic groups. Government participation in managing America's wealth has continually increased over the years as citizens and business groups have requested additional government intervention to deal with the broad economic, financial, social and political problems of the country.

How much is America worth and what is its wealth based upon?

According to recent US Department of Commerce data, our tangible assets (excluding cash, checking and savings accounts, and corporate stocks and bonds) are nearly $12.5 trillion in current prices: of our structures, equipment, housing, land and goods, the government owns 21 percent, the business sector (including owner-occupants) owns 68 percent, and households own 11 percent. The current growth rate of our wealth is approximately 1.7% annually.

The vast majority of the purchasers of the assets listed did not pay cash for them. Credit and borrowing were used.

Real estate plays a major role in the economy of our country, namely, *net worth, income flow, major employer,* and *appreciation and inflation*, briefly considered as follows:

Net worth. Real estate in the form of land and improvements makes up a very large portion of the total net worth of individuals in the United States (as opposed to the government).

Income flow. As we can see on the circular flow chart of our economy (see Figure 1.2), money is paid for the use of real estate (rent) and for the raw materials, labor, capital and management used in construction work of all kinds.

Major employer. The real estate industry (brokerage, construction, management, finance, etc.) is a major employer in this country. It provides

Figure 1.2
The Circular Flow of the National Economy

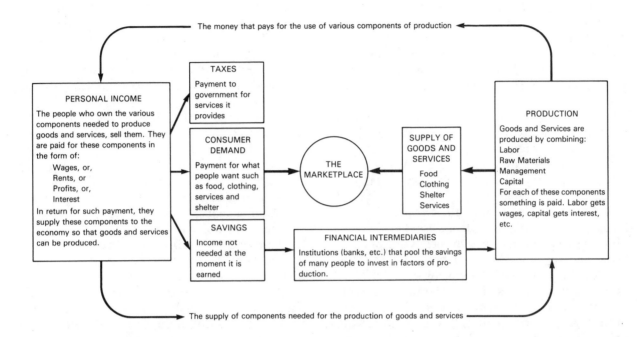

employment for a large segment of the population, accounting for billions of dollars in national income.

Appreciation and inflation. In recent years appreciation in the dollar value of real estate has outstripped the annual inflation rate and is the largest single contributor to inflation statistics. As the depreciation of the dollar has made passbook savings accounts, and most other forms of financial savings, increasingly unattractive, real estate with its increasing value has become a major means by which people save. Such savings are often referred to as *nonfinancial savings*. As the appreciation factor increases, the rate of savings may be adversely affected.

IMPORTANCE OF REAL ESTATE FINANCE

As stated in the *Real Estate Reference Book*,

Finance is the lifeblood of real estate development, sales, investment, brokerage and property management. The developer, contractor, real estate practitioner and property manager must understand how real estate is financed because most buyers are either financially unable to pay

cash for real property or are simply unwilling to buy unless most of the purchase price can be borrowed.

Successful real estate careers depend on currency of knowledge as to sources of available and affordable mortgage funds. In fact, this information and how to use it is vital to virtually all phases of real estate activity.

Traditional sources of funds include lending institutions such as savings and loan associations, mortgage lenders, banks, insurance companies and private sources such as individuals, pension funds, mortgage trusts and investment trusts. Yet some real estate finance experts predict that the fast developing secondary mortgage market (investors purchasing real estate loans originated by other lenders) may eclipse the traditional loan sources in the 1990s. Real estate agents should stay alert to the ever changing credit markets, mortgage sources and mortgage methods.

Probably no single transaction involves more money (often a buyer's life savings) for the average person than the purchase of a home or parcel of land. This investment in itself is ample justification for most individuals to become knowledgeable in the field of real estate finance.

The subject of finance will be considered in Chapters 7 and 8.

CALIFORNIA'S REAL ESTATE BACKGROUND

Inhabited first by nomadic Indians, then by Spaniards, Mexicans, and Americans, California became a state in the year 1850 with a thousand miles of coastline, the highest point in the contiguous United States (Mount Whitney, 14,495 feet), the lowest point (Bad Water, Death Valley, 282 feet below sea level), and some of the most scenic as well as the most fertile land anywhere in the world. It is a vast area, consisting of some 100,300,000 acres. Ownership rights to land in California are inextricably tied in with the state's history, so we start our study of California real estate principles by considering the historical background—first of land itself, then of land in California.

As we shall see, "under all is the land." The land, ever changing but changeless, has had significance to mankind since the beginning of time. It has been part of man's economic life from the time that land was used for grazing or for farming. In feudal times, people were born, lived their lives, and died on the same plot of ground which, in theory if not in actuality, belonged to the king or to a lesser chief. Since land was available and fertile, nobody was unduly concerned about it.

When people began to produce crops in abundance, beyond their capacity to consume at home, many moved to central places and specialized in making products that could be exchanged for food grown by someone else. Cities and concentrations of people resulted from this migration, a process we refer to today as *urbanization*. Gradually, certain land came to be looked upon as prized, not necessarily for its fertility, but for its location as the site of commerce, industry, or residence. Trading in land gave rise to a specialized group of people who bought, improved, and sold on their own account or as part of a service to others on a commission basis. Thus, the real estate business was born.

From the beginning of Western civilization, humans have explored and migrated into many parts of the world in search of land they could possess—land on which to build homes, raise crops, search for minerals, develop industries, or enjoy for recreational purposes such as fishing, hunting, hiking, and exploring. Where does California fit into this adventure? For the contemporary historian, California's story begins in 1513 when Vasco Núñez de Balboa first sighted the Pacific Ocean from the Isthmus of Panama, claiming it and the shores washed by it for the king of Spain.

But the year 1542, just fifty years after the discovery of the Americas by Columbus, is actually considered the first important date in the history of the settlement of California. In that year Juan Rodríguez Cabrillo, a Portugese navigator in the service of Spain, sailed into what is now San Diego harbor. Cabrillo's fleet, consisting of two small ships, sailed from Navidad on the west coast of Mexico in June 1542. After going northward along the coast of the present Baja California, the two ships arrived in September at what was described as a "very large" bay. Cabrillo named this bay San Miguel, and his sailors went ashore, took possession in the name of the king of Spain, and thus became the first white men to set foot on the coast of California. The name of the bay was later changed to San Diego, and a monument marks the landing spot (Figure 1.3).

After Cabrillo, many other explorers, including Sir Frances Drake, sailed along and landed on various parts of the California coast. It was in 1579 that Drake, commanding *The Golden Hind*, landed at Drake's Bay, north of the present city of San Francisco. Drake took possession of the land for England by setting up a post and nailing a sixpence to it. He christened his discovery New Albion. While ashore he held a Christian religious service, the first recorded in California.

From 1542 to 1769 was the period of exploration and discovery. It was not until 1769, starting with Gaspar de Portola's expedition, that the actual occupation of California by the Spaniards commenced. The Spanish occupation embraced a threefold plan for colonization:

1. Missionaries would establish a chain of *missions* to convert and civilize the Indians.
2. Soldiers would found frontier outposts or forts, called *presidios*, at strategic points along the coast to protect the colonizers.
3. Settlers would start communities or agricultural villages, *pueblos*, to raise food for the occupying forces.

By 1822 a chain of twenty-one missions had been established, together with four presidios (at San Diego, Santa Barbara, Monterey, and San Francisco) and three pueblos (at Los Angeles, San Jose, and Branciforte near Santa Cruz).

From 1769 until 1822 the land continued to be part of the Spanish realm. During the Spanish rule, the local government was patriarchal, with little regard for formal civil law. Military law prevailed, maintaining Spanish dominion over this vast, varied, but sparsely populated territory. All land in California was held in the name of the

Figure 1.3
Cabrillo Monument, Point Loma, San Diego

king of Spain, and technically it belonged to him. Ownership and transfer of land and property rights to the land were governed by the law prevailing in Spain. Spanish law recognized the rights of the Indians to use as much land as they needed for homes, tillage, and pasturage, but did not recognize the right of actual ownership. In practice the white man gave as little heed to the Indians' right of occupancy as the Indians themselves had given to the animals' right of occupation.

Under Spanish rule, the right to use specific land could be acquired only by political or military agencies of the king. The approximately thirty rancho grants made on behalf of the Spanish rulers were for grazing and agricultural purposes only. In modern terms, these were not grants of *fee simple absolute*, a term which signifies an owner's unrestricted title to his property. Although the grants did not actually result in private ownership, it was in some cases later recognized by the American government based on compliance with the laws in effect during the period that the Mexicans ruled California.

The missions did not acquire an absolute title to all of the lands they occupied. Their tenure was regarded as temporary, to be terminated with the completion of their task of Christianizing the Indians.

In 1822, Mexico, then a territorial possession of Spain, established her independence. Mexico encouraged the colonization of California. Governors were given absolute discretion in the selection of the persons who could receive grants of land. Under the Mexican regime, private ownership of land became a reality. An applicant for land filed a petition with the governor and, if approved, received a decree which was referred to the legislative body for ratification. Upon legislative approval, a formal grant of the land was made. This grant, known as the *expediente*, together with various related documents, was filed and recorded in the government archives. Other steps in the transfer of property from the government to the individual included the marking off of monuments—that is, fixed objects or points on the ground—and establishing the grantee in possession. The latter act was usually done by an officer with judicial capacity.

The governor was empowered to recognize the grants and possessory rights given under Spanish rule. In many cases boundaries were somewhat vague, and some persons failed to take the steps necessary to acquire perfect title, which later was to affect their rights under American law. In any event, grants were made in increasing numbers, with many of them running up to eleven square leagues (about 47,400 acres) in size. Some of the grantees were Americans who had become naturalized Mexican citizens in order to qualify for a grant. The grants of ranchos were stimulated by the secularization of the missions in 1834. By 1846 more than five hundred rancho grants had been made, embracing most of the suitable grazing and farming areas in California. The ranchos flowered during the Mexican period of California history.

In 1846 the Mexican War broke out, and California for a short time became the Bear Flag Republic. Then in 1848 the war ended with the signing of the Treaty of Guadalupe Hidalgo. California became a possession of the United States, but a provision in the treaty stated that existing property rights of Mexicans should be "inviolably respected." In 1851, to carry out the terms of the treaty, Congress passed an act providing for the appointment of a Board of Land Commissioners to which all claims were to be submitted. All titles and claims of title to land in California were to be determined by this commission. If claims to land titles were rejected by this commission, the case was appealable to the United States District Court and thence to the United States Supreme Court. When a claim was approved, the United States government issued a patent to the claimant. If a claim was not approved, title remained with the United States government.

Under Spanish and Mexican law, in addition to private rancho land grants, each of the pueblos received four square leagues of land without the necessity of formal government grant. A league under the old Spanish law consisted of about 4439 acres, a sizable area. Under Mexican law, the mayor of the pueblo, with the approval of the council, was empowered to grant house lots and farm lots to inhabitants. However, the Mexican government retained ultimate control over the disposition of the pueblo lands. Under the Treaty of Guadalupe Hidalgo, the sovereignty over pueblo lands passed to the United States, in trust for the future state of California. The city, however, was authorized to file a claim for the land. Upon confirmation of the claim, a patent was issued to the city; the city then held title in trust for the inhabitants. Subsequently, the cities conveyed portions of the former pueblo lands to inhabitants in accordance with provisions of local laws.

When California was admitted as a state in 1850, it became the owner of all lands lying under navigable streams and lakes, all swamp and over-flowed lands, together with the tidelands and submerged lands. The ownership of such lands passed from the United States without the formality of a grant. The state became the owner of the tidelands in trust for the people for such purposes as commerce, navigation, and fishing. Although the state cannot transfer these lands absolutely to private owners, it can lease such lands, and substantial revenues have been realized from the sale of oil and gas produced from these lands.

The United States continued to retain certain paramount rights in the territory involved. It retained as public lands all of the lands not specifically confirmed as Mexican or Spanish grants or not set apart as tidelands or as cities or towns. Thereafter title to public lands could be acquired only by specific grants from the United States in the form of a patent. A large part of this land has since been granted to the state of California for educational purposes and state parks. Large grants were also made to railroad companies as an inducement for the construction of a transcontinental railroad. Of the state's total area of some 100,300,000 acres, the federal government still owns about 44 percent. It is mostly part of the *public domain:* that part of the land originally acquired by the government and still vested in the government. Government-owned lands also include *acquired* lands, distinguishable from the public domain in that they have been acquired by the United States by purchase or gift from private landowners or from the state, or by condemnation proceedings under which private land is acquired for public purposes upon payment of just compensation.

The over 100 million acres of land in California vary widely in character. The chief value of more than one-third is for forest and watershed purposes. About one-fifth is barren desert land. About one-sixth is suitable for cultivation. Scenic and recreational resources—beaches, forests, lakes, mountains, and wildlife—have been outstanding in the past, but there is growing concern that these resources may be lost to future generations. Recent laws have sought to protect these lands.

CALIFORNIA'S PLACE IN THE WORLD

If you were asked the question, "Where in the world is California?" you could refer to its location in various ways: in the western part of the United States, on the Pacific Ocean, south of Ore-

Figure 1.4
Prime Meridian (0°)

Figure 1.5
Greenwich, England

gon, etc. But we can be more specific by referring to its exact location, as land is measured in the real estate profession, in terms of *longitudes* and *latitudes* that traditionally appear on a map or globe of the world. We will learn the importance of a good and sufficient legal description of land in a later chapter. But now let us describe California's location like that of a ship at sea. A ship at sea gives its position in terms of longitude and latitude. Similarly, the exact "world location" of any point on land may be so stated, naming the north-south lines and the east-west lines that cross at that point. Using such points as starting places and measuring in stated directions, we can describe land areas of any shape and size.

Longitude is measured by north-south meridians encircling the earth through the poles, counting from the prime meridian (0°) in Greenwich, England, just outside of London. This is the place where world measurements begin. This is graphically illustrated on a commemorative stamp issued by the British Post Office in 1984 (Figure 1.4). Greenwich is depicted on a companion issue (Figure 1.5). West longitude extends halfway

around the world, westerly from Greenwich. Each degree of longitude is 1/360th of the globe's circumference. At the equator, each degree measures 69.17 miles; the distance shortens as you travel toward the poles.

Latitude lines are called *parallels*: each point on a given parallel is the same distance from the equator as any other point on that parallel. North latitude is measured "up" from the equator (0°) to the North Pole (90°). Longitude and latitude are expressed in degrees (0°), minutes ('), and seconds(").

An atlas or globe of the world shows that California is located between longitude 114° west and longitude 125° west, and between latitude 32° north and latitude 42° north (Figure 1.6). We now know the exact location of California.

SOURCES OF RULES AND PRINCIPLES

For anyone going into the field of real estate, a knowledge of real estate law is essential. This is particularly recognized in California, where one

Figure 1.6
California's Place in the World

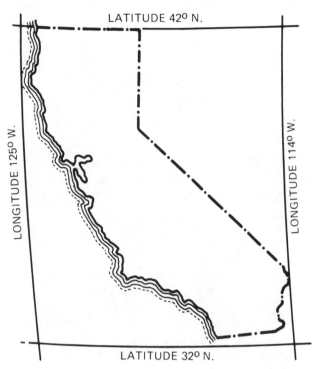

of the courses required to qualify for the real estate broker's examination is Legal Aspects of Real Estate. The law is a source of many of the rules and principles studied in this book, and a short review of the sources of the law will be helpful.

Although California inherited from Spain and Mexico certain laws relating to rights in property, the basic principles generally applied were derived from the *common law* of England. In the absence of some constitutional or statutory provision to the contrary, the common law generally applies in California as it does in most of the other states.

The common law is one of the two great systems of law in force in the Western world today; the other is the *civil law*. The common law was born in medieval England. It traces its origins to the experimental and practical temperament of the people who developed it. Early growth of this system of law was through legal recognition of local and popular customs, beliefs, and standards of conduct. As the courts were called upon to hear disputes and grievances, a body of rules and precepts was gradually developed, which in time established precedents for similar disputes in the future.

The Spanish and Mexican law, initially appli-

cable in California, was based on the civil law, which is an outgrowth of Roman law. The famous Code of Justinian is the basis for the legal codes of most present-day western European countries. Civil law is based on a code or rule of law created to cover every possible dispute that might arise, rather than on a gradual development of rules based on determination of individual cases as they arise. Civil law tends to be more formal, more dogmatic, and more resistant to change than the common law.

Regardless of the origins of the law, the most difficult part is the application of the law to a particular set of circumstances. The law represents a continuing attempt to feel the pulse of conduct; it is not a static, but a dynamic and vital force in the rights of the people, both personal rights (i.e., freedom) and property rights (i.e., ownership and use). The law, of course, involves *duties and responsibilities* as well as *rights and privileges*.

Where do we look to find the laws and other rules that affect these duties and responsibilities and rights and privileges? To answer this question, we must have in mind the dual nature of our system of government. This system embraces both federal law, applicable throughout the United States, and state law, applicable within the state.

The principal sources of law on the federal side are the Constitution of the United States, regarded as the supreme law of the land; treaties made under the authority of the United States government; statutes enacted by Congress; rules and regulations of federal agencies; and federal court decisions. The sources of the laws in the state of California are the Constitution of the state of California, adopted over one hundred years ago and amended from time to time; statutes enacted by the state legislature, which meets annually at the capitol in Sacramento; rules and regulations of state agencies; local ordinances enacted by cities and counties; and decisions of the California appellate courts.

CALIFORNIA COURT SYSTEM

Basically, there are two kinds of courts in the judicial system—*trial courts* and *appellate courts*. And since there are two separate systems of government in effect in the United States, there are two separate court structures, the federal and the state. Each one has a similar system,

Figure 1.7
Basic Court Structure

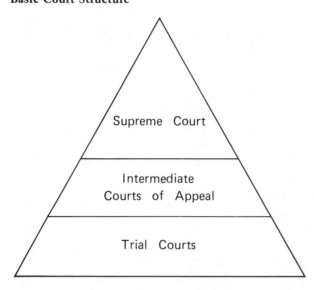

shaped somewhat like a pyramid. At the base are the trial courts and at the peak is the supreme court. In between are intermediate courts of appeal (see Figure 1.7). The appellate courts review cases heard by the trial courts and render opinions, many of which are published and can be found in bound volumes of decisions used as guides or precedents in other litigation. Basically, cases are divided into two classes, *civil* and *criminal*, although many types of cases are heard by the various courts, such as title litigation, damage actions, probate proceedings, domestic relations matters, etc.

For a judgment to be binding, the court must have jurisdiction over both the parties and the subject matter of the action. Jurisdiction means the power of a court to determine a matter brought before it.

LEGAL ASPECTS OF REAL ESTATE

The law is the source of many of the rules and principles discussed in this book. Some clarification is needed in this regard. The Department of Real Estate publishes, in addition to the *Real Estate Reference Book*, a volume entitled *Real Estate Law*. This latter affects the licensing and conduct of persons acting as real estate agents. The law is enforced at special administrative hearings by the Commissioner rather than by a court of law.

The California Real Estate Law or *license law*,

as it is sometimes referred to, has two principal purposes: (1) the protection of the general public from harm at the hands of dishonest and incompetent agents and (2) the protection of the reputation of honest agents against the adverse publicity and public resentment often caused by the unprincipled and unscrupulous who would infiltrate the agents' ranks. This aspect will be discussed in more detail in Chapter 5.

Real Estate Law must be distinguished from what is known as *real property law, general law of agency, contract law*, or other legal aspects of real estate ownership and conveyancing. Although these sets of laws interrelate and overlap, they are nevertheless different legal rules and should be separately understood. The law of contracts will be considered further in Chapter 4. A consideration of the general law of agency is included in Chapter 5. Rules of conveyancing are considered in Chapter 3. Real property law as such is reflected particularly in Chapter 2, and is encountered throughout the book. Two other aspects of the law need to be considered briefly at this point, namely, the law of torts and the impact of the criminal law.

The Law of Torts

Although contract law is applied more frequently in the practice of real estate than in any other body of law, the real estate licensee should be aware of the applications of tort law as well. A *tort* is a wrongful act or a violation of another person's legal rights. It is a civil wrong that arises independent of any contractual duty. It may be based on a willful act or a negligent or careless act. The law of torts is concerned with what individuals can or cannot do in their relations with other persons. It is also concerned with the use that persons can or cannot make of their property, and with the results that follow when they fail to comply with their legal obligations.

The broad area of torts includes such subjects as conversion or misappropriation of funds, false imprisonment, libel and slander, fraud and deceit, negligence, assault and battery, and so forth.

The law of torts can become applicable in the field of real estate in many situations, such as the following:

1. A neighbor boy climbs over a fence on your property and is bitten by your dog or is injured in your swimming pool.
2. An old oak tree on your property is blown

over in a windstorm and crashes onto your neighbor's porch.

3. A neighbor, in retaliation for excessive noise you make when carrying out the trash cans late at night, deposits refuse on your property or squirts water through your windows.

4. While you are trimming vines that extend over onto your property from your neighbor's yard, he knocks down your ladder.

5. The owner of the land over which you have an easement for ingress and egress puts up a barrier that prevents you from using the easement.

6. A seller of real property you have purchased misrepresented the location of the boundary or the income from the property.

Some of the risks of ownership or use of property can be covered by insurance. The subject of hazard and other types of insurance will be considered in Chapter 6.

Impact of the Criminal Law

Land sometimes becomes involved in criminal proceedings, and a person engaged in real estate transactions should be familiar with the criminal implications of land transactions. As mentioned in the *Real Estate Reference Book*, it is a tribute to the integrity of the thousands of real estate brokers and salespersons in California that comparatively few prosecutions are brought against persons in the real estate business for violating the criminal laws of the state. Nonetheless, the problems of violations of the Penal Code are of interest to all real estate practitioners, since offenses are sometimes committed by clients or others with whom brokers, escrow officers, lenders, etc., may come into contact.

A crime is classified as a felony, a misdemeanor, or an infraction. A felony is a crime punishable by imprisonment in a federal or state prison. Misdemeanors are punishable by imprisonment in a county jail or by a fine, or by both fine and imprisonment. Infractions do not include imprisonment as part of the penalty.

Following is a list of some of the crimes involving real property that may be encountered:

1. Theft, either *grand* theft or *petty* theft, depending upon the value of the property stolen or embezzled. (When the theft involves the land itself, it would be stolen "on paper," by means of fraud or other misrepresentation.)

2. Fraudulent sale of the same land to more than one party

3. Fraudulent sale of land by a married person without his or her spouse's consent

4. False statement about financial ability, in writing, with intent that others will rely upon it

5. Entering and removing part (such as a structure) of the property without right

6. Removal of property from mortgaged premises with intent to defraud

7. Forgery of a deed or other document

8. Fraudulent removal of an owner's personal property by a lessee

Finally, there is the matter of the unlawful practice of law. The Business and Professions Code specifically prohibits the practice of law by persons who are not members of the State Bar of California. Real estate licensees and others in the real estate field must have a knowledge of the law but must not attempt to practice it. The consequences of practicing law without a license are not only liability for damages, but also criminal sanctions and disciplinary proceedings.

ROLE OF THE DEPARTMENT OF REAL ESTATE

The real estate commissioner, appointed by the governor to serve at the governor's pleasure, is chief executive of the Department of Real Estate and presides at the meetings of the Real Estate Advisory Commission. It is the commissioner's duty to determine administrative policy and enforce the provisions of the real estate law in a manner which achieves maximum protection for the purchasers of real property and those persons dealing with real estate licensees.

The duties of the real estate commissioner are varied, but one of the main functions is the licensing procedure. The main purpose of Real Estate Law is to protect the public by regulating those in the real estate business who are acting as agents for others. Practically every activity in connection with a real estate transaction requires a real estate license when the activity is performed for another or others, and for compensation, a commission or a fee, or in expectation thereof.

As stated in the *Real Estate Reference Book*, five major fields of real estate testing have been established. These five major divisions are law, public control, valuation, finance, and real estate practice. As stated in the *Real Estate Reference Book* (1984–85 ed., pp. 36–37), applicants for a real estate license are expected to demonstrate knowledge in the following areas:

1. In law—a reasonable understanding of general real estate law and the laws pertaining to real estate licensees, and their applications to real estate transactions; the laws and regulations relating to the ethics of the profession. This area includes the analysis of listing and deposit receipts and other contracts used in real estate transactions.

2. In matters of public control—a general understanding of the impact of federal, state and local authorities in zoning, subdividing, exercise of the power of eminent domain, taxation, housing, construction, syndicates and franchises, and real estate transactions in general.

3. In valuation—a sufficient knowledge of valuation methods to enable the licensee to serve clients and the general public in a useful and dependable manner in application of appraised values in the real estate market.

4. In finance—a general knowledge of available financial resources, procedures, practices and government participation sufficient to assist clients in obtaining and utilizing credit in real estate transactions.

5. In real estate practice—an understanding of special fields pertaining to real estate with which the licensee should be sufficiently familiar in order to perform their duties and responsibilities competently, including land development (water supply, sewage, drainage, streets, community facilities), escrows (nature and purposes, requisites, obligations of parties), title insurance, construction factors, real estate office administration and advertising.

Figure 1.8 indicates the relative weight presently assigned in the respective licensing examinations. The weight shown is subject to variation from time to time.

QUESTIONS FOR CHAPTER 1

For each chapter there is a total of 50 questions. Except for Chapters 14 and 15, where the questions are all multiple choice, each chapter's questions fall into the following three categories:

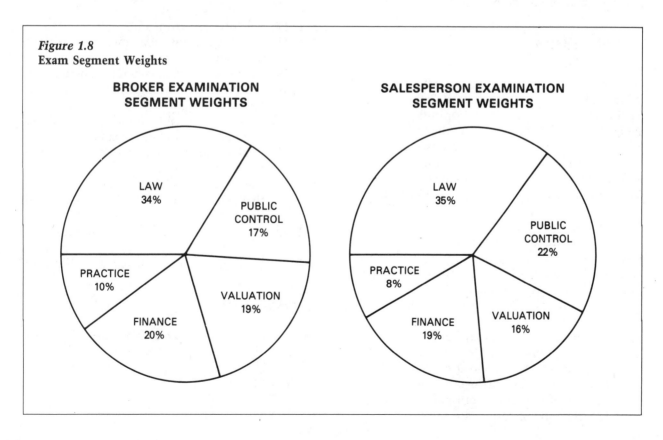

Figure 1.8
Exam Segment Weights

BROKER EXAMINATION
SEGMENT WEIGHTS

LAW 34%
PUBLIC CONTROL 17%
PRACTICE 10%
VALUATION 19%
FINANCE 20%

SALESPERSON EXAMINATION
SEGMENT WEIGHTS

LAW 35%
PUBLIC CONTROL 22%
PRACTICE 8%
VALUATION 16%
FINANCE 19%

The vital role of real estate in your life will be emphasized throughout this book. As a basic introduction to this role, refer to a booklet published by the California Association of Realtors entitled "Real Estate and Your Life." You will want to know as much as you can about

Ownership of real and personal property

Buying versus renting

Investing in real estate

Financing your home purchase

Selling your home

Your career in real estate

The Department of Real Estate and the Real Estate Commissioner are concerned with consumer protection in the real estate field. Awareness of the role of the DRE is vital.

Matching terms (15). The appropriate letter (a-o) should be written before the corresponding matching statement (1-15).

True/false (10). The letter T or F should be circled as appropriate.

Multiple choice (25). Of the 4 choices, only one selection should be made. The letter representing the best answer should be circled.

Matching Terms

a. property
b. raw land
c. longitude
d. latitude
e. tort
f. immobility
g. ownership
h. common law
i. civil law
j. Real Estate Commissioner
k. modification
l. Greenwich
m. encumber
n. finance
o. personal property

____ 1. physical characteristics of land
____ 2. measured by east-west parallels
____ 3. law originating in early England
____ 4. law originating in continental Europe
____ 5. land in its natural condition
____ 6. economic characteristic of land
____ 7. where world measurements begin
____ 8. anything which may be owned
____ 9. breach of the duty of care
____ 10. that which is not real property
____ 11. measured by north-south meridians
____ 12. one of the bundle of rights
____ 13. lifeblood of real estate sales
____ 14. chief executive of the Department of Real Estate
____ 15. exclusive right to the use and enjoyment of land

True/False

T F 16. There is no basic distinction between real and personal property.
T F 17. All torts are crimes.
T F 18. One of the rights of an owner is the right to exclude others.
T F 19. All property is considered to be unique.
T F 20. Scarcity is one of the economic characteristics of land.
T F 21. In the national economy, real estate ownership is not significant.
T F 22. Real estate plays a major role in the national economy.
T F 23. California was discovered by Cabrillo fifty years after Columbus discovered the Americas.
T F 24. California was part of Mexico from 1822 to 1846.
T F 25. California was admitted as a State in 1850.

Multiple Choice

26. California is a vast area, consisting of approximately
    a. 90,000 acres
    b. 100,300,000 acres
    c. 105,000,000 acres
    d. 110,000,000 acres

27. California became a part of the United States
in the year
   a. 1846
   b. 1848
   c. 1850
   d. 1852
28. The *bundle of rights* theory relates to
   a. use of property
   b. disposition of property
   c. enjoyment of property
   d. all of the above
29. Real property generally means
   a. the land itself
   b. things attached to land
   c. things appurtenant to land
   d. all of the above
30. Physical characteristics of land include
   a. immobility
   b. indestructibility
   c. homogeneity
   d. all of the above
31. Economic characteristics of land include
   a. scarcity
   b. situs
   c. fixity
   d. all of the above
32. In which of the following does real estate play
a major role in the economy?
   a. net worth
   b. income flow
   c. employment
   d. all of the above
33. In which year did Cabrillo discover California?
   a. 1513
   b. 1532
   c. 1542
   d. 1548
34. The actual occupation of California by the
Spanish began in the year
   a. 1669
   b. 1697
   c. 1749
   d. 1769
35. The number of missions established in California was
   a. 12
   b. 17
   c. 21
   d. 28
36. Mexico obtained its independence from Spain
in the year
   a. 1776
   b. 1796

   c. 1822
   d. 1846
37. The Treaty of Guadalupe Hidalgo was signed
in the year
   a. 1846
   b. 1848
   c. 1850
   d. 1851
38. Cabrillo first landed in California in what is
now
   a. San Pedro
   b. Santa Barbara
   c. San Diego
   d. Monterey
39. When California became part of the United
States, it adopted as its basic source of law
   a. Spanish law
   b. Common law of England
   c. Civil law of France
   d. Law of the Indies
40. Pueblos under Spanish or Mexican law
received 4 square leagues of land from the
government. A league under the old Spanish
law consisted of approximately
   a. 4439 acres
   b. 4349 acres
   c. 3940 acres
   d. 4040 acres
41. Sources of real property law in California
include
   a. U.S. Constitution
   b. Federal court decisions
   c. State court decisions
   d. all of the above
42. Sources of real property law in California also
include
   a. State statutes
   b. Federal statutes
   c. Administrative rules and regulations
   d. all of the above
43. Real property law in California is based on
   a. State law exclusively
   b. Federal law exclusively
   c. both state and federal law
   d. none of the above apply
44. The power of a court to hear and determine a
matter is called
   a. judicial discretion
   b. jurisdiction
   c. venue
   d. all of the above
45. The penalty for violation of the criminal law
may be
   a. fine

b. imprisonment
c. loss of license
d. any of the above

46. The relative weight of law on the salesperson's examination as compared with the broker's examination is generally
a. more
b. less
c. the same
d. neither cover the law

47. The relative weight of finance on the salesperson's examination as compared with the broker's examination is
a. more
b. less
c. the same
d. neither cover finance

48. The relative weight of public control on the salesperson's examination as compared with the broker's examination is
a. more
b. less
c. the same
d. neither include public control

49. The relative weight of practice on the salesperson's examination as compared with the broker's examination is
a. more
b. less
c. the same
d. practice is included only in the broker's examination

50. The relative weight of valuation on the salesperson's examination as compared with the broker's examination is
a. more
b. less
c. the same
d. only the broker's examination includes valuation

2
NATURE AND DESCRIPTION OF PROPERTY, ESTATES AND INTERESTS IN REAL PROPERTY

In the previous chapter we found that there are two types of property, real and personal. In this chapter we will consider the nature of each, and primarily the many ingredients of real property. We will discover that fixtures, although once personal property, become part of the real property to which they are affixed. Thus, property has a changeable character. Easements as an ingredient of real property will be discussed in detail. The importance of the distinction between real and personal property will be reviewed, and then we will explain how land is described and subdivided. In the area of land descriptions we will have an introduction into the mathematics of real

estate and realize the importance of basic arithmetic, a subject which will be detailed in Chapter 6. The chapter will conclude with an explanation of the various estates and interests in real property.

NATURE OF PERSONAL PROPERTY

As mentioned in the previous chapter, personal property is defined in the negative; i.e., it is defined as all property which is not real property. It includes such things as cars, goods, furniture, evidence of a debt in the form of a promissory note, money, etc. Personal property consists of property that is generally consumable and not durable; in other words, it is frequently "used up."

Personal property is either *tangible*—i.e., having physical existence, such as books, desks, lamps, motor vehicles, etc.—or *intangible*—i.e., a right of action against a third person. Personal property is sometimes referred to as *chattels* or *personalty*.

NATURE OF REAL PROPERTY

Real property basically consists of land, that which is affixed or attached to land, that which is incidental or appurtenant to land, and that which

17

Figure 2.1
Land includes the surface of the earth and the sky above and everything beneath the surface to the center of the earth.

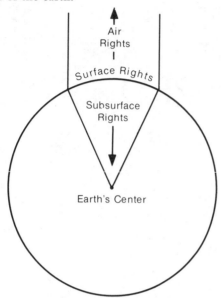

is immovable by law. Land includes the solid material of the earth, such as the soil, rock, gravel, or other substance. Used in a broad sense to reflect the common law concept, land also includes not only the surface of the earth, but the space beneath it and substances within it to the very center of the earth, and the air space above it to the periphery of the universe (see Figure 2.1).

In addition to land, real property consists of anything affixed to it in a permanent manner, such as buildings, fences, and other improvements on the land. Real property also includes items of personal property that are so attached to buildings and other improvements on the land as to become part of the real property. Such items are called *fixtures* (see later discussion in this chapter). Real property also includes that which is incidental or appurtenant to the land: anything that is used with the land for its benefit, such as a right of way over adjoining land to reach a public street. As another example, stock in a mutual water company that supplies water to the land might be appurtenant to the land. Also, real property consists of that which is immovable by law— for example, trees and other vegetation together with crops that have not been harvested.

In a grant or conveyance of real property in which only the legal description is given, the following elements of the property are included:

1. The land itself; i.e., the soil or earth

2. Minerals in place, such as gold, silver, iron, or coal, referred to as solid substances of the earth
3. The right to extract oil and gas from beneath the land, referred to as liquid or gaseous substances of the earth
4. The right of reasonable use of underground waters and streams or other watercourses
5. Air space above the land
6. Improvements such as buildings, swimming pools, etc., that are attached to the land
7. Trees and other vegetation, including crops not severed
8. Unaccrued rents due from a tenant in possession
9. Appurtenant easements
10. Right to acquire appurtenant water stock
11. Whatever the law declares real property interests to be

FIXTURES

Fixtures are items of personal property which have become attached to a building or other improvement on real property in such a manner that they become part of the real property, in absence of an agreement to the contrary. Examples of such items are plumbing or electrical fixtures, shelves, TV antennas, etc. Depending on the circumstances, personal property may become so integrated with the land or a building that it is regarded as part of the real property and belongs to the owner of the real property. A question as to whether or not a thing is a fixture frequently arises when real property is sold or when a tenant has installed improvements on the premises. In the sale of a home, such improvements as carpets, drapes, built-in appliances, and plants can become matters of contention between the buyer and the seller.

Various tests have been applied in determining whether or not a thing is a fixture, including the following:

1. The *method* by which property is attached, whether by nails, screws, glue, cement, or other means of keeping something in place.
2. The *agreement* of the parties. The existence of an agreement can avoid many problems, provided the agreement is clear and unambiguous.
3. The *relationship* of the person who adds or attaches the personal property *to* the real property. When a dispute arises between a

landlord and a tenant the law is inclined to favor the tenant. If a dispute arises between a buyer and seller of real property, the law is inclined to favor the buyer. This is also true in a dispute between a mortgagor and a mortgagee. The latter will usually be favored in the event of a later foreclosure of the mortgage.

4. The *intention* of the person in installing improvements to real property.

5. The *adaptability* of the personal property to the ordinary use in connection with the real property. If well adapted, especially if designed for a particular structure, it will probably be regarded as a fixture.

(As an aid to memory, the first letter of each of the above tests spells MARIA.)

In the case of *trade fixtures*, that is, items used for the purpose of engaging in business or manufacture, or for ornament or domestic use, a tenant can remove the items upon termination of the lease if the removal can be effected without injury to the premises.

CHANGEABLE CHARACTER OF PROPERTY

Property does not have a permanent status as real or personal, but is changeable in its character. Thus, a fir tree while part of a forest is real property. When cut and made into logs and eventually lumber, it becomes personal or movable property. Then when it is used as part of a building, it again becomes real property. If the building is later torn down, any lumber salvaged would again become personal property. This changeable status is true for many other elements of real property, such as solid minerals, bricks, oil, water, and so on, as illustrated in Figure 2.2.

IMPORTANCE OF THE DISTINCTION BETWEEN REAL AND PERSONAL PROPERTY

Different rules have developed relating to real and personal property, and in many situations it is important to determine whether property is real or personal in order to apply the proper law or to decide other rights. For instance, real property is regarded as exclusively subject to the laws and jurisdiction of the state in which it is located. On the other hand, personal property is usually regarded as situated at the domicile of its owner,

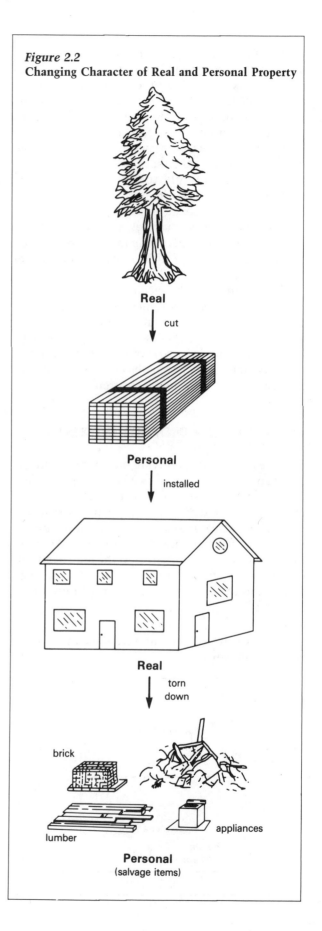

Figure 2.2
Changing Character of Real and Personal Property

Real

↓ cut

Personal

↓ installed

Real

↓ torn down

brick

lumber

appliances

Personal
(salvage items)

regardless of the actual location of the property, and is governed by the law of the owner's domicile. The distinction becomes particularly significant when the owner of property dies, since the jurisdiction of the probate court can be dependent upon the location of the property.

Another distinction between real and personal property relates to the method of transfer. A voluntary transfer of title to real property can be made only by an instrument in writing, called a *deed*. Title to personal property generally passes by delivery of possession, or, if a written document is used, by a *bill of sale* in the case of tangible property, or by an *assignment* in the case of intangible property.

The distinction between real and personal property is also of importance in connection with the recording of documents, property taxation, condemnation or eminent domain proceedings, levy and sale under a writ of execution, and probate distribution. These subjects will be considered further in subsequent chapters.

EASEMENTS AS A PROPERTY INTEREST

Most real property in private ownership is affected by an easement, either as a benefit or a burden. The subject is sometimes considered as an encumbrance and discussed as such, but it seems preferable to treat it as a property interest, since it is one of the ingredients of real property. An *easement* is defined as an interest in the land of another person that entitles the owner of the easement to use the other person's land for a limited pur-

Figure 2.3
An appurtenant easement for ingress and egress (driveway purposes)

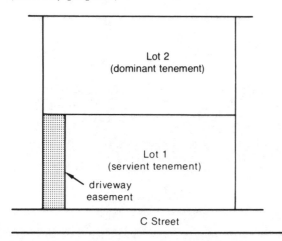

pose. It may be an *affirmative* easement, such as the right to cross over another person's property, or it may be a *negative* easement, such as the right to prevent the owner of adjoining land from constructing a building that exceeds a specified height (so as not to block the view).

Easements rights are frequently created so that the owner of adjoining land may have access or a right of way to get to and from his or her property, which otherwise might be landlocked, i.e., lacking a way to get to a public thoroughfare. For example, the owner of a back lot that does not have access to a public street might obtain an easement from the owner of the front lot in order to get to the street. The easement could be described as "an easement for driveway purposes over, along, and across the west 10 feet of Lot 1." This is illustrated by Figure 2.3.

Types

Easements are generally classified as either *appurtenant* or *in gross*. Appurtenant means *belonging to*. An appurtenant easement is one which is attached to a particular parcel of land for the benefit of that land. It is part of the real property. The land to which an appurtenant easement attaches is called the *dominant tenement*; the land burdened by the easement is called the *servient tenement*. With a driveway easement, for example, the land the driveway crosses is the servient tenement, and the land the driveway leads to is the dominant tenement.

An easement in gross is one which does not benefit any specific parcel of land. Although it is a right in another person's land, it is not created for the benefit of land owned by the easement holder but, rather, is a personal right. Typical examples of easements in gross are those granted public utility firms to install and maintain pole lines or pipelines for telephone, electricity, gas, and water. Such easements ordinarily have no dominant tenement, only the servient tenement. Figure 2.4 illustrates an easement in gross.

Whether an easement is appurtenant or in gross is determined mainly by the nature of the right and the intention of the parties. An easement is deemed appurtenant to land when it is used for the benefit of that land. An easement will not be presumed to be in gross if it can be fairly construed to be appurtenant. Once created, an appurtenant easement attaches (belongs) to the land of the owner of the easement, and title to the easement passes with a transfer of the land, even

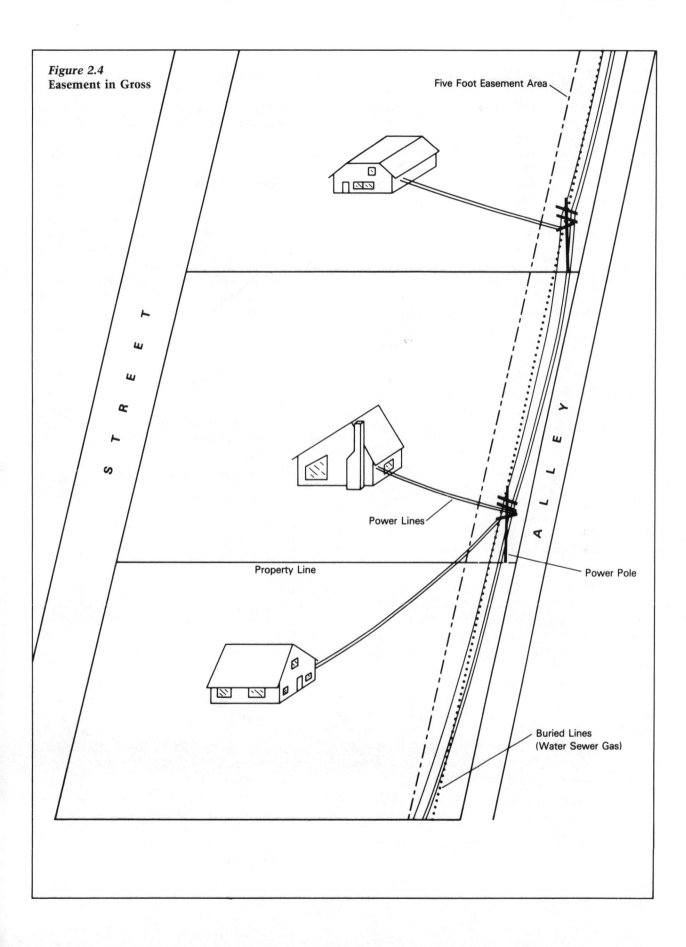

Figure 2.4
Easement in Gross

Five Foot Easement Area

Power Lines

Property Line

Power Pole

Buried Lines
(Water Sewer Gas)

STREET

ALLEY

though the easement is not specifically mentioned. Conversely, an easement in gross must be expressly transferred.

Purchasers of the servient tenement usually have no choice and take the title subject to the easement, either because the easement is recorded or because it is apparent on the ground. The owner of an easement, whether appurtenant or in gross, has an insurable interest in the land involved and may obtain a policy of title insurance insuring this ownership interest. This subject will be considered further in Chapter 6.

Creation

Easements may be created for a great many purposes, including rights of way, pasturage, hunting, fishing, and support of land. Although the Civil Code lists seventeen different land burdens that may be appurtenant to other land, there is actually no limit as to the purposes for which easements may be created. The following example of a recorded easement is of interest to golfers plagued by uncontrolled hooks or slices:

> A specific right of all easement way, ingress, egress and seizure for the immediate *search, recapture, retrieving,* and *recovery* of errant golf balls for a period of five minutes immediately following the departure of any golf ball from the confines of the club golf links, as reserved in the declaration of Virginia Country Club of Long Beach, California, a corporation, recorded in book 16402, page 291, Official Records.

Other easement rights include the following: flight of golf balls over an owner's property; shadow easements (to prevent structures from casting shadows on a motel's swimming pool area); noise easements; vibration easements; and avigation easements. An avigation easement is more than an easement for the flight of aircraft. It may include such additional items as a limitation on the height of buildings, and allowable noise, dust, fumes, or blinding lights.

Most property is subject to at least one easement, usually in gross, for public utility purposes. A typical example is the following:

> An easement in favor of Central California Edison Company, a corporation, for public utility purposes, including poles, lines, and conduits, over, under, along and across the south 6 feet of Lot 1, etc.

Such easements are technically land burdens, but they are also benefits, since electricity and other modern conveniences are vital to our way of life. Not only do easements affect small areas, like the typical residential property, but also easements cover mile after mile of area for high voltage transmission lines. Land beneath the lines is being used for such diverse purposes as vineyards, pastures, truck farming, growing Christmas trees, and raising ducks. Additional uses include public parks, picnic grounds, greenbelts, hiking paths, and equestrian trails. For example, the city of Monterey Park in southern California named one such parcel of land Edison Trails Park and added a winding, slightly graded hiking path designed for people with cardiac difficulties. In nearby Rosemead a minipark that has become popular with senior citizens occupies a portion of an Edison right-of-way. Even in such things as easements, then, there is concern for a better environment.

Easements may be created or acquired in many ways: by *grant*, either express or implied; by *reservation*, either express or implied; by *dedication*; by *necessity*; by *prescription*; and so on.

The following are examples of ways that easements may be created:

1. Express Grant: A, owner of Blackacre, grants B, owner of Whiteacre, the right to use a private road over Blackacre for the purpose of getting to and from Whiteacre. The easement is appurtenant to Whiteacre and burdens Blackacre. Whiteacre is the "dominant tenement." Blackacre is the "servient tenement."

2. Implied Grant: A, owner of lots 1 and 2, conveys lot 1 to B. At the time of the deed a driveway over lot 2 is openly used and is reasonably necessary to the beneficial use of lot 1. An easement for the driveway over lot 2 (the lot retained by A) would ordinarily pass by implication with the deed of lot 1.

3. Easement of Necessity: A, owner of a 50-acre parcel designated as lot 1, conveys the north 5 acres of lot 1 to B. The land conveyed has no access to a public road except over the remaining part of lot 1. As a rule B would have an easement of necessity over the land retained by A.

4. Easement by Prescription: This arises where a person has used another person's land for a continuous period of five years without permission. Payment of taxes by the easement claimant is not required.

In the creation of an easement, regard must be made for the sufficiency of the description. As a general rule, if a description is indefinite or uncertain, a conveyance is void. However, in the case of an easement, a description that does not identify the particular portion of the land burdened by the easement may be valid. Such an easement is usually referred to as a *floating* easement, for example "an easement ten feet in width for roadway purposes *over Parcel A*." Until the ten-foot strip is located, the easement encumbers the entire parcel, even though it is described as only a narrow strip of land.

Open-space easements provide for grants of open spaces by the landowner to counties and cities. Such easements restrict the property to open-space use for the benefit of the public and entitle the property to special tax consideration. Instruments conveying open-space easements are both a grant to the governmental agency and a dedication in favor of the public, relinquishing the right to construct improvements, extract resources, or remove natural growth, except as specifically reserved. Open-space easements may be granted for a minimum period, such as twenty years, and may be extended beyond the period specified in the grant. An open-space easement is effective after it is accepted by resolution of the governing agency. After this is done, no building permit is to be issued for a structure in violation of the terms of the easement.

Termination

Easements may be terminated or extinguished in a number of ways, including the following:

1. Express release; e.g., through a quitclaim deed by easement holder relinquishing the easement
2. Merger of the servient tenement and the easement in the same person (the owner of the servient tenement acquires legal title to the dominant tenement)
3. Nonuse of *prescriptive* easement for a continuous period of five years; however, nonuse of an easement created by grant does not extinguish the easement
4. Abandonment of the easement
5. Destruction of the servient tenement; e.g., building in which stairway easement was created is destroyed by fire

Sometimes a pipeline easement or other type of easement may seem to affect adversely a strategic portion of a parcel of land suitable for development, but often the problem can be resolved satisfactorily by an agreement for relocation of the easement. The holder of an easement cannot be arbitrary or unreasonable in the exercise of his or her rights, and this doctrine could be applicable in the event a need to relocate an easement became essential to the productive use of the land by the landowner.

HOW LAND IS DESCRIBED

There are many ways that land may be described. The three principal methods are *metes and bounds*, which describe the property by its actual boundaries or perimeter (*metes* meaning measurements, and *bounds* meaning boundaries); the *government survey*, which is a rectangular system adopted by the U.S. Congress in 1785 and still used in many areas throughout California; and *tract references* to lots and blocks in a recorded subdivision map as provided by the state's Subdivisions Map Act. Other methods sometimes encountered include reference to visible monuments such as a fence, a tree, a hill, etc.; assessor's parcel numbers, used for identifying property for tax purposes; the State Plane Coordinate System; and street and number (street address). These relate primarily to surface land descriptions. Although lines generally appear horizontally on a map or other drawing, the result on the ground is a vertical division. Land may also be described in terms of a horizontal division. This is accomplished by establishing a *datum*, a point from which a distance (up or down) is measured. The most commonly used datum in many places in the United States is mean sea level. Horizontal measurements are encountered when air spaces or subsurface areas need to be identified, such as in condominium developments or subsurface oil leases.

As we will see in the next chapter, the primary document used to transfer an interest in property is the *deed*. It is a fundamental rule that a deed must unmistakably identify the property that is the subject of the conveyance. Usually this is accomplished by what is called a "legal description." In title work this term is often shortened and referred to simply as the "legal."

The "unmistakable identification" test affects the very legality of a transaction, for without it there could be a void and uninsurable conveyance.

Because the three principal methods listed above are most frequently encountered and usually result in a sufficient legal description, particularly for title insurance purposes, they will now be considered in detail.

Metes and Bounds

Before the rectangular survey system (described in more detail later) was established, land was usually described by metes and bounds. This type of description begins at a certain well-defined point and then follows the exterior boundaries by *course* (or direction) and *distances*. The starting point — the point of beginning, or POB — is described in relation to a survey marker or monument, or to a natural marker such as the mouth of a stream, a bridge, a road, or a prominent outcropping of rock. The starting point is plainly marked on the ground with a pile of stones, a tree blazed on four sides, or in some other prominent way. Where it is not possible to give the starting point in relation to a survey monument or marker, then the latitude or longitude should be given with as much accuracy as possible. Latitude and longitude can be read from a good map of the area. The tract is then described by all of its boundaries. Properly prepared, metes and bounds can be an accurate and acceptable method of describing an irregularly shaped parcel of land.

In the early days of California's history, when land was plentiful and inexpensive, such descriptions were frequently colorful, if not always entirely accurate. References were made to such landmarks as "the dead oak tree with the skull of a steer set in its forks," or "the clump of sycamores springing from one root." Stones, houses, adobe walls, streams, and other such reference points were often used; people ignored the fact that time would destroy them or that their location might change. Today, of course, most such descriptions are based on accurate surveys; exact directions and distances are established by transits and other instruments and standard measuring devices. References, or "ties," are made to permanent monuments, such as streets, or to fixed points that have already been located and established by other surveys and recorded on a map.

Government Survey

Many boundaries established under both the Spanish and Mexican regimes in California had been so vague that they were a constant source of disagreement. Newly arrived Americans at the time California became a state found the metes and bounds descriptions too ambiguous. They lacked the precision of the familiar grid system of townships, sections, and quarter-sections used by the United States in the subdividing of public lands. Before such a system could be established, specific points of reference, called *initial points*, had to be determined. Three of them were established in California, as illustrated on Figure 2.5. The three principal bases and meridians in California are called the Humboldt Base Line & Meridian, the Mt. Diablo Base Line & Meridian, and the San Bernardino Base Line & Meridian, in the northern, central, and southern parts of the state respectively. As we learned in Chapter 1, these lines are all measured from Greenwich, England.

Mt. Diablo, in Contra Costa County, is a conspicuous landmark in the San Francisco bay area. When a person is flying in, sometimes the peak is the only visible sight above the fog bank. It is presently the site of a State Park, and a rock tower has been erected on the spot (see Figure 2.6).

A plaque was placed on the site in 1978 which reads in part:

> Mount Diablo, sacred to Native Americans who lived and worshipped there for over 5000 years, became a critical reference point for Spanish explorers in the 18th Century and American trappers and early California settlers in the 19th. In 1851 Colonel Leander Ransome established the crossing of the Mount Diablo base and meridian

Figure 2.5
The Three Principal Bases and Meridians in California

Figure 2.6
Rock Tower on the Site of the Mt. Diablo Base and Meridian Lines

lines from which most of California and Nevada are surveyed.

To develop a grid system, the latitude and longitude of the initial points are ascertained; then a true north-and-south line, called a *principal meridian*, is run through the initial point and marked on the ground. Next, a line is run east and west from the initial point. This line is called a *base line* and is at right angles to the principal meridian. On either side of the principal meridian the land is laid out in approximately square units, looking very much like a checker board. These units are called *townships*. Their boundary lines are six miles long, and run north-south and east-west. A tier of townships running north and south is called a "range." The townships are described as being so many townships east or west of a named principal meridian (see Figure 2.7.)

Each township is divided into thirty-six sections, each approximately one mile square, and containing 640 acres. The sections are uniformly numbered from one to thirty-six, starting in the northeast corner and moving alternately right to left, then left to right, ending in the southeast section (see Figure 2.8). This assumes that the section is regular in size. In some instances there is a shortage because the boundary line of the section at the time of the original survey was adjacent to rancho property vested in private ownership, or because of a river or some other natural cause. Each section can be located by its number, township, and range from the principal base and merid-

Figure 2.7
Townships and Ranges

								T3N R3E	TOWNSHIP 3 NORTH
		T2N R3W							TOWNSHIP 2 NORTH
									TOWNSHIP 1 NORTH

BASE MERIDIAN LINE

TOWNSHIP 1 SOUTH — T1S R2E

TOWNSHIP 2 SOUTH

←6 MI.→

PRINCIPLE MERIDIAN

RANGE 5 WEST RANGE 4 WEST RANGE 3 WEST RANGE 2 WEST RANGE 1 WEST RANGE 1 EAST RANGE 2 EAST RANGE 3 EAST RANGE 4 EAST

Figure 2.8
Sectional Map of a Township with Adjoining Sections

36	31	32	33	34	35	36	31
1	6	5	4	3	2	1	6
12	7	8	9	10	11	12	7
13	18	17	16	15	14	13	18
24	19	20	21	22	23	24	19
25	30	29	28	27	26	25	30
36	31	32	33	34	35	36	31
1	6	5	4	3	2	1	6

ian. So long as the principal base and meridian are shown, it is unnecessary to show the *county* where the property is located, since the location can be otherwise ascertained. Showing the county is customary, however. In other types of descriptions, the county must be shown.

Sections may be further divided into quarter-sections. Each quarter-section (160 acres) is identified by its compass direction—NE, SE, SW, NW. The corners of every section and quarter-section are permanently located on the ground by monuments. The exact location of the corner is stamped into a brass cap on the top of the monument.

A quarter-section can be divided into quarter-quarters of 40 acres. Quarter-quarters, or "40s" as they are often called, can be further subdivided into areas as small as 5 acres, or $2\frac{1}{2}$ acres, or $1\frac{1}{4}$ acres. These divisions are illustrated in Figure 2.9.

Because of the shape of the earth, principal meridians come closer together as they extend north toward the North Pole. To adjust to this, correction lines are run every twenty-four miles or, in some areas, every thirty miles.

Tract References

Reference to a map showing lot and block numbers in a tract is another method of describing land in California today. Under the Subdivision Map Act, (explained in the next section of this chapter), new subdivisions in California must be mapped or plotted. The map shows the relationship of the subdivision to other lands, and each parcel on the new subdivision is delineated and identified by a symbol. When accepted by the appropriate local regulatory authority, the map is filed in the county recorder's office and becomes official. Thereafter, any parcel in the subdivision is described in legal documents simply by reference to the lot and block number in the named or numbered tract, to which is added the name of the city and the county in the state of California, followed by a reference to the book and page of the *Official Records* where the map is on file. Following is an example of such a description:

> Lot 10 in Block 20 of the Ramona Tract, in the city of Rosemead, county of Los Angeles, state of California, as per map recorded in Book 7, Pages 21 to 25 of Maps in the office of the County Recorder of said County.

SUBDIVIDED LANDS

Two major state laws provide for the orderly development of parcels of land and maintain great control over every aspect of development while providing that development be consistent with the adopted local plan. The first of these is the Subdivision Map Act, now part of the Government Code. The primary objective of the Subdivision Map Act is to provide definitions of terms and to outline methods of map filing procedure applicable on a statewide basis.

Figure 2.9
Division of Section

The other law is known as the Subdivided Lands Law, part of the Business and Professions Code. The latter is administered by the real estate commissioner. Each of these laws was enacted for different purposes. The Subdivided Lands Law regulates the *sale* of subdivided lands, and the Subdivision Map Act controls *filing* of subdivision maps and enables cities and counties to enact ordinances as necessary to regulate local subdivision activity. Local ordinances also pertain to lot splits, where one parcel is divided into two, three or four parcels. A federal law, the Interstate Land Sales Full Disclosure Act, affects certain types of subdivisions offered in interstate commerce or by mail.

It has been found that the new problems created by the continued growth of population and the movement of people into the cities and suburbs can be solved only through governmental action. These problems and their solutions include the prevention of fraud, misrepresentation, and deceit in the sale of subdivided property; the regulation of lot designs and physical improvements; the construction of streets and highways and parking facilities; the creation of an adequate water supply; the protection of life and property by effective police and fire departments; the maintenance of pure air; the minimizing of noise; the disposal of sewage and waste products; and the providing of utility services, either under public or private facilities.

If communities grow haphazardly, old problems are aggravated and new ones added. Government agencies try to make each newly developed area as livable as possible through state laws regulating the subdivision of real estate and by means of master plans, zoning laws, and building codes. These latter subjects will be considered further in Chapter 12.

Subdivision Map Act

The primary objective of the California Subdivision Map Act is to prescribe a method of subdivision *filing* procedures on a statewide basis. Prior to 1929 there was no effective control over the filing of subdivision maps in California. As a result, coordination of land subdivision with overall community development plans was lacking.

The Map Act is an enabling act; it permits local governing bodies to enact the ordinances that have direct jurisdiction over subdivisions in their communities. Such ordinances must meet the limitations and scope set forth in the Map Act. Thus, the direct control of the kind and type of subdivisions to be created in each community, and the physical improvements to be installed, are left to the control of the local jurisdictions, but within certain general limits specified in the Map Act.

The Map Act has two major objectives:

1. To coordinate the subdivision plans—including lot design, street patterns, right of way for drainage and sewers, etc.—with the community pattern and plan, as laid out by the local planning authorities.
2. To insure that the areas dedicated for public purposes by the filing of the subdivision maps, including public streets and other public areas, will be properly improved initially by the subdivider so that they will not become an undue burden in the future upon the general taxpayers of the community.

Among the subjects of concern to the local governing authority are the following: location and boundaries of the property, physical features of the property as disclosed by a topographic map, availability of public utilities, general features of the area as disclosed by a site location map, natural features, accessibility, character of the neighborhood, drainage, flood hazard, geological report, sewage disposal, water supply, public utilities, public park and recreational facilities, and schools.

The process of obtaining approval for the subdivision involves the filing of a tentative map and ultimately the recording of a final map. A diagram showing the typical steps in subdivision procedures under the Map Act appears as Figure 2.10.

Subdivided Lands Law

This law, first enacted in 1933, is administered by the real estate commissioner. Its basic objective is to protect the purchasers of property in new subdivisions from fraud, misrepresentation, and deceit in the marketing of subdivided lots, parcels, units and undivided interests in the State of California.

In general, no subdivision can be offered for sale in California until the real estate commissioner has issued a subdivision public report on it. This restriction applies not only to tracts located in California, but also to subdivided lands lying outside the state's boundaries, but *offered for sale* in California. The public report is a factual

Figure 2.10   Basic Outline of Final Map Preparation and Approval

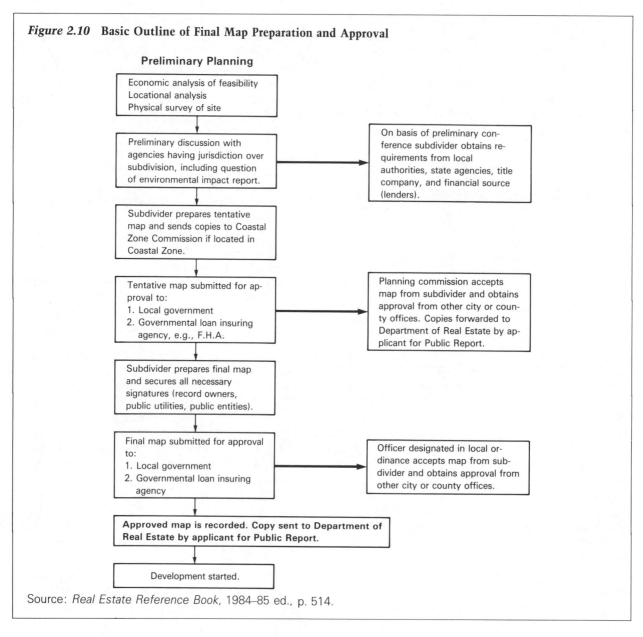

Source: *Real Estate Reference Book*, 1984–85 ed., p. 514.

account of the subdivided property, with emphasis on what might be considered its shortcomings. The report will not be issued until the commissioner is satisfied that the subdivider has met all statutory requirements with particular emphasis on the establishment of financial arrangements to assure completion and maintenance of improvements and facilities included in the offering, and a showing that the lots or parcels can be used for the purpose for which they are being offered.

Classification of Subdivisions

Basically, subdivisions may be classified as

1. *Standard:* a land division with no common or mutual rights of either ownership or use

among the owners of the parcels created by the division. A standard questionnaire is provided by the real estate commissioner for those subdivisions in which the interest to be conveyed is an individual improved or unimproved lot or parcel. Usually unimproved lots in a subdivision are developed with the necessary utilities installed. The market for lots in a standard subdivision generally consists of people interested in building their own homes or building contractors who purchase one or more lots for building and sale. Many developers construct the dwellings themselves, offering a "package" complete with financing arranged for the purchasers. In the standard subdivision, as well as in all other types of subdivisions, the commissioner inquires into not only the fundamental physical characteristics, but also into the matters of title, financing, handling of purchaser's deposit money, and methods of conveying the interest contracted for.

2. *Common interest:* individuals own or lease a separate lot or unit, or an interest therein, together with an undivided interest or membership interest in the common areas of the entire project. These common areas are usually governed by a homeowners' association. These subdivisions vary both in physical design and legal form. Condominiums, planned developments, stock cooperatives and community apartment projects are examples, as are time-sharing projects. Many of them are located in resort areas. Ownership aspects of these various types of multiple housing units will be considered further in Chapter 3.

3. *Undivided interests:* the purchaser receives an undivided interest in a parcel of land as a tenant in common with all the other owners. All owners have the nonexclusive right to the use and occupancy of the property. A recreational vehicle park, with campground and other recreational amenities, is an example.

4. *Land project:* briefly, a remote area subdivision of 50 or more parcels without onsite improvements, with less than 1500 registered voters residing within certain distances from the subdivision.

Questionnaire Forms

Certain minimum information concerning a new subdivision must be furnished to the Department of Real Estate prior to the issuance of a public report, and the Department has developed questionnaires which must be used by the subdivider for this purpose. Some of the information required by the questionnaire must be in documentary form, such as a preliminary report of title. Other information can be filled in from the subdivider's records.

Different questionnaire forms are supplied by the Department for the different types of subdivisions, such as standard subdivisions, "common interest" subdivisions, stock cooperatives and out-of-state subdivisions. Many common requirements apply to all subdivision filings, but the varying characteristics of each type of subdivision require special information and documentation.

Each form of questionnaire is designed to elicit information relating to the particular type of development involved, but in all cases the real estate commissioner is concerned with the following:

1. On- or off-site conditions which may affect the intended use of the land
2. Provisions for essential utilities, such as water supply and sewage disposal
3. The nature of the on-site improvements, existing or proposed
4. The condition of title, including any restrictions or reservations affecting building, use or occupancy
5. The financing of community, recreational or other common facilities, if any
6. The terms and conditions of sales or lease
7. The ability of the subdivider to deliver the interest contracted for
8. The method of conveyance
9. Any representations of "guarantees" or "warranties" made as part of a sales program.

The subject of subdivided lands in California is discussed in considerable detail in the *Real Estate Reference Book*, and is recommended reading for anyone desiring further information.

AREAS AND DISTANCES

A knowledge of basic arithmetic is essential for anyone going into the real estate field, and a good place to start is in land measurements. The mathematics of real estate will be considered further in Chapter 6. Figure 2.11 shows a list of linear and spatial measurements used in land descriptions.

Most purchasers of real property will want to know the size of the lot and structure. This computation usually is given in square feet. To measure a rectangular or square-shaped lot or structure, the formula is:

$$\text{Area} = \text{Width} \times \text{Length}$$

Suppose a lot measures 50 feet frontage and 200 feet in depth, as plotted below. What is its area?

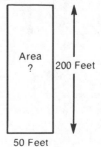

Figure 2.11
Measurements Used in Land Descriptions

Common Linear Measurements

One foot	= 12 inches.
One yard	= 3 feet or 36 inches.
One rod	= 16½ feet, 5½ yards.
One furlong	= 40 rods.
100 feet	= 6.6 rods.
One mile	= 5280 feet, 1760 yards, 320 rods, 80 chains.

Surveyors' Measurements

1 link	= 7.92 inches.
1 rod	= 25 links.
1 chain	= 4 rods, or 66 feet.

Special or Area Measurements (Length X Width)

1 square foot	= 144 square inches.
1 square yard	= 9 square feet.
1 square rod	= 30¼ square yards.
1 acre	= 10 square chains, 160 square rods, 4840 square yards, 43,560 square feet.
A section	= 1 square mile, 640 acres.
A township	= 36 square miles.
A quarter section	= 160 acres.
Area of a square or rectangle	= length × width in unit of linear measurement used.
Area of a triangle	= base × ½ altitude.

Cubic Measurements (Length X Width X Height)

| 1 cubic foot | = 1728 cubic inches. |
| 1 cubic yard | = 27 cubic feet. |

Substituting the numbers in the formula gives:

$$A = W \times L$$
$$A = 50 \text{ feet} \times 200 \text{ feet}$$
$$A = 10{,}000 \text{ square feet}$$

If the property is in the form of a triangle, take half the area of a rectangle or square-shaped parcel, as plotted below:

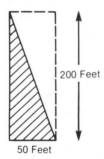

200 Feet

50 Feet

By filling in with broken lines, it is apparent that the triangular-shaped property is really half of a rectangle. Thus the formula for the area of a triangular-shaped property is:

$$A = \frac{\text{Width} \times \text{Length}}{2}$$
$$A = \frac{50 \text{ feet} \times 200 \text{ feet}}{2}$$
$$A = 5000 \text{ square feet}$$

Mathematicians use the terms "base" and "height" instead of width and length when computing the area of a triangle. The final results are identical, as illustrated below:

$$A = \frac{\text{Base} \times \text{Height}}{2}$$
$$A = \frac{50 \text{ feet} \times 200 \text{ feet}}{2}$$
$$A = 5000 \text{ square feet}$$

THE METRIC SYSTEM: ITS ROLE IN REAL ESTATE

At least 90 percent of the world's population uses the metric system to measure dimensions and areas, temperatures, distances, weights, volume, and so forth. The United States is one of the few countries that has not converted to the metric system. However, it appears likely that federal legislation will someday be passed to implement the system gradually.

Proponents claim that "going metric" will facilitate computations, that the metric system is simpler and more logical than our measuring systems, and that it is internationally accepted because of its more precise standards of measurement. Also, because world trade is carried on in metric measurements, the United States must facilitate the exchange of goods and services in order to remain competitive.

With the general increase in the use of the metric system and with its many advantages, the system would readily lend itself to use in map making, land descriptions, computing land and building sizes and dimensions, and so on. Figure 2.12 shows the approximate conversion between the English and metric system for measuring lengths and distances and for measuring areas and surfaces.

ESTATES AND INTERESTS IN REAL PROPERTY

The ownership interest a person has in land is called an *estate*, and the highest form or ownership is a fee simple absolute. The extent of a person's interest in real property can range all the

Figure 2.12 **Approximate Conversion Between the English and Metric Systems**

For Measuring Lengths and Distances			For Measuring Areas and Surfaces	
	1 inch	= 25 millimeters	1 meter	= 39.37 inches
12 inches	= 1 foot	= 30 centimeters		= 3.28083 feet
3 feet	= 1 yard	= 0.9 meter		= 1.0936 yards
1760 yards	= 1 mile	= 1.6 kilometers	1 square meter	= 10.764 square feet
	1 millimeter	= 0.04 inch		= 1.196 square yards
10 millimeters	= 1 centimeter	= 0.39 inch	1 square foot	= .0929 square meters
10 centimeters	= 1 decimeter	= 3.93 inches	1 acre	= .4046 hectare
10 decimeters	= 1 meter	= 1.1 yards	1 hectare	= 10,000 square meters
1000 meters	= 1 kilometer	= 0.62 mile		= 2.471 acres

way from a fee simple absolute to a mere tolerated possession, called a *tenancy at sufferance.*

An estate may be categorized either as real property or as personal property. Estates that are real property are determined by the fact that the duration of ownership is always indefinite. This grows out of the fact that since the 13th century *estates in fee* and *estates for life* have been referred to as *freehold estates*, because (1) their exact time of termination was uncertain, and (2) they were characteristics of the holdings of a "free man" under the English feudal system.

The term *real property* has been applied to these freehold estates. Lesser estates are categorized as *non-freehold estates*, and are regarded as personal property interests. This distinction becomes important in many situations, such as determining whether or not a judgment lien attaches (see Chapter 7), or what property is included in a devise by a general description, such as "all my real property to A, and all my personal property to B" (see Chapter 3).

The word *estate* is used to express the degree, quantity, nature, duration, or extent of an interest in land. There are various additional ways of classifying an estate, based on such factors as *quality*, i.e., whether absolute or subject to contingencies; *time of enjoyment*, i.e., whether there is a present right of possession or a future right of possession; *number of owners*, i.e., whether there is a sole owner or two or more owners; and *duration of enjoyment*, i.e., whether for a definite or an indefinite period of time.

As to duration of enjoyment, the Civil Code classifies estates as follows:

1. Estates in fee
2. Life estates
3. Leasehold estates (estates for years)
4. Estates at will

As we have seen, estates in fee and life estates are known as freehold estates. The uncertain duration of its existence is the distinguishing characteristic of a freehold estate. No one knows how long a fee simple estate will last, because the owner has the right to dispose of it whenever he desires. It is not an estate for any fixed period of time. A life estate depends on the duration of a person's natural life, and is terminated only on the death of the person whose life measures the duration of the life estate, which is an event uncertain as to time. A life estate can be measured by the life of the person owning the life estate, or it can be measured by the natural life of another person. It can be created either by grant or by reservation. Figure 2.13 compares these two methods.

As to *quality* of an estate, a fee simple estate can be classified as either a *fee simple absolute* or a *fee simple defeasible*.

An estate in fee simple absolute, often referred to as an "estate in fee" or merely a "fee," is the highest type of interest a person can have in land. It is restricted only by the rights of the adjoining owners, the duties of an owner regarding the exercise of his or her property rights, and the powers of the government (such as the power of taxation and the power of eminent domain).

A fee simple defeasible, sometimes referred to as a "qualified fee," is subject to limitations in

Figure 2.13
Creation of a Life Estate

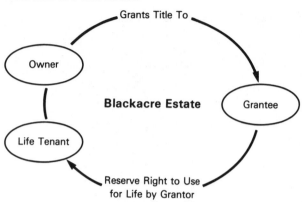

Life Estate Created by Reservation

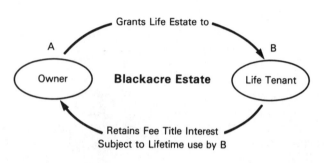

Life Estate Created by Grant

use that can result in a loss of title if the property is used in a manner that is inconsistent with whatever the use qualification is. For instance, a conveyance may be made on condition that the land shall not be used for the sale of intoxicating liquors, and further providing that title shall revert to the original grantor or his or her successors on breach of the condition. If there is a violation of the condition, the grantor or his or her successor has the right to terminate the estate. Or, land may be conveyed on condition that it be used for park puposes only. If the park use is abandoned, title may revert to the original grantor or his or her successors. Or conditions may be imposed in subdivision deed restrictions which can result in loss of title (see Chapter 11).

As to *time of enjoyment*, estates may be classified as either *possessory* or *nonpossessory*. In order for a right in real property to be an estate, it must be a present possessory interest or become possessory at some future time. Possessory and nonpossessory rights are often owned simultaneously by two or more persons in the same parcel

of land. The nonpossessory estate is known as a "future interest." At some time in the future it can ripen into a possessory interest. The following two examples explain this difference.

1. In a life estate, the person owning the life estate is called the life tenant. The person who will be entitled to the estate on the death of the life tenant is called the *remainderman*. The life tenant's estate is possessory. The estate of the remainderman is nonpossessory.

2. In the case of a lease of real property, the tenant has a possessory estate. The landlord has a *reversionary estate*, which is a nonpossessory interest. Upon the termination of the lease, the tenant's possessory interest will revert to the landlord.

A primary distinction based upon possessory and nonpossessory interest is illustrated by Figure 2.14.

As to *number of owners*, this is dependent upon whether there is only one person in ownership, called *ownership in severalty*, or whether ownership is in more than one person, called *co-ownership*. This aspect will be considered further in the next chapter.

The subject of estates, especially future interests in real property, can be complicated, and is treated in greater detail in *Real Estate Law in California*, 7th ed., by Arthur G. Bowman and W. D. Milligan, to which we refer the reader for additional information.

QUESTIONS FOR CHAPTER 2

Matching Terms

a. estate	**i.** appurtenant
b. movable	**j.** deed
c. tangible	**k.** bill of sale
d. intangible	**l.** base line
e. air rights	**m.** section
f. fixtures	**n.** contingent
g. easement	**o.** meridian
h. dominant	
tenement	

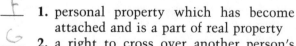

_F_ **1.** personal property which has become attached and is a part of real property

_G_ **2.** a right to cross over another person's property

_N_ **3.** dependent upon a future event

Figure 2.14
Interests in Real Property

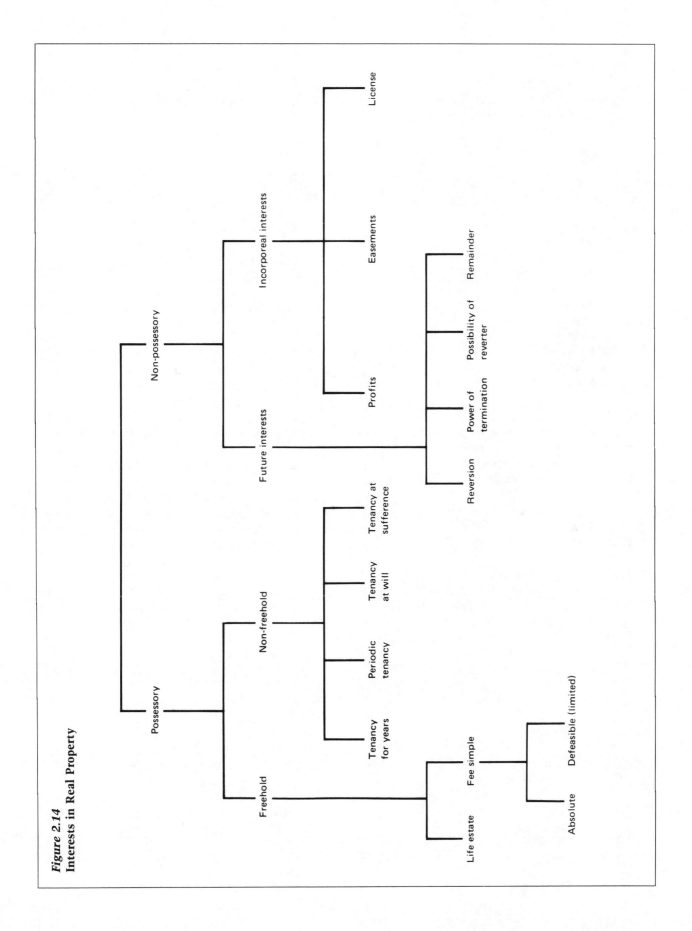

___ 4. document used to transfer title to real property

___ 5. property benefited by an easement

___ 6. line running east and west from which land measurements are made

___ 7. personal property which basically consists of a right, such as a cause of action

___ 8. line running north and south from which land measurements are made

___ 9. an ingredient of real property

___ 10. an area containing 640 acres

___ 11. property which has physical existence

___ 12. belonging to

___ 13. document used to transfer title to tangible personal property

___ 14. the degree, quantity, nature, duration, or extent of an interest in land

___ 15. characteristic of all personal property

True/False

T F 16. Basically, there is no distinction between real and personal property.

T F 17. The character of property, once determined, is not subject to change.

T F 18. An appurtenant easement is regarded as a part of real property.

T F 19. A section has a larger area than a township.

T F 20. The owner of the surface owns all oil and gas beneath the surface.

T F 21. Easements may be acquired only by written grant.

T F 22. In any description of land, an initial point of beginning is essential.

T F 23. All land in California is described by the government survey method.

T F 24. A metes and bounds description can no longer be used in California.

T F 25. Basically, there is no distinction between the Subdivision Map Act and the Subdivided Lands Law.

Multiple Choice

26. Which of the following are included in the definition of real property?
    a. easements
    b. licenses
    c. movables
    d. all of the above

27. Personal property includes which of the following?
    a. minerals in place

    b. air space
    c. potted plants
    d. flowing water

28. Real property ordinarily does not include the following:
    a. concrete block fence
    b. fruit trees
    c. built-in stove
    d. rugs

29. The distinction between real and personal property is of significance when
    a. buying a home
    b. obtaining a loan on real property
    c. leasing real property
    d. all of the above

30. Where land in California is in private ownership, the original source of title will ordinarily be evidenced by a
    a. patent
    b. quit claim deed
    c. rancho grant
    d. quiet title decree

31. Personal property that is attached to and made a part of real property is called a
    a. chattel real
    b. fixture
    c. riparian right
    d. profit a prende

32. Real property ordinarily does not include
    a. water rights
    b. minerals in place
    c. severed crops
    d. fixtures

33. Of the following, which one would most likely be deemed a fixture?
    a. patio furniture
    b. rugs
    c. flower pots
    c. carpeting

34. Personal property ordinarily includes the following
    a. growing crops
    b. air space
    c. furniture and furnishings
    d. gold or silver in place

35. There are two classes or kinds of property, real and personal. Both have certain characteristics that are similar. Of the following statements, which is incorrect?
    a. real property may become personal property
    b. personal property may become real property

c. personal property is defined as immovable property
d. crops may be either real or personal property

36. When a residence is sold, title is transferred by a deed that contains a legal description and a street address. Buildings and other improvements are generally not described, but would be included in the deed. Which of the following ordinarily would not be included in the transfer?
    a. growing trees
    b. appurtenant easement
    c. floor lamps and shades
    d. installed furnaces

37. Real property may be described by
    a. metes and bounds
    b. government survey
    c. tract reference
    d. any of the above

38. Principal base and meridian lines were originally established in California in
    a. four places
    b. three places
    c. three places including Sacramento
    d. three places including San Francisco

39. Townships are divided into the following number of sections:
    a. twelve
    b. twenty-four
    c. thirty-six
    d. forty-eight

40. The description of land as "the NW ¼ of Sec. 10, T2N, R4E, SBBM" is a description by
    a. metes and bounds
    b. courses and distances
    c. reference to a subdivision
    d. government survey

41. The description of land as "Lot 2 of the Smith Tract, as per map recorded in book 10, Page 61 of maps" indicates a description by
    a. metes and bounds
    b. courses and distances
    c. reference to a subdivision
    d. government survey

42. The SE ¼ of the NE ¼ of the SW ¼ of a theoretical section contains
    a. 2½ acres
    b. 5 acres
    c. 10 acres
    d. 20 acres

43. The NW ¼ of the SE ¼ of a theoretical section contains
    a. 20 acres

b. 40 acres
c. 80 acres
d. 120 acres

44. The NW ¼ of section 9 in a township would adjoin sections numbered
    a. 3, 4, and 10
    b. 10, 15, and 16
    c. 8, 16, and 17
    d. 4, 5, and 8

45. How many square miles are in a township?
    a. 6
    b. 16
    c. 26
    d. 36

46. California became a part of the United States in the year
    a. 1846
    b. 1848
    c. 1850
    d. 1851

47. Easements may be acquired by
    a. implied grant
    b. dedication
    c. express reservation
    d. any of the above

48. The dominant tenement is the property
    a. upon which the burden of an easement is imposed
    b. in whose favor an easement appurtenant is created
    c. owned by a tenant in common having the largest interest
    d. owned by the landlord

49. Smith used a path across Jones's property for a continuous period of five years without permission. He then claimed an easement. This is an example of an easement by
    a. dedication
    b. reservation
    c. prescription
    d. necessity

50. An owner sold a lot with a front footage of 120 feet and a depth of 300 feet for $3.50 per square foot. The selling price was
    a. $72,600
    b. $96,200
    c. $54,500
    d. $126,000

3

ACQUISITION AND TRANSFER OF TITLE, RECORDING, AND FORMS OF OWNERSHIP

This chapter first considers the various ways of acquiring title to real property and methods of transfer. Usually *acquisition* of property by one owner entails a *transfer* from another owner, so we consider these two aspects together. Because of the importance of deeds as a method of transfer, the subject is discussed at length, including the use of a power of attorney and the impact of the documentary transfer tax on conveyancing. After a discussion of several other methods of acquisition and transfer of real property, the recording system is explained. The chapter concludes with an examination of the various methods of ownership of real property in California, particularly ownership by two or more persons, or some type of entity ownership, and ownership rights and responsibilities in multiple housing

projects, including condominiums, co-ops, and own-your-own or community apartments.

Regarding the several ways of acquiring and transferring title to real property, we will find that many property transfers involve the transfer of a fee simple absolute interest in the property; that is, as we have learned in Chapter 2, the highest type of estate and interest a person may have in the property—sometimes referred to as the unlimited right to do as he or she pleases with it. However, it is not an absolute right, since various limitations do apply (as we shall learn in Chapter 12). There are, in fact, few absolute rights.

The California Civil Code lists five ways by which property may be acquired: by will, succession, accession, occupancy, and transfer. Transfer or acquisition by *will* or *succession* relates to disposition of an owner's property when he or she dies. *Accession* encompasses three different methods, i.e., *accretion*, *reliction*, and *annexation*. The latter is basically the improvement of land by the addition of *fixtures*. *Occupancy* as it relates to acquisition of *title* is called *adverse possession*; as it relates to acquisition of an *easement*, occupancy is referred to as *prescription*. Transfer includes *voluntary alienation*, such as a deed, or *involuntary alienation*, such as bankruptcy or an execution sale. Transfer can be made through a variety of methods, including private grant, public grant, dedication, eminent domain (or condemnation), escheat, execution sale, tax sale, mortgage or trust deed foreclosure sale, bankruptcy proceedings, abandonment, and forfeiture. A chart illustrating the several methods of acquisition and transfer of real property is shown as Figure 3.1.

The discussion that follows emphasizes deeds since this method of transfer is most frequently encountered. Also, for comparative purposes, we'll introduce a *bill of sale*, which is the document used to transfer tangible personal property, such as furniture, tools, and typical yard sale items. An *installment land sales contract* will transfer the *equitable* title to the buyer when duly executed, and will be discussed in Chapter 4, along with options to buy and preemptive rights (right of first refusal).

DEEDS AS A PRINCIPAL METHOD OF TRANSFER

There are a number of different types of deeds (See Figure 3.2), but basically the grant deed and the quitclaim deed are the forms of deeds ordinarily used in California. They will be illustrated later in this chapter. Printed forms of deeds are customarily used, with the blank spaces to be appropriately filled in by the person responsible for the preparation of the deed. Although from the illustration of various types of deeds it would appear that there are more than two forms in use, each one of these various types is either in the form of a grant deed or a quitclaim deed. The type of deed merely indicates who the person is that executes the deed, or, in the case of a gift deed, that no consideration was paid. Their use will be further explained as we proceed in the chapter.

Types of Deeds

Grant Deeds. The Civil Code provides that by the use of the word "grant" in any conveyance of real property, certain covenants, or warranties, are *implied* unless the deed provides to the contrary. These covenants are:

1. That the grantor has not previously conveyed the property or any interest therein to any other person
2. That the property is free from encumbrances made or permitted by the grantor or any person claiming under the grantor.

The warranty does not assure title or assure that the property is unencumbered; it relates to what

the *grantor* may have done with the property during the time he or she was the owner.

The grant deed has an additional distinguishing characteristic: it conveys the grantor's *after-acquired title*, unless a different intent is expressed. An example of this would be a situation in which a party conveys a parcel by grant deed before he or she actually acquires title. When the person does acquire title, it would immediately be transferred by the grant deed made earlier, and it would not be necessary for the grantee to obtain another deed.

In order to have a valid deed, in addition to the requirement of a written instrument, there are seven minimum requisites:

1. Competent grantor
2. Grantee capable of acquiring title
3. Operative words of conveyance, such as the word "grant"
4. Sufficient legal description (see Chapter 2)
5. Execution by the grantor
6. Delivery to the grantee
7. Acceptance by the grantee.

The only description needed is the legal description; this will be sufficient to transfer title to the improvements, water rights, minerals, and everything that is deemed to be real property, to the extent owned by the grantor. Although not essential, the street address can be used in addition to the legal description where the property is improved.

A form of individual grant deed appears in Figure 3.3. The circled numbers indicate those portions which should be filled in, as follows:

1. Insert name of person requesting recording. Often this is the title company.
2. Name and address of the person to receive deed after recording. Ordinarily this is the grantee. Tax statements will be mailed to that person unless otherwise shown.
3. Amount of documentary transfer tax is shown here. (This subject will be considered later in the chapter.)
4. Name of grantor appears here. Name should be shown the same way as grantor took title. If grantor's name has since been changed, new name should be shown, followed by the phrase "who acquired title as __(old name)__." If grantors are husband and wife, full name of each should be shown, not "John and Mary Smith." It is advisable to show status of grantor.

Figure 3.1
Methods of Acquisition and Transfer

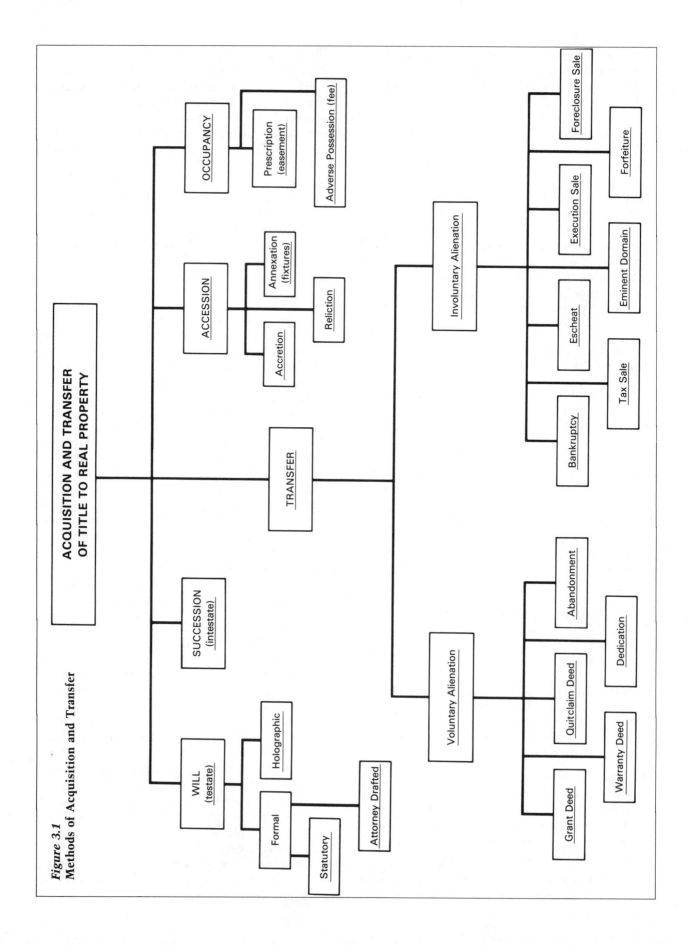

Figure 3.2
Types of Deeds

5. Name of grantee to be inserted here. Status and tenure of title should be shown.
6. Insert name of city if property is located in city limits.
7. Insert name of county where property is located.
8. Legal description is inserted here, with any exceptions or reservations to be shown. If property is improved, street address can be shown by language such as "which property is commonly known as 1234 First Avenue, [city], California."
9. If the conveyance is to be made subject to a mortgage, deed of trust or other encumbrance, an appropriate clause can be inserted here. Also, a recital showing the purpose of the deed can be inserted, such as, "The purpose of this deed is to terminate that certain joint tenancy created by. . . ."
10. The date when the deed is signed by the grantor should be inserted here. If a date isn't shown, it will be presumed that the deed was executed on the date it was acknowledged.
11. This is the place where the grantor or grantors sign.
12. This is filled in by the notary or other person taking the acknowledgment. The notary signs his or her name where shown, and affixes the notorial seal.

As a general rule, *consideration* is not essential; however, in certain types of conveyances, such as a deed by a guardian or an executor or a trustee or a governmental agency, consideration

is required. A *date* is not essential although recommended. An acknowledgment is not a prerequisite. However, if the deed is to be recorded, as is customary, then it must be acknowledged or proved. An acknowledgment is usually made before a notary public. This generally means that the grantor has personally appeared before the notary public and formally declared (acknowledged) that he or she did in fact execute (sign) the instrument (deed). As proof of this fact, the notary completes the printed form of certificate on the deed, signs it, and affixes his seal in the manner required by law. The form of acknowledgment differs depending on whether the grantor is an individual (natural person) or a corporation, partnership, or some other entity. (A form of individual acknowledgment appears on the deeds illustrated in Figures 3.3 and 3.4.)

A date, although advisable, is not essential to validity, nor is it essential that the status of the parties be shown, i.e., whether married or single, or widowed, etc. Tenure of title, i.e., how title is to be taken, ordinarily is not required to be shown, although necessary to create a valid joint tenancy if that is the way the grantees intend to take title. (This subject will be discussed later in the chapter.)

Quitclaim Deeds. A *quitclaim* deed generally uses the following words as operative words: "remise, release, and forever quitclaim." In some cases merely the word *quitclaim* is used. No warranties are implied. It is customarily used to clear some "cloud on the title" such as deed restrictions that are no longer enforceable, or an unused easement. In addition to being used to remove a cloud on the title, a quitclaim deed is frequently used by a spouse to convey his or her half of community or joint tenancy property to the other spouse. Deeds by representatives, such as a guardian or an administrator in probate proceedings, or by a sheriff in an execution sale, take the form of a quitclaim deed. A form of quitclaim deed is illustrated by Figure 3.4. It should be completed in the same manner as the grant deed in Figure 3.3.

Trust Deeds. A *trust deed*, also referred to as a *deed of trust*, is a form of deed in that it conveys the owner's title to a third party, the *trustee*. This type of deed is basically a security instrument, such as collateral for a real estate loan. When the obligation for which the trust deed was given has been satisfied, the owner of the property is entitled to a *deed of reconveyance*. If a default

Figure 3.3
Individual Grant Deed

RECORDING REQUESTED BY

①

AND WHEN RECORDED MAIL THIS DEED AND, UNLESS
OTHERWISE SHOWN BELOW, MAIL TAX STATEMENTS TO

NAME

STREET
ADDRESS   ②

CITY,
STATE
ZIP

Title Order No.............. Escrow No..............   This space for Recorder's use

GRANT DEED

THE UNDERSIGNED GRANTOR(s) DECLARE(s)
DOCUMENTARY TRANSFER TAX is $_____

③ ☐ computed on full value of property conveyed, or
    ☐ computed on full value less value of liens or encumbrances remaining at time of sale, and

FOR A VALUABLE CONSIDERATION, receipt of which is hereby acknowledged,

④

hereby GRANT(S) to   ⑤

the following described real property in the   ⑥
County of   , State of California:
                    ⑦

                    ⑧

⑨

Dated_____   ⑩   ⑪ _____

STATE OF CALIFORNIA
COUNTY OF_____ } SS.
On_____ before me, the under-
signed, a Notary Public in and for said State, personally appeared

⑫

known to me to be the person(s) whose name(s) is(are) subscribed
to the within instrument and acknowledged that........................
executed the same. Witness my hand and official seal.

Signature _____   (Space above for official notarial seal)

MAIL TAX STATEMENTS TO PARTY SHOWN ON FOLLOWING LINE; IF NO PARTY SO SHOWN, MAIL AS DIRECTED ABOVE

_____   _____   _____
      Name   Street Address   City & State

Figure 3.4
Individual Quitclaim Deed

RECORDING REQUESTED BY

AND WHEN RECORDED MAIL TO

Name

Street
Address

City &
State

MAIL TAX STATEMENTS TO

Name

Street
Address

City &
State

SPACE ABOVE THIS LINE FOR RECORDER'S USE

Quitclaim Deed

THIS FORM FURNISHED BY COMMONWEALTH LAND TITLE COMPANY

The undersigned grantor(s) declare(s):
Documentary transfer tax is $ _____
(   ) computed on full value of property conveyed, or
(   ) computed on full value less value of liens and encumbrances remaining at time of sale.
(   ) Unincorporated area: (   ) City of _____ , and

FOR A VALUABLE CONSIDERATION, receipt of which is hereby acknowledged,

hereby REMISE(S), RELEASE(S) AND FOREVER QUITCLAIM(S) to

the following described real property in the   county of
state of California:

Dated _____

STATE OF CALIFORNIA
COUNTY OF_____ }SS.
On _____ before me, the under-
signed, a Notary Public in and for said State, personally appeared
_____
_____
_____, known to me
to be the person____whose name____ subscribed to the within
instrument and acknowledged that_____executed the same.
WITNESS my hand and official seal.

Signature _____

Name (Typed or Printed)
*If executed by a Corporation the Corporation Form
of Acknowledgment must be used.*

(This area for official notarial seal)

Title Order No._____   Escrow or Loan No._____

CLT-D29(11/75)   MAIL TAX STATEMENTS AS DIRECTED ABOVE

occurred and the trustee were to sell the property at a trustee's sale, a *trustee's deed* would be issued to the buyer. Or if the owner of the property willingly gives up his interest to a beneficiary under the trust deed after a default occurs, then the owner would execute a *deed in lieu of foreclosure*. (The use of such documents will be considered further in Chapter 7.)

Other Deeds. A *sheriff's deed* is a deed given to the purchaser at an execution sale after the owner's redemption period has expired.

A *commissioner's deed* is a deed given in court proceedings by a court-appointed official, called a commissioner, to effect a sale of property, such as an action to foreclose a deed of trust by judicial foreclosure (instead of a foreclosure by trustee's sale) or a partition action.

Other Conveyancing Instruments

Bills of Sale. In the sale of residential property, the buyer may want to acquire some of the seller's personal property, such as furniture and furnishings. The document used to effect a transfer of such personal property is called a *bill of sale*, illustrated by Figure 3.5. Included with the illustration is a completion guide. A bill of sale transfers title to tangible personal property, whereas intangible personal property is transferred by a document called an *assignment*, discussed below.

Assignments. This is a type of document that may also be encountered in connection with a conveyance of real property; for example, of water stock. In the sale and purchase of city or suburban residential property, water for domestic use, along with other utilities, is generally supplied by the municipality; the availability of water is taken for granted. Throughout the state, however, there are areas, many of which are well planned and often improved with costly homes, that look to privately owned water companies for their supply of this essential commodity.

A mutual water company is a private corporation authorized under its bylaws to issue shares of water stock. These companies are sometimes organized as part of a tract development plan, with the shares issued to purchasers of a lot and the cost often being included in the purchase price of the lot. A *certificate of stock* is issued to the original purchaser evidencing his ownership of a certain number of capital shares of stock in the water company. To cover the operating expenses of the company, the property owner will generally be billed by the company for the water he uses. However, if these revenues are insufficient, or if special improvements are voted by the directors (elected by the stockholders), additional assessments may be levied. Such assessments, if unpaid, become a lien on the stock, not on the land.

Sometimes the stock certificate recites that the stock is appurtenant to a given parcel of land, and that it entitles the owner of the stock to water for use only on the parcel described. Such stock is transferable only with a transfer of the land. In other instances, the water stock may be sold separately from the land. In either case, when the water stock is to be transferred, the certificate must be surrendered to the water company with an *assignment* from the owners. The water company then transfers the ownership of the stock on its books and issues a new certificate to the purchaser. Generally, a charge is made for the transfer of the stock and the issuance of the new certificate; the water company usually requires also that all assessments and water bills be paid prior to the transfer.

Installment Land Sales Contracts. A real property sales contract, or *installment sales contract*, is an instrument by which the owner agrees to convey legal title to real property to a buyer after the buyer has complied with the terms of the contract. Such a contract is most popularly referred to as a "land contract."

The word *land* in the contract comes from the days when such contracts were used to sell raw and unimproved land and did not have much use in any other sale of real estate. Under the terms of such a contract, the buyer makes periodic payments over a specified length of time; when he or she has completed the obligation, he or she is entitled to a deed. Although *legal title* does not pass to the buyer until a deed has been delivered, the execution and delivery of the contract of sale will effect an *equitable transfer* of title, whereby the seller retains the legal title for security purposes, but the equitable title passes to the buyer. The purchaser may be able to encumber his or her contract interest, or transfer it, or declare a homestead on it, etc. The contract of sale will be considered further in Chapter 4, where an "Agreement for Sale of Real Estate" is illustrated in Figure 4.6 in connection with contracts.

Since it is also a financing vehicle as well as a contract for sale of real property, this topic will be covered again in Chapter 7.

Figure 3.5
Bill of Sale

BILL OF SALE

By delivery of this Bill of Sale, Seller,   ①

ratifies the fact of transfer of title to Buyer,   ②

of that personal property and goods identified as: ③

And warrants that title so conveyed is good, and its transfer rightful, and that the goods are free of any security

interest, lien or encumbrance of which Buyer, at the time of contracting had no knowledge.

Signed:_____④_____, 19_____

_____⑤_____

_____⑥_____

L-284 (G.S.) 6-69

1. Insert name of seller.
2. Insert name of buyer.
3. Include description of personal property sufficient to identify (show size, make, model, age, number, etc.).
4. Insert date.
5. Insert signature of seller.
6. Insert name of city.

Options. An option to purchase is a right given by a property owner to another party, called the optionee, to buy the property upon specific terms within a specified period of time. The option differs from other contracts in that the optionee can compel performance by exercising the option, but the owner of the property does not have the right to compel exercise of the option. Of course, once the option is exercised, contract rights arise in favor of both parties. The option itself does not result in a transfer of title until the option is exercised. Options to buy are often encountered in long-term leases.

An option to purchase is distinguishable from a *right of preemption* or right of first refusal. An option creates in the optionee a power to compel the owner of the property to sell it at a stipulated price, whether or not the owner at that time is willing to part with ownership. On the other hand, a right of preemption does not include the power to compel an unwilling owner to sell; it merely requires the owner, *when and if he decides to sell*, to offer the property first to the person entitled to the preemption at the stipulated price.

Patents. As mentioned in Chapter 1, where title is in the United States and a transfer is to be made to a private person pursuant to legislative authority, a patent is used instead of a deed. Most land in private ownership in California has a patent as its original source of title. A form of patent is shown in Figure 3.6.

USE OF A POWER OF ATTORNEY

Many transfers of real property are made by an attorney-in-fact subject to a power of attorney. Prior to World War II a power of attorney was not often encountered. But with military service, thousands of young people found it necessary to do business far from home. They had to sell, mortgage, or lease all kinds of property—houses, farms, cars, refrigerators, household goods, and so on. A document called a *power of attorney* made it possible for them to conduct their business back home while they were overseas.

A power of attorney is an instrument whereby one person, called the *principal*, authorizes another person, called the *attorney-in-fact*, to act as his or her agent. The attorney-in-fact is not necessarily an attorney. He or she may be a relative, a spouse, or any other qualified person. The powers granted are determined by the terms of the instrument itself, which may be either a *general* or a *special* power of attorney. Under a general power of attorney, the agent is authorized to transact all business on behalf of the principal or "do all things that the principal could do if present in person," including the transfer and conveyance of real property. Under a special power of attorney, the agent's acts are generally limited to those specified in the language of the particular instrument; for example, the attorney-in-fact may be authorized to convey only a particular parcel of land or enter into only a specific type of contract.

An attorney-in-fact is limited by law from doing certain acts. He or she is prohibited from making a gift deed; from making a deed, mortgage, or release without a valuable consideration; from conveying or mortgaging property on which a declaration of homestead has been recorded; from dealing with the principal's property for his or her own benefit; from deeding the property to himself or herself; from releasing any mortgage made by himself or herself to his principal; from mortgaging the principal's property to himself or herself; and so on.

For the purpose of dealing with real property, the power of attorney must be acknowledged and recorded. If a recorded power of attorney is later revoked, the revocation must be recorded in the same office where the power was originally recorded. Otherwise the power of attorney may stay in effect. A form of general power of attorney is illustrated in Figure 3.7.

For a long time the authority of an attorney-in-fact was terminated if the principal became mentally incapacitated. California has now adopted the Uniform Durable Power of Attorney Act under which a *durable* power of attorney may be created. Such a power is not affected by the principal's subsequent incapacity. Also, a form of *springing power of attorney* can be used which doesn't take effect unless and until the principal is no longer able to handle his or her own affairs because of lack of mental capacity.

DOCUMENTARY TRANSFER TAX

In almost all sales of real estate, the State of California, through the agency of the 58 counties, imposes a documentary transfer tax. Such taxes are imposed upon the net taxable equity of the property transferred at the rate of $.55 per $500

Figure 3.6
Patent

THE UNITED STATES OF AMERICA,

To all to whom these presents shall come, Greeting:

Certificate
No. 1450

Whereas *David Anderson of Los Angeles County California*
has deposited in the General Land Office of the United States a Certificate of the Register of the Land Office at *Los Angeles, California*
whereby it appears that full payment has been made by the said *David Anderson*
according to the provisions of the Act of Congress of the 24th of April, 1820, entitled "An Act making further provision for the sale of the Public Lands," and the
acts supplemental thereto, for *the lot numbered four of section six in township two south of range*
eight west of San Bernardino Meridian in California, containing thirty
nine acres and thirtytwo hundredths of an acre

according to the Official Plat of the Survey of the said Lands, returned to the General Land Office by the Surveyor General, which said Tract has been purchased
by the said *David Anderson*

Now know ye, That the United States of America, in consideration of the premises, and in conformity with the several Acts of Congress in such case made
and provided, **have given and granted,** and by these presents **do give and grant,** unto the said *David Anderson*
and to *his* heirs, the said Tract above described: **To have and to hold** the same, together with all the rights, privileges, immunities, and appurtenances,
of whatsoever nature thereunto belonging, unto the said *David Anderson* and to *his*
heirs and assigns forever; subject to any vested and accrued water rights for mining, agricultural, manufacturing, or other purposes, and rights to ditches and reservoirs used
in connection with such water rights, as may be recognized and acknowledged by the local customs, laws, and decisions of courts, and also subject to the right of the proprietor
of a vein or lode to extract and remove his ore therefrom, should the same be found to penetrate or intersect the premises hereby granted, as provided by law; and there reserved from the lands hereby granted a right of way thereon for ditches or canals constructed by the authority of the United States.

In testimony whereof, I, *Benjamin Harrison*, President of the United States of America, have caused these
letters to be made Patent, and the Seal of the General Land Office to be hereunto affixed.

Given under my hand, at the City of Washington, the *twenty-third* day of *September*, in the year of our Lord one thousand
eight hundred and *eighty nine*, and of the Independence of the United States the one hundred and *fourteenth*.

BY THE PRESIDENT: *Benjamin Harrison*

By *Ellen MacFarland Ast.* Secretary.

J. M. Townsend Recorder of the General Land Office.

Recorded, Vol. *4*, Page *490*

Figure 3.7 **Power of Attorney**

RECORDING REQUESTED BY

AND WHEN RECORDED MAIL TO

Name

Street
Address

City &
State

——— SPACE ABOVE THIS LINE FOR RECORDER'S USE ———

Power of Attorney
THIS FORM FURNISHED BY COMMONWEALTH LAND TITLE COMPANY

Know All Men by These Presents: That_____

_____

the undersigned (jointly and severally, if more than one) hereby make, constitute and appoint_____

_____,

my true and lawful Attorney for me and in my name, place and stead and for my use and benefit:

(a) To ask, demand, sue for, recover, collect and receive each and every sum of money, debt, account, legacy, bequest, interest, dividend, annuity and demand (which now is or hereafter shall become due, owing or payable) belonging to or claimed by me, and to use and take any lawful means for the recovery thereof by legal process or otherwise, and to execute and deliver a satisfaction or release therefor, together with the right and power to compromise or compound any claim or demand;

(b) To exercise any or all of the following powers as to real property, any interest therein and/or any building thereon: To contract for, purchase, receive and take possession thereof and of evidence of title thereto; to lease the same for any term or purpose, including leases for business, residence, and oil and/or mineral development; to sell, exchange, grant or convey the same with or without warranty; and to mortgage, transfer in trust, or otherwise encumber or hypothecate the same to secure payment of a negotiable or non-negotiable note or performance of any obligation or agreement;

(c) To exercise any or all of the following powers as to all kinds of personal property and goods, wares and merchandise, choses in action and other property in possession or in action: To contract for, buy, sell, exchange, indorse, transfer and in any legal manner deal in and with the same; and to mortgage, transfer in trust, or otherwise encumber or hypothecate the same to secure payment of a negotiable or non-negotiable note or performance of any obligation or agreement;

(d) To borrow money and to execute and deliver negotiable or non-negotiable notes therefor with or without security; and to loan money and receive negotiable or non-negotiable notes therefor with such security as he shall deem proper;

(e) To create, amend, supplement and terminate any trust and to instruct and advise the trustee of any trust wherein I am or may be trustor or beneficiary; to represent and vote stock, exercise stock rights, accept and deal with any dividend, distribution or bonus, join in any corporate financing, reorganization, merger, liquidation, consolidation or other action and the extension, compromise, conversion, adjustment, enforcement or foreclosure, singly or in conjunction with others of any corporate stock, bond, note, debenture or other security; to compound, compromise, adjust, settle and satisfy any obligation, secured or unsecured, owing by or to me and to give or accept any property and/or money whether or not equal to or less in value than the amount owing in payment, settlement or satisfaction thereof;

(f) To transact business of any kind or class and as my act and deed to sign, execute, acknowledge and deliver any deed, lease, assignment of lease, covenant, indenture, indemnity, agreement, mortgage, deed of trust, assignment of mortgage or of the beneficial interest under deed of trust, extension or renewal of any obligation, subordination or waiver of priority, hypothecation, bottomry, charter-party, bill of lading, bill of sale, bill, bond, note, whether negotiable or non-negotiable, receipt, evidence of debt, full or partial release or satisfaction of mortgage, judgment and other debt, request for partial or full reconveyance of deed of trust and such other instruments in writing of any kind or class as may be necessary or proper in the premises.

Giving and Granting unto my said Attorney full power and authority to do and perform all and every act and thing whatsoever requisite, necessary or appropriate to be done in and about the premises as fully to all intents and purposes as I might or could do if personally present, hereby ratifying all that my said Attorney shall lawfully do or cause to be done by virtue of these presents. The powers and authority hereby conferred upon my said Attorney shall be applicable to all real and personal property or interests therein now owned or hereafter acquired by me and wherever situate.

My said Attorney is empowered hereby to determine in his sole discretion the time when, purpose for and manner in which any power herein conferred upon him shall be exercised, and the conditions, provisions and covenants of any instrument or document which may be executed by him pursuant hereto; and in the acquisition or disposition of real or personal property, my said Attorney shall have exclusive power to fix the terms thereof for cash, credit and/or property, and if on credit with or without security.

The undersigned, if a married woman, hereby further authorizes and empowers my said Attorney, as my duly authorized agent, to join in my behalf, in the execution of any instrument by which any community real property or any interest therein, now owned or hereafter acquired by my spouse and myself, or either of us, is sold, leased, encumbered, or conveyed.

When the context so requires, the masculine gender includes the feminine and/or neuter, and the singular number includes the plural.

Witness my hand this_____day of_____, 19_____.

_____   _____

_____   _____

STATE OF CALIFORNIA

COUNTY OF_____ } SS.

On_____before me, the under-

signed, a Notary Public in and for said State, personally appeared

_____

_____

_____, known to me

to be the person _____whose name_____subscribed to the within

instrument and acknowledged that_____executed the same.

WITNESS my hand and official seal.

Signature _____

_____
Name (Typed or Printed)

(This area for official notarial seal)

CLT D-100 (1/76)

consideration, or $1.10 per $1000. Exceptions to the law include all transfers in which the consideration is less than $100. Any transfer by gift is excluded from the tax because, by definition, a gift involves no consideration.

To illustrate the law's application, assume that you are going to sell your property for $100,000, and that the buyer is to obtain a new loan. What is the documentary transfer tax liability?

$100,000	Sale price
– 0	Existing liens
$100,000	Net taxable equity
100	Number of thousands
$ 1.10	Tax rate per thousand
$110.00	Documentary transfer tax due

Note that the tax is due only on "new money." This is defined as the sales price less any *existing* loans to be taken over by the buyer. If in the above example there were an existing first trust deed loan of $32,000, the tax would be $74.80, computed as follows:

$100,000	Sale price
32,000	Existing liens
$ 68,000	Taxable equity
68	Thousands
$ 1.10	Rate per thousand
$ 74.80	Documentary transfer tax due

The tax is collected at the time the document is recorded in the county recorder's office, and an appropriate notation is made on the deed or on a separate paper if the party so desires.

RECORDING RULES AND PROCEDURES

Historical Background

In early times, the fact of one's ownership of land presented few problems. The person in possession of the land was the recognized owner as long as he could successfully defend his ownership against all others—by force, if necessary. Title to the land usually remained vested in one family from generation to generation, passing to the eldest son on the death of the patriarch of the family.

In 1677, England enacted the Statute of Frauds. Thereafter, title to land could be conveyed only by an instrument in writing. In addition to the deed from the seller, the buyer usually received a bundle of documents which included the evidences of ownership and transfers of titles from previous owners. This bundle of documents, known as a "chain of title," still prevails in England as the evidence of land ownership.

Although the American colonists used English law as the basis for many of their laws, the English method of using original documents to prove good title to the land was not practical. In 1640 the colony of Massachusetts enacted the first Registry Act. The resulting recording system (in some areas called the registration system) was later adopted in most of the other states, including California.

There were no registry or recording laws in California under the Spanish and Mexican governments. However, one of the first legislative acts of California as part of the United States was the adoption of a recording system. When California's first legislature met at San Jose on December 15, 1849, shortly after the first constitution had been ratified, it organized the state government, divided California into counties, provided for the incorporation of cities, and—to safeguard the ownership of land and facilitate land transfers—adopted the recording system. Basically the system was developed to protect against secret conveyances and liens and to allow property to be freely transferable.

Modern Practice

In the American recording system the public recording of a deed or other document gives *constructive notice*, i.e., notice implied by law as distinguished from *actual notice*, i.e., notice based on facts actually known to a person. All concerned persons are *conclusively presumed* (see Glossary) by law to have received notice of properly recorded instruments, whether or not these persons have examined the public record. A prospective buyer of real property is bound by any facts within his own knowledge relating to the property, and by any facts that can be ascertained by examining the public records. If the buyer doesn't examine the records, the law presumes that he or she has notice anyway. So a prudent buyer will not only look at the property to ascertain whatever facts can be found from a physical inspection of the land, but will also examine the public records (or have them examined by a title company or other expert).

The act of recording consists of the following procedures: Instruments to be recorded (along with the recording charges) are deposited with the county recorder in the county where the property is located. The recorder endorses the *time, filing number*, and *name of the person* requesting the recordation. The instrument is *copied* and then *indexed* in a set of books called the grantor-grantee index. Evidence of title or interest in real property is thus collected in a convenient and safe public place so that those planning to purchase or otherwise deal with land may be more fully informed as to the ownership and condition of title.

Following are some of the rules that apply to recording:

1. Instruments or documents that are entitled to be recorded are those affecting the *title* or *possession* of real property, such as a deed or a lease or a land sales contract, including those which are not technically instruments but which do affect title, such as notices under the mechanic's lien law, homestead declarations, etc.

2. The general purpose of the recording statutes is to *permit*, rather than *require*, the recordation of any instrument which affects the title to or possession of real property. However, certain documents are not effective unless recorded, such as a declaration of homestead.

3. Generally, there is no particular *time* within which an instrument must be recorded. However, time of recording may be very important from the standpoint of a bona fide purchaser or lender. Between conflicting claims to the same parcel of land, *priority of recordation* will ordinarily determine the rights of the parties. First in time will ordinarily be first in right.

4. A person who takes title with *actual notice* (see Glossary) of a previously executed though unrecorded instrument, such as a mortgage, does not benefit from the recording statutes.

5. *Possession* of land by a person other than the record owner will also give constructive notice of a possible claim of interest. As mentioned previously, a prudent buyer or lender will not only check the records in the county recorder's office, but also will make a physical inspection of the land.

6. An unrecorded instrument is *valid* between parties who have actual notice, but is rendered *void* as against a subsequent bona fide purchaser or encumbrancer who first records. The effect of the recording act is that a grantor has the *power* to defeat the first conveyance, because its existence won't show up in the records. However, this type of conduct is illegal, and the power to do a wrongful act doesn't give the person the right to do it.

OTHER WAYS OF ACQUIRING TITLE

Adverse Possession

Adverse possession is a method of acquiring fee title to real property based on hostile use and occupation of another person's property for a continuous period of five years and payment of taxes. If the use continues for a period of five years, but without payment of taxes, it may result in an *easement by prescription*.

In order to acquire title by adverse possession, five tests must be met:

1. The possession must be by actual occupation and must be *open* and *notorious*, i.e., it must be apparent to the true owner when inspecting his property.

2. It must be *hostile* (denying the validity) to the true owner's title.

3. It must be a *claim of right* or *color of title*. *Claim of right* means that a claim need not be valid as long as the claimant asserts a right to occupy the property. *Color of title* means that the occupant holds a deed which appears to be valid.

4. Possession must be *continuous* and uninterrupted for a period of five years.

5. Claimant must have paid all real property taxes assessed during the five-year period.

Adverse possession is not unique to California. Other states recognize title by adverse possession, the period of time varying with the laws of the particular state. A justification for this method of acquiring title is that it restores title to the tax rolls. The property otherwise would not be paying its fair share of the tax burden. Also, the property is being cared for, which lessens the chance that it will become an eyesore.

In order to obtain a marketable title, i.e., one that is traceable from the records, it is necessary for the claimant to bring a *quiet title* action against the record owner or his or her successors, and to record a quiet title decree in the office of the county recorder. This method of acquiring title is often encountered in cases where a nonresident owner cannot be found and the property is being neglected by the owner or his or her heirs.

Eminent Domain

Eminent domain (or condemnation) is the power of the government to take private property from individuals for public use, upon payment of just compensation based on the fair market value of the property taken. The state can take land from an owner only upon compliance with due process of law. Whether or not the owner wants to part with the land makes no difference, nor can the owner set his or her own price. A fair valuation fixed by expert appraisers is all that the owner is entitled to receive. However, because of the hardships involved, the trend today is to include, as part of the compensation in certain situations, such items as the refinancing costs in acquiring a new home, or replacement cost, or moving costs, and so on.

Land is frequently acquired by eminent domain for such uses as streets, highways, schools, parks and playgrounds, public buildings, airports and airport approach areas. The acquisition of property for freeways has been increasing in California. To explain the procedures and problems to the landowner, the State Division of Highways has published various booklets for the property owner with questions and answers concerning freeway land acquisition.

A type of condemnation that does not require the payment of compensation comes under "police power" designed to protect the public welfare. For example, if a building or other structure becomes unsafe or a menace to health, it can be condemned and ordered removed or destroyed. If, after proper notice, the owner fails to remove the structure, the government can do so. The cost of removal will then become a lien on the land on a parity with taxes and assessments. Such a lien takes priority over the lien of a previously recorded mortgage or deed of trust.

Dedication

Dedication is the donation or setting apart or the giving of the land by the owner for a public use. The dedication may be of a *fee estate*—land to which the dedicator has title and perhaps wants to see used as a park—or of an *easement*, such as a road.

There are two types of dedications: *common law* and *statutory*. Common law dedication requires that the landowner's *conduct* indicate an intent to devote land to some public use. The landowner's acquiescence can be shown by establishing open and continuous public use of the owner's land for a five-year period. Owners who permit public use of their property but do not

want to dedicate it can post signs saying something like, "Right to Pass Revocable at Any Time." In this way they establish their intent to give a revocable license, not lose their interest in the property.

Statutory dedication occurs under the California Subdivision Map Act when a landowner records a map, approved by local governing authorities, in which certain areas are expressly dedicated to the public use as, for example, streets and parks.

Dedication can also be accomplished by *deed* or by a person's *last will and testament*. In many such instances only an easement is transferred. This may be satisfactory in most cases. However, many local governmental agencies prefer to obtain the fee title rather than an easement so that they can still retain the title even if the public use of the dedicated property is abandoned at some future time.

Accession

Accession is defined briefly as the acquisition of property by its incorporation or union with other property. It may occur by the processes of *accretion*, *reliction*, or by *annexation*.

Accretion is the process of gradual addition of land bordering on a watercourse, such as a river or stream, caused by the action of the water in washing up sand, earth, or other such materials. The land formed as the result of accretion is called *alluvium*. Accretion is distinguished from *avulsion*, which occurs when a river, by sudden violence in a heavy storm, carries away a part of the bank and takes it to the opposite bank or to another part of the same bank. The owner of the land has a right to reclaim it.

Accession also occurs when land formerly covered by water is uncovered by the gradual recession of the water. This process is known as *reliction*. It frequently occurs with land fronting on the ocean. The added land becomes the property of the owner of the land to which it is added.

Annexation is the addition of improvements or fixtures to another person's land without an agreement permitting their removal. The things so affixed belong to the owner of the land. For instance, a tenant can fasten things to the real property of the landlord in such a way that they become permanently attached and part of the real property.

Foreclosure and Other Involuntary Transfers

Transfers of title to real property normally occur by virtue of the voluntary act of the record owner. However, there are a variety of situations in which title can be transferred involuntarily through the process of the law; in other words, title is transferred regardless of the desire of the owner. This is often referred to as *involuntary alienation*.

One of the most common methods is a *foreclosure* action. A person holding a lien upon property in the form of a mortgage or deed of trust may bring an action in court to foreclose the lien when a default occurs, and may then obtain a judgment authorizing sale of the property. After sale of the property by a court-appointed official, and after the redemption period has expired, a deed is issued to the purchaser. The deed transfers to the purchaser whatever interest the former owner had in the property at the time of the sale. In the case of a deed of trust, a trustee's sale may be held after proper notice. The purchaser of the property is entitled to a trustee's deed *immediately* following a sale by the trustee since there is no right of redemption.

An *execution sale* is another type of transfer by involuntary alienation. When a plaintiff in an action for money obtains a judgment against a defendant, the plaintiff can cause a *writ of execution* to be levied on property of the defendant, and the property can thereafter be sold by the sheriff to satisfy the judgment. A *certificate of sale* is issued to the purchaser at the sale. After the time for redemption has expired (one year), a *sheriff's deed* is issued to the holder of the certificate of sale.

Another type of sale that results in an involuntary transfer of an owner's property is a *tax sale*, where real property that is tax delinquent can be sold to satisfy taxes that are past due. A *tax deed* is issued to the purchaser at such a sale. This subject will be discussed further in the chapter on taxes and assessments.

Bankruptcy

Bankruptcy, still another method of transfer of title by involuntary alienation, is a proceeding initiated under federal law whereby an insolvent debtor may be adjudged bankrupt. The Bankruptcy Act is quite technical and complex. Basically, however, it involves the filing of a petition in bankruptcy, either by the debtor (voluntary pro-ceedings), or by the required number of his or her creditors (involuntary proceedings). The bankruptcy court then takes possession of the debtor's nonexempt property, liquidates the assets, and distributes the net proceeds, if any, proportionately among the bankrupt's creditors.

The primary purpose of a bankruptcy proceeding is to accomplish the following:

1. To satisfy the claims of creditors
2. To permit the bankrupt to acquire new property free of claims of former creditors to the extent allowed by the Bankruptcy Act. Once the bankrupt person has received a discharge in bankruptcy, he or she is given a fresh start, and perhaps the next time around will have better luck.

The effect of bankruptcy on title is this: title to all property of the debtor that is not exempt (such as under the California homestead law) *vests* in the trustee in bankruptcy, thus effecting a transfer of title by operation of law. If title is held by the bankrupt and another person in joint tenancy, bankruptcy severs or destroys the joint tenancy. The other person and the trustee in bankruptcy thereupon become owners as tenants in common.

Wills and Succession

An owner may dispose of his or her property by *will*. A will is commonly referred to as "a last will and testament"; it becomes effective upon death. The person making a will is called a *testator*. Persons over eighteen years of age and of sound mind have the right to make a will. When a person dies without a will, the person is said to die *intestate*, and his or her property then goes to his or her heirs in accordance with the laws of succession, subject to probate administration. The heirs are said to succeed to the estate of the deceased owner.

The three types of wills heretofore permitted in California are defined as the formal or witnessed will, the holographic will, and the nuncupative will.

The *witnessed* will is a formal written instrument, ordinarily prepared by an attorney, signed by the maker, and declared to be his or her will in the presence of two people who also sign the document as witnesses at the end. The witnesses are not necessarily aware of the contents of the will. They are witnesses to the fact of the execution of the document as a will, and of the mental state of the person making the will. Because of the reluctance of many people to have a will, especially one drafted by an attorney, the legislature has sanctioned the use of a *statutory* form of will which merely requires the insertion of necessary information.

The *holographic* will is entirely written, dated, and signed in the testator's own handwriting. No witnesses are required. Because testators frequently fail to use clear language or for other reasons, holographic wills often become invitations to lawsuits, and their use is not encouraged.

The *nuncupative* will was previously valid but is no longer recognized. It did not require writing or other formalities; it was an oral statement made in contemplation of death, and could only assign personal property up to $1000 in value.

Escheat

In the event a person dies without a will and without heirs, title to the property will *escheat* to the state of California. This is not an uncommon event. Unclaimed funds and abandoned property with a value of over $10 million have been received by the state controller's office in some years. This total has included unclaimed funds from more than 1,000 estates in California. Estates permanently escheat to the state if they are unclaimed after five years. The fact that an owner has died and that an estate is pending, with a possibility of escheat occurring, is given as much publicity as possible by the state during the period of the probate proceedings.

Abandonment and Forfeiture

Two other methods of transfer of title are sometimes encountered in title work: abandonment and forfeiture.

Although the fee ownership of real property technically cannot be abandoned, lesser interests can be, such as the interest of a tenant or lessee under a lease. *Abandonment* is primarily a question of intent. It is defined as the voluntary giving up of a thing by the owner because he or she no longer desires to possess it or to assert any right or dominion over it. It is the relinquishment of a right or the giving up of something to which one is entitled.

Forfeiture is the loss of property in consequence of a default. A forfeiture is distinct from an abandonment in that a forfeiture arises from the operation of facts independent of any question of intent, whereas an intention to part with ownership is a necessary element of abandonment.

Following are illustrations of ways in which an interest in property may be lost by forfeiture:

1. Breach of a condition in a deed, thereby causing the loss of *fee* title
2. Breach of a condition in a lease, thereby causing the loss of a *leasehold* estate
3. Breach of the provisions of a land sales contract, thereby causing the loss of an *equitable* title

A court proceeding is normally necessary to establish that a title has been forfeited; however, the courts look upon forfeiture with little favor.

FORMS OF OWNERSHIP

Ownership of property is defined as the right to the use and enjoyment of property to the exclusion of others. As we shall see in Chapters 11 and 12, this right is not absolute but subject to governmental control and regulations and also to private agreements imposing restrictions on the use of property.

In this section we consider *ownership* of real property—that is, how title may be held by one or more persons—and its consequences when there is *co-ownership*, i.e., ownership by two or more persons. You will recall in Chapter 2 (under the subject of estates and interests in land) that the number of owners is one of various ways by which interests are classified.

It should be noted at the outset that all real property in California must have an owner—either the government or private parties. Private ownership can be by one or more persons; either by *individuals* or *organizations*, such as corporations or partnerships. Title to property can be jointly owned, as is often the case between husband and wife. The way in which title is held many times is of vital importance, for not only does it affect taxes, but also management and control, disposition in the event of death, creditors' rights, convenience of transfer, and liability for repairs and maintenance. These and other aspects of ownership are explored in the material that follows.

Sole Ownership Versus Co-ownership

Property may be owned by one person only, referred to as *sole ownership* or *ownership in severalty*; or it may be owned by two or more persons, referred to as *co-ownership* or *joint ownership*. There are various forms of co-ownership in California, the most frequently encountered being *joint tenancy, community property*, and *tenancy in common*. In general, any two or more persons may own property as tenants in common. With certain limitations, any two or more persons may hold title to real property as joint tenants. Community property is another form of co-ownership, available only to a husband and wife, and then only during the period of their marriage to each other.

When two or more persons become common owners of property, then each person's ownership is subject to the rights, duties, and responsibilities of a co-owner.

A particular method of ownership is chosen for many reasons, including the following:

1. Relationship of the parties
2. Tax aspects
3. Continuity of ownership
4. Rights of creditors
5. Management and control
6. Individual responsibility and liability
7. Transfer of title
8. Homestead rights
9. Disposition when death occurs

TYPES OF CO-OWNERSHIP

Joint Tenancy

Joint tenancy ownership has been prevalent in California for a number of years, especially between husband and wife. The main reason for, and advantage of, joint tenancy is the *right of survivorship*. When one joint tenant dies, his or her interest vests in the survivor without the necessity for probate. In small estates, joint tenancies often offer advantages, particularly where the family residence is the most important asset, and where the husband and wife each intend that the survivor take all the property, regardless of other heirs. A married couple may also benefit from having a reasonable amount of money held in a joint tenancy bank or savings and loan account rather than in the husband's or wife's name alone in order to have liquidity when death occurs.

We can describe a joint tenancy interest as one

1. Created by a *single* will or transfer
2. Owned by *two* or *more* persons

3. Owned in *equal* shares
4. *Expressly declared* to be a joint tenancy

Four unities are essential to the creation of a valid joint tenancy: namely, unity of *time, title, interest,* and *possession*. This means that a joint tenancy *must* be created by the same instrument, at the same time, with each owner having an equal interest and the same right of possession.

The following is a sufficient expression of joint tenancy in a deed: "To A and B[add the status, such as husband and wife] as *joint tenants*." The following expressions are not sufficient for real property ownership. To "A and B jointly," or to "A and B," or to "A or B," or to "A and/or B." Most joint tenancy interests in real property are created by using a printed form of joint tenancy grant deed. The deed is similar in all other respects to the form of grant deed illustrated in the previous chapter except for the addition of the printed words "as joint tenants" after the names of the grantees. A joint tenancy can be created simply by filling in the names and status of the parties and otherwise completing the deed form. It is not necessary to show the words "with right of survivorship." However, in the case of personal property ownership, such as stock in a corporation, it might be essential, depending upon the law of the state of incorporation.

The following are some aspects a student of real estate should know about joint tenancies in California.

1. Ordinarily joint tenancy property is not subject to provisions in a will. The decedent's interest in the property passes instead by right of survivorship to the other joint tenant. The entire estate plan should be considered in light of this fact. Also, the mere fact that a person owns property in joint tenancy doesn't mean that he or she should not make a will. Joint tenants may die simultaneously (at the same moment of time, as in an airplane crash), in which event the joint tenancy property is subject to administration in the estate of each. Or, the joint tenancy may have been severed by a transfer of one joint tenant's interest in the property; either voluntarily, as by deed, or involuntarily, as by bankruptcy or by an execution sale. For example, if one joint tenant is declared a bankrupt, the joint tenancy is severed and the property is then vested in the remaining joint tenant and the trustee in bankruptcy (of the bankrupt joint tenant)

as tenants in common. And, as either joint tenant may end up being the survivor of the joint tenancy, each should have a will to direct the disposal of the property. Sometimes the survivor's death occurs a short time afterwards, with insufficient time to prepare a will.

2. Although joint tenancy may avoid probate costs and expenses, there may be other expenses in terminating a joint tenancy. The fact of death must be made a matter of record, either by a recorded affidavit or otherwise, in order to satisfy title insurance requirements; and evidence that no inheritance tax is due, or release of the inheritance tax lien if a tax is due, must be obtained. A form, "Affidavit—death of joint tenant," is frequently used to record the fact of death.

3. In a joint tenancy, usually there is no tax saving and, in many cases, taxes may be substantially increased. This is particularly true when a parent leaves to a child property that has had a substantial increase in value over its original cost. For capital gains tax purposes it is often desirable that the property go through probate in order to get a new tax base. The saving here can be considerably more than the cost of probate. Tax laws frequently change, which should always be taken into consideration when buying real property.

4. Your joint tenant, without informing you, may sell his or her interest in the property or even give it away. This act will prevent you from succeeding to the other person's interest in the property upon his or her death. Each co-tenant, whether a joint tenant or a tenant in common, may sell or encumber his or her interest in the property regardless of the knowledge, consent, or approval of the other co-tenants.

5. One joint tenant has the power to encumber his or her interest in the property without the knowledge or consent of the other joint tenant. However, a joint tenant interest is usually not considered attractive security for a lender. One joint tenant alone cannot lease a 100 percent interest in the property—it takes the consent of both. The other joint tenant, if absent, ill, incompetent, or uncooperative, may make it difficult to manage and maintain the property.

6. In the case of a joint tenant who disappears, i.e., becomes a "missing person," there is no adequate provision for handling his or her estate.

The question is often asked, "Is joint tenancy a substitute for a will?" or, "Should a joint tenant make a will?" To summarize, a will is essential for many reasons, including the following:

1. The survivor's will is effective to dispose of the property, and generally a joint tenant wouldn't know who the survivor will be.

2. The joint tenancy may be severed voluntarily at any time by a joint tenant.

3. There may be simultaneous death of the joint tenants, necessitating a probate for each estate.

4. One joint tenant may cause the death of the other joint tenant under circumstances which would automatically terminate the joint tenancy to prevent survivorship.

5. There may be some defect in the creation of the joint tenancy.

6. There may be other assets not owned in joint tenancy.

Community Property

Community property is a form of co-ownership between husband and wife which is recognized in California and a few other western states. It is based on the Mexican or Spanish law, and differs materially from the laws applicable in other states.

Property of a husband and wife in California is either *separate* property or *community* property. Community property is defined in the Civil Code in a negative way. It is defined as property acquired by husband and wife that is not separate property. Thus, we must know what separate property is. With certain exceptions, separate property is property of a husband or wife acquired *before* marriage, or acquired *after* marriage by gift. The statute uses the words "gift, bequest, descent, or devise," which means either a gift effective during the life of the donor, or a gift effective upon the death of the donor, either by will or under the laws of succession. The rents, issues, and profits from separate property are also considered to be separate property.

A husband and wife may enter into contracts with each other respecting property, and may alter their ownership rights. They may provide that property which is separate shall be community, or that property which is community shall be separate. Such agreements may apply to property presently in ownership by either one or both, and also to property subsequently acquired. The latter type is referred to as *after-acquired property*, i.e., property acquired by either one or both after the date of their agreement.

The basic concept of community property ownership is that husband and wife have *equal* interest and *equal* rights in property acquired after marriage and that such property is subject to the management and control of both the husband and wife. Neither husband nor wife has the right to transfer or encumber community real property without the signature of the other, and each one has the right of testamentary disposition over one-half of the community property. In the absence of a will, *all* of the community property goes to the surviving spouse.

A knowledge of community property rules in California is essential where married persons acquire an interest in real property because there are innumerable situations where problems may arise. Questions as to the character of the property are frequently raised in connection with actions for the dissolution of a marriage (formerly called divorce proceedings), and in probate proceedings where, for instance, a person may leave "community property" to the spouse and "separate property" to the children.

Many times husband and wife acquire property "as joint tenants" allegedly for purposes of convenience, but still regard it as community property. For purposes of marital separation, a single-family residence acquired by the spouses during marriage as joint tenants will be presumed to be community property, and set apart accordingly.

Tenancy in Common

A tenancy in common in California is defined in a negative way. It is created whenever an instrument conveying real property to two or more persons does not vest title in them as joint tenants, or as community property, or in partnership.

The important characteristics of a tenancy in common are:

1. Interests may be unequal or acquired at different times (unlike joint tenancy).
2. Normally there is no right of survivorship; the interest of a deceased tenant in common vests in his or her heirs or devisees.
3. As in a joint tenancy, there is an equal right of possession.

4. Each interest is freely transferable.
5. Ownership is of *undivided* interests—one tenant cannot transfer a specific part of the common land.
6. There is a right of contribution in favor of a co-tenant paying more than his or her share of taxes or liens on the common property.

When creating a tenancy in common, it is usually desirable that the deed recite the fractional interest that each grantee acquires. Following is an example:

> . . . to Benjamin Johnson, a married man, an undivided 1/4 interest, and to James Oliva, an unmarried man, an undivided 3/4 interest in the following described property . . .

Unless the deed recites the respective interest of each tenant in common, it is presumed that their interests are equal.

For title insurance purposes, the spouse of any married person acquiring an undivided interest must join in any conveyance or encumbrance of such interest, unless the interest is in fact separate property.

Tenancy by the Entirety Compared to Joint Tenancy

In some states, but not in California, another form of co-ownership is recognized, called a *tenancy by the entirety*. It is similar to joint tenancy, but differs from a joint tenancy in the following ways:

1. The owners must be husband and wife.
2. Neither owner can sever his or her interest without the consent of the other.
3. The interest of either owner cannot be reached by his or her creditors.

Corporations

Ownership of property may be by *corporations*, either domestic or foreign, private or public, or profit or nonprofit. A domestic corporation is one organized under the laws of the state of California. Foreign corporations are those organized under the laws of another state or country. A foreign corporation may own real property in California, or do business in the State, subject to compliance with the laws of California. Most corporations are private business corporations, organized for the purpose of making a profit. Since it is not a natural person, but an artificial being, a corporation may not hold title to property in joint tenancy. Nonprofit corporations are also permitted under the law and can obtain various tax benefits, and may own real property in California. A *public corporation* is a governmental agency, such as a municipality or other instrumentality of the government. Of concern when a corporation is an owner of real property is the authority to execute documents on behalf of the corporation. A special form of acknowledgment is used when a corporation executes a deed or other document. Other types of corporations may also be encountered, such as a *corporation sole*, consisting of a single person; i.e., the Roman Catholic Archbishop of a geographic area, and his successor in office, who is incorporated by law to permit ownership of property in perpetuity. Another type of corporation consisting of one person only is a professional corporation created under provisions of the income tax laws for the purpose of setting up an approved pension or retirement plan.

Partnerships

Property may also be owned by a *partnership*, which is a form of co-ownership, although title can be held in the name of the partnership as a single entity. A partnership is defined as an association of two or more persons to carry on a business for profit as co-owners. A partnership may be either a *general partnership* or a *limited partnership*. In a general partnership, each of the partners is liable for the debts of the partnership, whereas in a limited partnership the limited partner's liability is limited to the amount of his or her investment. Each limited partner also has limited responsibility in the management of the partnership. In order to qualify as a limited partnership, a statement of partnership describing the limitations must be recorded in the office of the county recorder in the county in which the partnership has its principal place of business.

Joint Ventures

Another form of co-ownership is a *joint venture*, which has characteristics of a partnership but is usually limited to a single enterprise, such as the development of a particular parcel of property. Unless designated as an unincorporated association, a joint venture (often referred to as a "joint adventure") is technically not a legal entity capable of taking title to or transferring real property in its name. The title is considered to be held by the venturers as tenants in common. A joint venture also has certain aspects of a partnership. Based on practical considerations, however, title companies have insured ownership in the name of the joint venture.

Unincorporated Associations

Unincorporated *benevolent*, *fraternal*, and *religious associations* and *labor organizations* can own and deal with real property to the extent necessary for the objects of the organization. Real estate syndicates and real estate trusts are included in these unincorporated associations. The association may record in any county in which it has an interest in real property a statement listing the name of the association, its officers and the title or capacity of its officers and other persons authorized on its behalf to execute conveyances of its real property.

Trusts

The trust form of ownership is often used, primarily for the purpose of providing for the comfort and well-being of another person. This is a method where title to real property (or personal property) is transferred by the owner to another party, called the trustee, who holds the title and manages the property for the benefit of another person (called the beneficiary) in accordance with the terms of the trust. There are two forms of trusts that are frequently encountered: the *inter vivos* trust (or living trust), and the *testamentary* trust, created by will. The living trust is effective during the lifetime of the creator, whereas the testamentary trust is effective upon the death of the one creating the trust.

Another form of trust that has proven to be popular over the years is the Real Estate Investment Trust (REIT). The REIT uses the funds of many investors for the purpose of acquiring real property. An REIT is primarily an attempt to combine the advantages of the corporate form of ownership with a single income tax status. REITs will be discussed further in Chapter 13.

MULTIPLE HOUSING PROJECTS AS STRUCTURAL DEVELOPMENTS

In the last few years there has been a dramatic increase in the number and types of multiple housing projects. They involve numerous co-ownership concerns and accordingly are dealt with here. Among the most frequently encountered types are condominiums, stock cooperatives, own-your-own apartments, and planned residential developments.

Condominiums

The word *condominium* has been used to define a form of real property ownership representing a combination of two distinct tenures: one being an exclusive or separate ownership and the other being an ownership shared in common with others. In its usual application, the ownership of a residence or apartment in a multioccupant residential structure is held in severalty while the ownership of the land, building, patios, balconies, swimming pool, etc., is held in common with other occupants. The composite of these two different tenures creates one ownership, estate, or interest, called a condominium.

Among the objectives of the condominium concept is the elimination of certain disadvantages of former programs by completely segregating all obligations, including taxes. The condominium involves a conveyance of the fee title to a particular residential unit, in addition to a proportionate interest in the common area. Units are conceived as cubes of space bounded by floor, ceiling, and wall surfaces. The common area, title to which is held by all owners as tenants-in-common, is ordinarily composed of the land together with all structural portions of the buildings, including plumbing, electrical pipes and conduits as well as all bearing walls, roofs, and foundations. Basically, only the enclosed cube of space above the surface of the land is separately owned.

Unlike the statutes in most states, California's condominium statutes were not intended to preempt or usurp the field governing multioccupant structures within the state. Rather, it was the intent of the legislature to enact and modify the law only as deemed necessary and desirable in order to create an easier working approach to this concept of real property ownership.

Essential Requirements of a Statutory Condominium. There are four essential requirements to the creation of a statutory condominium:

1. The interests created must conform to the statutory definitions.
2. A statutory condominium plan must be documented, consented to, and recorded.

3. A declaration of restrictions must be recorded.
4. There must have been at least one conveyance to a purchaser of a condominium severing the ownership of the common area.

Before considering the basic procedure required to create a statutory condominium, we should be familiar with the following words:

1. *Unit* means the elements of a condominium that are not owned in common with the owners of other condominiums in the project.
2. *Project* means the entire parcel of real property divided, or to be divided, into condominiums, including all structures thereon.
3. *Common area* means the entire project excepting all units therein granted or reserved to individual unit owners.

Duration and Type of Interest. With respect to the duration of its enjoyment, a condominium estate or interest may be (1) an estate of inheritance or perpetual estate, (2) an estate for life, or (3) an estate for years, such as a leasehold or a subleasehold.

Creation of Condominium. As stated above, in order to have a valid statutory condominium, a *condominium plan* must be recorded, which consists of the following:

1. A description or survey map
2. A diagrammatic floor plan
3. A certificate consenting to the condominium plan.

Regarding the description or survey map, the statutes provide that a project with two or more condominiums is a subdivision within the purview of the Subdivided Lands Law, discussed in Chapter 2. Accordingly, special condominium subdivision questionnaires must be prepared and submitted to the real estate commissioner. A public report must be obtained prior to the conveyance of a condominium. Condominium projects containing five or more units are subject to the same map filing requirements as are conventional surface subdivisions, under the Subdivision Map Act.

The diagrammatic floor plan should detail each unit in its relative location and must include approximate dimensions. The adequacy of the plan is normally tested by whether it identifies the units with sufficient accuracy for the purpose of a valid conveyance.

A condominium plan may be created encompassing structures already completed, or it may be created to embrace structures to be constructed in the future. The floor plan may thus be based upon an existing structure or upon an architect's drawings and specifications.

The certificate consenting to the condominium plan must be executed by all record owners of the property and by all record owners of a security interest in the property. This includes involuntary as well as voluntary security interests.

Transfer of Interests. Prior to the conveyance of a condominium, the owner of the project must have recorded a declaration of restrictions. The covenants, conditions, and restrictions contained in the declaration are those deemed necessary to the preservation of the legal concept of the project, to the management and maintenance of the common areas, and to the fostering of a harmonious communal environment. In the event that the project is to qualify for FHA financing, the appropriate governmental officials must be given the opportunity to approve the documentation prior to recording.

In conveying a condominium, care must be exercised in the preparation of the deed. The legislature has provided for a condominium to be conveyed by reference to the unit designation as shown upon the diagrammatic floor plan, in much the same manner that lots in surface subdivisions are conveyed. Normally, there are three minimum requisites for every condominium deed, as follows:

1. *The description must include an interest in the common area.* By statutory definition, the common area is presumed to be owned in equal shares by the various condominium owners. Essentially, the common area will be the entire project, except the units owned in severalty.
2. *A description of the unit or units to be acquired in severalty.* It will usually be sufficient to refer to the unit designations as they are shown on the diagrammatic map or on the subdivision map.
3. *The imposition of the declaration of restrictions.* It is the customary practice to incorporate and impose the declaration of restrictions in every deed by reference to the record of the declaration.

In summary, the nature of a condominium gives to each buyer in a multiple development an *undivided* interest in the land upon which the structure is built, and in addition gives the buyer a fee interest in a cube or unit of air space, i.e., the space or apartment enclosed by four walls, the lower surface of the ceiling, and the upper surface of the floor. Ownership of such dwelling unit is a *divided* interest, and if the structure qualifies as a statutory condominium, each owner is entitled to a separate tax bill and can obtain a separate encumbrance and a separate policy of title insurance covering his or her interest. Incidentally, the concept of condominiums applies not only to single-family homes, but also to office buildings, industrial parks, shopping centers, and other commercial developments.

Time Sharing

This form of ownership has received increasing attention, particularly in resort areas. Because of this, the law now requires that when there are twelve time-share ownerships or more in a given project, the subdivision act applies. Under time sharing, a person acquires the right to exclusive use of a unit in a condominium or other multiple housing development for a specified period of time each year, called an *interval*. In effect, each unit is owned by a number of persons, the number being dependent upon the number of time periods that make up a year. For example, if a unit is purchased on a two-week time share plan by twenty-six people, each of the owners has an exclusive right to occupy the premises during his or her two-week ownership period.

Stock Cooperatives

A form of multioccupant project often confused with a condominium is a *stock cooperative*. The latter is distinguished from a condominium in that the legal title to the entire project is vested in a single entity, which may be a cooperative association, a nonprofit corporation, or a cooperative housing corporation. An individual purchaser doesn't receive a deed, but instead receives a share of stock or a certificate of beneficial interest, with the right to occupy a particular apartment.

Such projects are normally financed by a blanket encumbrance constituting a lien upon the entire project. Heretofore, the real property taxes were assessed to the title-holding entity and were a lien upon the project as a whole. Now it is possible for the owners of stock cooperatives and other forms of multiple ownership to obtain separate assessments and tax bills.

The management of the title-holding entity is generally exercised by a board of directors composed of and elected by the owner-tenants. A disadvantage of the cooperative plan in the minds of some prospective residential owners is the fact that the purchaser has no evidence of title, such as a deed, nor does he or she have a land interest to hypothecate (offer as security) for his or her own mortgage—unless the lender is willing to accept a stock pledge or an assignment of the tenant's beneficial interest. Frequently, however, such stock or beneficial interest is subject to a prohibition against hypothecation.

Since the corporation or association is the sole legal owner of the entire cooperative project, it alone can mortgage the property, customarily under a "blanket" loan covering the land and the building which includes all of the living units. The corporation, being the owner, has the direct responsibility for payments on all encumbrances, which may include unsegregated taxes and assessments as well as mortgages. Thus, the purchaser in a cooperative project may be concerned about a possible loss of his or her investment through the foreclosure of an obligation arising out of defaults other than his own. Although each purchaser agrees to pay his or her proportionate amount of the mortgage and tax payments, the failure of any one to pay his or her share may result in a burden to be assumed by the other purchasers if foreclosure of the lien on the whole property is to be avoided. Hence, the reason for obtaining separate tax assessments. Increasingly, too, the trend is toward individual financing of individual units by each owner, occupier, or stockholder tenant.

Own-Your-Own or Community Apartments

These ventures are normally to be distinguished from a stock cooperative in that there is no single title-holding entity. The occupants usually own an undivided interest in the entire project, as tenants-in-common with the other owners, plus an exclusive right to possession of a specific unit or apartment. Each purchaser receives a deed describing his or her undivided or fractional interest in the whole project.

The control and management are generally provided for in a declaration of restrictions, which may also provide for maintenance assessments,

voting rights, and so on. As with condominiums and stock cooperatives, an association serves as a forum and governing body for the community apartment.

While the apparent intent of the own-your-own plan was to provide an arrangement by which purchasers could deal with their titles independently, the plan does not fully satisfy some prospective buyers. Although the purchaser can offer what he or she owns in the land and building as security for an individual mortgage, some institutional lenders have been unwilling to make loans on fractional interests.

Also, the advocates of these plans have not been able to segregate blanket encumbrances for the benefit of individual owners and lenders satisfactorily. Thus, as in the case of a stock cooperative, the purchaser of an own-your-own apartment could face a possible loss of the investment through foreclosure of obligations arising out of the other people's defaults on the unsegregated taxes and assessments as well as blanket encumbrances.

Planned Residential Developments

The ingenuity of real estate developers has been responsible for the creation of as many varieties of planned developments as there have been developers. These developments are designed to meet individual needs in areas of diminishing available land. Such projects have been designated by an equal number of names, such as "townhouse development" and "postage stamp subdivisions." Also called "PUD's" or Planned Unit Developments, this type of subdivision provides for high density housing, often with as many as eleven to fifteen or more units per acre. The more common form consists of separately owned parcels with additional parcels owned in common.

Usually, the commonly owned parcels are the areas or facilities shared and enjoyed by all residents, such as recreational areas. The management and control of the common areas is usually handled by an owners' association created in accordance with the provisions of a recorded declaration of restrictions, with each owner holding stock, shares, or a certificate of membership in the association.

Such projects are similar to a condominium in that the units are generally owned in severalty while ownership of the common area is shared.

Following is a list of the characteristics of planned residential developments:

1. Usually the boundaries of each owner's small lot coincide exactly with the limits of his or her apartment, which is in a building located upon several of these small lots.
2. A purchaser of any one such small lot acquires, in addition, title to that portion of the improvement located upon the lot (i.e., the apartment and that part of the structure enclosing it).
3. Side, rear, and front yard areas, which would otherwise be required for building setbacks under local ordinances, are usually pooled within large "green area" lots shown separately on the map.
4. Since these "green area" lots are designed for the common use and benefit of all residents in the development, and include within their confines the general landscaping, recreational and service facilities, it is customary that they be jointly owned.
5. Titles or ownerships in a planned residential development are vested in individual purchasers, much as in a conventional subdivision. Each such purchaser receives a grant deed describing a full interest in his or her particular lot (apartment), together with an undivided interest in the "green area" lots.

The difference between a unit in a planned residential development and a condominium is based on the *structural* characteristics of the two parcels: In a unit of a PUD (a "townhouse"), no one else owns an interest above or below the structure; therefore, the owner also holds title to the ground upon which the structure rests. On the other hand, a condominium may have individual owners living above or below each other, as in an apartment house, so the land under the structure must be considered part of the commonly owned area.

QUESTIONS FOR CHAPTER 3

Matching Terms

a. alienation
b. constructive
c. intestate
d. assignment
e. preemptive right
f. accretion
g. dedication
h. patent
i. deed
j. power of attorney
k. alluvium
l. forfeiture
m. common area
n. time sharing
o. unit

__j__ 1. document authorizing a person to act on behalf of another
__g__ 2. donation of land to the public
__h__ 3. document used to convey title from the United States
__n__ 4. interval ownership in a multiple housing project
__o__ 5. elements of a condominium in individual ownership
__m__ 6. elements of a condominium shared in ownership
__a__ 7. opposite of acquisition
__l__ 8. loss of property in consequence of a default
____ 9. document used to transfer title to intangible personal property
____ 10. to die without a will
____ 11. right of first refusal
____ 12. opposite of actual notice
__i__ 13. document used to transfer title to real property
__k__ 14. soil deposited by accretion
__f__ 15. process of gradual addition of land bordering on a water by natural means

True/False

T **F** 16. A quitclaim deed transfers after acquired title
T **F** 17. Four unities are essential in the creation of a tenancy in common
T F 18. A tenancy by the entirety form of ownership is not used in California
T F 19. A deed must be supported by consideration to be valid
T F 20. All deeds must contain a sufficient description of the property
T F 21. Recording imparts constructive notice
T F 22. Failure to pay a documentary transfer tax will nullify a deed
T F 23. A deed requires a competent grantee
T F 24. A durable power of attorney is not recognized in California
T F 25. Involuntary alienation of title to property is unconstitutional

Multiple Choice

26. A deed is not entitled to be recorded unless it is

a. acknowledged or proved
b. witnessed
c. verified
d. all of the above are true

27. A deed, to be effective, must
   a. contain a sufficient description of the property
   b. be signed by a legally competent grantee
   c. both (a) and (b) are necessary
   d. neither (a) nor (b) is necessary

28. Real property may be transferred voluntarily by
   a. quitclaim deed
   b. bill of sale
   c. assignment
   d. mortgage

29. Alienation expresses a meaning opposite to
   a. acceleration
   b. accretion
   c. acquisition
   d. conveyance

30. The following is essential to the validity of any deed:
   a. consideration
   b. description
   c. date
   d. all of the above

31. One who acquires title under a deed is known as the
   a. grantor
   b. optionee
   c. grantee
   d. trustor

32. Involuntary alienation of an estate means
   a. an estate cannot be transferred without the express consent of the owner
   b. aliens cannot own estates in fee simple in California
   c. ownership of estates may be transferred by operation of law
   d. a fee interest cannot be conveyed

33. Forms of co-ownership of property include
   a. joint tenancy
   b. tenancy in common
   c. community property
   d. all of the above

34. The unities of a tenancy in common include the following:
   a. time
   b. title
   c. interest
   d. possession

35. John is joint tenant with his brother Joe. When John dies, his interest goes to
   a. Joe
   b. his widow
   c. his children
   d. his parents

36. When a married person dies without a will, community property goes to the
   a. surviving spouse
   b. children
   c. surviving spouse and children equally
   d. parents of the deceased

37. Separate property consists of property acquired
   a. before marriage
   b. after marriage by gift
   c. after marriage by descent
   d. by any of the above

38. Severalty ownership of real estate means
   a. ownership by several persons
   b. there are several ways to own property
   c. ownership by one person
   d. property has been in several condemnation proceedings

39. Which of the following property is ordinarily not subject to testamentary disposition?
   a. community property
   b. a fee simple defeasible title
   c. joint tenancy property
   d. property owned as a tenant in common

40. The distinguishing feature of joint tenancy ownership is
   a. sole ownership
   b. availability to husband and wife only
   c. survivorship aspects
   d. unequal shares

41. A corporation can hold title to real property with another person in all except which of the following ways?
   a. tenants in common
   b. joint tenancy
   c. general partnership
   d. limited partnership

42. Certain unities are necessary to create a joint tenancy. These unities include:
   a. marriage
   b. relationships
   c. interest
   d. all of the above

43. The minimum period for obtaining title by adverse possession in California is
   a. twenty years
   b. five years
   c. seven years
   d. ten years

44. Escheat is a word meaning
   a. property subject to a mortgage has been released
   b. a fraudulent act has been committed
   c. property has reverted to the state
   d. an agent's license has been revoked
45. Ownership in an own-your-own apartment is
   a. in divided interests
   b. in undivided interests
   c. a restraint on alienation
   d. a violation of setback ordinances
46. Ownership under a statutory condominium is in
   a. divided interests exclusively
   b. undivided interests exclusively
   c. both divided and undivided interests
   d. neither divided nor undivided interests
47. In order to have a valid statutory condominium the following must be recorded
   a. a description or survey plan
   b. a diagrammatic floor plan
   c. a certificate consenting to the plan
   d. all of the above

48. Recording of a declaration of restrictions for a statutory condominium is
   a. optional
   b. mandatory
   c. illegal
   d. ineffective
49. If a condominium complies with statutory requirements, an owner may obtain a separate
   a. policy of title insurance
   b. tax bill
   c. encumbrance
   d. any of the above
50. Depending on the status of an owner, a unit of a condominium may be owned
   a. as community property
   b. as joint tenants
   c. in severalty
   d. all of the above are true

4
REAL ESTATE CONTRACTS

Practically every real estate transaction involves the use of at least one contract, and usually more than one. Probably no other phase of the law is as important to the parties entering into a real estate transaction as the law of contracts. It is essential, therefore, to understand the nature of contracts and to be familiar with some of the basic rules governing their creation and enforcement. In this chapter we will discuss the classifications of contracts, consider their essential elements, and become familiar with the impact of the Statute of Frauds and the Statute of Limitations. The use of common real estate contracts will be explained, as well as the ramifications of other contracts used in the real estate field.

Defined simply, a contract is an agreement, supported by considerations, between two or more persons to do or not to do a certain thing. Another definition of a contract is that it is a promise or set of promises for the breach of which

the law gives a remedy, or the performance of which the law in some way recognizes as a duty.

All promises do not create contractual rights. There are certain essential elements that must be present before a contractual right is created, which will be discussed later in the chapter.

CLASSIFICATION OF CONTRACTS

Various terms are commonly used to classify contracts. A contract may be either *express* or *implied*. In an express contract, the contracting parties create the terms and declare their intention in words, either oral or written. As we shall see, oral contracts are sufficient in some cases, but many types of contracts must be in writing in order to be enforceable. In an implied contract, the agreement of the contracting parties is shown by acts and conduct rather than words. As an example, you might enter a store, pick up a newspaper, wave it at the clerk at the back of the store, who nods, and you leave. There is an implied contract that you will pay for the item at a later time.

A contract may also be either *bilateral* or *unilateral*. A bilateral agreement is one in which a promise by one party is given in exchange for a promise by the other party. For example, "I promise to pay you $400 if you will promise to repair the roof on my house and replace all damaged tile

with new tile." A unilateral agreement is one in which a promise is made by one party to induce some actual performance by the other party but without the latter being obligated to act. If he does act, however, the party making the promise will be obligated to perform. An example of a unilateral agreement is the offer of a reward: a man offers a reward of $50 to anyone finding his lost dog Rover. No one is obligated to try and find the lost dog. However, if someone does find Rover and returns the dog to the man, the person returning the dog is then entitled to the reward.

A contract may also be either *executory* or *executed.* In an executory contract something still remains to be done by one or both of the parties. In an executed contract both parties have fully performed. This distinction becomes important, at times, in connection with an *oral* agreement to do an act where the law requires a *written* agreement. If the contract has been completely executed, then the fact that it was not in writing becomes immaterial.

Contracts may also be classified as *valid, partially void, void, voidable,* or *unenforceable.* A valid agreement is one that contains all the essential elements required by law and is enforceable by court action. A void agreement is not a contract at all; it lacks any legal effect whatsoever. An example would be an agreement to lease property for an unlawful purpose, such as gambling. A partially void contract would be one where only part of the contract is void and that part can be severed from the remaining part of the contract. Thus, if a person promises to pay $10,000 for the delivery of two kinds of goods, one legal and the other illegal, the contract will not be enforced since it is tainted with illegality in its entirety. But if a separate price was set out for each type of goods, then the valid part could be separated from the invalid part, and the contract then could be partially enforced. A voidable contract is one that appears to be valid and enforceable on its face, but is lacking in some required element, and can be voided by one of the parties if he or she so chooses. A contract by an incompetent person prior to an adjudication of incompetency is an example; a guardian appointed on the person's behalf could void the contract if he or she chooses. Another example is a contract induced by fraud; the victim can void such an agreement. An unenforceable contract is one that is valid but for some reason, such as a lapse of time, is not enforceable. *Statutes of limitation* impose a time period within which rights may be asserted in

court actions, and this could be a bar to an action on the contract. This will be discussed later in this chapter.

ESSENTIAL ELEMENTS

Under California law, the essential elements of a contract are as follows:

1. Parties capable of contracting, i.e., adult, competent persons
2. Mutual assent or consent (meeting of the minds)
3. Lawful object or purpose
4. Consideration

In addition, certain contracts, such as contracts to sell real property, must be in writing, as shown in Figure 4.1.

Capacity

Regarding the capacity of parties to enter into a contract, there are certain statutory limitations. Persons who may not enter into a contract include minors, persons of unsound mind, and persons deprived of civil rights, such as convicts, who lose their civil rights during the course of their imprisonment. A prisoner may, however, enter into an enforceable contract provided it is ratified by the California Adult Authority. Convicts do not forfeit their property or right to acquire property, such as by will or by inheritance, but they have a limited right to contract.

Figure 4.1
Elements of a Real Estate Contract

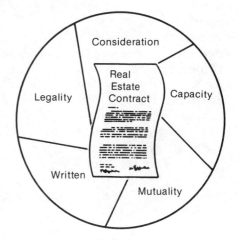

Parties Capable of Contracting

Minors. In California, a minor (unless emancipated) is a person under the age of eighteen years. Minors have not yet reached the *age of majority*, and their powers to deal with real property are severely limited. For a considerable period of time the age of majority was 21. The age of 21 still applies in connection with the sale or purchase of intoxicating liquor.

The Emancipation of Minors Act was enacted in California as part of the Civil Code. According to the *Real Estate Reference Book* (1984–85 ed., p. 119), an emancipated minor

> is a person under 18 years of age who has entered into a valid marriage (even though terminated by dissolution) *or* is on active duty with any of the armed forces of the United States of America *or* has received a declaration of emancipation by petitioning the superior court of the county where he or she resides. Emancipated minors have certain powers to deal with real property and are considered as being over the age of majority for certain purposes, including the following: to enter into a binding contract; to buy, sell, lease, encumber, exchange, or transfer any interest in real or personal property; and to convey or release interests in property.

Mental Incapacity. After a person's mental incapacity has been judicially determined, California law provides that no valid contract can be made with him or her until he or she has been restored to capacity. And if the person is "entirely without understanding," he or she has no power to contract and no valid contract can be made with the person whether or not he or she has been declared incompetent in judicial proceedings. In dealing with persons under disability, the usual procedure calls for the appointment of a guardian (or a conservator in some cases) and court approval of the transaction.

Both minors and legally-declared incompetents may *acquire* title to real or personal property by gift or by inheritance without having a guardian. It is only when their property is sold, encumbered, leased, exchanged, or otherwise disposed of that a guardian is required—or, in the case of an incompetent person, that another person has been authorized to act on his or her behalf, as under a durable power of attorney (see Chapter 3).

Intoxication. Intoxication of one of the parties to a contract may also result in a voidable contract.

If a person is so intoxicated as to be unable to understand the nature and consequences of his or her actions, or that he or she is unable to act in a reasonable manner, any contract made with that person is voidable. Slight intoxication will not necessarily destroy a person's contractual capacity, but neither is it a requirement for voiding a contract that a person be so drunk as to be totally without reason or understanding.

Mutual Consent and Assent

The next essential element of a valid contract is mutual consent, also called mutual assent. This is evidenced by an *offer* of one party and *acceptance* by the other party, and a "meeting of the minds" as to the terms and provisions of the agreement. The assent must be genuine and freely made. If it is clouded by such influences as fraud or mistake, the contract may be voidable at the option of one or both parties, depending on the circumstances.

The offer must express the offeror's willingness to enter into the contract. It must be *communicated* to the other party, and must manifest a *contractual intention*. Thus, under contract law a social invitation is not a legal offer which results in a binding contract when accepted; either party may change his or her mind. Nor is the usual newspaper or other advertisement an offer that becomes binding when accepted; it is merely an invitation to deal.

Basically, all essential matters must be agreed to before there can be a binding contract. Many times some terms of a proposed contract are left for future determination, or it is understood that the contract will not be deemed complete until reduced to writing, or there may be a condition that must be met before the parties become obligated to perform. In these situations there has not been a sufficient meeting of the minds for a binding contract to have come into existence. Such agreements are regarded as *illusory*. The courts may be unable to determine what the parties "mutually agree to" unless the terms of the contract are set out with sufficient clarity and detail. The offer must be definite and certain in its terms, and the precise acts to be done must be clearly ascertainable. In a contract for the sale of real estate, for example, there must be certainty and definiteness in the description of the property and in the terms of the sale, including the price and how it is to be paid.

Acceptance represents the proper assent by the offeree to the terms of the offer. The acceptance must be absolute and unqualified. If the acceptance modifies the terms of the offer in any material way, it becomes a counteroffer, and the original offer is terminated. Acceptance must be expressed or communicated. Ordinarily silence cannot be regarded as an acceptance of an offer, because the offeror cannot force the offeree to make an express rejection. For instance, if an owner of property sends a letter to another person stating, "I am selling the vacant lot I own on Third Street for $50,000 and unless I hear from you to the contrary, you have bought it", a failure to reply would ordinarily not be deemed an acceptance. However, silence may amount to an acceptance when the circumstances or previous course of dealing with the party receiving the offer place him under a duty to act or be bound. Acceptance of an offer must be in the manner specified in the offer, but if no particular manner is specified, then acceptance may be made by any reasonable and usual mode. A contract is legally made when the acceptance is *mailed* or put in the course of transmission by any other prescribed or reasonable method, for example, by deposit of a telegram for transmission. This is true even though the letter or telegram of acceptance is lost and never reaches the party who made the offer.

It is a fundamental rule that the offer and acceptance must be *genuine* in order that there be mutual consent. Principal obstacles to genuine or real assent are such factors as fraud, mistake of fact, mistake of law, menace, duress, or undue influence. If any of these obstacles is present, then the contract may be voidable and subject to cancellation or reformation depending upon the particular circumstances.

Lawful Object

The object of the contract is what the agreement of the parties requires them to do or not to do. Where the contract has but a single object and that object is unlawful, the contract is void. However, if there are several distinct objects, the contract is normally valid as to those parts which are lawful, and invalid only as to the unlawful objects. An object is unlawful if it is contrary to an express provision of the law, or contrary to the policy of the law, or if it is immoral. Since morality changes by judicial interpretation, largely dic-

tated by societal changes, it is difficult to define what constitutes "immoral" in contractual enforcement—it will be dependent upon the prevailing attitude of the particular period of time. Not only must the purpose of the contract be lawful, but the consideration must also be legal.

Consideration

Consideration is the price paid for a promise. In a contract the consideration may be either a *benefit* conferred upon the person making the promise, such as payment of money; or it may be a *detriment* to the person making the offer, such as a promise not to engage in a competing trade or occupation within a certain area, or some other act of forbearance, or a change in legal relations. Ordinarily the nature of the consideration is specified in the written agreement of the parties, although identifying the consideration in the agreement is not essential if consideration does in fact exist. The consideration must meet the test of legality. If the consideration required payment in contraband goods or performance of a criminal act, this would render the contract void.

A contract may fail if it lacks *sufficient* consideration. This means that the consideration must have some value, that it isn't worthless. Love and affection in some situations are sufficient considerations. However, when a person agrees to meet a purely moral obligation, there is not consideration involved.

Whether the consideration is *adequate* presents another problem. Adequacy of the consideration relates to value, and value is a matter of opinion. A person is free to contract on terms that he or she deems satisfactory. Thus, an option to purchase valuable property may be given in consideration of five dollars or some other nominal sum. However, if a person enters into a contract for the sale of land for a price that is substantially below market value, and thereafter changes his mind and refuses to sell and the buyer brings a court action to compel performance of the contract, the amount of the purchase price (or consideration) becomes important. The equitable remedy of specific performance will generally be denied unless the contract is supported by *adequate* consideration, in this case a price close to the fair market value. Also, under some circumstances, gross inadequacy of consideration may tend to show fraud or undue influence.

Breach of Contract

A breach of contract occurs when one party wrongfully fails to perform, which gives the other party a choice of remedies, as illustrated in Figure 4.2. When a breach of contract occurs, as a general rule the injured party is under a duty to take such steps as may be reasonably calculated to mitigate (lessen) the damages that he or she may sustain.

STATUTE OF FRAUDS

Contracts may be oral except those specifically required by law to be in writing. Any contract that the law requires to be in writing must be reduced to writing and signed by the parties in order to be valid and enforceable—regardless of how many witnesses a party has to an agreement. Such contracts are referred to as coming under the *Statute of Frauds*. This statute was first adopted in England in 1677; the principle later became part of the English common law. Subsequently, it was introduced in this country and has been adopted in California. The purpose of the statute is to prevent perjury and dishonest conduct with regard to certain types of contracts.

The types of contract that must be in writing to be enforceable usually deal with objects of considerable value or importance. The following are four common types.

1. Agreements for the sale of real property
2. Agreements for the leasing of real property for a period longer than one year
3. Agreements with a broker to find a buyer for a parcel of property and for payment of a commission
4. Agreements that are to be performed within a period longer than one year from the date of the contract

STATUTE OF LIMITATIONS

We have briefly considered the essential elements of a valid contract and the requirements of the Statute of Frauds. There are also many rules of law relating to the *interpretation, performance,* and *discharge* of contracts. These rules of law are ordinarily covered in business law and real estate law courses and need not be discussed here in detail. It will suffice for our purposes to consider one other statute that relates to, among other things, contract rights, i.e., the *statute of limita-tions.* If a person needs to go to court to enforce a right or redress a wrong, he or she must do so within a prescribed period of time. Actions can be properly commenced only within the periods prescribed by statute after the cause of action arose. The policy of the statute of limitations is to "aid the vigilant." The person who "sleeps on his rights" may find himself barred from relief by the statute of limitations. The amount of time given for redress depends on the nature of the action. For instance, an action to recover possession of real property by an owner must be brought within five years. An action for damages arising from a personal injury suit, such as assault and battery, must be brought within one year. The statute, based largely on public policy, takes as its premise that if a person has a just claim, he or she should assert it within a reasonable time. Stale claims are hard to prove or sometimes even harder to defend. Witnesses die, move away, forget; or evidence otherwise becomes unavailable. Basically it is a matter of fairness to parties involved in litigation.

The statute of limitations sets forth the *maximum* time limits for bringing a court action. In equitable cases, the statute of limitations may be shortened under the doctrine of *laches,* when an unreasonable delay in asserting a right would cause irreparable injury to the other party, such as purposely waiting to bring a lawsuit until after an important witness for the defense becomes unavailable.

COMMON REAL ESTATE CONTRACTS

As mentioned earlier in this chapter, a real estate transaction usually will involve a number of contracts. Because a *listing agreement* is usually the first type of contract entered into by an owner of real property who has decided to sell, it will be discussed at length, followed by an anlysis of a "Real Estate Purchase Contract and Receipt for Deposit" which becomes a binding agreement when duly executed by seller and prospective purchaser. Other types of real estate contracts frequently encountered will be mentioned later in the chapter.

Many of the contracts are known as contracts of *adhesion,* which is a printed form of contract, prepared by one party to a contract who is in a superior bargaining position, which the other party must accept without any modification. The other party must adhere to the terms, i.e., he or

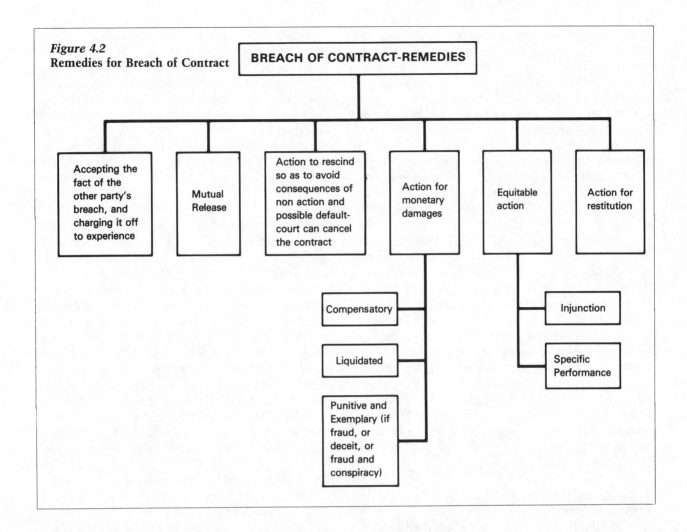

Figure 4.2
Remedies for Breach of Contract

BREACH OF CONTRACT-REMEDIES

- Accepting the fact of the other party's breach, and charging it off to experience
- Mutual Release
- Action to rescind so as to avoid consequences of non action and possible default-court can cancel the contract
- Action for monetary damages
  - Compensatory
  - Liquidated
  - Punitive and Exemplary (if fraud, or deceit, or fraud and conspiracy)
- Equitable action
  - Injunction
  - Specific Performance
- Action for restitution

she must either "take it or leave it." Any ambiguity or uncertainty in any of the terms in such a contract will be strictly construed against the party preparing the contract, and more liberally construed in favor of the other party, provided the latter's understanding or interpretation of the terms is reasonable.

There are several types of contracts of *sale*. The first kind, a form which we shall be analyzing later in the chapter, is a buy-and-sell-agreement that is intended to bind a bargain through escrow, at which time the buyer is entitled to a deed, and the contract is discharged by performance. The second kind is a long term installment contract where the buyer does not obtain a deed until sometime after close of escrow, depending on the exact terms of the contract. A third kind is basically a security device and has been used many times to avoid the consequences of an alienation or "due on sale" clause of a mortgage or deed of trust which the buyer desires to take subject to.

The latter type will be discussed further in Chapter 7.

Listing Agreements

A *listing agreement*, commonly referred to as a "listing," is basically an employment contract between an owner of real property, called the principal, and a real estate agent, authorizing the agent to perform services for the principal involving the latter's property. Listing agreements are normally entered into for the purpose of obtaining persons to buy, lease, or rent property. A prospective *purchaser* or *lessee* may also execute a listing agreement with a broker for the purpose of locating property for purchase or lease. A listing agreement must be in writing to be enforceable. To earn a commission, the broker must find a buyer ready, willing, and able to buy in accordance with the terms of the listing or with modifications of it that may be agreed to by the seller. Although there are several types of listings, basically they are either an open listing or an exclusive listing. The several specific types of listings used in real estate transactions are the open, exclusive agency, exclusive right to sell, multiple, net, and option listings. Following are brief descriptions of these most commonly used listings.

Open listing. More than one broker may have a listing under an "open" arrangement by separate listing agreements. The seller is obligated to pay a commission to the broker only if the broker or his or her salesperson is the first to procure a buyer who is ready, willing and able to buy the property on the seller's terms. This type of listing has no specific termination date and the seller can withdraw at any time. When oral, open listings are frequently referred to as back-pocket listings. Although this type of listing appears to be of great advantage to the seller, it is in fact not usually to the best interests of either brokers or sellers. The broker normally spends less time on it because of less of an assurance that he or she will be the one to earn a commission. They are generally used in the sale of vacant land that is located in more isolated areas. Putting a sign on the property and hoping prospects will show up at the office may be all the effort that the property is worth.

Exclusive agency listing. The seller designates a particular broker as the seller's exclusive agent for the sale of the property for a specified period, but retains the right to sell the property to a buyer procured by himself independently of the broker. If the seller through his or her own efforts sells the property, no commission is payable. However, if the property is sold by another broker, the broker with whom the listing agreement was made is entitled to a commission. By law, the agreement must contain a definite termination date.

Exclusive right to sell listing. One broker is designated as the listing agent. He or she is entitled to a commission if the property is sold during the period specified for the listing, regardless of whether the sale is made by the owner or another broker. The listing broker himself need not have procured the buyer. Also, the exclusive right to sell listing agreement often provides that, if the seller withdraws the property from the market, the broker is entitled to his or her full commission immediately, regardless of whether or not a buyer has been procured before the time of the

removal. Again, the real estate law requires that there be a definite termination date in this type of agreement.

Of these last two types of listing agreements, the exclusive right to sell is the most common and most advantageous for the broker. When entering into the exclusive right to sell, the broker should be sure the seller understands that the broker is entitled to his or her commission, regardless of who is responsible for the sale of the property.

Multiple listing. This is a type offered by realty boards having a multiple listing service whereby each board member agrees to refer listings to the other participating members through a central information exchange. Multiple listing is intended to give sellers a broader exposure in offering their property, and to give buyers a wider range of selection, thereby increasing the volume of transactions made and commissions earned by participating members. If the property is sold, the commission is split between the listing broker and the selling broker on a previously agreed-to percentage. Basically, this form of listing is a marketing tool, and is generally combined with an exclusive right to sell listing by agreement of the parties.

Net listing. The broker is entitled to receive as a commission any sum paid by the buyer in excess of a stated net price payable to the seller. Hence, this is actually a compensating tool rather than a listing agreement as such. If the property sells for less than the stated net price, then the broker is not entitled to a commission. Although the net listing is a valid contract, it is subjected to close scrutiny by the Real Estate Department. Use of the net listing is generally discouraged because it could give the broker an opportunity to take advantage of the seller and obtain a commission considerably in excess of the customary amount.

Option listing. Under prescribed conditions, the broker has the option to buy the property for his or her own account at a price specified in the listing agreement. The law imposes conditions in the use of an option listing. If the broker exercises this option and immediately resells the property for a profit, he or she must reveal to the principal in writing the full amount of the profit, either prior to or at the same time the option is exercised. The broker must also obtain the written consent of the principal approving the amount of the profit and make a full disclosure of all outstanding offers and other material information concerning the marketability of the property. The use of an option listing is generally discouraged, since it easily creates doubt as to whether or not the broker has at all times maintained the fiduciary role required in the broker-client relationship. (See Chapter 5 regarding the responsibilities of a broker to his principal.)

Preprinted Listing Agreements

Printed listing agreements are customarily used. Standard forms published by the CAR have statewide recognition and acceptance. The form, "Exclusive Authorization and Right to Sell," is illustrated in Figure 4.3. In using such a form it is essential, of course, that it be properly and completely filled in and properly executed in order that it evidence a binding agreement. In Figure 4.3, key provisions of the listing agreement are designated with circled numbers which are explained as follows:

1. The *type* of listing should be readily apparent, and the consequences of the use of this particular type should be explained to the principal. Better yet, the agent and the principal should read the agreement together point by point so that the principal has a thorough understanding of what it is he or she is signing.
2. The duration (time) of the listing should be specified with certainty. For instance, if an owner agrees to a ninety-day listing, it is important that the listing actually reflect termination in ninety days. The "exclusive right" and the "exclusive agency" type of listing must contain a definite termination date. If this is not provided for in the agreement, the agent risks disciplinary action.
3. The *description* of the property should be set forth with certainty, including the interest that is being sold, whether fee title or a lesser interest. The legal description may be obtained from the seller's deed or from his or her policy of title insurance. The tax bill ordinarily should not be used for this purpose. If the seller has previously sold a portion of the property or if he or she is selling only a part of a larger parcel, then an appropriate exception must be included in the description. The street address usually is given as further identification of property location. For more complete information, the type of property may be included, such as single-family dwelling.

In a suburban or rural area, the property may be difficult to locate by route and box number, but may be pinpointed by established landmarks and crossroads. If the property is subject to a mineral exception, it should be reflected in the description.

4. The *selling price* should be inserted in both words and figures.
5. The *exact terms* on which the seller agrees to sell the property should be accurately enumerated and described. Conditions or contingencies should be listed to avoid misunderstanding. It is the agent's obligation to make sure that the contract (listing agreement) is complete in all of its terms.
6. The amount of the *commission* should be reflected by writing, either as a fixed amount or as a percentage of the selling price; i.e., six percent (6%), if that is the agreed-to amount. The listing is an employment contract; therefore, the terms of compensation should be clear.

   Note in paragraph 3b that where the listing agent gives notice to the principal of prospective purchasers with whom the agent has negotiated, the agent may be entitled to a commission. This is known as a safety clause, designed to protect the listing agent who is the proximate cause of a later sale to one of those prospective buyers registered with the owner.
7. The *condition* of the title should be disclosed by enumerating matters to which the title is subject, such as covenants, conditions and restrictions, easements, rights and reservations of record. Such conditions are listed on the seller's policy of title insurance. Deed restrictions and other matters affecting use of property are discussed in Chapter 12.
8. Whether the *policy of title insurance* is *standard* coverage or *extended* coverage should be designated. The parties must agree on who pays for the policy of title insurance; local custom usually dictates the requirements here. (The subject of title insurance is treated in Chapter 6.)
9. The amount of the *deposit* should be indicated with certainty. Most standard forms of listing agreements specifically authorize the broker to accept a deposit from the buyer as "earnest money." If the broker loses or misappropriates the deposit, an express authorization to accept a deposit may place the risk of loss on the seller. In the absence of express

Figure 4.3
Exclusive Authorization and Right to Sell

EXCLUSIVE AUTHORIZATION AND RIGHT TO SELL ①
THIS IS INTENDED TO BE A LEGALLY BINDING AGREEMENT—READ IT CAREFULLY.
CALIFORNIA ASSOCIATION OF REALTORS® STANDARD FORM

1. **Right to Sell.** I hereby employ and grant _____
hereinafter called "Agent," the exclusive and irrevocable right commencing on _____ ② _____, 19_____, and expiring at
midnight on _____ ③ _____, 19_____, to sell or exchange the real property situated in_____,
County of __③_____, California described as follows:

_____
_____ ⑦ _____
_____

2. **Terms of Sale.** The purchase price shall be $_____ ④ _____, to be paid in the following terms:
_____
_____ ⑤ _____

(a) The following items of personal property are to be included in the above-stated price:
_____
_____
_____

(b) Agent is hereby authorized to accept and hold on my behalf a deposit upon the purchase price. ⑨
(c) Evidence of title to the property shall be in the form of a California Land Title Association Standard Coverage Policy of Title Insurance in
the amount of the selling price to be paid for by _____ ⑧
(d) I warrant that I am the owner of the property or have the authority to execute this agreement. I hereby authorize a FOR SALE sign to be
placed on my property by Agent. I authorize the Agent named herein to cooperate with sub-agents.

**3. Notice: The amount or rate of real estate commissions is not fixed by law. They are set by each broker individu-
ally and may be negotiable between the seller and broker.**
Compensation to Agent. I hereby agree to compensate Agent as follows: ⑥
(a) _____ % of the selling price if the property is sold during the term hereof, or any extension thereof, by Agent,
on the terms herein set forth or any other price and terms I may accept, or through any other person, or by me, or _____%
of the price shown in 2, if said property is withdrawn from sale, transferred, conveyed, leased without the consent of Agent, or made unmarketable by any voluntary act during the term hereof or any extension thereof.
(b) the compensation provided for in subparagraph (a) above if property is sold, conveyed or otherwise transferred within _____
_____ days after the termination of this authority or any extension thereof to anyone with whom Agent has had negotiations prior to
final termination, provided I have received notice in writing, including the names of the prospective purchasers, before or upon termination of
this agreement or any extension hereof. However, I shall not be obligated to pay the compensation provided for in subparagraph (a) if a valid
listing agreement is entered into during the term of said protection period with another licensed real estate broker and a sale, lease or
exchange of the property is made during the term of said valid listing agreement.
4. If action be instituted to enforce this agreement, the prevailing party shall receive reasonable attorney's fees and costs as fixed by the
Court. ⑪
5. In the event of an exchange, permission is hereby given Agent to represent all parties and collect compensation or commissions from
them, provided there is full disclosure to all principals of such agency. Agent is authorized to divide with other agents such compensation or
commissions in any manner acceptable to them.
6. I agree to save and hold Agent harmless from all claims, disputes, litigation, and/or judgments arising from any incorrect information
supplied by me, or from any material fact known by me concerning the property which I fail to disclose. ⑬
7. This property is offered in compliance with state and federal anti-discrimination laws. ⑫
8. Other provisions: ⑮
_____
_____ ⑩ _____
9. I acknowledge that I have read and understand this Agreement, and that I have received a copy hereof. ⑭
Dated_____, 19_____ _____, California

Owner_____ Address_____

Owner_____ City, State, Phone_____

10. In consideration of the above, Agent agrees to use diligence in procuring a purchaser.

Agent_____ Address_____ City_____

By_____ Phone_____ Date_____

NO REPRESENTATION IS MADE AS TO THE LEGAL VALIDITY OF ANY PROVISION OR THE ADEQUACY OF ANY PROVISION IN ANY
SPECIFIC TRANSACTION. IF YOU DESIRE LEGAL ADVICE, CONSULT YOUR ATTORNEY.
To order, contact—California Association of Realtors®
525 South Virgil Avenue, Los Angeles, California 90020
Copyright © 1978 by California Association of Realtors® (Revised, 1980)   FORM A-11   SALEMAN'S COPY

authorization, the broker holds the deposit as agent of the buyer, and the buyer bears the risk of loss; that is, the buyer would have to take action to recover the loss from the broker.

10. Where there are existing loans on the property, *loan information* should be precise as to amount, interest, and terms. It should include the current address of all lenders or loan-servicing agents, the loan numbers from the payment books, and any other pertinent information about the loan, especially if the loan is one of the alternative instruments described in Chapter 7, such as a Graduated Payment mortgage or a Variable Interest Rate mortgage.

11. If *attorney's fees* are to be payable to the agent in the event court action becomes necessary to collect the commission, the agreement must specifically so provide. Generally, it is provided that the prevailing party in a lawsuit will be entitled to attorney fees.

12. *Discrimination* in offering the property to prospective purchasers must be guarded against. The agreement should cover this, and the seller should be made aware of it.

13. If the agent is to represent *both parties* and collect a commission from both, an express agreement is required. The broker must disclose to each party the amount of compensation to be paid by the other.

14. The Real Estate Law provides that the licensee shall deliver a *copy* of any agreement relating to a real estate transaction to the person signing it at the time the signature is obtained. Failure to do so may jeopardize the agent's license.

Another form of employment contract, entitled "Exclusive Employment of Broker to Exchange, Sell, Lease, or Option," appears as Figure 4.4. This gives the broker much more latitude in dealing with the property.

Deposit Receipts

For a number of years brokers in California have customarily used a document commonly known as a *deposit receipt* when accepting "earnest money" from a prospective purchaser. The receipt constitutes an offer to buy real property according to the terms specified on the form by the prospective buyer. The deposit receipt is an extremely important document. It is not just a receipt for money deposited. When accepted by the seller, it is the basic contract for the purchase and sale of real property. Because it is usually the first evidence of a binding agreement between a buyer and a seller, extreme care must be exercised in its preparation.

Until a few years ago a more or less standard form of deposit receipt had been used for at least twenty-five years. After a period of extensive study and negotiation, representatives of the CAR and the State Bar of California formally approved a deposit receipt form entitled "Real Estate Purchase Contract and Receipt for Deposit" (see Figure 4.5) which is customarily used today. Because the deposit receipt, when properly executed, ordinarily results in a binding contract between a buyer and a seller, the rules of contract law apply: there must be competent parties, consideration, a meeting of the minds, a lawful object, and the form must be signed by both parties.

The standard form, completed with the aid of a licensed real estate agent, is ordinarily adequate for conventional and comparatively simply transactions. In complex transactions, however, the form should not be used without the assistance of an attorney, particularly when extensive riders or additions are needed. In this situation the attorney will normally prepare a hand-tailored document, perhaps patterned after a standard form, but designed to correspond precisely with the intent of the parties involved. The language used to express that intent must be absolutely clear.

Since you will be encountering the deposit receipt again in courses on real estate practice and real estate law, we will simply highlight some important points in the use of a deposit receipt.

As we saw with listing agreements, a printed form must be completed with extreme care. The utilization of a checklist, from the standpoint of both the buyer and the seller, will help ensure that all items of concern have been included. Every word printed on the form has meaning. The blank spaces also have meaning and should be carefully checked to make sure appropriate words and figures have been inserted.

The following list sets forth various items that need to be considered in the preparation of the deposit receipt. The circled numbers in Figure 4.5 locate these items. Items 1 through 19 constitute an offer to purchase, merely a bid, and therefore a unilateral contract until accepted, as explained in items 20 and 21, whereupon it ripens into a bilateral contract.

Figure 4.4
Contract of Employment Between Broker and Owner to Exchange, Sell, Lease, or Option

EXCLUSIVE EMPLOYMENT OF BROKER TO EXCHANGE, SELL, LEASE, OR OPTION
CALIFORNIA ASSOCIATION OF REALTORS ® STANDARD FORM

1. The undersigned, _____

(PRINCIPAL), hereby grants to _____

a licensed real estate broker, hereinafter called "agent," the EXCLUSIVE AND IRREVOCABLE RIGHT commencing on

_____ , 19_____ and terminating at midnight on _____ , 19_____ to advise, offer, solicit, and

negotiate for the disposition of the Principal's right, title, and interest, through sale, lease, option or exchange on terms

acceptable to Principal of the real and personal property described as follows:_____

_____

_____

_____

_____

_____

_____

_____

SUBJECT TO: _____

_____

_____

2. Agent is hereby authorized to accept and hold on my behalf a deposit from any offeror pending principals acceptance. No offer shall be submitted to Principal unless signed by the individual offeror or his authorized agent.

3. I warrant that I am the owner of or can obtain and deliver marketable title to the property described above. Evidence of title to the real property shall be in the form of a California Land Title Association Standard Coverage Policy of Title

Insurance to be paid for by _____ .

4. Agent may ☐ may not ☐ place a for sale or exchange sign on the property.

5. Compensation to Agent: I hereby agree to pay Agent a fee of $_____
upon any agreement for or transfer of title, during the term hereof or any extension thereof by agent, or through any other person, or by me, or if said property is withdrawn from exchange, sale, lease or option without the consent of Agent, or made unmarketable by my voluntary act during the term hereof or any extension thereof.

(a) If within _____ days after expiration hereof, or any extension thereof, Principal enters into an agreement with anyone with whom Agent has had negotiations prior to final expiration, provided I have received notice in writing thereof before or upon expiration of this agreement or any extension thereof.

6. If action be instituted to enforce this agreement, the prevailing party shall receive reasonable attorney's fees as fixed by the Court.

7. Agent may represent all parties and collect compensation or commission from them provided there is full disclosure to all principal's of such Agency. Agent may cooperate with sub-agents and may divide with other agents such compensation or commission in any manner acceptable to them.

8. Other Provisions:
_____

_____

_____

9. I acknowledge that I have read and understand this Agreement, and that I have received a copy hereof.

DATED: _____ , 19_____   _____ , California

_____   _____
                    OWNER   OWNER

_____
        ADDRESS   CITY   STATE   PHONE

10. In consideration of the above, Agent agrees to use diligence in the performance of his obligations.

_____
            AGENT   ADDRESS   CITY   STATE
BY _____
                                        PHONE   DATE

For these forms address California Association of Realtors,
505 Shatto Place, Los Angeles 90020. All rights reserved.
                                    EX-11   (Rev. 8-74)

1. The name of the city or town where the buyer signs should be inserted, together with the date.
2. The amount of deposit must be stated, and its form, whether cash, check, etc., should be indicated.
3. The total consideration must be shown.
4. A sufficient description of the real property is essential and, if personal property is included, this must also be described with certainty.
5. The escrow holder must be agreed upon by the buyer and the seller.
6. The terms of payment must be set out. To be enforceable they must be clear and concise, not vague or illusory. If all of the terms have not been agreed to, but are subject to later negotiation, the contract may not be enforceable.
7. Contingencies, if any, should be clearly set out, and should also designate the number of days for performance. Also, if there is a possibility the transaction will not be consummated because of failure to meet a contingency, the disposition of the deposit should be clearly set forth.
8. The condition or quality of the title should be agreed upon prior to execution. If all conditions are not known at that time, the buyer may insert a provision to the effect that his or her obligation to perform is contingent, for example, upon there being no prohibition against the intended use of the property by zoning regulations, deed restrictions, or other restrictions. This type of qualification may relate to other items as well.
9. The type of title insurance, the party responsible for payment, and the particular insurer should be shown. Selectivity in the choice of a title insurer can be very important, particularly from the buyer's viewpoint. In some sections of California it is customary for the buyer to pay for title insurance; in other sections the seller pays; in some areas they share the cost. In some cases the buyer may want to obtain, at his or her expense, additional assurances beyond that afforded by a standard coverage policy.
10. Items to be prorated should be spelled out with particularity.
11. If there are bonds or special assessments against the property, the party who is to pay or be responsible for them must be indicated. The matter of assessments can be a problem. The licensee should remember that special assessments do not ordinarily become a lien of record until bonds are issued to cover the cost of the work. Hence, they may not necessarily appear on the policy of title insurance, but often become a lien at a later time, and the buyer will be obligated to pay.
12. If the printed form refers to revenue stamps on the deed, as some still do, this should be changed to refer to the documentary transfer tax.
13. Careful attention should be given to the manner of possession. Any special arrangements should be spelled out with particularity.
14. The time of closing should be shown. Depending upon the information already available and the speed with which a report of title can be furnished, the time can be relatively long or short. A thirty-day escrow is customary, but there is no reason that a different time cannot be selected, depending upon the needs of the particular transaction and the condition of title.
15. The manner of vesting of title (for example, taking title as joint tenants) must be shown. A real estate agent can give *information* as to the various ways that property can be vested, but *advice* as to the way title is to be taken should be furnished only by an attorney for the buyer.
16. Risk of loss or damage to the improvements before close of escrow should be considered. Usually, risk of loss is to the person entitled to possession.
17. The effect of a default by the buyer and the resulting rights and liabilities of the parties should be covered. This is referred to as the "liquidated damages" clause, which changed in 1979 to provide for a maximum charge of 3 percent of the selling price for residential housing up to four units.
18. A time limitation for acceptance of the buyer's offer is often included in a deposit receipt. The number of days designated for acceptance is chiefly of psychological importance, as this receipt is not an option contract. The time period does not serve as a cutoff date for acceptance by the seller. Buyers and sellers should be aware that the buyer may withdraw his offer at any time before it is accepted by the seller and the acceptance is communicated to the buyer.
19. In the execution of the agreement by the buyer, it is necessary to obtain the correct signatures in addition to the signatures of *all* of the

Figure 4.5
Real Estate Purchase Contract and Receipt for Deposit

CALIFORNIA ASSOCIATION OF REALTORS® STANDARD FORM

REAL ESTATE PURCHASE CONTRACT AND RECEIPT FOR DEPOSIT

THIS IS MORE THAN A RECEIPT FOR MONEY. IT IS INTENDED TO BE A LEGALLY BINDING CONTRACT. READ IT CAREFULLY.

_____ (1) _____ , California. _____ (1) _____ , 19 _____

Received from _____
herein called Buyer, the sum of (2) _____ Dollars $ _____
evidenced by cash ☐, cashier's check ☐, or _____ ☐, personal check ☐ payable to _____
_____ , to be held uncashed until acceptance of this offer, as deposit on account of purchase price of
_____ (3) _____ Dollars $ _____
for the purchase of property, situated in _____ , County of _____ , California,
described as follows: _____ (4) _____

1.   Buyer will deposit in escrow with _____ (5) _____ the balance of purchase price as follows:

_____ (6) _____

_____ (7) _____

Set forth above any terms and conditions of a factual nature applicable to this sale, such as financing, prior sale of other property, the matter of structural pest control inspection, repairs and personal property to be included in the sale.

2.   Deposit will ☐ will not ☐ be increased by $ _____ to $ _____ within _____ days of acceptance of this offer.

3.   Buyer does ☐ does not ☐ intend to occupy subject property as his residence.

4.   The supplements initialed below are incorporated as part of this agreement.

Other

_____ Structural Pest Control Certification Agreement   _____ Occupancy Agreement   (16) _____   _____
_____ Special Studies Zone Disclosure   _____ VA Amendment   _____   _____
_____ Flood Insurance Disclosure   _____ FHA Amendment   _____   _____

5.   Buyer and Seller acknowledge receipt of a copy of this page, which constitutes Page 1 of **2** Pages.

X _____   X _____
  BUYER   SELLER

X _____   X _____
  BUYER   SELLER

A REAL ESTATE BROKER IS THE PERSON QUALIFIED TO ADVISE ON REAL ESTATE. IF YOU DESIRE LEGAL ADVICE CONSULT YOUR ATTORNEY.

THIS STANDARIZED DOCUMENT FOR USE IN SIMPLE TRANSACTIONS HAS BEEN APPROVED BY THE CALIFORNIA ASSOCIATION OF REALTORS® AND THE STATE BAR OF CALIFORNIA IN FORM ONLY. NO REPRESENTATION IS MADE AS TO THE APPROVAL OF THE FORM OF SUPPLEMENTS. THE LEGAL VALIDITY OF ANY PROVISION. OR THE ADEQUACY OF ANY PROVISION IN ANY SPECIFIC TRANSACTION. IT SHOULD NOT BE USED IN COMPLEX TRANSACTIONS OR WITH EXTENSIVE RIDERS OR ADDITIONS.

For these forms, address California Association of Realtors®
505 Shatto Place, Los Angeles, California 90020
(Revised 1978)

FORM D-11-1 NCR SHEETS

REAL ESTATE PURCHASE CONTRACT AND RECEIPT FOR DEPOSIT
The following terms and conditions are hereby incorporated in and made a part of Buyer's Offer

6. Buyer and Seller shall deliver signed instructions to the escrow holder within _____ days from Seller's acceptance which shall provide for closing within __(14)__ days from Seller's acceptance. Escrow fees to be paid as follows:
_____
_____

7. Title is to be free of liens, encumbrances, easements, restrictions, rights and conditions of record or known to Seller, other than the following: (1) Current property taxes, (2) covenants, conditions, restrictions, and public utility easements of record, if any, provided the same do not adversely affect the continued use of the property for the purposes for which it is presently being used, unless reasonably disapproved by Buyer in writing within _____ days of receipt of a current preliminary title report furnished at _____ expense, and (3) __(8)__ _____

(9) Seller shall furnish Buyer at _____ expense a standard California Land Title Association policy issued by _____ Company, showing title vested in Buyer subject only to the above. If Seller (1) is unwilling or unable to eliminate any title matter disapproved by Buyer as above, Seller may terminate this agreement, or (2) fails to deliver title as above, Buyer may terminate this agreement; in either case, the deposit shall be returned to Buyer.

8. Property taxes, premiums on insurance acceptable to Buyer, rents, interest, and __(10)__ _____ shall be pro-rated as of (a) the date of recordation of deed; or (b) _____ Any bond or assessment which is a lien shall be __paid/assumed__ by __(11)__ . _____ shall pay cost of (12) transfer taxes, if any.

9. Possession shall be delivered to Buyer (a) on close of escrow, or (b) not later than __(13)__ days after close of escrow or (c) _____

10. Unless otherwise designated in the escrow instructions of Buyer, title shall vest as follows: __(15)__ _____

(The manner of taking title may have significant legal and tax consequences. Therefore, give this matter serious consideration.)

11. If Broker is a participant of a Board multiple listing service ("MLS"), the Broker is authorized to report the sale, its price, terms, and financing for the information, publication, dissemination, and use of the authorized Board members.

12. **If Buyer fails to complete said purchase as herein provided by reason of any default of Buyer, Seller shall be released from his obligation to sell the property to Buyer and may proceed against Buyer upon any claim or remedy which he may have in law or equity; provided, however, that by placing their initials here Buyer: ( ) Seller: (17) ( ) agree that Seller shall retain the deposit as his liquidated damages. If the described property is a dwelling with no more than four units, one of which the Buyer intends to occupy as his residence, Seller shall retain as liquidated damages the deposit actually paid, or an amount therefrom, not more than 3% of the purchase price and promptly return any excess to Buyer.**

13. If the only controversy or claim between the parties arises out of or relates to the disposition of the Buyer's deposit, such controversy or claim shall at the election of the parties be decided by arbitration. Such arbitration shall be determined in accordance with the Rules of the American Arbitration Association, and judgment upon the award rendered by the Arbitrator(s) may be entered in any court having jurisdiction thereof. The provisions of Code of Civil Procedure Section 1283.05 shall be applicable to such arbitration.

14. In any action or proceeding arising out of this agreement, the prevailing party shall be entitled to reasonable attorney's fees and costs.

15. Time is of the essence. All modifications or extensions shall be in writing signed by the parties.

16. This constitutes an offer to purchase the described property. Unless acceptance is signed by Seller and the signed copy delivered to Buyer, in person or by mail to the address below, within __(18)__ days, this offer shall be deemed revoked and the deposit shall be returned. Buyer acknowledges receipt of a copy hereof.

Real Estate Broker __(19)__ _____   Buyer __(19)__ _____
By _____
Address _____   Address _____
Telephone _____   Telephone __(19)__ _____

ACCEPTANCE
The undersigned Seller accepts and agrees to sell the property on the above terms and conditions. Seller has employed _____ as Broker(s) and agrees to pay for services the sum of __(20)__ _____ Dollars ($ _____), payable as follows:
(a) On recordation of the deed or other evidence of title, or (b) if completion of sale is prevented by default of Seller, upon Seller's default or (c) if completion of sale is prevented by default of Buyer, only if and when Seller collects damages from Buyer, by suit or otherwise and then in an amount not less than one-half of the damages recovered, but not to exceed the above fee, after first deducting title and escrow expenses and the expenses of collection, if any. In any action between Broker and Seller arising out of this agreement, the prevailing party shall be entitled to reasonable attorney's fees and costs. The undersigned acknowledges receipt of a copy and authorizes Broker(s) to deliver a signed copy to Buyer.

Dated: _____ Telephone _____   Seller __(21)__ _____
Address _____   Seller _____

Broker(s) agree to the foregoing. Broker _____ Broker _____
Dated: _____ By _____   Dated: _____ By _____

For these forms, address California Association of Realtors® 505 Shatto Place, Los Angeles, California 90020 (Revised 1978)   D-11-2 NCR SETS   Page 2 of 2 Pages

parties where more than one has an interest. The licensee may be faced with problems respecting authority to sign if a corporation, partnership, or syndicate is the buyer. In such cases, a question may arise as to who has the authority to bind a group. If the buyers are a married couple, both husband and wife should sign.

20. Before the seller affixes his or her signature, the licensee should fill in the space relating to the commission. If the office has a listing agreement, the rights of the licensee may be more secure if he or she states that the commission is to be paid as per listing agreement dated _____, 19____. The commission may also be indicated in dollars or as a percentage of the selling price. This latter provides flexibility, particularly if the selling price is not determined at this time, since the seller may counter with a higher price than that offered by the prospective buyer.

21. When signed by the seller the agreement constitutes an acceptance of the offer and becomes a bilateral contract, fully executed and enforceable by both parties. It is recommended that consumers not sign a deposit receipt without having it explained to them. It is estimated that as many as thirty percent of the agents "sum up" highlights of the agreement instead of reading it thoroughly with the buyer and later with the seller.

Many more legal matters relating to contracts in real estate can be considered, but they are subjects for a course on legal aspects of real estate. Because of the continuing need for licensees and others to keep abreast of the changes in the law and to obtain an indication of the trends and developments in the law, an advanced course in real estate law, encouraged by the Department of Real Estate, is now being offered at several colleges. This course covers in detail the reasons that led to the present form of the deposit receipt.

OTHER COMMON CONTRACTS USED IN THE REAL ESTATE FIELD

Other contracts that are frequently encountered in real estate transactions include various forms of promissory notes secured either by mortgages or deeds of trust, installment sales contracts, escrow instructions, insurance policies, leases, and employment contracts between a broker and

salesperson. These will be discussed in detail in later chapters of this book. The following gives a brief introduction to the first two mentioned.

Promissory Notes

A written obligation containing a promise to pay a definite amount of money at or prior to a specified time is called a promissory note. They are usually negotiable. When secured by a mortgage or deed of trust (also called a trust deed) they become part of a security transaction containing many contractual obligations. Printed forms of notes, which are customarily used, are of various types, such as straight notes, installment notes with interest included, installment notes with interest excluded, and so on. The particular form used will be dependent upon the contract between the parties. The forms and purpose of the note will be discussed in depth in Chapter 7.

Mortgages and Trust Deeds

A mortgage is a form of security instrument whereby real property is pledged to secure repayment of a debt or performance of any lawful obligation, but without giving up possession of the property. They have been used for a long period of time. Trust deeds are instruments by which title to real property is transferred to a third party trustee as security for a debt or other obligation. They are often used in place of mortgages in California and other states, particularly in the West. These too will be discussed in detail in Chapter 7.

Installment Sales Contracts

A type of instrument that is sometimes used in lieu of a mortgage or deed of trust is a real property sales contract, referred to under various names, such as land contracts, contract for deed, land sales contracts, or installment sales contracts. However labeled, they have one thing in common: legal title initially stays with the seller-vendor. The owner agrees to convey title to real property to a buyer after the buyer has complied with the terms of the contract, particularly with the payment of the total purchase price. Under the terms of such a contract, the buyer makes periodic payments over a specified length of time, and when he or she has completed the obligation, he or she is entitled to a deed. Although *legal title* does not pass to the buyer until a deed has been delivered, the execution and delivery of the contract of sale will effect an *equitable transfer* of title, whereby the seller retains the legal title for security purposes, but the equitable title passes to the buyer. The purchaser may be able to encumber his or her contract interest, or to transfer it, or to declare a homestead on it, and so on. A form of contract, "Agreement for Sale of Real Estate," is illustrated in Figure 4.6.

QUESTIONS FOR CHAPTER 4

Matching Terms

a. mitigate	**i.** vendee
b. consideration	**j.** Statute of Frauds
c. executory	**k.** implied
d. breach	**l.** laches
e. liquidated	**m.** Statute of
f. rescission	Limitations
g. contract	**n.** listing agreement
h. restitution	**o.** mutual assent

____ **1.** an agreement to do or not do something for a consideration

____ **2.** return to an aggrieved party of the consideration for a contract

____ **3.** buyer under a contract for the sale of land

____ **4.** law which requires certain contracts to be in writing to be enforceable

____ **5.** law which sets forth a period of time within which an action in court must be filed

____ **6.** anything of value

____ **7.** contract between owner and broker authorizing the latter to find a buyer

____ **8.** a meeting of the minds

____ **9.** unreasonable delay in asserting a right

____ **10.** to lessen or reduce

____ **11.** that which is yet to be performed

____ **12.** cancellation

____ **13.** ascertained

____ **14.** failure to perform an obligation without justifiable excuse

____ **15.** presumed or inferred, rather than expressed

True/False

T F 16. All real estate contracts must be in writing to be enforceable.

T F 17. All promises create contractual rights.

T F 18. All essential matters must be substantially agreed to before there can be a binding contract.

T F 19. A bilateral agreement is a promise in exchange for an act.

T F 20. A voidable contract based on lack of capacity can be avoided at any time by either party to the contract.

T F 21. A guardian needs to be appointed before a minor can acquire title to real property.

T F 22. Both the purpose of a contract and the consideration must be lawful.

T F 23. A breach of contract is any failure to perform.

T F 24. Contracts of adhesion are invalid.

T F 25. Basically, a listing agreement is a contract of employment of an agent.

Multiple Choice

26. The essential elements of a contract include
   a. competent parties
   b. mutual consent
   c. lawful object
   d. all of the above

27. The statute that requires certain types of contracts to be in writing is known as the
   a. Statute of Frauds
   b. Statute of Limitations
   c. Statute of Uses
   d. Statute of Descent

28. An oral agreement to sell a parcel of real property for a commission is
   a. valid
   b. void
   c. unenforceable
   d. illegal

29. If an owner enters into an exclusive agency listing and thereafter sells the property through his or her own efforts,
   a. no commission is payable
   b. a full commission is payable
   c. the broker is entitled to half of the commission
   d. the sale is invalid

30. The amount of commission payable on a sale is ordinarily based on
   a. total price paid
   b. total price paid less costs of sale
   c. total price paid less any encumbrance
   d. listing amount, regardless of amount of sale

Figure 4.6
Agreement for Sale of Real Estate

AGREEMENT FOR SALE OF REAL ESTATE

THIS AGREEMENT, made in duplicate this_____day of_____, 19_____,

between_____herein called Seller,

and_____herein called Buyer,

WITNESSETH: that Seller, in consideration of the covenants and agreements of Buyer herein contained, agrees to sell and convey unto Buyer

and Buyer agrees to buy the real property situate in the_____

_____ _____, County of_____

State of California, hereinafter referred to as "said realty" and described as follows:

Subject to: Conditions, restrictions, reservations and easements of record, if any.

_____

_____ _____

for the principal sum of_____Dollars ($_____)
lawful money of the United States, of which principal sum Seller, by execution of this Agreement acknowledges receipt of_____

_____ _____Dollars ($_____)

and Buyer in consideration of the premises, promises and agrees to pay to Seller at_____

_____the remainder of said principal sum, together with interest on all deferred payments from

_____at the rate of_____per cent per annum, as follows:

_____

_____

and continuing until the full amount of principal and interest are paid. The number of years required to complete payment in accordance with the

terms of this agreement are _____
                              years   months

Each of said payments shall be credited, first, on the interest then due and the remainder on said principal sum.

Buyer agrees to pay_____taxes for the fiscal year_____

WOLCOTTS FORM 413—WITH ACKNOWLEDGMENT—REV. 6-66

Figure 4.6
Continued

and to pay during the life of this Agreement all taxes, assessments and charges of every kind now or hereafter assessed, levied, charged or imposed upon said realty, or any interest therein, at least ten days before the same become delinquent. Buyer further agrees to keep said realty free of all liens and encumbrances of every kind, except such as are incurred by Seller and not assumed by Buyer hereunder.

The basis upon which any tax estimate contained herein is made is

_____

Buyer and Seller further agree that time is of the essence of this Agreement and that full compliance by Buyer with all its terms is and shall be a condition precedent to Buyer's right to a conveyance here under, and should Buyer fail to comply with any of the terms hereof, then the whole unpaid balance of said principal sum and the interest thereon shall immediately become due and payable at the option of Seller; and thereupon Seller may at his option cancel and forfeit all of Buyer's rights under this Agreement and all his interest in said realty and its appurtenances, either by (a) service upon Buyer of a written declaration of default, forfeiture and cancellation, or (b) by depositing in the United States mail. postage prepaid, such written declaration addressed to Buyer either at the post office address Buyer shall have

caused to be filed with Seller, or if no such address be so filed, then addressed to Buyer at_____,

California, or (c) by recording such written declaration in the office of the Recorder of_____County; and such written declaration when served, mailed or recorded, shall be conclusive proof in favor of subsequent purchasers or encumbrancers in good faith and for a valuable consideration of such default, forfeiture and cancellation. Upon such declaration of default, forfeiture and cancellation by Seller according to any of the methods above provided, all rights, estates and interests hereby created or then existing in favor of Buyer, or anyone claiming under him, shall cease and become null and void; and the right of possession and all equitable and legal interests and estates in said realty, with all sums of money theretofore paid by Buyer, shall revert to, vest in and become the sole property of Seller in fee; and the money paid and any improvements erected shall be forfeited to and retained by, and become the sole property of Seller, as consideration for the execution of this Agreement, and also as liquidated damages for Buyer's failure to comply with the terms hereof, and not as a penalty.

Buyer and Seller further agree that no waiver by Seller of any failure of Buyer to comply with any of the terms hereof shall be construed to be a waiver of any subsequent failure of compliance by Buyer with the same or other terms; and that no delay or omission of Seller in exercising any right hereunder shall be construed as a waiver thereof; and that no acceptance by Seller of any payments made in a manner or at a time other than as herein provided shall be construed as a variation of the terms hereof.

Buyer and Seller further agree that in the event Seller cancels and forfeits Buyer's rights hereunder as provided above, Buyer will, at the option and upon demand of Seller, execute in favor of and deliver to Seller a good and sufficient Quit Claim Deed to said realty; and its acceptance by Seller shall operate as a full release of all of Buyer's obligations hereunder.

Seller agrees within a reasonable time after Buyer's compliance with all the terms hereof to execute and deliver to Buyer a good and

sufficient Deed, conveying said realty, and to furnish a Policy of Title Insurance of_____

_____, showing title to said realty vested in Buyer, both such Deed and Policy of Title Insurance to be and show subject only to encumbrances herein mentioned and to such other encumbrances as are not caused or created by Seller.

It is further agreed as follows:

Figure 4.6
Continued

1. Buyer agrees during the life of this Agreement, to keep all improvements on said realty fully insured with insurance companies acceptable to Seller and with loss payable to Seller as his interest may appear under this Agreement, and to deliver the policies to Seller together with receipts showing payment of premiums thereon.

2. That this Agreement shall apply to and be binding upon the respective successors in interest of Buyer and Seller.

3. That the terms Buyer and/or Seller wherever used in this Agreement shall include the plural as well as the singular number, and the masculine gender includes the feminine as well as the neuter. Furthermore, that said terms shall include respective successors in interest.

4. That no sale, transfer or assignment of any right or interest herein by Buyer shall be valid nor be binding upon Seller for any purpose without Seller's written consent thereto first having been obtained.

IN WITNESS WHEREOF, Seller and Buyer have, on the day and year first above written, set their hands and seals.

Address_____
(Buyer)

(Seller)

STATE OF_____
COUNTY OF_____ } ss.

SPACE BELOW FOR RECORDER'S USE ONLY

On_____,
before me, the undersigned, a Notary Public in and for said County and State, personally appeared

_____

known to me to be the person___ whose name_____ subscribed to the within instrument and acknowledged that _____ executed the same.
WITNESS my hand and official seal.

(Seal)_____

NAME (TYPED OR PRINTED)
Notary Public in and for said State.

WHEN RECORDED MAIL TO
_____

Title Order No._____

Escrow or Loan No._____

Figure 4.6
Continued

Under the Terms of This Agreement No Assignment can be Made without the Consent of the Seller
(**Note:** The marital status of the parties to any assignment must be shown and if Assignor is married the wife or husband must also sign.)

ASSIGNMENT

_____ Calif., _____, 19____

For value received, _____
do hereby grant and assign to_____

all_____right, title and interest in and to the
within Agreement and in and to the property therein described.

_____
_____

ASSIGNEE'S ACCEPTANCE

The undersigned assignee named in the Assignment of the foregoing Agreement, hereby approves, accepts and agrees to perform the same subject to all the terms, covenants and conditions thereof.

_____
_____

Address _____

SELLER'S CONSENT

The undersigned, seller of the real estate described in the within Agreement, hereby consents to the within Assignment, without warranty express or implied, as to the sufficiency thereof, as to the interest, if any, assigned thereby, or as to the existence or nonexistence of any prior Assignment, lien, encumbrance or other disposition of said Agreement or real property not endorsed thereon.

_____
(Seller)

31. Property subject to a $95,000 encumbrance is listed at $175,000 and sold for $170,000. The broker's commission is based on
    a. $175,000
    b. $170,000
    c. $170,000 less encumbrance
    d. $175,000 less encumbrance

32. To be enforceable as a contract, a deposit receipt must contain
    a. names and signatures of the parties
    b. consideration
    c. terms and manner of payment
    d. all of the above

33. A deposit receipt, when signed by the buyer only, is basically
    a. an offer
    b. a bilateral contract
    c. an option
    d. an acceptance

34. The amount of commission payable to a broker is determined by
    a. regulation of the corporations commissioner
    b. Fair Trade Laws
    c. regulation of the real estate commissioner
    d. contract between broker and seller

35. A listing agreement which entitles a broker to all proceeds in excess of the seller's asking price is called
    a. an open listing
    b. an option listing
    c. a net listing
    d. a multiple listing

36. A listing agreement which gives the broker the right to buy the property is called
    a. an exclusive right to sell
    b. an option listing
    c. a multiple listing
    d. a net listing

37. If an owner enters into an exclusive right to sell listing and thereafter sells the property through his or her own efforts
    a. the broker is entitled to a full commission
    b. the broker is entitled to one half of the commission
    c. no commission is payable
    d. the sale is unenforceable

38. If an owner enters into a net listing, and thereafter the broker sells the property for the net asking price
    a. the broker is entitled to a finder's fee
    b. the sale is invalid
    c. the broker is entitled to a reasonable commission
    d. no commission is payable

39. Payment of a commission to a broker under an oral listing is
    a. illegal
    b. contrary to public policy
    c. grounds for disciplinary action
    d. permissible if the seller chooses to do so

40. In an open listing, if more than one broker procures a buyer
    a. the broker who first procured a buyer acceptable to the seller is entitled to a commission
    b. each broker is entitled to a commission
    c. the commission is divided among the brokers
    d. no commission is payable

41. When properly executed, either buyer or seller can compel performance under a fully executed
    a. listing agreement
    b. net listing agreement
    c. multiple listing agreement
    d. deposit receipt and purchase contract

42. Which of the following is not required to be in writing?
    a. lease of real property for a period in excess of one year
    b. contract for employment of a broker for compensation ·
    c. commission agreement between cooperating brokers
    d. contract for the sale of real property

43. An offer to purchase real property may be terminated by
    a. lapse of time
    b. death of offeror
    c. death of offeree
    d. any of the above

44. A real estate broker obtained a listing on a vacant lot for $25,000. Knowing that the owner was anxious to sell, the broker had another party buy it for him without disclosing this fact to the seller, and thereupon the broker sold the property for $40,000. Under these circumstances, the broker is guilty of
    a. commingling
    b. double agency
    c. making a secret profit
    d. dilatory action

45. Broker Smith took a listing, after which the owner (principal) sold directly to a friend. To assure himself of a commission, what type of listing should Smith have bargained for?
    a. net
    b. open
    c. exclusive agency
    d. exclusive right to sell

46. If a broker is expressly authorized to accept earnest money as a deposit and does so and thereafter loses or misappropriates it, the party bearing the risk of loss is the
    a. seller
    b. buyer
    c. escrow holder
    d. all of the above

47. The broker ordinarily has earned his or her commission at such time as
    a. the listing agreement is signed
    b. the transaction is accepted by an escrow agent
    c. the property comes out of escrow free and clear
    d. he or she procures a buyer ready, willing, and able to perform on the agreed terms

48. To be enforceable, a deposit receipt must be
    a. executed by both buyer and seller
    b. subject to escrow conditions
    c. approved by the listing broker
    d. approved by the selling broker

49. The safety clause found in the CAR Exclusive Authorization and Right to Sell listing is designed to protect the
    a. selling broker
    b. listing broker
    c. seller
    d. buyer

50. Right of possession under a deposit receipt is determined by
    a. rules of the real estate commissioner
    b. regulations of the insurance commissioner
    c. agreement of the parties
    d. the escrow agent

5
AGENCY AND THE ROLE OF THE BROKER

In this chapter we will consider the agency relationship in general, and then discuss the agency status of a broker and a salesperson and that between an owner and a broker. The latter was considered briefly in Chapter 4 in our discussion of listing agreements. In a real estate transaction where the services of a broker are utilized we usually encounter two types of agency relationships, first, the one between an owner and the broker, and second, the one between the broker and the salesperson. Most brokers have salespersons assisting them, and in reality the latter become subagents in their relationship to the property owner.

The duties, rights, and responsibilities of any agent are explained, and the manner in which an agency relationship is terminated is discussed. This is followed by a consideration of the specific duties and responsibilities of real estate agents and their regulation by the State of California through the Department of Real Estate. The chapter concludes with a discussion of the many advantages of using the services of a real estate broker in the sale of a home.

Another type of agency will be considered in the next chapter, i.e., the role of the escrow agent.

AGENCY RELATIONSHIP

Agency

An agency is defined as the relationship between a *principal* and an *agent* whereby the agent represents or acts on behalf of the principal in dealings with a third party, i.e., any member of the public at large. From this simple relationship, a vast body of law has emerged governing the rights and duties of the principal, the agent, and the third party. The agency relationship is often referred to as a *triangular relationship*. It starts as a *dual* relationship, i.e., a matter of contract rights between a principal and his agent, and ripens into a triangular relationship when the agent makes contact with third parties on behalf of the principal. This can be illustrated as follows, using the mnemonic word PAT:

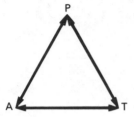

Figure 5.1
Triangular Nature of Agency

Each one of the three, principal, agent, and third party, will have rights, duties and responsibilities towards each other.

Creation of Agency

The relationship of the principal and the agent is normally created by express contract. When created in this way, the basic principles of contract law are applicable, with one principal exception. One may act as an agent without compensation, that is, gratuitously. Thus, consideration is not essential to the creation of an agency. Although based on contract and thus contractual, the relationship is often described as *consensual*. However, to undertake to act as an agent, even gratuitously, may subject the agent to certain obligations of an ordinary agent.

The agency relationship may also be created by ratification and by estoppel. *Ratification* means to accept the consequences of another person's acting on his or her behalf without prior approval. Occasionally a person may act as agent without any authority to do so, or an agent may act beyond the scope of his or her authority. In such cases the principal or alleged principal may, under certain circumstances, ratify the acts of the agent and thus become bound. *Estoppel* is a legal theory under which a person is barred from asserting or denying a fact because of previous inconsistent acts or words which another person relied on to his or her detriment.

Agency in Real Estate Transactions

The agency relationship is utilized in most real estate transactions when a property owner wishes to sell real property or sometimes when someone wishes to buy real property. As we have seen, the

document employed to create the relationship is a listing agreement, of which there are several types. If the listing agreement doesn't obligate the broker to use his or her best efforts to find a buyer but promises compensation for services by the agent if he or she procures a buyer, the contract is described as *unilateral*.

A contract may provide a *bilateral* agency relationship when the broker or salesperson enters into a counterpromise to "use due diligence" in finding a purchaser. The ultimate effect will, of course, be dependent upon the specific type of contract used. In most situations the preferable kind would be a bilateral agency.

In the ordinary sales transaction, the broker is the agent for the seller who is called the principal in dealing with a third party, the prospective buyer, either personally or by utilizing the services of a salesperson. Figure 5.2 illustrates the relationship.

Other Employment Relationships

Agency is distinguishable from two other types of relationships where a person is performing services on behalf of another, namely, the ordinary *employer-employee* relationship and the relationship between an *independent contractor* and his or her employer. An employee, sometimes referred to as the servant in a master-servant relationship, is one who is to render services to his or her employer and remains entirely under the con-

Figure 5.2
The Agency Relationship

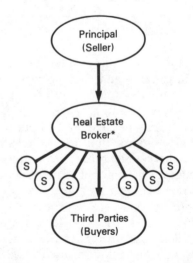

*The Broker-agent may have one or more licensed salespersons working under his/her broker's license

trol and direction of the employer. The doctrine of *respondent superior* applies to such a relationship and to a lesser extent to the agency relationship. The doctrine relates primarily to wrongs committed by the employee or the agent, and literally means "let the superior respond." It is referred to as a *vicarious* liability. The reason for this doctrine is that one who carries out his business activities through the use of other persons should be liable for their negligence in carrying out the services for which they were employed. This is a disadvantage in using an agent; on the other hand, if agents and employees were not utilized, there could be a stifling limitation on business activity.

The independent contractor relationship is often created in order to limit the liability of the person utilizing the services of another. The independent contractor *sells* final results rather than time; physical conduct is not subject to the control of another, since the one utilizing the services of the independent contractor maintains no control over mode or method in the completion of the work. An agent, in contrast, acts for and in the place of the principal for the purpose of making contracts, thus bringing the principal into a legal relationship with a third party.

AGENCY STATUS OF A BROKER AND SALESPERSON

A real estate broker is basically an agent and may, for compensation or expectation of compensation, do any one or more of a number of specified acts for another person—including selling, buying, soliciting purchasers, soliciting listings, or negotiating the purchase, sale or exchange of real property and used mobile homes.

Persons engaged in any of the foregoing activities must be licensed by the Department of Real Estate. Unlike most other states, the performance of even a single act or transaction requires a license in California. An unlicensed person who acts as a real estate broker or salesperson is guilty of a misdemeanor and also is not entitled to a commission. A licensed broker is not entitled to a commission in a transaction negotiated by an unlicensed salesperson in the broker's employ.

It is estimated that there are over 100,000 licensed real estate brokers in California and approximately 300,000 licensed salespeople. The scope and magnitude of broker activities range all the way from a one-person office to a tract builder-developer to a nationally known dealer in business and industrial properties. Real estate brokerage is a $40 billion business in California and over $200 billion in the United States.

Most real estate brokers use the services of a real estate salesperson. The latter is defined by the Department of Real Estate as an employee of the broker and cannot contract in his or her own name or accept money for services from any person other than the broker-employer. While the broker is authorized to contract in his or her own name, collect money, and perform other such services within the scope of the contract between the broker and the principal, the salesperson must work under the auspices of the broker's name or company.

A real estate broker must have a written employment contract with each of his or her salespersons, whether they are licensed as salespersons or brokers under a broker-salesperson arrangement. In the past questions have arisen as to whether or not a salesperson can be an independent contractor. As far as the Real Estate Law is concerned, salespersons are employees of the broker and cannot be independent contractors. This is primarily based on the reason that a salesperson is under the supervision and control of the broker. A contract between a broker and a salesperson in which the salesperson is characterized as an independent contractor does not make it so under the Real Estate Law. Whether such a relationship will be recognized under other laws is a question of fact. The broker-salesperson status under one law does not establish what the status is under different laws, rules, or circumstances. This can be of importance under the federal and state income tax laws, worker's compensation law, unemployment insurance or other matters. It has been established, however, that real estate brokers do not have to pay their salespersons the minimum wage required in the Labor Code.

Whereas an employer is liable for the salesperson's negligence and is responsible for worker's compensation, an independent contractor is liable for his or her own taxes, social security, and even his or her own negligence. Some of the factors bearing upon the issue of whether a person is an employee or an independent contractor are: limited or unlimited right of the employer to hire and fire, the extent to which the employment contract permits the employer to give orders about working time and other details, and the method of payment (whether by time or by job).

Special Agency Created

The relationship between a broker or salesperson and a client is that of agent and principal, but the broker or salesperson is considered a special rather than general agent in that the agent is authorized to perform only in a particular transaction. The fact that the agent is authorized to act in a number of transactions affecting various parcels of real property does not create a general agency since only limited authority is given in each of the transactions. As a general rule, the acts of the special agent do not bind the principal unless they are made strictly within the authority conferred.

Listing Agreement as Creation of Agency

The authority usually is spelled out in a contract called a listing agreement between the broker and the owner of property. There are various types of such agreements, many of which have become standardized. For example, The California Association of Realtors has printed several forms, including a form entitled "Exclusive Authorization and Right to Sell." Probably more real estate has been listed and sold on this form than any other in the state. The form was analyzed and explained in some detail in considering the contractual aspects in the previous chapter; a copy was used for illustrative purposes.

As far as the agency aspects of the listing are concerned, it should be understood that in general the broker's authority is limited to negotiating the transaction and does not include the authority to actually sell or purchase the property, or to enter into any agreements that would obligate the principal to convey title. The listing agreement merely authorizes the broker to solicit offers to buy the property on terms and conditions acceptable to the seller. Basically, it establishes a principal-agent relationship between the owner and the broker, and imposes on the broker certain fiduciary duties and responsibilities.

A listing agreement does not confer any power or right on a buyer to bind or commit the owner to sell his or her property, even if the buyer offers the exact terms of the listing agreement. In order to accomplish the sale, the owner and the buyer must enter into a contract between themselves, which is customarily in the form of a *deposit receipt* or the equivalent.

Of course, if the broker procures a qualified buyer willing to meet the terms of the listing agreement, but the owner refuses to enter into a contract with the buyer, the broker is still entitled to his or her commission.

Compensation of the Broker

One of the advantages of the present practice of paying a broker a percentage of the selling price as the commission is that a broker generally is entitled to payment only if he or she is successful in procuring a buyer ready, willing, and able to buy on the seller's terms. For a long time the percentage was fixed in an amount that was more or less uniform in a geographic area. The amount of a commission is now subject to negotiation between the broker and his principal; it is basically a matter of agreement between the parties. A sliding scale may be feasible in some situations based on the time and difficulty in selling a particular parcel of property, or on the selling price of more valuable property.

AUTHORITY OF AN AGENT

Once the agency relationship is created, the agent has authority to do everything necessary or proper or usual in the ordinary course of business for the purpose of the agency, and to make representations as to facts involved in the transaction in which he or she is engaged. There may be either an actual or an ostensible agency. Once there is in fact an agency the authority of an agent may be categorized also as actual or ostensible. Actual authority basically is that which the principal intentionally confers upon the agent. Ostensible authority is that which the principal unintentionally, or by want of ordinary care, causes or allows third persons to believe the agent possesses. The acts or declarations of the agent alone do not establish ostensible authority. But where the principal knows that the agent holds himself or herself out as clothed with certain authority which he or she does not have, and the principal remains silent, such silence can sometimes give rise to liability. For example, assume a broker pretends to be the agent of a seller, and with the seller's consent obtains a buyer with a valid offer to purchase the seller's property. Relying upon the broker's representations, the buyer borrows money for the purchase. Should the owner thereafter refuse to sell, the courts may rule that an ostensible agency, or agency by estoppel, was created. Thus, because of the buyer's reliance upon the broker's statements, the seller would be estopped from denying that an agency had been created, or that the broker had the authority to do what he or she did.

GENERAL DUTIES AND LIABILITIES OF AN AGENT

To the Principal

The duties owed by an agent to his or her principal in the real estate field are many. First of all, the agent owes a definite loyalty to the principal. A fiduciary relationship is created comparable to that of trustee and beneficiary under a trust. The law provides that in all matters connected with this trust, a trustee is bound to act in the highest respect toward the beneficiary, and may not obtain any advantage over the beneficiary by the slightest misrepresentation, concealment, duress, or adverse pressure of any kind. As a fiduciary, the agent in his or her relations with the principal is required to exercise the utmost good faith, loyalty, and honesty in the execution of the duties of the agency. It is the duty of the agent to make full disclosure of all material facts and circumstances within his or her knowledge relating to the transaction of the agency; any concealment of facts constitutes fraud. An agent also has an obligation to use reasonable *care, skill* and *diligence* in the performance of his or her duties. Further, an agent may not act for more than one party in a transaction without the consent of both of the parties.

To Third Parties

Regarding the duties and liabilities of an agent toward third parties, both contract law and the law of agency are applicable. In dealings with third parties the agent warrants that he or she has authority to act on behalf of the principal. If the agent acts with authority for the principal and in the name of the principal, the principal, not the agent, is bound by the act of the agent, and the principal alone can sue. Ordinarily the agent will not be liable under a written contract made in the name of the principal. When the agent acts without authority or in excess of his or her authority, he or she may be held liable personally. If an agent discloses the fact of agency but not the identity of the principal, the agent is not personally liable, but the undisclosed principal will be. It is a matter of obtaining the name of the principal. If, however, the fact of agency is undisclosed, the third party may hold either the agent or the principal liable, if and when he or she discovers the principal's identity.

An agent is always liable to third parties for his or her own wrongful acts (torts) whether the principal is liable or not, and in spite of the fact that the agent acts in accordance with the principal's directions. And an agent is liable to his or her principal for torts such as negligence, and for breach of contract in the event, for instance, he or she wrongfully abandons the employment before the end of the term.

TERMINATION OF AN AGENCY

An agency may be terminated voluntarily by the acts of the parties, or involuntarily by operation of law. Thus, the parties may voluntarily agree to terminate the relationship, or the agent may renounce the agency, or the principal may revoke it. An agency is also terminated by the expiration of its term, or by the extinction of its subject, or by the death or incapacity of either the principal or the agent. Schematically, agency terminations might be viewed as shown in Figure 5.3.

SPECIFIC DUTIES AND RESPONSIBILITIES OF REAL ESTATE AGENTS

The duties and responsibilities of a real estate agent are many. These matters are the subject of special study in a course on real estate practice and a course on the legal aspects of real estate. Some of the major responsibilities specified in the *Real Estate Reference Book* are the following:

1. The broker must not commingle the client's funds with his or her own.
2. The broker must keep a true record of all trust funds passing through his or her hands.
3. The broker must not make a secret profit on the concurrent resale of his or her principal's property, such as through a double escrow.
4. The broker may not collect a fee or commission from both buyer and seller without the written consent of each.
5. The broker must comply with provisions of California's Rumford Act and Unruh Act regarding discrimination in the sale or rental of real property.

Federal law barring discrimination in the sale or rental or financing of real property must also be complied with.

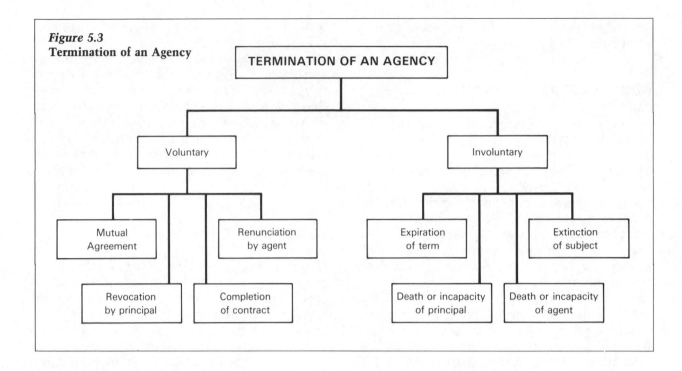

Figure 5.3
Termination of an Agency

Additionally it should be pointed out that although the seller's broker is not an agent of the buyer, there are duties owed to the buyer, not only to disclose material facts known to the seller and/or broker, but also to make an inspection of the property to ascertain that there are no defects—or, if defects are discovered, to so inform prospective buyers. Agents representing sellers now have the duty under a recent court decision, to conduct a "reasonably competent and diligent inspection of residential property listed for sale, and to disclose to prospective purchasers all facts materially affecting the value or desirability of the property that such an investigation would reveal." In other words, a seller and his or her agent can't hope that a potential buyer won't be too inquisitive. There is an affirmative duty to ascertain the condition of residential property before it is placed on the market.

Liability of Seller as Principal

The liability of a seller of real property, as principal, for the fraudulent statements of the broker as agent while negotiating a sale is substantially the same as the liability of the employer for the negligence of his employee who causes an accident while driving the employer's car. In each case, by virtue of the relationship of agent and principal, the latter may be liable to a third party. The prin-

cipal, in turn, may have a right to recover damages from his or her agent for breach of duty.

Liability of the Buyer as Principal

Generally a person seeking to purchase real property will not have entered into a written agreement with a real estate broker or salesperson. However, a buyer can have a formal written agreement spelling out the terms and conditions of an agreement to locate property, and such a written agreement may then be enforceable (whereas the verbal agreement regarding real property is not generally enforceable).

REGULATION OF REAL ESTATE AGENTS

California has been the leader among all the states in real estate regulation since the first license law was adopted in 1917. Today, California is not only recognized as having a model real estate license law, but also as having by far the largest and most effective educational, regulatory, and enforcement programs in the nation.

The Department of Real Estate, whose chief officer is the real estate commissioner, was created by legislative act in 1917. The first law of its kind in the United States, it provided for the licensing and regulation of real estate agents and has served as a pattern for similar legislation in many other states. The department administers that portion of the Business and Professions Code known as "the Real Estate Law."

The Real Estate Law was enacted for the purpose, among others, of raising the standards of the real estate profession, and requiring its members to act fairly and ethically with their clients and with the public. Before anyone can act as a broker or salesperson, the person is tested to determine whether or not he or she is qualified. On obtaining a license, the licensee must thereafter act in accordance with the law and the rules and regulations of the real estate commissioner, which means that he or she has the obligation at all times to be honest, trustworthy, and to show the utmost good faith and use the requisite care and skill in the performance of his or her duties. It is one thing to obtain a license, it is another thing to keep it.

To assist the real estate commissioner, a State Real Estate Board was established by legislative act in 1937; the name was changed to the State Real Estate Commission in 1957. It became known as the Real Estate Advisory Commission in 1976. This official body consists of the real estate commissioner and ten other members. Six of the advisory members must be licensed real estate brokers.

The real estate commissioner is appointed by the governor for a four-year term, and is the chief executive of the Department of Real Estate. It is his or her duty to determine administrative policy and enforce the provisions of the real estate law in a manner that will achieve the maximum protection for the purchasers of real property and persons dealing with real estate licensees.

California was not only the first state to enact a real estate license law; it also was a pioneer in providing, through legislation, a system whereby funds contributed by licensees are used to stimulate real estate education and research. As far back as 1949 the legislature, acting upon the recommendation of the real estate commissioner and the organized industry, appropriated money from this special fund for the University of California to aid the commission in developing a professional real estate education and research program. The growth and expansion of the program have been phenomenal; new services and aids to education are constantly being developed.

In 1963 the legislature renamed the Real Estate Education and Research Fund the Real Estate

Education, Research *and Recovery* Fund, reflecting another development in the concept of licensee responsibility. One portion of the fund is still allocated for education and research, and another portion now goes into a "recovery fund," which underwrites the payment of otherwise uncollectable court judgments obtained against licensees on the basis of fraud, misrepresentation, deceit, or conversion of trust funds in a transaction in which the judgment debtor participated as a licensee. In 1976, the Fund's lengthy name was abbreviated to the much simpler Real Estate Fund. Although the name has been changed, the functions remain identical.

The Department of Real Estate issues many publications, including the *Real Estate Reference Book*, *Real Estate Law*, and the quarterly *Real Estate Bulletin*. The *Reference Book* contains an extensive resume of the rules and regulations applicable to licensees, as well as material on other subjects related to real estate transactions. Because the *Reference Book* is actually compiled and distributed for the guidance of the entire real estate industry, it should be read and studied by anyone intending to make real estate his or her career, and should be required as a source of reference for all basic courses in real estate. In the years ahead the practice of real estate will become more and more complex to meet the demands and needs of the industry and the public. New laws will certainly be passed and others repealed. New policies will be established as the wise utilization of land becomes of paramount importance to the real estate industry and to the public alike.

Requirements for the real estate license examination, the procedure, and examination coverage are set forth in the *Reference Book*. Additionally the department publishes a booklet containing detailed instructions to license applicants, a copy of which is available upon request from the principal office of the department in Sacramento or from one of its regional offices.

Finally, the Department of Real Estate is vitally interested in eradicating racial discrimination in all areas of real estate. It has, for example, coined the phrase "color blind industry" in describing the real estate industry, defining that to mean that race, color, or creed shall not be considered in real estate dealings; that licensees should maintain an attitude free of racial prejudice, and to observe the "golden rule," namely, to do unto others as you would have them do unto you.

Licensing Requirements

Every real estate broker and salesperson must be licensed by the state of California. One of the requirements for a license is that the applicant take and pass an examination. In Chapter 1 we discussed the general content of the exam and the weight given to the principal subjects covered. We now consider the educational qualifications for taking the exam.

Prerequisites for the broker license examination administered by the Department of Real Estate include eight courses in three separate categories as follows:

I. All of the following four courses:
   A. Real Estate Practice
   B. Legal Aspects of Real Estate
   C. Real Estate Finance
   D. Real Estate Appraisal
II. plus *one* of the following:
   A. Real Estate Economics or a course in Accounting
III. plus *three* of the following:
   A. Real Estate Principles
   B. Advanced Legal Aspects of Real Estate
   C. Advanced Real Estate Finance
   D. Advanced Real Estate Appraisal
   E. Business Law
   F. Escrows
   G. Property Management
   H. Real Estate Office Administration

A candidate for a salesperson's license, on the other hand, takes a less extensive examination and is required to complete only one college level course before taking the salesperson's exam. Within 18 months after issuance of the license, the salesperson must also complete two additional basic real estate courses, selected from any of the three categories listed above (I, II and III).

Real estate licenses are issued for a period of 4 years. An original 4-year license is renewable without examination, but continuing education requirements must be satisfied. Most renewal applicants must attend 45 clock-hours of approved subjects within the 4-year period preceding license renewal, covering such topics as ethics, professional conduct, legal aspects of real estate, and consumer protection.

California Real Estate Commission's Code of Ethics

The State Department of Real Estate has adopted a code of ethics designed to advance the professional conduct of the real estate industry. As we shall see in the next section of this chapter, professional associations such as the National Association of Realtors and the National Association of Real Estate Brokers have adopted Codes of Ethics that apply to their members. Because many California real estate licensees do not belong to any such associations, the Real Estate Commissioner has adopted the California Code of Ethics and Professional Conduct for all California real estate licensees. It is reprinted in its entirety as Appendix A. The Code covers such areas as:

misrepresentation of market values for the purpose of securing listings or purchase by agents

misleading statements regarding commissions

failure to present all bona-fide offers

underestimating probable closing costs as an inducement for a principal to accept an agent's advice

refunding of a buyer's deposit without the approval of the seller

nondisclosure to a seller of a licensee's direct or indirect interest in a property being sold

representing services as free when in fact the services are covered by fees charged as part of the transaction

recommending use of a particular escrow or lender in which the broker has an undisclosed interest

claiming to be an expert in an area of specialization if the licensee has had no special training, preparation, or experience; i.e., appraisal, property management, industrial siting, etc.

failure to disclose to regulating agencies *redlining* and other discriminating practices by lenders

misrepresentation of the role of the *franchisor* in areas of shared responsibilities and liabilities

dishonest treatment of one or more parties to a transaction

inaccurate and misleading advertising

failure to keep current on factors affecting the real estate market

noncooperation with other licensees, including settling disputes through mediation or arbitration

PROFESSIONAL AND TRADE ASSOCIATIONS

Business and professional groups seek to attain public recognition, and one of the preferred methods is to form an organization which establishes ideals and ethics for its members. In the forefront of such organizations is the National Association of Realtors (NAR). Several specialized groups operate within this organization, some of which we will refer to in later chapters. State associations also work closely with the national board, as do local boards within the state.

In some areas the feeling still prevails that there are no ethics in business, let alone in some professions. This idea is both unfortunate and untrue. The average American businessman is perhaps many times more ethical than his predecessor. During the last fifty years there have been substantial advances in business ethics; many business methods that were taken as a matter of course a century ago are now generally condemned. Greater emphasis is being given to ethics than ever before.

It has been recognized since ancient times that no civilization can long survive the decay of ethical controls or the failure of ethical insight to grow with changing conditions. When an undisciplined profit motive expresses itself in greed, exploitation, and deceit, there can be neither business stability nor a high degree of general and lasting economic welfare. No just, stable government can exist when official life lacks ethical responsibility. A wholesome society finds its springs of action in sincerity and good will. These qualities are particularly important in the field of real estate, which is the very foundation of our stability and prosperity. The development of these qualities is a primary goal of professional and trade associations.

A trade association has been described as a voluntary nonprofit organization of independent and competing business units engaged in the same industry or trade, formed to deal with the industry's problems, promote its progress, and enhance its service. A real estate board is a voluntary organization whose members are involved in some phase of real estate activity. They are committed, among other things, to do everything in their power to insure the stability and dignity of the real estate business. Most boards also have *affiliate members* who work in banks, trust companies, title insurance companies, escrow companies, and other fields related to the real estate business.

The pioneer real estate organizations in California were the San Diego Realty Board, organized in 1887, and the San Jose Real Estate Board, organized in 1896. Other realty boards followed early in the 1900s—the Berkeley in 1902, the Los Angeles in 1903, and the San Francisco in 1905.

The California Association of Realtors (CAR) had its origins in the California Real Estate Association which was formed in Los Angeles in 1905. It is composed of the members of approximately 190 local real estate boards throughout the state, together with some individual members. When there is no board in a community, a broker desiring to belong to the California association may either join any local board or the association directly as an individual member.

The National Association of Realtors (NAR) came into being as The National Association of Real Estate Boards in 1908. The national association unifies the organized real estate interests throughout the country. It presents a common cause and program to Congress for national legislation affecting real property. All brokers are not necessarily *Realtors*. Only a real estate broker holding active membership in a real estate board affiliated with the National Association of Realtors is entitled to use the term *Realtor*. The word *should be spelled with a capital R* and pronounced "Reel-tor" (not "Realator"). Salespersons may qualify as Realtor-Associates by virtue of their employment with a Realtor and payment of dues.

Membership in NAR is important in that membership does imply a high level of competency and integrity. Even though competence in the field of real estate is now generally insured by requirements for obtaining a license, it alone does not qualify the practitioner as a Realtor. A candidate must establish competence, good character, and good standing in the community to be acceptable for membership in a Real Estate Board and must take the Realtor's Pledge: "I pledge myself to protect the individual right of real estate ownership and to widen the opportunity to enjoy it; to be honorable and honest in all dealings; to seek better to represent my clients by building my knowledge and competence; to act fairly towards all in the community, and through it my country; to observe the Realtor's Code of Ethics and conform my conduct to its lofty ideals."

NAR has adopted a Code of Ethics which is reprinted as Appendix B. The Code of Ethics is designed to protect individual rights of real estate ownership by requiring that all Realtors be honorable and honest in all their dealings. Implicit in such a requirement is that Realtors increase their knowledge and competency in every phase of real estate, and that they act for the betterment of their communities. The NATIONAL ASSOCIATION OF REALTORS® reserves exclusively unto itself the right to officially comment on and interpret the CODE and particular provisions thereof. For the NATIONAL ASSOCIATION'S official interpretations of the CODE, see INTERPRETATIONS OF THE CODE OF ETHICS; NATIONAL ASSOCIATION OF REALTORS®.

In 1947 another national association was created. The National Association of Real Estate Brokers (NAREB), composed of black real estate brokers, was formed in Miami, Florida and adopted the name *Realtist* for its members. This organization has local boards in the principal cities in forty states. The California Association of Real Estate Brokers (CAREB), organized in 1955, is affiliated with the national group. It has member boards in Sacramento, Oakland, Los Angeles, and San Diego.

A Realtist must be a member of a local board as well as a member of the national organization. Both nationally and locally, Realtists are working for better housing for the communities they serve. In many cases, individuals are both Realtors and Realtists, because they belong to both national associations. NAREB has also adopted a Code of Ethics which is reprinted as Appendix C.

California Association of Realtors Code of Practice

In connection with equal opportunity in housing, the CAR Code of Practices was adopted by all local Boards of Realtors in California, and reads as follows:

> The (name of Board of Realtors) subscribes to the policy that a favorable public attitude for equal opportunity in the acquisition of housing can best be accomplished through leadership, example, education and the mutual co-operation of the real estate industry and the public.
>
> The following is hereby stated as the Code of Practices of this Board:
>
> 1. It is the responsibility of a Realtor to offer equal service to all clients without regard to race, color, religion, or national origin in the sale, purchase, exchange, rental, or lease of real property.
>   a. A Realtor must stand ready to show property to any member of any racial, creedal, or ethnic group.
>   b. A Realtor has a legal and ethical responsibility to receive all offers and to communicate them to the property owner.

>   c. A Realtor should exert his best effort to conclude the transaction.
>
> 2. Realtors, individually and collectively, in performing their agency functions have no right or responsibility to determine the racial, creedal, or ethnic composition of any neighborhood or any part thereof.
> 3. Any attempt by a Realtor to solicit or procure the sale or other disposition in residential areas by conduct intended to implant fears in property owners based upon the actual or anticipated introduction of a minority group into an area shall subject the Realtor to disciplinary action. Any technique that induces panic selling is a violation of law and ethics and must be strongly condemned.
> 4. Each Realtor should feel completely free to enter into a broker-client relationship with persons of any race, creed, or ethnic group.
>   a. Any conduct inhibiting said relationship is a specific violation of the rules and regulations of this board and shall subject the violating Realtor to disciplinary action

ADVANTAGES OF USING A BROKER IN THE SALE OF A HOME

There are two disadvantages that may be applicable in using a broker in the sale of a home instead of the owner selling directly, namely, the payment of a commission, and the possibility of a vicarious liability. However, there are far more advantages than disadvantages, and it is generally far better to use the services of a real estate broker, perferably one who is a member of a Real Estate Board. The advantages are many, including the following:

1. A broker has knowledge of the market and available financing.
2. A broker will be able to qualify a buyer, i.e., determine whether or not the buyer is financially able to handle the purchase.
3. Setting the asking price, based on his or her valuation and appraisal knowledge.
4. Suggestions for presenting the property at the most favorable time.
5. Suggestions for any fixing up that may be needed.
6. Advertising the property and increasing the exposure by the use of a Multiple Listing Service.
7. Avoid wasting time with "sightseers" or curious neighbors.
8. Screening prospective buyers. A broker will

attempt to match potential buyers with the property.

9. Avoid any question of racial discrimination.
10. Obtaining the top price. A broker will know whether to hold firm on the asking price.
11. Broker can determine if a prospect is really a prospect. Sometimes a prospective buyer turns out to be a prospective burglar.
12. A broker can assist in arranging financing.
13. A broker can be of assistance in expediting the escrow.
14. A broker can arrange for new housing for the seller if needed.
15. Avoiding emotional stress and strain and around the clock concern and anxiety for fear of missing a prospect.
16. Disclosing any problems the property might have had, which can avoid later litigation.
17. Making an accurate record of the transaction for tax or other purposes.
18. Negotiation of terms and conditions of sale.
19. Owner can still sell under an exclusive agency (distinguished from an exclusive right to sell listing) and not be obligated to pay a commission.
20. Obtaining the services of a professional who is paid for success only.

QUESTIONS FOR CHAPTER 5

Matching Terms

a. license
b. broker
c. ethics
d. recovery fund
e. ratification
f. Realtor
g. salesperson
h. Real Estate Commissioner
i. agency
j. Realtist
k. principal
l. vicarious
m. deviation
n. gratuitous
o. consensual

____ 1. without compensation
____ 2. member of the National Association of Realtors
____ 3. characteristic of an agency
____ 4. member of the National Association of Real Estate Brokers
____ 5. departure from instructions
____ 6. one who employs an agent
____ 7. code of conduct requiring high standards
____ 8. source of payment for uncollectable judgements against licensees
____ 9. employee of a real estate broker
____ 10. enforcement officer of the Department of Real Estate
____ 11. a person authorized to act independently in conducting a real estate business
____ 12. liability arising from the wrongful act of an agent
____ 13. relationship by which one person acts in behalf of another
____ 14. affirmation of a previously unauthorized act
____ 15. requirement to sell real property as agent for a compensation

True/False

T F 16. When a real estate broker accepts a listing, a fiduciary relationship is created.
T F 17. A salesperson in his or her functions is indistinguishable from an independent contractor.
T F 18. Commingling is the mixing of an agent's personal funds with a client's funds.
T F 19. An agency, whether general or special, usually involves a triangular relationship.
T F 20. A principal is never liable when an agent violates the instructions of the principal.
T F 21. A listing agreement is a type of document that creates an agency relationship.
T F 22. In a listing agreement the broker occupies a position of trust and confidence.
T F 23. A broker is under a duty to use due diligence in performing his or her agency.
T F 24. The agent has no duty to disclose defects in property sold "as is."
T F 25. It is contrary to good ethics for a real estate broker to use a fictitious firm name.

Multiple Choice

26. The broker-client relationship is ordinarily created by the
    a. escrow instructions
    b. deposit receipt
    c. listing agreement
    d. land sales contract
27. An unlicensed person who acts as a real estate broker is
    a. permitted to do so for one transaction only
    b. guilty of a misdemeanor

c. entitled to a commission
d. entitled to a finder's fee only

28. A real estate salesperson may accept compensation directly from
   a. the buyer
   b. the seller
   c. the broker by whom he or she is employed
   d. any of the above parties

29. A real estate broker who employs a salesperson must execute a written agreement with each salesperson. The agreement must show the
   a. amount and type of supervision to be exercised by the broker
   b. duties of the parties
   c. compensation to be paid
   d. all of the above

30. Where a principal unintentionally, or by want of ordinary care, causes or allows third persons to believe the agent possesses authority to act as an agent, such authority is termed
   a. ostensible
   b. actual
   c. unilateral
   d. bilateral

31. The Real Estate Fund
   a. is maintained by the NAR
   b. is maintained by the CAR
   c. provides relief to victims of fraud by real estate licensees
   d. provides compensation to licensees defrauded by their principals

32. The agency relationship when operative ordinarily involves interaction between a minimum number of
   a. two persons
   b. three persons
   c. four persons
   d. five persons

33. The distinction between an employee and an independent contractor is based in part upon which of the following?
   a. existence of independent calling
   b. right to give orders
   c. supervision of work
   d. all of the above

34. The legal relationship between a seller and his or her real estate broker is that of
   a. attorney and client
   b. principal and agent
   c. agent and fiduciary
   d. none of the above

35. A real estate agent has a duty to use the following in the performance of his or her duties
   a. care, skill, and diligence
   b. dilatory practices
   c. care and imprudence
   d. all of the above

36. The parties referred to by the term *triangular agency relationship* are
   a. broker, salesperson, and principal
   b. agent, principal, and buyer
   c. broker, escrow agent, and seller
   d. broker, seller, and lawyer

37. Which of the following has a meaning similar to *fiduciary*?
   a. guaranty
   b. pecuniary
   c. trustee
   d. mercenary

38. If a salesperson misinforms a buyer as to deed restrictions
   a. there is no liability, as the restrictions are a matter of record
   b. the salesperson and broker may both be liable for damages
   c. the broker and not the salesperson is liable to the buyer
   d. the seller and not the broker is liable to the buyer

39. In order to use the title *Realtor*, a licensee must
   a. be a member of the National Association of Real Estate Brokers
   b. be licensed in two or more states
   c. be affiliated with the National Association of Realtors
   d. none of the above are true

40. If a listing held by a broker does not authorize the broker to accept a deposit, but he or she does accept one, he or she holds such deposit as agent for the
   a. seller
   b. buyer
   c. escrow company
   d. local realty board

41. A real estate salesperson
   a. must be licensed by the Department of Real Estate
   b. must be licensed by the Division of Corporations if employed by a partnership or corporation
   c. need not be licensed if he or she has five years experience
   d. need not be licensed if employed by a licensed broker

42. A broker may collect a commission from both buyer and seller when
   a. the listing agreement so specifies
   b. the buyer and seller both consent in writing
   c. the escrow agent approves
   d. under any of the above circumstances
43. The stated policy of the Department of Real Estate is to create a color-blind industry. What does this statement mean?
   a. maintain an attitude that is free of racial prejudice
   b. race, creed, or color is not a material fact in real estate dealings
   c. do unto others as you'd have them do unto you
   d. all of the above are true
44. The chief officer of the State Department of Real Estate is the
   a. corporations commissioner
   b. real estate commissioner
   c. savings and loan commissioner
   d. governor
45. An agency may be terminated by
   a. the agent, with the agreement of the principal
   b. the agent, without the agreement of the principal
   c. operation of law
   d. any of the above
46. At the time a listing agreement is executed, a copy must be
   a. delivered to the principal
   b. forwarded to the Department of Real Estate

c. delivered to the county recorder
   d. posted on the property
47. If a broker buys his or her client's property through a dummy or "strawman," he or she is
   a. relieved of any liability
   b. subject to disciplinary proceedings
   c. protected by the doctrine of "caveat emptor"
   d. all of the above
48. A licensee must
   a. respect the wishes of his or her principal regarding preferential treatment of certain races
   b. report to the police any buyer who discriminates against a seller
   c. show property to members of any racial, religious, or ethnic group
   d. strive to preserve the "ethnic purity" of neighborhoods where there is a concern
49. A person acting on behalf of another under a power of attorney is known as the
   a. principal
   b. attorney-in-fact
   c. attorney at law
   d. independent contractor
50. A person acting under a power of attorney may
   a. convey or mortgage property on which a homestead has been declared
   b. make a gift deed
   c. make a mortgage without valuable consideration
   d. dispose of property under terms of the instrument

6

REAL ESTATE MATHEMATICS, THE ROLE OF THE ESCROW, AND PROPERTY INSURANCE

In previous editions of this book the subject of real estate mathematics was included as a separate chapter. With the expansion of some of the other material, it has been included in this chapter on escrows and title insurance where basic mathematics is used extensively. Portions of the previous material on mathematics have been integrated into other appropriate chapters in the book, covering material such as descriptions, finance, valuation and appraisal, taxation, and investment.

When an escrow is opened, one of the first things the escrow holder usually does, in accordance with the instructions of the parties, is to order a preliminary report of title from a title insurance company. Hazard and public liability insurance is also encountered in an escrow transaction, either by way of proration of premiums or requesting insurance coverage for the new owner or borrower.

INTRODUCTION TO MATHEMATICS

For real estate work, knowledge is our stock in trade—a knowledge of words and their meaning, and a knowledge of figures and their use. As in many other businesses and professions, we also need to know people and have the ability to communicate with them. The glossary at the end of the book is intended to furnish the student with a broad real estate vocabulary. This section gives fundamental information about mathematics and applications of this information to the real estate field.

Just as law is inextricably tied to the study of real estate, so also is mathematics. The math we need to know for real estate work is basic arithmetic—how to add, subtract, multiply, and divide. This need is recognized in the requirements for a real estate license. The law provides that not only must an applicant for a real estate license have an appropriate knowledge of the English language including reading, writing, and spelling, but the candidate must also have a knowledge of arithmetical computations common to real estate and business practice.

Arithmetic is defined as the method or process of computation with figures, and is considered to be the most elementary branch of mathematics. Mathematics is defined briefly as the study of numerical quantities and the relationships among them, of spatial quantities and their relationships, and of various abstractions of these relationships. We need to be knowledgeable in such things as they relate to real estate.

Mathematic computations are necessary at many stages during a real estate transaction, including the following: land descriptions, from linear measurements to more complicated survey lines; escrow prorations, adjustments, and closing statements; interest, points and impound accounts; deposit receipts and trust accounts; the determination of square-foot areas in buildings and converting such figures into costs; determining zones and minimum lot sizes; calculating depreciation; computation of equity on encumbered property; interpretation and use of interest and amortization tables; and many others.

Real estate practitioners use numbers constantly in connection with measurements and dimensions, e.g., size, height, depth, area, distances, etc.; in connection with dollar amounts, e.g., price, taxes, etc.; and in connection with dates and the use of the calendar, e.g., in prorations and adjustments. This section explains the use and significance of numbers in the ordinary type of real estate transactions and sets forth some of the basic rules and principles that aid in a better understanding of this subject. We first discuss the nature and use of numbers and the numbering system, and then review the fundamentals of addition, subtraction, multiplication, and division. These subjects involve the use of the following four symbols:

$+$ plus (add)
$-$ minus (subtract)
$\times$ times (multiply)
$\div$ divided by

Another division indicator or representation is $\sqrt{}$, illustrated as follows: $2\overline{)8} = 4$.

Other symbols frequently encountered are:

$=$ equals, or equal to
$\%$ percent

Further in the section we consider fractions, decimals, and percentages. Then we discuss interest calculations and amortization of loans. The section includes a brief consideration of the importance of figures in prorations and adjustments, which we will encounter further in the chapter in the escrow discussion, and which we have already seen in Chapter 2 in relation to measurements and distances. The importance of figures in capitalization will be seen in Chapter 9.

The first part of this section deals with basic arithmetic. It is just that—very basic. Some readers skilled in math will want to jump directly into the discussion of interest, where basic arithmetic is applied to real estate matters, beginning at page 102.

BASIC ARITHMETIC

The Concept of Numbers

The Number System. Arithmetic is actually the science of numbers. It begins with the concept of the one and the many, or a single unit and plurality. It also considers the reduction of a unit into lesser parts.

A number is a unit or a collection of units. The operations of arithmetic are based on the assumption that we can pass from any number to the succeeding number. This generally involves counting, and the process of counting creates the number system.

The oldest records that show a systematic use of numerals are those of the ancient Babylonians and Egyptians. One of the important ancient systems has proved to be the Roman, as evidenced by the fact that we still use Roman numerals today for many purposes, particularly in dates and in outlines. However, our number system is based on the Arabic numerals; it was probably developed by the Hindus of India and subsequently introduced to Europe by the Arabs through Spain and Italy. Hence, we refer to our present numerals as Arabic or Hindu-Arabic.

All our numbers are made up from the ten digits, 0 through 9. These symbols are called digits from the Latin *digitus*, meaning finger. The fact that finger counting undoubtedly preceded any other counting method suggests the reason that numbers are collected in sets of ten. Thus, we have the ten digits 0, 1, 2, 3, 4, 5, 6, 7, 8, 9, with which we can write all possible numbers. This infinite variety is possible because, in our numerals, each has *intrinsic value*, i.e., its own value;

and *place value*, i.e., its position or location in the numeral. At a glance, we add the numbers together to get the total value. The following paragraphs explain and describe this automatic process.

The position of the digit in a numeral determines its value or size. Thus, starting at the left of the decimal point, the first digit tells how many ones or units are in the number; the next digit, immediately to its left, is ten times greater in value than the digit in the unit place and therefore represents the number of tens (10s); the next digit (immediately to the left of the digit in the 10s place) has a value ten times greater than ten and thus represents hundreds (100s); and so on. Let us consider the number 248, which represents the quantity two hundred and forty-eight. The 2 stands for two hundreds (200), the 4 for four tens (40), and the 8 for eight ones (8). When joined together they total two hundred and forty-eight.

As numbers go above the hundreds, punctuation is used for better understanding. For instance, the number 21278 is more readily understood when a comma is placed between the hundreds' and the thousands' positions, as follows: 21,278. Commas are inserted to separate groups of three digits, moving left.

To complete the description of the quantity, a word or symbol is added to show what the numeral or numerals represent, such as in the following illustrations: $100; 40 *acres*; 150 *feet*; 10 *percent*, etc.

To summarize the concept of numbers, then, we form our number symbols, or numerals, out of the ten basic digits. These numerals are used to write numbers, whereas words are used to name them. It is important to keep in mind that numbers are *ideas*; the words or figures that represent them are only *symbols*.

Fractions. So far we have illustrated whole numbers. Sometimes it is necessary to describe parts or portions of a whole. A fraction is simply a portion or part of a whole number. It is represented by two numbers, called the *denominator* and the *numerator*; the denominator is written *under* the numerator. The two terms are separated by a horizontal or oblique line. Thus, the fraction two-thirds would be written as $\frac{2}{3}$ or 2/3. In this illustration, the denominator is 3, the numerator is 2.

The numerator of a fraction (the number on top) may be either less than or greater than the denominator. If it is less than the denominator, the fraction is called a *proper* fraction. For example, 3/4 is a proper fraction. A fraction whose numerator is greater than its denominator is called an *improper* fraction. Thus, 6/4 is an improper fraction. A proper fraction is proper because it represents a number less than one; an improper fraction is improper because it represents a number greater than one.

A whole number *plus* a proper fraction is called a mixed number. Thus $1 + 3/4$ is written as 1-3/4 and is designated as a mixed number. In the preceding illustration of an improper fraction, if we divide the denominator (4) into the numerator (6), the answer is $1\frac{2}{4}$ or $1\frac{1}{2}$, a mixed number. Mixed numbers are often converted to improper fractions for ease of calculation. To convert a mixed number to an improper fraction, use the same denominator as in the fraction portion of the mixed number. To calculate the numerator for an improper fraction, multiply the denominator in the fraction portion of the mixed number by the whole number and add the numerator to that product. For example, if we took the improper fraction, $\frac{14}{4}$, and converted it into a mixed number, it would become $3\frac{2}{4}$ (or $3\frac{1}{2}$). Next, by multiplying the denominator portion, 4, by the whole number, 3, we would have $3 \times 4 = 12$. Finally, by adding the numerator portion, 2, to the 12, the total of 14 is produced. Thus, $3\frac{2}{4}$ becomes $\frac{14}{4}$.

In working with fractions it is usually helpful to reduce or simplify the symbol by finding numbers that will divide evenly into both the numerator and denominator. Thus, the fraction 4/16 can be reduced further by dividing both the numerator and the denominator by 4. The result is 1/4, a much easier number to work with than 4/16 (or 8/32 or 32/128, etc.). To the extent possible, fractions should be reduced to the point where no further division can be made.

Decimals. Decimals are directly related to fractions because they are also parts or portions of a whole number. Fractions are often not easy to work with; so, when possible, they are changed into decimals to eliminate the clumsiness of numerators and denominators. To use the decimal system, fractions are expressed in terms of parts of 10, 100, 1000, and so on. Fractions are often used with whole numbers. In the decimal system we separate the fraction from the whole number by using a decimal point, which is a period (.). Money is ordinarily expressed in decimal form such as 25 cents (or $.25), $1.25, $10.25, and so on. The amount $.25 is actually 25/100 of one dollar. Reduced to its lowest common denominator this becomes 1/4 or a quarter. Parts of a dollar usually are written with only two digits to the right of the decimal point. The numbers to the left of the decimal point represent the whole dollars, and there is no limit to how many digits can be used. Thus, whole numbers and parts are expressed simply in the decimal system.

The decimal system is used with all kinds of calculations. Before making the calculations, usually it is much easier to change a combination of fractions and whole numbers to the decimal equivalent. The change involves simple division and particular care in placing the decimal point. Thus,

$$\text{one quarter} = 1/4 = 4\overline{)1.00}^{\;.25} = .25 \text{ in decimal form.}$$

A fraction is thus expressed as a decimal by dividing the denominator into the numerator and placing a decimal point in the proper location. As illustrated above, the decimal point is placed on top in line with the end of the numerator. When a number being converted is a proper fraction, the digits in the answer will always be to the right of the decimal point. Where the number involved is an improper fraction or a mixed number, the decimal point separates the whole number from the fraction. Thus, the number $1\frac{1}{4}$ becomes 1.25.

The following data show the conversions of six of the most frequently used fractions into decimal fractions, decimals, and percentages:

Fraction	Fraction converted to decimal fractions	Fraction converted to decimal	Decimal × 100 to convert to percent
1/2 =	50/100 =	.50 =	50%
1/3 =	$\frac{33\frac{1}{3}}{100}$ =	.333 =	$33\frac{1}{3}$%
1/4 =	25/100 =	.25 =	25%
1/5 =	20/100 =	.20 =	20%
1/6 =	$\frac{16\frac{2}{3}}{100}$ =	.167 =	$16\frac{2}{3}$%

Percent. The results shown above have been expressed as percentages by multiplying the decimal form by 100. This is done simply by moving the decimal point two places to the right and adding a percent sign.

The importance of a decimal point is illustrated by the following:

2. =	200%	5. =	500%
.2 =	20%	.5 =	50%
.02 =	2%	.05 =	5%
.002 =	.2%	.005 =	.5%

Addition

Whole numbers, fractions, and decimals are all subject to the basic processes of arithmetic; that is, they can be added, subtracted, multiplied, or divided. Whole numbers are the easiest to work with, but fractions and decimals can become almost as workable by the application of a few basic rules or principles.

Addition is the process of combining smaller sets of numbers to form a larger set and determining the total numbers of the larger set. Thus, to find the total value of a set of numbers, they are *added* together. This can be done by writing them down in a column and adding them mentally, or by using an adding machine or calculator. The latter is one of the easiest and usually the most accurate way, but may not always be available. Therefore, it is important to know how to add as quickly and accurately as possible without the use of a machine.

Adding probably started as a process of counting, one by one; now it is a process of finding the sum of a group of numbers by using some basic laws. Memorizing the sums of any two digits makes the process easier. The basic laws of addition are:

1. The sum is a number of things similar to the things added; therefore, only similar things can be added.
2. The sum is the same regardless of the order in which the numbers are added.

Following are two columns of numbers that illustrate the addition of numbers of two or more digits:

$$
\begin{array}{r} 23 \\ 31 \\ +12 \\ \hline 66 \end{array}
\qquad
\begin{array}{r} 74 \\ 26 \\ +32 \\ \hline 132 \end{array}
$$

The unit of figures in the column at the right uses combinations of single digits whose sum is greater than ten $(4 + 6 + 2 = 12)$. Twelve is 10 + 2, two ones and one ten. You put the 2 in the ones place and then add one ten or 1 to the next column (tens place).

Let us add another group of numbers:

$$
\begin{array}{r}
694 \\
235 \\
+440 \\
\hline
1,369
\end{array}
\qquad
\begin{array}{r}
69.4 \\
23.5 \\
44.0 \\
\hline
136.9
\end{array}
$$

There are various ways to check addition. One way is to reverse the method and repeat the adding. The usual procedure in adding is to start at the bottom of the right-hand column and add upward. To check the answer, start at the top of the right-hand column and work down. If the same answer is found, then it is probably correct.

The addition of fractions is not easy unless we are using relatively simple fractions, which can be added by sight, such as $1/2 + 1/2 = 1$. In fact, it is easier to convert the fractions to decimals, but where there are relatively few fractions to be added and you wish to express the answer in the form of a fraction rather than a decimal, you will need to know how to add fractions with different denominators. For example, the sum of $7/8 + 5/6 + 3/4$ is not so easily figured. However, this addition may be accomplished by changing each fraction so that all have the same denominator. This is done by multiplying both numerator and denominator by the same number to obtain the desired denominator. The most useful denominator to select is the lowest one into which all of the original denominators will divide evenly. Of course, a common denominator can be found by multiplying all the denominators together: all denominators will divide evenly into it. But computation is easiest if you use the lowest common denominator.

In the fractions previously mentioned, $7/8 + 5/6 + 3/4$, the common denominator is 192; the lowest common denominator is 24. Note that the denominator 8 of the first fraction divides into 24 three times. We multiply both the numerator and the denominator by 3 to produce 21/24. The same process is followed for the other fractions. The value of the fraction remains the same when both the numerator and the denominator are multiplied by the same number. We then convert each fraction (7/8, 5/6, 3/4) to its equivalent in twenty-fourths:

$$
\frac{7}{8} = \frac{21}{24}
$$

$$
\frac{5}{6} = \frac{20}{24}
$$

$$
\frac{3}{4} = \frac{18}{24}
$$

Then we add the numerators:

$$
\begin{array}{r}
21 \\
20 \\
+18 \\
\hline
59
\end{array}
$$

Next divide the sum of the numerators by the common denominator to change the improper fraction to a mixed number:

$$
\begin{array}{r}
2 \\
24\ \overline{)59} \\
48 \\
\hline
11
\end{array}
$$

This will give us the sum of $2^{11}/_{24}$.

When adding decimals it is important to align all decimal points. For example, the addition of 22.3 plus 1.52 plus 369.16 is:

$$
\begin{array}{r}
22.3 \\
1.52 \\
+369.16 \\
\hline
392.98
\end{array}
$$

Subtraction

Subtraction is the reverse of adding. It involves the basic process of taking a number away from another number. Usually the smaller number is taken from the larger. Following is an example:

$$
\begin{array}{r}
\$24.00 \\
-\ 6.00 \\
\hline
\$18.00
\end{array}
$$

If the amount to be subtracted is *larger* than the amount from which it is to be deducted, the procedure is the same, except that the answer is no longer positive. Instead, the result is negative, a minus quantity.

To subtract fractions, the common denominator is used as in addition. Once each fraction has been changed so that all have the same denominator, which should be the lowest common denominator, you then subtract the numerators. The following is an example of how to subtract 3/10 from 7/8:

$$
\frac{7}{8} = \frac{35}{40}
$$

$$
-\frac{3}{10} = \frac{12}{40}
$$

$$
\frac{23}{40}
$$

To subtract decimals, it is important that the numbers be written so that the decimal points are all in a vertical line, the same as in addition. Once the numbers are lined up properly, then you subtract in the usual way. Following is an example:

$$625.43$$
$$- 275.18$$
$$350.25$$

A way to check the results is to add the bottom two rows to see if the total is the same as the number on the top row: 350.25 + 275.18 = 625.43.

Multiplication

Multiplication serves a purpose similar to addition, but the method is much faster. It is a shortcut to addition. The times sign (×) is used to indicate multiplication. When two numbers are multiplied, the result (or product) is the same as if the first number was added the number of times represented by the second number. Following is an example:

$$25 \times 5 = 125$$

This process is the same as adding 5 sets of 25:

$$25$$
$$25$$
$$25$$
$$25$$
$$+ 25$$
$$125$$

It actually does not matter which number is the multiplier. The number 25 added 5 times is the same as 5 added 25 times. However, for ease the smaller number is ordinarily used.

Memory is an aid to multiplication, and most students have memorized the multiplication tables at least from 1 to 9. The number 9 is an interesting number in this regard. When you multiply 9 by any other number and add the digits in the product, you always get 9. For example, picked at random are the following:

$$9 \times 7 = 63; \quad 6 + 3 = 9$$
$$9 \times 9 = 81; \quad 8 + 1 = 9$$
$$9 \times 12 = 108; \quad 1 + 0 + 8 = 9$$
$$9 \times 50 = 450; \quad 4 + 5 + 0 = 9$$

To multiply fractions, you simply multiply numerator by numerator and denominator by denominator, as follows:

$$3/4 \times 3/8 = 9/32$$

Mixed numbers are handled by changing them to improper fractions and multiplying as usual. Following is an example:

Mixed Numbers	Improper Fractions	Mixed Numbers
2 1/2 × 1 3/4 =	5/2 × 7/4 =	35/8 = 4 3/8

In multiplying decimals, the process is the same as for whole numbers. However, special care must be exercised in placing the decimal point in the appropriate place in the product. The number of decimal places in the product is the sum of the number of places in the multiplier and in the number being multiplied (multiplicand). Following is an example:

$$92.75$$
$$\times \quad 3.55$$
$$46375$$
$$46375$$
$$27825$$
$$329.2625$$

There were two decimal places in the multiplier, and two decimal places in the multiplicand, for a total of four decimal places, as shown in the answer, 329.**2625**

Division

Just as multiplication is a special case of addition in which the numbers added are all equal, division is a special case of subtraction in which the same number is successively subtracted. Division can be regarded as the process of finding the number of times that one number contains another; as such, it is the inverse of multiplication.

Small numbers can often be divided mentally, but usually a calculation involving larger numbers must be written. We have already shown a few examples of division. As we have seen, the division signs are ÷ and $\sqrt{}$.

A way to verify the result of dividing is to multiply the *quotient* by the *divisor* and if the product equals the *dividend*, the division is correct.

The quotient is the answer.

The divisor is the number to be divided into the other.

The dividend is the number into which the other is to be divided.

Following is an example of division and its verification:

375 ÷ 25 (this means three hundred and seventy-five divided by twenty-five)

<pre>
          15 quotient   15 quotient
divisor 25/375 dividend   ×25 divisor
        25   75
        125   30
        125   375 dividend
</pre>

To divide fractions, the divisor is inverted and the fractions are then multiplied. This is illustrated as follows:

$$\frac{7}{8} \div \frac{3}{4} = \frac{7}{8} \times \frac{4}{3} = \frac{28}{24} = 1\frac{4}{24} = 1\frac{1}{6}$$

In the division of decimals, the decimal point in the dividend is moved as many places to the right as there are decimal points in the divisor. This process is illustrated as follows:

$$1.25\,/\,10.750 \;=\; 125\,/\,1075.0$$
$$\begin{array}{r}8.6\\\hline1000\\750\\750\end{array}$$

When dividing a larger number into a smaller number, a decimal point followed by zeros is added to the dividend, and is illustrated as follows:

$$8\,/\,\underset{}{\overset{.25}{2.00}}$$
$$\begin{array}{r}16\\\hline40\\40\end{array}$$

INTEREST COMPUTATIONS

When you borrow money, you pay for its use. Interest is this payment. The amount paid is determined by the *rate* of interest, i.e., the percentage of the amount borrowed; by the *amount* borrowed; and by the length of *time* or the period for which it is borrowed.

There are two types of interest, *simple* and

Figure 6.1
Interest Calculations

INTEREST CALCULATIONS

RULE: Multiply the principal by as many one hundredths as there are days, and then divide as follows:

Per cent	4	5	6	7	8	9	10	12
Divide by	90	72	60	52	45	40	36	30

EXAMPLES: Interest on $100, for 90 days at 5 per cent.: *100 × .90 = 90.00 divided* by 72 = 1.25 (*one dollar and 25 cents*).

TABLE: Showing the number of days from any date in one month to the same date in any other month.

FROM	TO	JAN.	FEB.	MAR.	APRIL	MAY	JUNE	JULY	AUG.	SEPT.	OCT.	NOV.	DEC.
January		365	31	59	90	120	151	181	212	243	273	304	334
February		334	365	28	59	89	120	150	181	212	242	273	303
March		306	337	365	31	61	92	122	153	184	214	245	275
April		275	306	334	365	30	61	91	122	153	183	214	244
May		245	276	304	335	365	31	61	92	123	153	184	214
June.............		214	245	273	304	334	365	30	61	92	122	153	183
July		184	215	243	274	304	335	365	31	62	92	123	153
August		153	184	212	243	273	304	334	365	31	61	92	122
September		122	153	181	212	242	273	303	334	365	30	61	91
October		92	123	151	182	212	243	273	304	335	365	31	61
November		61	92	120	151	181	212	242	273	304	334	365	30
December		31	62	90	121	151	182	212	243	274	304	335	365

EXAMPLE: How many days from May 5th to October 5th? Look for May at left hand and October at the top; in the angle is 153. In leap year add one day if February is included.

compound. Simple interest is calculated solely on the principal sum (the amount borrowed) for the length of time of the loan. In installment notes when a partial payment is made on the loan, the interest to date of payment is deducted from the payment, and the balance of the payment is applied to the principal.

Compound interest is paid on savings deposits, and is generally not charged for extending credit. When compound interest is paid, the depositor receives interest on interest. In a bank, for example, each time interest is payable (on a quarterly or other basis), it is credited (added) to the amount of the deposit. If the depositor does not withdraw any of the funds, interest is payable on the increased amount at the end of the next interest period. Thus, the depositor receives interest on the previously credited interest. By allowing the interest to accumulate, a deposit can double in ten to twenty years depending on interest rates. A table showing interest calculations appears as Figure 6.1.

Computing Simple Interest

To compute simple interest, multiply the principal, i.e., the amount borrowed, by the selected interest rate; the product or result is the interest for one year. The rate charged for borrowing is a percentage of the amount borrowed, such as 8% or 9%, or 10%. Since a percentage cannot be multiplied in its regular form, it must be converted to the decimal equivalent before calculating the interest. Commonly used rates and their equivalents are: $6\% = .06$; $10\% = .10$; $14\frac{1}{2}\% = .145$, etc. Remember, then, that when the interest rate is expressed by a decimal, two points are marked off from the right of the percentage number.

There are 12 months in a year, or 365 days. Because 365 makes an awkward denominator, it is acceptable business practice, in computing interest, to assume 12 months of 30 days each, or 360 days to a year.

To avoid long computations which may involve cumbersome fractions, it is common to use prepared computations in the form of interest tables which may show the base (principal) as $1, $100 or $1,000 for various interest and time periods. From the interest table, we take the applicable factor and multiply it with the amount involved if it is over or under the base of the table. A factor is a predetermined number, based on computation, which is multiplied with the amount to be borrowed to obtain the product or particular interest we need to know.

Let us first illustrate the long method of determining the amount of interest before using a table. If we are asked, "What is the interest on $4,650 for 75 days at 9 percent?" we could figure it out in the following way:

$$\$4,650 \times .09 \times 75/360 = \$87.18$$

This process involves multiplying the amount of principal by the interest rate, and the product or result is the interest for one year. We then reduce this amount to the applicable amount for 75 days.

Now, for a shorter method, we will use an interest table like the one illustrated in Figure 6.2. Look in the table for 30 days at 9 percent.

We observe that the factor is 7.5000. We then add this factor and the number of days as follows:

$$\begin{array}{rcl} & 7.5000 &= 30 \\ & 7.5000 &= 30 \\ \text{Factor for 15 days} & \underline{3.75000} &= \underline{15} \\ & 18.75000 & \quad 75 \text{ days} \end{array}$$

$$\$4,650 = \$4.65 \text{ per } \$1,000$$

$$\text{Multiply } \$4.65 \times 18.75000 = \$87.18$$

Following are other shortcut methods for computing simple interest, which are all based on predetermined calculations:

10%: Multiply by the number of days and divide by 36. Remember to mark off two points from the right to reflect the fact that the interest rate is a decimal.

15%: Add the results of 10% plus 5% as calculated above.

20%: Double the figure obtained in computing for the 10% rate.

25%: Multiply the figure obtained in the 10% rate by 2 1/2 times.

4%: Multiply the principal by the number of days; cut off (or drop) the right-hand figure and divide by 9.

5%: Multiply the principal by the number of days and divide by 72.

6%: Multiply by the number of days; cut off (or drop) the right-hand figure and divide by 6.

7%: Compile the interest for 6% and add 1/6 of that.

8%: Multiply by the number of days and divide by 45.

9%: Multiply by the number of days; cut off (or drop) the right-hand figure and divide by 4.

Figure 6.2
Daily Interest Table Figured on $1,000

Days	5%	6%	7%	8%	9%	10%
1	0.1389	0.1667	0.1944	0.2222	0.2500	0.2778
2	0.2778	0.3333	0.3889	0.4444	0.5000	0.5556
3	0.4167	0.5000	0.5833	0.6666	0.7500	0.8334
4	0.5556	0.6667	0.7778	0.8888	1.0000	1.1112
5	0.6944	0.8333	0.9722	1.1111	1.2500	1.3890
6	0.8333	1.0000	1.1667	1.3333	1.5000	1.6668
7	0.9722	1.1667	1.3611	1.5555	1.7500	1.9446
8	1.1111	1.3333	1.5556	1.7777	2.0000	2.2224
9	1.2500	1.5000	1.7500	2.0000	2.2500	2.5002
10	1.3889	1.6667	1.9444	2.2222	2.5000	2.7780
11	1.5278	1.8333	2.1389	2.4444	2.7500	3.0558
12	1.6667	2.0000	2.3333	2.6666	3.0000	3.3336
13	1.8056	2.1667	2.5278	2.8888	3.2500	3.6114
14	1.9444	2.3333	2.7222	3.1111	3.5000	3.8892
15	2.0833	2.5000	2.9167	3.3333	3.7500	4.1670
16	2.2222	2.6667	3.1111	3.5555	4.0000	4.4448
17	2.3611	2.8333	3.3055	3.7777	4.2500	4.7226
18	2.5000	3.0000	3.5000	4.0000	4.5000	5.0004
19	2.6389	3.1667	3.6944	4.2222	4.7500	5.2782
20	2.7778	3.3333	3.8889	4.4444	5.0000	5.5560
21	2.9167	3.5000	4.0833	4.6666	5.2500	5.8338
22	3.0556	3.6667	4.2778	4.8888	5.5000	6.1116
23	3.1944	3.8333	4.4722	5.1111	5.7500	6.3894
24	3.2222	4.0000	4.6667	5.3333	6.0000	6.6672
25	3.4722	4.1667	4.8611	5.5555	6.2500	6.9450
26	3.6111	4.3333	5.0555	5.7777	6.5000	7.2228
27	3.7500	4.5000	5.2500	6.0000	6.7500	7.5006
28	3.8889	4.6667	5.4444	6.2222	7.0000	7.7784
29	4.0278	4.8333	5.6389	6.4444	7.2500	8.0562
30	4.1667	5.0000	5.8333	6.6666	7.5000	8.3340
31st day						

Loan Amortization

Amortization is a term used to indicate that partial payments are to be made to repay a loan at stated intervals, usually monthly, and that each payment includes a portion of interest and a portion to be credited to the principal. During the life of the loan, the payment amount remains the same. However, each month a smaller portion is charged for interest and a larger portion credited to the principal.

Special tables have been prepared to show the amount of monthly payments required to amortize a loan according to the rate of interest being charged. Many such tables are available to real estate practitioners, often furnished without charge by lending institutions and title insurance companies (see Figure 6.3).

Let's make sense of the table by applying it to a few problems:

1. Assume you are to borrow $100,000 at 12% interest per annum for 25 years. What will be your monthly payment?

First look up the number of years in the first column (Term of Years). Then look across the horizontal row until you reach the rate column desired, 12%. Where these two items intersect will be found the number (called a *monthly constant*) 10.54. Since this figure represents the combined principal and interest factor per thousand dollars, simply multiply 10.54 by 100, giving $1,054 as the monthly payment.

It should be noted that these monthly factors, or constants, are rounded to the nearest cent. In actual practice a more precise factor would be used, carried to six decimal places (10.532242 in the above example). Accordingly, the monthly payment that would be quoted by lenders is $1,053.23. For simplification purposes, however, we use the table provided in Figure 6.3.

Figure 6.3
Payments to Amortize $1000, Including Principal and Interest

Term of years	7%	7.2%	7¼%	7½%	7¾%	7.8%	8%	8.4%	8½%	9%	9½%	10%	11%	12%	13%	14%	15%	16%	17%	18%	19%	20%
5	19.81	19.90	19.92	20.04	20.16	20.19	20.28	20.47	20.52	20.76	21.01	21.25	21.75	22.25	22.76	23.27	23.79	24.32	24.86	25.40	25.95	26.49
6	17.05	17.15	17.17	17.30	17.42	17.44	17.54	17.73	17.78	18.03	18.28	18.53	19.03	19.55	20.07	20.61	21.15	21.69	22.25	22.81	23.38	23.95
7	15.10	15.20	15.22	15.34	15.47	15.49	15.59	15.79	15.84	16.09	16.35	16.61	17.12	17.65	18.19	18.74	19.30	19.86	20.44	21.02	21.61	22.21
8	13.64	13.74	13.76	13.89	14.01	14.04	14.14	14.35	14.40	14.66	14.92	15.18	15.71	16.25	16.81	17.37	17.95	18.53	19.12	19.72	20.33	20.95
9	12.51	12.61	12.64	12.77	12.89	12.92	13.02	13.23	13.28	13.55	13.81	14.08	14.63	15.18	15.75	16.33	16.92	17.53	18.14	18.76	19.39	20.03
10	11.62	11.72	11.75	11.88	12.01	12.03	12.14	12.35	12.40	12.67	12.94	13.22	13.78	14.35	14.94	15.53	16.14	16.76	17.38	18.02	18.67	19.33
11	10.89	10.99	11.02	11.15	11.29	11.31	11.42	11.64	11.69	11.97	12.24	12.52	13.09	13.68	14.28	14.89	15.51	16.14	16.79	17.44	18.11	18.79
12	10.29	10.40	10.42	10.56	10.69	10.72	10.83	11.05	11.11	11.39	11.67	11.96	12.54	13.13	13.75	14.37	15.01	15.66	16.32	16.99	17.67	18.37
13	9.79	9.89	9.92	10.06	10.20	10.22	10.34	10.56	10.62	10.90	11.19	11.48	12.08	12.69	13.31	13.95	14.60	15.27	15.94	16.63	17.35	18.04
14	9.36	9.47	9.50	9.64	9.78	9.80	9.92	10.15	10.20	10.49	10.79	11.09	11.69	12.31	12.95	13.60	14.29	14.95	15.64	16.34	17.05	17.77
15	8.99	9.11	9.13	9.28	9.42	9.45	9.56	9.79	9.85	10.15	10.45	10.75	11.37	12.01	12.66	13.32	14.00	14.69	15.40	16.11	16.83	17.56
16	8.63	8.79	8.82	8.95	9.11	9.14	9.25	9.49	9.55	9.85	10.15	10.46	11.09	11.74	12.40	13.05	13.77	14.47	15.19	15.91	16.65	17.39
17	8.40	8.52	8.55	8.69	8.84	8.87	8.99	9.23	9.29	9.59	9.90	10.22	10.85	11.51	12.19	12.87	13.58	14.29	15.02	15.76	16.50	17.26
18	8.16	8.28	8.31	8.45	8.60	8.63	8.75	9.00	9.06	9.37	9.68	10.00	10.65	11.32	12.00	12.70	13.42	14.14	14.88	15.63	16.38	17.15
19	7.95	8.07	8.10	8.25	8.40	8.43	8.55	8.80	8.86	9.17	9.49	9.82	10.47	11.15	11.85	12.56	13.25	14.02	14.76	15.52	16.29	17.06
20	7.76	7.88	7.91	8.06	8.21	8.25	8.37	8.62	8.68	9.00	9.33	9.66	10.33	11.02	11.72	12.44	13.17	13.92	14.67	15.44	16.21	16.98
21	7.59	7.71	7.74	7.90	8.05	8.08	8.21	8.46	8.53	8.85	9.18	9.51	10.19	10.89	11.60	12.33	13.07	13.82	14.59	15.36	16.14	16.93
22	7.44	7.56	7.59	7.75	7.91	7.94	8.07	8.32	8.39	8.72	9.05	9.39	10.07	10.78	11.50	12.24	12.99	13.75	14.52	15.30	16.09	16.88
23	7.30	7.43	7.46	7.62	7.78	7.81	7.94	8.20	8.27	8.60	8.93	9.28	9.97	10.69	11.42	12.16	12.92	13.69	14.46	15.25	16.04	16.84
24	7.18	7.31	7.34	7.50	7.66	7.70	7.83	8.09	8.16	8.49	8.83	9.18	9.88	10.60	11.34	12.10	12.86	13.63	14.42	15.21	16.01	16.81
25	7.07	7.20	7.23	7.39	7.56	7.59	7.72	7.99	8.06	8.40	8.74	9.09	9.81	10.54	11.28	12.04	12.81	13.59	14.38	15.18	15.98	16.78
26	6.97	7.10	7.14	7.30	7.46	7.50	7.63	7.90	7.97	8.31	8.66	9.01	9.73	10.47	11.22	11.99	12.76	13.55	14.34	15.15	15.95	16.76
27	6.88	7.01	7.05	7.21	7.38	7.41	7.55	7.82	7.89	8.24	8.59	8.95	9.67	10.41	11.17	11.95	12.73	13.52	14.32	15.12	15.93	16.75
28	6.80	6.93	6.97	7.13	7.30	7.34	7.47	7.75	7.82	8.17	8.52	8.88	9.62	10.37	11.14	11.91	12.70	13.50	14.30	15.11	15.92	16.73
29	6.73	6.86	6.89	7.06	7.23	7.27	7.40	7.68	7.75	8.11	8.47	8.83	9.57	10.33	11.10	11.88	12.67	13.47	14.28	15.09	15.91	16.72
30	6.66	6.79	6.83	7.00	7.17	7.20	7.34	7.62	7.69	8.05	8.41	8.78	9.53	10.29	11.07	11.85	12.65	13.45	14.26	15.08	15.89	16.71
35	6.39	6.53	6.57	6.75	6.93	6.96	7.11	7.40	7.47	7.84	8.22	8.60	9.37	10.16	10.96	11.76	12.57	13.39	14.21	15.03	15.86	16.69
40	6.22	6.37	6.40	6.59	6.77	6.81	6.96	7.26	7.34	7.72	8.11	8.50	9.29	10.09	10.90	11.72	12.54	13.36	14.19	15.02	15.85	16.68

2. Assume instead that you know the amount of loan, monthly payment, and the interest rate, but do not know how long the loan is to run. How is the term of loan computed?

Again we would look at an amortization table such as the one reproduced in Figure 6.3. Our task is to find the nearest monthly factor per thousand under a given rate of interest, then to look across to the Term of Years column to determine length of payoff. If the loan is for $100,000, payable $1,054 per month, including 12% interest per annum, can you compute what the term of repayment will be?

Answer: Divide $1,054, the monthly payment, by 100, the number of thousands of dollars of principal to get 10.54. Then look up 10.54 under the 12% column. Looking to the years column at the left, we find the 10.54 cell corresponds to 25 years.

The amortization table will be further discussed in Chapter 7, where it will be applied to other financial situations.

I = PRT

Interest and other amounts to be computed in many real estate transactions can be easily determined by simple formulas which are easy to memorize and to use. For example, I=PRT is a basic tool for the figuring of interest, principal, rate, and duration of payment (time). By plugging in known amounts or values, the unknown amount can be determined.

I=PRT is perhaps the most useful in real estate financing: *Interest equals Principal times Rate times Time.* It answers the central question, "how much of my monthly trust deed payment represents interest, and how much is for principal?"

Returning to the $100,000 example, if 12% is the rate of interest and 25 years the time for repaying the loan, the monthly payment of principal and interest is $1,053.23. To calculate the first month's interest, substitute the known values for the letters:

$$I = PRT$$
$$I = \$100,000 \times .12 \times 1/12$$
$$I = \$12,000 \div 12$$
$$I = \$1,000$$

Thus, $1,000 of the $1,053.23 monthly payment represents interest, and the remainder, $53.23 represents principal. After the first install-

ment, the balance of the loan will be $100,000 less $53.23, or $99,946.77.

You may wonder why we use 1/12 for time. This is because interest rates are computed on a yearly basis, and if a payment is made every month, the interest amount will be one twelfth (1/12) of a year. By contrast, if payments were made twice a year, the time rate would be 1/2; if every three months (quarterly payments), it would be 1/4; and so on.

Computing Total Interest

A question frequently asked is, "How do you figure the actual interest cost of a mortgage?" Multiply the monthly payment times the number of months your loan will run; then subtract the original loan from this figure, and you discover just how much you must pay to borrow a given amount of money for a certain period of time. For example, assume you want to borrow $100,000 at 12% for 25 years. Monthly payments are $1,053.23 for 300 months, including principal and interest.

$$
\begin{array}{r}
\$1,053.23 \text{ per month} \\
\times\ 300 \text{ monthly payments} \\
\hline
\$\ 315,969 \text{ to be paid in 25 years} \\
-\ 100,000 \text{ original loan} \\
\hline
\$\ 215,969 \text{ interest cost}
\end{array}
$$

After figuring the exact interest costs of various loans, you will discover that on a long-term loan, a slight drop in the interest rate can result in a big saving over the years. For example, if you took out the loan above at only 10%, your total interest payments would be $172,700 ($9.09 per $1000 × 300 months = $272,700 less $100,000 principal). A drop of only 2% in the interest rate would save you $43,269 during the time the mortgage runs.

You will discover, too, that even a small loan can be expensive: For example, only $5,000 for 5 years at 15% calls for monthly payments of $118.95, including principal and interest. Thus, the total payment of $7,137 includes interest expense of $2,139. When rates are high, interest payments can be a serious obstacle to home ownership, as could be seen since the spring of 1980, when rates soared and real estate sales plummeted.

PRORATIONS AND ADJUSTMENTS

In a sales escrow, there is usually a need to make various prorations or adjustments between buyer and seller. Included are such items as taxes, insurance, interest, and rent. Proration means a division or splitting of expenses and income on real estate in proportion to the period of ownership of the seller and the buyer, usually as of the date of closing escrow. If an item has been paid in advance by the seller, he or she is entitled to recover the unused portion from the buyer. Conversely, if items of expense have been incurred by the seller, but not paid, the buyer is entitled to credit for the seller's share. Prorations are usually made on the basis of a thirty-day month and are reflected in the escrow statement prepared for each of the parties.

As an example of proration, the seller's fire insurance policy may have cost $900.00 for a three-year term. If it is to be assigned to the buyer and, for instance, still has 1-1/2 years to run, the buyer will be charged one-half of the cost (or $450.00).

Adjustments or prorations can be computed in two ways: by working them out mathematically or by using escrow prorating tables. The mathematical computations provide a better understanding of the theory of adjustments and can be useful in explaining to a customer how an adjustment was calculated. However, the use of tables provides an accurate and faster method of making these computations and is favored by most escrow officers. The subject will be considered in further detail in a later section, which discusses the role of the escrow.

Another escrow responsibility relates to the computation of interest when a trust deed is to be paid off through escrow. Assume an escrow transaction is scheduled to close on February 11 as of 8:00 A.M. (time of recording). A bank holds a note secured by a trust deed with an unpaid balance of $3,965.18; interest is paid to February 1. The note is to be paid off through escrow. In its demand, the bank called for interest at 10% from February 1 to the date payment is received at the bank. The first step is to ascertain the amount of interest for one day. This is done by a simple arithmetic four-step method:

Principal balance	$3,965.18
Rate of interest	× .10
Interest for 1 year	$ 396.52
	12) 396.52
Interest for 1 month	$ 33.04
	30) 33.04
Interest for 1 day	$ 1.10

The bank's demand provides for the interest to be paid "to date payment is received by us." By this, the bank probably means that it will want to have the interest computed to include the day on which it receives the payment. This could be accomplished on February 11; accordingly, the escrow officer would be safe in providing the bank with eleven days' interest. The exact amount of interest is figured as follows:

$$11 \text{ days @ } \$1.10 \ldots . \$12.10$$

SOME HANDY FORMULAS

Three-Variable Formulas

The *Real Estate Reference Book* (1984–85 ed., p. 760) describes some handy three-variable formulas:

> In three-variable formulas, one variable is equal to the other two. Place this one variable in the top half of an imaginary circle. Place each of the other two variables in adjacent quarters in the bottom half of the circle. Divide the circle horizontally by a diameter line. This is a *division line* (÷). Divide the bottom quarters of the circle vertically by a radius line. This is a *multiplication line* (×). To find the unknown variable, cover with your finger the unknown variable and complete the calculation.

Figure 6.4
Three-Variable Formulas

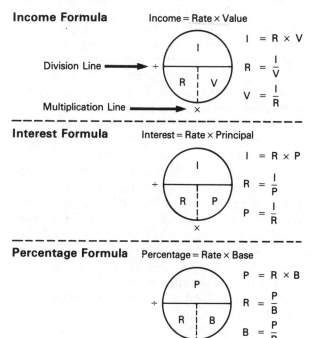

Other three-variable formulas:

Area = Length × Width (A = L × W)

Tax = Assessed Value × Rate (T = A × R)

Commission = Sales Price × Rate (C = S × R)

INTRODUCTION TO ESCROWS

Nature of an Escrow

Many persons buying a home for the first time wonder if they really need the services of an escrow. Once its role is understood, however, it is generally agreed that an escrow is quite essential to the satisfactory closing of a real estate transaction in California. In fact, escrows are used to effect a satisfactory closing of many transactions in addition to real estate sales: loans, exchanges, leases, sales of personal property including business opportunities or assets of a business (bulk sales), transfers of liquor licenses, sales of securities, and transfer of a vendee's interest under a contract of sale. There are also escrows involving permits issued by the corporations commissioner, the savings and loan commissioner, the state banking superintendent, and others.

In many respects the escrow officer often plays the most knowledgeable role in a real estate transaction. Therefore, the escrow business requires a very high degree of care, skill, and sophistication. Basically, an escrow is a *trust arrangement* between the principals in a transaction and the escrow holder.

After a person has agreed to buy property and is assured of financing, the next step usually is for the parties to "go into escrow." Escrow transactions are most commonly handled by escrow holders such as banks, title insurance companies, or independent escrow companies. In the escrow procedure, the parties to the transaction—seller, buyer, lender, mortgage holder, or other party—deposit their funds or documents, together with written instructions regarding their use, in the hands of an impartial "trustee," or disinterested third party, called the *escrow holder*, who becomes the *agent* of both parties to the transaction (a dual agency). The escrow holder will thereafter release the monies and documents only when all of the instructions and agreements have been fully complied with—which is referred to as the closing of escrow.

The word *stakeholder* is also used to designate the escrow agent. He or she becomes a *trustee* for the money and documents until they are distributed in accordance with the escrow instructions. This means that the escrow holder is the agent for the buyer, for instance, regarding the use of funds deposited by the buyer. The funds still belong to the buyer. But when the escrow closes, these funds become the property of the seller, and the escrow holder becomes a trustee of the funds for the seller's account.

In simple form, then, an escrow is the depositing of funds or documents by a buyer and a seller (or pledger and pledgee or other principal parties) with an impartial agent for delivery upon completion of the terms and provisions of the escrow instructions—which, when properly drawn, usually evidence a binding contract between the parties.

Buyer and seller are the *principals* in the escrow. The principals may also include a bank or other lending institution making a loan on the property. Each of the principals will give to the escrow holder written instructions (illustrated later in this chapter) setting out the conditions under which the ultimate delivery is to be made. These instructions are usually typed by the escrow officer or his or her secretary. They are prepared either from oral information supplied by the principals, which is usually transcribed by the escrow officer on a work sheet called an *escrow memo sheet*, or from a written agreement executed by the parties before they arrive at the escrow office.

Some escrow customers have had little experience in dealing with real estate and are not acquainted with the customary procedures. It requires considerable patience and understanding on the part of the escrow officer to be sure that the intent of the parties is expressed accurately and completely in the escrow instructions. The role of the escrow holder calls for a considerable degree of tact and diplomacy in addition to the requisite knowledge and skill.

The complexity of the escrow can depend not only upon the nature of the transaction (whether a sale, loan, exchange, lease, etc.) and the type of property involved (whether residential, commercial, industrial, etc.) but also upon the identity of the parties—whether individuals, corporations, partnerships, joint venturers, trustees, executors or administrators of a decedent's estate, guardians, attorneys-in-fact, government agencies, and so on.

Reason for an Escrow

The word *escrow* is derived from the French word *escroue*, meaning a scroll or a roll of writing. When an owner of real property executed an instrument in the form of a deed conveying land to a grantee, and delivered the deed to a third person with instructions that the instrument should be delivered to the grantee (with title passing to him) only upon the fulfillment of some condition, a separate legal designation for the document while held in abeyance was necessary. It could not be called "deed," since a deed is an instrument that legally is immediately operative. For this reason the instrument in the form of a deed was designated as an "escrow."

The technical definition of an escrow, denoting the *instrument* that is conditionally delivered to a third party, does not entirely reflect its modern meaning. Thus, when parties speak of "an escrow" or "going into escrow," they regard the "escrow" as the *transaction* itself.

More often than not real estate is the subject of an escrow transaction. Why is this so? Basically because of the difference between real and personal property. When a person wants to buy a piece of furniture or equipment, all he or she has to do is walk into a store, select the article, pay for it (or charge it), and either take it home or have it delivered. He or she obtains *possession*, and is ordinarily not concerned about the right of the store to sell it or about obtaining a written document to evidence his or her title.

In contrast, transactions involving real property are not so simple. Although in theory the owner of land can sign a simple form of conveyance and deliver it to the buyer upon payment of the purchase price, a prudent buyer wants assurances that he or she is obtaining the title bargained for. A transaction solely between the parties *might* be as safe as if the parties used the services of an escrow holder, but it also *might not be*. In most cases a transaction solely between seller and buyer would not be an acceptable procedure, either for the buyer or the seller.

To illustrate: *If* the deed is properly executed by the parties who actually own the land, *and if* title to the land is in fact unencumbered to the extent bargained for, *and if* the land is accurately described, *and* if the deed is recorded within the proper time, then the buyer may have nothing to worry about.

However, if the buyer is a prudent, careful person, he or she will realize that it is much safer to deposit his or her money with a responsible third party with instructions to pay it to the seller only when the title has been investigated and the sufficiency of the deed as a valid conveyance has been determined by a title insurance company. The buyer should not be expected to part with any money until it is certain that he or she is getting good title and that the condition of title is as represented and intended.

The buyer's instructions to the escrow holder will ordinarily specify that the buyer is to be furnished with written evidence that the title investigation has been completed, and that there are no encumbrances on the title other than those agreed upon with the seller. The buyer will require that the deed in his or her favor be recorded at the time the escrow is closed. The evidence of title to be furnished to the buyer will show that the deed has been recorded, and will assure the buyer that the title is vested in him or her and will be defended to the extent afforded by the coverage of the policy of title insurance issued to the buyer.

The seller will also benefit from this method of effecting completion of the agreement of sale. First of all, he or she will not want to convey title to a buyer until the consideration has been received, either in the form of cash, or part cash and the balance evidenced by a note secured by a deed of trust or other form of consideration. The seller will want the deed prepared by an experienced person and will want it delivered to the buyer only after the terms of the sale have been complied with. The escrow instructions that the seller signs will so provide.

Because of the special conditions involved in the sale of a mobile home—i.e., the mobility of the property, the law requires that the interests of the buyer and seller be protected by the services of an escrow holder.

In summary, the most common reason for an escrow is to enable the buyer and seller of real property to deal with each other without risk of loss, since all responsibility for handling funds and documents is placed squarely on the shoulders of the escrow holder.

Basic Characteristics of an Escrow

The importance of the escrow to the parties in a real estate transaction is reflected in the many purposes an escrow serves:

1. It is often a method of achieving a binding *contract*.
2. It affords an instrument to effect performance, but only upon compliance with *conditions*. It protects the seller in that his or her documents will not be used until the consideration is paid. It protects the buyer in that his or her funds will not be used until assurances have been obtained that title as bargained for will be conveyed to him or her.
3. It provides a *custodian* of funds and documents pending the closing of the transaction.
4. It affords a *clearing house* for the payment of demands.
5. It affords an *agency* to clear accounting details, such as prorations and adjustments.

Although an escrow in most transactions is not compulsory, it is the common practice in California, and we have seen that it does afford many advantages both from the standpoint of protection and convenience. However, this does not mean that the services of an attorney are not also needed. The role of attorneys is an important one, and their services and assistance are frequently desirable. The primary role of the attorney is to advise his or her client about the client's rights and duties, and to prepare necessary documentation that is beyond the scope of the escrow function. It is unlawful for an escrow officer to prepare documents or escrow provisions that go beyond the customary duties of an escrow holder. Parties frequently need to consult with their attorneys about the manner in which title is to be taken and about the tax aspects of the transaction. An escrow holder cannot perform legal services. When legal problems arise, the escrow holder should request the parties to consult with their attorneys.

There are many essential characteristics of escrows, including the following:

1. An escrow is *confidential*. Information in the escrow file must not be disclosed to third parties without the express permission of the principals. Only the principals to the transaction are entitled to see the escrow instructions and other documents pertinent to the escrow, and then only insofar as they apply and dovetail with each other's instructions.
2. The escrow officer must be *impartial*. He or she is a neutral or disinterested third party as far as any dispute between the parties is concerned.
3. The escrow officer *must not give legal advice*.
4. The escrow officer must do *only as directed*. He or she must follow the specific instructions of the parties, doing no more and no less.

The Escrow Business

In view of the public interest involved in the escrow business, and especially because of the trust aspects in the conduct of an escrow and the role of the escrow holder, legislation has been enacted in California to regulate various aspects of the escrow business. The main regulations are referred to as the Escrow Law, first enacted in 1947 and presently contained in the Financial Code of the state of California. The Escrow Law is designed to regulate the business of escrow agencies and their employees; to provide for their licensing, examination, and regulation by the commissioner of corporations; to specify exemptions from the law; and to prescribe penalties for violations of the law.

The Escrow Law contains several requisites for the incorporation, qualification, bonding, experience, audit, and other regulation of any person undertaking the performance of escrow agent services, unless exempt (see below).

An individual as such cannot be licensed as an escrow holder. The license must be held in the name of a corporation duly organized for the purpose of conducting an escrow business. The Escrow Law contains several exemptions from the licensing requirement, including

1. Banks, trust companies, building and loan or savings and loan associations, insurance companies, and title companies
2. Licensed attorneys not actively engaged in conducting an escrow agency
3. Any broker licensed by the Real Estate Commissioner while performing acts in the course of, or incidental to, a real estate transaction in which the broker is an agent or a party to the transaction and in which the broker is performing an act, for which a real estate license is required.

A real estate broker can handle escrows only in connection with his or her own real estate brokerage business, not transactions made by other brokers or by individuals acting without the benefit of a broker.

The reason for these exemptions is that the persons exempted are already subject to the jurisdiction of other licensing and regulatory authorities. Additional controls or regulations are deemed unnecessary as far as the public interest is concerned.

The escrow business in California has developed into a major undertaking. However, the method of handling escrows is not uniform throughout the state. The diversity in practice is based largely on local custom and experience. Differences relate principally to the form of escrow instructions and to the division of charges. Other differences may also be encountered, dependent upon the practices of the particular escrow company.

In southern California the prevailing practice has been to draft more or less formal escrow instructions. The escrow is a transaction independent from the issuance of a policy of title insurance, with a separate fee for each service. The escrow holder may be a title company, but often is not. The seller usually pays the fee for a standard coverage policy of title insurance.

In northern California generally, escrow instructions are inclined to be much less formal. The handling of an escrow and the issuance of a policy of title insurance were for a long time indivisible operations furnished by title companies only and for a single fee. The present practice is to charge separate fees. The buyer customarily pays the title policy fee.

In both regions, the recognized practice is to make the closing of a real estate transaction conditional upon the issuance of a policy of title insurance. The trend today is leading to a greater uniformity in the escrow practices, and it is anticipated that in time the practice will be considerably more uniform throughout the state.

Escrow Associations

Business and professional associations traditionally have played an important role in building up the image, prestige, status, and service standards of the members of their particular groups, and afford a means of cooperation among their members and related groups. In the escrow field the California Escrow Association performs this function. It was formed in 1957 as a state association, although the name had already been adopted by an escrow association in Los Angeles in 1956.

The Los Angeles group cooperatively changed its name to the Los Angeles Escrow Association in order that the first statewide group could be known as the California Escrow Association. Conferences stressing the importance of the continuing education of its members have been held annually since the inception of the association. It has sponsored an escrow certificate program offered at many of the state's community colleges.

A Code of Ethics delineating the professional standards and goals of the association was adopted in 1969. A copy appears as Appendix D.

THE ESCROW FUNCTION

Basic Steps in an Escrow

Stated simply, here are the mechanics of a typical escrow:

1. Buyer and seller agree upon the price, terms, and conditions for the purchase by the buyer of a parcel of real property owned by the seller.
2. They select an escrow holder. The law prohibits any person to require, as a condition precedent to entering into any transaction involving the transfer of real property containing a single family residence, that the escrow be conducted by any specified agency. However, a failure to comply with the act will not invalidate the transfer.
3. Buyer delivers to the escrow holder the funds required. The buyer's instructions to the escrow holder authorize and direct the escrow holder to deliver to the seller the stated sum of money when the escrow holder obtains from the seller a deed which, when recorded, will enable a title insurance company to issue a policy of title insurance in a stated amount (ordinarily the selling price of the property), vesting the title to the property in the buyer's name, subject only to restrictions or encumbrances approved by the buyer in the escrow instructions.
4. Seller deposits the deed and other necessary documents (if any) with the escrow holder, and authorizes and directs the escrow holder to deliver the deed to the buyer once he or she has deposited into escrow the necessary funds.

5. At the moment the deed is delivered to the buyer through escrow, the funds then become the property of the seller, from which the escrow holder will have paid any necessary amounts to clear the title in accordance with the seller's instructions. All these steps are accomplished in a single closing transaction.

Many escrow transactions involve a third-party lender such as a savings and loan association. Many times the buyer has agreed to purchase the property for cash to the seller, but will need to arrange financing with a third party, who will require the protection of the escrow process. The mechanics of such a transaction can be briefly summarized as follows:

1. Seller deposits the deed and other documents into escrow with the understanding that he or she is to receive the purchase price in cash.
2. Buyer deposits cash into escrow in an amount up to the loan, and authorizes the use of such cash, together with additional funds to be provided by a lender, in payment of the purchase price.
3. The lender deposits funds into escrow with instructions that such funds are to be dispersed only when his or her security interest has been perfected by the recording of a deed of trust on the property and the issuance of a lender's policy of title insurance insuring his or her lien as a first lien (or second, as the case may be), subject only to matters affecting the title that he or she has approved.
4. The transaction is completed when, simultaneously, the deed to the purchaser and the deed of trust in favor of the lender are recorded, and the funds become the property of the seller.

In taking an escrow through these basic steps, the functions of the escrow holder are many: ordering a search of title from a responsible title insurance company as the first step in obtaining the required policy of title insurance; obtaining clearance from the appropriate parties of any objectionable clouds on title, liens, and other encumbrances; drafting such documents as grant deeds, trust deeds, and promissory notes; paying demands of holders of loans being paid off through the escrow; procuring beneficiary statements, rent statements, and other offset statements as appropriate; adjusting and prorating such items as taxes, interest, rent, and hazard insurance premiums; and satisfying the require-

ments and conditions imposed by third-party lenders prior to their advancing loan funds.

When the preliminary report of title is received from the title insurance company, the report will be checked against the instructions of the parties to the escrow. The title insurance company will then examine the deed and other documents for legal sufficiency. When the escrow holder is satisfied that all of the conditions of the escrow have been met, it will so inform the title insurance company and will give recording instructions. The title insurance company will cause the deed and other necessary documents to be recorded, and will then issue the evidence of title in the form of a policy of title insurance for the buyer and for other parties, such as a lender, in accordance with their requirements.

Even in a relatively simple transaction, much coordinated effort and attention to detail will be required in order to make sure that there has been full compliance with the instructions of the parties. Figure 6.5 sketches the procedure in a flow chart format.

Use of the Memo Sheet

When the escrow officer first takes an escrow, he or she will ordinarily take the instructions of the parties verbally and will transcribe them (make a notation of them) on a memo sheet or *escrow work sheet*. From this information the escrow instructions will be typed on a printed form.

A typical escrow work sheet illustrates the type of information needed in order to carry out the necessary functions in an escrow (see Figure 6.6). The various parts of the work sheet have been numbered for convenience, and will be discussed by reference to these numbers.

1. *Type of transaction*, ordinarily the first bit of information the escrow officer will want to know. Sales, loans, and exchanges are most frequently encountered. Sometimes the transaction is a combination of two or more types.
2. *Total consideration*, the *total* sale price, not just the equity. In most home purchases, the buyer pays only part of the purchase price in cash. The portion of the total consideration not represented by cash may be in the form of a loan. This loan may be a purchase money trust deed, or it may be a loan already on the property on which the buyer takes over the

Figure 6.5
Life of an Escrow

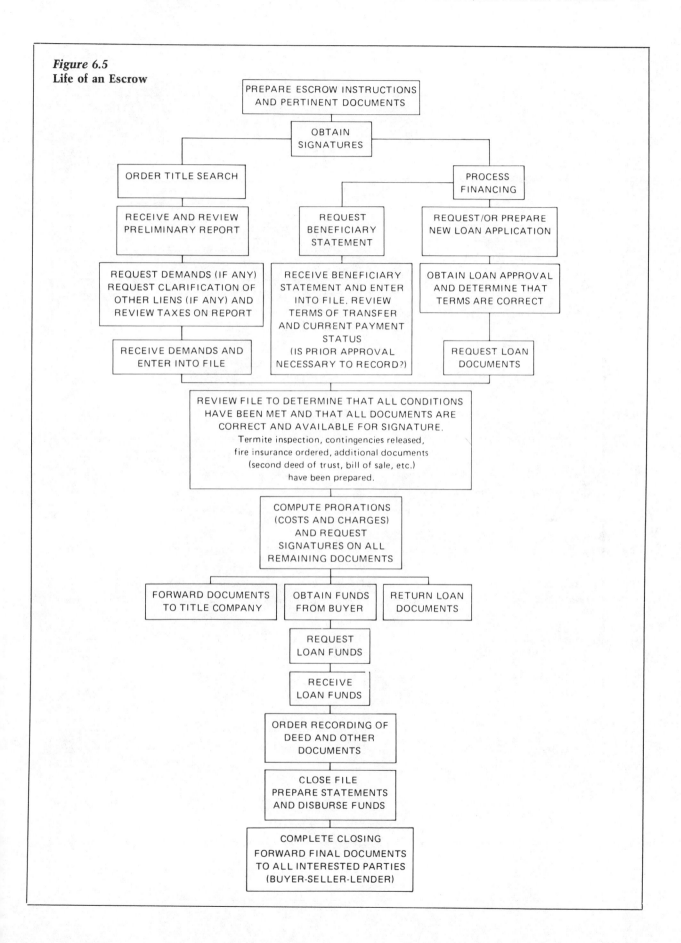

Figure 6.6
Escrow Work Sheet

payments, either by taking the property *subject to* the loan or by *assuming* the loan.

3. *Time limit* specifies the time within which the escrow is to be closed. It will be governed by any provisions in the escrow instructions authorizing an extension of time.

4. *First party*, the seller, one of the principals to the escrow.

5. *Second party*, the buyer, the other principal. Ordinarily it is preferable to use the words *seller* and *buyer*, rather than *first party* and *second party*.

6. *The type of policy of title insurance* could be a CLTA standard coverage policy or an ALTA loan policy or other form of policy. Title insurance policies are described in detail later in this chapter.

7. *Description of the property* should be the full legal description and not the street address alone.

8. *Vest in.* The names of the buyers of the property and the manner in which they are to hold title.

9. *Encumbrances.* This includes all matters that the buyer approves as liens or encumbrances against the property and that will be shown as matters affecting the title when escrow closes.

10. *Adjustments* are usually made on the theory that the seller is the owner of the property and is entitled to possession or the income from the property until title actually passes to the buyer. In such cases, the seller continues to bear the expenses of ownership, such as taxes, principal and interest on any mortgage, etc., until title has passed to the new owner. Accordingly, escrow instructions usually provide that the rent, interest, taxes, and hazard insurance shall be prorated between buyer and seller as of close of escrow, or any other date agreed to and designated by the parties.

11. *Charges* include the title policy premium, escrow fee, and any incidentals. These charges are usually divided according to local practice, but may be subject to other agreement between the parties.

12. *Transfer tax*, paid, if applicable, at the time of recording. In California the Documentary Transfer Tax Act requires payment of $1.10 for each $1,000 of taxable equity.

13. *Commission.* If a sale is made through the service of a real estate broker, the seller is usually obligated to pay a commission for these services. Normally the seller will direct that this payment be made from funds accruing to his or her account at close of escrow. The escrow officer will need to ascertain that the party receiving the commission is licensed.

14. *Other payments.* In order to comply with the terms of the sales agreement, the seller frequently will authorize payment of other encumbrances for which he or she is obligated. The seller may authorize these payments from funds deposited in the escrow by the buyer, but payable, of course, only when the escrow is ready to close.

15. *Water stock* in a mutual water company which furnishes water to the premises is sometimes the subject of an assignment through escrow.

16. *Drawing documents* refers to the documents, such as transfer deeds and trust deeds, that the escrow is to prepare.

17. *Remarks* are additional items to be covered in the escrow instructions, such as termite inspections or reports. A termite inspection is not mandatory, but a buyer will usually require it in areas where termite infestation is apt to occur. In such localities, termite inspection is often made a condition of sale, especially if the house is an older one. Many lenders traditionally require it. Who pays the cost varies. In some areas the seller will pay for the cost of the report, obtained from a licensed pest control operator, and for any *corrective* work that needs to be done. The buyer generally pays for any *preventive* work that he or she desires to have done. In any case, the cost for termite work is always by agreement of the parties to the transaction. Persons may request from the Structural Pest Control Board in Sacramento certified copies of inspection reports and completion notices filed during the preceding two years by any structural pest control operator. Copies are furnished for a nominal fee.

18. *Party opening escrow.* This information is necessary for the purpose of assuring payment of escrow costs. Who guarantees the escrow charges is a matter of agreement between the parties and the escrow company.

Escrow Instructions

From the information set forth in the memo sheet, the escrow officer will see that the escrow

Figure 6.7
Escrow Instructions

**Figure 6.7
Continued**

PAGE 2
ADDITIONAL ESCROW CONDITIONS AND INSTRUCTIONS

1. Your duty to act as escrow holder does not commence until these instructions, signed by all parties, are received by you. Until such time either party may unilaterally cancel and upon written request delivered to you, the party may withdraw funds and documents he previously handed to you.

2. All funds received in this escrow shall be deposited with a State or National bank with other escrow funds. Make disbursements by your check. checks not presented for payment within six months after date are subject to service charges in accordance with your schedule in effect from time to time. Make all adjustments and prorations on the basis of a 30 day month. "Close of Escrow" is the day instruments are recorded. All documents and funds due the respective parties herein are to be mailed to the addresses set out below their respective signatures, unless otherwise instructed. Our signatures on any documents and instructions pertaining to this escrow indicate our unconditional approval of same. Whenever provision is made herein for the payment of any sum, the delivery of any instrument or the performance of any act "outside of escrow," you as escrow holder shall have no responsibility therefor, shall not be concerned therewith and are specifically relieved of any obligation relative thereto.

3. You shall not be responsible or liable in any manner whatsoever for the sufficiency or correctness as to form, manner of execution or validity of any documents deposited in escrow. nor as to the identity, authority or rights of any person executing the same, either as to documents of record or those handled in this escrow. Your duties hereunder shall be limited to the safekeeping of such money and documents received by you as escrow holder, and for the disposition of the same in accordance with the written instructions accepted by you in this escrow. You shall not be required to take any action in connection with the collection, maturity or apparent outlaw of any obligations deposited in this escrow, unless otherwise instructed.

4. Seller guarantees, and you shall be fully protected in assuming, that as to any insurance policy handed you each policy is in force, has not been hypothecated and that all necessary premiums therefor have been paid. You will transmit for assignment any insurance policy handed you for use in this escrow, but you shall not be responsible for verifying the acceptance of the assignment and policy by the insurance company. ESCROW HOLDER WILL MAKE NO ATTEMPT TO VERIFY THE RECEIPT OF THE REQUEST FOR ASSIGNMENT BY THE ISSUING COMPANY. You are hereby placed on notice that if the insurance company should fail to receive said assignment, the issuing company may deny coverage for any loss suffered by Buyer. IT IS THE OBLIGATION OF THE INSURED OR HIS REPRESENTATIVE TO VERIFY THE ACCEPTANCE OF THE ASSIGNMENT OF THE POLICY BY THE ISSUING COMPANY.

5. The adjustments and prorations called for, shall be computed as set forth below, or as otherwise amended in writing.
    (a) Taxes, including all tax bill items, except taxes on personal property not conveyed through this escrow, based on current year's taxes, or between July 1st and November 1st of each year based on immediately preceding year's taxes. In each case, use the figures from the tax bill handed you by the seller or figures furnished you by title company, without liability on your part as to their correctness. Seller agrees to pay prior to delinquency, any taxes on real and personal property not being sold herein, which is a lien on the real property being conveyed. You are not to be concerned with same.
    (b) Interest on Mortgages and/or Trust Deeds of record, mortgage insurance premiums, funds accrued in Impound Account for future payment of taxes, fire or mortgage insurance as disclosed by any beneficiary statement received in escrow. If any beneficiary statement discloses that the unpaid PRINCIPAL AMOUNT DUE ON ANY TRUST DEED OF RECORD IS MORE OR LESS THAN THE AMOUNT HEREIN SET FORTH, adjust the difference in cash through this escrow, unless otherwise provided for herein.

6. Deliver assurances of title, and insurance policies, if any, to holder of senior encumbrance or his order, or if there be no encumbrances, then to the buyer or his order.

7. If the conditions of this escrow have not been complied with prior to the expiration of time provided for herein, or any extension thereof, you are nevertheless to complete the escrow as soon as the conditions, except as to time, have been complied with unless written demand shall have been made upon you not to complete it. Following receipt of such written demand not to complete the escrow, you are to promptly mail a copy of said demand to the other party. Unless written objection thereto from such other party shall be received by you within 7 business days after mailing, you may comply with such written demand and return all monies and documents, upon payment of your cancellation fees. costs and expenses, to the party or parties depositing the same with you. If written objection is received within the time stated, you may proceed in accordance with the provisions of paragraph 8 hereof.

8. NO NOTICE, DEMAND OR CHANGE OF INSTRUCTIONS SHALL BE OF ANY EFFECT IN THIS ESCROW UNLESS GIVEN IN WRITING BY ALL PARTIES AFFECTED THEREBY. In the event conflicting demands or notices are made or served upon you or any controversy arises between the parties hereto or with third person growing out of or relating to this escrow, you shall have the absolute right to withhold and stop all further proceedings in, and performance of, this escrow, until you receive written notification satisfactory to you of the settlement of the controversy by agreement of the parties thereto, or by final judgment of a court of competent jurisdiction. All of the parties to this escrow hereby jointly and severally promise and agree to pay promptly on demand, as well as to indemnify you and to hold you harmless from and against all litigation and interpleader costs, damages, judgments, attorney's fees, expenses, obligations and liabilities of every kind which, in good faith, you may incur or suffer in connection with or arising out of this escrow whether said litigation. interpleader, obligations, liabilities or expenses arise during the performance of this escrow, or subsequent thereto, directly or indirectly notwithstanding, you are authorized at your discretion to accept written instructions by one seller on behalf of all sellers and same by one buyer or behalf of all buyers and to act thereon as though same was signed by all parties.

9. You are hereby authorized to deposit any funds or documents handed you under these escrow instructions, or cause the same to be deposited with any duly authorized sub-escrow agent, subject to your order at or prior to close of escrow, in the event such deposit shall be necessary or convenient for the consummation of this escrow.

10. All parties agree that as far as your rights and liabilities are involved, this transaction is an escrow and not any other legal relation and you are an escrow holder only on the within expressed terms, and you shall have no responsibility of notifying me or any of the parties to this escrow of any sale, resale, loan, exchange, or other transaction involving any property herein described or of any profit realized by any person, firm or corporation (broker, agent and parties to this and any other escrow included) in connection therewith regardless of the fact that such transaction(s) may be handled by you in this escrow or in another escrow.

11. You are not to be concerned with the giving of any disclosures required by Federal or State law, specifically but not exclusively, RESPA (Real Estate Settlement Procedures Act). Regulation Z (Truth in Lending disclosures) or other warnings, or any warranties express or implied. Neither are you to be concerned with the effect of zoning ordinances, land division regulations, or building restrictions which may in any manner affect the land or improvements that are the subject of this escrow. Such requirements shall be the responsibility of the parties and their agents.

12. The parties to this escrow will satisfy themselves outside of escrow that the transaction covered by this escrow is not in violation of the Subdivision Map Act or any other law regulating land division, and you as escrow holder are relieved of any responsibility and/or liability in connection therewith, and are not to be concerned with the enforcement of said laws.

13. In the event any Offer to Purchase, Deposit Receipt or any other form of Purchase Agreement is deposited in this escrow, it is understood that such document shall be effective only as between the parties signing said document. You as escrow holder are not to be concerned with the terms of such document and are relieved of all responsibility and or liability for the enforcement of such terms and your only duty being to comply with the instructions set out in this escrow. In connection with any loan transaction involving an FHA, or VA loan you are authorized to deliver a copy of any such document to FHA, VA or lender as the case may be.

14. Time is of the essence of these escrow instructions. In the event of failure to pay fees or expenses due you hereunder, on demand, I agree to pay a reasonable fee for any attorney's services which may be required to collect such fees or expenses.

15. If a party to this escrow unilaterally assigns or orders the proceeds of this escrow to be paid to other than the original parties to this escrow, such assignment or order shall be subordinated to the expenses of this escrow, liens of record on the subject property, and payments directed to be made by original parties together. If the result of such assignment or order would be to leave the escrow without sufficient funds to close, then you may but you are not required to close nevertheless, and to pay such assignments or orders only out of the net proceeds due except for such assignments or orders, and to pay them in the order in which such assignments or orders are received by you. You are to furnish a copy of these instructions, amendments thereto, closing statements and/or any other documents deposited in this escrow to the lender or lenders and/or the real estate broker or brokers involved in this transaction upon request of such lenders or brokers. In the event of an assignment or transfer of interest by operation of law, with or without the approval or consent of any or all of the parties hereto, you shall retain the right to deduct any and all escrow costs, fees and expenses provided for herein from said assigned or transferred funds, properties or rights, said assignment or transfer notwithstanding.

16. These instructions may be executed in counterparts, each of which shall be deemed an original regardless of the date of its execution and delivery. All such counterparts together shall constitute one and the same document.

17. The parties to these escrow instructions authorize you to destroy these instructions and all other instructions and records in this escrow at any time after five (5) years from date of the last transaction concerning this escrow.

instructions are typed on a printed form and thereafter executed (signed) by the principals. There is no standard form of escrow instructions. Each escrow company ordinarily has its own printed form. However, there are many similarities in the various forms used since many of the procedures have become more or less standardized. A form of escrow instructions used by a company in Southern California is illustrated in Figure 6.7. The front side, when properly completed, sets forth the details of the particular escrow transaction. The reverse side sets forth additional printed instructions and the terms and conditions under which the escrow company agrees to handle the escrow. The parties should be familiar with the particular form to be used in their transaction, and should be guided by the advice of their own counsel about any provisions that are not understood or that may be questioned.

Prorations

One aspect of an escrow that frequently gives rise to inquiries by the parties is *proration*. The buyer and the seller will be concerned with what it is and what effect it has on them. A proration is defined briefly as "a dividing, assessing, or distributing proportionately." Prorations in escrow result in various *adjustments (charges and credits)* to the buyer's and seller's accounts. Such items as taxes, interest, hazard insurance, rents (including prepaid rents and security deposits), and impounds are usually subject to proration. Some transactions call for normal prorations, some call for no prorations, and others call for specific prorations only. The decision is a matter for agreement between the parties. Prorations can be made as of a designated date, agreed to at the time of the negotiations, or they can be set for a date that is not known for sure at the time the escrow is first opened, such as the date "escrow closes" or the "date of possession." The particular date does not matter, since the principle of prorating will be the same, but the actual date to be used must be ascertainable from the parties' instructions.

The application of the rules for prorations and adjustments is illustrated below, using a proration date of May 1 of the current year (with one exception as noted):

Taxes. Real property taxes in all counties in California run on a fiscal year from July 1 through June 30, and are payable in two installments, due on or before December 10 and April 10. Therefore, by May 1, the taxes should already be paid. In such a case, the proration of the taxes calls for a credit, which would accrue to the seller, of two months (May and June) or two-twelfths (2/12) of the total tax for that fiscal year. This "credit" naturally is a charge against the buyer's account during escrow.

As another example, if the escrow closes on October 1, the taxes for that part of the fiscal year are probably not yet paid; therefore, the seller is charged for three-twelfths (3/12) of the year's taxes (July, August, and September). However, the amount of taxes for that year may be unknown at that time, so the tax proration would ordinarily be based on the previous year's taxes.

Interest. If a loan of record is being taken over by the new buyer, the provision for proration of interest probably would apply. Let us assume that the loan of record has monthly payments due on the fifteenth of each month, and that the last payment was made on April 15. Interest normally is post paid (seldom paid in advance). The seller in our case has paid interest only until April 15, and therefore should be charged (and the buyer credited) with the interest from April 15 until May 1. When the buyer makes his first monthly payment on May 15, he has already had a part of that payment—specifically, the interest that accrued from April 15 to May 1—credited to his account through the escrow.

Another example of an interest proration is a street improvement bond of record. Once in a while, a bond remains of record, the buyer taking title subject to that special debt. The interest is such that it would be proratable. Normally, bond payments are made in two installments—principal on (or before) January 2 of each year, and interest on January 2 and July 2 of each year. Let's assume that the interest on the bond taken over by the buyer on May 1 is paid to the following January 2. The seller's portion of that obligation would be approximately four-sixths (January, February, March, April) of the interest that will become due on July 2 for the period of January 2 through July 2. This prorated amount would be a charge to the seller and a credit to the buyer.

Insurance. Let us assume that the existing fire insurance policy is to be transferred to the new buyer through the escrow and that it is a three-year policy, running from May 1 of the current

Figure 6.8   Table for Proration of Personal Property Taxes or One Year Insurance and Interest

Days＼Mos.	0	1	2	3	4	5	6	7	8	9	10	11
0		.0833	.1667	.2500	.3333	.4167	.5000	.5833	.6667	.7500	.8333	.9167
1	.0028	.0861	.1694	.2528	.3361	.4194	.5028	.5861	.6694	.7528	.8361	.9194
2	.0056	.0889	.1722	.2556	.3389	.4222	.5056	.5889	.6722	.7556	.8389	.9222
3	.0083	.0917	.1750	.2583	.3417	.4250	.5083	.5917	.6750	.7583	.8417	.9250
4	.0111	.0944	.1778	.2611	.3444	.4278	.5111	.5944	.6778	.7611	.8444	.9278
5	.0139	.0972	.1806	.2639	.3472	.4306	.5139	.5972	.6806	.7639	.8472	.9306
6	.0167	.1000	.1833	.2667	.3500	.4333	.5167	.6000	.6833	.7667	.8500	.9333
7	.0194	.1027	.1861	.2694	.3528	.4361	.5194	.6028	.6861	.7694	.8528	.9361
8	.0222	.1055	.1889	.2722	.3556	.4389	.5222	.6056	.6889	.7722	.8556	.9389
9	.0250	.1083	.1917	.2750	.3583	.4417	.5250	.6083	.6917	.7750	.8583	.9417
10	.0278	.1111	.1944	.2778	.3611	.4444	.5278	.6111	.6944	.7778	.8611	.9444
11	.0306	.1139	.1972	.2806	.3639	.4472	.5306	.6139	.6972	.7806	.8639	.9472
12	.0333	.1167	.2000	.2833	.3667	.4500	.5333	.6167	.7000	.7833	.8667	.9500
13	.0361	.1194	.2028	.2861	.3694	.4528	.5361	.6194	.7028	.7861	.8694	.9528
14	.0389	.1222	.2056	.2889	.3722	.4556	.5389	.6222	.7056	.7889	.8722	.9556
15	.0417	.1250	.2083	.2917	.3750	.4583	.5417	.6250	.7083	.7917	.8750	.9583
16	.0444	.1278	.2111	.2944	.3778	.4611	.5444	.6278	.7111	.7944	.8778	.9611
17	.0472	.1306	.2139	.2972	.3806	.4639	.5472	.6306	.7139	.7972	.8806	.9639
18	.0500	.1333	.2167	.3000	.3833	.4667	.5500	.6333	.7167	.8000	.8833	.9667
19	.0528	.1361	.2194	.3028	.3861	.4694	.5528	.6361	.7194	.8028	.8861	.9694
20	.0556	.1389	.2222	.3056	.3889	.4722	.5556	.6389	.7222	.8056	.8889	.9722
21	.0583	.1417	.2250	.3083	.3917	.4750	.5583	.6417	.7250	.8083	.8917	.9750
22	.0611	.1444	.2278	.3111	.3944	.4778	.5611	.6444	.7278	.8111	.8944	.9778
23	.0639	.1472	.2306	.3139	.3972	.4806	.5639	.6472	.7306	.8139	.8972	.9806
24	.0667	.1500	.2333	.3167	.4000	.4833	.5667	.6500	.7333	.8167	.9000	.9833
25	.0694	.1528	.2361	.3194	.4028	.4861	.5694	.6528	.7361	.8194	.9028	.9861
26	.0722	.1556	.2389	.3222	.4056	.4889	:5722	.6556	.7389	.8222	.9056	.9889
27	.0750	.1583	.2417	.3250	.4083	.4917	.5750	.6583	.7417	.8250	.9083	.9917
28	.0778	.1611	.2444	.3278	.4111	.4944	.5778	.6611	.7444	.8278	.9111	.9944
29	.0806	.1639	.2472	.3306	.4139	.4972	.5806	.6639	.7472	.8306	.9139	.9972
30	.0833	.1667	.2500	.3333	.4167	.5000	.5833	.6667	.7500	.8333	.9167	1.0000
	=	=	=	=	=	=	=	=	=	=	=	=

year to May 1 three years later. There are still two years to run on the policy. The seller is entitled to a credit of two-thirds of the total premium already paid for the policy. This charge is made against the buyer's account. It should be observed that most fire insurance policies are written for one year, and that because of increasing values and lender requirements, such policies are rarely assumed by the buyer. Instead, a new policy is usually issued to the new owner.

Rents. Normally, rents are paid in advance, and therefore are already collected by the seller. Let's say that the property being sold is rented and the rents cover the period from the 15th through the 14th of the following month. The buyer is entitled to one-half of the rent that the seller collected on April 15 (sale as of May 1). Therefore, this charge is made against the seller's account and a corresponding credit given to the buyer.

Sometimes there is a cleaning deposit, security

deposit, or prepaid rent charge already collected by the seller. Such deposits are also charged against the seller's account and credited to the buyer.

Impounds. Impounds, also known as loan trust funds or escrow accounts, are collected from the owner by various lenders, and are required on all FHA and VA loans. Then, when due, the taxes or insurance premiums on the property are paid from the funds accumulated in the impound account. In reality, these funds are a special savings account built up by the owner over a period of months or years. When the property is sold, the seller is entitled to receive a credit for the balance in the account. The lender simply keeps the funds for the buyer, if he or she is assuming the loan. When real property is sold, impounds are a matter of crediting and debiting (charging) the funds through escrow.

Figure 6.9
Escrow Checklist—How to Speed Up Your Escrow

YOUR ESCROW WILL CLOSE FASTER
If you will follow these suggestions

Bring this with you when you open an escrow . . .

√ when completed

1 CORRECT LEGAL DESCRIPTION
IF POSSIBLE BRING THE EXISTING DEED. (DO NOT USE DESCRIPTIONS FROM TAX BILLS NOR THE STREET ADDRESS.) DO NOT BRING YOUR TITLE POLICY: KEEP IT FOR YOUR FUTURE PROTECTION. ☐

2 FULL NAMES OF PARTIES TO THE DEAL
INITIALS ARE NOT SUFFICIENT: GET FULL NAMES. ☐

3 STATEMENT OF HOW BUYER WANTS TO MAKE TITLE
– AND NAME IN WHICH TITLE IS TO BE TAKEN. ☐

4 NAMES OF ALL HOLDERS OF MORTGAGES OR TRUST DEEDS
GET ADDRESSES, PHONE NUMBERS AND LOAN NUMBER TOO. ☐

5 TERMS OF NEW ENCUMBRANCES
AND TERMS OF EXISTING ENCUMBRANCES AND UNPAID BALANCES OF EACH. ☐

6 ALL FIRE POLICIES
IF HELD BY SOME MORTGAGEE, BRING HIS NAME AND ADDRESS. ☐

7 CURRENT TAX BILLS AND RECEIPTS
– IF AVAILABLE. ☐

8 COMPLETE LIST OF TENANTS
– INCLUDING AMOUNTS AND PAYMENT DATES FOR EACH AND AMOUNTS PAID IN ADVANCE, IF RENTS ARE TO BE PRORATED. BRING IN ALL LEASES. ☐

Bring all the facts – You get faster service and greater protection when you follow these simple suggestions. A complete agreement between the parties on all essential points, in the beginning, is your best assurance of an early and certain closing of your escrow. Please do not telephone the escrow officer unless important, and then please save your time and his by giving him the correct escrow number.

Proration tables that give the percentage of an annual payment for any given day are customarily used by escrow officers (see Figure 6.8).

How to Speed Up Your Escrow

Once an escrow transaction is under way, the parties ordinarily become anxious to see that the escrow closing is expedited. Sometimes delay is the result of oversights that can easily be avoided if a check list is maintained, particularly by the broker, on each transaction, to be sure that everything that will be needed is brought into the escrow at the time of opening (see Figure 6.9).

Summary of Escrows

The subject of escrows may be summarized by reviewing, step by step, the duties of the escrow officer in a real property sales transaction:

1. Take information and any initial deposit.
2. Prepare (type) instructions, documents, and water stock assignments, if any.
3. Obtain signatures on instructions, documents, etc.
4. Receive signed instructions and documents.
5. Open title order and transmit documents to title company.
6. Request any necessary beneficiary's statement, reconveyance and demand, or water company information.
7. Receive and review carefully the title report.
8. Receive mortgagee statement and/or reconveyance and demand, and submit for approval.
9. Submit reconveyance documents, if any, to title company.
10. Figure estimated closing costs, due from buyer and/or seller.
11. Request closing funds.
12. Receive and deposit closing funds.
13. Order recording when all checks have cleared.
14. Receive confirmation of recording and charges (from title company).
15. Compute final closing and disbursements.
16. Type settlement statements and checks.
17. Type fire insurance assignments and transmit to agent, as well as sending any water stock assignments to water company.
18. Write closing letters.
19. Receive and check thoroughly policy of title insurance; send to insured.
20. Close file.

REAL ESTATE SETTLEMENT PROCEDURES ACT (RESPA)

According to the *Real Estate Reference Book* (1984–85 ed., p. 192, 337),

[b]oth the buyer and seller, in transactions involv-

ing "federally related" first mortgage loans for one-to-four family dwellings (including VA, FHA, and lenders whose deposits are federally insured or which make government related loans) must be furnished a settlement statement which conforms to requirements of the Federal Real Estate Settlement Procedures Act (RESPA). The law

---

Figure 6.10
Good Faith Estimates of Closing Costs

The charges listed below are our Good Faith Estimate of some of the settlement charges you will need to pay at settlement of the loan for which you have applied. These charges will be paid to the title or escrow company that conducts the settlement. This form does not cover all items you will be required to pay in cash at settlement, for example, deposit in escrow for real estate taxes and insurance. You may wish to inquire as to the amounts of such other items. You may be required to pay other additional amounts at settlement. This is not a commitment to make a loan.

Services		Estimated Fees
Loan Origination Fee _____% + $_____		$
Loan Discount %		$
Appraisal Fee		$
Credit Report		$
Mortgage Insurance Application Fee		$
Assumption Fee		$
Tax Service Fee		$
Interest		$
Mortgage Insurance Premium		$
Settlement or Closing Fee		$
Notary Fees		$
Title Insurance Lender's	List only those items Buyer will pay	$
Title Insurance Owner's		$
Recording Fees		$
County Tax		$
City Tax		$
Pest Inspection		$
Building Inspection		$
		$
TOTAL		$

requires that all closings of home sales and other transactions covered by this law use a uniform settlement statement and that lender, or the party performing the closing, give borrower-buyer and seller advance information and estimates of closing costs.

Figure 6.10 illustrates the information contained on such an estimate.

A form of Settlement Statement prepared by HUD is also used by the person conducting the settlement, containing a summary of all charges to be paid by the borrower (buyer) and the seller in connection with the settlement. The borrower has the right to inspect the Uniform Settlement Statement one business day before the date of closing.

Among its many provisions, RESPA limits the amount which a lender may collect for establishing new insurance and tax reserves, prohibits kickbacks and the practice of seller alone directing the transaction to a title company. (See Chapter 7 for additional information on the lender's requirements.)

More information can also be obtained in a free HUD booklet available from lenders, entitled *Settlement Costs and You.*

INSURANCE RELATED TO REAL PROPERTY

In this section we discuss three types of insurance related to real property ownership and use. Title insurance is commonly used in California to obtain assurance against title defects that might result in a loss of title or diminution in the value of the title. Hazard insurance protects a property owner from losses due to fire or other action of the elements; and liability insurance, against injury to persons or other damages arising from the condition of the property or from activities conducted on the property.

Insurance is broadly defined as coverage by contract in which one party (the insurer) agrees to indemnify or reimburse another party (the insured) for loss or damage that may occur under the terms of the contract. Assurances are given in the form of an insurance policy; most policies are on printed forms. For this protection, the insured pays a consideration, called a *premium.*

The amount of the premium not only covers the cost of producing the insurance policy, but is also based on the need for the insurance company to set up reserves to cover the risk factor. In addi-

tion to indemnifying against loss, an insurance policy also contains an agreement whereby the insurer is obligated to pay attorneys' fees and litigation costs in the event a claim for damages is asserted against an insured by a third party.

TITLE INSURANCE

Nature of Title Insurance

The use of title insurance policies in California is widespread. In fact, it is unusual for a buyer of real property or a lender obtaining a lien on real property in the form of a mortgage or deed of trust not to obtain a policy of title insurance.

Basically, a policy of title insurance is an insured statement of the condition of the "title," i.e., the *ownership* of a particular parcel of land, according to those public records that give *constructive notice,* i.e., notice implied by law. Such a policy also shows what the title is subject to by way of taxes, mortgages, and other liens and encumbrances, including deed restrictions, easements, and other similar rights or reservations of record.

In order to give such assurances, a title insurer will *gather information* from the public records affecting a parcel of land. After *interpreting* the effect of such information on ownership, the insurer can then *issue its policy* of title insurance. Such a policy insures against loss in the event that the search of the record and its *interpretation* proves to be incorrect, thus causing potential loss or damage to the insured. In brief, a policy of title insurance is a contract to indemnify against specified loss or damage occasioned by defects in the title. The process of insuring the title to real property can be summarized in the flow chart in Figure 6.11.

The person obtaining the benefit of such insurance may be the purchaser of a parcel of real property, such as a home, raw land, or commercial or industrial property. Or he or she may be a lender who has obtained as security a mortgage or deed of trust on real property. Or the insured may be the owner of an oil and gas lease or other leasehold estate, or may be a contract purchaser under a recorded land sales contract.

An *owner's policy* of title insurance insures the title to the land. A *lender's policy* insures the *priority* and *validity* of the mortgage or deed of trust on the land. Both an owner and a lender can be

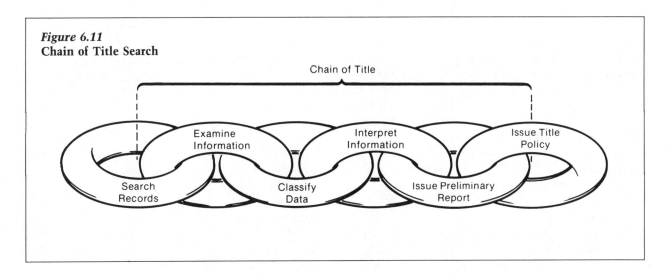

Figure 6.11
Chain of Title Search

insured in the same policy, which is then referred to as a *joint protection* policy of title insurance.

Regarding the *extent of coverage*, a policy of title insurance may be either a *standard coverage* policy or an *extended coverage* policy. The difference between these types of coverage will be discussed later in this section, as will the further extension of coverage by way of *special endorsements*.

In addition to the issuance of policies of title insurance, a title insurance company offers many other forms or assurances including subdivision guarantees, litigation guarantees, and trustee sale guarantees.

Unlike other types of insurance (life, fire, automobile, etc.), which insure against loss in the event of a future happening, title insurance protects the insured against the possibility of loss resulting from a defect in the title that may have occurred in the *past*. Another important distinction is that life and casualty insurance are written for a specific period of time and must be renewed to remain in effect. Title insurance is written for a *one-time* premium; the protection continues until the interest of the insured is transferred during his or her lifetime. When an insured owner dies, his or her heirs or devisees remain protected under the terms of the policy.

The amount of liability which a title insurance company assumes under a policy of title insurance is determined by the type of policy issued and the value of the property or the amount of the loan. An owner's policy is ordinarily written for the market value, i.e., the selling price of the land. The amount can be increased as the value of the land increases. Some policies even contain automatic cost-of-living-increase clauses. A lender's policy is written for the amount of the loan.

Historical Development

The insurance of land titles in California started early when the California Pacific Title Insurance Company was organized in 1886. Prior to that time, people relied upon abstracts which traced the chain of title to the property in question, and upon attorneys' opinions as to the validity of ownership and the effect of matters shown in the abstract. It is true that, ever since the adoption of the recording system in California in 1850, the records have been available to the public. But over the years, as more and more documents were recorded, it became increasingly difficult for the average person to search the public records and obtain the necessary information regarding property. As a result, persons with a special aptitude for examining records began to specialize in title searching and developed the business of furnishing summaries, called "abstracts," of the pertinent information contained in the documents that formed the chain of title for a particular parcel of property. These early-day title searchers, known as "abstractors," adopted the practice of keeping duplicate copies of their abstracts so that, if they were employed to search the title to the same property again, they could start with the previous work rather than re-search the title from the beginning again. From this practice stemmed the modern-day issuance of title insurance policies.

The attraction of mortgage loan funds to California from the eastern seaboard in the twenties was an important factor in bringing to the attention of the large eastern lenders and other financial institutions the speed, efficiency, and safety with which their mortgage transactions could be completed, utilizing the title insurance system in California. Most of these lenders were familiar only with the abstract-and-lawyer-opinion service. As the volume of business increased, they found it almost impossible to complete their loans rapidly on an abstract-and-opinion basis because the examination of abstracts was too time-consuming, and the storage of their records was too expensive.

The stability of the title insurance industry had been enhanced by the formation of the California Land Title Association (CLTA) in 1907 as a nonprofit trade organization. Throughout its history the association has stressed that its members can produce the most accurate title report possible at the least cost to the customer. The association requires that all its members maintain title plants, which are extensive physical collections of documents, maps, and other data which may be pertinent to future title searches. The title plant is the most efficient and accurate method of producing a title report yet devised. CLTA officers and committees have produced uniform forms of title insurance policies and endorsements. Uniformity in the forms has been, of course, vital to landowners and lenders; the same form of policy of title insurance is available to the customer regardless of which of the fifty-eight counties in California the real property is located in.

The American Land Title Association (ALTA) is the trade association for title insurance and related companies doing business throughout the country. In the title industry ALTA is a familiar term, because it designates an extended coverage policy of title insurance developed to meet the requirements of national lenders.

Through the efforts of both ALTA and CLTA, the owner's policy has been made uniform throughout the United States. One reason for this development was the lender's requirements, arising from sale and lease-back arrangements, for an owner's policy that would be substantially uniform throughout the country. Although designated as a CLTA form, it is based on the standard form approved by the ALTA. These forms have undergone changes from time to time to meet current needs and developments, and, of course, are subject to constant review and changes to meet future needs.

Types of Policies

Standard Coverage Policies. Most buyers and many lenders in California use and rely on the policy known as the "standard coverage" form. Its full title is California Land Title Association Standard Coverage Policy Form. As we have observed above, this form has been standardized by the CLTA to comply with requirements recommended and approved by the ALTA for use throughout the United States.

The standard coverage policy insures single or multiple estates or interests in land and such combinations thereof as may be brought within the coverage given by the policy. It is an *owner's policy* when the owner is insured, a *loan policy* when the lender only is insured, a *joint protection policy* when both owner and lender are insured, a *leasehold policy* or *subleasehold policy* when a lessee or sublessee is insured, and an *easement policy* when the owner of an easement is insured.

The most commonly used standard coverage policy insures the ownership of an estate or interest in the described land and insures the priority and validity of the lien of the insured mortgage (which by definition includes deed of trust) upon that estate or interest. Its coverage is not limited solely to matters revealed by public records. This coverage also includes protection against such defects as forged instruments in the chain of title; acts of minors and incompetents whose disability is undisclosed; instruments made void because drawn by an attorney-in-fact acting under powers already terminated by the death of the principal; or undisclosed rights of husband or wife when recorded instruments falsely state that a person in the chain of title is unmarried. If the land covered by the policy abuts upon one or more physically open streets or highways, it further insures the ordinary rights of access to one of these streets or highways.

Excluded from the coverage of this type of policy are mining claims, reservations in patents, water rights, and certain matters and potential claims not shown by public records. Also excluded from this, and from all other forms of title insurance, are matters contained in governmental regulations including zoning and, with certain express exceptions, the exercise of the power of eminent domain and the exercise of rights under the police power. In addition, the standard coverage policy does not insure its owners against the provisions in such laws as consumer credit protection and truth in lending.

Since the insuring company does not ordinarily make an inspection or survey of the land or premises involved in a standard coverage policy, the reasons for most of these general exceptions are largely self-explanatory. The average buyer or lender, who is personally familiar with the land, does not object to these exceptions. Such exceptions have their counterparts in fire, automobile, life, and other insurance policies. If desired and to the extent feasible, these exceptions may be eliminated by extended coverage policies or, in some cases, by special endorsements.

A copy of the California Land Title Association Standard Coverage Policy Form is included as Figure 6.12. The first or "cover" page states the basic terms of the insurance contract, subject to the conditions and stipulations and the schedules set forth on the pages following.

Schedule A shows the amount for which the title company is liable, the name of the parties insured, the effective date, and sets forth the nature of the interest of the insured in the land. The policy is designed to insure *any* estate or interest in land, including fee, leasehold, life estate, etc.

Schedule B has two parts. Part I sets forth the printed exceptions contained in a standard coverage form. Part II sets forth the specific exceptions resulting from an examination of the record title to the property in question. In its combined parts, Schedule B sets out the encumbrances and other matters against which the title company does *not* insure.

Schedule C describes the land; this schedule is referred to as the "legal description" for the property in question.

The Conditions and Stipulations contain definitions of terms and also the contract provisions that generally apply.

Extended Coverage Policies. Extended coverage policies are available to both owners and lenders, although their use by lenders is more prevalent. Generally speaking, these policies afford the coverages of the standard coverage policies and also such matters as rights, interests, or claims not shown by the public records, but which would be ascertained from an *inspection* of the land itself, or from a correct *survey*, or from making *inquiry* of persons in possession of the land, or from other public records that technically do not give con-

structive notice. The latter would include a proposed assessment for a local improvement, such as sidewalks or street lighting, which has not yet become a lien on the land but may become a lien when the work is completed. Of course, rights of third parties revealed by the title company's "off record" investigation of the title are shown as specific exceptions in the policy. However, every effort is made to keep these exceptions to a minimum.

The ALTA loan policy originated because eastern life insurance companies, not equipped to do so, were obligated to make local inspections (and possibly surveys) of the land upon which a loan was being requested. They called upon the title companies to satisfy this requirement. In the ALTA loan policy, insurance is given that the lender has a valid and enforceable lien, subject only to the exclusions from coverage and to such defects, liens, and encumbrances on the title as are shown therein. In addition, the policy expressly includes priority insurance to cover mechanic's liens and assessments for street improvements. It also insures that the land has a right of access.

Because of the additional work involved (at least in an inspection of the land) and the additional risk assumed, the cost of extended coverage policies is proportionately greater. As in the case of other forms of insurance, the greater the coverage in a title policy, the higher the premium.

The cost of the ALTA loan policy is based on the amount of the loan and is about 25 percent higher than the standard coverage loan policy. In the ALTA loan policy, a survey may be required. When an owner or lessee is insured, the cost is about double that of a standard coverage policy, and a survey is normally required, a cost incurred in addition to the policy fee. The survey charge is not made by the title company, but by the licensed surveyor who makes the survey.

Special Endorsements

Assurances in addition to the coverage afforded by a policy of title insurance may be given by way of *special endorsements*. Through such endorsements, which expand or supplement the coverage of either extended or standard form policies of title insurance, insured owners and lenders may obtain a variety of specific benefits. For this available additional coverage, a commensurate extra premium is charged.

Over one hundred different endorsements are

Figure 6.12   **Policy of Title Insurance**

**TITLE INSURANCE
AND TRUST**

A TICOR COMPANY

Policy of Title Insurance

SUBJECT TO SCHEDULE B AND THE CONDITIONS AND STIPULATIONS HEREOF, TITLE INSURANCE AND TRUST COMPANY, a California corporation, herein called the Company, insures the insured, as of Date of Policy shown in Schedule A, against loss or damage, not exceeding the amount of insurance stated in Schedule A, and costs, attorneys' fees and expenses which the Company may become obligated to pay hereunder, sustained or incurred by said insured by reason of:

1. Title to the estate or interest described in Schedule A being vested other than as stated therein;

2. Any defect in or lien or encumbrance on such title;

3. Unmarketability of such title; or

4. Any lack of the ordinary right of an abutting owner for access to at least one physically open street or highway if the land, in fact, abuts upon one or more such streets or highways;

and in addition, as to an insured lender only;

5. Invalidity of the lien of the insured mortgage upon said estate or interest except to the extent that such invalidity, or claim thereof, arises out of the transaction evidenced by the insured mortgage and is based upon

    a. usury, or
    b. any consumer credit protection or truth in lending law;

6. Priority of any lien or encumbrance over the lien of the insured mortgage, said mortgage being shown in Schedule B in the order of its priority; or

7. Invalidity of any assignment of the insured mortgage, provided such assignment is shown in Schedule B.

Title Insurance and Trust Company

by

                    President

Attest

                    Secretary

TO 1012 TI (10-75) California Land Title Association Standard Coverage Policy-1973

Figure 6.12   **Continued**

Schedule B Part I

1. Taxes or assessments which are not shown as existing liens by the records of any taxing authority that levies taxes or assessments on real property or by the public records.

Proceedings by a public agency which may result in taxes or assessments, or notices of such proceedings, whether or not shown by the records of such agency or by the public records.

2. Any facts, rights, interests or claims which are not shown by the public records but which could be ascertained by an inspection of the land or by making inquiry of persons in possession thereof.

3. Easements, liens or encumbrances, or claims thereof, which are not shown by the public records.

4. Discrepancies, conflicts in boundary lines, shortage in area, encroachments, or any other facts which a correct survey would disclose, and which are not shown by the public records.

5. (a) Unpatented mining claims; (b) reservations or exceptions in patents or in Acts authorizing the issuance thereof; (c) water rights, claims or title to water.

6. Any right, title, interest, estate or easement in land beyond the lines of the area specifically described or referred to in Schedule C, or in abutting streets, roads, avenues, alleys, lanes, ways or waterways, but nothing in this paragraph shall modify or limit the extent to which the ordinary right of an abutting owner for access to a physically open street or highway is insured by this policy.

7. Any law, ordinance or governmental regulation (including but not limited to building and zoning ordinances) restricting or regulating or prohibiting the occupancy, use or enjoyment of the land, or regulating the character, dimensions or location of any improvement now or hereafter erected on the land, or prohibiting a separation in ownership or a reduction in the dimensions or area of the land, or the effect of any violation of any such law, ordinance or governmental regulation.

8. Rights of eminent domain or governmental rights of police power unless notice of the exercise of such rights appears in the public records.

9. Defects, liens, encumbrances, adverse claims, or other matters (a) created, suffered, assumed or agreed to by the insured claimant; (b) not shown by the public records and not otherwise excluded from coverage but known to the insured claimant either at Date of Policy or at the date such claimant acquired an estate or interest insured by this policy or acquired the insured mortgage and not disclosed in writing by the insured claimant to the Company prior to the date such insured claimant became an insured hereunder; (c) resulting in no loss or damage to the insured claimant; (d) attaching or created subsequent to Date of Policy; or (e) resulting in loss or damage which would not have been sustained if the insured claimant had been a purchaser or encumbrancer for value without knowledge.

10. Any facts, rights, interests or claims which are not shown by the public records but which could be ascertained by making inquiry of the lessors in the lease or leases described or referred to in Schedule A.

11. The effect of any failure to comply with the terms, covenants and conditions of the lease or leases described or referred to in Schedule A.

Conditions and Stipulations

1. Definition of Terms
The following terms when used in this policy mean:
(a.) "insured": the insured named in Schedule A, and, subject to any rights or defenses the Company may have had against the named insured, those who succeed to the interest of such insured by operation of law as distinguished from purchase including, but not limited to, heirs, distributees, devisees, survivors, personal representatives, next of kin, or corporate or fiduciary successors. The term "insured" also includes (i) the owner of the indebtedness secured by the insured mortgage and each successor in ownership of such indebtedness (reserving, however, all rights and defenses as to any such successor who acquires the indebtedness by operation of law as described in the first sentence of this subparagraph (a) that the Company would have had against the successor's transferor), and further includes (ii) any governmental agency or instrumentality which is an insurer or guarantor under an insurance contract or guaranty insuring or guaranteeing said indebtedness, or any part thereof, whether named as an insured herein or not, and (iii) the parties des-

ignated in paragraph 2(a) of these Conditions and Stipulations.
(b.) "insured claimant": an insured claiming loss or damage hereunder.
(c.) "insured lender": the owner of an insured mortgage.
(d.) "insured mortgage": a mortgage shown in Schedule B, the owner of which is named as an insured in Schedule A.
(e.) "knowledge": actual knowledge, not constructive knowledge or notice which may be imputed to an insured by reason of any public records.
(f.) "land": the land described specifically or by reference in Schedule C, and improvements affixed thereto which by law constitute real property; provided, however, the term "land" does not include any area excluded by Paragraph No. 6 of Part I of Schedule B of this Policy.
(g.) "mortgage": mortgage, deed of trust, trust deed, or other security instrument.
(h.) "public records": those records which by law impart constructive notice of matters relating to the land.

(CONDITIONS AND STIPULATIONS Continued on the inside of the Last Page of This Policy)

Figure 6.12   **Continued**

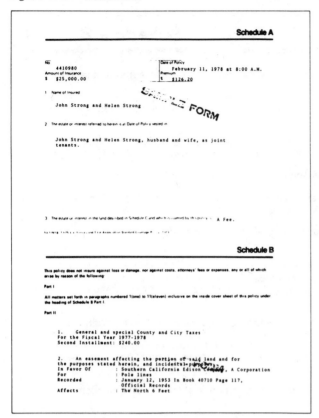

available. Those most frequently encountered relate to the following subjects: mechanic's lien priority insurance (mostly limited to lenders); violations of covenants, conditions, and restrictions; assignments of trust deeds; encroachment of improvements onto easements; and right of surface entry under existing oil leases or outstanding mineral interest.

Preliminary Reports of Title

The preliminary report of title is a report issued by a title company, usually prior to issuing a policy of title insurance. As we have seen, in most cases the preliminary report is issued in connection with an escrow transaction and is forwarded to the escrow company. The report identifies the particular property which is to be the subject of the title policy and shows the present vesting and liens and encumbrances as disclosed by an examination of the record title. The report is not a policy of title insurance, but rather is issued for information purposes and generally as a prelude to the issuing of a title policy. If a title policy is issued, the title company makes no additional charge for the preliminary title report, since the cost is

included in the policy fee. However, if a policy is not issued, a charge is ordinarily made for the report, perhaps 50 percent of the policy fee.

Additional Services of a Title Insurer

In addition to reports and policies and guarantees, a title insurance company may also furnish limited information through its title plant services, such as the name of the record owner, or whether or not a homestead has been recorded against a particular parcel of property. It may also furnish tax services, particularly to institutional lenders, by providing current tax information on property subject to a loan.

Persons dealing with real property in California have adopted the practice of depending on a title insurance company to examine and interpret the public records and to ensure the correctness of its findings by the issuance of a policy of title insurance or other appropriate evidence of assurance. These assurances and other services are accepted throughout California as helping to make it safe to buy or sell land—and are also relied upon throughout the United States by those who invest in California land or who lend money and take as security a deed of trust on land in California.

HAZARD INSURANCE

The basic coverage of hazard insurance relating to real property involves risks related to the four ancient Greek elements: earth, air, fire, and water. Any of these elements at times can cause property damage. Although some of the risks are excluded from the ordinary policy, a homeowner might desire protection not only from fire, wind, rain and hail, but also from earth movement or earthquakes. Contrary to popular belief, earthquake insurance is available in all of California for an extra premium. It may be specifically excluded from the printed form of homeowners' policies, but such type of insurance can be included, by adding an *endorsement* to the owner's policy.

The danger of fire is perhaps the biggest factor in hazard insurance. Persons living in what has been declared a "brush hazard area" of southern California, mainly the foothill regions, following the disastrous fire of 1970 were unable to obtain fire insurance under their normal homeowners' policies. However, they have been able to obtain coverage from a privately organized and state-sponsored group of insurance companies called the California F.A.I.R Plan. Each company writing fire insurance policies in California is a member of the F.A.I.R. Plan and is responsible for losses in proportion to the amount of fire insurance policies it carries.

Another area of major concern to owners in the fire areas is the future possibility of floods and mud slides which will occur when the rains begin pouring over the vegetation-stripped hills. Flood coverage is ordinarily excluded under homeowners' policies, as is seepage due to rising waters. The reason for the exclusion is that only those persons in areas prone to flooding and mud slides would be interested in the insurance. Persons living in areas never affected by flooding would not purchase the insurance and thereby would not become part of the overall risk pool that is fundamental to insurance philosophy. To fill the need for flood and mud-slide coverage, the federal government now subsidizes the rate.

Several forms of homeowner's policy are available, and all provide coverage for personal liability as well as property damage. The most popular homeowner's policy in California is a broad, nom-inally all-risk policy on building structures; it also covers personal property on the premises as well as off the premises, living expenses, medical payments, as well as personal liability.

An owner of property that is free and clear may choose to be a self-insurer and not maintain any insurance on the property and save the premiums. However, the lack of insurance creates a risk that most persons would not wish to assume. Where property is subject to a mortgage or deed of trust, the lender traditionally requires the borrower to maintain insurance coverage on his or her property in a form and amount prescribed by the lender, and written by an insurance company acceptable to the lender. Most FHA, VA, and conventional mortgages require that monthly deposits be made by borrowers to pay hazard insurance premiums. This creates an *impound account*, already mentioned in this chapter.

The main purpose of hazard insurance from the lender's point of view is to provide funds for repairing damaged property, thus restoring the primary value on which the security of a mortgage loan depends, and protecting the lender against loss in case the value of a mortgaged property is reduced by fire or other casualties.

An item that should also be included in the coverage is the cost of removal of a damaged structure that is beyond repair.

LIABILITY INSURANCE

In addition to protecting the property itself from various hazards, a landowner also wants to maintain liability insurance to protect against claims for damages from persons who may be injured by an activity on the property. The owner also wants to obtain protection from liability for damage to other property caused by a condition of or activity on his or her property. This type of insurance is similar to the public liability insurance that an owner of a motor vehicle normally has.

The need for adequate public liability and property damage insurance has increased in California because of the adoption of new concepts about a landowner's liability for injuries to third parties while on the land. Distinctions in the past were made as to the degree of care that the owner or possessor of land owed a person on his or her land. The degree of care depended on the particular status of the person on the land—whether he was a *trespasser*, a *licensee* (someone permitted to be on the property temporarily, such as a ticketholder

---

BUYERS AND LENDERS BEWARE OF TITLE TROUBLE SPOTS:

1. Impersonation of true owner
2. Forgeries
3. Deeds by minors
4. Deeds by persons of unsound mind
5. Deeds by a married person who claims to be single
6. Executions under duress/menace
7. Deeds by trustees exceeding powers
8. Children left out of will
9. Deeds to or from defunct corporations
10. Recording errors
11. Unrecorded mechanics' liens
12. Unrecorded easements

---

at a sporting event), or an *invitee*. For instance, a lesser duty of care was owed to a trespasser than to a licensee or an invitee. However, the California Supreme Court has formulated new tests to be applied to the liability of the owner or possessor of land for negligence or for the want of ordinary care or skill in the management of property. The supreme court has ruled that the status of the injured party as a trespasser, licensee, or invitee does not determine liability; that each of us is responsible, not only for the result of our own willful acts, but also for any injury occasioned to another person by reason of our want of *ordinary care or skill* in the management of our property. The court has stated that the proper test to be applied to the liability of the possessor of land for the injury to another person is whether, in the management of his or her property, the owner has acted as a reasonable person in view of the probability of injury to others.

The trend in California today, as far as liability to third parties is concerned, is to return to the feudal concept of the individual, i.e., the courts have become less sensitive to the action of the tort-feasor (committer of the tort) and more sensitive to the injury to the tort victim. The increase in danger to the individual from the incidents of technology, and the new emphasis upon the protection of the individual, have combined to shift the determination of liability from the nature of the wrong committed to the nature of the harm done.

QUESTIONS FOR CHAPTER 6

Matching Terms

a. closing statement
b. fiduciary
c. premium
d. arithmetic
e. number
f. prorate
g. contract of indemnity
h. prime number
i. endorsement
j. fraction
k. escrow
l. marketable title
m. priority
n. mixed number
o. interest

____ 1. the process of computation with figures
____ 2. an amendment to an insurance policy
____ 3. portion of a whole number
____ 4. divisible by no number except itself
____ 5. deposit of a deed or other instrument with a third party for delivery upon condition
____ 6. title that is free from reasonable doubt in law and in fact
____ 7. whole number plus a fraction
____ 8. state or quality of being earlier in point of time or right
____ 9. payment for the use of money
____ 10. a unit or a collection of units
____ 11. policy of title insurance
____ 12. an accounting of funds to the buyer and seller at the completion of a real estate transaction
____ 13. held or founded on trust
____ 14. to divide proportionately to the time of use
____ 15. the amount of money paid for insurance coverage

True/False

T F 16. Each numeral has intrinsic value only.
T F 17. A whole number plus a fraction is called a mixed number.
T F 18. Subtraction is the reverse of adding.
T F 19. 3/8 is the equivalent of 37½ percent.
T F 20. All number symbols are formed out of the ten basic digits.
T F 21. In a fraction, the denominator is written above the numerator.
T F 22. Interest equals principal times rate times time.

T F 23. An ALTA extended form of title policy affords greater protection than a CLTA standard coverage form.

T F 24. All insurance policies call for an annual premium.

T F 25. Hazard insurance relates to risks involving the four ancient Greek elements.

Multiple Choice

26. The sum of 1/4 + 1/3 + 1/2 + 1/6 is
  a. 1-3/4
  b. 1-1/8
  c. 2
  d. 1-1/4

27. 20 percent is the same as
  a. 2.0
  b. 0.2
  c. 0.02
  d. 0.002

28. 5% is the same as
  a. .5
  b. .05
  c. .005
  d. .0005

29. A mixed number is
  a. a combination of percentages
  b. a whole number plus a fraction
  c. the sum of the numerator and the denominator
  d. none of the above

30. The number .25 expresses a
  a. percentage
  b. fraction
  c. mixed number
  d. decimal form

31. To multiply fractions, you multiply
  a. numerator by denominator
  b. denominator by numerator
  c. numerator by numerator and denominator by denominator
  d. none of the above

32. In division the answer is known as the
  a. quotient
  b. dividend
  c. percentage
  d. divisor

33. The total amount of interest to be paid on a loan is determined by
  a. rate of interest
  b. principal amount borrowed
  c. duration of the loan
  d. all of the above

34. Escrow companies are subject to regulation by the
  a. real estate commissioner
  b. corporations commissioner
  c. banking commissioner
  d. attorney general

35. When a deed is delivered into escrow by the seller,
  a. title then passes to the buyer
  b. it must be recorded the same day
  c. title remains with the seller until the escrow is ready to close
  d. the buyer must deposit his or her funds immediately

36. An escrow holder may be utilized in connection with
  a. a loan transaction
  b. a sale of a business
  c. an exchange of real property
  d. any of the above

37. To be enforceable, escrow instructions for the sale of real property must contain
  a. names of the parties
  b. consideration
  c. property description
  d. all of the above

38. An escrow holder must be
  a. partial
  b. impartial
  c. a principal to the transaction
  d. able to act without regard to instructions

39. An escrow holder is not permitted to
  a. furnish legal advice
  b. draft subordination agreements
  c. suggest the way to acquire title
  d. do any of the above

40. If a dispute arises in a sales escrow, the escrow holder should
  a. favor the buyer
  b. favor the seller
  c. favor the broker
  d. remain neutral

41. Breach of a fiduciary duty by an escrow holder
  a. is excusable
  b. is immaterial
  c. may incur liability for damages
  d. is inconsequential

42. The buyer's instruction: "You may use my funds when you have assurances that title to the subject property is vested in me" is an illustration of a
  a. covenant
  b. condition
  c. waiver
  d. release of liability

43. In an insurance policy the party who obtains the benefit of the insurance is called the
   a. insurer
   b. insured
   c. indemnitor
   d. assignor
44. Which of the following would give the greatest amount of protection?
   a. abstract of title
   b. certificate of title
   c. guarantee of title
   d. policy of title insurance
45. A standard coverage policy of title insurance excludes from its coverage
   a. forged deeds
   b. competency
   c. authority of a trustee
   d. zoning regulations
46. Which one of the following is included in the coverage of a standard policy of title insurance?
   a. failure of consideration
   b. fraud in the execution of a document
   c. imprudent investments
   d. matters not of record but known to the insured

47. The following interests are insurable under a policy of title insurance
   a. vendee's interest under a contract
   b. condominium
   c. life estate
   d. all of the above
48. Which of the following is not included in the coverage of a standard coverage policy of title insurance?
   a. false personation
   b. lack of capacity of grantor
   c. rights of persons in possession
   d. recorded court judgments and decrees
49. An extended coverage policy of title insurance does not include assurances as to
   a. access
   b. market value
   c. mechanic's liens
   d. encroachments
50. A policy of title insurance assures the sufficiency of
   a. subordination agreements
   b. court decrees
   c. joint tenancy deeds
   d. any of the above

7
REAL ESTATE FINANCE

As mentioned in Chapter 1, the subject of finance is of vital importance in the real estate field. Basically it involves the use of credit, and involves a borrower and a lender. In Shakespeare's play *Hamlet* (I.iii), the advice is given, "Neither a borrower nor a lender be." But that admonition, if followed, would create havoc in the financial world today. Having a choice, which would you rather be, a borrower or a lender? The latter might

be preferable, but Rabelais gives the opposite viewpoint where one of his characters flings down the challenge to thrift and counsels prodigality:

> The Lord forbid that I should be out of debt, be still indebted to somebody or other, that there may be somebody always to pray for you; that the giver of all good things may grant unto you a blessed, long, and prosperous life, fearing if Fortune should deal crossly with you that it might be his chance to come short of being paid by you; he will always speak good of you in every company . . . to the end that . . . you may make a shift by borrowing from Peter to pay Paul. . . . Believe me, your creditors with a more fervent devotion will beseech Almighty God to prolong your life; they being afraid of nothing more than that you should die.

The subject of finance will always be of interest and concern. In this chapter we consider primarily the instruments of real estate finance. In the following chapter we discuss real estate lenders and the role of the government in real estate finance. It should be obvious that we cannot tell you everything about real estate finance, but the chapter thoroughly covers the basics and will give you a strong foundation for continuing your studies in this important subject.

More specifically this chapter deals primarily with the multitude of legal documents used to secure and encumber real property. This can be done in a variety of ways for a variety of reasons. Each particular instrument has a very specific purpose but often any one of several instruments can be used to accomplish the same or similar purposes. It is therefore important that anyone dealing with real estate transactions be familiar with the different types of instruments and be ready to enlist expert help in selecting the best one for a particular set of circumstances. Protection of future rights, reduction or deferring of taxes, estate planning, and many other considerations must be a part of the basis for selection.

A mortgage or deed of trust or other security instrument creates a lien on real property. We will first discuss liens, then consider briefly the characteristics and types of promissory notes that are secured by such a lien. We then explain the nature and types of several different varieties of security instruments, along with practical aspects. The chapter concludes with brief discussions of a long term contract of sale as a security device and personal property security instruments.

LIENS AS CHARGES ON THE LAND

A lien is characterized as an encumbrance on land. An encumbrance may be of two types: one that imposes a lien and one that restricts the use or enjoyment of the property. The latter type will be considered in Chapter 12. We will find that all liens are encumbrances, but not all encumbrances are liens. A lien may be classified as either voluntary or involuntary. In this chapter we will consider voluntary liens, i.e., those created by voluntary act of the property owner. These liens were created for the purpose of securing a promise—either a promise to pay a debt or to perform some other obligation. Involuntary liens, i.e., those created by operation of law or by the creditor of a property owner exercising statutory rights, will be the subject of Chapter 10. Frequently encountered voluntary liens include mortgages or deeds of trust given to secure payment of a promissory note or other obligation, long term land sales contracts, and land contracts primarily in the form of a security device.

VOLUNTARY LIENS

In California the most frequently encountered

type of voluntary encumbrance is the *deed of trust*, which is used in place of the *mortgage*. In some states, mortgages are used as security for loans. Because mortgages are seldom used in California, we'll consider mortgages principally by way of comparison with deeds of trust. We'll discuss deeds of trust in considerable detail, including the procedures applicable in the event of a default in payment of the debt or default in performance of the obligation secured by the deed of trust.

PROMISSORY NOTES AS PRIMARY EVIDENCE OF DEBT OBLIGATIONS

Mortgages and trust deeds are given in most cases to secure payment of a *promissory note*. This note is usually in the form of a *negotiable instrument*, to which special rules apply.

Essentially a negotiable instrument is a written *promise* or *order* to pay money. It can be in the form of a promissory note, illustrated in Figure 7.1, or a check, or a certificate of deposit, or a draft or bill of exchange. Bank checks are the most common type of negotiable instrument. A check is an *order* on a third party (the bank) to pay money to the person so entitled, either the payee or an endorsee. Checks and drafts are referred to as "three-party paper," whereas a note is a "two-party paper."

Negotiable instruments are freely transferable in commerce. Because of the need for substantial uniformity in commercial paper throughout the United States, a uniform negotiable instruments law was adopted by all the states many years ago. It was adopted in California in 1917 and is now part of the Uniform Commercial Code. When properly prepared, negotiable instruments are ordinarily accepted as the equivalent of cash. This facilitates trade and commerce and is the reason for the enactment of the Negotiable Instruments Law. To be regarded as a negotiable instrument under this law, the note or other document must conform strictly to each of the following requirements. It must be

1. An unconditional promise or order
2. In writing
3. Made by one person to another
4. Signed by the maker or drawer
5. Agreeing to pay on demand or at a definite time

Figure 7.1
Straight Note

PROMISSORY NOTE

$5,000.00   Los Angeles, California   June 30, 1986

One year after date, for value received, I promise to pay [name of creditor], or order, at Los Angeles, California the sum of Five Thousand Dollars with interest from date until paid, at the rate of fifteen (15) percent per annum, payable in quarterly installments, commencing September 20, 1986.

Should interest not be so paid it shall thereafter bear like interest as the principal, but such unpaid interest so compounded shall not exceed an amount equal to simple interest on the unpaid principal at the maximum rate permitted by law. Should default be made in payment of interest when due the whole sum of principal and interest shall become immediately due at the option of the holder of this note. Principal and interest payable in lawful money of the United States. If action be instituted on this note I promise to pay such sum as the Court may fix as attorney's fees.

/s/

_____   _____

_____   _____

6. A certain sum in money
7. Payable to order of a named payee or to bearer.

The note illustrated by Figure 7.1 complies with all the above requirements.

If any one of the listed elements is missing, the document may still be valid, but it will be transferable like any ordinary contract right. As such, the transferee gets no more than the transferor had, and defenses that were good against the original payee are good against the assignees.

However, when the document is a valid negotiable instrument, a subsequent owner, or transferee, may derive more benefit from it than the transferor had. In general a third-party transferee enjoys a favored position if he takes the note as a *holder in due course*. A person is a holder in due course if he or she has taken a negotiable instrument for value, in good faith, and without notice that it is overdue or has been dishonored. Also, the person must be without notice of any defense against it or claim to it on the part of any other person. Such defenses and claims cannot be asserted against a holder in due course.

The negotiability of a promissory note is not affected by the fact that it is secured by a mortgage or deed of trust. To be sure, the fact that it is secured makes the note even more attractive as an instrument because the creditor may foreclose on the property to satisfy the debt. Similarly, the negotiability of the note is not affected by the inclusion of a clause, as in the note illustrated, adding attorney's fees or court costs in the event litigation becomes necessary to collect, nor by inclusion of an *acceleration clause* which provides that the entire amount of the loan is immediately due at the election of the holder under certain prescribed conditions. When the property is sold, the type of acceleration clause that applies is sometimes called a *due-on-sale*, or *alienation clause*. Types of obligations subject to an acceleration clause include defaults in loan payments, failure to maintain the property, or failure to pay insurance premiums. The three terms—acceleration, alienation, and due-on-sale—are often used interchangeably. However, *acceleration* is a general term, whereas an *alienation* or *due-on-sale* is a type of acceleration clause which becomes operative in the event of a transfer of the property to a third person.

Promissory notes are usually prepared on printed forms, and can be either *straight notes* or *installment notes*. The latter can provide that interest is to be either *included* or *excluded* from the monthly payments, or can contain a balloon payment provision. The basic differences among these forms of notes are illustrated by Figure 7.2.

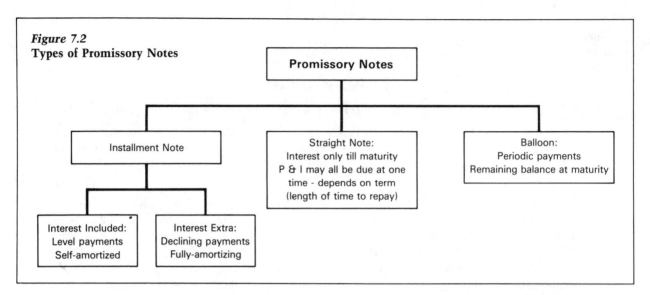

Figure 7.2
Types of Promissory Notes

The differences may be briefly summarized as follows:

1. *Straight note.* All principal is due at one stated time, although the interest may be paid at stated times (quarterly, annually, etc.), depending upon the terms of the loan.
2. *Installment note-interest extra.* A specific sum (or installment) must be paid on the principal at stated intervals. Interest is collected *in addition to* the principal payment. Interest is computed on the principal balance prior to the credit of the principal payment. Thus, as payments on the principal are made, the amount of the interest payment is reduced, and the total amount of the payment due on each payment date becomes less, since less interest is required as the note is paid down.
3. *Installment note-interest included.* In this form of note (fully amortized) the amount of the monthly payment remains constant. The interest is computed on the principal balance of the note as of the date of each payment. The amount of the interest is subtracted from the amount of the payment, and the remainder of the installment is credited on the principal, as was illustrated in Chapter 6. The installment payments continue until the full amount of principal and interest has been paid. Figure 7.3 illustrates this form of note.
4. *Installment note–interest included (balance due date).* This form is basically the same as the interest-included note described above, except that the installment payments continue until a stated date, at which time the entire remaining unpaid principal and inter-

est become due and payable. This lump sum is the balloon payment referred to earlier. This is also known as a partially amortized note.

MORTGAGES AND TRUST DEEDS AS SECURITY FOR DEBTS OR OTHER OBLIGATIONS

Historical Development of Mortgages

The mortgage actually started a long time back in English history with early Saxon law, when an owner, desirous of borrowing money from someone, would put his land up as security for the loan. The borrower (mortgagor) conveyed the legal title to the land to the lender (the mortgagee), with the written understanding that up to a certain date the mortgagor could get the land back by repaying the loan. Meanwhile, the lender could actually possess the land and collect any rents or profits from it. Thus, the earliest mortgage was actually a *deed* which contained a defeasance clause, that is, a clause providing that upon repayment of the loan on the due date, the title would be conveyed back to the borrower. The word *mortgage* originates from two French words, namely *mort* meaning *dead*, and *gage* meaning *pledge.*

With time the mortgage was increasingly recognized as a security device rather than a conveyance of title. In California, as in most western states, the mortgage is now recognized as merely a lien. Thus, with a modern-day mortgage, the *borrower* retains legal title to the property and

Figure 7.3
Note Secured by Deed of Trust

DO NOT DESTROY THIS NOTE: When paid, this note and the Deed of Turst must be surrendered to the First American Title Company of Los Angeles with request for reconveyance.

INSTALLMENT NOTE
(INTEREST INCLUDED)
(This note contains an acceleration clause)

$ _____   _____ , California, _____

In installments and at the times hereinafter stated, for value received _____

promise _____ to pay to

or order, at _____

the principal sum of _____

with interest from _____ Dollars,

_____ on the amounts of principal remaining from time

to time unpaid, until said principal sum is paid, at the rate of _____ per cent, per annum. Principal and interest

due in monthly installments of _____ Dollars,

($ _____), or more on the _____ day of each and every month, beginning on the _____ day

of _____ , 19 _____

and continuing until said principal sum and the interest thereon has been fully paid. AT ANY TIME, THE PRIVILEGE IS RESERVED TO PAY MORE THAN THE SUM DUE. Each payment shall be credited first, on the interest then due; and the remainder on the principal sum; and interest shall thereupon cease upon the amount so credited on the said principal sum. Should default be made in the payment of any of said installments when due, then the whole sum of principal and interest shall become immediately due and payable at the option of the holder of this note.

If the trustor shall sell, convey or alienate said property, or any part thereof, or any interest therein, or shall be divested of his title or any interest therein in any manner or way, whether voluntarily or involuntarily, without the written consent of the beneficiary being first had and obtained beneficiary shall have the right, at its option, to declare any indebtedness or obligations secured hereby, irrespective of the maturity date specified in any note evidencing the same, immediately due and payable.

Should suit be commenced to collect this note or any portion thereof, such sum as the Court may deem reasonable shall be added hereto as attorney's fees. Principal and interest payable in lawful money of the United States of America. This note is secured by a certain DEED OF TRUST to the First American Title Company of Los Angeles, a California corporation, as TRUSTEE.

_____   _____

_____   _____

_____   _____

FATCOLA 85

can continue to use and enjoy it. If he or she fails to pay up at the agreed time, foreclosure proceedings must be undertaken before he or she loses title. And even after the foreclosure sale, the mortgagor has the right to possess the property until his or her right to *redeem* his property has expired, normally after *one year*, or three months in the event the property is sold for the entire amount of the debt owing, i.e., in the event there is no deficiency.

Nature of a Deed of Trust

A deed of trust, commonly referred to as a trust deed or TD, is a written instrument by which title to land is transferred to a third party, as trustee, to secure payment of a debt or performance or some other obligation owing to another person. A trust deed imposes a *lien* on real property and serves a purpose similar to a mortgage, but differs in some important respects. First of all, the mortgage is a two-party agreement, whereas the deed of trust involves three parties, the *trustor*, the *beneficiary*, and the *trustee*. The trust deed differs from the Grant Deed described in Chapter 3 in that a Trust Deed is an instrument of security, while a Grant Deed conveys title in a sale or exchange of real property.

The *trustor* is comparable to the mortgagor, and executes both the promissory note and the trust deed. The *beneficiary* in the deed of trust is the lender—the person or lending institution to whom the obligation is owed and to whom payment is due. In a mortgage the lender should be the *mortgagee*. The *trustee* is the third party who is said to stand between the trustor and the beneficiary. Usually the trustee is a corporation, often a title insurance company or financial institution, that holds the legal title *in trust with power of sale* to secure the debt. The trustee's powers are confined primarily to two functions:

1. If the debt is not paid in accordance with the terms of the note, upon the beneficiary's request the trustee is empowered *to sell the property* at public auction in satisfaction of the debt.
2. After the loan is repaid in full, the trustee is authorized *to execute a reconveyance deed* or release of the property from the lien of the deed of trust.

Each of these functions can be performed, of course, only in accordance with the applicable laws and the provisions of the instrument itself. Figure 7.4 illustrates the procedures involved at two stages of the loan transaction.

The terms of the trust deed disclose that *title* to the property is *conveyed* or transferred to the trustee. Since the deed of trust recites that the "trustor irrevocably grants, transfers and assigns" the property to the trustee, the trustor seems to be divested of all title, including the right of possession. However, this is not the case. The trust deed merely provides security for the performance of the obligation, and the law considers that the trustee acquires *only such title* as is necessary to accomplish this purpose, and that title is vested in the trustee only to expedite the real estate loan.

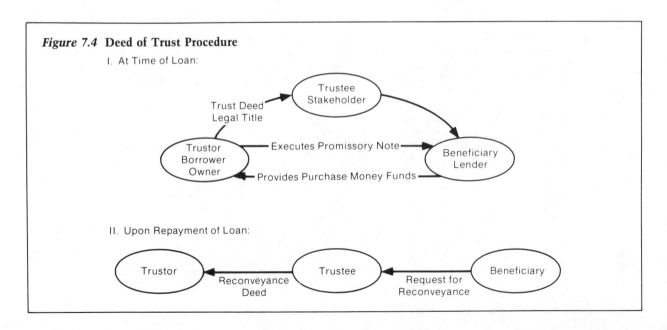

Figure 7.4 **Deed of Trust Procedure**

I. At Time of Loan:

Trustee
Stakeholder

Trust Deed
Legal Title

Trustor
Borrower
Owner

—Executes Promissory Note—▶

Beneficiary
Lender

—Provides Purchase Money Funds—

II. Upon Repayment of Loan:

Trustor   ◀— Reconveyance Deed —   Trustee   ◀— Request for Reconveyance —   Beneficiary

In addition to a difference in the number of parties, there are other differences between a mortgage and deed of trust, several stemming from the type of *remedy* available in the event of a default. The ordinary mortgage can be foreclosed only by court action, whereas the common method for foreclosure of a trust deed is a nonjudicial sale by the trustee. When a situation warrants, however, a trust deed can be foreclosed by court action, the same as a mortgage. As stated earlier, there is a *right of redemption* after the sale of property by court action; on the other hand, there is *no* redemption period following a trustee's sale under a deed of trust. Also, in a judicial foreclosure—but not in a trustee's sale—the *defaulted party* may be able to obtain a *deficiency judgment*. These matters will be discussed more thoroughly later in this chapter under "Foreclosure Procedures."

Mortgages and trust deeds are also differentiated by the effect the *statute of limitations* has on each. The power of sale under a deed of trust can still be exercised even though the statute has run out on the obligation. The enforcement of a mortgage is barred when the statute of limitations runs out on the underlying obligation.

The chart shown as Figure 7.5 summarizes the principal differences between the mortgage and

Figure 7.5
Comparison of Trust Deeds and Mortgages

Deed of Trust	Comparison	Mortgage
Trustor — Borrower Beneficiary — Lender Trustee — Neutral third party	*Parties*	Mortgagor — Borrower Mortgagee — Lender
Rests in — Trustee	*Title during loan term*	Rests in — Mortgagor
Trust Note — Evidence of debt Trust Deed — Conveyance of title to trustee as security for the debt	*Loan Documents*	Mortgage Note — Evidence of debt Mortgage Contract — Hypothecation of real property as security for debt
Court Action *or* Trustee's Sale	*Foreclosure*	Court Action Only

If Foreclosure by Court Action: Same as for Mortgage
 	
Trustee's Sale—
  Notice of Default—Owner may redeem by bringing payments current within *three months*
  Notice of Sale—Owner may redeem only by paying entire indebtedness in full
  Trustee's Sale—Sale final. No redemption
	Owner's Rights of Redemption	Before Decree of Foreclosure—
		  Owner may redeem anytime by bringing payments current
		After Decree of Foreclosure and Sale—
		  Owner has one year "Equity of Redemption"
		  Must pay indebtedness in full to redeem

If Foreclosure by Court Action: Same as for Mortgage Trustee's Sale—No Deficiency Judgment Possible	*Lender's Rights*	Possible Deficiency Judgment
Grant Deed	*Conveyance*	Warranty Deed
Policy of Title Insurance	*Protection*	Abstract of Title or Certificate
Deed of Reconveyance—Recorded	*Receipt for Payment*	Certificate of Discharge—Recorded
Trust Note—Outlaws four years after due date Trust Deed—Never Outlaws—Lender can always have trustee sell to recover unpaid balance	*Statute of Limitations*	Mortgage note and contract both outlaw four years from due date, or from date of last payment. No relief. Monies involved not collectable.

trust deed. A close study of it will reveal why the trust deed is favored over the mortgage instrument as a security device in California. The deed of trust is a more flexible security device than the mortgage; the rules for foreclosure by trustee's sale have been firmly established, with the result that the deed of trust is widely used in California in preference to a mortgage. It is possible to use a mortgage with a power of sale in California; this type of mortgage does give some of the flexibility found in a deed of trust. However, it still has been used very little.

At the present time there is no standard form for the deed of trust, and the provisions do vary, depending upon the requirements of the particular lender. Most deeds of trust are prepared on forms, preprinted either by or on behalf of a designated beneficiary or as an accommodation by companies authorized to act as a trustee, such as a title company.

A deed of trust may be given to secure not only payment of a promissory note, but also performances of any other type of lawful obligation, such as an indemnity agreement or a bail bond obligation. The purpose of the deed of trust is the same as that of a mortgage, i.e., to create a lien on real property. In California, counties sometimes employ mortgages to secure obligations owing to the county, many times for hospital care. These are commonly referred to as "indigent mortgages." However, most lenders prefer the deed of trust, and it is the usual type of security instrument employed in the real estate loan transactions.

A Short Form Deed of Trust is shown in Figure 7.6. It is designed to save recording expenses, in that the general provisions appearing on its reverse side are not recorded. To obtain the benefit of this procedure, a fictitious deed of trust is recorded in each county where the short form is to be used, setting forth the full provisions of the agreement between parties using this particular form. The "general provisions" are then *incorporated by reference* into the abbreviated form that is executed by the trustor. This identical text is printed on the reverse side of the short form for information, but is not transcribed into the records. A Long Form Deed of Trust, by contrast, is recorded in full (both sides), resulting in additional recording charges.

Most printed forms of trust deeds used today also include a provision for an *assignment of rents* in the event the trustor defaults in any payments of the indebtedness secured by the deed of trust. In the form illustrated, this provision is contained in the paragraph immediately following the description of the property. To exercise this right, usually a receiver must be appointed by appropriate court action.

Each of the trustee's functions is performed in accordance with the provisions of the instrument itself and the laws relating to trustee's sales and reconveyances. Before looking at the general provisions, observe that the reverse side of Figure 7.6 also includes a form used by the beneficiary to direct the trustee to execute a reconveyance of the deed of trust. This form is designated as a Request for Full Reconveyance. In order to execute a reconveyance (or "deed of reconveyance," as it is sometimes called) the trustee will require that the original note and deed of trust be delivered to him and that the Request for Reconveyance be properly executed. If the original note or deed of trust becomes lost or destroyed, it can be costly and time-consuming to replace it. Thus, the admonishment appears on the note. *"Do Not Destroy This Note."*

The general provisions appearing on the reverse side of Figure 7.6 cover more or less standardized covenants, rights, and duties, including the following:

1. Trustor promises to keep the property in good repair and promises not to do anything with the property which would impair the security.
2. Trustor agrees to maintain fire insurance on the property.
3. Trustor agrees to defend the title against others attempting to gain an interest in the property that might affect the lender's rights (normally via title insurance).
4. Trustor agrees to pay taxes and other obligations, including those incurred prior to the lien of this deed of trust. If trustor fails to do so, then the beneficiary may advance funds for this purpose and add such advances to the amount due.
5. Trustor agrees to reimburse beneficiary for any advances or other sum paid on account of the deed of trust.
6. Condemnation action awards are payable to beneficiary, up to amount of outstanding loan.
7. The beneficiary's acceptance of payments after the due date is not a waiver of his or her rights under the deed of trust.
8. Trustee may reconvey a portion of the prop-

Figure 7.6
Deed of Trust and Assignment of Rents

RECORDING REQUESTED BY

AND WHEN RECORDED MAIL TO

NAME
ADDRESS
CITY &
STATE
ZIP

Title Order No............................Escrow No...........................

SPACE ABOVE THIS LINE FOR RECORDER'S USE

DEED OF TRUST AND ASSIGNMENT OF RENTS

BY THIS DEED OF TRUST, made this   day of   , 19   , between

, herein called **Trustor**, whose address is

(number and street)   (city)   (state)   (zip)

and **SAFECO TITLE INSURANCE COMPANY,** a California corporation, herein called **Trustee,** and

, herein called **Beneficiary,**

Trustor grants, transfers, and assigns to trustee, in trust, with power of sale, that property in
County, California, described as:

Trustor also assigns to Beneficiary all rents, issues and profits of said realty reserving the right to collect and use the same except during continuance of default hereunder and during continuance of such default authorizing Beneficiary to collect and enforce the same by any lawful means in the name of any party hereto.

For purpose of securing:

(1) Payment of the indebtedness evidenced by one promissory note in the principal sum of $
of even date herewith, payable to Beneficiary, and any extensions or renewals thereof; (2) the payment of any money that may be advanced by the Beneficiary to Trustor, or his successors, with interest thereon, evidenced by additional notes (indicating they are so secured) or by endorsement on the original note, executed by Trustor or his successor; (3) performance of each agreement of Trustor incorporated by reference or contained herein.

On October 25, 1973, identical fictitious Deeds of Trust were recorded in the offices of the County Recorders of the Counties of the State of California, the first page thereof appearing in the book and at the page of the records of the respective County Recorder as follows:

COUNTY	Book	Page	COUNTY	Book	Page	COUNTY	Book	Page	COUNTY	Book	Page
Alameda	3540	89	Kings	1018	394	Placer	1528	440	Siskiyou	697	407
Alpine	18	753	Lake	743	552	Plumas	227	443	Solano	1860	581
Amador	250	243	Lassen	271	367	Riverside	1973	139405	Sonoma	2810	975
Butte	1870	678	Los Angeles	T8512	751	Sacramento	731025	59	Stanislaus	2587	332
Calaveras	368	92	Madera	1176	234	San Benito	386	94	Sutter	817	182
Colusa	409	347	Marin	2736	463	San Bernardino	8294	877	Tehama	630	522
Contra Costa	7077	178	Mariposa	143	717	San Francisco	B820	585	Trinity	161	393
Del Norte	174	526	Mendocino	942	242	San Joaquin	3813	6	Tulare	3137	567
El Dorado	1229	594	Merced	1940	361	San Luis Obispo	1750	491	Tuolumne	396	309
Fresno	6227	411	Modoc	225	668	San Mateo	6491	600	Ventura	4182	662
Glenn	565	290	Mono	160	215	Santa Barbara	2486	1244	Yolo	1081	335
Humboldt	1213	31	Monterey	877	243	Santa Clara	0623	713	Yuba	564	163
Imperial	1355	801	Napa	922	96	Santa Cruz	2358	744		File No.	
Inyo	205	660	Nevada	665	303	Shasta	1195	293	San Diego	73-299568	
Kern	4809	2351	Orange	10961	398	Sierra	59	439			

The provisions contained in Section A, including paragraphs 1 through 5, and the provisions contained in Section B, including paragraphs 1 through 9 of said fictitious Deeds of Trust are incorporated herein as fully as though set forth at length and in full herein. The undersigned Trustor requests that a copy of any notice of default and any notice of sale hereunder be mailed to Trustor at the address hereinabove set forth, being the address designated for the purpose of receiving such notice.

STATE OF CALIFORNIA,   SS.
COUNTY OF_____

On this the _____ day of _____ 19 ___, before me, the undersigned, a Notary Public in and for said County and State, personally appeared _____

_____

_____ , personally known to me or proved to me on the basis of satisfactory evidence to be the person(s) whose name(s) is (are) subscribed to the within instrument and acknowledged that _____ executed the same.

FOR NOTARY SEAL OR STAMP

Notary Signature

SAFECO Stock No. **CAL-0092** (Rev. 1-85)

Figure 7.6
Continued

DO NOT RECORD — Provisions incorporated from Recorded Fictitious Deed of Trust.

A. TO PROTECT THE SECURITY HEREOF, TRUSTOR AGREES:

[1] To keep said property in good condition and repair, preserve thereon the buildings, complete construction begun, restore damage or destruction, and pay the cost thereof; to commit or permit no waste, no violation of laws or covenants or conditions relating to use, alterations or improvements; to cultivate, irrigate, fertilize, fumigate, prune, and do all other acts which the character and use of said property and the estate or interest in said property secured by this Deed of Trust may require to preserve this security.

[2] To provide, maintain and deliver to Beneficiary fire insurance satisfactory to and with loss payable to Beneficiary. The amount collected under any fire or other insurance policy may be applied by Beneficiary upon any indebtedness secured hereby and in such order as Beneficiary may determine, or Beneficiary may release all or any part thereof to Trustor. Such application or release shall not cure or waive any default or notice of default hereunder or invalidate any act done pursuant to such notice.

[3] To appear in and defend any action or proceeding purporting to affect the security hereof or the rights or powers of Beneficiary or Trustee; and to pay all costs and expenses, including cost of evidence of title and attorney's fees in a reasonable sum, in any such action or proceeding in which Beneficiary or Trustee may appear.

B. IT IS MUTUALLY AGREED THAT:

[1] Any award of damages in connection with any condemnation for public use of or injury to said property or any part thereof is hereby assigned to Beneficiary, who may apply or release such moneys received by him in the same manner and with the same effect as provided for disposition of proceeds of fire or other insurance.

[2] By accepting payment of any sum secured hereby after its due date, Beneficiary does not waive his right either to require payment when due of all other sums so secured or to declare default for failure so to pay.

[3] At any time or from time to time, without liability therefor and without notice, upon written request of Beneficiary and presentation of this Deed and said note for endorsement, and without affecting the personal liability of any person for payment of the indebtedness secured hereby, Trustee may: reconvey any part of said property; consent to the making of any map thereof; join in granting any easement thereon; or join in any agreement extending or subordinating the lien or charge hereof.

[4] Upon written request of Beneficiary stating that all sums secured hereby have been paid, and upon surrender of this Deed and said note to Trustee for cancellation and retention and upon payment of its fees, Trustee shall reconvey, without warranty, the property then held hereunder. The recitals in such reconveyance of any matters or facts shall be conclusive proof of the truthfulness thereof. The grantee in such reconveyance may be described as "the person or persons legally entitled thereto."

[5] Upon default by Trustor in payment of any indebtedness secured hereby or in performance of any agreement hereunder, Beneficiary may declare all sums secured hereby immediately due and payable by delivery to Trustee of written declaration of default and demand for sale and of written notice of default and of election to cause said property to be sold, which notice Trustee shall cause to be duly filed for record. Beneficiary also shall deposit with Trustee this Deed, said note and all documents evidencing expenditures secured hereby.

Trustee shall give notice of sale as then required by law, and without demand on Trustor, at least three months having elapsed after recordation of such notice of default, shall sell said property at the time and place of sale fixed by it in said notice of sale, either as a whole or in separate parcels and in such order as it may determine, at public auction to the highest bidder for cash in lawful money of the United States, payable at time of sale.

[4] To pay: at least ten days before delinquency all taxes and assessments affecting said property, including assessments on appurtenant water stock; when due, all incumbrances, charges and liens, with interest, on said property or any part thereof, which appear to be prior or superior hereto; all costs, fees and expenses of this Trust.

Should Trustor fail to make any payment or to do any act as herein provided, then Beneficiary or Trustee, but without obligation so to do and without notice to or demand upon Trustor and without releasing Trustor from any obligation hereof, may: make or do the same in such manner and to such extent as either may deem necessary to protect the security hereof. Beneficiary or Trustee being authorized to enter upon said property for such purposes; appear in and defend any action or proceeding purporting to affect the security hereof or the rights or powers of Beneficiary or Trustee; pay, purchase, contest or compromise any incumbrance, charge or lien which in the judgment of either appears to be prior or superior hereto; and, in exercising any such powers, pay necessary expenses, employ counsel and pay his reasonable fees.

[5] To pay immediately and without demand all sums so expended by Beneficiary or Trustee, with interest from date of expenditure at seven per cent per annum, and to pay for any statement provided for by law regarding the obligations secured hereby in the amount demanded by Beneficiary, not exceeding the maximum amount permitted by law at the time of the request therefore.

Trustee may postpone sale of all or any portion of said property by public announcement at such time and place of sale, and from time to time thereafter may postpone such sale by public announcement at the time fixed by the preceding postponement. Trustee shall deliver to such purchaser its deed conveying the property so sold, but without any covenant or warranty, expressed or implied. The recitals in such deed of any matters or facts shall be conclusive proof of the truthfulness thereof. Any person, including Trustor, Trustee, or Beneficiary as hereinafter defined, may purchase at such sale.

After deducting all costs, fees and expenses of Trustee and of this Trust, including cost of evidence of title in connection with sale, Trustee shall apply the proceeds of sale to payment of: all sums expended under the terms hereof, not then repaid, with accrued interest at seven per cent per annum; all other sums then secured hereby; and the remainder, if any, to the person or persons legally entitled thereto.

[6] This Deed applies to, inures to the benefit of, and binds all parties hereto, their legal representatives and successors in interest. The term Beneficiary shall include any future owner and holder, including pledgees, of the note secured hereby. In this Deed, whenever the context so requires, the masculine gender includes the feminine and/or neuter, and the singular number includes the plural.

[7] Trustee accepts this Trust when this Deed, duly executed and acknowledged, is made a public record as provided by law. Trustee is not obligated to notify any party hereto of pending sale under any other Deed of Trust or of any action or proceeding in which Trustor, Beneficiary or Trustee shall be a party unless brought by Trustee.

[8] The Trusts created hereby are irrevocable by Trustor.

[9] Beneficiary may substitute a successor Trustee from time to time by recording in the Office of the Recorder or Recorders of the county where the property is located an instrument stating the election by the Beneficiary to make such substitution, which instrument shall identify the Deed of Trust by recording reference, and by the name of the original Trustor, Trustee and Beneficiary, and shall set forth the name and address of the new Trustee, and which instrument shall be signed by the Beneficiary and duly acknowledged.

REQUEST FOR FULL RECONVEYANCE

To be used only when note has been paid

To SAFECO Title Insurance Company, Trustee: Dated_____

The undersigned is the legal owner and holder of all indebtedness secured by this Deed of Trust. All sums secured by said Deed of Trust have been paid, and you are requested, on payment to you of any sums owing to you under the terms of said Deed of Trust, to cancel all evidences of indebtedness, secured by said Deed of Trust, delivered to you herewith and to reconvey, without warranty, to the parties designated by the terms of said Deed of Trust, the estate now held by you under the same.

Mail Reconveyance to:

_____
_____   By_____
_____   By_____

Do not lose or destroy this Deed of Trust OR THE NOTE which it secures. Both must be delivered to the Trustee for cancellation before reconveyance will be made.

---

erty covered by the deed of trust or perform other acts when requested to do so by beneficiary.

9. This paragraph provides a procedure for issuance of a full reconveyance.

10. Relates to the "assignment of rents" provision appearing on the face of the deed of trust. It applies only where the property is rented and then only after occurrence of default by trustor.

11. In the event of default in the payment of an installment, beneficiary may accelerate the

due date by declaring *all* sums immediately due and payable. This clause is subject to a statutory right of reinstatement for a period of three months after a notice of default is recorded. The clause further relates to the power and duties of the trustee in connection with a trustee's sale proceedings.

12. Provides a method for substituting another trustee for the one named in the deed of trust.

13. States that the provisions of the deed of trust are binding on successors in interest to any of the parties.

14. Provides for acceptance of the trust by the named trustee.

As mentioned above, the general provisions of trust deeds do vary, depending upon the particular beneficiary or trustee. Some trust deed forms contain printed alienation clauses, or prepayment privilege clauses, or variable interest clauses that can be of vital concern to a borrower. Prudent persons will familiarize themselves with all the general provisions of the particular form of deed of trust to be used in their transactions as well as any added special clauses.

Special Clauses

A deed of trust may contain any number of special clauses. It will suffice for our purposes to discuss some of these clauses only briefly. The enforceability and effect of such clauses are considered further in the course on real estate law. The following is a list of the special clauses frequently encountered:

Open-end provision. Some deeds of trust provide that additional sums of money be loaned or advanced by the lender; these additional sums may be either *obligatory* or *optional*, depending upon the content of the clause, and are also secured by the deed of trust. They are evidenced by an additional note or notes. The loans are obligatory if the lender has no choice but to make them, usually in a specified amount, if the trustor so demands. Obligatory advances normally arise in construction loans, where the proceeds of the loan are advanced as the construction project progresses. Open-end provisions should be distinguished from advances made under the provisions of the deed of trust to protect the security, such as payment of real property taxes, insurance premiums, or sums due under prior encumbrances. Different rules of priority apply under these conditions.

Alienation or due-on-sale clauses. Most deeds of trust provide that in the event of a transfer of the property by the trustor, the beneficiary may, at his or her discretion, accelerate (cause to be paid immediately) the entire unpaid balance due on the note. The validity of alienation clauses has been the subject of much litigation and legislative action, both on the state and federal levels. In 1976 the California Supreme Court held that a sale by land sales contract does not necessarily violate a due-on-sale clause of a prior trust deed (*Tucker* v. *Lassen*), provided the seller retained a sufficient interest in the property by way of an unpaid balance owing to the seller. The rationale was that there was not such a threat to the lender's security to justify an enforcement of the due-on-sale clause. This brought on new forms of contracts of sale intended primarily to be security devices (see further discussion later in this chapter). This was followed by another significant decision (*Wellenkamp* v. *Bank of America*) in which the California Supreme Court held, in essence, that a sale of property does not automatically trigger the acceleration or due-on-sale clause by lenders. In order to enforce the clause, the lender must demonstrate that such enforcement is necessary to protect the lender from default or impairment to its security.

Subsequently the United States Supreme Court ruled that federally chartered savings and loan associations were not bound by the California state court decision, and have the right to enforce alienation clauses since they are exclusively regulated by the Federal Home Loan Bank Board. This was followed by federal legislation which allows virtually all types of lenders to enforce alienation clauses contained in loans secured by real property. This subject is treated at more length in a course on real estate law.

Prepayment privileges. A trustor does not have the right to prepay an installment note at any time if the note does not give such a right. Prepayment is a matter of contract between the parties. The beneficiary may require a bonus for such privilege unless the note permits payment at any time. In Figure 7.3, the privilege to pay more is reserved. Such language clearly authorizes the trustor to pay off the note in full at any time, without penalty. A prepayment privilege, however, usually provides that the trustor must pay additional interest if the loan is paid off early. Such a charge is referred to as a *prepayment privilege* (sometimes unwisely referred to as a *prepayment penalty clause*) and usually amounts to 6 months' interest.

As an example, suppose a loan has been issued for $100,000 at 13½ percent interest per annum. In California, a borrower may pay off up to 20 percent of the original loan balance each year if the loan is on an owner-occupied dwelling of up to four units. The maximum penalty may not exceed six months of unearned interest after first deducting 20 percent of the original balance. No penalty may be charged after five years. What would be the amount a lender could assess you for paying off the loan before its maturity, within the first five years?

In the example below, assume that you are paying off the loan three years after the loan was made, and that there remains a balance of $95,000. The steps for computing the penalty are as follows:

1. $ 100,000   Original loan balance
    × ____20%   Statutory prepayment privilege
    $ 20,000   Amount exempt from
                prepayment privilege

2. $ 95,000   Existing loan balance
    − 20,000   Statutory exemption
    $ 75,000   Loan balance subject
                to prepayment privilege

3. × 13.5%   Interest rate
    $ 10,125   Interest computed on
                annualized basis

4. × ____50%   Half year's interest
    $5,062.50   Prepayment amount for
                six months

The reason that the word *penalty* should be avoided is that it is not the policy of the courts to enforce a penalty. There should be some reasonable relationship between the amount paid for the privilege of early payoff and the detriment to the lender.

Variable interest rates. In a market where interest rates have been on the increase, many loans provide for an automatic increase in their rates, geared to the prime rate or other similar factor. The security instrument is known as a variable rate mortgage (VRM) or more recently as an adjustable rate mortgage (ARM). In a fluctuating market there is generally a need for both parties to protect themselves. A variable interest rate, now subject to certain legislative controls, is considered to be a fair way to cover the situation from the standpoint of both parties. See a later discussion in this chapter which shows many types of variation in adjustable rate mortgages. Normally provisions for variable interest rates are found in the promissory note, and may also be contained in the trust deed.

Late charges. The courts have also sustained the validity of late charges. They are considered to be simply an agreement to pay a higher rate of interest in the event of late payment, rather than an illegal penalty.

Partial release clauses. Trust deeds frequently include partial release clauses. They are intended to effect a release of part of the security before the obligation is paid in full. Partial release clauses are commonly used in subdivision developments, and are known as *blanket encumbrances*. The following is illustrative of such a clause:

> Provided the trustor is not in default under this deed of trust, a partial reconveyance from the lien or charge of this deed of trust will be given of any one or more of the lots hereinbefore described at any time, and from time to time, prior to the maturity of the note secured hereby, upon payment of an amount (to apply on the principal of said note) based on the rate of $_____ for each lot to be so reconveyed.

Where acreage is being released, care must be exercised in identifying the location of the particular acreage being released.

Subordination clauses. Subordination clauses have created numerous problems and have been the subject of much litigation. These clauses provide that a prior deed of trust be subordinated to, i.e., *made junior to*, another specific lien, charge, or encumbrance. Subordination clauses or agreements are generally of two types: specific or future (or future automatic). A specific subordination clause subordinates to a present, existing encumbrance. An example would be when an existing first trust deed note matures, and the borrower wishes to renew the note. Under a specific subordination clause, the renewed first note would retain its priority position even against an existing junior loan that otherwise would have assumed a higher priority because it was recorded first. A future subordination clause subordinates to an encumbrance placed on the property at some future time. The usual reason for including a subordination clause is that the buyer intends to improve the property at a later date and wants the seller's purchase money trust deed (to be discussed later in this chapter) to be subordinated to a construction loan. The fact that the construction loan will have priority will make it easier for the buyer to obtain such a loan.

TYPES OF TRUST DEEDS AND MORTGAGES

Purchase Money Trust Deeds

A purchase money trust deed or mortgage is one given to secure payment of all or a portion of the purchase price of a parcel of property. Purchase money trust deeds have certain special characteristics, including the following:

1. A purchase money deed of trust has a special *priority* by statute. The California Civil Code provides that a mortgage or trust deed given for the price of real property, at the time of its conveyance, has priority over all other liens against the purchaser. This means that judgments and other liens against the buyer, even though of record prior to the purchase money trust deed, are inferior; i.e., subordinate to the trust deed.
2. Generally the purchaser is not liable for a *deficiency* on a foreclosure of a purchase money trust deed under California law. This rule is not applicable, however, for federally backed loans, such as FHA or VA.
3. There can be more than one purchase money deed of trust, in which case priority is established by the dates of recordation. We might think of a purchase money deed of trust as one given only to the *seller* to secure a portion of the purchase price. However, a deed of trust executed in favor of a third-party lender, to enable the buyer to finance the purchase of the property, is also a purchase money deed of trust as far as the rules of priority and antideficiency legislation are concerned.
4. The usury law does not apply to a purchase money trust deed in favor of the seller.

The special priority feature of a purchase money trust deed protects lenders from claims general creditors may make on the property. Lenders are thus encouraged to make loans on property because they know their investments will be protected.

Non-Purchase Money Trust Deeds

In contrast to purchase money, a non-purchase money trust deed, sometimes called a "hard money" trust deed loan, is a loan secured by a trust deed that is *not* used in the purchase or acquisition of real estate. For example, if you had a free

and clear property and wished to borrow using the property as collateral, the loan would be deemed non-purchase, or hard.

So why the distinction between purchase money and non-purchase money? Most importantly, non-purchase-money loans are subject to deficiency judgments in the event of foreclosure (if accomplished through a court sale). Second, interest rates for non-purchase money trust deed loans are limited to the FRB discout rate plus 5 percent, unless transacted through a real estate broker.

All-Inclusive Deed of Trust (AITD)

This type of deed of trust, sometimes referred to as an "overriding" or "wraparound" deed of trust, has become more popular in recent years (See Figure 7.7). It is a form of *junior* trust deed; one that is inferior or subordinate to another trust deed on the same property. Basically, it includes not only the obligation owed by the trustor to the beneficiary in the particular transaction that gives rise to its use, but also includes an obligation owed under a prior deed of trust. An all-inclusive deed of trust is created by a clause reading somewhat as follows:

> This is an all-inclusive deed of trust, securing a note for $138,000, which includes within said sum an $80,000 obligation of trustor to X bank . . . or other lender. . . . Beneficiary hereby agrees with trustor to discharge said $80,000 obligation in accordance with its terms from payments received from trustor, and to hold trustor harmless from any liability resulting from the failure of beneficiary to so discharge said obligation.

Figure 7.8 illustrates an example of an all-inclusive note.

A similar provision is usually contained in the note. In order to avoid difficulties in connection with foreclosure by trustee's sale, a special recital is also needed governing the rights of the parties in the event a default occurs.

This form of trust deed requires special care in its preparation, and it is unlikely that a standard form can be used. The deed must be tailored to fit the facts in each particular case. The provisions of the prior deed of trust must be considered, and special concern must be given to all of its provisions, particularly as to whether or not it contains an alienation clause or provides for prepayment privileges.

Figure 7.7
Wraparound Deed of Trust

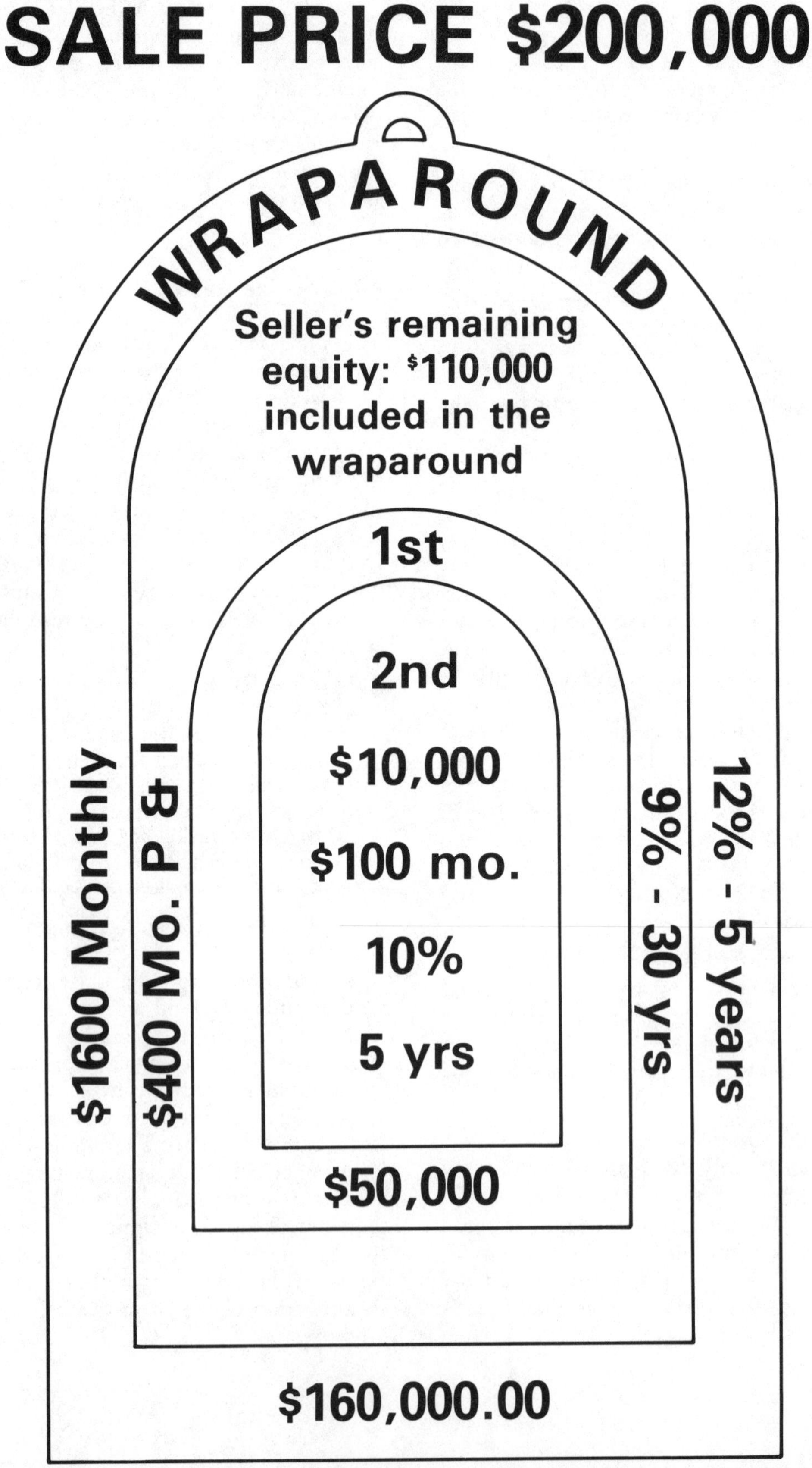

SALE PRICE $200,000

WRAPAROUND

Seller's remaining equity: $110,000 included in the wraparound

1st

2nd

$10,000

$100 mo.

10%

5 yrs

$50,000

$160,000.00

$1600 Monthly

$400 Mo. P & I

9% - 30 yrs

12% - 5 years

Figure 7.8
All-Inclusive Note Secured by All-Inclusive Deed of Trust

DO NOT DESTROY THIS ORIGINAL NOTE: When paid, said original note, together with the Deed of Trust securing same, must be surrendered to Trustee for cancellation and retention before reconveyance will be made.

ALL INCLUSIVE PURCHASE MONEY PROMISSORY NOTE SECURED BY ALL-INCLUSIVE PURCHASE MONEY DEED OF TRUST
(INSTALLMENT NOTE, INTEREST INCLUDED)

$ _____   _____ , California, _____ 19 _____

In installments as herein stated, for value received, I/We ("Maker") promise to pay to _____

_____

("Payee") or order, at _____

the principal sum of _____ DOLLARS, with interest

from _____ on unpaid principal at the rate of

_____ per cent per annum; principal and interest payable in installments of _____

or more on the _____ day of each _____ month, beginning

on the _____ day of _____ 19 _____ , and continuing until said principal and

interest have been paid.

Each installment shall be applied first on the interest then due and the remainder on principal; and interest shall thereupon cease upon the principal so credited.

The total principal amount of this Note includes the unpaid principal balance of the promissory note(s) ("Underlying Note(s)") secured by Deed(s) of Trust, more particularly described as follows:

1. (A) PROMISSORY NOTE:
   Maker: _____
   Payee: _____
   Original Amount: _____
   Date: _____

   (B) DEED OF TRUST:
   Beneficiary: _____
   Original Amount: _____
   Recordation Date: _____
   Document No. _____ Book _____ Page _____
   Place of Recordation: _____ , County, California

2. (A) PROMISSORY NOTE:
   Maker: _____
   Payee: _____
   Original Amount: _____
   Date: _____

   (B) DEED OF TRUST:
   Beneficiary: _____
   Original Amount: _____
   Recordation Date: _____
   Document No. _____ Book _____ Page _____
   Place of Recordation: _____ , County, California

By Payee's acceptance of this Note, Payee covenants and agrees that, provided Maker is not delinquent or in default under the terms of this Note, Payee shall pay all installments of principal and interest which shall hereafter become due pursuant to the provisions of the Underlying Note(s) as and when the same become due and payable. In the event Maker shall be delinquent or in default under the terms of this Note, Payee shall not be obligated to make any payments required by the terms of the Underlying Note(s) until such delinquency or default is cured. In the event Payee fails to timely pay any installment of principal or interest on the Underlying Note(s) at the time when Maker is not delinquent or in default hereunder, Maker may, at Maker's option, make such payments directly to the holder of such Underlying Note(s), in which event Maker shall be entitled to a credit against the next installment(s) of principal and interest due under the terms of this Note equal to the amount so paid and including, without limitation, any penalty, charges and expenses paid by Maker to the holder of the Underlying Note(s) on account of Payee failing to make such payment. The obligations of Payee hereunder shall terminate upon the earliest of (i) foreclosure of the lien of the All-Inclusive Purchase Money Deed of Trust securing this Note, or (ii) cancellation of this Note and reconveyance of the All-Inclusive Purchase Money Deed of Trust securing same.

Should Maker be delinquent or in default under the terms of this Note, and Payee consequently incurs any penalties, charges or other expenses on account of the Underlying Note(s) during the period of such delinquency or default, the amount of such penalties, charges and expenses shall be immediately added to the principal amount of this Note and shall be immediately payable by Maker to Payee.

Notwithstanding anything to the contrary herein contained, the right of Maker to prepay all or any portion of the principal of this Note is limited to the same extent as any limitation exists in the right to prepay the principal of the Underlying Note(s). If any prepayments of principal of this Note shall, by reason of the application of any portion thereof by Payee to the prepayment of principal of the Underlying Note(s), constitute such prepayment for which the holders of the Underlying Note(s) are entitled to receive a prepayment penalty or consideration, the amount of such prepayment penalty or consideration shall be paid by Maker to Payee upon demand, and any such amount shall not reduce the unpaid balance of principal or interest hereunder.

At any time when the total of the unpaid principal balance of this Note, accrued interest thereon, all other sums due pursuant to the terms hereof, and all sums advanced by Payee pursuant to the terms of the All-Inclusive Purchase Money Deed of Trust securing this Note, is equal to or less than the unpaid balance of principal and interest then due under the terms of the Underlying Note(s), Payee, at his option, shall cancel this Note and deliver same to Maker and execute a request for full reconveyance of the Deed of Trust securing this Note.

Should default be made by Maker in payment of any installments of principal, interest, or any other sums due hereunder, the whole sum of principal, interest and all other sums due from Maker hereunder, after first deducting therefrom all sums then due under the terms of the Underlying Note(s), shall become immediately due at the option of the holder of this Note. Principal, interest and all other sums due hereunder payable in lawful money of the United States. If action be instituted on this Note, I/we promise to pay such sums as the Court may fix as attorney's fees. This Note is secured by an ALL-INCLUSIVE PURCHASE MONEY DEED OF TRUST to Lawyers Title Insurance Corporation, a Virginia corporation, as Trustee.

_____   _____
(Maker)   (Maker)

The undersigned hereby accept(s) the foregoing All-Inclusive Purchase Money Promissory Note and agree(s) to perform each and all of the terms thereof on the part of Payee to be performed.

Executed as of the date and place first above written.

_____   _____
(Payee)   (Payee)

(THIS NOTE IS FOR USE ONLY IN PURCHASE MONEY TRANSACTIONS. IT IS RECOMMENDED THAT, PRIOR TO THE EXECUTION OF THIS NOTE, THE PARTIES CONSULT WITH THEIR ATTORNEYS WITH RESPECT THERETO.)

061-4-284-0000
FORM T284   THIS FORM FURNISHED BY LAWYERS TITLE INSURANCE CORPORATION

ALTERNATIVE MORTGAGE INSTRUMENTS

Home buyers have many choices of loans besides the traditional fixed-rate, fixed-term, level-payments, fully-amortized trust deed. The smorgasbord of financing choices is limited only by the lenders' and the borrowers' imaginations. Following are brief descriptions of several of the choices.

1. *Rollover Mortgage* (or *Renegotiable*). Here the rate of interest is fixed, as are the monthly payments, but the loan is renegotiated at the end of a relatively short term, typically five years. Because of this feature it is also called a renegotiable mortgage. Principal, interest rates and the term are rolled over or renegotiated at stated intervals. Thus if market rates are higher at the end of the term, the borrower can expect to pay more for the loan.

   The chief advantage to the borrower is the potential for a lower going-in interest rate, with corresponding lower payments and overall reduced interest expense. Another advantage: renegotiation is usually guaranteed, thus avoiding the usual expenses of refinancing. But a serious drawback lurks in the background: What if market interest rates at the time of rollover are so high that the borrower is unable to meet the high payments? The ultimate penalty of foreclosure and loss of the property may result.

2. *Adjustable Rate Mortgages (ARM)*. Instead of a fixed interest rate, this loan carries a rate that changes up or down from time to time during the life of the loan, reflecting changes in market rates for money. For example, a lender may offer an initial interest rate of 10 percent, with adjustments every six months, up to a 5 percent cap. This means that the 10 percent loan could eventually increase to 15 percent; if the lender limits the increase to no more than $\frac{1}{2}$ percent every six months, it would take at least five years before the 10 percent loan would reach the 15 percent cap. As shown in Figure 7.9, on a $100,000, 30-year loan, payments could start at only $878 per month by the time the interest rate peaks.

   Advantages to the borrower include lower going-in rate, with corresponding initial lower monthly payments, easier qualifying and the possibility of rates and payments actually declining. The Federal Reserve Board and the Federal Home Loan Bank Board have published a booklet entitled *Consumer Hand-book on Adjustable Rate Mortgage*, designed to help explain this subject.

3. *Graduated Payment Mortgage (GPM)*. Monthly payments under this type of loan start out low, but enlarge gradually over specified intervals, such as every 12 months. The interest rate and term of the loan remain the same, only the payments change. The GPM differs from the ARM in the following ways: the GPM payments go in only one direction, up. Because the rate remains fixed under the GPM, this means that during the low initial payment years the borrower's payments may not even be covering the interest portion of the loan, resulting in an *increasing* outstanding loan instead of diminishing. This condition is referred to as *negative amortization*, or deferred interest. (In Figure 7.9, the principal curve slopes downward for a diminishing, positively amortizing loan; the curve would slope upward for an increasing, negatively amortizing loan such as the GPM.)

   The chief advantages to the borrower are the lower initial payments and, therefore, easier qualifying for the loan, just as with the ARM. But this is offset by the inevitable increase in monthly payments later, even though market interest rates may actually be lower. (Of course, if the spread between the two rates is significant, the owner may want to refinance.) Unless the borrowers anticipate income increases to offset the payment increases, they may be advised to shop for a fixed rate, or at least a fixed payment loan. The GPM is designed largely to appeal to younger borrowers whose income is expected to be constantly on the increase.

4. *Shared Appreciation Mortgage (SAM)*, sometimes called a Shared Equity Mortgage (SEM), is at a below-the-market interest rate and has lower monthly payments in exchange for a share of profits when the property is sold on a specified date, such as 10 years from date. There are many variations of this type.

5. *Reverse Annuity Mortgage (RAM)* is a type where the borrower owns mortgage-free property and would like to generate income without selling and reinvesting the proceeds. The lender makes monthly payments to the borrower, using the property as security. This can have an appeal to an older person who doesn't want to sell his or her home, but would like to enjoy some of the appreciated

value for travel or other purposes. Like the other types discussed above, there are many variations.

The Federal Trade Commission has published a booklet entitled "The Mortgage Money Guide," subtitled "Creative Home Financing" which explains most of the various types and has many valuable suggestions.

INTEREST RATES AND THEIR IMPACT ON COSTS

In deciding how to finance real property, the all-important question of cost must be addressed. Indeed, the housing market took a severe downturn from 1980 and 1985 because interest rates reached skyscraping levels.

To show the effects of varying costs of borrowing, the following table compares interest rates at 10 percent and 15 percent; the example uses a $100,000 loan repayable over a 30-year period.

10%		15%
$125,000	Sale price	$125,000
− 25,000	Down payment	− 25,000
$100,000	Loan amount	$100,000
$878	Monthly payment of principal and interest	$1,265
$316,080	Total of P & I over 360 months	$455,400
$216,080	Interest cost (total payments less $100,000 principal)	$355,400

The comparison between 10 percent and 15 percent as the cost of renting money is summarized graphically in Figure 7.9.

QUESTIONS OF USURY

Usury has been one of the vexing problems in commercial law since ancient times. It has been held by the courts to be the conscious and voluntary taking of more than the maximum legal rate of interest. No specific intent to violate a statute regulating interest is necessary to constitute usury. And even where the form of a transaction makes it appear to be nonusurious, it can nonetheless be held to be usurious. Substance is more important than form, and the label given to excessive payments is immaterial.

Interest is defined as compensation for the use of money. Prior to 1918 there was no statute in California limiting the rate of interest, except in

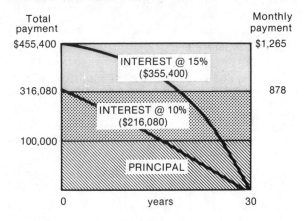

Figure 7.9
Comparison of Monthly Payments and Interest Costs over a 30-Year Loan Term

the cases of pawnbrokers and the personal property brokers. The usury law enacted in 1918 and modified by a constitutional amendment in 1934 limits the rate of interest to 10 percent per annum with certain exceptions including banks, building and loan associations, and other institutions that are governed by other statutes. This 10 percent maximum rate does not include normal service charges and commissions charged by brokers.

In order for usury to exist, there must be a *loan* of money or *forbearance* to collect money. It has been held by the courts in California that a *sale* or purchase money transaction is not a loan or forbearance, but a matter of contract between buyer and seller; the parties can agree on one price for cash and another and perhaps much larger price on credit without regard for the usury law. A loan of money is a contract by which one delivers a sum of money to another person, and the latter agrees to return it at a future time. *Forbearance* is a time of waiting to collect the debt or granting of additional time to pay. Thus, a seller of real estate carrying back a trust deed may charge whatever interest rate the buyer is willing to pay—subject, however, to the rule relating to unconscionable contracts which a court might refuse to enforce, and the attitude of the Internal Revenue Service in allowing interest deductions for income tax purposes.

Proposition Two

Sweeping changes were made as a result of Proposition 2, passed by the California voters in 1979. Accordingly, the State Constitution has been amended to include the following changes:

1. Loans originated by real estate brokers, whether as principals or agents, are exempt from usury, provided such loans are secured by real property.

2. Loans made by other than brokers and secured by real property are limited to the greater of 10 percent *or* the sum of the discount rate charged by the Federal Reserve Board in San Francisco plus 5 percent. Thus, if the FRB charges borrowing member banks 11 percent, the maximum interest that could be charged by third party lenders would be 16 percent, provided the loan was secured by real property.

3. All other loans, such as for personal, family, and household goods, are still limited to 10 percent. Thus a personal loan for $10,000 made by an individual and secured by an automobile could not cost more than 10 percent.

The Constitutional Amendment is subject to legislative implementation. See *Real Estate Law in California*, 7th ed., by Bowman and Milligan for further information on this subject.

SOME PRACTICAL ASPECTS OF TRUST DEEDS

Protecting the Holder of a Junior Trust Deed

As already indicated, real property may be encumbered by several deeds of trust, each of which has different priority, such as a first, a second, a third or even a fourth. A first deed is, of course, in the paramount position; a foreclosure of the first trust deed eliminates the junior liens. The holder of a junior lien, in order to be promptly informed of a notice of default under a prior deed of trust, will ordinarily record a "request for notice of default" in the office of the county recorder in the county where the real property is located. He or she will then be entitled by law to receive notice of default under the prior deed of trust within ten days of the recording of the notice of default. The junior lienholder can then determine what the best course of action is. A sample form, Request for Notice, is illustrated in Figure 7.10.

Questions of Priority

Questions of priority frequently arise under deeds of trust. *Priority* means the quality of being *prior* or preceding in order of time. Priority gives superiority or seniority in position, the opposite of inferiority or subordination.

Priority as far as real property rights are concerned is generally dependent upon *time of recording*, but not always. The principal exceptions relate to the following:

1. Real property taxes and assessments. Real property taxes are afforded priority from year to year by law.
2. Mechanic's lien. Priority is dependent upon the date when the work of improvement actually commences on the ground and not upon the date of recording the mechanic's liens.
3. Actual notice of an unrecorded lien. If the beneficiary under a deed of trust has *knowledge* of an earlier but unrecorded interest, his or her lien will be junior even though recorded earlier in point of time.
4. The lien in favor of a municipality or other agency for the cost of removing an unsafe or hazardous structure. The hazard may be caused by fire, earthquake, or other calamity. Municipal ordinances in many communities provide for the manner in which such a lien may be created. If a structure is deemed substandard or unsafe, the governmental agency having jurisdiction may give notice to the owner and to holders of encumbrances to correct the situation or to remove the structure. If the owner fails to comply, the government agency may then cause the removal of the structure, and the cost thereof becomes a lien and is on a *parity*, i.e., of equal rank, with the lien of state, county, and municipal taxes. A foreclosure of such lien would eliminate the lien of a previously recorded mortgage, deed of trust, or abstract of judgment. This points up the need for adequate hazard insurance, not only for the cost of replacing a structure but also for the additional cost of making the land suitable for rebuilding.

FORECLOSURE PROCEDURES

A right to foreclose a mortgage or deed of trust arises when a default occurs, either by the trustor's failure to make payment in accordance with the terms of the note; or by failure to perform the terms of any other obligation that may be secured by the mortgage or deed of trust; or by failure to perform any of the terms and provisions of the

Figure 7.10
Request for Notice

RECORDING REQUESTED BY

AND WHEN RECORDED MAIL TO

Name

Street
Address

City &
State

————— SPACE ABOVE THIS LINE FOR RECORDER'S USE —————

Request for Notice
UNDER SECTION 2924b CIVIL CODE

TO 422 C (9-67)

In accordance with Section 2924b, Civil Code, request is hereby made that a copy of any Notice of Default and a copy of any Notice of Sale under the Deed of Trust recorded as Instrument No._____ on_____ _____, in book_____, page_____, Official Records of_____ County, California, and describing land therein as

Executed by_____, as Trustor, in which_____is named as Beneficiary, and_____, as Trustee, be mailed to_____ at_____
Number and Street

City and State

Dated_____

STATE OF CALIFORNIA,
COUNTY OF_____ }SS.
On_____before me, the under-signed, a Notary Public in and for said State, personally appeared

_____, known to me to be the person__ whose name_____subscribed to the within instrument and acknowledged that_____executed the same.
WITNESS my hand and official seal.

Signature_____

Name (Typed or Printed)
If executed by a Corporation the Corporation Form of Acknowledgment must be used.

(This area for official notarial seal)

Title Order No._____ Escrow or Loan No._____

deed of trust, such as the obligation to pay taxes, or to properly maintain the property.

As stated previously, trust deeds and mortgages with power of sale can both be foreclosed by judicial or nonjudicial action. The remedy of nonjudicial sale is most often used, due to the following advantages to the lender:

1. It is a relatively fast procedure. Usually a final sale can be effected in approximately four months, which includes a three months' right of reinstatement after notice of default is recorded, plus the prescribed time for a notice of sale, which is at least twenty days prior to the sale.
2. There is no right of redemption after a trustee's sale, except a limited right in favor of the United States, if there is a junior tax lien. The sale is a final sale. A trustee's deed is issued in favor of the purchaser immediately. A form of trustee's deed is illustrated in Figure 7.11.
3. The statute of limitations is not a bar to a trustee's sale, even though the note may be outlawed.
4. There is a considerable element of certainty in the proceedings. The procedure is well established and has been so recognized in numerous court decisions. The trustee's deed conveys the title of the trustor free of any inferior liens.

The disadvantages to the lender of a trustee's sale over a judicial foreclosure include the following:

1. No deficiency is recoverable following a trustee's sale: If, after the sale of the property, the trustee has not recovered the entire debt, a deficiency judgment against the trustor to pay the remainder of the debt cannot be obtained.
2. There is no determination as to priority of liens where more than one lien exists. It is sometimes necessary to establish priority in a later court suit such as an action to quiet title.

Although a trustee's sale seems so much simpler, there are occasions when foreclosure by action of the court may be necessary or desirable:

1. When the trustee wants to obtain a deficiency judgment (however, if the deed is a purchase money deed of trust, deficiency cannot be had).
2. When it is necessary to determine relative priorities in a case, for instance, where mechanic's liens are of record; or where two deeds of trust were recorded concurrently but without priority clauses; or where one trust deed was recorded later than another but *executed* earlier and this fact was known to the beneficiary on the trust deed recorded earlier.
3. Where the alleged default is other than the payment of money, and the trustee cannot determine whether or not a default has in fact occurred, or he or she is unwilling to resolve the matter out of court.
4. Where the note appears to be usurious and the trustee is unwilling to act.
5. Where the trustee is incapable of acting—in the case of a defunct corporation or a deceased individual trustee, and substitution of another trustee is not feasible.
6. When the note has been lost, and it is necessary to bring an action to prove a lost instrument.
7. When irregularities have been found in the note or deed of trust, such as
   a. The amount of the note is not set forth in the trust deed, or the amounts do not coincide.
   b. The trustee identified on the note is not the same as the trustee on the deed of trust.
   c. A discrepancy exists between the date of the note and the date of the deed of trust.
   d. Description of the property may be defective.

In instances such as these, an action to foreclose is often combined with an action to reform the note and/or deed of trust.

Sequence of Events in a Trustee Sale

1. Default by borrower
2. Beneficiary orders trustee to foreclose via a "Request to Prepare a Notice of Default"
3. Trustee records a "Notice of Default"
4. During the required three-month waiting period that follows step 2, the borrower has reinstatement rights, i.e., to repay the delinquency and penalties.
5. Trustee advertises the date, time, and place of sale three weeks in succession in a newspaper of general circulation. (The trustee can postpone the sale at the direction of the beneficiary so long as there is no collusion involved.)

Figure 7.11
Trustee's Deed Upon Sale

RECORDING REQUESTED BY

AND WHEN RECORDED MAIL TO

SPACE ABOVE THIS LINE FOR RECORDER'S USE

The undersigned declares under penalty of perjury that the following declaration is true and correct:

1) The grantee herein (was) (was not) the foreclosing beneficiary
2) The amount of the unpaid debt together with costs was . . . . $________
3) The amount paid by the grantee at the trustee's sale was . . . . $________
4) The documentary transfer tax is . . . . $________
5) Said property is in ( ) unincorporated area; ( ) City of ________

________, county of ________ T.D. SERVICE COMPANY

Date ________ By ________

TRUSTEE'S DEED UPON SALE

Loan No.:
T.S. No.:
This Indenture is made with reference to the Deed of Trust hereinafter described and is made between

(herein called Trustee), and the Grantee hereinafter named.

TRUSTOR:

BENEFICIARY:

Recorded as instr. No. in book page of Official Records in the office of the Recorder of County;
said deed of trust describes the following property:

Whereas, the above named trustor did, by the trust deed referred to above, grant and convey to the trustee named therein, the property heretofore described to secure, among other obligations, payment of a note or notes with interest according to the terms thereof; and Whereas, the holder of said note did execute and deliver to trustee written declaration of default and demand for sale and notice of default and election to cause the undersigned to sell said property which notice was
Recorded as instr. No. in book page of said Official Records.

Thereafter, a notice of trustee's sale, stating that said trustee would sell the above described property at public auction to the highest bidder for cash on

MAIL [illegible]TATEMENTS TO THE ADDRESS SHOWN ABOVE

Figure 7.11
Continued

said notice was posted for not less than twenty days before the date of sale therein fixed, as follows: In one public place in the said city of

wherein said property was to be sold, to wit: on a bulletin board

and also in a conspicuous place on said property to be sold; and said Trustee did cause a copy of said Notice to be published once a week for twenty days before the date of sale therein fixed in

a newspaper of general circulation printed and published in the city or district in which said real property is situated, the first date of such publication being   ; and

Said notice was also recorded at least 14 days prior to the sale in the office of the county recorder of the county in which the property heretofore described is located.

Whereas, copies of said recorded Notice of Default and of said Notice of Sale were mailed, served or published in accordance with Section 2924b of the Civil Code to or upon all those who were entitled in compliance with all requirements of law; and

Whereas, all applicable statutory provisions of the state of California and all of the provisions of said Deed of Trust have been complied with as to acts to be performed and notices to be given; and

Whereas Trustee did at the time and place of sale fixed as aforesaid, then and there sell, at public auction, to said Grantee, being the highest bidder therefore, the property hereinafter described, for the sum of $
paid in cash, lawful money of the United States by the satisfaction   of the indebtedness then secured by said Deed of Trust.

Now, therefore, Trustee in consideration of the premises recited and of the sum above mentioned bid and paid by Grantee, the receipt whereof is hereby acknowledged, and by virtue of the authority vested in it by said Deed of Trust, does, by these presents GRANT AND CONVEY without any covenant or warranty, express or implied all that certain property hereinbefore described, to

In Witness Whereof, the undersigned caused its corporate name and seal to be hereunto affixed

Dated_____   By _____

                                                              By _____

STATE OF CALIFORNIA
COUNTY OF_____ } SS.

On _____ 19_____ ,
before me, the undersigned, a Notary Public in and for said County
and State, personally appeared_____
_____ ,
☐ personally known to me
☐ proved to me on the basis of satisfactory evidence
to be the _____ and _____
_____ ,
☐ personally known to me
☐ proved to me on the basis of satisfactory evidence
to be the_____of the
corporation that executed the within instrument, and known to
me to be the persons who executed the within instrument on
behalf of the corporation therein named, and acknowledged to
me that such corporation executed the within instrument pursuant
to its by-laws or a resolution of its board of directors.

Signature_____
              Notary Public in and for said State.

FOR NOTARY SEAL OR STAMP

6. The property goes to the successful bidder at an auction (trustee's) sale.
7. Trustee's Deed is issued to the successful bidder (see Figure 7.11). The sale is final and the borrower has no right of redemption.

These steps can be shown in a flow chart form as illustrated by Figure 7.12.

Deed in Lieu of Foreclosure

Foreclosure proceedings are not only time-consuming, but they can also be expensive. Suppose a trustor is in default, can't cure the default, and is willing to give a deed to the beneficiary. Wouldn't it be prudent for the beneficiary to accept such a

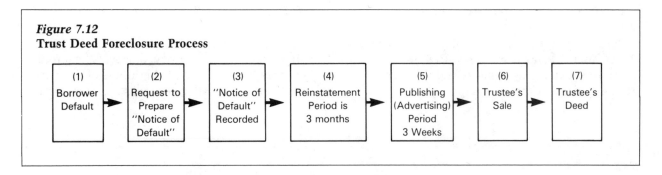

Figure 7.12
Trust Deed Foreclosure Process

(1)	(2)	(3)	(4)	(5)	(6)	(7)
Borrower Default	Request to Prepare "Notice of Default"	"Notice of Default" Recorded	Reinstatement Period is 3 months	Publishing (Advertising) Period 3 Weeks	Trustee's Sale	Trustee's Deed

deed? The answer to the question depends upon the particular facts and circumstances.

The beneficiary, prior to the acceptance of such deed, will need to ascertain by a title search the condition of the title to the property. This requirement arises from the fact that junior liens—which would be eliminated by a trustee's sale—will still attach as liens against the property after delivery and acceptance of the deed in lieu of foreclosure. When such a deed is given, a merger of the legal title and the equitable interest under such deed of trust ordinarily results. However, liens, encumbrances, and matters affecting title that intervene are not eliminated. Thereafter, the grantee (the former beneficiary) stands in the shoes of the grantor (the former trustor), and the grantee's title becomes subject to all liens against the grantor.

Although there is a merger of the legal title and the equitable interest in the acceptance of the deed in lieu of foreclosure, it is still necessary to obtain a full reconveyance of the deed of trust in order to eliminate it from the records. The note or other evidence of the obligation secured by the deed of trust should be canceled, and thereafter surrendered to the trustee together with the deed of trust and a request for full reconveyance. Upon payment of a fee, a full reconveyance will be issued, which should, of course, be recorded.

Where the trustor is permitted to remain in possession either under a lease or an option to purchase or otherwise, this circumstance may cast doubt on the sufficiency of the deed in lieu of foreclosure, and may prevent a title insurer from treating such deed as an effective satisfaction of the deed of trust and termination of the interest of the trustor in the property. If the trustor is to remain in possession, it should be under an established tenancy relationship which leaves no doubt that his or her sole interest is that of a tenant, and that the deed in lieu of foreclosure is not in fact merely a mortgage in the form of a deed.

CONTRACT OF SALE AS A SECURITY DEVICE

We have already considered a contract of sale in Chapter 4 in connection with conveyancing, and learned that the equitable title passes to the buyer-vendee upon execution and delivery of the contract. Legal title is still retained by the seller-vendor. However, the retention of title by the vendor is for security purposes, and for all practical purposes the vendee is the owner of the property. Sometimes a contract will provide that the vendee must make full payment before he or she is entitled to a deed, or the vendee may be entitled to a deed, or the vendee may be entitled to a deed upon payment of a specified sum, perhaps 25 or 30 percent of the total purchase price. The buyer would then execute a deed of trust in favor of the seller to secure payment of the balance of the purchase price.

The advantage of a contract as a security device to the vendor is the relative ease with which he or she may terminate the interest of the vendee in the event of a default. However, the following question arises many times: If the vendee is unable to continue to make the payments, and the vendor then seeks to cancel the contract, what effect does this have on the payments already made under the contract? The courts in California have held that, to the extent that the vendor would be "unjustly enriched" by retaining such payments, he or she must refund them to the vendee. A distinct advantage to holding a trust deed as a security device is the fact that this unjust enrichment doctrine does not apply in the foreclosure. Other advantages and disadvantages of land sales contracts are considered in detail in a course on real estate law.

As mentioned previously, following the decision in the *Tucker* v. *Lassen* case, a new form of contract (three-party contract) was created, primarily as a security device. It is compared with the conventional two-party contract in Figure 7.13.

Figure 7.14 contains a Long Form Security (Installment) Land Contract with Power of Sale that often is used by vendors and vendees transacting under a contract of sale.

DEED AS A SECURITY DEVICE

What purports to be a conveyance of the fee title can in fact be a security device. The problem becomes one of proof of the intent of the parties in the event the alleged lender (grantee) were to

---

Figure 7.13
Two-Party and Three-Party Contracts of Sale

Two-Party Land Contract

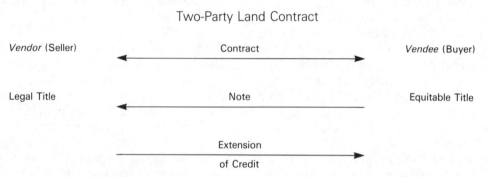

Under the two-party land contract, there is no protection for the vendor should the vendee default in his or her payments; nor for the vendee, should the vendor not be around to issue a grant deed once the contract is paid off.

Three-Party Land Contract

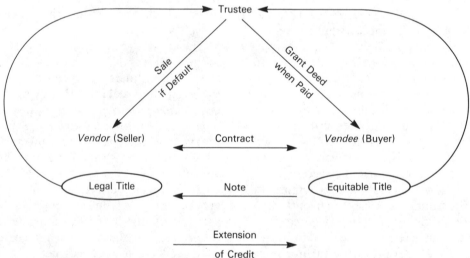

Under the three-party land contract, both the vendor and the vendee give their interest to a trustee with power of sale, usually a title insurance company. The contract is recorded, and when the vendee finishes paying, he or she gets a grant deed from the trustee. (Vendee can make payments to the vendor or the trustee, according to the agreement.) If the vendee defaults, there is a foreclosure by trustee's sale, as with a trust deed.

claim that it was a conveyance of the fee title. Proof could consist of such factors as

1. Relationship of the parties
2. Whether there were previous loans between the parties (past transactions could be important)
3. Value of the property as compared with the consideration for the deed
4. Possession and payment of taxes and insurance and maintenance by the grantor
5. Documentation in the form of receipts, cancelled checks, etc.

PERSONAL PROPERTY SECURITY INSTRUMENTS

A form of security agreement that covered personal property, including growing crops, used to be known as a *chattel mortgage*. This agreement could be recorded in the office of the county recorder for the purpose of giving constructive notice to third parties. It has been replaced by a form of agreement called a personal property *security agreement*, provided for in the Uniform Commercial Code, which was adopted in California in 1965. This code establishes a unified, comprehensive scheme for the regulation of security transactions in personal property, and supersedes the former statutes on chattel mortgages, conditional sales, trust receipts, and so on. Its object is to protect purchasers of certain types of personal property and creditors who have rights in such personal property.

Unlike a chattel mortgage, the security agreement itself is not the document that is filed or recorded. The code provides a simplified filing system using *financing statements*. If a financing statement is not filed when a personal property security agreement is made, subsequent purchasers without knowledge of the agreement take the property free of the prior security interest. On the other hand, if a secured party does file, he or she is in most cases protected from the interests of subsequent purchasers. Local filing in the county recorder's office is permitted only for specific types of agreements. In all other cases, financing statements must be filed with the secretary of state in Sacramento. A form of financing statement is illustrated in Figure 7.15.

QUESTIONS FOR CHAPTER 7

Matching Terms

a. priority
b. foreclosure
c. covenants
d. trust deed
e. mortgagee
f. beneficiary
g. due-on-sale clause
h. notice of default
i. mortgage
j. deed-in-lieu of foreclosure
k. trustor
l. usury
m. security agreement
n. subordinate
o. promissory note

___ 1. a three-party security instrument
___ 2. an acceleration clause
___ 3. must be recorded as a condition of a trustee's sale
___ 4. the lender under a mortgage
___ 5. evidence of a debt
___ 6. creates a lien on personal property
___ 7. charging more interest than the law allows
___ 8. promises contained in a mortgage or deed of trust
___ 9. to make inferior
___ 10. ranking of a lien as it relates to another lien
___ 11. the lender under a deed of trust
___ 12. a two-party security instrument
___ 13. method of enforcing rights under a mortgage or trust deed
___ 14. substitute for foreclosure
___ 15. owner of property who executes a deed of trust

True/False

T F 16. The word *hypothecate* means to pledge property without giving up possession.
T F 17. An acceleration clause in a note secured by a mortgage is unenforceable since it is contrary to public policy.
T F 18. A junior mortgage is always one that is subordinate to another mortgage or other real property lien.
T F 19. The mortgagor is the person who lends money and takes a mortgage as security.
T F 20. Priority of a mortgage or other lien can be changed by the use of a subordination agreement.

Figure 7.14
Land Contract as a Security Device

RECORDING REQUESTED BY

AND WHEN RECORDED MAIL TO

NAME

ADDRESS

CITY &
STATE
ZIP

Title
Order
No.

Escrow
No.

——— SPACE ABOVE THIS LINE FOR RECORDER'S USE ———

LONG FORM SECURITY (INSTALLMENT) LAND CONTRACT WITH POWER OF SALE
AND REQUEST FOR NOTICE OF DEFAULT
(PRIOR LOAN PAYMENTS INCLUDED*)

THIS AGREEMENT, made and entered into this   day of   , 19   among

herein called VENDOR, and

herein called VENDEE, and

SAFECO TITLE INSURANCE COMPANY, a California corporation, herein called TRUSTEE.

The signature of Vendor and Vendee of this contract shall also constitute their signature of the

REQUEST FOR NOTICE OF DEFAULT

In accordance with Section 2924(b), Civil Code of California, request is hereby made by the undersigned Vendor and Vendee that: (1) a copy of any Notice of Default and a copy of any Notice of Sale under Deed of Trust recorded_____ _____ in Book___ __ ___, Page_____, Document No. _____ _____, Official Records of__ _ _ ____ _____ County, California as affecting the herein described property, executed by___ ___ ___ _____ ___ __ ____ __ ___ ___ ___ ___ ___ _____ _____ _____ _____ _____ _____ _____ as Trustor, in which _ . __ _ _____ __ ___ ___ is named as beneficiary, and _____ as Trustee, be mailed to Vendor and Vendee at address immediately below; and (2) a copy of any Notice of Default and a copy of any Notice of Sale under Deed of Trust recorded __ _ __ _____ in Book _____, Page _____, Document No. _____, Official Records of _____ _____ __ _____ County, California as affecting the herein described property, executed by __ _ _ _____ as Trustor, in which __ _ _____ is named as beneficiary, and _____ ___ _____ ___ ___ _____ Trustee, be mailed to Vendor and Vendee at address below.

Vendee __ _ _ _____   Vendor _____

Address_ _ _ _____   Address _____

To secure the obligations of Vendee herein, Vendor and Vendee hereby grant, transfer and assign to Trustee, in trust, with power of sale, their right, title and interest in the real property situated in the County of _____, State of California, and described as follows:

Reserving unto Vendor the power to convey title to the Vendee or the Vendee's successors or assigns upon the performance of Vendee's obligation under this agreement, Any recorded deed executed and acknowledged by the Vendor or his successors, to the Vendee or his successors of the real property described herein, or any portion thereof, shall be deemed executed pursuant to this power, which dee shall be free and clear of, and terminate, the right, title, interest and the powers of the Trustee.

Reserving unto Vendee the right of possession subject, however, to the power of sale herein granted to the Trustee.

WITNESSETH:

WHEREAS, Vendor has agreed to sell, and Vendee has agreed to buy said real property upon the terms and conditions set forth herein, and
WHEREAS, Vendee agrees, that if Vendor elects to enforce the Vendor's security interest in the real property by exercising the power of sale, as herein provided, such sale shall discharge and terminate any and all rights of the Vendee arising out of this agreement, whether in the form of restitution, redemption or otherwise.

CAL-321 (8—78)
* ALL INCLUSIVE FORM

Figure 7.14
Continued

NOW, THEREFORE, VENDOR AND VENDEE DO HEREBY AGREE AS FOLLOWS:

1. Payment of purchase price (Loan payments included).

    A. Vendee shall pay to Vendor forthwith the sum of $_____ _____ as a down payment.

    B. And Vendee promises to pay to Vendor or order at _____ the sum of $_____ with interest thereon at the rate of _____% per annum commencing _____, principal and interest payable _____

    _____

    _____

    _____

    _____

    Payment shall be in lawful money of the United States and shall be applied first to the interest accrued hereon and then to the principal of this Contract and Vendor promises to pay the installments (due or becoming due prior to the next installment date hereunder) upon the notes secured by the existing deeds of trust referred to in the Request for Notice set forth on page 1 of this Contract.

    C. Vendee agrees to pay to Vendor such additional amounts as may be required by the holders of the notes secured by the deeds of trust identified in such Request for Notice for tax or insurance premium impounds accounts.

    Should Vendor fail to pay any installments when due on such existing deeds of trust, Vendee may make such payments directly to the holder of such notes, and the amount thereof shall be credited to the next installment or installments due or becoming due under this contract.

    Any prepayment of all or a portion of the unpaid principal balance of this contract permitted by the terms of this contract may be made upon the written requirement by the Vendee that Vendor prepay a proportionate amount of the unpaid balance of the notes secured by such existing deeds of trust, provided however, that the obligation of Vendor to do so is conditioned upon the right of Vendor to prepay such notes, and is further conditioned upon the payment by Vendee to Vendor of any additional amount required by the holders of such existing notes as a penalty or consideration for such prepayment.

    D. At any sale for the enforcement of this contract, the bid by the Vendor upon the credit of the money obligation secured by this contract shall be reduced in an amount equivalent to the then unpaid principal balance of the notes secured by such existing deeds of trust.

This agreement will require _____years and _____ months to complete payment in accordance with its terms.

2. **TITLE INSURANCE**

    Upon recordation of this security land contract, SAFECO TITLE INSURANCE COMPANY, shall issue a joint protection policy of title insurance (lender's - owner's) insuring the Vendor's (lender's) and Vendees's (owner's) interest herein.

3. **POSSESSION**

    (a) Vendor grants to Vendee the possession of said real property, for the term of this agreement, or until the earlier termination of this agreement.

    (b) Vendor hereby reserves the right, power and authority to collect the rents, issues and profits of said real property. However, Vendor assigns to Vendee the right, prior to any default by Vendee in payment of any indebtedness secured hereby, or in performance of any agreement hereunder, to collect and retain such rents, issues and profits as they become due and payable. Upon any such default, Vendor may at any time without notice, either in person, by agent, or by a receiver to be appointed by a court, and without regard to the adequacy of any security for the indebtedness hereby secured, enter upon and take possession of said property or any part thereof, in his own name, sue for or otherwise collect such rents, issues and profits, including those past due and unpaid, and apply the same, less costs and expenses of operation and collection, including reasonable attorney's fees, upon any indebtedness secured hereby, and in such order as Vendor may determine. The entering upon and taking possession of said property, the collection of such rents, issues and profits and the application thereof, as aforesaid, shall not cure or waive any default or notice of default hereunder or invalidate any act done pursuant to such notice.

4. **RISK OF LOSS**

    (a) Vendee assumes all hazards of damage to or destruction of any improvements now or hereafter placed upon said real property and of the taking of such real property or any part thereof for public use, and agrees that no such damage, destruction or taking shall constitute a failure of consideration under this contract.

    (b) Any award of damages from any taking for public use, or from any damage to said real property or any part thereof is assigned to Vendor with the right to apply or release such monies in the same manner and effect as provided for disposition of proceeds of fire insurance.

    (c) Vendee does hereby indemnify Vendor and Trustee against any and all claims by third parties for personal injury or property damage, and agrees to provide public liability insurance on the premises in an amount not less than $_____ naming Vendor as an additional insured.

5. **TO PROTECT VENDOR'S SECURITY INTEREST, VENDEE AGREES:**

    (a) To keep said property in good condition and repair, preserve thereon the buildings, complete construction begun, restore damage or destruction, and pay the cost thereof; to commit or permit no waste, no violation of laws or covenants or conditions relating to use, alterations or improvements; to cultivate, irrigate, fertilize, fumigate, prune, and do all other acts which the character and use of said property and the estate or interest in said property secured by this agreement may require to preserve this security.

    (b) To provide, maintain and deliver to Vendor fire insurance satisfactory to and with loss payable to Vendor. The amount collected under any fire or other insurance policy may be applied by Vendor upon any indebtedness secured hereby and in such order as Vendor may determine, or Vendor may release all or any part thereof to Vendee. Such application or release shall not cure or waive any default or notice of default hereunder or invalidate any act done pursuant to such notice.

    (c) To appear in and defend any action or proceeding purporting to affect the security hereof, or the rights or powers of Vendor or Trustee, and to pay all costs and expenses, including cost of evidence of title and attorney's fees in a reasonable sum, in any such action or proceedings in which Vendor or Trustee may appear.

    (d) To pay, at least ten days before delinquent, all taxes and assessments affecting said property, including assessments on appurtenant water stock when due, as well as all encumbrances, charges and liens, with interest, on said property or any part thereof, which appear to be prior or superior hereto, except as agreed to be paid by Vendor, all costs, fees and expenses of this agreement.

    Should Vendee fail to make any payment, or to do any act as herein provided, then Vendor, but without obligation to do so and without notice to or demand upon Vendee and without releasing Vendee from any obligation hereof, may make or do the same in such manner and to such extent as Vendor may deem necessary to protect the security hereof. Vendor is authorized to enter upon said property for such purposes; appear in and defend any action or proceeding purporting to affect the security hereof or the rights or powers of Vendor or Trustee; pay, purchase, contest or compromise any encumbrance, charge or lien which in the judgment of either appears to be prior or superior hereto; and, in exercising any such powers, pay necessary expenses, employ counsel and pay his reasonable fees.

    (e) To pay immediately and without demand all sums so expended by Vendor, with interest from date of expenditure, at ten percent per annum.

6. **VENDOR AGREES:**

    (a) Upon the performance in full by the Vendee, to execute and have acknowledged a Grant Deed, in recordable form, of the real property described in this agreement, vesting the fee title in Vendee, or the Vendee's successors or assigns, subject only to the liens to be paid by the Vendee, and such other encumbrances accepted, made by or suffered by the Vendee, and to deliver such deed as directed by the Vendee, or his successors or assigns.

    (b) To pay Vendee any transfer tax required by law.

    (c) During the existence of this contract, and upon the written demand of the Vendee or his authorized agent made at any time before or within two months after the recording of a notice of default under this contract, or thirty days prior to the entry of a judgment for the enforcement of this contract, and upon the payment of fifteen dollars ($15.00) therefore, to cause to have prepared and delivered to the person demanding it, a written statement materially setting forth the information required to be supplied by a mortgagee or beneficiary by Section 2943 of the Civil Code of the State of California.

    (d) To keep current all payments due the underlying Deed(s) of Trust.

Figure 7.14
Continued

7.   DEFAULT AND ACCELERATION

Time is of the essence in the payments agreed to be paid Vendor, and the performance of the agreements made for the protection of the Vendor's security, and should Vendee fail to make such payment or tender such performance when due, such failure shall constitute a default.

Upon the occurrence of any such default, Vendor may declare all sums secured unto Vendor by this agreement immediately due and payable.

8.   ELECTION TO SELL

Upon the election by Vendor to proceed by Trustee's Sale, Vendor may elect to declare all sums immediately due and payable by delivering to the Trustee a written declaration of default and demand for sale, Vendor's copy of this agreement; and all documents evidencing expenditures by Vendor, secured by this agreement.

9.   NOTICE OF DEFAULT

Vendor shall further deliver to Trustee a written Notice of Default and Election to Sell, which notice shall identify the contract by stating the names of the Vendor and Vendee, and the date of recording, and the recording reference and shall contain a description of the real property. Such notice shall also contain a statement that a breach of the obligations secured by such agreement has occurred, and shall set forth the nature of such breach and the election by the Vendor to sell or cause such property to be sold to satisfy the obligations secured by this agreement. If the default is curable under the provisions for reinstatement set forth in this agreement, such Notice of Default shall further contain a statement substantially in the form set forth in paragraph (1) of subdivision (b) of Section 2924(c) of the Civil Code of the State of California.

10.   POWER OF SALE

The only power the Trustee has under this agreement is to exercise the power of sale in the event of a default by the Vendee. The Trustee shall have no power to convey Vendor's interest to Vendee upon fulfillment of Vendee's obligations hereunder.

11.   PROCEDURE FOR SALE

(a)   Trustee shall cause to be filed for record in the office of the Recorder of each county wherein the real property, or some part or parcel thereof, is situated an executed copy of the Notice of Default.

(b)   Any person desiring a copy of any notice of default and/or of any notice of sale under this Contract may, at any time subsequent to recordation of this Contract, and prior to recordation of notice of default thereunder, cause to be filed for record in the office of the recorder of any county in which any part or parcel of the real property is situated, a duly acknowledged request for a copy of such notice of default and of sale. This request shall be signed and acknowledged by the person making the request, specifying the name and address of the person to whom the notice is to be mailed, shall identify the Contract by stating the names of the parties thereto, the date of recordation thereof and the book and page where the same is recorded or the recorder's number and shall be substantially in the form set forth in Civil Code's section 2924(b).

The Vendor, Trustee or other person authorized to record the notice of default, shall, within 10 days following recordation of such notice of default, deposit, or cause to be deposited, in the United States Mail, an envelope, registered or certified and with postage prepaid, containing a copy of such notice with the recording date shown thereon, addressed to the Vendee, at the address set forth in this agreement and to each person, including Vendee, whose name and address is set forth in a duly recorded request therefor, directed to the address designated in said request. And at least 20 days before date of sale the Vendor, Trustee or other person authorized to make the sale shall deposit, or cause to be deposited, in the United Sates Mail, an envelope registered or certified and with postage prepaid, containing a copy of the notice of the time and place of the sale, addressed to each person whose name and address is set forth in a request therefor recorded, within the time herein provided.

(c)   Whenever all or a portion of the principal sum of any obligation secured by this Contract has, prior to the maturity date fixed in such obligation, become due, or been declared due by reason of default in payment of interest or of any installment of principal, or by reason of failure of Vendee to pay, in accordance with the terms of such obligation or of such Contract, taxes assessments, premiums for insurance or advances made by Vendor in accordance with the terms of such obligation or of such Contract, the Vendee or his successor in interest in the property or any part thereof, or any beneficiary under a subordinate deed of trust, or any other person having a subordinate lien or encumbrance of record thereon, at any time within three months of the recording of the notice of default under this Contract, may pay to the Vendor or successors in interest, respectively, the entire amount then due under the terms of such Contract and the obligation secured hereby including costs and expenses actually incurred in enforcing the terms of such Contract and Trustee's or attorney's fees actually incurred (not exceeding fifty dollars ($50), or one half of one percent of the unpaid principal sum secured whichever is greater), other than such portion of principal as would not then be due had no default occurred and thereby cure the default theretofore existing, and thereupon, all proceedings theretofore had or instituted shall be dismissed or discontinued and the obligation and Contract shall be reinstated and shall be and remain in force and effect the same as if no such acceleration had occurred.

(d)   Before any sale of property can be made under the power of sale contained in this Contract, notice of the sale thereof must be given by posting a written notice of the time and place of sale, and describing the property to be sold, at least 20 days before the date of sale, in one public place in the city where the property is to be sold, if the property is to be sold in a city, or, if not, then in one public place in the judicial district in which the property is to be sold, and publishing a copy thereof once a week for the same period, in some newspaper of general circulation published in the city in which the property or some part thereof is situated, if any part thereof is situated in a city, if not, then in some newspaper of general circulation published in the judicial district in which the property or some part thereof is situated, or in case no newspaper of general circulation is published in the city or judicial district, as the case may be, in some newspaper of general circulation published in the county in which the property or some part thereof is situated. A copy of such notice of sale shall also be posted in some conspicuous place on the property to be sold at least 20 days before date of sale. In addition to any other description of the property, the notice shall describe the property by giving its street address, if any, or other common designation, if any; but if a legal description of the property is given, the validity of the notice shall not be affected by the fact that the street address or other common designation recited is erroneous or that the street address or other common designation is omitted. The term newspaper of general circulation is used herein is as defined in Article 1 (commencing with Section 6000) of Chapter 1, Division 7, Title 1 of the Government Code.

(e)   All sales of property under the power of sale contained in this Contract shall be held in the county where such property or some part thereof is situated, and shall be made at auction, to the highest bidder, between the hours of 9 in the morning and 5 in the afternoon. When the property consists of several known lots or parcels they shall be sold separately upon request of Vendee or any lien creditors with liens junior to Vendor, or when such portion of such property is claimed by a third person, and he requires it to be sold separately, such portion may be thus sold. The Vendee if present at the sale, may also direct the order in which property shall be sold, when such property consists of such several known lots or parcels which may be sold to advantage separately, and the Trustee shall follow such direction. After sufficient property has been sold to satisfy the indebtedness no more can be sold. The remainder of the property shall then be conveyed by Vendor to Vendee.

If the property under the power of sale is in two or more counties, the public auction sale of all of the property under the power of sale may take place in any one of the counties where the property, or a portion thereof, is located.

There may be a postponement of the sale proceedings at any time prior to the completion of the sale thereof at the discretion of the Trustee, or if the Vendor instructs the Trustee to postpone the sale proceedings. The notice of each postponement shall be given by public declaration by the Trustee at the time and place last appointed for sale. Such public declaration of the postponement shall also set forth the new date, time, and place of sale, which place of sale shall be the same place as originally fixed by the Trustee for the sale. No other notice of postponement need be given.

(f)   (i)   Each and every bid made by a bidder at a trustee's sale under the power of sale contained in this Contract shall be deemed to be an irrevocable offer by that bidder to purchase the property being sold by the Trustee under such power of sale for the amount of the bid. Any second or subsequent bid by the same bidder or any other bidder for a higher amount shall be a cancellation of the prior bid.

(ii)   At the Trustee's sale the Trustee shall have the right (1) to require every bidder to show evidence of his ability to deposit with the Trustee the full amount of his final bid in cash, or the equivalent of cash in a form satisfactory to the Trustee prior to and as a condition to the recognizing of such bid, and to conditionally accept and hold these amounts for the duration of the sale, and (2) to require the last and highest bidder for deposit, if not deposited previously, the full amount of his final bid in cash, or the equivalent of cash in a form satisfactory to the Trustee, immediately prior to the completion of the sale, the completion of the sale being so announced by the fall of the hammer or in any other customary manner.

(iii)   If the Trustee has not required the last and highest bidder to deposit the cash or equivalent in the manner set forth in subparagraph (ii) of subparagraph (f) above, the Trustee shall complete the sale. If the last and highest bidder then fails to deliver to the Trustee, when demanded, the amount of his final bid in cash, or the equivalent of cash in a form satisfactory to the Trustee, such bidder shall be liable to the Trustee for all damages which the Trustee may sustain by the refusal to deliver to the Trustee the amount of the final bid, including any court costs and reasonable attorney's fees.

(iv)   Any postponements or discontinuance of the sale proceedings shall be a cancellation of the last bid.

(g)   Any person, including the Vendor, Trustee and Vendee may purchase at such sale.

(h)   Trustee shall deliver to such purchaser its deed conveying the real property so sold but without any covenant or warranty, expressed or implied. The recitals in such deed of any matters or facts shall be conclusive proof of the truthfulness thereof.

Figure 7.14
Continued

12. SUBSTITUTION OF TRUSTEES

   Vendor, or any successor in ownership of any indebtedness secured hereby, may from time to time, by written instrument, substitute a successor or successors to any trustee named herein or acting hereunder, which instrument, executed by the Vendor and duly acknowledged and recorded in the office of the recorder of the county or counties where said property is situated, shall be conclusive proof of proper substitution of such successor trustee or trustees, who shall, without conveyance from the predecessor trustee, succeed to all its title, estate, rights, powers and duties. Said instrument must contain the name of the original Vendee, Trustee and Vendor, hereunder, the book and page or Document No. where this Security Land Contract is recorded and the name and address of the new trustee.

13. BINDING EFFECT

   This agreement binds the parties hereto, their heirs, legatees, devisees, administrators, executors, successors and assigns, and may be executed in duplicate.

.4. CONSTRUCTION

   All words used in this agreement, including the words "Vendor" and "Vendee" shall be construed to include the plural as well as the singular number and words used herewith in the present tense shall include the future as well as the present, and words used in the masculine gender shall include the feminine and neuter gender.
IN WITNESS WHEREOF, the parties have hereunto executed this agreement as of the date first above written.

15. ATTORNEY'S FEES

   If any party to this Agreement or any assignee of any party hereunder shall bring an action in any court of competent jurisdiction to enforce any covenant of this Agreement, including any action to collect any payment required hereunder, or to quiet his title against the other party to this Agreement, it is hereby mutually agreed that the prevailing party shall be entitled to reasonable attorney's fees and all costs and expenses in connection with said action, which sums° shall be included in any judgment or decree entered in such action in favor of the prevailing party.

_____   _____

_____   _____
Vendor(s)   Vendee(s)

NOTE: THE PARTIES HERETO ARE CAUTIONED THAT BY COMPLETING AND EXECUTING THIS AGREEMENT, LEGAL RIGHTS AND DUTIES ARE CREATED. THEY ARE ADVISED TO SEEK INDEPENDENT LEGAL COUNSEL AS TO ALL MATTERS CONTAINED IN THIS DOCUMENT.

STATE OF CALIFORNIA
COUNTY OF _____   ss.

On _____, before me, the undersigned, a Notary Public in and for said State, personally appeared _____

known to me to be the person(s) whose name(s) is/are subscribed to the within instrument and acknowledged that _____
executed the same.

WITNESS my hand and official seal

_____
NOTARY PUBLIC
In and for said County and State

STATE OF CALIFORNIA
COUNTY OF _____   ss.

On _____, before me, the undersigned, a Notary Public in and for said State, personally appeared _____

known to me to be the person(s) whose name(s) is/are subscribed to the within instrument and acknowledged that _____
executed the same.

WITNESS my hand and official seal

_____
NOTARY PUBLIC
In and for said County and State

Figure 7.15
Financing Statement

STATE OF CALIFORNIA
UNIFORM COMMERCIAL CODE—FINANCING STATEMENT—FORM UCC–1 (REV. 1/76)
IMPORTANT—Read instructions on back before filling out form

WOLCOTTS FORM UCC-1CA

This FINANCING STATEMENT is presented for filing pursuant to the California Uniform Commercial Code.

1. DEBTOR (LAST NAME FIRST—IF AN INDIVIDUAL)	1A. SOCIAL SECURITY OR FEDERAL TAX NO.
1B. MAILING ADDRESS 1C. CITY, STATE	1D. ZIP CODE
2. ADDITIONAL DEBTOR (IF ANY) (LAST NAME FIRST—IF AN INDIVIDUAL)	2A. SOCIAL SECURITY OR FEDERAL TAX NO
2B. MAILING ADDRESS 2C. CITY, STATE	2D. ZIP CODE
3. DEBTOR'S TRADE NAMES OR STYLES (IF ANY)	3A. FEDERAL TAX NUMBER

4. SECURED PARTY NAME MAILING ADDRESS CITY STATE ZIP CODE	4A. SOCIAL SECURITY NO FEDERAL TAX NO. OR BANK TRANSIT AND A.B.A. NO.
5. ASSIGNEE OF SECURED PARTY (IF ANY) NAME MAILING ADDRESS CITY STATE ZIP CODE	5A. SOCIAL SECURITY NO FEDERAL TAX NO. OR BANK TRANSIT AND A.B.A. NO.

6. This FINANCING STATEMENT covers the following types or items of property **(include description of real property on which located and owner of record when required by instruction 4).**

7. CHECK ☒ IF APPLICABLE   7A. ☐ PRODUCTS OF COLLATERAL ARE ALSO COVERED

7B. DEBTOR(S) SIGNATURE NOT REQUIRED IN ACCORDANCE WITH INSTRUCTION 5(a) ITEM: ☐ (1)   ☐ (2)   ☐ (3)   ☐ (4)

8. CHECK ☒ IF APPLICABLE   ☐ DEBTOR IS A "TRANSMITTING UTILITY" IN ACCORDANCE WITH UCC § 9105 (1) (n)

9.
►
SIGNATURE(S) OF DEBTOR(S)   DATE:

TYPE OR PRINT NAME(S) OF DEBTOR(S)

►
SIGNATURE(S) OF SECURED PARTY(IES)

TYPE OR PRINT NAME(S) OF SECURED PARTY(IES)

CODE
1
2
3
4
5
6
7
8
9
0

10. THIS SPACE FOR USE OF FILING OFFICER (DATE, TIME, FILE NUMBER AND FILING OFFICER)

11. *Return copy to:*

NAME
ADDRESS
CITY
STATE
ZIP CODE

(1) FILING OFFICER COPY

FORM UCC-1—FILING FEE $3.00
Approved by the Secretary of State

T F 21. As a general rule, there is a right of redemption for a limited time after a foreclosure sale under a mortgage.

T F 22. A mortgage customarily has three parties, whereas a deed of trust has only two.

T F 23. To be valid, a mortgage, like any contract, must be signed by both the mortgagor and the mortgagee.

T F 24. Like a deed, a mortgage must contain a sufficient description of the property.

T F 25. To be enforceable, a mortgage must be recorded.

Multiple Choice

26. The trustee under a deed of trust is the party who
  a. makes the loan
  b. signs the note
  c. holds the title as security
  d. executes the deed of trust

27. A promissory note providing for payment of principal in one sum is
  a. a straight note
  b. an installment note
  c. an amortized note
  d. an installment note with interest included

28. A mortgage customarily has the following number of parties
  a. one
  b. two
  c. three
  d. four

29. A deed of trust to be enforceable must be
  a. witnessed
  b. executed
  c. acknowledged
  d. recorded

30. When a note secured by a deed of trust is paid, the note should be
  a. recorded
  b. destroyed
  c. reconveyed
  d. delivered to the trustee when reconveyance is requested

31. After the foreclosure of a deed of trust by trustee's sale, the owner has a right of redemption for
  a. three months
  b. six months
  c. one year
  d. none of the above or any other period

32. A right of reinstatement exists (after a notice of default under a trust deed is recorded) for a period of
  a. 30 days
  b. 60 days
  c. 90 days
  d. 3 months

33. The time within which to reinstate a deed of trust commences to run from the date
  a. the beneficiary requests the trustee to foreclose
  b. a default first occurs
  c. a request for notice of default is recorded
  d. the notice of default is recorded

34. In event of foreclosure, a deficiency judgment is never permitted under or for
  a. court action
  b. trustee's sale
  c. non-purchase money loans
  d. junior trust deed loans

35. A form of financing instrument in which the seller retains legal title is called
  a. mortgage
  b. all-inclusive trust deed
  c. land contract of sale
  d. deed in lieu of foreclosure

36. A "request for notice" is intended to protect primarily the
  a. property owner
  b. first trust deed holder
  c. junior trust deed holder
  d. county taxing agencies

37. When you use real property as security for a loan, you
  a. pledge it
  b. hypothecate it
  c. assign it
  d. warrant it

38. A trustor is to a beneficiary as a
  a. donor is to donee
  b. vendor is to vendee
  c. trustor is to trustee
  d. mortgagor is to mortgagee

39. A security device on the sale of real property can be in the form of
  a. contract of sale
  b. deed of trust
  c. mortgage
  d. any of the above

40. A deed of trust is regarded as
  a. a charge (lien)
  b. an encumbrance
  c. both a and b
  d. neither a nor b

41. An instrument by which an earlier recorded deed of trust is made junior or inferior to a later recorded deed of trust is called
   a. an acceleration clause
   b. an alienation clause
   c. a subordination clause
   d. an escalator clause

42. The instrument used to remove the lien of a trust deed from the records is called a
   a. partial satisfaction
   b. release of mortgage
   c. deed of reconveyance
   d. certificate of redemption

43. Which of the following is ordinarily not essential to obtain a reconveyance of a trust deed?
   a. a copy of the note
   b. original trust deed or certified copy
   c. original note or bond if the note is lost
   d. signed request for reconveyance

44. A purchase money trust deed has the following characteristic
   a. not subject to foreclosure
   b. seller entitled to deficiency judgment
   c. has priority over judgment liens previously recorded against the buyer
   d. subject to foreclosure by court action only

45. A deed of trust may be foreclosed
   a. by the beneficiary selling under the power of sale
   b. by trustee's sale only
   c. by court proceeding only
   d. either by trustee's sale or court action

46. A clause in an installment note which permits the payee, in the event of default, to declare the entire amount immediately due is called
   a. a priority clause
   b. an open-end clause
   c. a due-on-sale clause
   d. an acceleration clause

47. Notice given by recording a trust deed with the county recorder is called
   a. actual
   b. constructive
   c. conditional
   d. contingent

48. To be valid, a deed of trust must be signed by the
   a. trustor
   b. trustee and beneficiary
   c. trustor and beneficiary
   d. trustor and trustee

49. The instrument that is used to secure a loan exclusively on personal property is called a
   a. security agreement
   b. bill of sale
   c. negotiable instrument
   d. mortgage

50. A personal property security instrument that may be filed or recorded to give notice to third parties is called a
   a. financing statement
   b. request for notice
   c. trustee's deed upon sale
   d. personal property statement

8

LENDERS AND THE ROLE OF THE GOVERNMENT IN REAL ESTATE FINANCE

As we saw in the previous chapter a knowledge of mortgages and trust deeds is essential for a basic understanding of how real estate is encumbered. A person should also be familiar with current institutional practices in extending mortgage loan credit and the role of the government in lending operations.

Broadly speaking, mortgage markets are classified as *primary* and *secondary*. The primary market is made up of lenders who supply funds directly to borrowers, bear risks with long-term financing, and who, as a rule, hold the mortgage until the debt is paid in full. The secondary market is one in which existing mortgages are bought, sold, or borrowed against. Lenders or investors in the secondary mortgage market buy mortgages as long-term investments in competition with other types of securities, such as government or corporate bonds.

Before discussing specific types of lenders and how they differ from one another, the reader may be asking, "Where does money for real estate loans come from? I know about banks, savings and loan associations, and other kinds of lenders, but where and how exactly do they obtain the money?"

Perhaps the easiest way to answer is in the form of a flow chart. A close inspection of the chart will reveal that savings deposits account for vitually all of the capital that enters the mortgage market.

SOURCES OF FUNDS

As can be seen from the chart (Figure 8.1), capital that is floated in the mortgage market comes from three principal sources: (1) fiduciary, popularly called "institutional" lenders, which provide the largest portion by far of all monies invested in real estate loans; (2) semifiduciary, popularly called "noninstitutional" lenders; and (3) nonfiduciary, or "private" lenders.

Fiduciary lenders are those directly responsible to their depositors or premium payers; semifiduciary lenders are responsible principally

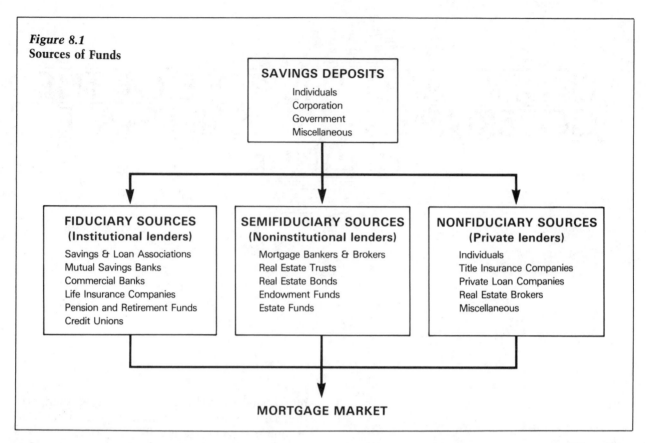

Figure 8.1
Sources of Funds

SAVINGS DEPOSITS

Individuals
Corporation
Government
Miscellaneous

FIDUCIARY SOURCES
(Institutional lenders)

Savings & Loan Associations
Mutual Savings Banks
Commercial Banks
Life Insurance Companies
Pension and Retirement Funds
Credit Unions

SEMIFIDUCIARY SOURCES
(Noninstitutional lenders)

Mortgage Bankers & Brokers
Real Estate Trusts
Real Estate Bonds
Endowment Funds
Estate Funds

NONFIDUCIARY SOURCES
(Private lenders)

Individuals
Title Insurance Companies
Private Loan Companies
Real Estate Brokers
Miscellaneous

MORTGAGE MARKET

to their owners, partners, or those they represent as agents. Nonfiduciary lenders invest their own funds and owe no duty to others as such. Again, regardless of the type of lender, the ultimate source for mortgage funds is savings.

INSTITUTIONAL LENDERS

The great majority of loans on all types of property are made by *institutional lenders*. They provide the principal source of funds for mortgage lending. The financial institutions falling into this category include life insurance companies, savings and loan associations, commercial banks, savings banks, and mortgage companies.

Savings and Loan Associations

Among institutional lenders, savings and loan associations account for the greatest share of the *home loan* market. They include both federally chartered and state-licensed associations. All federally-chartered savings and loan associations and all state-licensed associations are members of the Federal Home Loan Bank System, and savings

deposits are insured by the Federal Savings and Loan Insurance Corporation (FSLIC).

California's savings and loan business began in San Francisco in 1865. It has grown to some $50 billion in assets, which make California the "number one" savings and loan state in the nation. The savings and loan industry serves as a financial link or intermediary, gathering savings from the public and lending the bulk of these savings to home builders and buyers. Savings and loans associations may make long-term home loans, junior trust deed loans, home improvement loans, and consumer loans.

Commercial Banks

Commercial banks are "general purpose" lenders. The activities of state-chartered banks are covered by the State Banking Law, while those of national banks come under the National Bank Act. Commercial banks may lend on the security of a first lien on real property or a first lien on a leasehold under a lease which does not expire for at least ten years beyond the maturity date of the loan, subject to certain other requirements. In general, there are four types of bank real estate financing:

1. Long-term loans for the purchase of real estate already improved or to be improved.
2. Construction loans to finance the construction of land improvement, to be repaid when building is completed.
3. Interim financing of mortgage companies, i.e., business loans to mortgage companies to conduct their mortgage brokerage operations, pending "takeouts" by permanent lenders.
4. Home improvement loans (ordinarily classified as consumer loans rather than as mortgage loans) for repairing and modernizing existing improvements.

A *conventional* loan is one which is not insured or guaranteed by a governmental agency, such as FHA or VA (to be discussed later in this chapter).

Life Insurance Companies

Life insurance companies make *conventional* loans on most types of property, and supply most of the loans where large amounts are required, such as for large commercial properties, hotels, shopping centers, and industrial properties.

Besides making conventional loans, insurance companies quite commonly invest funds through mortgage companies which are appointed as loan correspondents.

Mortgage Companies

Mortgage companies make mortgage loans in the area where they do business and, when completed, sell these loans to the life insurance companies. Frequently, the mortgage companies thereafter act as service agencies for such loans on a fee basis.

Mortgage companies operate primarily as mortgage loans correspondents of life insurance companies, pension funds, and other financial institutions. They may furnish mortgage loans to these institutions from a single metropolitan area, or exclusively from one state, or sometimes from several states. The mortgage companies, with their loan brokerage functions, are one of the prime sources for mortgage loans. They make loans on homes, on income property, and under Federal Housing Administration (FHA) and Veterans Administration (VA) programs, which will be discussed later in this chapter.

The general procedure followed by a mortgage banking office in arranging real estate loans is as follows:

1. The customer fills out a loan application, assisted by a loan officer.
2. A credit report is ordered.
3. An appraiser from the mortgage banking firm evaluates the property. At this stage the particular investor has been determined, and the appraiser is guided by standards important to the investor, for example, three- or four-bedroom homes only, etc.
4. The application package is mailed to the investor (lender). This includes the application form, the borrower's financial statement, the credit report, the appraisal, photographs of the property, and a copy of the sale agreement or building contract.
5. The investor (the supplier of funds) examines the application to decide whether or not to approve and accept.
6. If the investor decides to accept, approval is sent to the mortgage banker.
7. When specific conditions are met, the mortgage banker forwards the investor's funds to escrow for closing.
8. After closing, the loan documents are sold to the investor, and the mortgage banker is ready to commence servicing the loan—collecting payments, keeping records, etc. Servicing, or *loan administration*, is carried out under a contract between the mortgage banker and the investor.

Figure 8.2 illustrates this procedure in the form of a flow chart. Figure 8.3 summarizes the principal differences between savings and loan associations, commercial banks, life insurance companies, and mortgage companies.

PRIME RATE

The prime rate is probably more closely watched than any other indicator of economic activity. Its movement up and down determines the cost of all borrowing, the interest paid by thrift institutions, and the gyrations of the stock and bond markets. The rate is a reflection of loan demand which economists, in turn, interpret as an indicator of general economic activity.

The prime rate had its origin just after the depression in the 1930s. It was evolved by banks who used it as a floor above which they pegged their interest rates in order to assured of a positive return on loans and to curb cut-throat competition for loan business. Until 1970, the rate changed about once a year. Since then, it has

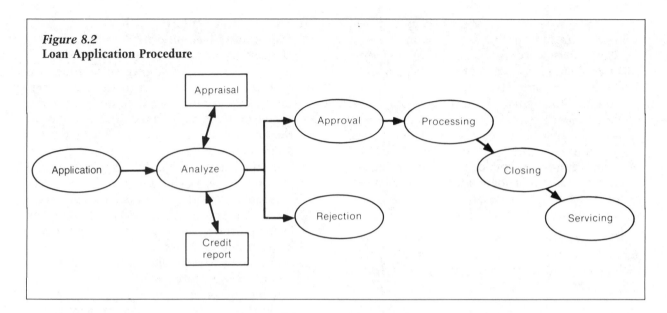

Figure 8.2
Loan Application Procedure

changed more than 300 times because banks decided that it should be more reflective of money market interest rates such as those on commercial paper. Today, unlike the early days of the prime rate, not all borrowers need to pay a premium above the prime rate since banks will make loans to preferred borrowers at lower rates.

POINTS

For making a loan, institutional lenders charge *points* to a buyer; points are also referred to as discount points, loan fees, service charges, or commitment fees. The amounts charged may vary considerably, depending upon the particular lender. Lenders or investors are, of course, concerned with yield (the amount of return which they will receive on their investment). Many investors are only willing to invest in real estate loans if their yield will be higher than that of corporate or government bonds. These investors feel that a mortgage yield should be at least one percent more than the ordinary investment yield to offset expenses caused by delinquencies and the necessity to institute foreclosure proceedings. Since the interest rates on FHA and VA loans are established by the respective agencies, and the amount of interest charged is not sufficient to return the required yield, such mortgages can only be sold at a discount. Discount points paid to lenders or investors are in effect prepaid interest, and are used to adjust the effective interest rate so that it is equal to or nearly equal to the prevailing

market rate, i.e., the rate charged on conventional loans.

A buyer in an FHA or VA transaction can be charged one percent as a service charge or obligation fee, but the seller in a VA transaction has to absorb (pay) the discount points. Otherwise FHA interest rates are now freely negotiable between borrower and lender, and the points may be paid by either buyer (borrower) and seller.

The discount rate fluctuates, depending upon current market conditions. For example, if the market is paying 98 percent of the face value of the note, the seller will be charged a two-point (2 percent) discount fee by the investor to buy the loan. If the market is paying only 95 percent of the face value of the loan, the seller will be charged a five-point (5 percent) discount fee. This can be illustrated as follows:

$100,000	Loan amount
5%	Points expressed as a percentage
$ 5,000	Points expressed as a dollar amount
$100,000	Face value of loan
$ −5,000	Discount points
$ 95,000	Funds committed by lender

It should be noted that while the example shows $95,000 of funds committed, the borrower would be receiving the $100,000 loan amount. The difference of $5,000—that is, $100,000 face amount less $95,000 actually committed by the lender—would, in this example involving 5 points, be absorbed by the seller who is paying the points.

Finally, for FHA loans on dwelling units containing up to four units, points may be capital-

Figure 8.3
Institutional Lenders

	Savings and Loan Associations	Commercial Banks	Life Insurance Companies	Mortgage Companies
Control agency	Federal Home Loan Bank	Federal and state banking laws; Federal Reserve Bank	California Commissioner of Insurance	State laws (varying from state to state)
Character of Loans	First loans; junior loans for home improvements	First loans; second loans for home improvements	First loans only	First loans and junior loans
Type of loans	Conventional, FHA, VA	Conventional, FHA, VA	Conventional primarily	Conventional, FHA, VA
Maximum term (other than FHA-VA)	30 years	30 years	Not limited by statute	5-10 years, brokerage; 25 years correspondent
Maximum ratio of loan to appraised value	95% to $108,300 with innumerable variations thereafter. Most often 80%.	Lesser of 90% of market or appraised value	No legal restriction. Usually follows markets for other groups; usually not over 90%	No legal restriction. Usually follows markets for other groups; usually not over 80%
Risks usually accepted in order of value of investment	Residential Income-producing	Commercial Industrial Agriculture Multiple Dwelling Units Single-family dwelling Other residential	Commercial Lease-back Other income-producing Single-family dwellings	Residential Income
Interest rates (other than FHA-VA)	10%-16%—fixed or variable Follows market	10%-15%—fixed or variable Follows market	10%-14%—fixed or variable Follows market	10%-16%—fixed or variable Follows market
Points or discounts	Depends on money market and risk, usually 1-5 points plus flat fee	Depends on money market and risk: 1-5 points plus flat fee of $50 to $150	Depends on money market and risk: 1-5 points	Depends on money market and risk, plus 1 point brokerage commission To lender: 1-5 points
Prepayment penalties for	Up to six months' interest common practice, except where restricted by law			
Availability of funds	Generally unlimited. Lendable funds cannot exceed given percent of the amount on deposit.	Portfolio basis. Percentage of total lendable funds established by the *Federal Reserve Bank.*	Portfolio basis. Percentage of available funds. Each company sets it own program. Wide variation caused by fluctuating reserves.	Selective. Most are also correspondents for S&L's and insurance companies as well as loan brokers.

ized, that is, added to the loan and repaid over the life of the loan if the points are paid by the buyer-borrower.

THE GOVERNMENT'S ROLE IN REAL ESTATE FINANCE

There are various ways that the government, principally the federal government, participates in real estate finance. As we have seen, various types of lenders engage in activities that constitute the primary mortgage market. A very important adjunct of the primary market is a secondary one whose members, that is, those large agencies that call themselves secondary buyers, such as the Federal National Mortgage Association, do not make direct loans, but assist in buying or discounting loans already made or insure the lenders against losses from possible foreclosures.

Buying or discounting may be done by private institutions or by an agency of the federal government. Private individuals may also buy but, due to the large capital involved, seldom do.

The insuring program is carried on by the federal government through the Federal Housing Administration (FHA), a division of the Housing and Urban Development Agency (HUD). A guarantee program falls under the jurisdiction of the Veterans Administration. Under the California Farm and Home Purchase Program (Cal-Vet), the state of California is a direct lender. Another agency of the federal government, the Farmer's Home Administration (FmHA), provides loans in rural areas to finance homes and building sites. Rural areas include open country and places with population of 10,000 or less, and, under certain conditions, towns and cities between 10,000 and 20,000 population. It is an agency of the US Department of Agriculture, and serves the entire United States through a system of local offices. The state office in California is located in Woodland, California.

The most frequently encountered of these agencies and the roles they play may be summarized as follows:

FHA Mortgage Insurance

FHA mutual mortgage insurance (MMI) was initiated in 1934 to bring investors back into a depressed home mortgage market and to reduce the use of second and third mortgages. The insurance protection enables the investor to grant the borrower a larger first mortgage for a longer term. FHA does not lend money to buy or remodel homes. Its main function is the *insurance* of mortgages in order that borrowers may receive liberal terms in financing.

Cost for MMI—now called MIP (Mortgage Insurance Premium)—is as high as 1/2 percent of the unpaid loan balance. It may be paid by the borrower on a "pay-as-you-go" basis, that is, with the monthly loan payments; or the MMS may be paid "up front," that is, in one lump sum through escrow.

Here is how the insurance works. When an incurable default occurs, the investor (lender) must first acquire marketable title to the real estate either through foreclosure or by deed in lieu of foreclosure. The investor then has the option of retaining the property and canceling the FHA insurance, or transferring title and custody of the property to FHA and filing a claim under the insurance. If the investor chooses to retain the property, he or she assumes any profit or loss resulting from its eventual sale or other disposition. If the investor elects to convey the property to FHA, he or she files a claim for the unpaid principal balance on the loan, plus other reimbursable expenses incurred in obtaining title through foreclosure or deed in lieu of foreclosure.

When the loan is paid off on a long standing FHA insured loan, the owner of the property at the time of the payoff may be entitled to a refund, called a *distributive share*. This refund or rebate represents extra money left in a pool of mortgage insurance premiums.

Veterans Administration

Rather than insuring loans like the FHA, the Veterans Administration usually guarantees the lender against loss up to certain limits. Benefits under the program are available to World War II veterans and veterans of subsequent hostilities. The law establishing such benefits is known as the GI Bill.

The difference between a guaranteed and an insured loan is this: If there is a default on a guaranteed loan, the government pays the lender a specified maximum amount, which is reduced proportionately as the loan is paid. When the VA does insure a loan, it will pay the lender's net loss up to the amount of his or her insurance account.

VA loans are made only on homes where the borrower has the intent of being an owner-occupant. However, after living in a home that has been financed by a VA loan, the veteran can move out and rent it without affecting the loan. Veterans' guaranteed and direct loan benefits extend beyond conventional housing to include mobile homes and condominiums. Condominums are also covered under the FHA program.

Federal National Mortgage Association

The Federal National Mortgage Association (FNMA), popularly known as Fannie Mae, is engaged in the business of expanding the amount of capital available to finance home building and home buying. Its primary function is to buy FHA-insured and GI-guaranteed mortgages made by private lenders. This paper is purchased at discount rates as explained previously. Fannie Mae also deals in the conventional mortgage market, and buys hundreds of millions of dollars worth of conventional mortgages each year.

Government National Mortgage Association

The Government National Mortgage Association (GNMA), popularly known as Ginny Mae, is also engaged in the business of expanding the amount of capital available to finance home building and home buying. Its primary function is to issue a commitment to buy a mortgage upon completion of a project and to purchase the mortgage at par.

Cal-Vet

The Department of Veterans Affairs (DVA) is an agency of the state of California which administers the California Veterans Farm and Home Purchase Program (Cal-Vet loans). This department was originally created in 1921. Its purpose is to assist qualified California veterans in acquiring suitable farm or home property at low financing costs. The amount advanced by the state is repaid by the veteran at a low rate of interest through uniform monthly payments over a period of years. These monthly payments cover all costs including bond issuance, redemption, and interest to bond-holders, and costs of administering the program; therefore, there is no expense to the taxpayer. This program utilizes a contract of sale rather than a mortgage or deed of trust as the security instrument.

Figure 8.4 outlines and compares the three principal government loan programs—FHA, VA, and Cal-Vet.

Cal-First Homebuyers Program

This is a more recent program established in California. Now, through the California Housing Finance Agency, qualified first-time home buyers can secure low, graduated payment mortgage financing to purchase an existing or new home. This could be a single dwelling, condominium, or cooperative.

To qualify, buyers must be first-time buyers who have not owned a principal residence in the preceding three years, and they must occupy the dwelling for at least two years.

The program uses California tax-exempt mortgage bonds to provide a graduated buydown of the interest rate on the buyer's fixed-rate, first mortgage loan. The buydown is graduated over the first six years of the loan so that the buyer's monthly payment increases each year as their income grows. The monthly payment continues to rise until the ninth year of the loan, after which it levels out and the buyer makes the entire mortgage payment, including the repayment of the buydown.

The program provides help with monthly payments in the earlier years of ownership, when the first-time home buyer needs it most. While there are no income eligibility requirements, buyers must earn enough to qualify for financing at the buydown rate. Also, there are maximum purchase prices that vary according to the area, which are subject to change. For example, the purchase price cap in the Los Angeles area is $126,000 as of this writing.

SECONDARY OR JUNIOR FINANCING

Very often the sale of real estate requires secondary financing in order to complete the transaction. Although the term *secondary* is used in both cases, secondary financing has no particular relation to the secondary mortgage market. Secondary financing is any financing that is *junior* to the prime or first loan. It may consist of a second trust deed, third, etc. Junior loans have a secondary claim behind the first trust deed loan; thus, in the event of foreclosure, the first trust deed is paid off first, the second paid off next, and so forth.

Secondary financing is normally obtained from nonfiduciary sources (see Figure 8.1), most often from individuals who make up the category of "private" lenders. Sellers, for example, will often "carry back" a second trust deed when a buyer is

Figure 8.4 Comparison of FHA, VA, and Cal-Vet Financing (Existing rates and loan amounts are subject to change at any time.)

	Federal Housing Administration	Veterans Administration (GI)	Cal-Vet
Purpose of Loan	Single-Family Dwellings, Condominiums Multiple Housing	Homes, Farms, Capital Improvements, Mobile homes, Condominiums	Single-Family Residences, Farms Mobile Homes
Eligibility	Any U.S. Resident	W.W. II, Korean, "Cold War" Vets	California Veterans (except periods from 2-1-55 to 8-4-64 and since 5-7-75)
Maximum Loan	1 unit: Lesser of $108,300 or 95% of median price in area 2 units: $138,500 3 units: $167,200 4 units: $207,900	None-Controlled by market conditions. Common practice: 4 × maximum guarantee amount	$75,000 Home, Condominium $200,000 Farm + $5,000 for solar heating devices
Down Payment	3% of first $25,000 appraisal value (FHA may raise to 50,000) 5% of balance 100% of excess of selling price over appraised value	None, But Loan Limited to CRV (Certificate of Reasonable Value)	Home—3% of first $35,000 5% of balance Farm— 5% 100% over appraised value
Maximum Term	30 Years Existing Dwelling 35 Years New Construction	30 Years Home 40 Years Farm	25 Years—may extend to 40 Years
Secondary Financing	None allowed concurrent with first loan	Allowed under prescribed conditions	Allowed if combined liens do not exceed 90% of value
Interest Rate	Not regulated but includes M.M.I. (Mutual Mortgage Insurance) Negotiable: floats with market	Statutory rate varies according to market (fixed at time of purchase)	8% (Floating Rate) Rates on junior loans 2% higher
Prepayment Penalty	None	None	2% during first 2 years on original loan amount
Loan Origination Fee	Negotiable: may be paid by either buyer or seller	1% of loan maximum charge to buyer	$530
Loan Security	Deed of Trust or Mortgage	Deed of Trust or Mortgage	Conditional Sales Contract (Land Contract)
Lender Security	1/2% Mutual Mortgage Insurance	Guarantee—60% of Loan Balance with 30,000 Maximum	State retains title until loan repaid. Life Insurance on Buyer
Source of Funds	Approved Lending Agencies	Approved Lending Institutions	State Bonds (bonded indebtedness)
Assignment and Assumption of Loan	Anyone	Anyone	Cal-Vets at prevailing rate Other Vets—2% higher
Monthly Payment	P & I, 1/2% M.M.I. 1/12 Annual Tax 1/36 of 3-Year Fire Insurance Policy	P & I, 1/12 Taxes, 1/36 of 3-Year Fire Insurance	P & I, Life Insurance Premium, Disability Insurance Premium, 1/12 Annual Tax
Minimum Salary Required	4 × Fixed Monthly Payments	4 to 4-1/2 × Fixed Monthly Obligations	4-1/2 × Monthly Charges, plus property tax
Controlling Governmental Agency	FHA—Department of Housing and Urban Development	VA-U.S. Government	State of California—Department of Veterans Affairs, Division of Farm and Home Purchases

Figure 8.5 Mortgage Loan Disclosure Statement

MORTGAGE LOAN DISCLOSURE STATEMENT

....

(Name of Broker/Arranger of Credit)

....

(Business Address of Broker)

I. SUMMARY OF LOAN TERMS

A. PRINCIPAL AMOUNT OF LOAN . . . . **$**................

B. ESTIMATED DEDUCTIONS FROM PRINCIPAL AMOUNT

   1. Costs and Expenses (See Paragraph III-A) . . . . **$**................

   2. Brokerage Commission (See Paragraph III-B) . . . . **$**................

   3. Liens and Other Amounts to be Paid on
      Authorization of Borrower (See Paragraph III-C) . . . . . . **$**................

C. ESTIMATED CASH PAYABLE TO BORROWER (A Less B) . . . . **$**................

II. GENERAL INFORMATION CONCERNING LOAN

A. If this loan is made, you will be required to pay the principal and interest at ....% per year, payable as follows:

..........................., ... payments of **$**.. and a **FINAL/BALLOON** payment
  (number of payments)   (monthly/quarterly/annual)

of *$... to pay off the loan in full.

> ***CAUTION TO BORROWER:** If you do not have the funds to pay the balloon payment when due, it may be necessary for you to obtain a new loan against your property for this purpose, in which case, you may be required to again pay commission and expenses for arranging the loan. Keep this in mind in deciding upon the amount and terms of the loan that you obtain at this time.

B. This loan will be evidenced by a promissory note and secured by a deed of trust in favor of lender/creditor on

   property located at (street address or legal description): ....

....

....

C. Liens against this property and the approximate amounts are:

Nature of Lien	Amount Owing
....	....
....	....
....	....

D. If you wish to pay more than the scheduled payment at any time before it is due, you may have to pay a **PREPAYMENT PENALTY** computed as follows:

....

....

....

....

E. The purchase of credit life or credit disability insurance is not required of the borrower as a condition of making this loan.

(CONTINUED ON REVERSE SIDE)

FORM 134-CAL   (7-10-74)   PROFESSIONAL PUBLISHING CORP., 122 PAUL DRIVE, SAN RAFAEL, CALIFORNIA 94903

Figure 8.5
Continued

III. DEDUCTIONS FROM LOAN PROCEEDS

A. ESTIMATED COSTS AND EXPENSES to be paid by borrower out of the principal amount of the loan are:

PAYABLE TO

	Broker	Others
1. Appraisal fee		
2. Escrow fee		
3. Fees for policy of title insurance		
4. Notary fees		
5. Recording fees		
6. Credit investigation fees		
7. Other Costs and Expenses:		

TOTAL COSTS AND EXPENSES . . . . $................................

B. LOAN BROKERAGE COMMISSION . . . . $................................

C. LIENS AND OTHER AMOUNTS to be paid out of the principal amount of the loan on authorization of the borrower are estimated to be as follows:

PAYABLE TO

	Broker	Others
1. Fire or other property insurance premiums		
2. Credit life or disability insurance premiums		
3. Beneficiary statement fees		
4. Reconveyance and similar fees		
5. Liens against property securing loan:		
6. Other:		

TOTAL TO BE PAID ON AUTHORIZATION OF BORROWER . . . $................................

The undersigned certifies that the lender for this loan will not be the broker or designated representative, either directly or indirectly, and that the loan will be made in compliance with the provisions of the California Real Estate Law.

OR

....	....
(Broker)	(Designated Representative)
....	....
(License Number)	(License Number)

NOTICE TO BORROWER

DO NOT SIGN this statement until you have read and understood all of the information in it. All parts of the form must be completed before you sign.

The broker will rely on the INFORMATION ON LIENS in Paragraph II-C which was supplied by you. Be sure that you have stated all liens accurately. If you contract with the broker to arrange this loan and if the loan cannot be made because you did not state these liens correctly, you may be liable for payment of commission, fees and expenses.

The commission to be paid by you to the broker as shown in Paragraph III-B is customarily a percentage of the principal amount of the loan. The percentage that may be charged as a commission increases with the length of the loan. Keep this in mind in deciding upon the term for repayment of the loan.

Borrower hereby acknowledges the receipt of a copy of this statement.

DATED:..   ....
(Borrower)

....
(Borrower)

unable to pay cash to the existing or new first loan.

Mortgage Loan Brokers in Secondary Financing

Another important source of secondary financing is the so-called loan brokers, whose role in the financing process is so important that special laws regulate their activities. Licensees (real estate salespersons or brokers) who are employed by private lenders to find borrowers, and are compensated for their efforts, come under the Real Property Loan Law, also known as the Loan Brokerage Law. They may be viewed as middlemen, or loan arrangers.

The purpose of the Real Property Loan Law is to protect borrowers by requiring full disclosure of all the particulars of a loan, and to limit commission rates and other costs. The law requires that all loan charges be detailed on an approved form signed by the borrowers, and that a copy be furnished them. Figure 8.5 is an example of a Mortgage Loan Disclosure Statement.

The law applies only to first liens of less than $20,000, and to junior liens of less than $10,000. Figure 8.6 outlines the maximum commission and other costs and expenses that may be charged the borrower.

In addition to placing limits on loan charges, the law also stipulates that installment loans of six years or less may not contain any balloon payments. In other words, the installments must be substantially equal, with the exception of purchase money loans. Finally, it should be noted that California law limits interest charges to 10 percent; if secured by real property, however, the

interest rate may be the greater of 10 percent *or* the sum of the 5 percent plus the discount rate charged by the Federal Reserve Bank in San Francisco. Thus, if the FRB is charging its member banks 12 percent, individual lenders may charge 17 percent for trust deed loans. If arranged by a licensed real estate broker, whether as a principal or agent, Proposition 2 passed in 1979 does not limit loans secured by real estate.

Otherwise anything in excess of these rates is considered usury. The usury rate is not to be confused, however, with the so-called legal rate of 7 percent. This is the amount that a lender would be limited to charging in the unlikely event that a promissory note failed to state an interest rate.

TRUTH IN LENDING

The federal Truth in Lending Act has great impact on certain types of real property transactions.

The fundamental purpose of the law is to aid and encourage the consumer to become more aware of the interest rate and costs that are being exacted from him for the privilege of deferring payment for a period of time. It is presumed that the more knowledge the consumer has and, consequently, the more sophisticated he or she becomes, the more he or she will shop around for better credit terms. This law requires creditors to *disclose* in writing the cost, terms, and conditions of credit in a prescribed and uniform manner. The act does not establish or limit the *cost* of credit.

Responsibility for *administration* of the law is vested in the board of governors of the Federal Reserve System. Responsibility for the *enforcement* of the law, insofar as it relates to real estate

Figure 8.6
Maximum Commissions for Loan Brokers and Other Costs

Maximum Commissions	First Loans	Less than 3 years, 5%	3 years and over, 10%		Loans of $20,000 and over, exempt
	Junior Loans	Less than 2 years, 5%	2 years, but less than 3, 10%	3 years and over, 15%	Loans of $10,000 and over, exempt
Miscellaneous Costs and Expenses	Loan Amount	Under $3,901	$3,901 to $6,999	$7,000 to $19,999	First loans of $20,000 and over Junior loans of $10,000 and over
	Maximum Charges	$195	5% of loan	$350	No legal limitations
		Not to exceed actual costs and expenses			

and allied fields, is vested in the Federal Trade Commission. The act is implemented by a set of regulations known as "Regulation Z."

The law is intended for the protection of *natural persons*, in contrast to artificial "persons" such as corporations, in transactions in which credit is extended *primarily for personal, family, household, and agricultural purposes.* All persons who, in the ordinary course of their businesses, regularly *extend* or arrange for the extension of consumer credit, or who *offer* to arrange for the extension of consumer credit, are deemed to be creditors under the act and are required to disclose the cost of the credit they extend.

The impact of the law on real property transactions is particularly significant in connection with a right of rescission. A borrower is given a right to rescind a credit transaction and avoid a security interest retained or acquired in real property used or expected to be used as the *borrower's residence.* Figure 8.7 shows a filled in Notice of Right to Cancel. As a general rule, the right of the borrower to rescind must be exercised within three business days following the *consummation* of the contract to extend credit. Exceptions to the right to rescind apply in the case of a first lien created for the purpose of financing purchase of a residence for the borrower.

Security interests in which a right of rescission is recognized include real estate *mortgages* and *deeds of trust* encumbering the principal residence of the borrower. *Contracts for the sale of real property* also qualify as a security interest which is subject to the right to rescind.

REAL ESTATE SETTLEMENT PROCEDURES ACT (RESPA)

Another disclosure law relative to financial transactions is RESPA, designed to show borrowers exactly what costs are involved during the escrow (settlement) period. This law was first encountered in Chapter 6.

This federal statute covers most residential mortgage loans used to finance the purchase of one to four family properties, such as a house, condominium or cooperative apartment unit, a lot with a mobile home, or a lot on which a house is to be built or a mobile home placed using the loan proceeds.

The law requires that the lender furnish the borrowers a uniform settlement statement at or before settlement, showing a good faith estimate of likely charges. Figure 8.8 is an example. An escrow information booklet must also be furnished by the lender.

The administration and enforcement of RESPA is the responsibility of the U.S. Department of Housing and Urban Development.

OTHER BORROWER PROTECTIONS

Anti-Discrimination—Equal Credit Opportunity

On loan applications, the Federal Equal Credit Opportunity Act prohibits discrimination based on age, sex, race and marital status, color, religion or national origin. Senior citizens, young adults, and single persons must be considered on the basis of income adequacy, satisfactory net worth, job stability and satisfactory credit rating, the same as anybody else. Credit guidelines are to be applied to each potential borrower in the same manner.

Redlining

Redlining was the practice—now illegal in California—of denying real estate loans on property in older, changing urban areas, usually with large minority populations, because of alleged higher lending risks without due consideration being given by the lending institutions to the credit worthiness of the individual loan applicant.

Questions for Chapter 8

Matching Terms

a. conventional loan   i. Fannie Mae
b. point   j. CRV
c. impound account   k. redlining
d. loan to value ratio   l. Ginnie Mae
e. rescission   m. mortgage broker
f. principal   n. PMI
g. mortgage banker   o. discount
h. PITI

____ 1. name associated with the Federal National Mortgage Association
____ 2. a requirement of a VA loan

Figure 8.7
Notice of Right to Cancel

NOTICE OF RIGHT TO CANCEL

Transaction I.D. No.   Loan Number   24100663-5
Borrowers: JOE P. GROSSNICKLE AND SHARON L. GROSSNICKLE

Property Address: 1993 DAYLIGHT COURT
                     THOUSAND OAKS, CALIFORNIA 91362

YOUR RIGHT TO CANCEL:

You are entering into a transaction that will result in a mortgage, lien, or security interest on/in your home. You have a legal right under federal law to cancel this transaction, without cost, within three business days from whichever of the following events occurs last:

1. the date of the transaction, which is   ; or
2. the date you receive your Truth in Lending disclosures; or
3. the date you receive this notice of your right to cancel.

If you cancel the transaction, the mortgage, lien, or security interest is also cancelled. Within 20 calendar days after we receive your notice, we must take the steps necessary to reflect the fact that the mortgage, lien, or security interest on/in your home has been cancelled, and we must return to you any money or property you have given to us or to anyone else in connection with this transaction.

You may keep any money or property we have given you until we have done the things mentioned above, but you must then offer to return the money or property. If it is impractical or unfair for you to return the property, you must offer its reasonable value. You may offer to return the property at your home or at the location of the property. Money must be returned to the address below. If we do not take possession of the money or property within 20 calendar days of your offer, you may keep it without further obligation.

HOW TO CANCEL:

If you decide to cancel this transaction, you may do so by notifying us in writing,

Name of Creditor   ADVANCED SAVINGS
                          AND LOAN ASSOCIATION
at   15720 VENTURA BLVD. #200
                          ENCINO, CALIFORNIA 91436

You may use any written statement that is signed and dated by you and states your intention to cancel, or you may use this notice by dating and signing below. Keep one copy of this notice because it contains important information about your rights.

If you cancel by mail or telegram, you must send a notice no later than midnight of   (or midnight of the third business day following the latest of the three events listed above.) If you send or deliver your written notice to cancel some other way, it must be delivered to the above address no later than that time.

I WISH TO CANCEL

_____   _____
        date   Consumer's Signature

ON THE DATE LISTED ABOVE I/WE UNDERSIGNED EACH RECEIVED TWO (2) COMPLETED COPIES OF THE NOTICE OF RIGHT TO CANCEL IN THE FORM PRESCRIBED BY LAW ADVISING ME/US OF MY/OUR RIGHT TO CANCEL THIS TRANSACTION.

_____   _____
        JOE P. GROSSNICKLE   SHARON L. GROSSNICKLE

_____   _____

Figure 8.8
RESPA Disclosure Settlement

HUD-1 Rev. 5/76	Form Approved OMB NO. 63-R-1501

A.

U. S. DEPARTMENT OF HOUSING AND URBAN DEVELOPMENT

SETTLEMENT STATEMENT

B. TYPE OF LOAN

1. ☐ FHA   2. ☐ FmHA   3. ☐ CONV. UNINS.
4. ☐ VA   5. ☐ CONV. INS.
6. File Number: 7. Loan Number:

8. Mortgage Insurance Case Number:

C. NOTE: *This form is furnished to give you a statement of actual settlement costs. Amounts paid to and by the settlement agent are shown. Items marked "(p.o.c.)" were paid outside the closing; they are shown here for informational purposes and are not included in the totals.*

D. NAME OF BORROWER: **E. NAME OF SELLER:**   **F. NAME OF LENDER:**

G. PROPERTY LOCATION: **H. SETTLEMENT AGENT:**   **I. SETTLEMENT DATE:**

PLACE OF SETTLEMENT:

J. SUMMARY OF BORROWER'S TRANSACTION		K. SUMMARY OF SELLER'S TRANSACTION	
100. GROSS AMOUNT DUE FROM BORROWER:		**400. GROSS AMOUNT DUE TO SELLER:**	
101. Contract sales price		401. Contract sales price	
102. Personal property		402. Personal property	
103. Settlement charges to borrower *(line 1400)*		403.	
104.		404.	
105.		405.	
Adjustments for items paid by seller in advance		*Adjustments for items paid by seller in advance*	
106. City/town taxes to		406. City/town taxes to	
107. County taxes to		407. County taxes to	
108. Assessments to		408. Assessments to	
109.		409.	
110.		410.	
111.		411.	
112.		412.	
120. GROSS AMOUNT DUE FROM BORROWER		**420. GROSS AMOUNT DUE TO SELLER**	
200. AMOUNTS PAID BY OR IN BEHALF OF BORROWER:		**500. REDUCTIONS IN AMOUNT DUE TO SELLER:**	
201. Deposit or earnest money		501. Excess deposit *(see instructions)*	
202. Principal amount of new loan(s)		502. Settlement charges to seller *(line 1400)*	
203. Existing loan(s) taken subject to		503. Existing loan(s) taken subject to	
204.		504. Payoff of first mortgage loan	
205.		505. Payoff of second mortgage loan	
206.		506.	
207.		507.	
208.		508.	
209.		509.	
Adjustments for items unpaid by seller		*Adjustments for items unpaid by seller*	
210. City/town taxes to		510. City/town taxes to	
211. County taxes to		511. County taxes to	
212. Assessments to		512. Assessments to	
213.		513.	
214.		514.	
215.		515.	
216.		516.	
217.		517.	
218.		518.	
219.		519.	
220. TOTAL PAID BY/FOR BORROWER		**520. TOTAL REDUCTION AMOUNT DUE SELLER**	
300. CASH AT SETTLEMENT FROM/TO BORROWER		**600. CASH AT SETTLEMENT TO/FROM SELLER**	
301. Gross amount due from borrower *(line 120)*		601. Gross amount due to seller *(line 420)*	
302. Less amounts paid by/for borrower *(line 220)*	( )	602. Less reductions in amount due seller *(line 520)*	( )
303. CASH (☐ FROM) (☐ TO) BORROWER		**603. CASH (☐ TO) (☐ FROM) SELLER**	

Figure 8.8
Continued

–2–

L. SETTLEMENT CHARGES			
700. TOTAL SALES/BROKER'S COMMISSION based on price $ @ % =		**PAID FROM BORROWER'S FUNDS AT SETTLEMENT**	**PAID FROM SELLER'S FUNDS AT SETTLEMENT**
Division of Commission (line 700) as follows:			
701. $ to			
702. $ to			
703. Commission paid at Settlement			
704.			
800. ITEMS PAYABLE IN CONNECTION WITH LOAN			
801. Loan Origination Fee %			
802. Loan Discount %			
803. Appraisal Fee to			
804. Credit Report to			
805. Lender's Inspection Fee			
806. Mortgage Insurance Application Fee to			
807. Assumption Fee			
808.			
809.			
810.			
811.			
900. ITEMS REQUIRED BY LENDER TO BE PAID IN ADVANCE			
901. Interest from to @ $ /day			
902. Mortgage Insurance Premium for months to			
903. Hazard Insurance Premium for years to			
904. years to			
905.			
1000. RESERVES DEPOSITED WITH LENDER			
1001. Hazard insurance months @ $ per month			
1002. Mortgage insurance months @ $ per month			
1003. City property taxes months @ $ per month			
1004. County property taxes months @ $ per month			
1005. Annual assessments months @ $ per month			
1006. months @ $ per month			
1007. months @ $ per month			
1008. months @ $ per month			
1100. TITLE CHARGES			
1101. Settlement or closing fee to			
1102. Abstract or title search to			
1103. Title examination to			
1104. Title insurance binder to			
1105. Document preparation to			
1106. Notary fees to			
1107. Attorney's fees to			
(includes above items numbers:)			
1108. Title insurance to			
(includes above items numbers:)			
1109. Lender's coverage $			
1110. Owner's coverage $			
1111.			
1112.			
1113.			
1200. GOVERNMENT RECORDING AND TRANSFER CHARGES			
1201. Recording fees: Deed $; Mortgage $; Releases $			
1202. City/county tax/stamps: Deed $; Mortgage $			
1203. State tax/stamps: Deed $; Mortgage $			
1204.			
1205.			
1300. ADDITIONAL SETTLEMENT CHARGES			
1301. Survey to			
1302. Pest inspection to			
1303.			
1304.			
1305.			
1400. TOTAL SETTLEMENT CHARGES (enter on lines 103, Section J and 502, Section K)			

HUD-1 Rev. 5/76

✿ US GOVERNMENT PRINTING OFFICE:1976:690-033/577

_____ 3. name associated with the Government National Mortgage Association

_____ 4. person who makes a mortgage loan and then sells it to an investor

_____ 5. specializes in bringing together borrowers and lenders

_____ 6. arbitrarily defining a neighborhood as high risk

_____ 7. insures against loss based on default of a loan

_____ 8. to pay less than face or market value

_____ 9. one percent of the loan amount

_____ 10. reserves for payment of taxes and insurance premiums

_____ 11. principal, interest, taxes, and insurance

_____ 12. a right to cancel

_____ 13. a real estate loan not insured by the FHA or guaranteed by the VA

_____ 14. percentage of value that lender will loan

_____ 15. amount borrowed or remaining balance due on a loan

True/False

T F 16. The prime rate is always constant.

T F 17. The loan to value ratio is higher in a conventional loan than in a government-insured loan.

T F 18. FHA loans normally call for a short term and high interest.

T F 19. FHA and VA loans are available to anyone who applies.

T F 20. A mortgage banker and a mortgage broker basically perform the same acts.

T F 21. Hazard insurance and private mortgage insurance assume the same risk.

T F 22. The Cal-Vet program lends money directly to a person who qualifies.

T F 23. FHA primarily is a lending agency.

T F 24. Two certificates are required in a GI loan.

T F 25. The Farmer's Home Administration and the Federal Housing Administration are parts of the same agency.

Multiple Choice

26. Real property loans are classified as either "conventional" or "government-insured or -guaranteed." The latter type may be
    a. VA
    b. FHA
    c. Cal-Vet
    d. any of the above

27. The "legal" rate of interest in California is
    a. 7 percent
    b. 10 percent
    c. 17 percent
    d. none of the above

28. The role of the FHA is to
    a. lend money
    b. insure borrowers
    c. insure loans made by approved lenders
    d. create secondary money markets

29. Advantages of "government" loans over "conventional" when buying a home include the following:
    a. fewer points
    b. lower down payment
    c. longer repayment period
    d. all of the above

30. Federally chartered savings and loan associations doing business in California are regulated by the
    a. Federal Reserve Bank
    b. Federal Home Loan Bank Board
    c. California Savings and Loan Commissioner
    d. Corporations Commissioner of California

31. A discount loan means that
    a. no interest is payable
    b. no interest is paid until due date
    c. lender collects interest on loan in advance
    d. the loan is usurious

32. "Balloon payment" is a term commonly associated with
    a. negotiable instruments
    b. junior loans
    c. most institutional loans
    d. government-backed loans

33. An example of a conventional loan is one made by
    a. FHA
    b. Cal-Vet
    c. VA
    d. Private lender

34. In a "tight money" market, the lowering of interest rates will normally increase
    a. real estate sales activity
    b. new construction
    c. lending activities
    d. all of the above

35. Under California law, the maximum rate that a party, not exempt under the usury law, can charge for an unsecured loan is
    a. 7 percent
    b. 10 percent
    c. 12 percent

d. any rate mutually agreed to by the borrower and lender

36. The largest source of funds for home loans comes from
  a. commercial banks
  b. private lenders
  c. life insurance companies
  d. savings and loan associations

37. Noninstitutional lenders include
  a. banks
  b. insurance companies
  c. savings and loan associations
  d. real estate trusts

38. The ultimate source of mortgage capital comes from
  a. taxation
  b. savings
  c. bonds
  d. stock

39. The maximum FHA loan available for the purchase of a single dwelling is
  a. $67,500
  b. $90,000
  c. $95,000
  d. none of the above

40. Secondary financing is not permissible, at the time of purchase, under (refer to Figure 8.4)
  a. FHA
  b. VA
  c. Cal-Vet
  d. conventional loans

41. A "floating" or variable interst rate is most frequently subject to change under the following program:
  a. FHA
  b. VA
  c. Cal-Vet
  d. conventional loans

42. Under the Real Estate Law, any loan other than a trust deed taken back by a seller, made by any person and secured directly by a lien on real property, requires subtantially equal payments over the life of the loan if the term is for six years or less. This section of the law

  a. applies to all real estate loans
  b. means that payments on the loan must be made monthly
  c. does not apply to a six-year loan
  d. applies only if a trust deed is used to secure the loan

43. Bonded indebtedness is usually associated with which of the following (see Figure 8.4)
  a. Cal-Vet
  b. FHA

c. VA
d. conventional loans

44. Looking at the Mortgage Loan Disclosure Statement in Figure 8.5, it can be demonstrated that
  a. the broker violated the law by charging excess commission
  b. the broker violated the law by charging excess costs and expenses
  c. one or more other provisions of the law has been violated
  d. there has been no violation of the law

45. The Real Estate Settlement Procedures Act is designed to
  a. control interest rates
  b. set prices of settlement services
  c. require disclosure of all loan costs
  d. all of the above

46. Ordinarily the best source for obtaining construction financing is the
  a. savings and loan association
  b. life insurance company
  c. private lender
  d. commercial bank

47. The provisions of the Real Estate Law limiting the amount of commission a broker may charge for negotiating real property loans apply to junior liens of up to (see Figure 8.6):
  a. $9,999
  b. $15,999
  c. $19,999
  d. none of the above

48. Which of the following commission rates applies to a junior loan of $4,000 to be repaid in 2-1/2 years?
  a. 5 percent
  b. 10 percent
  c. 15 percent
  d. any amount agreed to by the borrower

49. The interest rate for a conventional loan secured by a first trust deed is usually
  a. the same as for an FHA loan
  b. more than an FHA loan
  c. the same no matter what the source of funds
  d. the maximum rate allowed by law

50. As one of the major sources of conventional loans, life insurance companies
  a. restrict their operations to the immediate area of their home office
  b. have only a minor portion of investments in mortgages and trust deeds
  c. generally do not use the services of loan correspondents
  d. lend money for large commercial projects

9

VALUATION AND APPRAISAL

Real estate appraisal, a complex art under the best of circumstances, plays a critical role, particularly in times of wild economic fluctuation when market conditions vary substantially, literally from day to day. A thorough and thoughtful investigation by an expert becomes a practical necessity in nearly any transaction involving real estate since it is unlikely that everyone can be sufficiently knowledgeable to arrive at an accurate value of a given parcel. Property valuation is at the heart of much, if not all, real estate activity. Valuation and appraisal go hand in hand. For various reasons the *value* of property must be ascertained; to obtain an opinion as to value we must ordinarily go through the *appraisal process*.

This chapter introduces basic concepts of valuation and appraisal techniques. Although there

may be no real difference between the words *valuation* and *appraisal*, *valuation* is a somewhat broader term, which tends to be economic in origin and emphasizes theory. *Appraisal* refers more to practice, methods, and techniques.

The importance of appraisal in the real estate field is demonstrated by the fact that all applicants for the real estate broker's examination must satisfactorily complete a college course on real estate appraisal. A practical understanding of real estate values enables real estate licensees to carry out their functions in a useful and dependable manner. Even though they may not qualify as expert appraisers, real estate licensees should be familiar with the theoretical concepts of value, the forces which influence it, and the methods by which it may best be estimated.

An appraisal is defined briefly as an estimate and opinion of *value*, based on facts and conclusions. *Value* is briefly defined as the amount or price a property will command from a reasonable buyer in the open market. Actually, anyone can make an appraisal, even a lay person, but the *worth* of an appraisal is determined by the experience, knowledge, qualifications, and motives of the person who makes it. Figure 9.1 shows the steps involved in the appraisal process.

Because the appraisal process is basically a matter of forming an opinion, it is not an exact science. Even expert real estate appraisers will

Figure 9.1
The Appraisal Process

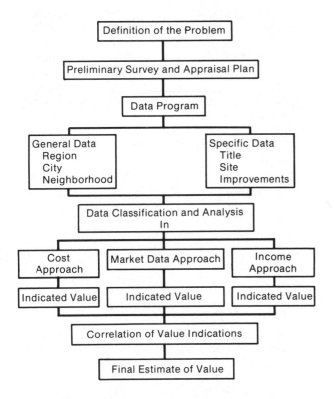

assign different values to the same piece of property, depending on various factors.

Clients ask the real estate practitioner questions about appraising property every day: the worth or the fair price, or a fair rental, or a fair basis for trade, or a proper insurance coverage. Licensees need to know how to answer such questions intelligently. For one thing, they must determine whether or not they can profitably spend time trying to sell a property at a listing price set by the owner; the owner's estimate of the property's value could be entirely unrealistic. In this regard brokers must bear in mind that in accepting listings, they obligate themselves to put forth their best efforts the find a buyer for the property. If the asking price is substantially out of line with market value, the broker's efforts could be for naught.

In our discussion of real estate appraisal, we first consider the various needs for an appraisal. We then discuss the concepts of value and the forces that influence value. The appraisal process is reviewed, including the three principal methods of appraising property and the impact of depreciation. The role and responsibilities of the professional appraiser are discussed. The chapter concludes with a summary of the factors that influence the value of a home.

NEED FOR AN APPRAISAL

Appraisals are needed for a variety of purposes, including the following:

1. Purchase of property, either for present use or as an investment
2. Sale of property
3. Loan secured by a mortgage or trust deed on real property
4. Taxation of real property (*ad valorem* taxes)
5. Inheritance or federal estate tax purposes
6. Condemnation actions (eminent domain)
7. Insurance purposes
8. Rental purposes, including computing a fair return on the investment
9. Exchange or trade of properties

Appraisals are required by lenders, and the values obtained are used in determining loan amounts—an essential fact of life for real estate salespersons.

An appraisal can be an opinion about the fair market value, the fair rental value, the separate value of land and improvements, the replacement cost of a structure, or about other factors.

An appraiser furnishes an appraisal report that sets forth such information as

The purpose of the appraisal
The type of value sought
The property rights involved
An adequate description of the property
The estimate of value
The date of the estimate of value
Any limiting conditions.

The appraisal report may be submitted in many forms, including any one of the following depending upon the needs of the client:

1. *Narrative report*: A complete description and discussion of all pertinent facts about the area and the subject property, with reasons and computations that support the appraised value. The report may include photographs, charts, maps, and plot plans. The narrative report is ordinarily used in a condemnation action, for instance.
2. *Short form report*: A check sheet or printed form indicating the important facts and data to be filled in by the appraiser. It is frequently used by lending institutions such as banks, savings and loan associations, etc.

3. *Letter report*: A brief description and analysis without inclusion of supporting data. It is generally used where the client is already familiar with the area, but needs an expert's views as to value.

PRINCIPLES OF VALUATION

A knowledge of the basic assumptions or premises that underlie appraisal methods is essential to an understanding of the purpose, methods, and procedures of valuation. The *Real Estate Reference Book* (1984–85 ed., pp. 417–419) sets forth the following principles of value influences that are important for a general understanding of the appraisal process.

Principle of Conformity. Holds that maximum value is realized when land uses are compatible and a reasonable degree of architectural harmony is present. Zoning ordinances help set comformity standards.

Principle of Change. Real property is in a constant state of flux and change, affecting individual properties, neighborhoods and cities.

The appraiser follows trends and influences and is sensitive to changes in conditions that affect the value of real estate. Economic, environmental, government, and social forces in constant change, affect all markets, especially real estate.

Principle of Substitution. This principle is the basis of the appraisal process. Simply stated, value will tend to be set by the cost of acquiring an equally desirable substitute. The value of a property to its owner cannot ordinarily exceed the value in the market to persons generally, when it can be substituted without undue expense or serious delay. In a free market the buyer can be expected to pay no more and a seller can expect to receive no less than the price of an equivalent substitute.

A property owner states that owner's house is worth $100,000. Buyers in the market can obtain a substitute property with the same features and utility for only $90,000. The seller's house, therefore, has a value of approximately $90,000, not $100,000.

Principle of Supply and Demand. Holds that price varies directly, but not necessarily proportionately, with demand, and inversely, but not necessarily proportionately, with supply. Increasing supply or decreasing demand tends to reduce price in the market. The opposite is also true.

Principle of Highest and Best Use. The best use of a parcel of land, known as its highest, best and most profitable use, is that which will most likely produce the greatest net return to the land over a given period of time. This net return is realized in terms of money or other amenities.

The application of this principle is flexible. It reflects the appraiser's opinion of the best use for the property as of the date of his appraisal. At one period of time, the highest and best use of a parcel of land in the downtown business district might be for the development of an office building, at another time, a parking lot may be the highest and best use.

A single-family house on a commercial lot may not be the highest and best use for the site. A four-unit apartment on multiple zoned land suitable for 30 units is probably not the long term highest and best use of the land.

It is also useful to understand highest and best use may no longer be only economic or profit making in character. Environmental, aesthetic, and historical considerations are increasingly important in governmental views of highest and best use.

Determining highest and best use includes assessing buyers' motives, the existing use of the property, potential benefits of ownership, the market's behavior, community or environmental factors, and special conditions or situations which come to bear on appraisal conclusions of value.

Principle of Progression. The worth of a lesser valued object tends to be enhanced by association with many similar objects of greater value.

Principle of Regression. The worth of a greater valued object is reduced by association with many lesser valued objects of the same type.

Principle of Contribution. A component part of a property is valued in proportion to its contribution to the value of the whole property or by how much that part's absence detracts from the value of the whole. Maximum values are achieved when the improvements on a site produce the highest (net) return, commensurate with the investment.

Principle of Anticipation. Value is created by anticipated future benefits to be derived from the property. In the Fair Market Value Analysis appraisers estimate the present worth of future benefits. This is the basis for the income approach to value. Simply stated, the income approach is the analysis of the present worth of: (1) projected future net income, and (2) future resale value anticipation. Historical data are relevant as they aid in the interpretation of future benefits.

Principle of Competition. Competition is created where substantial profits are being made. If there is a profitable demand for residential construction, competition among builders will become very apparent. This could lead to an increase in supply in relation to the demand, resulting in lower selling prices and unprofitable competition, leading to renewed decline in supply.

Principle of Balance. Value is created and sustained when contrasting, opposing, or interacting elements are in equilibrium, or balance. Proper mix of varying land uses creates value.

Imbalance is created by an *over improvement* or an *under improvement*. Balance is created by developing the site to its highest and best use.

Principle of Three Stage Life Cycle. In due course all material things go through the process of wearing or wasting away and eventually disintegrating. All property is characterized by three distinct stages described as *development, maturity, and old age* (or *growth, stability,* and *decline*).

Single properties, districts, neighborhoods, etc., tend generally to follow this pattern of growth and decline. It is also evident this process can be reversed as neighborhoods and individual properties in older residential areas are renewed and restored.

Revitalization and modernization in inner-city older neighborhoods may result from organized government programs or as a result of changing preferences of individual buyers. Most neighborhoods remain in the mature or stable stage for many years with decline being hardly noticeable.

Figure 9.2 illustrates some of these principles of valuation.

CONCEPTS OF VALUE

There are many different designations or definitions of value. For our purposes we will consider two principal classifications:

1. *Utility value*: The value to an owner in his or her use and enjoyment of property. Frequently termed a *subjective* value, it includes a valuation of *amenities* that may attach to a parcel of property. Amenities are those intangible benefits in real property ownership arising from such factors as pride of ownership, desirable social or cultural environment, architectural excellence, or uniqueness.
2. *Market value*: The value of the property in exchange for money or other property ordinarily means the amount of money at which property can be sold or exchanged at a given time or place as the result of market conditions. Frequently termed the *objective* value.

Other types of value that have been designated from time to time for specific purposes include the following: book value, tax value, cash value, sentimental value, capital value, speculative value, par value, time value, exchange value, investment value, rental value, cost value, etc.

When reference is made to the value of property, people generally mean market value. The market value may be based on a "willing buyer" and a

---

Figure 9.2
Some Principles of Valuation

Principle of:	Example
Substitution	Mr. A. has his house for sale for $135,000. Comparable houses in the area with the same features and utility can be purchased for $100,000. Mr. A's house would generally be considered to be worth closer to $100,000 (substitute property).
Change	Ms. B. purchased a residence in the early 1940s. Over the next 40 years the neighborhood had deteriorated to cheap apartments, rooming houses, etc.
Supply and Demand	Mrs. C. owns a large parcel of desert land. There is no development near the property. The demand for land in the area is negligible. The supply is excessive.
	Mr. D. owns a parking lot one-half block from the 100% commercial corner in a major city. The demand for his property is steadily increasing.
Highest and Best Use	Miss E. has a new residence in a recently developed subdivision of comparable homes. This is the highest and best use of the land.
	Mr. F. owns a single-family residence situated on a commercial lot. This is *not* the highest and best use of the land, provided that there is a need and demand for commercial property.

"willing seller" concept. Under this concept market value is the price in terms of money for which the property would sell in the open market when

1. The seller is not obliged to sell.
2. The buyer is not obliged to buy.
3. There is a reasonable length of time within which to effect a sale.
4. Both the seller and the prospective buyer are fully informed of all purposes to which the property is adapted and for which it is capable of being used.

Market value, then, is what the property is worth to the typically informed buyer. Price is what one might get from the sale of the property in terms of money. Sometimes value and price are the same. Under certain circumstances, however, there is a wide difference between the market value of a property and the actual sales price.

The real estate broker must always be particularly aware that no two parcels of land are exactly alike; the particular location of a plot of ground on the earth's surface always makes that plot unique. Accordingly, there are no precise means of making a positive comparison between properties. Whereas market value is governed by the actions of many buyers and sellers of similar type properties, the circumstances of a particular buyer and a particular seller may drastically affect the ultimate price of a specific parcel of property. For example, assume two identical houses are for sale. One owner will sell on conventional terms (i.e., 20 percent down payment, 80 percent first trust deed), while the other will sell under VA terms (i.e., no down payment, 100 percent financing). The VA-financed house would generally command the greater selling price, because of the appeal to a larger number of buyers.

Value, Cost, and Price

Value can be distinguished from *cost* as well as from *price* in the following principal ways:

1. *Value* has to do with the combined factors of present and anticipated enjoyment and profit. In appraising property, the value is the *discounted worth* of all desirable benefits that may accrue from the maximum use of the property. A conclusion in regard to these benefits will, of course, be a matter of opinion, an intelligent estimate based on a complete analysis of all available influencing factors and on reasonable, warranted assumptions.

2. *Cost* represents a measure of past expenditures for labor, material, and other improvements. While cost is frequently a factor upon which value is at least partially based, cost does not control present and future value. As an example, the cost of a mansion and the cost of an apartment structure may be the same, but in time the mansion may become a white elephant with substantially less value. The apartment structure, meanwhile, may increase in value because the owner gets income from renting it.

3. *Price* is what is actually paid for property, and usually means the amount of money involved in a transaction. Whether or not a person gets value for what he or she buys depends on many factors, including the soundness of the appraisal and the events that occur in the future. Under an efficient market structure, price will tend to equal value.

Elements of Value

Four essential elements make up value: *utility, scarcity, demand,* and *transferability.* None alone creates value. For example, a thing may be scarce, but if it has no utility, there is no real demand for it. Other things, such as air, for instance, may have utility and may be in great demand, but are so abundant as to have little or no commercial value. Also, the commodity must be transferable or reasonably available.

Implicit in these four elements is the concept of supply and demand. In the housing market, for example, *supply* means that at any time there will be a given number of housing units available for sale. *Demand,* on the other hand, means that at any time there will be a given number of buyers. If there is a large supply of housing units in relation to demand, we have what is popularly called a *buyer's market,* and prices tend to be driven downward. If there is a small supply of housing units relative to demand, this condition is known as a *seller's market,* and prices trend upward.

Inflation is a factor that must be kept in mind when considering value. Inflation causes a rise in price but not necessarily in value. There can be *real-cost* inflation or there can be *runaway* inflation. Real-cost inflation is caused, basically, by the increased effort to produce the same quantity of goods or services. Runaway inflation is caused by a number of factors, including monetary policies, supply of money, and psychological reactions. Inflation can also be categorized as *cost-push* or *demand-pull* inflation. The former results from higher prices due to increased costs of labor and supplies; the latter results from a shortage of supply with buyers bidding against each other.

Highest and best use, a fundamental concept of value, is implicit in these four elements. As we have seen, the highest and best use of land is that use which is most likely to produce the greatest net return over a given period of time. This period may be dependent upon the purpose for which the property is desired. For example, the "given period" to be studied and analyzed would be shorter for a speculative venture than for a long-term investment.

FORCES THAT INFLUENCE VALUE

As is frequently observed, the value of real estate is created, maintained, modified, and nullified or destroyed by the interplay of the following four forces:

1. *Social ideals and standards.* Examples include attitudes toward population growth and decline; toward birth, marriage, divorce and death rates; toward education, recreation, and other human desires, yearnings, and instincts

2. *Economic factors.* Examples include location, quantity, and quality of natural resources, industrial and commercial trends, employment trends, wage levels, availability of money and credit, interest rates, tax rates, etc.

3. *Governmental regulations.* Examples include zoning ordinances, building codes, public health measures, fire regulations, govern-

ment housing policies, credit controls, etc.

4. *Physical factors.* Examples include size and shape of the lot, soil and geologic conditions, climate, and specific location.

Another way to view the elements of value—that is, how values are created—and the forces that influence value or how values are changed, is by way of the flow chart depicted in Figure 9.3.

These forces are interrelated and are also in a constant state of flux. Each one of them to some degree has an effect on cost, price, and value. A chart which shows the factors that influence the value of real estate is shown in Figure 9.4. Specific factors that influence value include the directional growth of a community, exact location of a particular parcel of property, utility of the land, the size and shape of the parcel, street and highway conditions, the business climate, character of the soil, topography of the land, and obsolescence caused by economic changes or decreasing functional utility of the property. For valuation purposes, property is classified into various categories: residential, residential income, commercial, industrial, recreational and agricultural or farm property.

In making an estimate of the value of residential property it is usual to evaluate the lot and the present value of the building based on an estimate of the cost of replacing the building, in addition to checking recent sales of similar properties in the neighborhood. These represent two of the three methods of appraising property which we will discuss further below.

Industrial lands are usually valued on an *area* basis, either so much a square foot or so much an acre, because the industrial parcel is generally all usable, right up to the boundary lines. The term *plottage value*, which often arises in connection

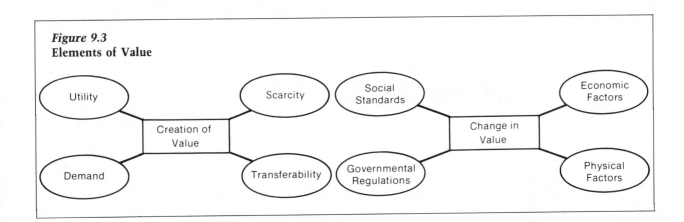

Figure 9.3
Elements of Value

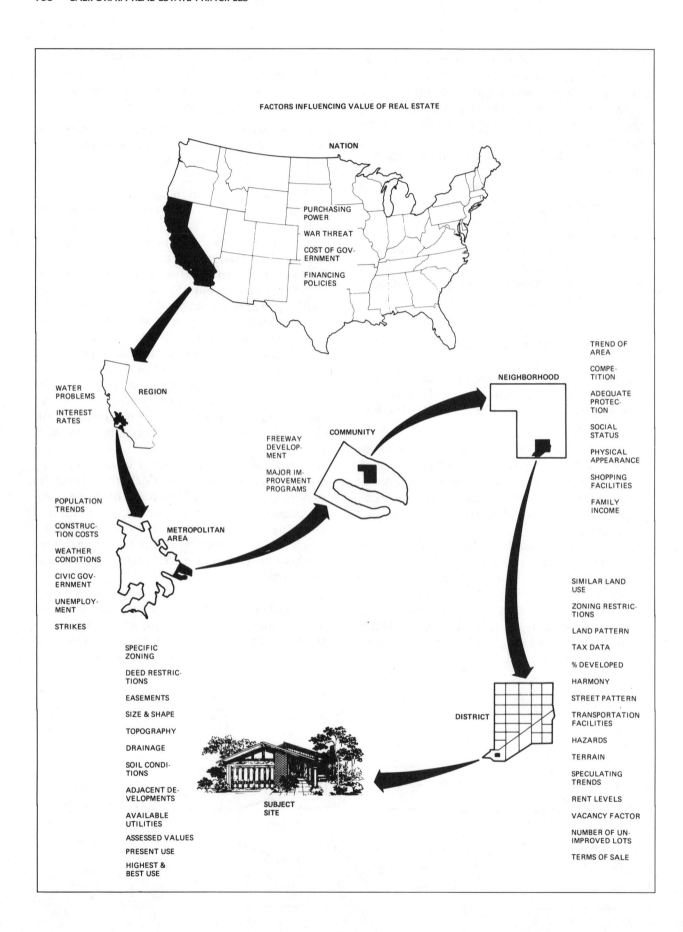

FACTORS INFLUENCING VALUE OF REAL ESTATE

NATION

PURCHASING POWER

WAR THREAT

COST OF GOV-ERNMENT

FINANCING POLICIES

REGION

WATER PROBLEMS

INTEREST RATES

METROPOLITAN AREA

POPULATION TRENDS

CONSTRUC-TION COSTS

WEATHER CONDITIONS

CIVIC GOV-ERNMENT

UNEMPLOY-MENT

STRIKES

COMMUNITY

FREEWAY DEVELOP-MENT

MAJOR IM-PROVEMENT PROGRAMS

NEIGHBORHOOD

TREND OF AREA

COMPE-TITION

ADEQUATE PROTEC-TION

SOCIAL STATUS

PHYSICAL APPEARANCE

SHOPPING FACILITIES

FAMILY INCOME

DISTRICT

SIMILAR LAND USE

ZONING RESTRIC-TIONS

LAND PATTERN

TAX DATA

% DEVELOPED

HARMONY

STREET PATTERN

TRANSPORTATION FACILITIES

HAZARDS

TERRAIN

SPECULATING TRENDS

RENT LEVELS

VACANCY FACTOR

NUMBER OF UN-IMPROVED LOTS

TERMS OF SALE

SUBJECT SITE

SPECIFIC ZONING

DEED RESTRIC-TIONS

EASEMENTS

SIZE & SHAPE

TOPOGRAPHY

DRAINAGE

SOIL CONDI-TIONS

ADJACENT DE-VELOPMENTS

AVAILABLE UTILITIES

ASSESSED VALUES

PRESENT USE

HIGHEST & BEST USE

with industrial or commercial property, means an added increment of value gained by assembling the individual parcels in an urban area into a larger-sized industrial site. A shopping center is a typical example of plottage value.

In the case of agricultural or farm lands, one important factor in determining the value is the nature and long-term price trend of the crop grown, or intended to be grown, on the land. By way of example, when the property is to be used as a dairy farm, factors to consider include the character of the soil, particularly the type and condition of the topsoil; whether the land is in fact suitable for hay and grain; available water for the cattle and crops; climatic conditions such as heat, dampness, and winds; proximity to markets; labor conditions in the area; etc. Other types of farm uses would necessitate other considerations. Farm land valuation is actually a highly specialized field which usually requires the assistance of soil and crop experts. In spite of the urbanization trends in California, there is still a tremendous amount of farming and ranching in the state.

METHODS OF APPRAISING PROPERTY

General Considerations

The appraisal of real estate has become more or less standardized by virtue of the experience and practice of qualified people in all parts of the country who encounter the same or similar types of valuation problems, and who attempt to solve them in an equitable manner by the adoption of various methods.

Three commonly adopted ways to approach an estimate of market value are the *market comparison*, the *replacement cost*, and the *capitalization* approach. Figure 9.5 illustrates these three approaches. Under the comparison method, sales of similar properties in the area are analyzed to form an opinion of value. The replacement cost method considers the value of the land, assumed to be vacant, added to the *depreciated replacement cost* of the improvements. Under the capitalization approach, the estimated potential net income is capitalized into an indication of value, as will be detailed later. No single method can always be depended upon to produce a reliable estimate. Frequently the knowledgeable appraiser will use all three methods to appraise a given

piece of property. A simplified application of these three methods is shown in the filled-in Residential Appraisal Report in Figure 9.6, and is appropriately analyzed in a course on real estate appraisal.

The first step in any appraisal procedure is to have a clear understanding of the reason for making the appraisal. There are many different purposes for which an appraisal may be made, and each variation of purpose could result in a considerable, yet logical, variation of estimated value. Factors which influence the selection of proper methods and the result include the following:

1. Nature of the property, whether investment, noninvestment, or service
2. Purpose of the purchase, whether for use, investment, or speculation
3. Purpose of the appraisal, whether for a sale, or loan, or taxation, or insurance, etc.
4. Adequacy and reliability of available data
5. Weight to be given to a particular method, based on its adaptability to the specific problem

Often appraisers use a procedure known as *correlation*, in which each approach method is used independently to reach an estimated value. The final step is to apply to each separate value a weight proportionate to the merit of using its approach in that particular instance. Conclusions are then reached as to one appropriate value.

Market Comparison Approach

This approach uses comparable sales as its principal tool. It is most generally adaptable for use by real estate brokers and licensees. It particularly lends itself to the appraisal of land, residences, and other types of improved property which are very much alike and for which a ready market exists.

The market comparison approach uses market data of all kinds in order to compare closely the property being appraised with other similar properties which have been sold recently or are currently being offered for sale. The sources used for determining value include actual sales prices, listings, offers to purchase, properties being leased or rented, as well as an analysis of social and economic factors affecting marketability. The greater the number of comparable sales used, the better the result, provided a proper analysis is made. Figure 9.6 illustrates a convenient method

Three Approaches to Appraisal

Cost Approach

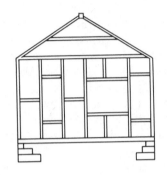

Income Approach

Market Approach

of setting forth this information by professional appraisers, outlining all three approaches to value. Figure 9.7 is a filled-in form which licensees use, called a Competitive Market Analysis. It focuses on the market comparison approach and is especially helpful in the marketing of real property. Figure 9.8 illustrates the application of the market approach.

Market data is obtained from many sources including banks, title insurance companies, county assessor's office, realty boards, financial news services, classified advertisements, and so on. The market approach is based on the assumption that property is worth what it will sell for in the open market in the absence of undue stress and if a reasonable time is given to find a buyer. For this

Figure 9.6
Market Comparison Appraisal

Figure 9.6
Continued

VALUATION SECTION

Purpose of Appraisal is to estimate Market Value as defined in Certification & Statement of Limiting Conditions (FHLMC Form 439/FNMA Form 1004B). If submitted for FNMA, the appraiser must attach (1) sketch or map showing location of subject, street names, distance from nearest intersection, and any detrimental conditions and (2) exterior building sketch of improvements showing dimensions.

COST APPROACH

Measurements	No. Stories	Sq. Ft.
26.5 x 70	x 1	= 1855
x	x	=
x	x	=
x	x	=
x	x	=
x	x	=

Total Gross Living Area (List in Market Data Analysis below) 1855

Comment on functional and economic obsolescence: NONE

ESTIMATED REPRODUCTION COST – NEW – OF IMPROVEMENTS:

Dwelling 1855 Sq. Ft. @ $ 45	=	$ 83,475
Sq. Ft. @ $	=	
Extras	=	
Special Energy Efficient Items	=	
Porches, Patios, etc.	=	
Garage/Car Port 400 Sq. Ft. @ $ 13	=	5,200
Site Improvements (driveway, landscaping, etc.)	=	2,000
Total Estimated Cost New	= $	90,675
Less Physical 8,000	Functional	Economic
Depreciation $ 8,000 $	$	= $(8,000)
Depreciated value of improvements	= $	82,675
ESTIMATED LAND VALUE (If leasehold, show only leasehold value)	= $	20,000
INDICATED VALUE BY COST APPROACH	$	102,675

MARKET DATA ANALYSIS

The undersigned has recited three recent sales of properties most similar and proximate to subject and has considered these in the market analysis. The description includes a dollar adjustment, reflecting market reaction to those items of significant variation between the subject and comparable properties. If a significant item in the comparable property is superior to, or more favorable than, the subject property, a minus (-) adjustment is made, thus reducing the indicated value of subject; if a significant item in the comparable is inferior to, or less favorable than, the subject property, a plus (+) adjustment is made, thus increasing the indicated value of the subject.

ITEM	Subject Property	COMPARABLE NO. 1		COMPARABLE NO. 2		COMPARABLE NO. 3	
Address	5480 Booster	5601 Booster		1760 Morale		1804 Granite	
Proximity to Subj.		½ Block		3 Blocks		4 Blocks	
Sales Price	$100,000	$105,000		$9,000		$120,000	
Price/Living area	$53.91	$58.02		$50.84		$62.34	
Data Source	Buyer	Appraiser		Appraiser		Appraiser	
Date of Sale and Time Adjustment	DESCRIPTION	DESCRIPTION	+(-)$ Adjustment	DESCRIPTION	+(-)$ Adjustment	DESCRIPTION	+(-)$ Adjustment
	7-82	12-81	+6000	4-82	+2250	1-82	+4500
Location	Good	Equal		Equal		Superior	-3000
Site/View	Good	Superior	-2000	Inferior	+2000	Superior	-2000
Design and Appeal	Good	Equal		Inferior	+4000	Superior	-4000
Quality of Const.	Good	Equal		Equal		Equal	
Age	6	5		7		7	
Condition	Good	Superior	-2500	Inferior	+1500	Superior	-1000
Living Area Room Count and Total	Total 7 B-rms 2 Baths 2½	Total 6 B-rms 3 Baths 2½	+2500	Total 6 B-rms 2 Baths 2	+3000	Total 7 B-rms 3 Baths 3	-7000
Gross Living Area	1855 Sq.Ft.	1810 Sq.Ft.		1790 Sq.Ft.		1925 Sq.Ft.	
Basement & Bsmt. Finished Rooms	NONE	NONE		NONE		NONE	
Functional Utility	Average	Ave		Ave		Ave	
Air Conditioning	Adequate	Ade		Ade		Ade	
Garage/Car Port	Double Attached	DA		DA		DA	
Porches, Patio, Pools, etc.	NONE	NONE		NONE		NONE	
Special Energy Efficient Items	NONE	Heavier Insulation	-1500	EQUAL		Heavier Insulation	-1500
Other (e.g. fire-places, kitchen equip., remodeling)	Fireplace	Fireplace		No Fireplace	+1500	Fireplace	
Sales or Financing Concessions	Conventional	VA	-6000	Conv		Seller A1TD	-5000
Net Adj. (Total)		☐ Plus; ☒ Minus $ 5500		☒ Plus; ☐ Minus $ 14250		☐ Plus; ☒ Minus $ 19000	
Indicated Value of Subject		$100,500		$105,250		$101,000	

Comments on Market Data   SALES 1 AND 3 MOST NEARLY LIKE SUBJECT PROPERTY

INDICATED VALUE BY MARKET DATA APPROACH	$100,000
INDICATED VALUE BY INCOME APPROACH (If applicable) Economic Market Rent $ 750 /Mo. x Gross Rent Multiplier 130	= $ 97,500

This appraisal is made ☒ "as is" ☐ subject to the repairs, alterations, or conditions listed below ☐ completion per plans and specifications.

Comments and Conditions of Appraisal:

Final Reconciliation: SUFFICIENT DATA TO SUPPORT VALUE OF $100,000 PLUS OR MINUS 2%

Construction Warranty ☒ Yes ☐ No   Name of Warranty Program   HOW   Warranty Coverage Expires 12/31/86

This appraisal is based upon the above requirements, the certification, contingent and limiting conditions, and Market Value definition that are stated in ☒ FHLMC Form 439 (Rev. 10/78)/FNMA Form 1004B (Rev. 10/78) filed with client ___ 19 ___ ☒ attached.

I ESTIMATE THE MARKET VALUE, AS DEFINED, OF SUBJECT PROPERTY AS OF August 14 1986 to be $ 100,000

Appraiser(s) Eva Luston   Review Appraiser (If applicable) Assi Stance

☒ Did   ☐ Did Not Physically Inspect Property

FHLMC Form 70 Rev. 7/79   REVERSE   FNMA Form 1004 Rev. 7/79

Figure 9.7
Competitive Market Analysis

COMPETITIVE MARKET ANALYSIS

CALIFORNIA ASSOCIATION OF REALTORS® STANDARD·FORM

PROPERTY ADDRESS 13515 Tennis Lane, Sylmar _____ DATE. 6-2-81 _____

FOR SALE NOW:	BED-RMS.	BATHS	DEN	SQ. FT.	1ST LOAN	LIST PRICE	DAYS ON MARKET	TERMS
13431 Tennis	3	1	FK	1450	52021	99950	59	10000 c/1, c/nl
13404 Sunshine	2	1	YES	1350	66258	97900	33	700 c/nl
13501 Humor	3	1	FR	1400	58198	89900	12	10% c/1, va
13612 Smile	4	1	CD	1600	69866	95900	44	20% c/nl
4901 Spring	4	1	NO	1500	75784	99000	19	10,000 c/nl
13598 Mellow	3	1	CD	1450	57038	93900	4	9390 c/1 or va or FHA

SOLD PAST 12 MOS.	BED-RMS.	BATHS	DEN	SQ. FT.	1ST LOAN	LIST PRICE	DAYS ON MARKET	DATE SOLD	SALE PRICE	TERMS
13543 Tennis	3	1	FK	1450	46486	95900	9	11/15/80	93000	10%/3300
13546 Tennis	3	1	NO	1450	53322	86900	27	10/1/82	8400	FHA
13613 Tennis	3	1	NO	1400	43962	82950	32	9/11/80	8000	c/1
4915 Ocean	4	1	CD	1450	61680	93900	18	8/14/80	90000	c/nl
13602 Mellow	3	1	NO	1400	54820	86900	12	7/4/80	79950	c/nl
13697 Sunshine	3	1	CD	1400	47238	84000	21	12/18/80	83500	GI

EXPIRED PAST 12 MOS.	BED-RMS.	BATHS	DEN	SQ. FT.	1ST LOAN	LIST PRICE	DAYS ON MARKET	TERMS
4924 Ocean	2	1	AREA	1300	44224	85900	90	ALL CASH
4954 Ocean	2	1	ADDON	1300	53362	86900	120	C/EL
4950 Carefree	3	1	NO	1350	48906	89900	60	C/NL
4902 Carefree	4	1	CD	1450	54240	99000	30	10,000
13630 Tennis	3	1	CD	1400	47538	88000	90	C/NL OR SUBMIT
13911 Mellow	4	1	NO	1400	39224	89500	30	5000 C/NL

F.H.A. ---- V.A. APPRAISALS

ADDRESS	APPRAISAL	ADDRESS	APPRAISAL
13531 Tennis	92000	13602 Mellow	95000
4922 Spring	88000	13516 Humor	90000
13546 Tennis	94000	13777 Sunshine	93500

BUYER APPEAL   MARKETING POSITION

(GRADE EACH ITEM 0 TO 20% ON THE BASIS OF DESIRABILITY OR URGENCY)

1. FINE LOCATION Walk to Fashion Square   20 %
2. EXCITING EXTR. Garage Conv. to playroom 10 %
3. EXTRA SPECIAL FINANCING_____ 20
4. EXCEPTIONAL APPEAL_____ Well Maintained 5 %
5. UNDER MARKET PRICE_____YES____NO_ 0 ,

1. WHY ARE THEY SELLING. Job Transfer _____ 20
2. HOW SOON MUST THEY SELL 90 Days _____ 5
3. WILL THEY HELP FINANCE.................YES 20% ,____ %
4. WILL THEY LIST AT COMPETITIVE MARKET VALUE...YES 20% o____ %
5. WILL THEY PAY FOR APPRAISAL.............YES____NO_ 0 %

RATING TOTAL _____ 55 %   RATING TOTAL _____ 65

ASSETS_ Centrally located to complete shopping facilities, schools, large playroom, pool
DRAWBACKS. No air conditioning, unrepaired damages in pool area_____
AREA MARKET CONDITIONS.Very active, most sales averaging less than one month if priced _____
_competitively
RECOMMENDED TERMS_ 10% down, seller to finance difference between down payment plus new loan and selling price, possible FHA Financing. _____

TOP COMPETITIVE MARKET VALUE.................................$ 88000 to 97000 ____

PROBABLE FINAL SALES PRICE.....................................$ 95000 _____

SELLING COSTS

BROKERAGE	$ 5700	
LOAN PAYOFF	$ 42832	
PREPAYMENT PRIVILEGE	$ 1684	
FHA ---- VA POINTS	$	
TITLE AND ESCROW FEES IRS STAMPS RECONS RECORDING	$ 950	
TERMITE CLEARANCE	$ 160	
MISC PAYOFFS 2ND T D. POOL. PATIO. WTR SFTNR. FENCE. IMPROVEMENT BOND.	$	
	$	
	$	
TOTAL	$	

TOTAL ....$____ 51326

NET PROCEEDS $__ 43674 _____ PLUS OR MINUS $_ 950 _____

For these forms, address California Association of Realtors, 505 Shatto Place, Los Angeles 90020. All rights reserved.

FORM CM 14
REV. 9/64

Figure 9.8
Application of Market Approach

Facts: Good quality 12 year old home, 3 bedrooms, 2 baths, 7 rooms, 1850 square feet; double attached garage, 400 square feet. Three other houses of similar size that sold within the last few months are compared to the subject property.

Comparable Sales

Item:	Property 1	Property 2	Property 3
Price	$114,000	$131,500	$148,000
Location	worse	equal	better
Lot Size	smaller	same	larger
Rooms	6	7	8
Condition	worse	equal	better

Assuming differences of $3,000 for location, $2,000 for lot size, $7,500 for additional rooms, and $2,500 for condition, the following adjustments are made:

Adjusted Prices

Item:	Property 1	Property 2	Property 3
Sale price	$114,000	$131,500	$148,000
Location	+ 3,000	—	− 3,000
Lot Size	+ 2,000	—	− 2,000
Rooms	+ 7,500	—	− 7,500
Condition	+ 2,500	—	− 2,500
Adjusted price	$129,000	$131,500	$133,000

(The adjusted price is the price at which the comparables would have been sold if identical with the subject property).

---

reason the appraiser will look behind sales and transfers to ascertain what influences may have affected sales prices, particularly if only a few comparisons are available.

Some of the advantages of using the market comparison approach are:

1. It is the most easily understood method of valuation and is the most common practice among real estate licensees.
2. It is particularly applicable in the sale or exchange of single-family residences and to financing of such property. These operations make up the bulk of real estate transactions.

Some of the disadvantages of the comparison approach method are:

1. It can sometimes be difficult or impossible to locate enough similar properties which have recently sold.

2. Adjusting amenities and other characteristics to make them comparable with the subject property is often difficult.

Cost Approach

The cost approach is an estimate of the cash amount required to duplicate the property in its present condition. People ordinarily will not pay more for a piece of property than it would cost to replace it, or more than it would cost to obtain an equally satisfactory substitute property. The cost approach, therefore, has a tendency to set the upper limit of value. The application of the cost approach is shown in Figure 9.9.

When using the cost approach, there is a distinction between *replacement* cost and *reproduction* cost. Replacement cost means the cost of replacing the subject improvement with a structure having the same utility and amenities. Reproduction cost is generally regarded as mean-

Figure 9.9
Application of Cost Approach

Facts: Home is 12 years old, estimated life is 40 years.
        Cost per square foot: House: $60
                              Garage: $25
        Lot, 50′ × 100′, $10.00 per square foot

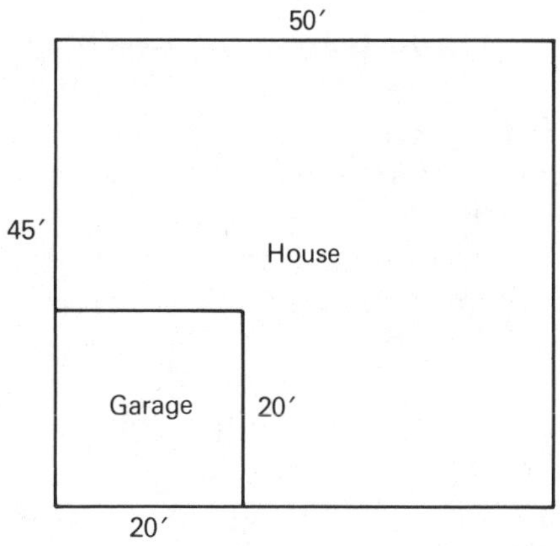

1. House Size: 50′ × 45′ = 2250 sq. feet
      Less   20′ × 20′ = 400

                            1850 sq. feet
   Cost per sq. foot   × $ 60
   Replacement cost new $111,000

2. Garage size: 20′ × 20′   400 sq. feet
   Cost per sq. foot   × $ 25
   Replacement cost new $10,000

3. $111,000 Replacement cost of house
     10,000 Replacement cost of garage
   $121,000 Total replacement cost
   − 36,300 Depreciation: $\frac{100\%}{40 \text{ yrs}}$ = 2.5% annually, × 12 yrs = 30%

4. $ 84,700 Depreciated cost of improvements
     50,000 Lot value: 5000 sq. feet × $10,00
   $134,700 Combined property value (say $130,000)

50′ — House — 45′ — Garage 20′ — 20′

ing the cost that would be incurred if the improvement were to be reproduced exactly. Exact reproduction might well involve materials and construction practices long since outmoded, and thus it is impracticable to estimate such costs. Consequently the cost approach is more appropriately designated the "replacement cost method." However, some appraisals are based on exact reproduction costs, such as those that might be made to determine insurance values.

Let us see how this approach is used to determine the value of residential property. In California the estimate of the cost of replacing buildings is ordinarily made by the square-foot method. This method requires measuring the building and dividing it into units, each usually a rectangle. Multiplying the length of each rectangle by its width produces the square-foot area of that segment. The total square-foot area of the residence is obtained by adding together the square-foot area of all the rectangular segments. The sum obtained is then multiplied by an appropriate con-

struction cost per square foot, depending upon the type of construction involved. The result is considered the replacement cost of the residence. Depreciation is then taken from the replacement cost to give the present value of the improvements. The present value added to the land represents the value of the subject property or at least gives us a fairly accurate indication of the value.

Construction costs are obtainable from local contractors as well as from numerous services which publish building cost data. Actually, building costs vary considerably, based on such factors as the efficiency of the builder and the amount of profit included in such costs. The quality and design of the structures also vary widely.

The cost approach method is frequently used to get a ceiling upon the value established by the other two appraisal methods. Is is particularly appropriate for appraising newly built improvements where the construction represents the highest and best use of the land. It is also the most appropriate method for appraising service-type properties such as public schools, city halls, libraries, etc., since this type of property has no active market and thus lacks market data which could be used for a comparison approach. Further, the income or capitalization approach cannot be used because there is no income on which to base it.

Capitalization or Income Approach

The income approach is concerned with the present worth of future benefits that may be derived from the property and is particularly important in the valuation of income-producing property. An important consideration in this approach is the net income which a fully informed person using good management is warranted in receiving, assuming the property will be productive during the remaining useful life of the improvement.

The procedure used in this approach involves three steps:

1. A net annual income is derived by deducting the total annual expenses from the annual gross income after making proper allowances for vacancies and rental collection losses.
2. A selection is made of an appropriate capitalization rate, i.e., the rate of interest which is considered a reasonable return on the investment. The greater the risk of recapturing the investment price, the higher the capitalization rate should be.
3. The final step, after having determined the net income and the capitalization rate, is to capitalize the income. If the income is considered to be in perpetuity, this step may be merely the mathematical calculation of dividing the income by the rate. By way of example, the valuation of property which has an assumed perpetual annual income of $40,000 and a capitalization rate of 8 percent is $500,000. This figure is obtained as follows:

$$\frac{\$40,000}{.08} = \$500,000$$

The general formula reads

$$\frac{\text{Income}}{\text{Yield Rate}} = \frac{\text{Capitalized Value}}{\text{(Market Value)}}$$

The lower the rate, the greater the valuation and the greater the assumed security of the investment. Conversely, the higher the rate, the lower the indicated value.

There are many technical procedures involved in this as well as other methods of appraisal. The foregoing is a brief introduction to real estate appraisal, and acquaints you with the basic terms and techniques in the appraisal process.

Figure 9.10 illustrates the application of the income approach.

Other appraisal terms that should be familiar to the real estate broker and salesperson are *gross annual multiplier, gross monthly multiplier,* and *gross rent multiplier (GRM).* The terms are used in connection with older residential property, and are based upon the market relationship between rental value and the sale price of such properties. For instance a certain type of property may be sold at 100 times the monthly gross income. Accordingly, a property with a projected gross income of $2000 per month would have an indicated value of $200,000.

The multiplier is more commonly stated in annual terms such as "8 times gross." If the income from a property is $24,000 per year, the indicated value is 8 × $24,000, or $192,600. Gross multipliers are simply a device to compare one investment property to others, based upon *quantity* of income only. GRMs do not say anything, however, about the *quality* of the income (i.e., the net income).

Gross *monthly* multipliers are frequently used as part of the appraisal process for single-family residential properties and for small income-producing properties. Gross *annual* multipliers, in contrast, are commonly used to estimate the value of larger income-producing properties, particularly apartment houses.

Metric Conversions

The appraisal process involves the use of measurements to a considerable extent. Figure 9.11 is a sample of an appraisal including metric conversion computations.

DEPRECIATION

Depreciation is a factor in the appraisal process, and we should know its meaning. It is briefly defined as a loss in value from any cause. It is customarily measured by estimating the difference between the current replacement cost new and the estimated value of the property as of the date of appraisal.

Figure 9.10
Application of Income Approach

Facts: Ten-unit apartment building, each apartment renting for $500. Vacancies and collection allowances are 5 percent of the gross scheduled income.

Operating Expenses: Management $3,000
Insurance $2,000
Property tax $4,500
Utilities $2,500
Maintenance and repairs $2,800
Miscellaneous (licenses, supplies, etc.) $1,200
Depreciation $7,000

Assume a capitalization rate of 8 percent.

Steps:

1. Gross scheduled income ($500 × 10 units × 12 months)	$60,000
2. Less: vacancies and collections allowances ($60,000 × 5 percent)	3,000
3. Gross operating income (or effective gross)	$57,000
4. Less: Operating expenses (management, utilities, maintenance and repairs, insurance, property taxes)	$16,000
5. Net operating income	$41,000

6. Indicated Value $= \dfrac{\text{Net operating income}}{\text{Capitalization rate}} = \dfrac{\$41,000}{8\%} =$ $512,500

Note: Depreciation has been ignored in the computation. While depreciation is used in determining taxable income, it is not an operating expense.

Depreciation includes all the influences that reduce the value of a property below its replacement cost new. The principal influences are usually grouped under three general headings and futher divided as follows:

1. Physical deterioration, resulting from
   a. Wear and tear from use
   b. Negligent care
   c. Severe changes in temperature
   d. Damage by termites, dry rot, etc.
2. Functional obsolescence, resulting from
   a. Poor architectural design and style
   b. Lack of modern facilities
   c. Out-of-date equipment
   d. Changes in styles of construction
   e. Changes in construction methods and materials
   f. Changes in utility demand
3. Economic and social obsolescence, resulting from
   a. Misplacement of improvements
   b. Zoning or other legislative limitations in use
   c. Detrimental influence of supply and demand
   d. Change of location demand
   e. Excessive property tax rates

Figure 9.12 is illustrative of these three principal influences.

When applying the depreciation factor to residential property, an appraiser will pay special attention to such items as the overall condition of the building; the interior fixtures, plans, and workmanship; interior decoration; plumbing and heating; type of roof; landscaping; foundation and underpinnings; damp areas, etc. The difficulties of correctly estimating depreciation tend to increase with the age of the improvement. Experience and good judgment are among the necessary qualifications for making a realistic estimate of depreciation.

In this chapter we have discussed depreciation from an appraisal point of view. In Chapter 13 another type of depreciation will be introduced in connection with income taxation and investments. Then we will be concerned with the

WHICH PROPERTY IS WORTH MORE?

Home A

Home B

1. While Home B may appear to be the better of the two, it may be in a poor area, or about to topple over due to a mudslide.
2. Home A may be located in a prestigious neighborhood surrounded by $200,000 houses.

Conclusion: One cannot judge a property's value *solely* by its appearance.

Figure 9.11
Sample of Appraisal Including Metric Conversion Computations

SALE			PARCEL AREA				INDICATED PRICE PER UNIT			
Sale No.	Time of Sale	Price	Square Feet	Square Meters	Acres	Hectares	$ Per Sq. Ft.	$ Per Sq. Meter	$ Per Acre	$ Per Hectare
1	1/81	$105,000	228,690	21,246	5.25	2.12	$0.46	$4.94	$20,000	$49,530
2	12/80	$72,500	137,200	12,747	3.15	1.27	0.53	5.69	23,000	57,080
3	2/81	$68,000	126,300	11,734	2.90	1.17	0.54	5.80	23,450	58,100
4	1/81	$18,750	32,650	3,033	0.75	0.30	0.57	6.18	25,000	62,500
5	3/81	$17,000	27,000	2,508	0.62	0.25	0.63	6.78	27,400	68,000
6	2/81	$93,400	180,750	16,794	4.15	1.68	0.52	5.56	22,500	55,600
SUBJECT PARCEL 260' × 500' or 79.25 Meters × 152.40 Meters			130,000	12,078	2.98	1.21	$0.55	$5.92	$24,000	PARCEL VALUE $71,500* $59.200

*Note: After analysis and adjustments for time of sale, location, size and shape etc., appraiser concluded that the effective unit value for the subject parcel is $24,000 per acre (equivalent to $59,200 per hectare, $0.55 per square foot or $5.92 per square meter). Extending those unit values to the parcel area leads to an estimated parcel value for the subject property of $71,500.00

1 Sq. Meter = 10,764 Sq. Ft.   1 Acre = 0.4046 Hectares   1 Hectare = 2,471 Acres   1 Acre = 43,560 Sq. Ft.

Figure 9.12
Depreciation

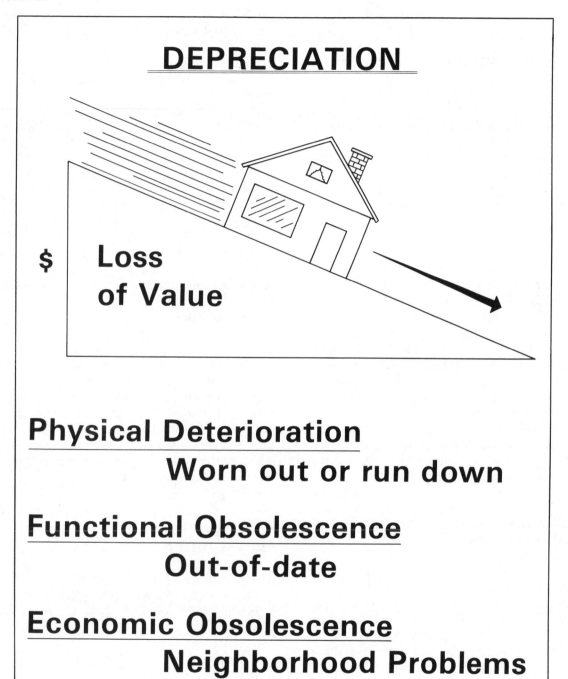

DEPRECIATION

$ | Loss of Value

Physical Deterioration
Worn out or run down

Functional Obsolescence
Out-of-date

Economic Obsolescence
Neighborhood Problems

accountant's treatment of depreciation, which involves bookkeeping entries that may bear no correlation to an actual loss in value.

ROLE OF THE PROFESSIONAL APPRAISER

Importance of Accurate Appraisals

The importance of the appraisal in our economy cannot be overemphasized. Accurate appraisals are of vital concern in many areas of real estate. As in many other businesses and professions, there have been times when real estate appraisers have been under attack. Government officials, lenders, and real estate people at times have asserted that many appraisers were giving in to the unrealistic demands of their clients and setting excessive values on property. Such appraisals were used in attempts to bring owners of condemned property inflated awards from government agencies, or to enable borrowers and lenders to get around legal restrictions on the size of real estate loans. In most states, as in California, the size of mortgage loans made by banks and other lending institutions is limited to a certain percentage of the appraised value of the property. Some lenders in the past have been known to urge appraisers to build up property values to support larger loans. Some lenders allegedly were even "shopping around" for liberal appraisals. Evidently some were finding them, as it became necessary at one time for the California savings and loan commissioner to order a number of state-chartered lending institutions to set aside substantial reserves against possible losses on mortgage loans they had made.

In response to the criticisms, the appraiser's own professional societies stepped up their efforts to prevent ethical violations among their members. Actually, flagrant abuses of their responsibilities by members of professional groups are rare. Appraiser groups have attempted to ward off any future criticism by setting their own house in order. The first such groups were formed as long ago as the 1930s when the general collapse of real estate values also provoked a wave of criticism of appraisers and their standards. Today, there are professional associations pledged to maintain the highest ethical standards in the appraisal process.

Professional Associations

The American Institute of Real Estate Appraisers was founded in 1932 as an affiliate of NAR. Its members use the designation MAI (Member, Appraisal Institute). The institute is dedicated to the furtherance of the art and skill of appraising, has adopted a code of ethics, and publishes a magazine called the *Appraisal Journal*. It has also pioneered the development of appraisal texts and college courses in appraisal throughout the United States.

Another professional group is the Society of Residential Appraisers, founded in 1935. The society was sponsored by member organizations of the United States League of Savings and Loan, which is primarily concerned with mortgage loans on residential properties throughout the United States.

Still another appraisal group is the Society of Real Estate Appraisers. Its members use the designation SRA. It was founded with the following purpose: "To elevate the standards of the appraisal profession, to aid in the solution of the many problems of the profession in appraising real estate, and to designate certain members as having attained certain skills and knowledge." The members are pledged to maintain a high level of trust and integrity in their practice.

The Society of Real Estate Appraisers has adopted a Code of Ethics and Standards of Professional Practice, which is included as Appendix E. It serves as an excellent summary of the appraisal process, the caliber of the professional appraiser, and the ethical concepts applicable to members of a professional organization.

SUMMARY OF FACTORS INFLUENCING THE VALUE OF A HOME

There are innumerable factors that influence the value of a home or its selling price, and the following list includes many of these items (not necessarily in the order of their importance, except for item 1):

Location—location—location
Size (area)
Age of the structure
Condition of the improvements
Style of architecture and type of construction
Scarcity, i.e., supply and demand
General economic condition
Economic base of the area, i.e., the ability of the area to support itself economically
Quality of the environment—air, water, noise, etc.
Quality of the neighborhood

Accessibility
Water—source, quality, quantity, cost
Tax rate
Utilities, including TV reception—cost
Cost of maintenance, repairs and upkeep
Sewers and drainage
Security—police and fire protection
Insurance rates in the area, both for home and auto
Amenities, such as sauna or pool, workshop, etc.
Prevailing weather conditions—how they will affect the property
Political environment

QUESTIONS FOR CHAPTER 9

Matching Terms

a. value
b. to appraise
c. adjustments
d. amenities
e. comparables
f. appraisal
g. market approach
h. capitalize
i. physical deterioration
j. plottage
k. cost-push inflation
l. economic base
m. functional obsolescence
n. demand-pull inflation
o. economic obsolescence

____ 1. an expert's opinion as to the value of a parcel of property
____ 2. establishing value by ascertaining what other properties have sold for
____ 3. depreciation resulting from wear and tear of the improvements
____ 4. loss of value due to external forces or events
____ 5. joining of two or more adjacent parcels of land to form a single, larger parcel
____ 6. higher prices due to buyers bidding against each other
____ 7. higher prices due to increased cost of labor and materials
____ 8. to estimate a property's value
____ 9. depreciation resulting from outmoded improvements
____ 10. properties similar to property being appraised that are used to determine value
____ 11. corrections made to comparable properties in the market value approach to account for differences
____ 12. ability of a region to exchange goods or services with other regions
____ 13. to convert future income to current value
____ 14. intangible or other benefits in real property ownership that add to value or enjoyment
____ 15. what property is worth to an owner

True/False

T F 16. Economic obsolescence is loss of value resulting from wear and tear of the improvements.
T F 17. To capitalize is basically to convert future income to current value.
T F 18. Economic obsolescence is loss of value resulting from improvements that are inadequate or improperly designed for today's needs.
T F 19. Functional obsolescence is loss of value due to external forces or events.
T F 20. Corrosion of metals (rust) is an example of physical deterioration.
T F 21. Ancient plumbing is an example of economic or social obsolescence.
T F 22. Population decrease is an example of functional obsolescence.
T F 23. In order to ascertain value by the capitalization approach, you multiply the rate of return by the annual income.
T F 24. Replacement cost of a destroyed building is generally much higher than reproduction cost.
T F 25. Properties similar to the subject property that are used to estimate the value of the subject property are called *comparables*.

Multiple Choice

26. Functional obsolescence basically is caused by
    a. directional growth
    b. zoning
    c. outmoded improvements
    d. structural damage
27. In using the market data approach, which one of the following comparisons would have the least value in appraising a single-family home?
    a. sales in other parts of the town
    b. new homes in the area
    c. old homes in the area
    d. distress sale of a home in the area

28. "Value of the whole is greater than the sum of the individual parts" is a concept best illustrated by
    a. zoning
    b. obsolescence
    c. plottage
    d. directional growth
29. Value in use, that is, subjective value, best describes
    a. market value
    b. cash value
    c. book value
    d. utility value
30. In the appraisal of residential property, the cost approach is most appropriate in the case of
    a. new property
    b. property constructed ten years ago
    c. property constructed twenty years ago
    d. property constructed over fifty years ago
31. Which of the following is the best example of physical deterioration?
    a. zoning change
    b. termination of deed restrictions
    c. neighborhood decline
    d. termite and dry rot damage
32. The income approach would be most appropriate in the case of
    a. raw land
    b. apartment house
    c. owner-occupied home
    d. governmental building
33. Which of the following is ordinarily not a purpose for making an appraisal?
    a. condemnation
    b. commission
    c. mortgage loan
    d. insurance
34. In appraising a home, you are asked to specify the square footage. This represents the
    a. interior measurement of each room
    b. exterior dimensions of the building
    c. size of the lot
    d. length, width, and height of the building
35. An apartment house contains five units, each renting for $400 per month. The vacancy factor is 7 percent. Operating costs total $7,200. At 8 percent capitalization, the value of the property is
    a. $189,000
    b. $158,250
    c. $205,000
    d. $192,000

36. An appraisal is an estimate of value
    a. for a period of six months
    b. as of a specified date
    c. for a reasonable period
    d. for a period of one year
37. The rate of return on property costing $100,000 and yielding a net return of $8,000 is
    a. 10 percent
    b. $12\frac{1}{2}$ percent
    c. 15 percent
    d. 8 percent
38. The market comparison approach is most suitable for the appraisal of
    a. apartment projects
    b. commercial properties
    c. single dwellings
    d. schools
39. An appraisal report which details all pertinent facts and includes charts and photographs is a
    a. letter report
    b. narrative report
    c. short form report
    d. none of the above
40. Essential elements or characteristics of value would not include
    a. scarcity
    b. utility
    c. transferability
    d. conformity
41. A roof that leaks in rainy weather is a typical example of
    a. economic obsolescence
    b. curable obsolescence
    c. social obsolescence
    d. amenity value
42. Valuation of real property is important in connection with
    a. taxation
    b. insurance
    c. condemnation
    d. all of the above
43. Determining the value of property by considering net income and percentage of reasonable return on the investment is known as
    a. amortization
    b. depreciation
    c. appreciation
    d. capitalization

44. Fundamental to the concept of value is the *highest and best use*. This can be best defined as
    a. contributing to the best interest of the community
    b. complying with zoning and deed restrictions
    c. producing the highest gross income
    d. producing the greatest net return on an investment over a given period of time
45. Value of property is generally comparable to
    a. cost
    b. price
    c. use
    d. worth
46. The value of property that earns a net income of $540 per month capitalized at 5 percent is
    a. $108,000
    b. $129,600
    c. $ 64,000
    d. $115,000
47. The integration of a much more expensive home into a neighborhood of smaller, modest homes will most likely
    a. greatly increase the value of the smaller homes
    b. bring the value of the more expensive home down to the exact amount as the smaller homes
    c. severely reduce the value of the more expensive home when compared to location in a neighborhood of similar homes
    d. not exert any influence that might result in economic obsolescence
48. Market value is the price for which property can be sold in the open market if there is a
    a. willing buyer and willing seller
    b. reasonable time period to effect a sale
    c. sufficient knowledge by buyer and seller
    d. all of the above
49. An example of economic obsolescence is
    a. excessive tax rates
    b. change in construction style
    c. outmoded fixtures
    d. cracked foundation
50. A loss in value from any cause is referred to as
    a. wear and tear
    b. deflation
    c. depreciation
    d. obsolescence

10

INVOLUNTARY LIENS, HOMESTEADS, AND REAL PROPERTY TAXES

A lien is an encumbrance on land. All liens are encumbrances but not all encumbrances are liens. Real property is subject to two basic types of encumbrances: those of a financial nature which give a creditor a security interest, and those which in some way limit or have an effect on the physical use of the land. Two frequently encountered use limitations—private deed restrictions and zoning—will be discussed in Chapter 12. Another type of use limitation is an easement, which we already encountered in Chapter 2 when we considered ownership interests in real property.

In this chapter we will discuss various types of liens that can attach to real property; liens, however, that are not voluntarily created by the owner, as in the case of a mortgage or trust deed which we considered in Chapters 7 and 8, but that are imposed or created by operation of law. In this latter category are real property taxes and assessments. Priority becomes of primary importance in the case of a foreclosure of a lien, and we will find that taxes and assessments have ongoing priority over later recorded liens. We will also discuss the protection afforded a homeowner under the state homestead laws with respect to certain types of liens.

CLASSIFICATION AND TYPES OF LIENS

A lien is a charge imposed on property by means of which the interest in the property becomes security for the performance of an act, usually the payment of money.

Liens are ordinarily classified by the manner in which they are created, either by voluntary action, such as a trust deed, or by operation of law, such as taxes and assessments, judgments, attachments, executions, and mechanics' liens. Liens created by operation of law are known as *involuntary* liens.

As we saw in Chapter 7, one of the most frequently encountered liens, apart from real property taxes, is created by the deed of trust (traditionally used in California in lieu of a mortgage). Other liens in the involuntary category frequently encountered are execution liens, judgment liens and mechanic's liens, and less frequently encountered are attachment liens. Figure 10.1 illustrates these various types of liens.

INVOLUNTARY LIENS

There are several types of involuntary liens, as is apparent from Figure 10.1. Discussion of some of these follows.

Judgment Liens

A *judgment lien* is a statutory lien that is created by recording an abstract or certified copy of a money judgment in the office of the county recorder. A *judgment* is described as the decree of a court of law setting out the final determination of the rights of contending parties in a court action. The kind of judgment we are concerned with here is one resulting from an action for money.

Before the judgment can constitute a lien on property, an abstract or certified copy of the judgment will need to be recorded. As a rule, the judgment does not describe any specific property. However, immediately upon recording, the judgment becomes a lien on all real property, not exempt, owned or acquired by the debtor in the county where the judgment is recorded. The lien continues for a period of ten years from date of entry of the judgment, and can be renewed if the judgment is not satisfied during that period.

Attachment Liens

An *attachment lien* is obtainable in certain types of actions prior to a judgment being entered by levy of a *writ of attachment*. Under this procedure, the plaintiff may cause property of the defendant to be seized and retained in the custody of the law any time after the filing of a complaint. The attachment is a lien upon the property seized for a period of three years after the day of levy of the writ of attachment. The property cannot be sold under a writ of attachment; it can only be retained in the custody of the court pending the outcome of the lawsuit.

At one time attachments were quite common, but changes in the law have limited the remedy substantially. Attachment without notice to the property owner and a hearing held before the property is levied upon violate due process of law, and such procedure is unconstitutional.

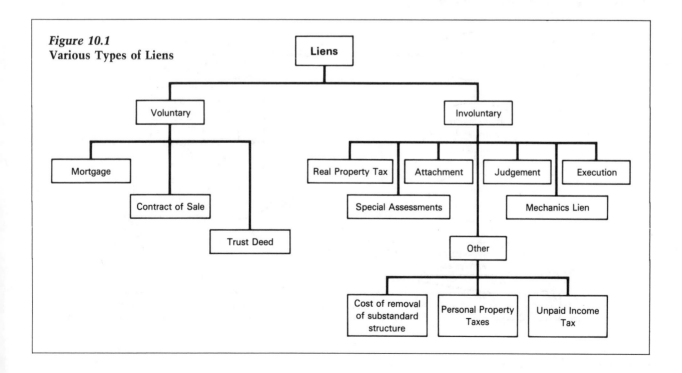

Figure 10.1
Various Types of Liens

Execution Liens

An *execution lien* is obtained by the levy of a *writ of execution* on specific property of the defendant. It can be levied *after* a judgment has been entered. Unless the property is exempt from execution, the property can be sold by the sheriff under the writ and the proceeds used to satisfy the judgment in full or in part, depending on the value of the property and the amount bid at the sale. A *certificate of sale* is issued to the purchaser at the execution sale and, if redemption is not made within a year, a *sheriff's deed* is issued to the holder of the certificate. If, after levy of a writ of execution, the property for some reason is not sold, the execution nonetheless continues as a lien for a period of one year.

Mechanics' Liens

A mechanic's lien is a statutory lien in favor of persons who furnish labor or materials and who have thus contributed to a work of improvement on someone else's property. The mechanic's lien law is based on the theory that improvements contribute additional value to land. Therefore, it is only equitable to impose a charge on the land equal to such increase in value in favor of those who performed services or furnished materials. Accordingly, an unpaid contractor or a craftsman employed by the contractor may protect his or her interest by filing a lien against the property in the manner and within the time prescribed by law. Lien claimants have a period of *ninety days* after completion of the improvement within which to file a lien. This ninety-day period can be shortened to *sixty days* for the general contractor and *thirty days* for other lien claimants if the owner of the land records a *notice of completion* within ten days after completion of the structure. If the lien claimant is not paid, he or she has the right to file an action to foreclose the lien within ninety days after the date of filing his or her lien. The property can then be sold in satisfaction of the judgment in a manner similar to an execution sale.

In order to obtain the benefit of the mechanic's lien law, the potential lien claimant must give a written preliminary notice to the landowner, the general contractor, and the construction lender within twenty days of the furnishing of labor, equipment, or materials.

The priority of the lien goes back to the date when the work of improvement first commenced

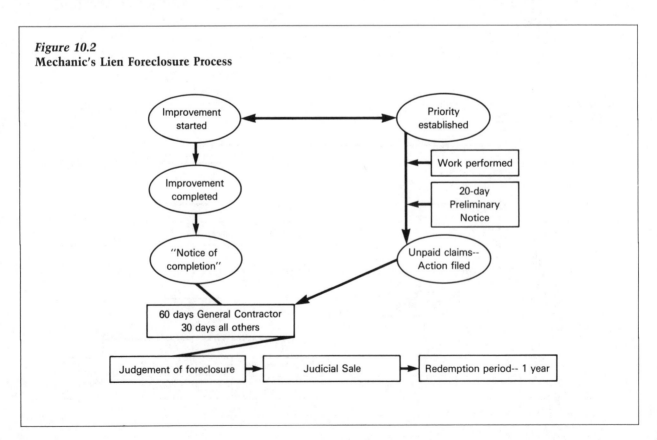

Figure 10.2
Mechanic's Lien Foreclosure Process

on the ground. Thus, the date of recording a lien doesn't determine priority. Priority of a mechanic's lien relates back to the date when the work of improvement first began, including preliminary clearing of the land. In legal language this is referred to as the "doctrine of relating back."

If a lessee or a contract purchaser causes the property to be improved, the legal owner may be relieved of responsibility for payment of the cost of improvement by recording a *notice of nonresponsibility* within ten days from the time he or she first finds out that the property is being improved. The lien claimants can then look only to the interests of the people who hired them and not to the legal owner's interest in the real property for payment of their lien. Figure 10.2 briefly shows the mechanic's lien foreclosure process.

IMPACT OF THE HOMESTEAD LAW ON CERTAIN LIENS

A homestead is a right or privilege given by the California Constitution and state statutes to provide shelter for the family and its members, and to prevent the forced sale of such dwelling for the payment of certain unpaid obligations. It is a matter of public policy and a right recognized for a long period of time in this state. The rationale seems to be that it is better for a creditor to wait for payment rather than have a family forced out into the street. The principal purpose is to shield the home against creditors of certain types whose claims might be exercised through judgment lien enforcement.

At one time, in order to obtain protection the homeowner was required to record a Declaration of Homestead *prior* to the recordation of an abstract or certified copy of a judgment. Figure 10.3 illustrates such a form of homestead. You will notice that it must be both *acknowledged* and *verified*.

Today there are two types of homesteads: the *Declared Homestead* and the *Dwelling House Exemption*. The latter can be claimed after proceedings are undertaken by a judgment creditor to effect a sale of the property, and is available to everyone qualifying without having previously recorded a declaration of homestead. The amount of protection afforded by each type of homestead is basically the same.

Some people think that a recorded homestead will absolutely protect against a sale of the property; it doesn't. Certain liens can still be enforced, such as mechanics' liens, the lien of a mortgage or trust deed, and real property taxes and assessments. Nor does it totally save a person's equity in the property. What it does protect is the amount of a homeowner's equity over and above recorded liens on the property up to the amount of the applicable exemption. A creditor might still be able to force the sale of homesteaded property if the creditor can establish that there is surplus equity in excess of liens and the amount of the exemption.

The exemption amounts have increased substantially over the years and are presently $45,000 for a member of a family unit and $30,000 for other persons, with an increase to $55,000 if the claimant is 65 years of age or older or is under a disability and unable to work.

A *dwelling* within the meaning of the homestead law is a place where a person actually resides, and may include a house, a mobile home, a boat or other waterborne vessel, a condominium, a planned unit development, a stock cooperative, or a community apartment project.

The definition of a "dwelling" means an interest in real property that is in fact a dwelling place, but excludes a leasehold estate with an unexpired term of less than two years at the time of filing a homestead declaration.

The validity of a declared homestead cannot be assumed solely from the recordation of a Declaration of Homestead that appears to be in proper form, because its validity depends on certain off-record matters. A Declared Homestead is considered to be invalid if

1. The declarant was not actually living on the property at the date of selection of the homestead
2. The property is not, in fact, a proper subject of homestead
3. In the case of a marital homestead, the purported husband and wife were not legally married

A declared homestead continues until the property is sold or an abandonment of homestead is recorded. A homestead declaration does not restrict or limit the right to convey or encumber the declared homestead.

Another type of homestead is referred to as a *Probate Homestead*. This type may be created in probate proceedings by court order in the absence of a recorded homestead in order to protect those in protective custody of the court, such as widows with minor children, those unable to care for

Figure 10.3
Declaration of Homestead

RECORDING REQUESTED BY

Real Estate Clinic

AND WHEN RECORDED MAIL TO

Name
Street
Address
City &
State

Real Estate Clinic
6511 Van Nuys Blvd.
Van Nuys, CA 91401

─── SPACE ABOVE THIS LINE FOR RECORDER'S USE ───

DECLARATION OF HOMESTEAD

(JOINT DECLARATION OF HUSBAND AND WIFE)

◆

Charles Hart   and   Shirley Hart
(Name of Husband)   (Name of Wife)

do severally certify and declare as follows:

(1) They are husband and wife.

(2) Charles Hart   is the head of a family, consisting of himself and
(Name of Husband)

Shirley Hart
(Name of Wife)

(3) They are now residing on the land and premises located in the City of   North Hollywood

County of   Los Angeles   , State of California, and more particularly described as follows:

Lot 3, Block 7, Tract 1492, recorded in Maps,
Book 2, Page 16, in L.A. County on July 14, 1948

and commonly known as   6835 Bellaire St., No. Hollywood, CA

(4) They claim the land and premises hereinabove described together with the dwelling house thereon, and its appurtenances, as a Homestead.

(5) No former declaration of homestead has been made by them, or by either of them, except as follows:[1]

(6) The character of said property so sought to be homesteaded, and the improvements thereon may generally be described as follows:[2]
A single family dwelling
IN WITNESS WHEREOF, they have hereunto set their hands this 2d   day of   May   19 86

Charles Hart
(Husband)

Shirley Hart
(Wife)

Footnotes 1 and 2: See Reverse Side.

STATE OF CALIFORNIA }
                      } ss.
COUNTY OF_____ }

On_____, 19_____
before me, the undersigned, a Notary Public in and for said State,
personally appeared_____
_____
_____
and_____
_____

known to me to be the persons whose names are subscribed to the within instrument, and severally acknowledged to me that they executed the same.
Witness my hand and official seal.

_____
Notary Public in and for said State.

STATE OF CALIFORNIA }
                      } ss.
COUNTY OF_____ }

and_____
husband and wife, each, being first duly sworn, deposes and says: That he/she is one of the declarants in the foregoing declaration of homestead; that he/she has read the foregoing declaration and knows the contents thereof, and that the matters therein stated are true of his/her own knowledge.

_____
(Husband)

_____
(Wife)

Subscribed and Sworn to before me on

_____, 19_____

_____
Notary Public in and for said State.

themselves, and certain others whom the court believes should be protected.

Homesteads under the state law are distinguishable from the term "homesteading" as applied to filings on federal lands whereby a person acquired title to acreage by establishing residence or making improvements upon the land. The purpose of the federal homestead laws was to encourage settlement of the nation, but today, except for Alaska, homesteading has been discontinued on federal lands.

Application of the Homestead Exemption

1. Persons who are married or head of a family unit (head of household) with certain exceptions noted above, are exempt for up to $45,000 of the equity. In the examples which follow, the first shows an equity below $45,000 so that the equity would be insufficient for creditors to reach. In the second example, there is an equity surplus, so that the excess is reachable by creditors.

   a. Insufficient equity:

Fair market value of residence	$100,000
Less amount of loans secured by home	− 70,000
Equity	$ 30,000

   b. Sufficient Equity:

Fair market value of residence	$100,000
Less amount of loans secured by home	− 30,000
Equity	$ 70,000

2. For all other parties, that is, for those who are single and under the age of 65 (and not head of household), the exemption is $30,000 of the equity.

   a. Insufficient Equity:

Fair market value	$100,000
Liens	− 75,000
Equity	$ 25,000

   b. Sufficient Equity:

Fair market value	$100,000
Liens	− 25,000
Equity	$ 75,000

INTRODUCTION TO THE TAXING PROCESS

In this section we consider real property taxation and other taxes that have an impact on real property ownership. Property taxation is one of the main sources of funds for operating the govern-

ment, and there is an ever present need to raise more funds because costs of operating the government constantly increase.

Two of the main contributing factors to increased governmental costs are population growth and urbanization. An urban industrial society places much greater responsibilities on state and local governments than did the agricultural society of the past. In California, more than 85 percent of the population is concentrated in ten urban centers. This concentration of people means increased demand for police, fire, and health protection.

People have come to expect and demand more services available through centralized or governmental operation, and perhaps to realize many social benefits possible through such cooperative aid. Increased pressure for police, fire, and health protection, and well-maintained streets and public facilities result in the need for greater revenues. Government also suffers the effects of inflation when obsolete or vandalized facilities must be replaced at an increasing rate and at an ever-higher cost.

It has been estimated that each new household unit in an urban area of California creates a demand for at least $30,000 worth of equipment and facilities for classrooms, police, fire protection, freeways, water, sewage, waste disposal, recreation, and other social services.

It is generally agreed that if orderly community and economic growth are to be realized, private citizens and business must be willing to allocate a share of their income to finance the services of the government. There are four main sources of taxes:

1. From property, including special assessments
2. From income
3. From business and franchises
4. From gift and estate or inheritance taxes

Others, such as documentary taxes discussed in Chapter 3, play a very minor role in the total revenue picture.

A big problem today is how to spread the taxes to a point where everyone bears a fair share of the tax burden. One issue is what role real property taxes should play in financing local government, including the schools. Another major problem is that of people on fixed incomes who own real property on which they must pay taxes. These people have difficulty in meeting the rising cost of living since their incomes fail to rise as well. The pressure of inflation on such people is

Figure 10.4
Where Do Taxes Go? Typical County Expenditures

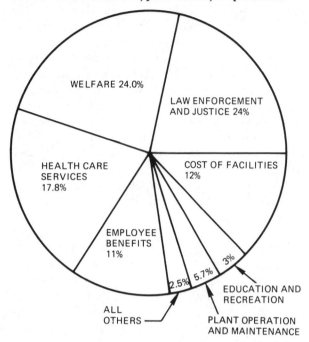

WELFARE 24.0%

LAW ENFORCEMENT AND JUSTICE 24%

HEALTH CARE SERVICES 17.8%

COST OF FACILITIES 12%

EMPLOYEE BENEFITS 11%

2.5% 5.7% 3%

ALL OTHERS

EDUCATION AND RECREATION

PLANT OPERATION AND MAINTENANCE

reflected in the continued trend toward exempting and crediting their real estate taxes.

Los Angeles County property owners paid approximately one billion dollars in property taxes for the fiscal year 1977-78, immediately after which the Jarvis-Gann Amendment, or Proposition 13, became effective. This amendment to the state constitution thereafter placed strict limitations to taxing practices, as noted later. Figure 10.4 shows typical allocation of taxes for local government services.

THE GENERAL NATURE OF TAXES

A tax is defined as a *burden* or *charge* imposed on persons or property by the sovereign authority, to raise money for the support of the government. By virtue of taxes the authority is able to discharge its functions. In a sense, taxes are part of what we pay to maintain a civilized society. Stated briefly, a tax is a *levy* (collection of assessment), under authority of law, for governmental purposes. Because of their importance to the government, some taxes are paramount to all other claims and liens against property.

The exercise of the taxing authority has long been a source of concern. You will recall that "taxation without representation" was a primary complaint in colonial times in America and was a moving factor in the American Revolution. Even today we hear of tax revolt.

However, the authority to tax is an essential aspect of government, and there is no escape from the need to tax property, real and personal. In order to have a valid tax, four essentials must be present:

1. A duly constituted taxing authority
2. Property within the jurisdiction of the taxing authority
3. The property legally subject to tax (not exempt)
4. Due process of law, which means notice and opportunity for a hearing

The source of the taxing authority in California is the state constitution. The constitution provides that all property in the state, not exempt under the laws of the United States, shall be taxed in proportion to its value, except as otherwise provided. The word *property* means money, credits, bonds, stocks, dues, franchises, and all other things—real, personal, and mixed—capable of private ownership, except mortgages or trust deeds or other security transactions affecting land. Various exemptions are contained in the state constitution, including property used for free public libraries and free museums; public schools and church or parochial schools; religious, hospital, and charitable institutions. Various other exemptions are applicable, including those for military service and for certain households. Ordinarily, exemptions must be claimed annually by filing a prescribed affidavit prior to a specified date.

REAL PROPERTY TAXES

The concept of land as the basis of taxation began to take shape in the Middle Ages. It was assumed that taxes should be assessed in accordance with a person's ability to pay. In those times, the extent and quality of a man's agricultural holdings were a dependable index of his ability to pay taxes, because his income was derived almost entirely from agricultural products. It therefore followed that land became a guide for determining the amount of tax to be levied. Other reasons for the popularity of real property taxation are the facts that land is easily assessable, its ownership cannot be effectively concealed, and it always remains within the locale.

In California both cities and counties are

empowered to levy and collect property taxes. Real property taxes are levied annually by each county on taxable property within its borders, and by each city on the taxable property within the city. Most cities delegate the levy and collection of their taxes to the county, and the general procedures for assessment and collection are substantially the same. Only one city in Los Angeles County, namely Pasadena, continues to do its own assessing, rather than utilizing the assessing, collecting, and assessment appeals service of Los Angeles County.

County Assessor's Role

The first step in the taxing of property is the determination of its value in relation to the value of all other property to be taxed, so that no substantial inequality or unfairness will result. This job is performed by the *county tax assessor*, an elected official whose legal responsibility requires him or her each year to discover, list, and appraise all taxable property in his or her jurisdiction. This assessment is made *annually* to the person owning, claiming, possessing, or controlling the property on the *lien date*. The lien date in California is March 1 of each year.

The assessor is not the tax collector and has nothing to do with the total amount of taxes collected. The assessor's function is to ascertain the fair market value of taxable property within the county. To do this, all property to be assessed is reviewed, then valued. Finding the market value of property is basically a matter of discovering the price most people would pay for it.

The assessor maintains an *assessment roll*, which lists and shows the assessed value of all taxable property within the assessor's jurisdiction. The assessor prepares this from all available data with respect to the property, and establishes the values in detail and under the appropriate divisions, i.e., land, improvements, mineral interest (if separately owned), etc.

The assessor can find the market value of any piece of property in at least three different ways, subject only to the limitations of Proposition 13, discussed later in this section.

The first way is to find similar properties that were sold recently. Their selling prices, however, must be analyzed very carefully to make sure the comparison is reasonable. Another property may have been sold for more than it was really worth because the buyer was in a hurry to occupy the property and would pay a greater price to be able to move in right away. Conversely, a seller may have sold his or her property for less than it was actually worth in order to cash out in a hurry.

A second way is based on how much money it would take, at current material and labor costs, to replace the property with one just like it.

A third way is applicable where the property produces rental income, such as an apartment house, a store, or a factory. The assessor then considers such dollar factors as the owner's operating expenses, taxes, insurance, maintenance costs, the degree of financial risk the owner takes in earning income from the property, and, finally, the return most people would expect to get on this kind of property.

As we can see, the assessor uses methods of determining value similar to the principal methods of appraising property considered in Chapter 9.

Proposition 13

On June 6, 1978 one of the most sweeping and radical changes to property assessment and taxation practices was voted into law. Proposition 13, the so-called Jarvis-Gann initiative, provided for a rollback in assessed value of real property to the March 1, 1975 lien date, subject to an annual increase by an inflationary factor of 2 percent. The 2 percent is fixed into the state constitution, and the taxable value is not affected by depreciation or appreciation. This valuation is also subject to an adjustment in the event that a purchase, new construction, alterations which change the use of the land or existing improvements, major rehabilitation, or a change in ownership has taken place since the 1975 lien date. If the property had undergone such a change, it is reappraised. If the new value is higher, the tax will be increased; if the reappraisal is lower, the tax will be decreased.

New Construction. New construction means any addition or improvement to land, including alterations of existing improvements if the alterations result in conversion to another use or an extension of the economic life of the improvement. An example of a taxable alteration would be anything that increases the usefulness of the structure, such as the addition of a bedroom or bathroom. Construction, reconstruction, or alteration performed for the purpose of routine or normal maintenance and repair would not trigger Proposition 13. Thus, interior or exterior painting, replacement of roof coverings, or the addition of aluminum siding would not be taxable. An example of an alteration which does *not* result in an increased usefulness of existing facilities is the modernization of a kitchen.

The second major provision of "Prop 13" is the tax itself. Prop 13 limits the maximum amount of any tax on real property to one percent of the market value (plus the amount needed to pay for any bonded indebtedness approved by the voters).

Guidelines for Reappraisal. What constitutes a "change" for purposes of establishing a new valuation is not always easy to define. However, guidelines have· been established by the State Board of Equalization. Among the types of transfers and changes that call for a reappraisal of the property are the following: sale or exchange of property; transfer by gift or inheritance; transfer of one spouse's separate property to other spouse as separate property, since no joint tenancy or community property interest exists; creation of joint tenancy interest between non-spouses; deed from joint tenants to a third party; transfer of a condominium unit, where the unit plus the undivided fractional interest in the common areas is appraised; transfer of stock in a housing co-op; creation of a trust for the benefit of another person; transfer of interest by a tenant-in-common to another tenant-in-common; transfer of interest of a partner in a general partnership; creation of a life estate; foreclosure sale, whether by trustee or court action; tax sale; a lease of property in excess of 35 years; and new construction.

Among the transfers which do not trigger a reappraisal are: creation or transfer of a security interest, such as a trust deed or mortgage; interspousal transfer to create or terminate a joint tenancy or community property interest; termination of joint tenancy via death of a joint tenant; deed from one joint tenant to another joint tenant as sole owner; change from joint tenancy to tenancy in common and vice-versa; transfer of corporate stock in real estate, since this is transfer of the stock and not of the asset; replacement of property taken by eminent domain; and where there is a change of name only.

Equalization of Assessments

Just as important in assessing value is the *equalization* of the assessment. The assessor must be sure that no parcel of property is assessed on a different basis than any other parcel similarly situated, subject to the provisions of Proposition 13.

Generally, the county board of supervisors—sitting as a Board of Equalization and vested with the power and authority to adjust any manifest inequalities in assessments—serves this function. The board of supervisors meets annually for this purpose, commencing in July.

Periodically during the month of June, taxpayers receive a notice of their property's assessed value from the county assessor's office. Taxpayers must take the initiative in processing an appeal if they feel their property has been assessed at more than market value. A suggested test is for the homeowner to consider whether he or she would accept the assessed value as a fair selling price. Normally one will find the assessor has been fair. If the property assessment still appears out of line, then the taxpayer has a right of appeal. The Board of Equalization may increase or lower any individual assessment, but not the entire roll. In accordance with recent legislation, all counties are authorized to create "assessment appeals boards" for the purpose of equalizing assessments. A State Board of Equalization performs a similar function respecting property subject to taxation by the state.

The next step in the taxing process is to determine the amount of revenue that needs to be raised that year to finance the government and its services, and then to establish the *tax rate*. The amount of tax revenue needed, together with the *tax base*, determine a year's tax rate. The *tax base* is the total assessed value in a given taxing district. The *tax rate* is a levy per each one hundred dollars of assessed value. The tax rate fluctuates each year, depending upon the needs of the government and changes in the county's tax base. A property owner's tax increases are thus determined not only by the assessed value of the property, but also by the year's tax rate. Again, the rate cannot exceed 1 percent of market value, adjusted for an annual 2 percent inflation factor.

Following is the way the amount of your property tax is computed. If the assessor has determined the market value of your property to be $100,000, the assessed value is likewise $100,000. If the tax rate in your county has been set at the maximum 1 percent, you will be assessed $1000. This is the same as 1 percent of the assessed value, or $1 for every $100 of assessed value. By dividing the assessed value of the property ($100,000) by $100, you will get the figure of $1000. Then you multiply by $1. The amount of your tax is thus $1000. Note in the illustrated tax bill in Figure 10.5, the old 4 percent rate which

Figure 10.5
Tax Bill

JOINT CONSOLIDATED TAX BILL

CITIES, COUNTY, SCHOOLS AND ALL OTHER TAXING AGENCIES IN LOS ANGELES COUNTY

SECURED PROPERTY TAX FOR FISCAL YEAR JULY 1, 1980 TO JUNE 30, 1981

H. B. ALVORD, TAX COLLECTOR
225 N. Hill Street, Los Angeles, California
P. O. Box 2102 Term. Annex Los Angeles, CA 90051

TELEPHONE INFORMATION
SEE PARAGRAPH 1 ON
REVERSE SIDE

OWNER OF RECORD AS OF MARCH 1, 1980

SAME AS BELOW

2042 017 005   SEQ 335145
BOND,ROBERT J
13515 ADDISON ST
SHERMAN OAKS CA   91423

PROPERTY LOCATION AND/OR PROPERTY DESCRIPTION
22844 LEONORA DR   LOT 393   WOODLAND
TRACT # 9545

ADDRESS CHANGE FORM

IF YOUR MAILING ADDRESS IS DIFFERENT FROM THAT ABOVE FILL IN THE
BOXES ON THIS FORM, DETACH AND RETURN WITH YOUR PAYMENT.
2042 017 005 BOND,ROB

NAME   BOND,ROBERT J
HOUSE NUMBER AND STREET NAME

CITY   STATE   ZIP CODE

CURRENT DATE

FOR UNPAID TAXES, SEE PARAGRAPH NO. 15 ON BACK
OF THIS BILL FOR INSTRUCTIONS TO REDEEM

SOLD TO STATE IN YEAR 1980

1ST INSTALLMENT
6% Penalty After
Dec. 10, 1980   505.37

2ND INSTALLMENT
6% Penalty & $3.00 Cost
After Apr. 10, 1981   505.36

TOTAL TAX
Penalties Apply
When shown   1010.73

GENERAL TAX LEVY, VOTED INDEBTEDNESS AND DIRECT ASSESSMENTS		
TAXING AGENCY	RATE	AMOUNT
GENERAL TAX LEVY ALL AGENCIES	4.0000	886.40
VOTED INDEBTEDNESS		
CITY-LOS ANGELES	.1352	29.05
COUNTY	.1972	42.70
UNIFIED SCHOOLS	.0775	33.00
COMMNTY COLLEGE	.1059	22.85
FLOOD CONTROL	.0550	11.90
METRO WATER DIST		
TOTAL VOTED INDEBTEDNESS		**
DIRECT ASSESSMENTS FLOOD CONTROL		5.37
TOTAL DIRECT ASSMTS		5.37
TOTAL TAX	4.5371	1010.73

LOCALLY ASSESSED VALUES IN THIS COUNTY ARE DETERMINED BY THE LOS ANGELES COUNTY ASSESSOR
AT 25% OF FULL VALUE EXCEPT AS OTHERWISE PROVIDED BY LAW.

ACCOUNT NO.   SEQUENCE NO.   REG   DIVISION INDEX   MAP BOOK   PAGE   PARCEL   TRA
335145   02   2042   017:005   0016

	FULL VALUE	EXEMPT. TYPE	EXEMPTION VALUE	NET ASSESSED VALUE
1 LAND	9920			
2 IMPROVEMENTS	12240			
3 FIXTURES				
4		H		22160
5 TOTAL REAL PROPERTY	22160		88640	22160
6 PERSONAL PROPERTY				
7 BUSINESS INVENTORY				

ASSESSED VALUE OF REAL PROPERTY.......
HOMEOWNER'S EXEMPTION ....
TOTAL APPLICABLE TAX RATE ....
GROSS TAXES BEFORE APPLICATION OF HOMEOWNERS' EXEMPTION ...
TAX REDUCTION ATTRIBUTABLE TO STATE-FINANCED HOMEOWNERS' TAX
RELIEF PROGRAM *** SEE PARAGRAPH NO. 6 ON REVERSE SIDE
TOTAL TAX AFTER ALLOWANCE FOR HOMEOWNERS' EXEMPTION
PERSONAL PROPERTY, DIRECT ASSESSMENT OR SPECIFIC LAND LEVY ...
TOTAL TAXES DUE ....

YOUR CANCELLED CHECK IS YOUR BEST RECEIPT

KEEP THIS UPPER PORTION OF THE BILL FOR YOUR RECORDS

IF YOU NEED A RECEIPT CHECK HERE ◯ AND RETURN ENTIRE TAX BILL WITH YOUR PAYMENT

TO PAY TOTAL TAXES SEND BOTH STUBS WITH YOUR PAYMENT

THE COUNTY OF LOS ANGELES IS REQUIRED BY LAW TO COLLECT THE TAXES FOR ALL SCHOOL DISTRICTS, CITIES AND OTHER TAXING AGENCIES.

BOND,ROBERT J
13515 ADDISON ST
SHERMAN OAKS CA

FOR EXPLANATION OF CHARGES AND SYMBOLS SEE PARAGRAPH NO. 6 ON REVERSE SIDE

1ST STUB (1)

USE THIS NUMBER ON ALL CHECKS & CORRESPONDENCE

Map Book	Page	Parcel
2042	017	005

1ST INSTALLMENT

DUE NOV 1, 1980
DELINQUENT DEC. 10, 1980

TAX	505.37
6% Penalty	30.32
Total with Penalty	

91423   80
1010-73

Please make checks payable to:
LOS ANGELES COUNTY TAX COLLECTOR.
Upon payment, appropriate distribution will be made to the various
taxing agencies, which require the County to make this collection.

20420170050000503570000535695910000

DETACH AND MAIL THIS STUB WITH 1ST INSTALLMENT PAYMENT
6% PENALTY IF NOT PAID BY DEC. 10, 1980

MAIL EARLY - AVOID PENALTY

2ND STUB (2)

USE THIS NUMBER ON ALL CHECKS & CORRESPONDENCE

Map Book	Page	Parcel
2042	017	005

2ND INSTALLMENT

DUE FEB 1, 1981
DELINQUENT APR 10, 1981

TAX	505.36
6% Penalty	
Cost	
Total with Penalty	

91423   33-32   80
1010-73

Please make checks payable to:
LOS ANGELES COUNTY TAX COLLECTOR.
Upon payment, appropriate distribution will be made to the various
taxing agencies, which require the County to make this collection.

20420170050000503600005386504200000

DETACH AND MAIL THIS STUB WITH 2ND INSTALLMENT PAYMENT
6% PENALTY + $3.00 COST IF NOT PAID BY APR. 10, 1981

MAIL EARLY - AVOID PENALTY

1980   2nd INSTALLMENT

applied on the assessed valuation is labeled General Tax Levy—All Agencies. This is to conform to Proposition 13, so that the total of all of the funds sought by all of the agencies listed thereafter do not exceed the 1 percent of market value limitation.

The final step is to levy and collect the tax. The board of supervisors actually "levies" the tax; i.e., formally determines that the taxes be collected. The county auditor then extends the tax against each parcel or item subject to taxation by applying the rate fixed by the board of supervisors against the assessed value of each parcel of property. The assessment roll is then delivered for collection to the tax collector, who prepares and mails the tax bills sometime in November of each year.

County taxes are levied on all real property that is not exempt, and they become a lien, annually, as of the first day in March *preceding the fiscal year* for which such taxes are levied. The fiscal year begins on July 1, and ends on June 30 of the following calendar year. For instance, taxes that became a lien on the first day in March 1986 are levied for the fiscal year July 1, 1986 to June 30, 1987.

County taxes for each fiscal year, and city taxes in areas where city taxes are collected with the county taxes, are due and payable in two installments. The first installment is due on November 1, and becomes delinquent if not paid on or by December 10. The second installment is due on February 1 and becomes delinquent if not paid on or by April 10. If these dates fall on Saturday, Sunday, or a holiday, the time for payment is extended to the close of business on the next regular business day.

If taxes for the fiscal year are not paid, the real property is shown on the tax rolls as "sold to the state." This action occurs on or about June 30. If the taxes are delinquent for five years, the title is transferred by deed to the state of California by the tax collector. Unless the tax-delinquent property is wanted by an agency of the state, it may be sold by the county tax collector at a tax sale to the highest bidder. Prior to the tax sale there is a statutory right of redemption for a five-year period. After the five years have elapsed, the owner or his or her successor has the privilege of redemption any time before the tax sale if the property is not to be retained in governmental ownership.

Taxes on real property are afforded a special priority by law. If they are not paid, the lien created on the property for them automatically takes priority over trust deeds and mortgages and similar liens; ultimately the lender, even though his or her deed of trust was recorded before the tax lien date, could lose his security as the result of a sale for nonpayment of taxes. A lender can be protected through a tax service or by checking tax rolls regularly.

A pie chart showing the important tax dates appears as Figure 10.6.

In order to continue all the community services needed to take care of the people, other taxing agencies in addition to the county must levy taxes. These agencies include school and flood control districts. The amount needed for such purposes is shown separately on the owner's tax bill.

EXEMPTIONS

Veteran's Exemption

California law provides certain exemptions from real property taxes to certain homeowners. Under the California Constitution, a California resident who has served in the armed forces in time of war is entitled to a veteran's exemption of $4000 on the market value. The same advantage is given to the widow, widowed mother, or pensioned father or mother of a deceased veteran. However, if the veteran or others entitled to the exemption own property valued at $20,000 or more ($40,000 if

Figure 10.6.
Real Property Tax Year

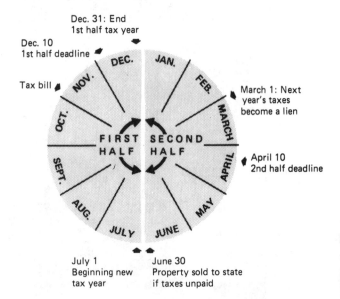

Figure 10.7
Property Tax Exemption Notices

Dear Homeowner,

Once you have filed a Homeowners' Claim with my office and I have allowed the exemption, it is not necessary to file each year. The Homeowners' Exemption will remain in effect until you sell the property, or it is no longer your principal place of residence. The law provides that you must notify my office when you are no longer eligible.

The enclosed form shows your Homeowners' Exemption claim information. Please do ONE of the following:
1. Return the form SIGNED ONLY if you are no longer eligible for the Homeowners' Exemption on this property. Your exemption will be canceled.
2. Return the form UNSIGNED if you are using the form to report an error in this exemption information.
3. DO NOT RETURN the form if you are still eligible and all information is correct. Your exemption will remain in effect.

Very truly yours,

Philip E. Watson

1981

TELEPHONE NUMBER
974-3211
THIS FORM VOID IF NOT SIGNED
FOR ASSESSOR'S USE ONLY

**1981 CLAIM FOR HOMEOWNER'S PROPERTY TAX EXEMPTION
COUNTY OF LOS ANGELES • OFFICE OF ASSESSOR**
500 WEST TEMPLE STREET
LOS ANGELES, CALIF. 90012

ASSESSOR'S IDENTIFICATION NUMBER		
MAP BOOK	PAGE	PARCEL
2215	026	0013

044-1	706	712	801
737		841-1	845

Please line out and correct any incorrect printed data
LOCATION OF PROPERTY
14526 Haynes St.

Van Nuys, CA 91411

If eligible, sign and file this form with the Assessor on or before April 15, 1981.

See enclosed instructions before completing.

Enter your Social Security number here ———————> 118 - 24 - 9046

If you are married and this property is both your and your spouse's principal residence,
enter your spouse's Social Security here ———————> __ - __ - ____
(This exemption claim is not subject to public inspection.)

I declare under penalty of perjury, that to the best of my knowledge the statement on the reverse side of this form and all entries on this form are true and correct.

Date __ January 2   1982 ____

Signed *Robert J. Bond* in _ Los Angeles __ County

Only the owner or a co-owner of the above described property (including a purchaser under contract of sale) or his legal representative may sign.

Daytime (8 a.m. — 5 p.m.) Telephone No. (213) 781-1200

MAILING ADDRESS
Bond, Robert J.
LAST NAME   FIRST NAME   MIDDLE INITIAL
14526 Haynes St.

Van Nuys, CA 91411

DO NOT FOLD, MUTILATE OR SPINDLE THIS FORM

---

married), they cease to become eligible. These values are equivalent to $20,000 and $40,000 respectively, based upon full cash value, as determined by the county assessor. This exemption cannot be applied on the same property for which a homeowner exemption has been allowed. However, if a veteran owns another property, a Veteran Exemption may be filed on it.

Homeowner's Exemption

A homeowner's exemption is also presently available, in the amount of $1750. This corresponds to $7000 full cash value, or to four times the assessed value. A claim of exemption must be filed to obtain this benefit. At one time it was necessary to claim the exemption each year, but now, once a claim has been filed and allowed, it is no longer necessary to reclaim the exemption each year. The notice from the assessor's office to the homeowner regarding any changes in exemption status is illustrated in Figure 10.7.

Senior Citizen's Exemption

Homeowners who are senior citizens—sixty-two years of age or older—are also entitled to state assistance on part of their property taxes under prescribed conditions. This notice from the assessor's office appears in Figure 10.8. Filing for property tax assistance will not reduce the amount of property taxes owed to the county, nor will it result in a lien being placed on the property. The procedure involves a rebate of a portion of the taxes to qualified seniors.

Under the provisions of another law (Senior Citizen Property Tax Postponement Act) senior citizens, if they wish, are able to defer payment of property taxes on their homes until sold, which could be after the homeowners' deaths. Actually, the state pays the taxes and collects them later by placing a lien on the property for the amount of the taxes plus a seven-percent yearly interest charge. To be eligible for this tax relief, a homeowner must be at least sixty-two years old, have at least a 20 percent equity in the home, and have a household income not exceeding $20,000 a year. The income limit will be increased each year to match inflation. A claim form must be filed for each year the owner desires to have property taxes postponed.

Individuals who qualify for postponement may also qualify for property tax assistance.

SPECIAL ASSESSMENTS

Special assessments differ from property taxes: taxes are levied for the support of the general functions of the government, whereas special assessments are levied for the cost of *specific local improvements* such as streets, lighting, sewers, weed abatement, irrigation, and drainage. In some instances, a special improvement district may be formed which includes all real property within the area obtaining the benefit of the improvement. When the cost of the work is determined, assessments are levied on the property in the district and become a lien on the property. The assessments may be paid over a period of years in equal annual installments. In other

instances where the cost is relatively small, the assessments are levied only once by the city or county for a particular work of improvement. A sidewalk, for example, might fall in this latter category.

The liens created by special assessments are usually on a *parity* with general tax liens, which means that they are of equal rank. The foreclosure of one does not ordinarily eliminate the other. For instance, a purchaser at a tax sale acquires the title subject to special assessments that are on a parity with the taxes.

Quite frequently self-governing districts, such as irrigation or sanitation districts, are the sources of special assessments. These districts are created under state law by a city or county or by the vote of the inhabitants in the locality. Upon activation, the district becomes a separate legal entity governed by a board of directors, and possesses many of the characteristics of a municipality, particularly in the revenue-raising field.

As a rule, the district issues its own bonds to finance the cost of particular improvements, such as water distribution systems, drainage structures, irrigation works, parking facilities, and many other types of developments. To repay the funds borrowed through the issuance of the bonds, these districts have the power to assess all lands included in the district on an *ad valorem* basis, i.e., according to the value. Such assessments constitute liens on the land in the district until paid. These liens can be foreclosed by sale similar to a tax sale, and are prior and superior to mortgages and deeds of trust or other private security interests.

When improvements are to be located completely within the boundaries of one city or county, an alternative to establishing a special improvement district is available: The city or county establishes an "improvement area" and then proceeds to assess the lands contained within the area on the basis of benefits to be received from the proposed improvement.

Many assessment acts have been enacted in California, dating as far back as 1885. The Street Improvement Act of 1911 is one that appears to be utilized more than any other for street improvements. Under this act the total assessment against each parcel of property is determined at the time the work is done and becomes a lien against the property at that time. The cost of the improvement against each parcel may be paid to the contractor within thirty days after completion of the work, or may be paid to the municipal-

Figure 10.8
Senior Citizens Property Tax Relief

ATTENTION HOMEOWNERS 62 OR OLDER

You may be eligible for additional property tax relief. Under the Senior Citizens Property Tax Relief Act, homeowners 62 years of age or older with incomes of $12,000 or less are eligible for a State rebate of part of their property taxes. This relief is available for the taxes you pay in December and in April. You also qualify if you are blind or disabled.

This assistance will afford you an additional and substantial reduction in your property taxes as shown in the table below. You may file for this property tax relief on or after this coming May 15th and claims will be paid on or after July 1st.

For further information, contact one of the sixteen offices of the Franchise Tax Board located throughout the state.

HOMEOWNER ASSISTANCE SCHEDULE

If your total household income is:		Your Percentage of Assistance is:	If your total household income is:		Your Percentage of Assistance is:
From	To		From	To	
	$3,000	96%	$ 6,601	$ 6,800	41%
$3,001	3,200	94%	6,801	7,000	37%
3,201	3,400	92%	7,001	7,200	34%
3,401	3,600	90%	7,201	7,400	31%
3,601	3,800	88%	7,401	7,600	28%
3,801	4,000	86%	7,601	7,800	25%
4,001	4,200	84%	7,801	8,000	22%
4,201	4,400	82%	8,001	8,200	20%
4,401	4,600	80%	8,201	8,400	18%
4,601	4,800	78%	8,401	8,600	16%
4,801	5,000	76%	8,601	8,800	14%
5,001	5,200	73%	8,801	9,000	12%
5,201	5,400	69%	9,001	9,500	10%
5,401	5,600	65%	9,501	10,000	8%
5,601	5,800	61%	10,001	10,500	7%
5,801	6,000	57%	10,501	11,000	6%
6,001	6,200	53%	11,001	11,500	5%
6,201	6,400	49%	11,501	12,000	4%
6,401	6,600	45%	Over	12,000	0

ity. If the cost of the work is not paid when the work is completed, bonds are issued to represent the assessment. Assessments may be paid in equal installments during the term of the bonds, usually a ten-year period. The local legislative body determines the rate of interest which the bonds will bear. The amount of the assessment may be paid along with local taxes, and the amounts due will appear on the property owner's tax bill.

OTHER TAXES THAT MAY BECOME A LIEN ON REAL PROPERTY

Various types of state taxes may become a lien on real property when a certificate of tax or an abstract of judgment is recorded in the office of the county recorder of the county where the taxpayer's property is situated. Such certificates or abstracts create a lien having the same effect and priority as an ordinary money judgment. Once the certificate or abstract is recorded, it gives constructive notice to the world of the tax lien. Subsequent purchasers and encumbrancers of the property will take the property subject to the effect of the recorded tax lien. Included in such types of taxes are the sales tax, the use tax, the state income tax, the unemployment tax, and many others.

Although not a tax lien as such, another type of lien may be created under prescribed conditions that is on a parity with real property taxes. This is a lien that secures the cost of removal of a substandard or dangerous structure which the owner and/or mortgagee fails to remove after notice, and a government agency incurs the expense of removal.

There are also several federal taxes which, under the provisions of a general lien statute, can constitute a lien in favor of the United States upon all property and rights to property belonging to the taxpayer. However, as a general rule, such liens are not valid against good-faith purchasers and encumbrancers of real property, unless a notice of lien is recorded by the federal government in the office of the county recorder in the county where the property is located. The federal income tax is the most frequently encountered tax of this type. Federal estate and gift taxes are two others. Federal tax liens may be enforced by seizure and sale of the property in what are referred to as distraint proceedings. Or the lien may be enforced by judicial sale under proceedings initiated by the district director of Internal Revenue in the local United States District Court.

PERSONAL PROPERTY TAXES

Certain types of personal property, such as business inventories and boats, are subject to taxation. Unsecured personal property taxes are normally due on March 1 (payable upon assessment) and are delinquent after August 31. However, personal property taxes can be secured by becoming a lien on the owner's real property. They may then be paid in two equal installments at the time the real property taxes are paid, although not every county permits this method of payment. Los Angeles County and one or two smaller counties require payment of all personal property taxes with the first installment of real property taxes. For the owner of the personal property, unsecured personal property taxes of course do not constitute a lien on his or her real property.

QUESTIONS FOR CHAPTER 10

Matching Terms

a. parity	i. tax certificate
b. ad valorem	j. tax deed
c. assessed value	k. redemption
d. lien	l. tax rolls
e. special assessments	m. homestead
f. tax base	n. tax
g. tax rate	o. mechanic's lien
h. exemption	

_____ 1. evidence that property was not redeemed following a tax sale

_____ 2. a levy, under authority of law, for governmental purposes

_____ 3. issued to the purchaser at a tax sale

_____ 4. right to buy back one's property after an execution sale

_____ 5. levy per each $100 of assessed value

_____ 6. special right afforded laborers and suppliers of materials for construction

_____ 7. value placed on property for purposes of taxation

_____ 8. protection afforded owners of a dwelling

_____ 9. a charge or hold on property to secure payment of a debt

_____ 10. value of all taxable property within a county

_____ 11. according to value

_____ 12. of equal rank

_____ 13. charge for cost of local work of improvement

_____ 14. immunity from some burden or obligation

_____ 15. books maintained by county tax assessor

True/False

T F 16. An involuntary lien means that a debt was created involuntarily.

T F 17. As a general rule, property is subject to sale under an attachment lien.

T F 18. A judgment lien continues for a five-year period.

T F 19. Homesteads are not favored by the law.

T F 20. A lien is an encumbrance on land.

T F 21. All encumbrances are liens, but not all liens are encumbrances.

T F 22. An execution lien is obtainable only after a judgment is entered.

T F 23. The priority of a mechanic's lien is exclusively based on date of recording.

T F **24.** Real property taxes and special assessments are generally on a parity.

T F **25.** To obtain homestead benefits, a declaration of homestead must be recorded prior to entry of a judgment.

Multiple Choice

26. A writ of execution permits property of a defendant to be sold
   a. before an action is filed
   b. before judgment is entered
   c. after judgment is entered
   d. after judgment is satisfied

27. A writ of attachment permits property of a defendant to be seized
   a. before an action is filed
   b. after an action is filed but before judgment
   c. after judgment is entered
   d. after judgment is satisfied

28. The judgment lien is for a period of
   a. three years
   b. five years
   c. ten years
   d. twelve years

29. The priority of a mechanic's lien is determined by the date
   a. the work of improvement commences
   b. the work of improvement is completed
   c. the claim of lien is recorded
   d. an action to foreclose the lien is filed

30. The following is essential to the validity of a declared homestead
   a. bona fide residence at the time the declaration is recorded
   b. properly recorded declaraton of homestead
   c. ownership interest with right of possession
   d. all of the above

31. A homestead declaration is abandoned by
   a. a sale and transfer of the property
   b. moving from the property
   c. moving from the state
   d. renting the property

32. A homestead when properly recorded takes priority over
   a. a deed of trust recorded after the homestead
   b. real property taxes for subsequent years
   c. a mechanic's lien
   d. a judgment recorded after the homestead

33. A married person is entitled to a homestead exemption in the amount of
   a. $25,000
   b. $45,000
   c. $60,000
   d. none of the above

34. A single person under sixty-five and not the head of a household is entitled to a homestead exemption in the amount of
   a. $45,000
   b. $25,000
   c. $30,000
   d. none of the above

35. Real property in California is taxed in
   a. proportion to its area, regardless of value
   b. proportion to its value, subject to provisions of Proposition 13
   c. accordance with the owner's ability to pay
   d. accordance with the rate prevailing in the United States

36. Real property taxes are levied
   a. semiannually
   b. monthly
   c. annually
   d. in odd-numbered years

37. The fiscal year for real property taxation commences on
   a. January 1
   b. March 1
   c. June 1
   d. July 1

38. The lien date for real property taxes in California is
   a. March 1
   b. first Monday in March
   c. March 15
   d. April 15

39. The tax assessor is charged with the duty of
   a. collecting taxes
   b. determining taxable value
   c. fixing the tax rate
   d. selling tax-delinquent property

40. The first half of real property taxes is due on November 1, and becomes delinquent if not paid on or by
   a. November 15
   b. February 1
   c. December 10
   d. April 10

41. The second half of real property taxes is due on February 1, and becomes delinquent if not paid on or before
   a. February 10
   b. March 10
   c. April 10
   d. April 15

42. An assessment roll is maintained by the
    a. county tax collector
    b. county tax assessor
    c. state treasurer
    d. state auditor
43. The total assessed value in a taxing district is called the
    a. tax rate
    b. tax base
    c. tax equalization
    d. tax deed
44. The levy per each $100 of assessed value is known as the
    a. tax rate
    b. tax base
    c. tax equalization
    d. tax exemption
45. Property taxes and special assessments are ordinarily
    a. on a parity with each other
    b. subordinate liens
    c. inferior to a purchase money trust deed
    d. inferior to a mechanic's lien
46. Special assessments are charges against real property for the cost of local improvements such as
    a. sidewalks
    b. sewers
    c. street lighting
    d. any of the above

47. If real property taxes become delinquent, the property may be sold at a tax sale. There are actually two tax sales, one a "paper sale" *to* the state at the end of the first year, and the other an actual sale *by* the state after
    a. two years
    b. three years
    c. four years
    d. five years
48. The requisites for a valid tax on real property include
    a. duly constituted tax authority
    b. notice and opportunity for hearing
    c. nonexempt property within the jurisdiction of the taxing authority
    d. all of the above
49. A sale of proprty for nonpayment of taxes is an example of
    a. voluntary alienation
    b. involuntary alienation
    c. condemnation
    d. prescription
50. Which of the following best describes the characteristics of a property tax?
    a. privity
    b. priority
    c. on a parity with trust deeds
    d. all of the above are true

LEASES, THE LANDLORD-TENANT RELATIONSHIP, AND PROPERTY MANAGEMENT

Historically, the three L's—landlords, lenders, and lawyers—have been perhaps the most maligned class in the world, going back to ancient times and down to the present. One reason is their opportunity to take advantage of another person's distress or necessitous circumstance.

Unfortunately, some of the criticism has been justified. However, landlords and the others do perform necessary services for which they should be adequately (but not exorbitantly) compensated.

The history of the landlord-tenant relationship occasionally has been one of virtual warfare. What should be a compatible relationship in order to meet the needs of both parties has been one of constant battle, with the pendulum swinging largely in favor of the tenant in this age of consumer protection.

Basically, the landlord is furnishing the tenant with a vital need; i.e. shelter, for which is paid a consideration in the form of rent. The tenant holds certain expectations with regard to meeting his or her needs and comfort, while the landlord is entitled to prompt payment for the value of the shelter he or she is furnishing. In many situations, especially when the interest on trust deed loans is very high, it is desirable that the landlord receive these payments on time in order to meet his or her own financial obligations in a timely fashion.

In the material that follows, consideration will be given to the many areas of conflict in the landlord-tenant relationship. The subject of leases will be discussed, including the nature of a lease, types of leasehold interests, and the requisites of a valid lease. Rights and duties of the landlord as well as those of the tenant will be reviewed, including a brief discussion of eviction proceedings. These topics are becoming increasingly important in today's society, particularly when the shortage of affordable housing units has increased the tenant population as fewer people can afford to buy. The chapter will conclude with a discussion of some of the important aspects of property management.

NATURE OF A LEASE

The nature of a lease can be briefly summarized as follows: it is a *conveyance* of a *limited* estate in the land by the owner (called the lessor or landlord) to another party (called the lessee or tenant). It is also a *contract* between the lessor and lessee for the lessee to pay rent. A lease contains numerous other promises made by both the lessor and lessee. No particular form of lease is required. However, a lease must include the names of the parties, a description of the premises, operative words, consideration and its manner of payment, and the term or period of time for the lease to run. Numerous contractual provisions are usually included, often in the form of either covenants or conditions, many of which are more or less standard clauses, such as the effect of condemnation, bankruptcy of the lessee, etc. A form of lease is illustrated in Figure 11.1. This form was created by the California Association of Realtors for the convenience of its members.

If it is desired to place the lease on record, a *short form* of the lease may be prepared and recorded, incorporating by reference the terms and provisions of the unrecorded original lease. This is quite frequently done to reduce recording charges.

When considering estates and interests in land in Chapter 2, we learned that a basic distinction is made between *freehold* estates and estates less than a freehold. Leases fall within the latter category. By executing a lease, the owner of the land has given to another person part of the interest he or she has in the land; i.e., his or her right of possession for the term of the lease. Thus, technically, two estates or interests in the property are created, a *leasehold estate* in favor of the lessee or tenant, and a *reversion* in favor of the lessor or landowner. The lessor still retains ownership of the fee, but has granted a lesser estate to another party for a period of time.

A leasehold estate is considered a *chattel real*. Although the tenant has an estate or interest in the land for a limited period of time, the interest is a form of personal property ownership, and many rights are governed by laws applicable to personal property.

Hotel guests are *not* considered lessees. Although they may also be privileged to use a given space under certain contractual conditions, they do not ordinarily have the exclusive right of possession of the premises. Accordingly, they are not governed by the ordinary rules regulating the relationship of landlord and tenant.

TYPES OF LEASEHOLD (TENANCY) INTERESTS

Generally speaking, there are four types of leasehold interests, based on the length or duration of the tenancy, illustrated in Figure 11.2 and described as follows:

1. *Estate for years.* To continue for a specified and definite period of time. The period is fixed in advance by agreement between the lessor and lessee. The phrase *estate for years* is somewhat misleading, since the period of time may be less than a year; it may be for a specified week or for a specified month or for any other fixed period of time. Both residential and commercial leases may fall in this category.

2. *Periodic tenancy.* To continue from a specified period to a specified period, such as from year to year, or month to month, or week to week, as determined by agreement of the lessor and lessee. It can be terminated at the conclusion of any of the periods by an appropriate notice from either party to the other.

3. *Tenancy at will.* Has no designated period of duration and is terminable at the will of either party at any time. However, notice of termination is required by either party prior to termination.

4. *Tenancy at sufferance.* Here a lessee or tenant who has rightfully come into possession of the land remains in possession after the expiration of his or her term.

Leases are also classified according to the type of property involved. The three types most commonly used are the residential lease, the commercial lease, and the oil and gas lease. Additionally, in some areas of the state timber leases are

Figure 11.1
Standard Residential Lease Form

RESIDENTIAL LEASE

THIS IS INTENDED TO BE A LEGALLY BINDING AGREEMENT – READ IT CAREFULLY

CALIFORNIA ASSOCIATION OF REALTORS® STANDARD FORM

_____ , California _____ 19_____
_____ , Landlord, and
_____ , Tenant, agree as follows:

1. Landlord leases to Tenant and Tenant hires from Landlord those premises described as: _____
_____
_____

together with the following furniture, and appliances, if any, and fixtures: _____

(Insert "as shown on Exhibit A attached hereto" and attach the exhibit if the list is extensive.)

2. The term of this lease shall be for a period of _____ months; _____ years
commencing _____ 19 _____ and terminating _____ 19___.
3. Tenant is to pay a total rent of $ _____ , payable as follows: _____
_____
_____
_____

The rent shall be paid at _____
or at any address designated by the Landlord in writing.
4. $ _____ as security has been deposited. Landlord may use therefrom such amounts as are reasonably necessary to remedy Tenant's defaults in the payment of rent, to repair damages caused by Tenant, and to clean the premises upon termination of tenancy. If used toward rent or damages during the term of tenancy, Tenant agrees to reinstate said total security deposit upon five days written notice delivered to Tenant in person or by mailing. Balance of security deposit, if any, together with a written itemized accounting shall be mailed to Tenant's last known address within 14 days of surrender of premises.
5. Tenant agrees to pay for all utilities and services based upon occupancy of the premises and the following charges: _____
_____
_____

except _____
which shall be paid for by Landlord.
6. Tenant has examined the premises and all furniture, furnishings and appliances if any, and fixtures contained therein, and accepts the same as being clean, in good order, condition, and repair, with the following exceptions: _____
_____

7. The premises are leased for use as a residence by the following named persons: _____
_____

No animal, bird, or pet except _____
shall be kept on or about the premises without Landlord's prior written consent.
8. Any holding over at the expiration of this lease shall create a month to month tenancy at a monthly rent of $_____
payable in advance. All other terms and conditions herein shall remain in full force and effect.
9. Tenant shall not disturb, annoy, endanger or interfere with other Tenants of the building or neighbors, nor use the premises for any unlawful purposes, nor violate any law or ordinance, nor commit waste or nuisance upon or about the premises.
10. Tenant agrees to comply with all reasonable rules or regulations posted on the premises or delivered to Tenant by Landlord.
11. Tenant shall keep the premises and furniture, furnishings and appliances, if any, and fixtures which are leased for his exclusive use in good order and condition and pay for any repairs to the property caused by Tenant's negligence or misuse or that of Tenant's invitees. Landlord shall otherwise maintain the property. Tenant's personal property is not insured by Landlord.
12. Tenant shall not paint, wallpaper, nor make alterations to the property without Landlord's prior written consent.
13. Upon not less than 24 hours advance notice, Tenant shall make the demised premises available during normal business hours to Landlord or his authorized agent or representative, for the purpose of entering (a) to make necessary agreed repairs, decorations, alterations or improvements or to supply necessary or agreed services, and (b) to show the premises to prospective or actual purchasers, mortgagees, tenants, workmen or contractors. In an emergency, Landlord, his agent or authorized representative may enter the premises at any time without securing prior permission from Tenant for the purpose of making corrections or repairs to alleviate such emergency.
14. Tenant shall not let or sublet all or any part of the premises nor assign this lease or any interest in it without the prior written consent of Landlord.
15. If Tenant abandons or vacates the premises, Landlord may at his option terminate this lease, and regain possession in the manner prescribed by law.
16. If any legal action or proceeding be brought by either party to enforce any part of this lease, the prevailing party shall recover in addition to all other relief, reasonable attorney's fees and costs.
17. Time is of the essence. The waiver by Landlord or Tenant of any breach shall not be construed to be a continuing waiver of any subsequent breach.
18. Notice upon Tenant shall be served as provided by law. Notice upon Landlord may be served upon Manager of the demised premises

at _____ . Said Manager is authorized to accept service on behalf of Landlord.
19. Within 10 days after written notice, Tenant agrees to execute and deliver a certificate as submitted by Landlord acknowledging that this agreement is unmodified and in full force and effect or in full force and effect as modified and stating the modifications. Failure to comply shall be deemed Tenant's acknowledgement that the certificate as submitted by Landlord is true and correct and may be relied upon by any lender or purchaser.
20. The undersigned Tenant acknowledges having read the foregoing prior to execution and receipt of a copy hereof.

Landlord _____   _____ Tenant

Landlord _____   _____ Tenant

NO REPRESENTATION IS MADE AS TO THE LEGAL VALIDITY OF ANY PROVISION OR THE ADEQUACY OF ANY PROVISION IN ANY SPECIFIC TRANSACTION. A REAL ESTATE BROKER IS THE PERSON QUALIFIED TO ADVISE ON REAL ESTATE. IF YOU DESIRE LEGAL ADVICE CONSULT YOUR ATTORNEY.

For these forms, address – California Association of Realtors®
505 Shatto Place, Los Angeles, California 90020
Copyright ©1977-1978 California Association of Realtors® (Revised 1978)   **LR-14**

Figure 11.2
Leasehold Estates

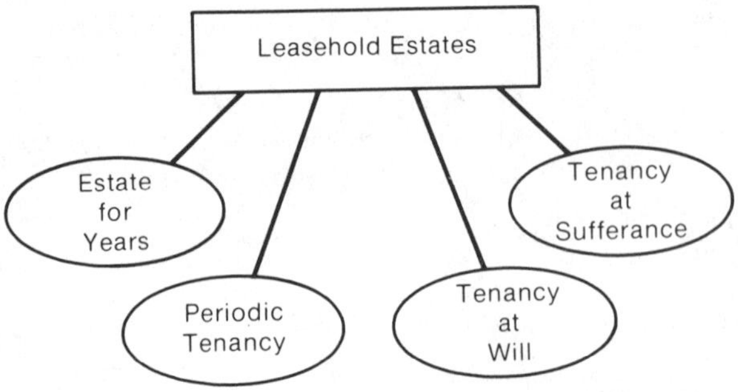

encountered covering forest lands for the right to log and related incidental purposes. An oil and gas lease ordinarily runs for a specified period of time, such as five years, plus an indeterminable period designated by language such as the following: "for such additional period as oil and gas are produced in paying quantities." Since California is one of the largest oil-producing states, the use of oil and gas leases has been widespread in this state. Rent payable under an oil and gas lease is called a *royalty*.

In a lease for a definite period of time, the interest of the lessee, as we have seen, is a chattel real and as such is personal property. In an oil and gas lease for an indefinite period of time, the interest of the lessee is referred to as an *incorporeal hereditament* and is regarded as real property. Another distinction is that in addition to the ordinary lease of the surface, the lessee has the right to take something (oil and gas) from the soil. This right is referred to as a *profit à prendre*.

Various types of oil and gas leases are encountered. The owner of a single parcel of land may lease it individually. Or he or she may join in a *community* oil and gas lease in which several owners of different parcels of land join in the execution of a single lease (or counter parts) for the development of oil from all of their lands. Each owner will be entitled to receive a percentage of the oil (or value thereof) produced from all of the parcels, the exact amount measured by his or her proportionate ownership of the surface.

REQUISITES OF A VALID LEASE

In order to create a leasehold interest, no particular language is required so long as the intention to rent the property is expressed unambiguously. Since a lease is both a conveyance and a contract, the requisites of each must be present. According-

ly, in order to have a valid lease the following requirements must be met:

1. The parties must be named: each must be competent.
2. Description of the property must be set forth; a street address or other informal description may suffice, depending upon the type of premises.
3. Operative words of a lease must be used; such words are usually expressed as "let and demise" or "lease and demise."
4. Consideration is required; this is ordinarily the amount of rent payable under the lease.
5. If for a period longer than one year, the lease must be in writing.
6. Lawful term must be set forth. A lease term cannot exceed fifty-one years for agricultural or horticultural lands; other property can be leased for ninety-nine years. Shorter periods apply in the case of government-owned lands.
7. Like a deed, the lease must be executed, delivered, and accepted. If the lease is in writing, it must be signed by the lessor to be effective. However, it is not necessary that the lessee actually sign the lease; delivery to and acceptance by the lessee is regarded as sufficient without his or her signature. Acceptance by the lessee is also evidenced by his or her entering into possession of the property and paying rent.

As a general rule, the rental of real property is presumed to be from month to month unless otherwise designated in writing by the parties.

A number of matters affecting the rights of the landlord and the tenant (or lessor and lessee) are normally considered before the parties enter into a lease agreement. Many times these matters may be relatively unimportant in the oral month-to-month tenancy, but become increasingly important in the case of written leases for a longer period of time. Some of these matters, ordinarily covered even in the simpler types of leases, are the following:

1. Duration of the lease and any extensions in the term
2. Rent, including any adjustment on renewal of the lease
3. Possession and repairs, maintenance, and improvements
4. Liability of the parties for injuries resulting from the condition of the premises
5. Transfer or assignment by the lessee, including approval by the lessor
6. Special provisions, such as rights of the parties in the event of the destruction of the premises, in whole or in part.

LONG-TERM LEASES IN LIEU OF SALE

Where property is appreciating in value, an owner contemplating its sale may choose instead to use a long-term lease in lieu of a deed, so that he or she may continue to benefit from the property's appreciation. Leases can provide a source of income which can be adjusted periodically to changing property values or the cost of living. Long-term leases not uncommonly provide that taxes, insurance, maintenance, and repairs are to be paid by the tenant. The result is, in effect, an annuity to the owner (landlord) or for his or her heirs or devisees for the leasehold term. At the end the owner will be entitled to regain possession of the property, which may at that time be much more valuable. In the absence of prepayment of rent in any substantial amount, a lease often has an income-tax advantage to the owner, since it creates only a small amount of current cash as compared with what may be derived from a sale. Thus, a lease can be and is used as a device to accommodate a great number of purposes.

ENCUMBERING THE LEASEHOLD ESTATE

Just as the fee estate may be encumbered, a leasehold estate may also be the subject of an encumbrance, such as a mortgage or deed of trust. Ordinarily it is not a requirement that the lessor subordinate his or her interest to the mortgage. However, matters of special concern to a prospective mortgagee of the leasehold estate will include such factors as the following:

1. The lessee's ability to encumber his or her estate or interest; i.e., whether there is any provision against encumbering or a requirement for the landlord's consent.
2. The marketability of the leasehold estate in the event foreclosure (of the leasehold mortgage) becomes necessary; i.e., whether there is someone other than the mortgagee who will be an interested bidder at the foreclosure sale in the event of a default by the lessee-mortgagor.
3. Adequate protection from defaults or rights of termination and modifications of the lease.
4. Adequate protection from termination of the lease by the foreclosure of a prior mortgage or deed of trust on the fee.

Usually the lender will require a policy of title insurance insuring the priority and validity and perhaps enforceability of the encumbrance. A leasehold estate can be insured by a policy of title insurance, and an encumbrance on the leasehold estate can also be insured.

ENCUMBERING THE FEE ESTATE SUBJECT TO A LEASE

A favorable lease on property can materially enhance the loan value of a parcel of property. As an instrument furnishing credit support for a mortgage loan, the lease of commercial real estate to a responsible tenant is generally looked upon by mortgagees as assurance of a flow of cash to the fee owner (landlord/mortgagor) sufficient to enable him or her after paying all maintenance, management, and operating costs, to pay the mortgage debt satisfactorily. The quality of the tenant's credit, the term of the lease, and the amount of the rent the landlord will net out of the lease are among the principal factors considered by the lender in placing a value on the property and determining how much he or she is willing to lend.

TRANSFERS OF LEASEHOLD INTERESTS

In the absence of a provision in the lease to the contrary, the tenant may transfer his or her interest in a leasehold estate. This may be accomplished by two different types of instruments: by an *assignment* of the lease or by a *sublease*.

An assignment is a transfer of the entire leasehold, whereas a sublease is a transfer of less than the leasehold estate with the reversion in the original lessee who is now also a sublessor. These differences can be better understood by graphic illustrations (see Figure 11.3).

Figure 11.3
Assignment Compared with a Sublease

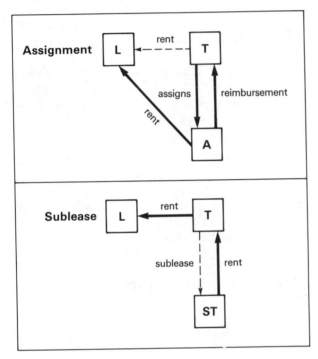

L: Lessor
T: Tenant
A: Assignee
ST: Subtenant

As an example, suppose three years of a five-year lease remain in effect. The original lessee might assign his leasehold interest to a third party for the remaining term and retain no further interest in it himself. Or he might sublet his rights for a period less than the three years remaining under the lease, say for a period of two years. He still retains an interest in it himself. He would have the right to reoccupy the premises or sublet again for the remaining year of the lease. During the term of the sublease, the interest created is referred to as a *sandwich lease*—the leasehold interest which lies between the primary lease and the operating lease.

TERMINATION OF LEASES OR TENANCIES

A tenancy for a specified term (an estate for years)

ends at the expiration of the term and without notice.

Periodic tenancies may be terminated by either the landlord or by the tenant by a written notice. The notice given must be at least as long as the term in the lease, but not exceeding one month. Thus, if a tenant pays rent on a weekly basis, one week's notice of termination is sufficient. If the tenancy is on a two-week basis, then two weeks' notice is required. However, parties may agree that another period for such notice will be sufficient, but not less than seven days.

A minimum of thirty days' written notice is required in order to terminate tenancies at will. This notice can be given at any time during the rental period.

A tenancy at sufferance does not require notice of termination for any prescribed period.

In addition to the expiration of the term of the lease by its written provisions, there are other grounds for termination, such as the following:

1. By the tenant if the landlord breaches his or her duty to place the tenant in quiet possession of the property.
2. By the tenant if the landlord breaches his or her duty to repair the premises
3. By the tenant if the landlord breaches his or her duty to maintain the premises in an inhabitable condition
4. By either party upon the destruction of the premises if the lease has no covenant to repair
5. By either party upon breach of a condition of a lease by the other party
6. By the landlord if the tenant uses the premises for an illegal or unauthorized purpose
7. By the landlord if the tenant fails to pay rent when due.

Figure 11.4 illustrates these various ways a lease may be terminated.

SECURITY DEPOSITS

It is common practice in the preparation of a lease to require a security deposit or to provide for advance rent payments of a sufficient amount to assure compensation to the lessor in the event he or she is unable to collect rent or damages from the tenant. The common characterization of all such payments as "security deposits" is often misleading. The courts have broken down such deposits or advance payments into four categories:

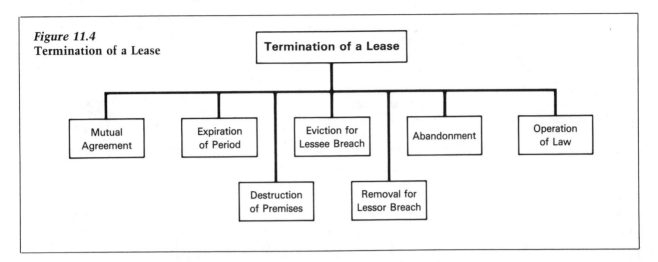

Figure 11.4
Termination of a Lease

1. Advance payment of rent, usually for the last month of the term
2. Payment expressly stipulated to be a bonus or consideration for the execution of the lease
3. Payment of an amount as anticipated liquidated damages
4. Payment as a deposit to secure the tenant's faithful performance of the terms of the lease

If the deposit under the lease falls within the first two classes, it may be retained by the lessor. When the deposit was made as liquidated damages, if the amount paid does not correspond to the actual damages done, the payment may be ruled invalid as such and may be recovered by the lessee. If a deposit falls within the fourth class, it may be retained by the lessor only to the extent of damages actually suffered by the lessor. The advance money that can be taken on an unfurnished apartment or house is first month's rent, advance rent (last month's) equal to one month's rent, and a security deposit equal to two months' rent. In a furnished unit, the security can be equal to three months' rent. The law says that the deposits can only be used for unpaid rent and damages.

Security deposits usually cover such items as cleaning costs and the return of keys. They are trust funds and the landlord is held strictly accountable regarding their use and disposition. The landlord is required to furnish a tenant with an itemized written statement of the basis for, and the amount of, any security received from the tenant and the disposition of such security made by the landlord. An accounting and the return of any unclaimed portion of the security deposit must be made to the tenant no later than two weeks after the tenant vacates the premises. It should be noted that a security deposit in a lease or rental agreement may not be characterized as "nonrefundable."

RIGHTS, DUTIES, AND RESPONSIBILITIES OF LANDLORDS AND TENANTS

Both landlord and tenant have certain rights and duties that the law recognizes. The landlord has the duty to keep a building intended for human occupancy in a fit condition, and to repair dilapidations that render it untenable, except for damages caused by the tenant. However, by agreement the tenant can make repairs for which the landlord is responsible.

If the tenant has a legitimate complaint regarding the condition of the premises and notifies the landlord to make repairs, there are certain remedies available if the landlord fails to act within a reasonable time: The tenant may either abandon the premises and have no further liability for payment of rent, or he or she may spend up to one month's rent to make repairs. This option is available only twice in any twelve-month period, and then only if the tenant is not in default in rent. Another possible remedy for the tenant is a reduction in the amount of rent corresponding to the relative reduction in the usefulness of the premises based on the landlord's breach of duty.

As is true in the case of most contracting parties, the lessor and lessee can agree, in writing, to arbitrate any controversy relating to a condition of the premises.

In addition to the express legal duty placed upon a lessor to maintain a property, there is also an implied duty to keep the premises safe and healthy. This duty is called the *implied warranty of habitability* and is implied by law in all residential leases. This warranty cannot be waived.

In the past, if tenants exercised their legal rights, they were many times subjected to retaliatory eviction by landlords. The law now is more protective of the tenant's rights. A landlord is prohibited from recovering possession, raising the rent, or decreasing services if his or her main purpose is retaliation against a tenant for exercising his or her right to repair or for reporting the landlord for housing code violations. In other words, tenants cannot be deprived of their homes because they exercise a statutory right. This protection extends for a period of sixty days following the date of notice or the taking of other specified action. Further, the landlord is expressly prohibited from interrupting a utility service of a tenant. All actual damages for such an interruption can be awarded to the tenant plus $100 for each day the tenant is deprived of the service, plus attorney's fees.

Although a landlord can enter the tenant's premises in the event of an emergency, such as a fire or broken pipe, the landlord must respect the tenant's right of privacy. Even though the landlord is the owner of the property, he or she does not have the right to enter the premises without the tenant's permission. The landlord will retain a key, but its use should be limited to emergency situations. The adage that "a man's home is his castle" applies equally to rental housing as far as the tenant's rights are concerned.

Rights and duties of both the landlord and tenant are illustrated in Figure 11.5.

In the past, a tenant in a large apartment house—a house often owned by a syndicate as part of an investment project—was uninformed as to who the owner was and who to complain to if something needed attention. Often the only person the tenant had contact with was a person in a glorified clerical capacity who was responsible for filling vacancies and collecting the rent. The law now provides for disclosure information for the benefit of the tenant. As stated in the *Real Estate Reference Book* (1984–85 ed., p. 186),

> The owner of every multi-unit dwelling of more than two units or a party signing a rental agreement on such owner's behalf must disclose the name and address of each person authorized to manage the premises and to receive process for notices and demands on behalf of the owner.
>
> In the case of an oral rental agreement, the owner or person acting on the owner's behalf must furnish the tenant with a written statement containing the above information on written demand by the tenant.

The law provides for optional methods of disclosure. A printed or typewritten notice containing the required information may be placed in every elevator and in one other conspicuous place. Where there are no elevators, notices must be posted in at least two conspicuous places.

The information must be kept current. Moreover the statutory requirement to furnish a tenant with this information is enforceable against a successor owner or manager.

If the party who enters into a rental agreement on behalf of the owner fails to comply with the above provisions, such person is deemed an agent of each person who is an owner for the purpose of service of process, notices and demands and for the purpose of performing the obligations of the owner under the law and the rental agreement.

Inspection of the premises by the parties to the rental agreement can be important to each of the parties, both at the commencement of the term and at the termination of the tenancy. A tenant should not agree as to the condition of the premises without a thorough inspection.

Many landlords require references of a prospective tenant, and a prudent tenant will also want to know the past history and experience of the landlord.

The relationship of landlord-tenant is often misunderstood. As a public service, many local Bar Associations and others have published pamphlets on the subject "What You Should Know About Landlord-Tenant Rights and Responsibilities," available upon request and without charge.

EVICTION PROCEDURE

If a tenant falls behind in paying rent, a landlord cannot resort to self-help such as turning off utilities, keeping the tenant from possessing the property by changing locks, or seizing the tenant's property. If a tenant is in default in the payment of rent, the landlord can serve him or her with a three-day written notice to quit. The notice will direct the tenant either to pay the rent or give up possession. The notice to quit does not automatically terminate the lease, but it is the first step in the process of recovering possession. If the tenant fails to comply with the notice, the landlord can bring an *unlawful detainer* action and obtain relief by judgment of the court. The tenant is liable not only for past due rent but also for rent that accumulates during the pendency of the action. The remedy of unlawful detainer is also available against a tenant who holds over after the expira-

Figure 11.5
Rights and Duties of Landlords and Tenants

Landlord	Tenant
1. Provide premises that are "fit for human habitation"	1. Pay rent on time
2. Keep the premises up to code	2. Keep unit clean and sanitary
3. Maintain roof, exterior walls, and structural components	3. Properly use fixtures and appliances
4. Keep common areas reasonably safe and clear	4. Refrain from illegal activities
5. Adequately control insects and pests in premises as a whole	5. Refrain from loud and disturbing noises
6. Maintain electrical, plumbing, and heating facilities	6. Respect the rights of other tenants
7. Provide adequate locks	7. Report promptly the need for any repairs or replacements
8. Maintain all appliances furnished with rental units	8. Refrain from dangerous activities
9. Respect the tenant's right of privacy	9. Control the actions of his or her guests
10. Comply with duties imposed by local laws	10. Don't damage the landlord's property
11. Give advance notice before entering tenant's unit, unless a real emergency	11. On termination, restore the landlord's property to condition received
12. Promptly return deposits on termination if tenant has complied with terms	12. Vacate premises on time when term expires

tion of the term of the lease, or who continues in possession after neglecting or failing to perform covenants or conditions of the lease. Figure 11.6 is a typical three-day notice to pay rent or quit, based on cause, i.e., nonpayment of rent. Figure 11.7 is a form of a thirty-day notice to quit, not based on any special cause, such as tenant's default, but based on the landlord's desire to regain possession of the premises.

APPLICATION OF FAIR HOUSING LAWS

In the past, discrimination has been a problem not only in connection with the sale of residential housing, but also in the case of rentals. It has meant that many persons were denied the right to live in an area of their choice. Although some discrimination still exists, discrimination in rental housing on the basis of sex, race, religion, marital status, age, or physical disability is specifically forbidden by law. It is essential that anyone who is a landlord or property manager stay abreast of the Fair Housing Laws.

The government, both state and federal, constantly emphasize these rights. Persons who believe they are a victim of discrimination in rental housing may contact the nearest office of the California State Department of Fair Employment and Housing. The United States Department of Housing and Urban Development handles complaints concerning racial or religious discrimination. Victims of discrimination may also seek remedies in a court of law. This applies to discrimination both in rentals and evictions.

CONDOMINIUM CONVERSIONS

Because of the frequency of conversions of apart-

Figure 11.6
Three-Day Notice to Pay or Quit

To
_____
_____(NAME OF TENANT)_____
_____
_____

NOTICE TO PAY RENT
OR SURRENDER POSSESSION

NOTICE IS HEREBY GIVEN that, pursuant to the agreement by which you hold possession of the above-described premises, there is now due and unpaid rent for the premises in the total sum of $_____, being the rent that became due on _____ for the period from _____, at a monthly rental of $_____.

WITHIN THREE DAYS after service of this notice on you, you are required to pay the rent in full, or to deliver up possession of the premises to the undersigned, or legal proceedings will be commenced against you to recover possession of the premises, to declare the agreement forfeited, and to recover TREBLE RENTS AND DAMAGES for the unlawful detention of the premises.

Dated: _____

_____
(LANDLORD)

Figure 11.7
Thirty-Day Notice to Quit

To
_____
_____(NAME OF TENANT)_____
_____
_____

This is to give you notice that pursuant to California law which gives landlords the right to retake possession of their property on thirty days written notice to a renter, whether or not the renter is in default in payment of rent, you are to vacate the premises at _____ on or before

_____

Failure to vacate the premises by said date may lead to legal proceedings being commenced against you to recover possession, and to recover treble damages for the unlawful detention of said premises beyond said date.

Dated: _____

_____
(LANDLORD)

ment houses into condominiums or other forms of multiple ownership and the problems encountered by tenants in finding other suitable accommodations in some communities, the right was afforded to tenants to purchase their units under prescribed conditions. City ordinances prescribe the time during which a tenant of an apartment subject to conversion into a condominium, community apartment, or stock cooperative may exercise an exclusive right to contract for the purchase of his or her unit after the date of issuance of the subdivision public report. A landlord may be required to assist tenants in finding other housing if they elect to move rather than buy their unit. And, depending upon the age or health of the majority of tenants and the availability of rental housing, the application for conversion may be denied by a municipality. The criteria for apartment conversion will vary from community to community, thus a property owner must check carefully into local ordinances. For example, some criteria may consider the need to bring the individual units into conformity with standards for any other owner-occupied housing as to number of units for the zone, number of parking spaces per unit, and fees for recreation/open space usual in homes. The important thing to understand is that conversions are not automatic and that considerable rights are afforded tenants. Cities with specific ordinances include Los Angeles, San Francisco, Berkeley, Beverly Hills, and Santa Monica.

RENT CONTROL

During times of an extreme scarcity of rental units available at prices the average person can afford, or a scarcity of total available units that has caused rental prices to increase dramatically, there is much discussion about rent control as a means of protecting renters. World War II was just such a time, and rent controls were instituted in some locations. In the late 1970s, sharply rising housing costs attributed to higher costs of building materials, higher costs for skilled manpower, higher energy costs, and higher costs for construction and home purchase loans began to price a very large segment of the population out of the housing market. The same higher costs were reflected in rentals, and with the increasing demand for rental housing by people leaving their parents' home at a younger age, dividing households, or moving into already heavily populated areas, the rental squeeze became critical in many communities. Local governments found themselves imposing rent controls or regulations in a variety of ways to protect those no longer able to compete in the existing housing market. Some controls or regulations were imposed for a limited period of time or until the number of rental units increased. There are many concerns about the efficacy of controlling the amount of rent a private property owner can charge for housing—the belief that a commodity should be priced at whatever the traffic will bear, and that rentals must

fairly reflect increasing costs of providing the rental (such as insurance, more frequent repairs, higher prices for replacement items, higher costs for services, greater demands by tenants for higher quality housing and services, and higher energy costs). There is also the fear that, rather than protecting the general public, such controls or regulations reduce the long term increase in housing units available because investors are unwilling to build in what they consider to be a no-win market. Others point out that the regulations guarantee an annual increase in rents that is actually higher than former annual increases in the market average.

On the other hand, the controls or regulations do provide some measure of stability to tenants, who are then able to compute their maximum allowed rent increase, although the problems of protecting any "right" to remain in a unit are many as landlords seek relief from the controls. Landlords may seek to evict tenants and then begin charging new higher rents for the unit. The control is on the higher level, then, rather than the old amount. The controls or regulations are in many cases a product of political action and so may change as new organizations form and impress their concerns on local government. Again, as in condominium conversions, any rent control measures are detailed and specific from community to community and you must familiarize yourself with the ordinances in your area.

MOBILE HOME SPACE TENANCY

Because of the distinction between the ordinary tenant and a tenant of space in a mobile home park, special rules apply to this type of tenancy. For example, a tenancy may not be terminated for the purpose of making the space available to someone purchasing a mobile home from the park owner. Termination of mobile home tenancies creates great problems for the tenants: they have to find new quarters not only for themselves but for their mobile homes as well—not an easy task at times. A mobile home tenant cannot be evicted from the park, except for the following reasons:

1. Failure of the tenant to comply with local and state laws and regulations
2. Conduct by the tenant that constitutes an annoyance to other tenants
3. Failure of the tenant to comply with reasonable rules and regulations

4. Nonpayment of rent and other proper charges
5. Condemnation or other change in use of the park

In the notice to evict a tenant, the reason for termination must be set forth with specific facts, including the date, place, names of witnesses, and the circumstances concerning the reason or reasons for termination. If a mobile home cannot be moved to another location without a permit, the tenancy may not be terminated unless written notice of not less than sixty days is given.

REAL PROPERTY MANAGEMENT: AN INTRODUCTION

Property management is related to the subject of leases, but constitutes a special branch of the real estate business. In order to manage property, brokers and others who specialize in it need to be familiar with many aspects of both business and real estate: agency, contracts, ownership, insurance, taxation, and other subjects we have already considered. Naturally, a knowledge of rentals and leasing is also vital. The real estate manager also must know about business administration, merchandising, purchasing, credits, accounting, advertising, repairs and maintenance, and public relations. The extent of knowledge and experience necessary will, of course, vary depending on the size or extent of management operations carried out by the individual manager.

What Is It and Who Needs It?

An owner of income-producing property wants to rent or lease all or part of it at a rate which will secure sufficient return to pay his or her expenses—operating and fixed (taxes, insurance, capital retirement)—and still show a reasonable profit or return on the money invested in the property. On the other side of the coin, a tenant wants to lease or rent desired space at a rental within his or her income and at a rate which will allow the use of the space at a reasonable profit to the landlord. Property owners have found that they can employ experienced property managers to satisfy both their requirements and those of the tenants. Scientific property management achieves smooth operation and actually results in a saving for the owner.

Properties that need management are office buildings, store buildings, apartment houses and other multiple-housing complexes, single-family residences, public housing, factories, garages, parking lots, hotels and motels, shopping centers, theater buildings, restaurant chains, churches, hospitals, service stations, public buildings, and any other properties in which people live, work, study, or play. Property managers are employed more and more to manage industrial parks, mobile home parks, marinas, airports and their varied facilities, and high-rise parking structures. Even in mobile home parks, a person responsible for the operation and maintenance of the park must be available to the tenants. If the park has over fifty units, a manager must reside in the park.

Properties need a "management plan" that sets forth the desired goals and objectives to be accomplished for each property. An owner must decide, whether formally or informally, just what it is that his or her property will do or provide.

Although most people might prefer to buy their homes, and on a long-range basis will ordinarily find it an effective means of saving, there will always be a need for rental properties. Students and vacationers, for example, need temporary residences. There is the convenience of not having ownership duties and responsibilities, particularly for retired people who plan to travel and for executives who are transferred frequently; there are young married couples who aren't ready to buy a home; and many other potential renters.

Functions of a Property Manager

General Responsibilities. The property manager normally has a dual responsibility: to the owner and to the tenants. The owner is his or her employer and is interested in the optimum return from the property. Thus, in considering the owner's investment objectives, the manager must rent to desirable tenants without undue delays and at a maximum rent. He or she must strive for proportionately feasible costs, utilizing every means to reduce deterioration or material alterations, yet preserving the building in a desirable condition. The owner ordinarily will also be concerned with the enhancement of the physical value of the property as well as the prestige of the building.

The property manager must also serve and satisfy the tenant to the best of his or her ability. Tenants, of course, are interested in the best value they can get for their rental dollar. Tenants want to be assured that everything possible is being done for their personal safety, especially if they are families with children. Such social obligations are becoming more important every day for the property manager; he or she has a continuing interest in the civic life of the community—the communal safety measures, building restrictions, and the general welfare. The property manager takes responsibility in making the community a desirable place in which to live.

A successful property manager must

1. Be a leasing expert
2. Have maintenance know-how
3. Be a specialist in purchasing
4. Understand accounting procedure as well as cost accounting
5. Be knowledgeable in taxation
6. Know the various facets of insurance as it relates to buildings
7. Be a credit expert
8. Be adept in psychology
9. Have foresight and the ability to plan
10. Be an efficiency expert

Specific Duties. The specific duties of a manager depend upon the agreement made with the owner.

Included among the property manager's specific duties are the following:

1. Merchandise the space and collect the rents
2. Establish and supervise maintenance schedules and repairs
3. Supervise all purchasing
4. Develop a tenant-relations policy
5. Develop employee policies and supervise their operation
6. Maintain proper records and make periodic reports to the owner
7. Investigate a prospective tenant's credit
8. Prepare and execute leases
9. Prepare decorating specifications and obtain estimates
10. Hire, instruct, and maintain satisfactory personnel to staff the building
11. Audit and pay bills
12. Advertise vacancies through selected media
13. Plan alteration and modernizing programs
14. Inspect vacant space periodically
15. Pay insurance premiums and taxes and recommend tax appeals when warranted
16. Keep abreast of the times and be informed on competitive market conditions

Establishing the Rental Schedule. Managers need to know how to establish rental schedules. In order to do this properly, they must know how to make an appropriate neighborhood analysis and must actually make such an analysis. In general, rent levels are established on the basis of scarcity and comparability of values. The property manager must first know his or her own building thoroughly, and must be able to assess its values objectively. He or she must survey the buildings in the neighborhood within whatever limits he or she has set. Then the manager must analyze the following:

1. Character of the neighborhood
2. Economic level, family size, and age group
3. Domestic status and trends
4. Availability of transportation, recreation, shopping, churches, and schools
5. Physical aspects of structures as well as lot coverage
6. Extent and growth of local industries
7. Population growth trends
8. Personal income range, financial capacity, and stability of income
9. Growth of the community
10. Condition of the housing market in terms of inventory on the market, sales price range, new construction, and vacancy factors

Types of Real Property Managers

There are four basic types of real property managers:

1. *General manager*, often referred to simply as a property manager. A property manager may be in business alone as a managing agent, or he or she may be one of a number of managers in the management department of a large real estate organization that has many clients and many properties under its care. In the latter case, particularly in large cities, the property manager may manage a particular type of building, such as office buildings or apartment buildings, or he or she may manage two types, such as apartment buildings and outlying store structures, or office and store buildings located in the business district. Property management agencies ordinarily pay their general managers on a commission basis; i.e., a percentage of the rent collected.
2. An *individual building manager* may be employed either by a general property manager or directly by the owner. A building manager usually manages a single large property such as a high-rise building. He or she is usu-

ally hired on a straight salary basis. Normally this type of manager is used for nonresidential properties.

3. The *resident manager* is employed by a real estate agency or an owner or a managing agent to live in and manage an apartment building. The resident manager is usually in charge of a large building with many small apartments where the change in tenancy is frequent. As the value of apartment structures increases, the tendency is to utilize a resident manager with special training and experience.

4. A *building superintendent* is usually employed by an agency to supervise an office building and be the agency's representative on the premises. Often, a building superintendent is employed directly by the owner. The superintendent is concerned chiefly with maintenance and operation. He or she hires and supervises the janitorial staff, elevator operators, and maintenance personnel.

Property managers who handle several properties or who otherwise represent themselves as professionals in the field must be licensed real estate brokers. A live-in manager who manages only the building in which he or she lives need not be licensed.

Historical Development

Real-property management, like many other enterprises, had humble beginnings. In the eighteenth century, with the industrial revolution, many people were able to make more money than they needed to support themselves, so they purchased homes not to live in, but to rent to others for a profit. The owners needed assistance in handling their properties but, during the early period, this assistance came primarily from rent collectors, not property managers as we know them today.

Three things occurred at almost the same time which gave birth in this country to real estate management in its modern form: the assembly line, the steel building frame and elevator, and the depression. The increase in industrialization made possible by the assembly line brought men and women into the cities in ever increasing numbers.

At first, city people were housed in two- and three-story buildings. Construction at that time was limited in height because of building support problems. In wood-frame and stucco construc-

tion, the weight of buildings and roof is carried by the walls and bearing partitions, which are able to bear only a limited amount of weight. However, with the invention of the steel frame and the modern elevator, the height of buildings depended only upon man's ingenuity and imagination. The walls were no longer needed to carry weight, only for enclosure. Modern cities sprang up all over the country; in fact, all over the world. California was no exception, although for many years the height of buildings in certain areas was limited because of the possibility of earthquakes. But these restrictions no longer apply—California is seeing a tremendous increase in skyscrapers that use modern earthquake-resisting design and engineering. With the increase in the size and height of buildings, owners found that management problems also increased. As the problems became more complex, they began to seek the advice and services of qualified property managers.

The depression added to the need for property managers. Mortgage companies and banks and other lenders found it necessary to foreclose their secured loans. As a result they acquired title to large properties in wholesale numbers. The law in many places required disposition of such properties by the lending institutions within a period of five years. Because of the short time they were to own the properties, it was impractical for the institutions to set up their own building management departments, so they sought others to manage their properties for them.

The numbers of persons engaged in property management increased rapidly. Many persons became property managers virtually overnight, and, as a result of inexperience and lack of professional standards, failures and embezzlements occurred. To prevent this and to provide an ever-expanding source of data on management experience, real-property management was organized in 1933 by a group of brokers, all of whom were members of the National Associaton of Realtors (NAR). In that year they founded the Institute of Real Estate Management (IREM) as a division of NAR.

Membership in the original institute was open to private firms engaged in real-property management. In order to be a member, each firm was required to certify that it would follow certain ethical standards of trade practice. A few years later, some of the men who originally had established the institute realized that it was failing in many respects to provide a background of professionalism. It was generally recognized that the primary "management" qualities could be possessed only by a person as an individual and not by a firm. Having agreed upon this fundamental principle, the institute abandoned the firm and replaced it with the individual as its basis for membership. With this change in concept the institute reorganized into a truly professional group.

The institute grants the designation of CPM (certified property manager) to duly qualifed members. It also conducts courses of study for its members and publishes a trade journal, the *Journal of Property Management*.

Real estate management is a comparatively new profession, but much progress is being made toward developing professional standards and toward gaining public recognition as a profession. Within the past few years a number of universities have added courses in real estate management, and several colleges are offering specialized majors in property management. The subject of real property management is considered briefly again in Chapter 15.

QUESTIONS FOR CHAPTER 11

Matching Terms

a. lease
b. constructive
c. reversionary interest
d. escalator clause
e. security deposit
f. assignment
g. unlawful detainer
h. rent
i. eviction
j. sublet
k. lessor
l. term
m. chattel real
n. royalty
o. tenant

____ **1.** landlord under a lease
____ **2.** leasehold estate
____ **3.** consideration for a lease payable by lessee
____ **4.** period or duration of a lease
____ **5.** ousting of tenant from possession
____ **6.** transfer of a portion of a tenant's interest
____ **7.** rent under an oil and gas lease
____ **8.** a contract and a conveyance
____ **9.** assurance of performance by tenant
____ **10.** owner of possessory interest
____ **11.** provision in a lease for rental adjustments, upward or downward
____ **12.** implied or inferred from conduct
____ **13.** transfer of all of lessee's interest under a lease

____ **14.** interest of the landlord under a lease
____ **15.** court action by landlord to regain possession of rented property

True/False

T F 16. All leases of real property must be in writing to be enforceable.
T F 17. A lease is both a contract and a conveyance.
T F 18. Consideration is essential in order to have a valid lease.
T F 19. An assignment of a leasehold estate must be in writing.
T F 20. A guest at a hotel is considered to be a lessee.
T F 21. A lease must be recorded to be effective.
T F 22. An estate for years can be for a period less than a year.
T F 23. Notice of termination is unnecessary in a periodic tenancy.
T F 24. Fair Housing Laws apply to sales but not to tenancies.
T F 25. A leasehold estate cannot be encumbered by a mortgage or deed of trust.

Multiple Choice

26. Smith leased a mountain cabin from Brown for the period from October 1 to October 31 of the current year. Smith has
   a. periodic tenancy
   b. an estate for years
   c. a tenancy from month to month
   d. a tenancy at sufferance
27. The maximum term for a lease of land for agricultural purposes is
   a. fifteen years
   b. twenty-five years
   c. fifty-one years
   d. ninety-nine years
28. The maximum term for a lease of a town or city lot is
   a. one year
   b. twenty-five years
   c. fifty-one years
   d. ninety-nine years
29. Which of the following is not essential to the validity of any lease:
   a. consideration
   b. lawful object
   c. mutual assent
   d. signatures of both parties

30. A leasehold estate gives the lessee
    a. nonpossessory interest
    b. possessory interest
    c. reversion
    d. remainder
31. The following lease must be in writing to be enforceable:
    a. term in excess of one month
    b. term in excess of six months
    c. term in excess of twelve months
    d. periodic tenancy
32. If a tenant fails to pay rent when due, he or she may be
    a. summarily evicted without notice
    b. served with a three-day notice to quit or pay rent
    c. locked out of the premises
    d. taken to jail
33. Notice of a tenant's rights under a lease may be imparted by
    a. possession by tenant
    b. recording a memorandum of lease
    c. recording the lease
    d. any of the above
34. In order to be recorded, a lease must be acknowledged by the
    a. lessor
    b. lessee
    c. lessor and lessee
    d. county recorder
35. A tenant who continues in possession of property after the expiration of his or her lease without an express agreement is called a
    a. life tenant
    b. tenant for years
    c. tenant by sufferance
    d. periodic tenant
36. The landlord's interest under an estate for years is called a
    a. leasehold estate
    b. reliction
    c. chattel real
    d. reversion
37. The validity of a lease is dependent upon
    a. competent parties
    b. description of the premises
    c. mutual assent
    d. all of the above
38. Of the following, a lease to the lessee is comparable to that of
    a. a trust deed to a trustee
    b. an option to an optionee
    c. a land contract to the vendee
    d. a mortgage to a mortgagee
39. The holder of a life estate entered into a five-year lease as lessor of the property. The lessee went into possession, but after two years the lessor died. The owner of the remainder interest now wants possession. Which of the following statements is correct?
    a. the lease is invalid for any period
    b. the lease is terminated when the owner of the life estate dies
    c. the lease is valid for the five-year period
    d. the lease is invalid as it was for longer than one year
40. Of the following, who is considered to have the greatest right of possession?
    a. lessee
    b. licensee
    c. lodger
    d. easement holder
41. A leasehold interest lying between the primary lease and a sublease is referred to as
    a. a percentage lease
    b. a sandwich lease
    c. an inactive lease
    d. an inoperative lease
42. A and B signed an agreement for the use and possession of real property for a prescribed period of forty-five days. This is
    a. an estate for years
    b. an estate at sufferance
    c. a periodic tenancy
    d. an estate at will
43. An assignment of a lease is
    a. a transfer of the entire leasehold
    b. a transfer of less than the leasehold
    c. the same as subletting the leasehold
    d. not permissible
44. An action to evict a tenant for nonpayment of rent is known as
    a. specific performance
    b. unlawful detainer
    c. abatement
    d. partition
45. A lease of real property is
    a. both a contract and a conveyance
    b. a contract but not a conveyance
    c. a conveyance but not a contract
    d. neither a contract nor a conveyance
46. Which of the following designations is given by the Institute of Real Estate Management (IREM)?
    a. MRE
    b. REM
    c. CPM
    d. CMP
47. Rent payable under an oil and gas lease is called
    a. security deposit
    b. reversion

c. royalty

d. *profit à prendre*

48. Factors that assure a continuous need for rental units include

    a. schooling away from home

    b. RVs and campers

    c. infrequent job transfer

    d. all of the above

49. A month-to-month tenancy in an apartment may be terminated at any time by giving

a. three days' notice

b. thirty days' notice

c. two weeks' notice

d. no notice

50. The goal of a manager of rental property is to

    a. keep vacancies at a minimum

    b. keep cost of maintenance at a minimum

    c. keep collection of rents at a maximum

    d. all of the above

12

LIMITATIONS ON THE USE OF LAND

As we saw in Chapter 2, real property ownership includes three principal rights: the right to use and enjoy the land, the right to transfer and dispose of it, and the right to exclude others from it. Such rights comprise what was referred to as the *bundle of rights*. All property owners have certain responsibilities to other persons regarding the use they can make of their property. The owner's bundle of rights is not absolute but is subject to various limitations or burdens arising from private contracts or relationships with other parties, including adjoining landowners, and from governmental restrictions and controls, particularly zoning.

These limitations on use are commonly regarded as encumbrances, of which there are two basic types: those of a financial nature, which are in the form of a lien, either voluntary or involuntary, already considered (see Chapters 7, 8 and 10); and those that limit the physical use of the land, such as private deed restrictions, easements, encroachments, zoning and other public controls. Easements were considered in Chapter 2 along with one phase of public control, the regulation of subdivided lands. The latter topic was also considered in Chapter 5 in connection with the role of the Department of Real Estate.

Traditionally, governmental controls have mainly been in the form of local zoning regulations. Now much broader controls also exist, with the goal of preserving the natural environment.

Other rights or duties that impose a limitation on the use that property owners may make of their land relate to lateral and subjacent support, nuisances, trespass, waste, the impact of a mortgage or deed of trust, and the impact of insurance coverage on real property. These later topics are discussed in some detail throughout the chapter. Figure 12.1 graphically illustrates encumbrances or burdens that limit the physical use of property.

The wise use and development of land has probably been a concern since humans first realized that land provided much more than just

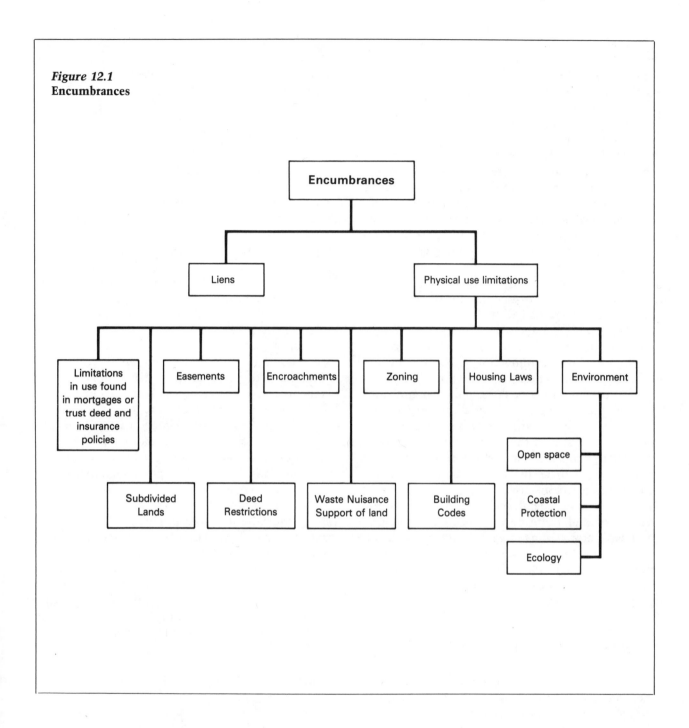

Figure 12.1
Encumbrances

something to walk on, lie on, and sit on. Even so, our ignorance of natural forces, our lack of foresight, determination to get out all wealth as quickly as possible from the land, and a lack of private or collective goals for the quality of life (or perhaps even a lack of confidence in our ability to make a difference in land use and productivity)

make it remarkable that we still have the land as a foundation and giver of life.

Though different individuals and groups have at different times declared a concern for the utilization and protection of land as a resource of priceless value, perhaps only in recent years has there come a collective and determined concern for and interest in land, both in its natural condition and when fully developed. Individuals and organizations are more able and willing to work with government, and government is willing to work with the people, in determining standards for land utilization, zoning, and methods of protecting the land for present and future generations. Along with an increasing awareness that the land itself must be protected, the air above the land, water on and within the land, and life forms on land and in water are being given new consideration. Earth's total ecological system must be protected; the protection of land cannot be separated from the protection of air, water, soil, plants, and animals.

In the past decade, countless new laws have evolved at all levels of government to reflect this collective concern and desire for the protection of our lands, cities, and our nation so that we may enjoy an improved quality of life, free from poisons, pollution, overcrowding, urban blight, and excessive noise. These new laws interface with the other thousands of laws, policies, and ordinances that determine what a property owner may or may not do with his or her land. Laws to protect the rights of the property owner, laws to protect the consumer and the surrounding community, as well as those laws that protect our environment are discussed in this chapter. Along with the many federal and state laws governing the use of land, there are very specific ordinances, policies, and customs in each community. Landowners, developers, buyers and real estate agents must become familiar with those items of specific concern within the community containing the property of interest.

TRENDS IN LAND USE

Trends in land use can evolve slowly or swiftly depending on a great number of factors: the influx of people to a given area; changing public tastes in housing and shopping preferences; customs and habits of people in the community; an increase or decrease in spendable income in an area; costs of land, money, materials, gradual changes in the age of residents; local taxing methods; and local requirements (or lack of them) to maintain property in a safe, neat condition. Local building codes also change requirements for use of materials, types of structures allowed, types of uses permitted, and control of off-site advertising signs and new industries. Planners, demographic special-

ists, census analysts, large lending institutions, major builders, and suppliers will try to project trends as accurately as possible so that changing needs and desires can be in an orderly fashion.

Residential Land

In residential units, laws are expanding to accommodate a greater variety of houses and apartments. Governing bodies seek ways to encourage the development of new housing stock at a greater variety of prices, streamline the processing of the various permits, and encourage the rehabilitation of older housing stock. Many cities have declared a willingness to work with developers and the housing industry to find new ways to provide desperately needed moderately priced housing. Real estate professionals must keep abreast of these constantly changing regulations, since ignorance can prove very costly if building plans have to be redrawn to accommodate new standards of insulation, fire-resistant materials, hard wire smoke detectors, etc.

Another example of a change that will have a great impact on real estate activity is the state provision that mobile homes can no longer be automatically barred from land zoned for single-family dwellings.

Frequent changes in government housing subsidies must be followed diligently. Newspapers, trade periodicals, and industry newsletters are the best sources for this information.

New types of home ownership have also had an impact on the housing industry. Among the most frequently encountered types are condominium, stock cooperative, own-your-own apartment, and planned residential development, discussed previously in Chapter 3.

Commercial Development

In commercial development and redevelopment, the most significant change affecting the real estate profession is the return to the inner city: the rehabilitation of older structures deemed to be sound and having some significance to the community. Even huge new enclosed malls are finding their way into what had been crowded and blighted areas. Most of these seem to be built in conjunction with other redevelopment projects. Whether this activity will continue without federal grants and various kinds of assistance is not known. It is clear, however, that increasing numbers of people in a variety of professions are becoming interested in preserving historical buildings, in recycling or finding new uses for sturdy older buildings, and in enticing new tenants to opt for buildings with history and character. The American Film Institute, Los Angeles Conservancy, and the Society for Architectual Historians are among those organizations working diligently and successfully to attract new owners and tenants for buildings that for a time were no longer considered to be in a good commercial location or condition. People have demonstrated that buildings can be successfully recycled, but first the incredible morass of conflicting regulatory agencies had to be brought together to streamline procedures for safely reopening older buildings. Many government departments must be brought into the act to make redevelopment work.

In some communities, whether by luck or design, older shopping areas have successfully reemerged with energetic new tenants after the traditional shops moved out. Again, success in real estate activity means staying acquainted with your community, watching commercial openings and closings, and finding helpful landlords, supportive chambers of commerce, and local lenders. A commercial area that is allowed to die will very quickly infect an increasingly large area with unsightly and costly blight. Perhaps obsolete commercial areas can be used for new housing developments; again, it is necessary to work with city planners on possible land use changes to reflect current needs.

Condominium ownership is available for commercial property as well as residential units. Both new developments and older, recycled commercial buildings may offer the opportunity to purchase space in a condominium arrangement.

Industrial Development

In industrial development, land use rules and other government regulations are becoming increasingly reflective of people's feelings about activities and materials involved in the manufacturing process. More control is being exerted over where certain plants can operate, how materials are transported and stored, safety devices to protect employees and surrounding areas, and safe disposal of dangerous waste products. Also, as people begin living or working closer to dirty, noisy, malodorous plants, they tend to complain successfully for the plant to reduce operation or

even relocate. More industrial areas are being zoned for "clean" or "light" manufacturing. Yet "heavy" (noisy, dirty, smelly) manufacturing processes are still important in the economic base and must be within commuting distance for employees and close to transportation arteries.

Industry continues to move into new areas, seeking new labor markets at lower costs, greater relocation incentives, and lower property costs. Real estate professionals need to work with industry to assure an adequate supply of properly zoned land to accommodate a full range of manufacturing activities and that the land will have the needed amenities such as railroad spurs and adequate water and power supplies. The professional may even assist a firm in getting acquainted with the community and local social resources which can attract and aid employees. Many communities are allowing industrially zoned land to be used for a variety of other uses, a practice which may prove to be a serious future economic blow.

Development of relatively large land areas exclusively for industrial use has been a growing trend for several decades. There are over 500 developments in California alone that cater exclusively to industrial users. Such developments are commonly referred to as "industrial parks." Although the term "industrial park" has no single meaning, an accepted definition might be the following: a contiguous land area planned exclusively for lease or sale to multiple industrial users. The key word in the definition is "planned."

The typical park will be developed with custom-designed facilities tailored to the needs of each user. Because industrial uses vary so widely, there is as much variation in the size of parcels as there is in design specifications. A recent survey disclosed that industrial parks range in size from three to three thousand acres.

Recreation/Open Space

Recreation and open space needs change but never diminish. Despite higher gasoline costs, Californians still expect lots of play space, close to both home and work; close enough for frequent weekend visits and interesting, varied, and active for periodic vacations. Real estate professionals know of the coordinated efforts by many to persuade government to acquire huge tracts of land for a variety of recreation and open space areas throughout the state. Purchase of land for such public use may change or increase the demand for developable land around the public recreation area. Also, more and/or different people are going to visit the new site, creating a whole new demand for services in the surrounding communities as well. That pressure will quickly be reflected in zone applications and building permits as property owners and developers seek to take advantage of the increased and changing demand. Real estate people must be aware of the time sequence for park purchases and development so as to be able to utilize the information in their work. Commercially zoned land may suddenly be at a premium as all the fast-food chains and sporting good stores seek to find sites to serve the new market. Residential needs may increase too as new employees seek homes closer to work and visitors decide they must have a vacation home adjacent to the park. Many communities are working hard to open bicycle routes, equestrian trails, hiking paths, wilderness parks, active sports complexes, and rock climbing training grounds. Any such activity will bring regulatory forces to bear as traffic increases, there is more competition for less land, and so on.

In California, state bond acts have passed every few years to enable state and local governing bodies to acquire special sites. State enabling legislation—the Quimby Act—has provided a mechanism whereby a city or county can charge a builder fees and/or a piece of land as a cost of developing residential units. The land and fees are for park and recreation purposes within the area generating the funds. Since some people find life near parks a nuisance and others find it a bonus, it behooves realtors to know how, when, and where government will charge the fees and where parks are planned.

Special-use recreation sites owned and developed by both the public and private sector are becoming more popular, more elaborate, and more costly. Equestrians are finding new communities designed to accommodate their life style and their need for trails, stables, and trailer storage. Boat lovers will find continuing competition for boat slips despite both private and public development of marinas along the coast and inland waters. Other homesites, whether single-family detached or multiple units, are continuing to answer the demand for a variety of recreational facilities as a part of the package—weight rooms, play courts, saunas, and jacuzzis along with the inevitable pool. Even par courses for running and exercising are a part of the scene as Californians take their exercise and play ever more seriously. Keeping up on recreation and leisure-oriented periodicals will help realtors and those interested in various aspects of the profession informed about trends in preferred activities and locations.

Remember, too, more real estate activity will invariably bring more government controls to protect against the unscrupulous on behalf of the unwary.

Agricultural Land

The 1965 Land Conservation Act (also known as the Williamson Act) was enacted to preserve agricultural land by affording tax benefits to the owner. The time may come when all remaining farm land in California will be voluntarily placed in agricultural preserves in order to retain a productive land resource base for food and fiber products. More than seven million acres of prime California agricultural land are already in land preserves. One of the basic problems in trying to arrive at a fair land-conservation program had been the conflict between what is in the short-range interest of a community and what is better in the long range for all the residents of a larger area.

CITY AND COUNTY PLANNING AND ZONING

City planning has existed since the first human said, "I want the path between our two caves to be HERE!" The ensuing argument over alignment, elevation, materials, thickness, curvilinear properties, color, scenic controls, signing, and traffic control continues to this day. City planning is the method by which we expect to realize the total concern for the protection and use of land and environment. It means, in part, providing a guide for development and redevelopment in an existing city. In most communities, early structures were erected and the first streets paved in a haphazard manner, with little concern as to use, population density, number of units, or impact on the surrounding community. The change from this unplanned manner of development to a concern for city planning has become more pronounced in the past decade in California. Using the catchwords, "the public health, safety, and general welfare," city planning is the means of authorizing a pattern for future growth and the orderly placement of living units, work units, and play units and the paths between all these units. The plan also calls for needed public services such as waste collection and disposal and fire protection.

Although we have used the term city planning, the county also has authority to enact zoning ordinances that apply to the unicorporated areas within the county.

New approaches to zoning and planning have resulted from the expansion of cities substantially beyond their original boundaries. At one time the suburbs were separated from the main city and had their own distinctive role. With the constant growth of the past two decades, smaller communities have been absorbed, and many urban areas have become, for all practical purposes, one large city—a megalopolis.

Perhaps the greatest influence for change in the planning process has been the demand by individual citizens to have an effective voice in all phases of community development from the initial base plan through development of implementation devices, establishment of adequately publicized public hearings, and systematic review of all parts of the process.

There has been an evolving collective concern for a broader consideration of the impact of any development on time and place, and planning has come to involve greater citizen participation in establishing goals and objectives. Citizens have even gone so far as to chain themselves to trees, rocks, and a variety of structures to focus attention on issues of concern. Such highly publicized events accomplished this objective and forced legislators to listen to their constituents. At the same time, citizens proved they were willing to do the necessary homework to provide serious input on confusing and controversial matters.

General Plan

Before a general plan can be implemented, the community must study its needs for housing, job sites, services, recreation and open space, transportation/circulatory systems, more efficient or multiple uses of land, the cost benefits of structural rehabilitation, renovation of neighborhoods, acceptable standards of noise control and air and water quality, slope density, special use districts, and waste disposal, and methods of fulfilling these needs. Citizen input demands that government take a greater responsibility for providing wisely and safely for these needs. And, from the extremes of "asphalt and concrete are progress"

to "protect our environment; stop development," a balance is slowly evolving.

Community plans provide for placement of physical facilities, workable interaction of the facilities and attendant streets, and utilities to ensure reasonable accommodation of the needs of the residents, and also provide a time frame for development. The general plan provides for a given mix of land uses, a range of densities, and the routes of major streets. The person interested in real estate should be aware that the general plan may show only the planned density or use and not the existing allowed density or use. Care should be taken to study both the general plan and the engineering maps to determine exactly what can be done with a specific property at what time.

Specific Plan Elements. Land use, recreation and open space, circulation, housing, seismic safety, noise pollution, scenic corridors, hiking and equestrian trails, bicycle trails, horsekeeping districts, and specific neighborhood plans are among the elements of a community plan. Copies of the plan maps and texts are a vital resource to those interested in any aspect of real estate.

With the adoption of plans allowing certain land uses and a prescribed number of units in a given area, buyers, sellers, and developers of land find themselves more easily able to do business: by reviewing a land use plan, one can determine what parcels may allow a particular use, and be fairly confident that the surrounding parcels will protect and enhance the parcel of interest. There is then the promise of systematic provision for the many services needed for any residential, commercial, or industrial activity. Traffic flow will have been considered, proximity of related uses, compatibility of adjacent uses, orderly installation of streets, sewers, storm drains, utility lines and easements, etc. The buyer, seller, and developer will be able to proceed with a particular project knowing that protective land use controls are in place.

Implementation Devices and Procedures. When general and specific plans have been adopted by the governing body, provisions must be set forth for the implementation of the plan. Planners, engineers, or other public employees, and even citizens' commissions, may be authorized by a governing body to make formal decisions on applications for development. Procedures are very specific for each locality and must be checked carefully.

The past has demonstrated that when an area develops without the guidance of adequate zoning, undesirable conditions, very difficult to correct, may result. Some cities have built up an amazing complex of very detailed rules and regulations covering details such as the size, height, color, and weight of a building, ratio of building size to lot size, and the location of the building on the lot. Everyone involved in real estate should be aware of these details, if only to appreciate the concerns of the governing body on behalf of the public, and the time and expense necessary to accomplish any project that is covered by these regulations.

When someone decides to begin a construction project, a parcel of land of a legally acceptable size to accommodate the required setbacks from the street, width of sidewalks, number of parking spaces, and orientation to streets must be found in a location either currently zoned or master planned for the particular use.

Zoning. Zones are designated on the land use plans by numbers, colors, or letters to symbolize the use and density to be permitted on a particular site. These restrictions on the use of land may be imposed by governmental regulations as well as by private agreement. Governmental regulations are normally imposed by cities or counties through *ordinances* which are enforced under the *police power* of the state. The uses and densities might be described as in the Los Angeles Summary of Zoning Regulations (see Figure 12.2). Other communities may have different titles, different groupings of uses, or different range of units, or a different means of measuring acreage. City, county, and state provisions may seem to overlap and be contradictory and confusing, so it is necessary to learn which level of government has jurisdiction over the parcel being considered.

Some of the specific considerations of zoning to protect community health, safety, and general welfare are:

1. Assuring sufficient light and air through control of building height and yard area and setback requirements. Height and orientation of buildings will become of greater importance as cities take up the matters of air and solar rights.
2. Providing a proper space for various types of activity and separating uses that might be incompatible.
3. Requiring off-street parking in various areas to help reduce traffic congestion.

New Zone Categories. Zoning regulations must be substantially uniform in operation. They cannot be discriminatory or created for the benefit of any particular group.

A relatively new branch of zoning is population density control in residential areas. For example, a zoning ordinance in San Francisco limits the number of dwelling units that may be built on a site; zoning authorities employ a sliding scale that ranges from one dwelling unit for every 1500 square feet of site ground area in a two-family area to one dwelling unit for every 125 square feet of site ground area in a high-density multiple dwelling area.

The environmental problems of many residential hillside communities have led planners to propose project concepts that depart from traditional planning controls. For instance, in Glendale more than one-third of the area is mountainous, as is true in many other areas of the state. In that community the city planning division submitted to the city council a number of ordinances designed not only to curtail the scarring of the hills, but also to preserve the vistas and to assure adequate open space and traffic circulation. One of the proposals, similar to those adopted elsewhere, provided for a planned residential development (PRD) which would create a new overlay zone in which a limited number of living units are permitted on larger land plots, and the open space is shared by the individual lot owners.

The PRD concept applies only to a total development project, not to the traditional individual lot concept. Traditional zoning in the past has been geared to control the placement of a single structure on a single lot. This type of zoning was fostered in the 1920s when the gridiron street pattern was paramount and when development usually occurred one lot at a time. The zoning then in effect was noted for its rigid separation of different uses in the different zones. Single and two-family houses were segregated from multiple houses, with few exceptions. The PRD, a substantial departure from the traditional scheme, provides for flexibility in location and construction of varying types of residential structures in a tract development.

In this type of development—commonly known as "garden clusters"—people own their own lots or parcels separately and share ownership of common areas and recreational facilities. The concept has proved useful both to developers and to buyers. Developers gain by being able to place fifteen units or more on an acre, compared to five units on conventional plans. Savings are

Figure 12.2
Example of Zoning Regulations

SUMMARY OF ZONING REGULATIONS
CITY OF LOS ANGELES

CLASSIFICATION	ZONE	USE	MAXIMUM HEIGHT STORIES	MAXIMUM HEIGHT FEET	REQUIRED YARDS FRONT	REQUIRED YARDS SIDE	REQUIRED YARDS REAR	MINIMUM AREA PER LOT	MINIMUM AREA PER DWELLING UNIT	MINIMUM LOT WIDTH	PARKING SPACE	EAGLE PRISMACOLOR PENCIL CHART
AGRICULTURAL	A1	AGRICULTURAL ONE-FAMILY DWELLINGS-PARKS-PLAY-GROUNDS-COMMUNITY CENTERS GOLF COURSES-TRUCK GARDENING-EXTENSIVE AGRICULTURAL USES	3	45 FT.	25 FT.	25 FT. MAXIMUM 10% LOT WIDTH 3 FT. MINIMUM	25 FT.	5 ACRES	2½ ACRES	300 FT.	TWO SPACES PER DWELLING UNIT	909 GRASS GREEN
	A2	AGRICULTURAL A1 USES	3	45 FT.	25 FT.	25 FT. MAXIMUM 10% LOT WIDTH 3 FT. MINIMUM	25 FT.	2 ACRES	1 ACRE	150 FT.	TWO SPACES PER DWELLING UNIT	912 APPLE GREEN
	RA	SUBURBAN LIMITED AGRICULTURAL USES	3	45 FT.	25 FT.	10'-1&2 STORIES 11'-3 STORIES	25 FT.	✱ 17,500 SQ. FT.	✱ 17,500 SQ. FT.	✱ 70 FT.	TWO GARAGE SPACES PER DWELLING UNIT	910 TRUE GREEN
ONE FAMILY RESIDENTIAL	RE40	RESIDENTIAL ESTATE ONE-FAMILY DWELLINGS PARKS PLAYGROUNDS COMMUNITY CENTERS TRUCK GARDENING	3	45 FT.	25 FT.	10 FT.	25 FT.	✱ 40,000 SQ. FT.	✱ 40,000 SQ. FT.	✱ 80 FT.	TWO GARAGE SPACES PER DWELLING UNIT	950 GOLD
	RE20				25 FT.	10 FT.	25 FT.	✱ 20,000 SQ. FT.	✱ 20,000 SQ. FT.	✱ 80 FT.		
	RE15				25 FT.	10 FT. MAXIMUM 10% LOT WIDTH 5 FT. MINIMUM	25 FT.	✱ 15,000 SQ. FT.	✱ 15,000 SQ. FT.	✱ 80 FT.		
	RE11				25 FT.	5'-1&2 STORIES 6'-3 STORIES	25 FT.	✱ 11,000 SQ. FT.	✱ 11,000 SQ. FT.	✱ 70 FT.		
	RE9				25 FT.	5 FT. MAXIMUM 10% LOT WIDTH 3 FT. MINIMUM	25 FT.	✱ 9,000 SQ. FT.	✱ 9,000 SQ. FT.	✱ 65 FT.		
	RS	SUBURBAN ONE-FAMILY DWELLINGS-PARKS PLAYGROUNDS-TRUCK GARDENING	3	45 FT.	25 FT.	5'-1&2 STORIES 6'-3 STORIES	20 FT.	7,500 SQ. FT.	7,500 SQ. FT.	60 FT.	TWO GARAGE SPACES PER DWELLING UNIT	911 OLIVE GREEN
	R1	ONE-FAMILY DWELLING RS USES	3	45 FT.	20 FT.	5'-1&2 STORIES 6'-3 STORIES	15 FT.	5,000 SQ. FT.	5,000 SQ. FT.	50 FT.	TWO GARAGE SPACES PER DWELLING UNIT	916 CANARY YELLOW
	RW1	ONE-FAMILY RESIDENTIAL WATERWAYS ZONE	2	30 FT.	10 FT.	• 4' PLUS 1' EACH STORY ABOVE 2ND 10% LOT WIDTH	15 FT.	2,300 SQ. FT.	2,300 SQ. FT.	28 FT.	TWO GARAGE SPACES PER DWELLING UNIT	914 CREAM
MULTIPLE RESIDENTIAL	RW2	TWO-FAMILY RESIDENTIAL WATERWAYS ZONE	3	45 FT					1,150 SQ. FT.			
	R2	TWO-FAMILY DWELLING R1 USES TWO-FAMILY DWELLINGS			20 FT.	5'-1&2 STORIES 6'-3 STORIES	15 FT.	5,000 SQ. FT.	2,500 SQ. FT.	50 FT.	TWO SPACES ONE IN A GARAGE	917 YELLOW ORANGE
	RD1.5	RESTRICTED DENSITY MULTIPLE DWELLING ZONE TWO-FAMILY DWELLING APARTMENT HOUSES MULTIPLE DWELLINGS	HEIGHT DISTRICT NO. 1 3 STORIES 45 FT. / HEIGHT DISTRICT NOS. 2,3 OR 4 6 STORIES 75 FT.		20 FT.	6 FT.	20 FT.	6,000 SQ. FT.	1,500 SQ. FT.	60 FT.	ONE SPACE EACH DWELLING UNIT OF LESS THAN THREE ROOMS / ONE AND ONE HALF SPACES EACH DWELLING UNIT OF THREE ROOMS / TWO SPACES EACH DWELLING UNIT OF MORE THEN THREE ROOMS / ONE SPACE EACH GUEST ROOM (FIRST THIRTY)	940 SAND
	RD2							8,000 SQ. FT.	2,000 SQ. FT.	60 FT		
	RD3								3,000 SQ. FT.			
	RD4				20 FT.	10 FT.	25 FT.	12,000 SQ. FT.	4,000 SQ. FT.	70 FT		
	RD5								5,000 SQ. FT.			
	RD6								6,000 SQ. FT.			
	R3	MULTIPLE DWELLING R2 USES APARTMENT HOUSES MULTIPLE DWELLINGS			15 FT.	5'-1&2 STORIE 6'-3 STORIES	15 FT.	5,000 SQ. FT.	800 TO 1,200 SQ. FT.	50 FT.		918 ORANGE
	R4	MULTIPLE DWELLING R3 USES CHURCHES HOTELS-SCHOOLS	UNLIMITED ✱		15 FT.	5' PLUS 1' EACH STORY ABOVE 2ND 16 FT. MAX.	15' PLUS 1' EACH STORY ABOVE 3RD 20 FT. MAX.	5,000 SQ. FT.	400 TO 800 SQ. FT.	50 FT.		943 BURNT OCHRE
	R5	MULTIPLE DWELLING R4 USES CLUBS-HOSPITALS LODGES-SANITARIUMS	UNLIMITED ✱		15 FT.	5' PLUS 1' EACH STORY ABOVE 2ND 16 FT. MAX.	15' PLUS 1' EACH STORY ABOVE 3RD 20 FT. MAX.	5,000 SQ. FT.	200 TO 400 SQ. FT.	50 FT.		946 DARK BROWN

✱ SEE HEIGHT DISTRICTS AT THE BOTTOM OF PAGE 2

• FOR TWO OR MORE LOTS THE INTERIOR SIDE YARDS MAY BE ELIMINATED, BUT 4 FT. IS REQUIRED ON EACH SIDE OF THE GROUPED LOTS.

✱ "H" HILLSIDE OR MOUNTAINOUS AREA DESIGNATION MAY ALTER THESE REQUIREMENTS IN THE RA-H OR RE-H ZONES,
SUBDIVISIONS MAY BE APPROVED WITH SMALLER LOTS, PROVIDING LARGER LOTS ARE ALSO INCLUDED. EACH LOT MAY BE USED
FOR ONLY ONE SINGLE-FAMILY DWELLING. SEE MINIMUM WIDTH & AREA REQUIREMENTS BELOW.

ZONE COMBINATION	MINIMUM TO WHICH NET AREA MAY BE REDUCED	MINIMUM TO WHICH LOT WIDTH MAY BE REDUCED
RA-H	14,000 SQ. FT.	63 FT.
RE 9 -H	7,200 SQ. FT.	60 FT.
RE11 -H,	8,800 SQ. FT.	63 FT.
RE15-H	12,000 SQ. FT.	72 FT.
RE 20-H	16,000 SQ. FT.	72 FT.
RE 40-H	32,000 SQ. FT.	NO REDUCTION

SHEET 1 OF 2

CP FORM 10

PREPARED BY CITY PLANNING DEPARTMENT

NOVEMBER 1980

Figure 12.2
Continued

SUMMARY OF ZONING REGULATIONS
CITY OF LOS ANGELES

CLASSIFICATION | EAGLE PRISMACOLOR PENCIL CHART

ZONE	USE	MAXIMUM HEIGHT (STORIES)	MAXIMUM HEIGHT (FEET)	REQUIRED YARDS (FRONT)	REQUIRED YARDS (SIDE)	REQUIRED YARDS (REAR)	MINIMUM AREA PER LOT AND UNIT	MINIMUM LOT WIDTH	LOADING SPACE	PARKING SPACE	
CR	LIMITED COMMERCIAL — BANKS, CLUBS, HOTELS, CHURCHES, SCHOOLS, BUSINESS & PROFESSIONAL OFFICES, PARKING AREAS	6	75 FT.	10 FEET	5'-10' CORNER LOT, RESIDENTIAL USE OR ADJOINING AN "A" OR "R" ZONE, SAME AS R4 ZONE	15' PLUS 1' EACH STORY ABOVE 3rd OTHERWISE NONE	SAME AS R4 FOR DWELLINGS OTHERWISE NONE	50 FEET FOR RESIDENCE USE OTHERWISE NONE	HOSPITALS, HOTELS INSTITUTIONS, AND WITH EVERY BUILDING WHERE LOT ABUTS ALLEY	ONE SPACE FOR EACH 500 SQ. FT. OF FLOOR AREA	939 FLESH
C1	LIMITED COMMERCIAL — LOCAL RETAIL STORES, OFFICES OR BUSINESSES, HOTELS, LIMITED HOSPITALS AND/OR CLINICS, PARKING AREAS				3'-5' CORNER LOT OR ADJOINING AN "A" OR "R" ZONE	15' PLUS 1' EACH STORY ABOVE 3rd RESIDENTIAL USE OR ABUTTING AN "A" OR "R" ZONE	SAME AS R3 FOR DWELLINGS EXCEPT 5000 SQ. FT. PER UNIT IN C1-H ZONES — OTHERWISE NONE		MINIMUM LOADING SPACE 400 SQUARE FEET	ONE SPACE FOR EACH 500 SQUARE FEET OF FLOOR AREA IN ALL BUILDINGS ON ANY LOT	929 PINK
C1.5	LIMITED COMMERCIAL — C1 USES — DEPARTMENT STORES, THEATRES, BROADCASTING STUDIOS, PARKING BUILDINGS, PARKS & PLAYGROUNDS				RESIDENTIAL USE SAME AS R4 ZONE	OTHERWISE NONE			ADDITIONAL SPACE REQUIRED FOR BUILDINGS CONTAINING MORE THAN 50,000 SQUARE FEET OF FLOOR AREA	MUST BE LOCATED WITHIN 750 FEET OF BUILDING	928 BLUSH
C2	COMMERCIAL — C1.5 USES — RETAIL BUSINESSES WITH LIMITED MANUFACTURING, AUTO SERVICE STATION & GARAGE, RETAIL CONTRACTORS BUSINESSES, CHURCHES, SCHOOLS	UNLIMITED ✳		NONE	NONE FOR COMMERCIAL BUILDINGS	NONE FOR COMMERCIAL BUILDINGS	SAME AS R4 FOR DWELLINGS OTHERWISE NONE				922 SCARLET RED
C4	COMMERCIAL — C2 USES — (WITH EXCEPTIONS, SUCH AS AUTO SERVICE STATIONS, AMUSEMENT ENTERPRISES, CONTRACTORS BUSINESSES, SECOND-HAND BUSINESSES)								NONE REQUIRED FOR APARTMENT BUILDINGS 20 UNITS OR LESS		924 CRIMSON RED
C5	COMMERCIAL — C2 USES — LIMITED FLOOR AREAS FOR LIGHT MANUFACTURING OF THE CM - ZONE TYPE				RESIDENTIAL USES — SAME AS IN R4 ZONE	RESIDENTIAL USES — SAME AS IN R4 ZONE				SEE CODE FOR ASSEMBLY AREAS, HOSPITALS AND CLINICS	925 CRIMSON LAKE
CM	COMM'L MANUFACTURING — WHOLESALE BUSINESSES, STORAGE BUILDINGS, CLINICS, LIMITED MANUFACTURING, C2 USES - EXCEPT HOSPITALS, SCHOOLS, CHURCHES						SAME AS R3 FOR DWELLINGS OTHERWISE NONE				905 AQUA-MARINE
MR1	RESTRICTED INDUSTRIAL — CM USES — LIMITED COMMERCIAL & MANUFACTURING USES, HOSPITALS, CLINICS, SANITARIUMS, LIMITED MACHINE SHOPS			15 FT.	NONE FOR INDUSTRIAL OR COMMERCIAL BUILDINGS	NONE FOR INDUSTRIAL OR COMMERCIAL BUILDINGS		50 FEET FOR RESIDENCE USE OTHERWISE NONE	HOSPITALS, HOTELS INSTITUTIONS, AND WITH EVERY BUILDING WHERE LOT ABUTS ALLEY	ONE SPACE FOR EACH 500 SQUARE FEET OF FLOOR AREA IN ALL BUILDINGS ON ANY LOT	901 INDIGO BLUE
MR2	RESTRICTED LIGHT INDUSTRIAL — MR1 USES — ADDITION INDUSTRIAL USES, MORTUARIES, AGRICULTURE				RESIDENTIAL USES — SAME AS IN R4 ZONE	RESIDENTIAL USES — SAME AS IN R4 ZONE	NONE EXCEPT FOR DWELLINGS		MINIMUM LOADING SPACE 400 SQUARE FEET	MUST BE LOCATED WITHIN 750 FEET OF BUILDING	906 COPEN-HAGEN BLUE
M1	LIMITED INDUSTRIAL — CM USES — LIMITED INDUSTRIAL & MANUFACTURING USES — NO "R" ZONE USES, NO HOSPITALS, SCHOOLS OR CHURCHES	UNLIMITED ✳		NONE					ADDITIONAL SPACE REQUIRED FOR BUILDINGS CONTAINING MORE THAN 50,000 SQUARE FEET OF FLOOR AREA		904 LIGHT BLUE
M2	LIGHT INDUSTRIAL — M1 USES — ADDITIONAL INDUSTRIAL USES, STORAGE YARDS OF ALL KINDS, ANIMAL KEEPING — NO "R" ZONE USES								NONE REQUIRED FOR APARTMENT BUILDINGS 20 UNITS OR LESS	SEE CODE FOR ASSEMBLY AREAS, HOSPITALS AND CLINICS	902 ULTRA-MARINE
M3	HEAVY INDUSTRIAL — M2 USES — ANY INDUSTRIAL USES — NUISANCE TYPE - 500 FT. FROM ANY OTHER ZONE — NO "R" ZONE USES				NONE	NONE	NONE —NOTE— "R" ZONE USES PROHIBITED	NONE			931 PURPLE
P	AUTOMOBILE PARKING — SURFACE & UNDERGROUND — PROPERTY IN A "P" ZONE MAY ALSO BE IN AN "A" OR "R" ZONE PARKING PERMITTED IN LIEU OF AGRICULTURAL OR RESIDENTIAL USES						NONE UNLESS ALSO IN AN "A" OR "R" ZONE	NONE UNLESS ALSO IN AN "A" OR "R" ZONE	—	—	967 COLD GREY LIGHT
PB	PARKING BUILDING — AUTOMOBILE PARKING WITHIN OR WITHOUT A BUILDING	✳✳	—	0', 5', OR 10' DEPENDING ON ZONING IN BLOCK AND ACROSS STREET	5' PLUS 1' EACH STORY ABOVE 2nd IF ABUTTING OR ACROSS STREET FROM "A" OR "R" ZONE	5' PLUS 1' EACH STORY ABOVE 2nd IF ABUTTING AN "A" OR "R" ZONE, TO A 16' MAXIMUM	NONE	NONE	—	—	936 SLATE GREY
SL	SUBMERGED LAND ZONE — COMMERCIAL SHIPPING, NAVIGATION, FISHING, RECREATION										919 SKY BLUE
(T)	TENTATIVE CLASSIFICATION — USED IN COMBINATION WITH ZONE CHANGE ONLY - DELAYS ISSUANCE OF BUILDING PERMIT UNTIL SUBDIVISION OR PARCEL MAP RECORDED										
(F)	FUNDED IMPROVEMENT CLASSIFICATION — AN ALTERNATE MEANS OF EFFECTING ZONE CHANGES AND SECURING IMPROVEMENTS (WHEN NO SUBDIVISION OR DEDICATIONS ARE INVOLVED)										
(Q)	QUALIFIED CLASSIFICATION — USED IN COMBINATION WITH ZONE CHANGES ONLY EXCEPT WITH RA, RE, RS OR R1 ZONES - RESTRICTS USES OF PROPERTY AND ASSURES DEVELOPMENT COMPATIBLE WITH THE SURROUNDING PROPERTY										

(Vertical classification labels: COMMERCIAL; RESIDENTIAL USES PROHIBITED IN ALL INDUSTRIAL ZONES / INDUSTRIAL; PARKING; SPECIAL)

SUPPLEMENTAL USE DISTRICTS: G ROCK AND GRAVEL • O OIL DRILLING • S ANIMAL SLAUGHTERING • RPD RESIDENTIAL PLANNED DEVELOPMENT
K HORSE-KEEPING • CA COMMERCIAL AND ARTCRAFT
(ESTABLISHED IN CONJUNCTION WITH ZONES)

HEIGHT DISTRICT ✳

N° 1	FLOOR AREA OF MAIN BUILDING MAY NOT EXCEED THREE TIMES THE BUILDING AREA OF THE LOT
N° 1L	SAME AS N° 1 AND MAXIMUM HEIGHT - 6 STORIES OR 75 FT.
N° 1-VL	SAME AS N° 1 AND MAXIMUM HEIGHT - 3 STORIES OR 45 FT.
N° 1-XL	SAME AS N° 1 AND MAXIMUM HEIGHT - 2 STORIES OR 30 FT.
N° 2	FLOOR AREA OF MAIN BUILDING MAY NOT EXCEED SIX TIMES THE BUILDABLE AREA OF THE LOT
N° 3	FLOOR AREA OF MAIN BUILDING MAY NOT EXCEED TEN TIMES THE BUILDABLE AREA OF THE LOT
N° 4	FLOOR AREA OF MAIN BUILDING MAY NOT EXCEED THIRTEEN TIMES THE BUILDABLE AREA OF THE LOT

MAXIMUM PB ZONE HEIGHTS ✳✳

N° 1	2 STORIES AND ROOF
N° 2	6 STORIES
N° 3	10 STORIES
N° 4	13 STORIES

NOTE: ALL INFORMATION GENERAL - FOR SPECIFIC DETAILS CHECK WITH DEPARTMENT OF BUILDING AND SAFETY

SHEET 2 OF 2

PREPARED BY CITY PLANNING DEPARTMENT   NOVEMBER 1980

made on construction costs by use of common walls, enabling the developer to locate on higher-priced land within more favorable commuting range. Buyers benefit from reduced prices and correspondingly lower down payments; in addition, monthly assessments for shared recreational facilities are substantially less than the upkeep of individually owned facilities. The development has an appeal to the community because less land is used for buildings; therefore, fifty percent more of the land can be set apart as "green areas" and be professionally landscaped.

Preserving the beauty of the landscape in California and other aesthetic considerations have gradually become legitimate purposes of zoning. For example, recent cases have sustained the validity of ordinances that require the removal of billboards from specified areas, such as along Highway 101, designated on the state's master plan as a "scenic highway" requiring "special scenic conservation treatment."

Zoning regulations change constantly, primarily because ours is a dynamic society. For instance, to the extent that the city of Los Angeles continues to grow and change—through economic, social, and population pressure—there is a need to revise the intensity or type of real estate development that takes place. Such revision is often accomplished through procedures provided in a municipality's *Comprehensive Zoning Plan*.

Zone Modification. Zoning strives for uniformity but cannot be enforced with excessive rigidity. Thus, provision is usually made for departures from the general rules. Applications for a change of zone or modification of existing zones usually fall into three major categories:

1. *Zone change or reclassification.* Applies where land is unsuited for the uses permitted under the present zoning, or could better serve the public interest if used for other purposes.
2. *Variance.* Applies where an unintended hardship would result from strict enforcement of the regulations and where special circumstances apply to a specific parcel of land for intended use.
3. *Conditional use.* Applies where certain special uses may be permitted but only in limited locations approved by the zoning authorities, and subject to appropriate conditions regarding design and operation.

Under both the variance and conditional use procedures, the zone classification remains the same; they are exceptions to the general rule. Many zoning offices publish pamphlets, booklets, and guides, available to the public, that explain the procedures applicable to the particular area.

Plan and Check, Check, Check

Additionally, many more mini-plans, ordinances, and provisions weigh on any development: Now that a particular use at a particular density has been approved for a particular parcel, a developer must consider the actual design of the tract. Rules govern side-yard requirements, depth of front and rear yards, nearness to neighboring structures, nearness of equestrian areas, location for driveways, surface of the driveway at equestrian trail crossings, width of required sidewalks, bicycle trails, equestrian trails, number and placement of utility easements, number of covered spaces for autos, minimal buildable lot size to protect trees or other environmental features, building height, archeological sites, permissible grading, placement of excess soil, energy conservation requirements, fencing of attractive nuisances, structural standards, etc. For buildings to be used by the public, physical accessibility may be regulated by both federal and state laws. Specifications covering the width of restroom doors, height of sinks and drinking fountains, ramps or elevator access from parking areas to the principal building access are all part of the standards to insure that people in wheelchairs can get into a building, reach all the floors, and use the restrooms. Also, it may be required that lots be partially landscaped or otherwise be shielded from view. "A place for everything and everything in its place" is the phrase; there are code sections to cover everything and a variety of agencies review plans to see that all codes are complied with. Other codes may apply on sites adjacent to areas having scenic controls or designated special-use districts such as areas zoned for horses.

Although these rules may seem detailed, cumbersome, and expensive, they exist to protect and enhance the community. Where a development is built without following the codes, it is important to see if the implementation process is lacking in detail, or if the problem lies with a faulty system for approving new developments and inspecting the work. Codes are continuously updated to insure that the general plan is being followed. Plan and code changes may be initiated by government or because of citizens' requests. Such changes or additions are carefully processed for maximum input by all concerned and to insure that the changes are in keeping with the intent of the general plan. It is evident that all those in real estate need to keep informed about revisions of city codes on building development.

ENVIRONMENTAL PROTECTION

The past decade has seen a remarkable upsurge of laws designed to protect, preserve, and enhance the environment. Most construction projects require an environmental impact statement that declares whether the proposed project will have no impact, some impact, or great impact on the immediate area. When assessing the impact of a project, traffic patterns, noise, air quality, flora, fauna, soil, topography, proximity to faults, and public services such as fire protection and school capacity are all considered. Unless a project is determined to have no adverse impact or to be "categorically exempt," a documented detailed report is required, covering each of the categories and showing the impact of the project, alternatives to the project, and possible mitigating measures to offset any adverse impact. More than one department, agency or commission may have authority to consider the findings and approve or disapprove the project. Conditions for development may also be spelled out that satisfy the concern for the environment. The applicant is expected to bear the cost of the report; a whole new industry has sprung up to provide the engineers and statisticians necessary to compile such data, though much of the information is readily available through the governing body for inclusion in the plans. Consultants in the field of report preparation are often called to court to testify as to their findings in disputes over noise levels or the presence or absence of air or water pollution.

Some of the basic laws relating to environmental concerns are the National Environmental Policy Act of 1970, the California Environmental Quality Act of 1970 (since amended several times), and the California Coastal Zone Conservation Act, first approved in 1972. The impact of these and related laws is further considered in the course on real estate law.

In addition to general environmental protection groups, in the last 15 to 20 years a number of environmental action groups have been formed with highly specific goals and programs, concerned with one or more of such environmental issues as air pollution, airport impact and noise, freeways and transportation, ocean and coastal preservation, open space and land use, waste disposal and recycling, wildlife habitats, and archeological site protection. The impact that such groups can make on development plans should not be overlooked.

DEED RESTRICTIONS

When the subdivision method of developing land for residential purposes came into use, the need arose to protect the economic value of the land by some kind of private control over its improvement and use. Such controls were necessary to induce purchasers and lenders to move into and to make loans in subdivisions or tract areas. It was apparent that purchasers and lenders could not be expected to make substantial investments in homes of a particular level of value and quality unless some protection was afforded them—for example, to prevent construction of a lower quality and value in the immediate neighborhood.

In addition to the need for controls of home construction, similar protection is needed against the encroachment of industry or business construction and uses. Some protection of this kind may be available in the form of zoning ordinances. But zoning controls are generally not considered fully adequate. The additional need may be properly filled by private controls.

Creation

As the name implies, an encumbrance in the form of a restriction in some way limits or restricts the use of the land by an owner. Restrictions are created by private agreement of property owners, typically by appropriate clauses in deeds, in agreements, or in a general plan affecting an entire subdivision. They are usually referred to as "covenants, conditions, and restrictions" or CC&R's.

The generic term is *restrictions*, which may be in the form of a *covenant* or in the form of a *condition*. The main difference between a convenant and a condition relates to the right of enforcement when a breach occurs. A covenant is a promise to do or not to do a certain thing. If a breach occurs, the remedy is either an action for money damages or an action to enjoin or prevent a violation; or both remedies may be available. On the other hand, if an owner breaches a condition, it may result in a loss of title with the title reverting back to the creator of the condition.

Because breach of condition has the rather extreme result of forfeiture of title, the courts generally construe restrictions as covenants, not as conditions.

Restrictions may be created for any legitimate purpose in limiting the use or occupancy of land. The right to acquire and possess property includes the right to dispose of all or any part of it, and to impose upon the grant any reservations or restrictions or conditions that the grantor may see fit, provided they are not contrary to the express or implied policy of the law. For example, restrictions prohibiting the use of property by certain races are now not merely unenforceable—they are void.

Restrictions may cover a multitude of matters, including limitations in use for either residential or business purposes. Following is a list of subjects often embodied in typical residential area restrictions:

1. Land use and building type, such as a one-story single-family residence
2. Dwelling cost, quality, and size
3. Lot area and width
4. Set-back lines
5. Planting and fencing
6. Sight distance at intersections
7. Slope-control areas
8. Easements
9. Signs on the property
10. Livestock, poultry, and pets
11. Nuisances
12. Temporary structures
13. Oil and mining operations
14. Architectural control.

Deed restrictions, in contrast to zoning ordinances, need not necessarily promote public health or the general public welfare. They are often intended to create a particular type of neighborhood deemed desirable by the tract developer—such as a Spanish or Mediterranean atmosphere—and may be based solely on aesthetic considerations.

The most common use of restrictions today is in new subdivisions where *general plan* restrictions are customarily employed. General plan restrictions are to be distinguished from *single plan* restrictions. A single plan restriction is ordinarily created for the benefit of the grantor's remaining land after he or she has sold a portion of it. A general plan restriction, on the other hand, is usually in the form of an extensive set of provisions that relate to an entire tract in multiple

ownership; such a plan gives every lot owner in the tract a right of enforcement. General plan restrictions are both mutually burdensome and mutually beneficial.

Restrictions under a general plan can be created in either of two ways. The restrictions may be set forth in full in all of the deeds, in which event there need not be any recorded declaration of restrictions preceding the deeds. Or a declaration of restrictions may be used for this purpose, the terms of which can be incorporated into each deed by reference. Following is the type of language usually contained in the deeds to accomplish this purpose:

> This conveyance is made subject to all of the covenants, conditions, and restrictions contained in that certain Declaration of Restrictions executed by the grantor herein and recorded on _____ in book _____, page _____, Official Records of the county of _____, state of California, which are incorporated herein and made a part of this deed the same as if set forth in full.

By incorporating the terms of a recorded set of restrictions by reference, the deed will be much shorter and the recording charges will be less. Also, there is an assurance that the restrictions will be identical in all cases.

In many instances the deed restrictions may provide for the formation of a perpetual property owners' association, such as may be found in a condominium. Such associations are often given the power to amend tract restrictions from time to time to correspond with community growth. They may be given the power to revise building restrictions pertaining to certain blocks of lots in the development, or to impose architectural restrictions, or to impose other requirements from time to time.

A *mortgage savings clause* is considered an essential part of a set of deed restrictions if the property is to be subject to a deed of trust in the future, as is usually the case. Such a clause may read as follows:

> A breach of any of the foregoing conditions, restrictions, covenants or reservations, or any reentry by reason of such breach, shall not defeat or render invalid a lien of any mortgage or deed of trust made in good faith and for value on the property or any part thereof, but said conditions, restrictions, covenants and reservations shall be binding upon and effective against any owner of the property or any part thereof whose title is acquired by foreclosure, trust deed sale or otherwise.

Without such a provision, the security could be lost to a lender through the acts of the borrower. A prudent lender will either require that the restriction contain a mortgage savings clause, or that the right of enforcement of any condition in the restrictions be subordinated to the lender's deed of trust. Such a clause means that if the owner of the property violates a condition of the deed restriction that may permit the grantor to regain title, the grantor or his or her successor will be subject to the obligation to pay the amount due under the deed of trust. Conversely, if the owner of the property defaults under the terms of the deed of trust and the property is sold to the beneficiary or other party at a foreclosure sale, the purchaser will acquire the title subject to the covenants and conditions of the deed restrictions.

The following illustrates deed restrictions and some of the usual provisions:

Provided, however, that this conveyance is made and accepted on each of the following express conditions:

That said premises shall be used for residence purposes only.

That no building or structure whatever other than a first-class private residence with the customary outbuildings shall be erected, placed, or permitted on the said premises or any part thereof, and that said residence shall cost and be fairly worth not less than $_____. *Note: A limitation based on a dollar amount is not too realistic in an inflationary period. A reference to minimum square footage could be more appropriate.*

That any such residence shall be located not less than _____ feet from the front line of said premises, and said building shall face the front line of said premises.

That no intoxicating liquor of any character shall be bought, sold, or kept for sale on said premises or any part of thereof.

PROVIDED THAT a breach of any of the foregoing conditions shall cause said premises to revert to the said grantor, his or her heirs or assigns, each of whom shall have the right of immediate re-entry upon said premises in the event of any such breach.

PROVIDED ALSO THAT a breach of any of the foregoing conditions or reentry by reason of such breach shall not defeat or render invalid the lien of any mortgage or deed of trust made in good faith and for value as to said premises or any part thereof, but said conditions shall be binding upon and effective against any owner of said premises whose title thereto is acquired by foreclosure, trustee's sale, or otherwise.

PROVIDED FURTHER THAT all and each of the restrictions, conditions and covenants herein contained shall in all respects terminate and end and be of no further effect either legal or equitable and shall not be endorseable after [date].

Termination

Restrictions may have either a designated termination date or a date of termination that becomes effective upon recording a cancellation notice by a given percentage of the lot owners. Many subdividers insert a clause in the deed restrictions which permits modification or alteration of the restrictions with the consent of a specified number of lot owners. Unless such a provision is contained in the deed restrictions, all lot owners in the tract would need to enter into modification agreements or give releases or quitclaim deeds before the restrictions became unenforceable.

Although deed restrictions are usually effective for the specified period of time set forth, they may be held unenforceable because of various factors, including a gradual change in the character of the neighborhood. Courts have held deed restrictions to be unenforceable where conditions in the neighborhood have changed so much that the purpose of the restrictions has become obsolete. However, where the original purpose of the covenant can still be realized, it will be enforced even though the unrestricted use of the property would be more profitable to its owner.

ENCROACHMENTS

Related to encumbrances on land use are encroachments, which occur when an improvement—such as a building or a wall or a fence—is located or extends onto a property of an adjoining owner. Ordinarily this constitutes a *trespass*. An appropriate action by the landowner whose property is encroached upon is to enjoin or compel the removal of the encroachment. However, the party who is encroaching on his or her neighbor, and thereby reducing the usable portion of the neighbor's property, may be doing so with legal justification. He or she may have gained title to the strip encroached upon by adverse possession, or may have obtained an easement by prescription or possibly by implication.

If the encroachment is wrongful, the party encroached upon may sue for damages and for removal of the obstruction. However, where the encroachment is slight and the cost of removal is great, and the encroachment resulted from an honest mistake and was not intentional, the courts, acting in their sound discretion, may award money damages—often only a nominal amount—in lieu of requiring removal of the structure. An example of an encoachment is shown in Figure 12.3.

Figure 12.3
Encroachment

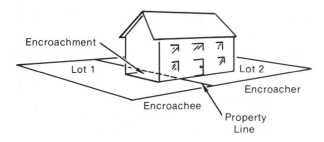

HOUSING AND BUILDING REGULATIONS

The housing and construction industry is regulated by three different laws:

1. State Housing Law
2. Local building codes
3. State Contractors' License Law

The State Housing Law is administered by the Division of Building and Housing Standards of the Department of Housing and Community Development. It is designed to provide minimum construction and occupancy requirements for all apartment houses and hotels throughout the state and all dwellings located in cities. Any city or county may impose more stringent requirements if it wishes. Incidentally, according to the official publication of the Department of Housing and Urban Development, the first building code in the United States dates back to 1626; it prohibited thatched roofs in the Plymouth colony, presumably because they would have been targets for flaming arrows.

Construction regulations under the statewide act are handled by local building inspectors. Occupancy and sanitation regulations are enforced by local health officers. Typically, procedures for new construction or building alterations require an application to the office of the local building inspector for a building permit. The application must ordinarily be accompanied by plans, specifications, and a plot plan. After approval of the application, a building permit is issued. No construction or alteration can be commenced before the building permit is issued.

Any city or county may supplement and strengthen the basic State Housing Law requirements by establishing additional construction and occupancy requirements for all structures within the local jurisdiction. These regulations are designated as local building codes. They do not take the place of the state law, but both may operate in the same area. Property owners must comply with the most stringent of the two applicable laws.

The State Contractors' License Law represents another approach to construction regulation. Protection against unqualified building contractors and subcontractors is achieved by requiring construction to be done only by licensed persons. This includes subcontract work as well as general contract and engineering work. Jurisdiction to enforce the law vests in the contractors' State License Board, which also concerns itself with the solvency of the license applicant.

An additional indirect regulation of housing construction is in effect by virtue of the various governmental financing roles under the FHA, VA, and Cal-Vet programs. These agencies require, as a prerequisite to participation in the programs, that the structure involved meet rather elaborate requirements referred to as *Minimum Property Requirements* (MPR's). These requirements are more demanding, in many details, than either the State Housing Law or local building codes.

Another state agency that exercises a degree of control over housing and construction is the State Department of Public Health. State law requires the appointment of a local health officer in every county and city. In most cases the officer enforces both state and local health laws, and uses the State Department of Public Health as an advisory agency. Drainage, plumbing, sewage disposal, and water supply fall under the jurisdiction of both the local health officer and the State Department of Public Health. These officers can require the halting of any proposed development that may result in contamination of the water supply or impairment of the drainage system, or that may result in improper sewage disposal. The sanitary condition of all housing is also subject to control by the health authorities.

On the subject of housing, Figure 12.4 projects the housing demands in the United States for the period from 1985 to the year 2000.

Figure 12.4
Estimated Housing Demands

WHAT FACTORS WILL CHANGE HOUSING DEMANDS FOR THE YEARS 1985–2000?

A report from the Joint Center for Urban Studies of the Massachusetts Institute of Technology and Harvard University, made in the early 1980s, pointed out four factors that they believed would affect housing over the decade:
1. The government was neglecting housing.
2. Average-income families were less able to afford houses now than they were ten or even five years before.
3. The make-up of the American family was changing, and that, along with the slower rate of growth in real income, would change housing requirements.
4. Migration to the warmer climates of the U.S. was increasing.
Thus far, each point has continued to prove true in this decade. We estimate that 25.3 million to 28.6 million new housing units will be needed by the year 2000. Low-income families will be hit hardest if the government doesn't take positive action to improve the housing situation.

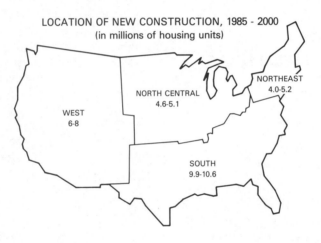

LOCATION OF NEW CONSTRUCTION, 1985 - 2000
(in millions of housing units)

NORTHEAST
4.0-5.2

NORTH CENTRAL
4.6-5.1

WEST
6-8

SOUTH
9.9-10.6

OTHER FACTORS INFLUENCING THE USE OF LAND

Not only are there legal limitations in the use that an owner can make of his land, but there are also limitations based on such factors as the land's size, shape, contour, type, location, and so on. In this section we look at some of these factors.

The availability of *water* affects the usability of land. Water can pose two problems—not having enough or having too much. One landowner in California may be fighting off flood waters when the rains are unusually heavy, while another, whose land is located in an arid or semi-arid area, can't get enough water to use his land properly.

Conservation of water has been of paramount importance in California as well as in other western states. This is especially true in view of the critical drought that affected California from 1976 to 1978. Because of the need for conservation, the doctrine of the reasonable user has developed. Under this doctrine the right of a riparian owner to the use of water is limited to such water as shall be reasonably required for the beneficial use of the land, but no more.

Another matter of concern relates to the *stability of the earth's surface*. California, like many parts of the world, is subject to earthquakes, and the proximity of land to a known fault obviously will have an effect on its usability. Relevant fault information is now part of the public report on subdivisions built after 1966. Earthquakes are a fact of life like any other natural phenomenon, and they should be taken into consideration when buying and building. The location of faults will influence not only the type of structure and the method of construction, but also the manner of installing fixtures. Experts seem to agree that there is literally no place in Caifornia, as is true in many parts of the world, where one can be completely "safe" from earthquakes, although some places may be safer than others.

Another matter of concern is that of *access*. Access right is the right of an owner to have ingress and egress to and from his or her property to a public street. There is no absolute right to access. Under certain situations, it is possible to have "land-locked" land in California. If a parcel of property does not abut on a public street, then the owner will ordinarily be dependent upon an easement, and whether he or she has a right or can obtain a right will be dependent upon all the circumstances.

Does the public have the right of access to the beaches and other recreational areas in California? The theory of *implied dedication* has been recognized in California. It has been held by the State Supreme Court that there is an implied public dedication of access to beaches and inland waterways when the public has used such routes for a period of five years. This ruling has had a tremendous impact on the use of land located near the beaches as well as near other recreational areas. The problem has been the subject of legislative study in an attempt to make compatible, to the extent possible, the conflicting rights of private property owners and of the public to access and use of beaches and other recreational areas. There is growing concern that the rights of the public be met in this regard. (This subject is discussed further in the course on real estate law.)

Lateral and Subjacent Support

All land is affected by the rights of adjoining owners, since all land at some point is bounded by property owned by others. A landowner is entitled to have the soil on his or her land remain in a natural position, undisturbed by excavation or other activities on adjoining property. This right is to the support of the land in its natural state, without the added weight of a building on it. If an adjoining owner desires to make excavations on his or her property that could affect neighboring property, he or she may do so after giving notice

and taking precautions as required by provisions of the Civil Code.

A similar situation occurs when one person owns the surface of the land and another person the subsurface or the minerals below the surface. The owner of the surface is entitled to have it remain in its natural condition without any subsidence caused by the withdrawal of land or minerals under it by the subjacent owner. Remedies include injunctions or restraining orders.

Nuisance

An owner of real property may not use his or her property in such a manner that it will interfere substantially with the use and enjoyment of real property by another person or interfere with the rights of the general public. Activities on one's land may result in obnoxious fumes or odors or other detriments. If an adjoining owner is affected, then the nuisance is said to be private, and the adjoining owner could maintain an action to enjoin (abate) the nuisance and to obtain damages.

If the disagreeable activity affects a larger segment of the community, it is considered a public nuisance, giving the right in the public body to maintain an action to enjoin or for other appropriate relief.

Waste

Where two or more persons have rights in the same parcel of land, such as a life tenant and the holder of the remainder interest, or a tenant and landlord under a lease agreement, the person having the right of possession has a duty to the other owners not to commit any act which might impair the value of the land, such as the unauthorized removal of timber or minerals from the land or permitting structures on the land to deteriorate through lack of reasonable care and maintenance. This duty applies to a life tenant, a tenant under a lease, or a tenant in common or other co-owner in possession.

Impact of a Mortgage or Deed of Trust

Where land is encumbered, the usual form of mortage or deed of trust contains provisions that the owner will permit no waste of the property, will keep the property in good condition and repair, and will not remove any of the improvements without the consent of the lender.

Impact of Insurance Coverage

Improved real property is customarily covered by hazard insurance. As a condition for coverage, the landowner agrees to do or not to do a variety of things that he or she might otherwise have the right to do, such as storing combustible material on the property. An owner should be aware of all the terms and provisions of the hazard policy in this regard so as not to impair its validity. Thus, because of a contractual obligation, there can be a compulsion to be more prudent in the use that is made of real property. And, to the extent that the owner does exercise greater care (e.g., the installation of smoke detectors), benefits may be obtained through a reduction in the size of insurance premiums.

QUESTIONS FOR CHAPTER 12

Matching Terms

a. lateral	i. capricious
b. encroachment	j. covenant
c. waste	k. deed restrictions
d. subjacent	l. general plan
e. zoning	m. condition
f. encumbrance	n. access
g. variance	o. nuisance
h. arbitrary	

_____ 1. limitations on the use of land imposed by governmental authorities

_____ 2. an exception to zoning

_____ 3. subject to whim

_____ 4. a promise

_____ 5. private restrictions imposed on an entire subdivision

_____ 6. dependent upon something occurring or not occurring in the future

_____ 7. bothersome activity

_____ 8. right to have ingress and egress to and from a public street

_____ 9. to the side

_____ 10. a charge or burden on land

_____ 11. act of a life tenant that could adversely affect the interest of the holder of the remainder interest

_____ 12. underneath

_____ 13. unauthorized extension of an improvement from one parcel of land onto a parcel owned by another person

_____ 14. decisive but unreasoned

_____ 15. limitations on use of property imposed by private agreement

True/False

T F 16. Ordinarily, private deed restrictions are more restrictive than zoning.

T F 17. Zoning may be arbitrary if uniformly applied.

T F 18. Planning and zoning are both aspects of public control.

T F 19. All encumbrances are liens.

T F 20. A hazard insurance policy may impose limitations on the use of real property.

T F 21. Wildlife preservation is of diminishing concern.

T F 22. Deed restrictions may not be based on aesthetic considerations.

T F 23. Zoning and deed restrictions must be consistent with each other.

T F 24. A PRD is not affected by zoning.

T F 25. All liens are encumbrances, but not all encumbrances are liens.

Multiple Choice

26. There is increased concern in California for the relation of land development to the following:
    a. ecology
    b. open space
    c. preservation of scenic areas
    d. all of the above

27. The first endeavor to control city directional growth and land use was in the form of what type of enactment?
    a. conditional use
    b. nonconforming use
    c. variance
    d. zoning

28. The manner in which improvements are to be constructed on land is ordinarily regulated by what type of code?
    a. zoning
    b. civil
    c. building
    d. real estate

29. Future planning and development of the state is least likely to include a consideration of
    a. coastal use
    b. air pollution
    c. mass transportation
    d. special interest groups

30. The movement away from the metropolitan area was basically influenced by the production of
    a. apartments
    b. automobiles

c. new roads

d. utility facilities

31. Zoning ordinances are unenforceable if
    a. arbitrary
    b. capricious
    c. unreasonable
    d. all of the foregoing apply

32. A subdivider and developer must be aware of many cost factors in developing new property. Which of the following would need to be considered in estimating the costs?
    a. topography
    b. zoning laws
    c. construction trends
    d. all of the above

33. The word *megalopolis* refers to
    a. subdivisions
    b. freeway system
    c. large city
    d. large recreational area

34. In planning and developing a shopping center, uppermost in the mind of the developer would be
    a. architectural design
    b. population growth
    c. competition
    d. topography

35. City planning commissions are empowered to:
    a. fix city boundaries
    b. restrict low-income families to designated areas
    c. plan for orderly growth and development of the community
    d. enforce building and safety codes

36. Referring to the sample "Summary of Zoning Regulations" in Figure 12.2, the zoning that permits the land use for the conduct of a real estate school would be found in:
    a. CR
    b. R3
    c. A2
    d. PB

37. Which of the following laws affect the manner in which improvements on property may be constructed?
    a. State Housing Act
    b. Health and Safety Code
    c. local building ordinances
    d. all of the above

38. A subdivider may place restrictions on individual lots in a subdivision by or through
    a. enacting zoning regulations
    b. covenants in a deed
    c. police power

d. eminent domain

39. Deed restrictions are considered to be
    a. a benefit
    b. a burden
    c. both a and b
    d. neither a nor b

40. The type of structure that an owner can build can be controlled by
    a. deed restrictions
    b. zoning
    c. both a and b
    d. neither a nor b

41. If deed restrictions prohibit a use permitted by zoning
    a. zoning is controlling
    b. restrictions are controlling
    c. restrictions are illegal
    d. the zoning is invalid

42. If zoning prohibits a use permitted by deed restrictions
    a. zoning is controlling
    b. the restrictions are controlling
    c. the zoning is invalid
    d. the restrictions are illegal

43. Deed restrictions are usually placed on property by the
    a. local planning commission
    b. original subdivider
    c. state of California
    d. city council

44. The term "CC&R" relates to
    a. zoning regulations
    b. building codes
    c. city and county regulations
    d. private deed regulations

45. A restriction which limits the square footage of a building creates
    a. an easement
    b. a lien
    c. an encumbrance
    d. a license

46. An owner wants to place a six-foot fence around his or her property to keep a dog in. He or she should check
    a. zoning regulations
    b. deed restrictions
    c. both a and b
    d. neither a nor b

47. Deed restrictions in a large subdivision are usually created by
    a. recording a "declaration of restrictions"
    b. including a set of restrictions in each deed
    c. recording a quitclaim deed
    d. filing a copy with the local planning commission

48. The extension of an improvement onto the land of an adjoining owner is referred to as
    a. an abatement
    b. a redemption
    c. an encroachment
    d. a preemption
49. A community driveway ordinarily benefits
    a. husband and wife
    b. all residents of a city
    c. noncontiguous owners
    d. adjoining land owners
50. The land of an adjoining owner of real property is entitled to
    a. subjacent support
    b. lateral support
    c. support of land
    d. all of the above

13

INTRODUCTION TO REAL ESTATE INVESTMENT

Real Property as an Investment

Impact of Income Taxes on Investment

Types of Investment Property

Factors that Influence Investments

Real Estate Investment Organizational Forms

Guidelines for Protecting the Public

In this chapter we will consider some basic rules that apply to real estate as an investment. Unless the investor is knowledgeable, the investment can turn out to be very good, with luck, or very bad. All real property is not necessarily a good investment. Many factors need to be taken into consideration, including the investor's own status. This area has become a highly specialized field, and most people need experts to assist them. A knowledge of the impact of taxes, especially income taxes, on the investment is also vital.

The word *return* is of primary concern. Many people consider return to mean only *yield*, i.e., the rate of return they can expect *on* the investment. But return has another meaning, one which involves an understanding of the risk factor.

Basically, an investment is the use of funds to make a profit. Unless there is growth in the value of the investment in a period of inflation, then a return of the original amount invested, even a percentage of interest as a yield on the investment, can actually result in a loss. When recovering the original amount of the investment, the investor has to be concerned with the amount's purchasing power *then*, i.e., when the investment was made, versus *now*, i.e., when the investment is returned. It is a matter of understanding the difference between dollars and value. Dollars don't change—a dollar is still a dollar—but its purchasing power can change drastically. Income taxes on the yield or earnings during the period of the investment can also reduce the net return.

A basic rule to follow is this—own a home for as long as you can. It isn't necessarily an investment as such, but it can prove over time to be a good investment while providing shelter. If a person doesn't have sufficient resources for a single family residence, then he or she may start with a duplex and obtain additional income tax advantages over a single family unit.

Speculation in real estate can involve a high risk. Generally, the higher the yield, the greater the risk—and conversely, the lower the yield, the lower the risk. There is no easy answer as to what is a good investment. Primarily it depends on intelligently made decisions, and not on unfounded hope.

REAL PROPERTY AS AN INVESTMENT

Land is regarded as the most important item in man's economic life. Most of our values, in terms of money, are based on land. Theodore Roosevelt said many years ago, "Every person who invests in well-selected real estate in a growing section of a prosperous community adopts the surest and safest method of becoming independent, for real estate is the basis of wealth." And Andrew Carnegie's words are as true today as when he said, "Ninety percent of all millionaires become so through owning real estate. More money has been made in real estate than in all industrial investments. The wise young man or wage earner of today invests his money in real estate."

Actually, many people who have made money in real estate did not look upon their land as an investment—rather, it was a means of livelihood, acquired for the primary purpose of growing crops or raising animals. Eventually, as a result of the population boom, its value substantially increased. Today, more and more people are motivated to acquire land primarily as an investment. Although land, more than any other commodity in the world, has probably made more people economically secure, there is still much misunderstanding about land values. Actually, no *one* factor makes land valuable.

Land value derives more from a series of factors: supply, use, and location. First, of course, there is only so much land and no more. The *amount* was fixed when the earth took shape. We cannot manufacture land as we manufacture items of personal property like cars, television sets, and other consumable commodities. Inevitably, following the law of supply and demand, as greater calls put upon the supply of land, its value goes up.

The second factor to assess in determining land value is the *use* to which the land is put. Will it be suitable for an apartment, home, motel, recreational area, store, business, arcade, or will it serve some other use?

The third factor is the *location* of the land. Is it near a city, good transportation, schools, shopping, a lake or resort area?

All of the foregoing factors play a vital part in the value of land. Today, people who purchase a home or any other essential property also look upon it as an investment and expect the value to increase over the years. A basic knowledge of the requirements for a sound investment is essential for success in buying real estate. However, there is a simple decisive answer to the question, "When is a good time to invest in property?" For many people the answer is, "When you have the money and can afford to have it tied up in real property."

Figure 13.1 illustrates many of the advantages of real estate as an investment.

Utilizing the services of a Certified Financial Planner or Certified Public Accountant is generally an indispensable part of financial and tax planning today. As a public service, CFPs and CPAs offer useful information to the public by way of newspaper advertisements, pamphlets, or other means. Figure 13.2 contains some basic suggestions for investing in rental property.

IMPACT OF INCOME TAXES ON INVESTMENTS

[Note: As this book went to press, 1986 federal tax legislation was still pending, and some of the following information may change due to tax reform.]

Both the federal government and the state of California impose an income tax, with returns to be filed on or before April 15 each year. California income tax law is patterned generally after the federal income tax laws, although there are differences. There are no immediate income tax effects resulting merely from acquiring property; however, the method in which it is acquired and the use to which it is put may have significant consequences upon later tax liabilities.

Three kinds of property have received favorable tax consideration for a number of years under the income tax law because of their importance to the economy and governmental needs, namely, housing, oil, and cattle. Housing, as we have seen, is a basic need for everyone, including those in the armed services. Oil is vital, and for years the government has encouraged exploration and development through tax incentives in an effort to maintain adequate reserves. And we've heard the expression "An army moves on its stomach," hence the need to favor cattle raising, which is always a high risk venture at best.

One aspect of taxation, especially true of income tax, is that it is subject to constant change. The present discussion is based on the tax laws today. Although the rules and procedures

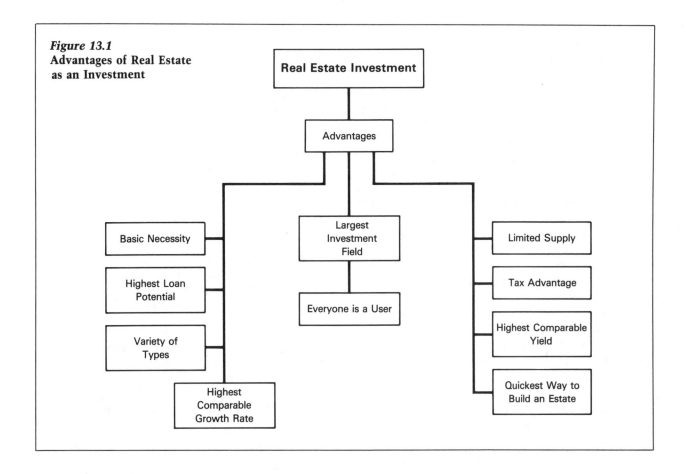

Figure 13.1
Advantages of Real Estate as an Investment

may change, the basic principles remain more or less constant.

For example, although *capital gains* were once given more favorable tax treatment than *ordinary gains*, both are now treated as ordinary income. Yet the tax code retains the label of *capital assets*.

Real estate transactions can be utilized in several ways to lessen the adverse consequences of taxation. Adverse tax consequences many times can be *avoided* by careful tax planning, or payment of tax can be *deferred* by utilizing such devices as tax-free exchanges. Avoidance must be distinguished from evasion. To avoid taxes is legitimate, but to evade taxes is illegal and is subject to severe penalties.

Concepts of Income Taxation

Because the subject of taxation is so complex, it suffices here to briefly summarize some of the principles that apply in this field and some of the terms you will encounter:

1. *Tax planning* can play a significant role in many real estate transactions because of the fact that the government is in effect a partner in the sharing of profits and losses. In buying and selling property, the price of a parcel of property may be less important than the tax position of buyer and seller.

2. During ownership, a given piece of real property will aquire, by virtue of the nature of its use, a certain character for tax purposes. This character vitally affects profit and loss upon disposition of the property. The character of real estate can be classified, for tax purposes, as follows:
   a. Taxpayer's personal residence
   b. Vacant land held for investment
   c. Inventory of dealers and subdividers
   d. Rental and business properties.
   Upon such classification rests the determination of whether and how much gains or losses are involved when the property is transferred; what expenses may be deductible; and whether depreciation is figured.

3. For owner-occupied single-family dwellings, which represent the largest number of real estate sales, possible deductions are considered during the three stages of ownership: the time of acquisition, the time of ownership (occupancy), and the time of sale. Costs

Figure 13.2
Suggestions for Investing in Rental Propety

REAL ESTATE INVESTING

(Get Rich Quick?)

You've probably seen the dozens of books and seminars with variations on the title "How To Make A Million Dollars In Real Estate." Could you really get rich quick by investing in real estate? Investing in real estate takes knowledge, time, energy—and a bit of luck. If you have those things and some perseverance, investing in real estate won't make you rich quick, but as one writer said, it might make you rich slowly.

Investing in residential rental property is probably the most attractive real estate investment for individuals. Your return will include the rents you receive, the tax writeoffs you get, and any appreciation in the property over a period of time.

If you decide to buy rental property for an investment, here are some suggestions:

1. Buy property where you live rather than in some other part of the country. You can manage your property more easily and will probably have a better feel for property values.

2. Look for a bargain. Find a piece of property that needs only cosmetic repair to appreciate in value. Don't buy property needing major repairs such as new wiring, plumbing, or structural renovating.

3. Select property where the rents will cover the mortage payment, taxes, insurance and other costs. You don't need a tax writeoff that drains cash out of your pockets, no matter what your tax bracket.

4. Invest only if you have the financial resources to stay with the investment if there is a downturn. If real estate values decline temporarily or if you have a series of vacancies, you should be able to stay with the investment until the situation improves.

5. Sell at the right time. Experience and perhaps a little professional assistance will help you decide when to sell. Take your profits and reinvest them in an even larger piece of rental property.

---

involved in acquiring a home—such as escrow fees, loan points, title search fee, title insurance premium, and professional fees—are *not* deductible, but are added to the base price of the property. During the time of ownership, interest paid on the loan, property taxes, and casualty losses over $100 are tax deductible. At the time of sale, the seller will be taxed on any capital gain, but losses resulting from the sale of one's residence are not deductible.

4. Capital assets consist primarily of a taxpayer's personal residence and vacant land held for investment. These assets are given the same ordinary income treatment when sold at a gain, regardless of how long the property was owned.

5. Passive loss rules allow offsets against active income for qualified taxpayers. Figure 13.3

illustrates the computation of gains. A special rule applies when the taxpayer reinvests in another residence within 24 months. In such case no gain is recognized except to the extent that the selling price of the old residence exceeds the cost of the replacement dwelling.

6. As for ordinary income, tax rates for married couples filing joint returns are graduated in an ascending scale depending upon the amount of taxable income. Earned income, such as wages or salary, along with so-called "unearned income," such as interest and rental income, are both subject to the same maximum tax rates.

Corporate tax rates are fixed at 15 percent on the first $50,000 of net income and thereafter graduate to 39 percent on amounts in excess of $100,000. These amounts are, of

Figure 13.3
Computation of Capital Gains

		Example*
Step 1:	Original Purchase Price (unadjusted basis)	$100,000
	+ Closing Costs (acquisition costs)	+ 2,000
	= Acquisition price (at close of escrow)	$102,000
Step 2:	+ Capital improvements (capital additions)	+ 18,000
	= Total cost of property	$120,000
Step 3:	− Depreciation (accumulated depreciation)	− 10,000
	= Adjusted Basis (cost basis)	$110,000
Step 4:	Gross Sales Price (unadjusted sales price)	$160,000
	− Sales Expenses (costs of sale)	− 12,000
	= Amount Realized (realized gain)	= $148,000
Step 5:	− Adjusted Basis	− 110,000
	= Potential Gain	$ 38,000
Step 6:	× Taxable Portion	× 40%
	= Recognized Gain (Addition to taypayer's reportable income)	$ 15,200

* Assume the property had been rented for at least a portion of the time. Capital additions included a room addition and extensive landscaping. The taxable portion, step 6, would be lower in event of a qualified replacement or exchange.

course, subject to change as amendments to the tax laws occur.

7. A tax-free exchange is an exchange of real property in which gain or loss is not attributable to the taxpayer at that time. Actually the term *tax free* is a misnomer. The situation created is actually *tax deferring*, and is accomplished by transferring the taxpayer's old cost basis to the newly acquired property.

8. Ownership of real property normally produces income or expenses or both. All payments received for the use of property must be included in the owner's gross income. All ordinary and necessary expenses of operation of the income or investment property are deductible. Additionally, for business and income-producing property, a deductible *depreciation* is allowable for wear, tear, and obsolesence; thus, the taxpayer can recover his or her original cost over a term as prescribed by the Internal Revenue Code.

The taxation of real estate is an important factor in real estate investment, and will probably always remain so. Figure 13.4 is illustrative of the income tax incentives for investors.

TYPES OF INVESTMENT PROPERTY

There are three basic types of real estate investment properties: (1) raw land, (2) land to be developed by the investor, and (3) improved real property that is income-producing. The type of property in which to invest is determined by the specific investment goal of the investor. Once the investor has decided on the type of property, consideration must be given to the economics of real estate investment as it relates to the particular parcel, including such additional factors as population studies and projections, supply and demand, and the effect of changes in money supply and costs. Also, regardless of the particular type of property, a location analysis should be made including such elements as a neighborhood survey, a specific use study, and the relationship to zoning, access, convenience, and so on.

One advantage of an investment in *raw land* is that it rarely presents management problems. However, since raw land generally produces no income, the investor must be able to carry the debt from some other source of funds such as excess income from a trade or profession. The down payment might range from 10 to 29 percent of the total cost of the land, although there is no exact figure in this regard. The down payment can be more or less than this range, depending upon the terms of the seller. The balance of the purchase price is ordinarily paid in regular payments, usually monthly, until the entire debt is paid. The key to making a good land investment is predicting land needs for the future, as well as the direc-

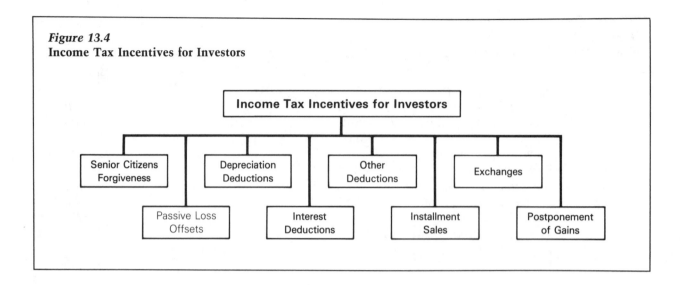

Figure 13.4
Income Tax Incentives for Investors

tion of the line of growth the community will take to meet those needs. It takes careful study to be able to predict the right direction.

The second type of investment property, *development property*, is usually best suited to the full-time real estate investor. The profit in this type of venture comes from improving the property, which involves the installation of streets, utilities, and buildings. This work requires time and talent as well as money. But the profit potential is high, and the satisfaction of having played a role in the development of the community can be considerable. Ventures in this category include shopping centers, mobile home parks, marinas, industrial parks, and planned residential developments.

The third type of property for investment purposes, *income property*, probably attracts the greatest number of investors in real estate. This category includes all types of real property that produce rent for the owner, including apartment buildings, office structures, shopping centers, motels and hotels, and commercial buildings. Two principal attractions of income property are depreciation and cash flow. For persons with a fixed amount to invest and without another source of income, income property is usually the most appropriate investment.

When deciding whether or not to invest in income property a prospective purchaser may first determine the desired rate of return on investment, which is called the capitalization rate. The purchase price is thus based on the percentage of return required by the investor. Here's how to help the investor reach a decision, based on a formula we already encountered in Chapter 9:

1. Determine the net operating income. For a parcel of property, calculate by deducting the total operating expenses from the annual gross income, making reasonable allowance for vacancies and rental collection losses.
2. Select an appropriate capitalization rate. Choose the rate of interest on the investment, such as 7 to 10 percent or more. The greater the risk of recouping the investment, the higher the capitalization rate should be.
3. Find the value of the property by "capitalizing the income." In other words, divide the income by the capitalization rate. For example, assume an annual net income of $30,000 and a rate of 5 percent. The valuation, or *capitalized value*, of the property is $600,000. This figure is obtained by dividing the net income of $30,000 by the rate (5 percent) as follows:

$$.05\overline{)\,30,000\,} = 5\overline{)\,30,000.00\,}^{600,000}$$

On the other hand, if an investor desires to ascertain the rate of return, then the following formula would apply:

$$\text{Return} = \frac{\text{Net Income}}{\text{Price}}$$

Sources of additional information on this subject are voluminous. For an easy introduction, the National Association of Realtors has prepared a booklet entitled *How to Make a Good Investment in Real Estate*, which has many helpful suggestions for those interested in real estate as an investment.

FACTORS THAT INFLUENCE INVESTMENTS

There are many important considerations when thinking of real estate in terms of investment, including the following:

1. Safety
2. Return or yield
3. Status of the investor, such as age, dependents, attitude toward risk, etc.
4. Kind of property
5. Source of investment funds
6. Short-term or long-term view
7. Amount needed to buy in
8. Liquidity

A word frequently encountered in connection with real estate investment, often misunderstood or misapplied, is *leverage*. Simply stated, leverage is to real estate transactions what margin is to stock. Leverage is the use of borrowed funds with the anticipation that the property being acquired will increase in value to the extent that the investor will realize not only his or her cash investment, but also the interest he or she has paid for the use of other people's money.

Leverage enables investors to acquire an interest in real property with a minimum number of their own dollars. Real property generally offers greater use of borrowed funds than any other type of investment. Stocks and bonds offer a good comparison. For instance, stock margin requirements have been increased over the years so that an investor is now able to borrow only 30 to 35 percent (or less) of the funds necessary to purchase listed securities. However, an investor in real property may be able to borrow as much as 75 to 80 percent of the purchase price by way of a first encumbrance, and up to 90 percent or even more by way of secondary financing. The amount of cash paid to a seller is essentially a matter of negotiation between buyer and seller.

The effect of leverage is illustrated in Figure 13.5.

In this figure the investor who used leverage has realized a considerably higher rate of return on his original $20,000 investment. With the same opportunity in other parcels of real property, he could spread an investment fund of $100,000 among five comparable parcels and thus realize a substantial increase in his return by the utilization of leverage.

As we have discussed, ordinary income and capital gains tax factors will also have a material

Figure 13.5
Effect of Leverage

	Without Leverage	With Leverage
Purchase price of land	$100,000	$100,000
Amount invested	100,000	20,000
Amount borrowed	—	80,000
Selling price after three years	150,000	150,000
Mortgage transferred	—	80,000
Equity	150,000	70,000
Interest cost for 3 years at 8 percent	—	19,200
Net cash to investor	150,000	50,800
Original investment	100,000	20,000
Profit before taxes	50,000	30,800
Rate of return on investment before tax on profit (yield)	50%	154%

effect on investment planning, and need to be taken into consideration. The relationship between carrying charges and the growth rate is also of vital concern. For instance, if the carrying charges—interest, property taxes, upkeep expenses, etc.—are equal to or exceed the increase in the value of the property for the contemplated holding period, there is obviously no leverage in the debt financing. The rate of growth and the length of time the investment is held are most important factors in determining its yield.

In assessing the growth factor, remember that both undeveloped land and fully developed land appreciate slowly. When land is fully developed, the values are generally on a much higher plateau. The most rapid appreciation normally occurs between these two stages. The acquisition of land at the time it has started its development, then, can yield the greatest advantage of leverage on debt financing, since the land will normally be in its period of most rapid appreciation.

For improved property, another vital element is *depreciation*, which is an important aspect of tax planning. Much of the romance of real estate investment has arisen out of the tax shelter generated from the availability of income-tax deductions for depreciation as well as interest payments. Those with modest incomes ordinarily do not obtain the benefits of a tax shelter. It is primarily an opportunity for those with considerable expendable income to effect income tax savings. The income-tax law for a number of years had permitted a tax savings through the conversion of income taxable at the regular rate into capital gain by first taking *accelerated depreciation* of real property used in a trade or business or held for the production of income, and then having profits from the later sale taxed as a capital gain. The Tax Reform Act enacted by Congress in 1986 as part of the economic recovery program provides many opportunities for investors, particularly in residential rental properties and in federally assisted low-income housing projects. The government still recognizes a need to stimulate construction in this field, hence the tax advantages allowed. However, as mentioned earlier, the tax laws are subject to constant change, and the investor must keep up with this important aspect of real estate investing.

It should be pointed out that depreciation for income tax purposes is entirely different from actual depreciation, which we considered in Chapter 9. It has aspects of a fictional type of depreciation, and isn't subject to the same rules as actual depreciation based on wear and tear and obsolescence. The latter, however, will still be going on.

Another word about the shelters—many investors have been duped by dubious or outright fraudulent tax shelters. And worse, the penalties today for fraudulent deals reach all the way down to the investor, and they can be severe. The three major areas of tax shelter abuse are farming, mining and real estate. Audit problems alone can be of concern. Every tax shelter must be registered with the IRS. If you invest in one, you must report it by registration number, which gives the IRS much greater control over tax shelters.

Before one invests in a tax shelter, one should assess the economic soundness of the venture on which the shelter is based. Too many people let the tax advantage of an investment blind them to the underlying soundness (or lack of soundness) of the venture.

The tax aspects of real estate investment are of course subject to constant change, and real estate people need to keep abreast of these changes by consulting the latest publications and by attending educational seminars and conferences frequently sponsored by realty boards and the local colleges. Professionals who may be consulted on specific questions include attorneys, Certified Financial Planners (CFPs), and Certified Public Accountants (CPAs). The California Association of Realtors has also published a number of timely books on this subject, including *The Dynamics of* *Real Estate Investment, Real Estate Investment Opportunities*, and *Real Estate Investment: Analysis and Programming*.

REAL ESTATE INVESTMENT ORGANIZATIONAL FORMS

Real Estate Syndicates

The term *real estate syndicate* encompasses a variety of arrangements through which investors may join together and pool their capital for investment in real estate, such as an apartment building, an office building, a shopping center, or raw land. The popularity of syndication is constantly increasing as more and more members of the investing public become aware that, through syndication, they can own a share of a large real estate development for a comparatively nominal investment.

In the past, many investors were reluctant to enter the real estate field, but the possibilities now offered by syndication have overcome their resistance to this type of investment. Reluctance was heretofore based on such factors as lack of experience, inability to obtain an appropriate analysis, management problems, and the matter of liquidity. And although it was generally recognized that the larger transactions offered better opportunities, the average investor was not in a position to compete for the big transaction. Syndication affords this opportunity, and it is generally considered that through syndication the lay investor can now participate at the professional level.

The word *syndicate* actually has no specific meaning as far as the form of association is concerned. It is a generic term indicating that a group of persons, either natural persons or legal entities such as a partnership or a corporation, have joined together for the purpose of acquiring an ownership interest in real property. The legal aspects of ownership are determined by the type of association adopted for the syndicate.

A favored form is a *limited partnership*, which, if properly devised, will limit the liability of the investor to the amount of his or her investment. Also, there may be tax benefits, since the limited partnership is *not* treated as a separate taxable entity (as a corporation is). In order to obtain the benefits of a limited liability, the limited partners cannot participate in management functions—which ordinarily is one of the responsibilities they wanted to avoid anyway.

Syndication is not new, but the regulation of syndicates is. California was the first state in the union to adopt a real estate syndicate law. The California Real Estate Syndicate Act applies to both incorporated and unincorporated investment groups formed for the purpose of investing in, or obtaining a gain from an interest in, real property. A permit must be obtained from the corporations commissioner before real estate syndicate securities may be advertised, offered for sale, or sold to the public.

The act vests the corporations commissioner with jurisdiction over certain types of real estate syndicate interests: corporate, general or limited partnerships, joint ventures, associations, or other entities formed for the sole purpose of, and engaged solely in, investment in or gain from an interest in real property. The act exempts certain operations from its jurisdiction, including planned developments, community apartment projects, condominium projects, stock cooperatives, and transactions not involving a public offering. These are already under the jurisdiction of the California Department of Real Estate.

In brief, the organizers of a real estate syndicate falling within the purview of the act are required to file with the corporation commissioner a request to offer shares in the syndicate to the public. A permit will not be issued unless the commissioner finds the offering to be "fair, just, and equitable." To be "fair" requires that each investor receive a fair share according to the amount of his or her individual investment. For the investment to be considered "just," the individual investor must be aptly suited to the particular investment and to its inherent risk factors. The word "equitable" relates to the merits of the product and the investment itself. Evidence is required that the land does have value. The commissioner retains a staff of professional appraisers for this purpose. These appraisers review the materials submitted by the promoter for evidence of value and may physically inspect the individual properties involved to obtain assurances.

Real Estate Investment Trusts

Another form of ownership interest that has an appeal for investors is known as the *real estate investment trust* (REIT), briefly encountered in Chapter 3. By virtue of federal legislation, such trusts can obtain certain tax benefits. The first basic requirement to qualify as a real estate investment trust under the federal law is that the trust must hold property "for *investment* and not primarily for *sale* to customers in the ordinary course of business." It must consist of at least 100 investors.

Using the general definition of *real estate syndicate* (not the specific one in the Real Estate Syndicate Act), a real estate investment trust is but one form of a real estate syndicate, and typically is utilized by a group of many investors who want to pool their capital into a trust for the purpose of acquiring a large tract of land usually priced too high to be purchased by a single individual, but not so high as to discourage the prospect of a considerable profit on a later resale. Because of the pooled interests, REITs have been called the "mutual funds of real estate investment." The trust device has proved popular because it provides for a responsible, impartial entity that holds title to the property and accounts for the funds, and because federal legislation extends favorable tax treatment to real estate investment trusts; for example, unlike the case of a corporation, the profits of a REIT are not taxed until they have been distributed to the individual investors.

During the holding period between acquisition and sale of the land, the members will be faced with the usual problems of real estate investors. They must decide when to sell, what the terms will be, and whether the sale should be in parcels or as a unit. They may even decide to develop and subdivide at the risk of jeopardizing their capital gains position. Other questions, sometimes perplexing, which can arise include the following:

1. Should the trustee be considered a mere agent holding legal title to the land and following the investors' directions, or should the trustee be granted the absolute power to sell?
2. Should the power to direct a sale be delegated to a few of the investors?
3. Should the investors' interests be transferable, and should the trust continue despite the transfer of an interest or the death of an investor?
4. Should restrictions be placed on the transfer of a beneficial interest, such as a right of first refusal in the remaining investors?

The wrong answer to these questions can make a substantial difference, both from a practical as well as a tax standpoint. As is true in many other areas of real estate practice, the advice of qualified counsel on all legal and tax problems should be obtained before proceeding with a venture of this type.

GUIDELINES FOR PROTECTING THE PUBLIC

Because of the history of fraudulent and unsound schemes that lure investors into the real estate field and the need to protect the gullible, the Department of Real Estate publishes pamphlets and other publications that have as their theme, "Investigate Before You Invest." The information that follows concludes our consideration of basic rules that apply to investments in real estate.

Buying Land? Investigate Before You Invest

Everyone wants to own land . . . part of the American heritage. Too often dreams of second homes, recreational retreats, retirement homes or sound land investments "go up in smoke" because the buyer failed to investigate before he invested.

Department of Real Estate

Department of Real Estate wants to be sure you receive what you bargain for . . . that California citizens have utmost protection when buying lot or parcel in a subdivision whether the subdivision is located in this state or anywhere in the world.

To give you this protection, this state has developed one of the most comprehensive subdivision laws in the nation.

In addition to regulating all California subdivisions, these laws give the California Real Estate Commissioner jurisdiction over subdivisions located anywhere in the world if they are offered for sale or lease in California.

What Is a Subdivision?

A subdivision, essentially, is improved or unimproved land divided for the purpose of sale, lease, or financing, whether immediate or future, into five or more parcels.

Types of Subdivisions

California subdivisions, generally, are comprised of quality urban, residential, commercial and industrial properties . . . in these offerings, few problems exist. Most sales agents act in good faith, with your best interest in mind.

What about resort or "recreational" or "second home" subdivisions? . . . usually highly advertised.

Some California subdivisions located in remote, sparsely populated areas . . . called "land projects" . . . commonly advertised for purpose of "second homes" or "recreation." Investigate!

Should you buy a lot or parcel in a land project?

To help you make such an important decision, the commissioner issues a subdivision public report on all subdivisions offered for sale or lease in California . . . includes "land projects" and out-of-state filings as well as ordinary urban residential subdivisions, condominiums, community apartments, stock cooperatives, apartment complexes and subdivisions known as "planned developments."

Subdivision Public Report

The commissioner's staff investigates every subdivision before issuing the subdivision public report. No subdivider (in or out-of-state) may legally offer any lot in a subdivision for sale in California until this report has been issued.

Basically, the public report is a disclosure instrument for you—in a sense, it constitutes the developer's "permit" to sell. It is not, however, a recommendation—pro or con. It does mean that the subdivider has made arrangements that should result in the buyer getting "what he bargained for" as to the physical characteristics of the land—such as its size, location, arrangements for off-site and recreational facilities, etc.

The subdivider or his or her agent must furnish you with a copy of the public report . . . give you an opportunity to read it before you commit yourself to purchase. Important! Do not buy a lot or interest in any subdivision unless you are given a copy of the public report. Read It! If it raises questions in your mind, check them out.

Pitfalls

When you buy an unimproved lot, its value largely depends on the developer fulfilling his or her promises. Base your decision on facts—don't be impressed with "get-rich-quick" promises.

What utilities will be or are available? Will they be installed at subdivider's expense? Must you pay and provide for installation of all or any utility services? If so, how much?

Has a "special district" been formed to install roads, or provide utility service such as water? Find out the costs to you.

In some areas fire protection service, public transportation and school facilities are minimal, distant, or nonexistent.

Do you intend to build? If so, explore financing and insurance costs. Most lending institutions require large down payments for construction loans to build on remote property. Fire insurance premiums can be costly. Is there a good pattern of growth in subdivision development? *How much land* is provided for open space? Will your house be built on filled ground? Has developer met required environmental measures?

Additional costs to be considered. Real property taxes ... service district taxes, e.g. sewer bonds, etc., (not included with county property tax) ... *assessments* for maintenance of common areas and homeowners associations (subdivision public report will set forth the amount of these assessments). Examine these costs carefully. Are they more than you can afford? If you don't make your monthly payments, there is danger of foreclosure.

Mountainous areas require snow removal, another expense. A wise buyer would ask: Who removes the snow? What will it cost me? How do I get to my lot in the winter? Are routes kept open by the state or county? You need to know this.

If the property is located on a flood plain, what safeguards are there against flooding? Proper drainage facilities can be expensive. Is water supply sufficient? How much will *water* connection *cost?* If there is no water supply, you may have to drill a well and install your own system. *Drilling, casing and pump could cost more than the lot.* Investigate!

Sewerage arrangements are important ... if septic tanks are required, installation costs would normally be the responsibility of the lot owner. How much will it cost? Some soils are not suitable for septic tank systems because of shallow soil conditions, tight substrata, and a high water table. *Does the county have laws banning or restricting septic tanks?* Check out!

Is the Subdivision Located Outside California?

Before it can be offered for sale or lease in California, the developer must apply and qualify for a subdivision public report and permit. Even though developers of out-of-state lands must comply with stringent requirements and arrangements must have been made to assure that the buyer will receive that for which he bargains, buyers should always personally examine any property they plan to buy. If you can't afford to visit the site before you buy it, can you afford to buy it? Buying property sight unseen opens the door to exaggerated descriptions, misrepresentations and deceptions, and may lead to major dissatisfaction when you finally see the property. If you go out of state to look at your subdivision lot, *beware* of a "lot switch" that may occur when the subdivider's agent shows you parcels *not covered by a California Subdivision Public Report and Permit.* Be sure you ask to see a California Subdivision Public Report and Permit that pertains to the *tract and parcel* you are considering purchasing.

Real Estate Contracts and Other Papers (Read the Small Print!)

Time to ask questions about your rights and obligations is before you sign ANY PAPERS. Real estate papers include such agreements as Deposit Receipts, Agreement of Sale, Land Contracts, Lease Rental Agreement, Option, Escrow Papers, etc. These documents, normally contracts or parts of contracts, can limit your rights and extend your obligations. A good rule to follow is read and understand all papers before signing. Don't be rushed.

Rescission Rights

Aggressive sales methods practiced by some salesmen to "get your name on dotted line" have led the California Legislature to pass laws granting "rescission rights" to purchasers of parcels in a land project ... they must be attached by the subdivider to the front page of the land project public report. You can cancel a purchase in a land project for any reason within 14 days from the date your contract was executed. These "rescission rights" (right to cancel agreement) are not granted purchasers of parcels in ordinary urban subdivisions.

Beware of Aggressive Sales Tactics

Don't let a salesman pressure you into a hasty decision, despite intensity and skill of sales pitch.

In unimproved land sales, some salesmen operate on the theory that if prospects have time to think things over, chances are they won't be back.

You may be transported to a subdivision at subdivider's expense and assigned to a salesman both during the trip and during the time you are at the subdivision. Some salesmen attempt to create an atmosphere of buyer hysteria by use of gimmicks—for instance, on a tour of the site, the two-way radio in the salesman's car may crackle incessantly with announcements: "lot 86 and 87 sold ... deposit taken on lots 971, 972 and 973." The salesman may point out to you that these persons realize land will quickly appreciate in value, and since it is a surefire investment they are buying several lots before prices go up and choice lots are still available. Don't fall for such sales patter. Do not allow high-pressure, hard-sell tactics to influence you.

Although it would probably be difficult on trips to a subdivision which are provided by the subdivider, it is recommended that if possible you do some comparative shopping locally. It is good sense in real estate as in anything else.

A reputable sales agent would not pressure you with any of these tactics. Remember, there are still millions of acres of undeveloped land in California.

Consumer Information

If you are not given a copy of a subdivision public report ... Or, if you believe you are the victim of fraud, misrepresentation or deceit in purchase of any lot in any subdivision, send copies of your papers and a written report of any conversation you had with the agent relative to the transaction to the nearest office of the Department of Real Estate.

QUESTIONS FOR CHAPTER 13

Matching

a. tax shelter
b. prospectus
c. gullible
d. leverage
e. liquidity
f. cash flow
g. appreciation
h. yield

i. risk
j. accelerated depreciation
k. speculation
l. cost basis
m. straight-line depreciation
n. equity build-up
o. negative cash flow

____ 1. use of debt financing of an investment to maximize the return per dollar investment

____ 2. cash paid out to carry a property exceeds income from property

____ 3. increase of the owner's percentage interest in a property based on mortgage reduction and price appreciation

____ 4. method of depreciation for tax purposes that achieves a faster rate than straight-line

____ 5. possibility that an investment will not be returned

____ 6. depreciation for tax purposes in equal amounts each year over the life of an asset

____ 7. opposite of a sound investment

____ 8. disclosure statement that describes an investment opportunity

____ 9. dollar amount assigned to property at the time of acquisition

____ 10. return on an investment

____ 11. income tax savings that an investment can produce for its owner

____ 12. increase in value from any cause

____ 13. easy to cheat or defraud

____ 14. number of dollars remaining each month after collecting rents and paying operating expenses and mortgage payment

____ 15. ability to convert assets to cash or its equivalent

True/False

T F 16. Generally, the higher the risk the greater the return on the investment.

T F 17. Return of and return on an investment are not distinguishable.

T F 18. Liquidity is an advantage in a real estate investment.

T F 19. Any investment in real estate will make money for the investor.

T F 20. Generally, an investor is safer by investing after a building project is completed.

T F 21. As a rule of thumb, raw land as an investment must double in value within five years.

T F 22. The further away an investment property is from the investor's home base, the greater the yield.

T F 23. An unsophisticated investor should choose a general partnership rather than a limited partnership.

T F 24. A limited partnership limits the liability of a general partner.

T F 25. Status of an investor is immaterial in determining risk factors.

Multiple Choice

26. Increase in value of property due to general appreciation of all property in an area is called
    a. leverage
    b. plottage
    c. unearned increment
    d. apportionment

27. A real estate syndicate may be composed of one or more
    a. corporations
    b. partnerships
    c. natural persons
    d. any of the above

28. Status of an investor relates to
    a. age
    b. occupation
    c. sophistication
    d. all of the above

29. Which of the following best describes the impact of a tax shelter on income-tax liability?
    a. avoidance
    b. evasion
    c. deferral
    d. cancellation

30. A syndication may be composed of several types of entities. A ceiling on the liability of an investor is ordinarily obtained by using a
    a. joint venture
    b. limited partnership
    c. general partnership
    d. unincorporated association

31. Under the Real Estate Syndicate Act, real estate syndication activity is primarily subject to the jurisdiction of the
    a. corporations commissioner
    b. real estate commissioner
    c. public utilities commissioner
    d. California building commissioner

32. Depreciation taken as a deduction on annual income tax is a form of
    a. tax shelter
    b. tax evasion
    c. tax increment
    d. all of the above

33. Depreciation is a factor in determining capital-gain taxes on the sale of
    a. income property
    b. the owner's residence
    c. raw land
    d. all of the above

34. A Real Estate Investment Trust (REIT) can be created under federal law and obtain tax advantages. This means that it and its members
    a. are taxed the same as corporations
    b. both pay income taxes as entities
    c. reduce income tax consequences
    d. none of the above apply

35. Real Estate Investment Trusts are characterized as either
    a. equity trusts
    b. mortgage trusts
    c. balanced trusts (combination)
    d. any of the above

36. Advantages of a REIT include which of the following?
    a. income tax benefits
    b. pooling of interests
    c. diversification
    d. all of the above

37. Which of the following offers the best advantage to an investor in real property?
    a. long-term capital gains
    b. short-term capital gains
    c. loss on the sale of a residence
    d. receipt of "boot" in an exchange of property

38. Investments in which of the following are frequently made primarily for tax purposes?
    a. oil and gas exploration and production
    b. real estate
    c. cattle
    d. any of the above

39. An investor in the acquisition of potential industrial property should be concerned with which of the following?
    a. transportation
    b. power supply
    c. tax aspects
    d. all of the above

40. Such an investor (question 39) should also be concerned with which of the following?
    a. expansion space
    b. local pollution laws
    c. supply of skilled labor
    d. all of the above

41. A person desires to invest a sum of money that would produce a monthly income of $250, paying 8 percent interest. Approximately how much would the person need to invest?
    a. $25,000
    b. $30,000
    c. $37,500
    d. $42,500

42. An apartment house with a net income of $7200 is purchased for $120,000. The percentage return on the buyer's investment is
    a. 4 percent
    b. 6 percent
    c. 8 percent
    d. 10 percent

43. A sixty acre parcel of desert property was purchased for $300 per acre and thereafter divided into three twenty-acre tracts. Each tract sold for $7500. What was the percentage of return on the purchase price?
    a. 15 percent
    b. 20 percent
    c. 25 percent
    d. 30 percent

44. When investing in land, the investor will be concerned with
    a. condition of the title
    b. boundary location
    c. mineral rights
    d. all of the above

45. Which of the following are of concern to an investor in real property?
    a. encroachments
    b. access
    c. abutter's rights
    d. all of the above

46. Additional matters for consideration when investing in land include
    a. legacy
    b. liquidity
    c. laches
    d. all of the above

47. Real estate investment property includes
    a. raw land
    b. land to be developed
    c. apartments
    d. all of the above

48. Syndication is an advantageous form of investment for a large number of investors to acquire an interest in a large parcel of property. However, regulations are considered necessary in the public interest because of such factors as
    a. possible conflict of interest
    b. excessive compensation to promoters
    c. insufficient disclosure of economic risks of the project
    d. any of the above

49. Investment techniques which persons in high income brackets use for the purpose of reducing income tax liability are known as
    a. tax assessments
    b. tax shelters
    c. tax impounds
    d. tax evasions

50. A Real Estate Investment Trust under federal law, in order to qualify for certain tax benefits, must have as members at least
    a. 20
    b. 50
    c. 75
    d. 100

14

GUIDELINES FOR ACQUIRING A HOME

There are many matters of concern to a buyer of real property, especially the first-time home buyer. In this chapter we will consider a number of these matters, and recommend the use of a checklist to ensure that the buyer's expectations will be met.

COMMON SENSE IN THE PURCHASE OF REAL PROPERTY

The marketing in California of huge land developments and housing subdivisions, particularly to inexperienced buyers who often accept colorful brochures and dramatic display advertisements at their face value, has created the need for a concise guide to sensible land buying. The Department of Real Estate has sought to meet this need by publishing brochures explaining how buyers can protect themselves. The Department of Real Estate has pointed out that, because of California's tremendous growth and spectacular real estate development, the public may well have been conditioned to the idea that investment in property in California—any kind of property—will return considerable profits. But this is not true. It has been found for example that extravagant advertising and self-serving opinions of present and future values can create an artificial market for lots in speculative subdivisions, often in remote areas in the state. The buyer of such a parcel, when he or she wishes to resell, may find that there is little or no market for his or her individual parcel at the price that was paid for it.

Prospective buyers of such lots should remember that the purchase of land for which there is no apparent present need or use can be a highly speculative proposition, depending for success on many factors that are difficult to estimate, even when one is completely familiar with a given area. It is wise to conduct a thorough personal investigation, and to base one's decision on the facts thus developed, rather than to rely on the rosy claims of promoters.

Whether one is buying for investment or for personal use, it is wise to have a checklist of those items of concern not only to ensure that the acquisition is actually what the purchaser wants or needs, but also to assure a satisfactory closing of the transaction once the terms are agreed upon.

Such a checklist allows one to consider both legal and practical matters before the execution of a contract. Because the buyer and seller have different concerns, it is customary to use a separate list for each, but the items are not necessarily exclusive. The same thing can be of concern to both, but many times for different reasons. The list for the buyer is usually much longer than the list for the seller, but the latter will also be concerned with the buyer's checklist in anticipation of finding a buyer who will be attracted to what the seller has to offer. If all such matters are properly considered at the outset, and if the seller is in a position to disclose to the buyer, at an early stage in the negotiations, all matters that would be of concern to the buyer, the possibility of the transaction's proceeding to a satisfactory close is considerably increased.

The checklist below indicates many of the matters of concern to the buyer and to the seller or to both of them. From it an individual checklist can be prepared for use in a particular transaction with the objective that all parties, including the broker, will be able to fill their roles efficiently. Speed can be particularly important for a buyer-investor because, by making a commitment on one parcel, he or she may lose the opportunity to invest in another equally good parcel.

Following is the list of most items to be considered in the sale and purchase of real property:

1. Nature of seller's ownership
   a. Fee or lesser interest
   b. Rights of co-owners, if any
   c. Limitations on right to transfer
      (1) Deed restrictions
      (2) "Due-on-sale" clause in encumbrance
      (3) Consent of lessor or vendor where interest is less than a fee
2. Income-tax consequences of sale or purchase
3. Method of selling
   a. Employment of broker
   b. Type of listing agreement
   c. Payment of commission
4. Type of agreement
   a. Deed
   b. Land contract (installment)
   c. Long-term lease with option to purchase
   d. Exchange
5. Land and improvements
   a. Exact description, and possible need for a survey
   b. Mineral rights
   c. Water rights
   d. Air space
   e. Size (acreage or square footage)
   f. Boundary lines (exact location)
   g. Topography
   h. Condition of improvements (age, cost maintenance)
   i. Surrounding neighborhood—signs of deterioration
   j. Architectural style (See Figure 14.1 for examples of residential styles)
6. Location, either for privacy or convenience (or both)
   a. Distance from employment, i.e., time and expense considerations
   b. Distance from freeways
   c. Distance from shopping, schools, church, hospital, airport, etc.
   d. Distance from friends or relatives (social life)
   e. Distance from recreation
      (1) Parks and playgrounds
      (2) Boating, golf, tennis, or other interests
      (3) Spectator sports (stadiums, ball parks, etc.)
   f. Distance from cultural outlets (museums, music centers, etc.)
   g. Proximity to neighbors
   h. Aesthetics—greenbelts, scenic value, etc.
   i. Trees and other vegetation (shade or windbreak)
7. Personal property and fixtures
   a. Right of removal
8. Encroachments
   a. Onto adjoining property
   b. Onto subject property from adjoining property (trees, walls, etc.)
9. Access to public streets
10. Abutter's rights if property abuts on a public street
    a. Any limitation by deed or agreement
11. Easements
    a. As a benefit
    b. As a burden
12. Outstanding mineral interest
    a. Surface drilling rights
    b. Drill site locations
13. Covenants, conditions, and restrictions
    a. As a benefit
    b. As a burden
14. Zoning, including future use
15. Building code requirements
16. Open housing laws—need for compliance
17. Consumer protection laws, including truth in lending.
18. Taxes and tax rate

Figure 14.1
Some Residential Styles

California Bungalow

Spanish

Monterey

California Cape Cod

Colonial

English

Rustic

Modern

19. Special assessments—present or future
20. Annexation charges (if property in unincorporated territory)
21. Water connection charges
22. Condemnation possibilities of this or adjoining property

24. Fire and police protection
25. Atmospheric conditions (weather)
    a. Wind, fog, rain, smog, etc. (clean air; wet or dry)
    b. Dust, fumes, etc.
26. Hazards from adjoining property
    a. Drainage
    b. Flooding
    c. Fire
    d. Party-wall agreements
    e. Land bordering on the ocean or navigable river
    f. Lateral support
27. Soil
    a. Compactness and grading
    b. Suitability for intended use
    c. Cuts and fills
    d. Geology—earth movement
28. Water
    a. Source and cost
    b. Quality and quantity for intended use
       (1) Domestic use (drink, wash, landscaping)
       (2) Agricultural use
       (3) Industrial use—source of power
29. Termites and other types of infestation
30. Identity of purchaser
    a. Entity, if other than individual
    b. Manner of taking title
    c. Substitution of third party (nominee)
31. Selling price
    a. Appraised value
32. Terms of sale
    a. Cash
    b. Deferred payments
    c. Method of financing
    d. Allocation of price between land and improvements
33. Possession
34. Escrow holder
    a. Selecting
    b. Functions to be performed
    c. Cost and expenses—payment
35. Title insurer
    a. Selecting
    b. Type of policy
    c. Cost—payment
36. If default occurs
    a. Seller's remedies—measure of damages
    b. Buyer's remedies—measure of damages
    c. Rights of the broker
    d. Status of the escrow

WHAT CAN YOU AFFORD?

Have you ever heard the expression, "I couldn't afford to buy the house I'm in!"? Actually, people who say this aren't complaining; what they're really saying is that the value of their house has gone up so much since they originally purchased it that if they were in the market today, they simply could not afford to buy that same house.

The seller's good fortune may, or course, be viewed as the misfortune of the person trying to buy a house. On the other hand, the buyer, too, can enjoy the profits being made in housing if inflation or other factors keep driving prices upward after he or she buys. The problem most people face, however, is that their incomes may not be rising as fast as home values. That is, housing costs can rise faster than incomes.

At the outset of his or her search for a house, the prudent buyer will ask, "Exactly how do I determine how much I can afford for housing?" Perhaps more to the point, "How much of my income can I comfortably set aside for housing expenses?" and "How large a down payment can I afford to make?" The buyer can answer these questions by following the simple four-step method that follows.

Step 1: What I Can Spend for Monthly Housing

The first step is to compare the amount which one can comfortably spend for housing, ignoring for the time being such things as down payment, financing, and average housing expenses. A simplified formula might appear as shown below, with a brief explanation following:

Step 1: A.   Monthly Income
         B. − *Payroll Deductions*
         C. = Take-Home Pay
         D. − *Non-Housing Expenses*
         E. = Available for Housing Expenses

Explanation

A. Monthly Income—Wages, salary, overtime pay, fees, commissions, rents, dividends, interest, and bonuses
B. Payroll Deductions—Federal and state income tax, social security taxes, disability insurance, unemployment insurance, contributions toward pensions and retirement plans

C. Take-Home Pay—What's left after payroll deductions.

D. Non-Housing Expenses—Foods, clothing, medical costs and insurance other than payroll deductions; life and casualty insurance; automobile insurance; commuting, transportation, and travel; installment payments, including interest charges; recreation and hobbies; telephone; contributions; personal items (barber, laundry and dry cleaning, toiletries); savings and investments; and household supplies. Not included here are rental payments, since we are only concerned with non-housing expenses.

E. Available for housing expenses—Net amount remaining for housing.

To illustrate, assume your gross monthly income is $3000, and that payroll deductions amount to $700. Your take-home pay is the difference, or $2300. Assume further that your non-housing expenses total $1100. What's left, $1200, is available for housing.

Step 2: Down Payment I Can Afford

Now that you know how much of your monthly income can be comfortably allocated to housing, the next step is to compute the amount of down payment that is available. Without a knowledge of this figure, it would be extremely difficult to determine how much financing will be needed to complete the purchase of any house which you may want to acquire.

> Step 2: A.   Available Funds
> B. – *Cash Reserves*
> C. = Adjusted Available Funds
> D. – *Cash Expenses*
> E. = Down Payment

Explanation

A. Available Funds—All cash on hand; cash in savings and checking accounts; cash value of life insurance, mutual funds, and other investments; personal loan. These will also include the net equity in your present home if you're selling it.

B. Cash Reserve—Money set aside for emergencies

C. Adjusted Available Funds—After allowance for emergencies

D. Cash Expenses—Includes closing and settlement costs; any necessary furniture; alterations, repairs, and landscaping; moving expenses; and other expected expenses

E. Down Payment—What's left. Suppose you had savings from all sources amounting to $40,000, and that you reason that you ought to have at least three months of earnings set aside for that proverbial rainy day—in other words, $9000 (3 × $3000). Your adjusted available funds, then, will represent the difference, $31,000. Cash expenses attributable to the purchase of a house are estimated at $6000. This leaves $25,000 for the down payment.

Step 3: How Much Financing I Will Need

The next step is to translate the down payment into financing, since financing will represent the difference between purchase price and down payment.

> Step 3: A.   Sales Price
> B. – *Down Payment*
> C. = Financing

Explanation

A. Sales Price—Gross Purchase Price, including points and other costs associated with borrowing, not included in the closing and settlement costs from Step Two

B. Down Payment—The figure obtained on the bottom line of Step Two

C. Financing—The amount needed for purchase will be in the form of one or more trust deeds secured by the property you are contemplating buying. Suppose the house you plan to buy has a price tag of $100,000. How much will you require? Deducting $25,000 available for down payment from the $100,000 leaves a balance of $75,000 to be financed.

Step 4: My Average Housing Expenses

Finally, compute what your average housing outlay per month would be to determine whether the house you're considering purchasing is affordable. To do this, you will need to determine your loan payment from amortization tables, such as found in Chapter 6.

Step 4: A.   Loan Payment
B. + Insurance
C. + Property Taxes
D. + Utilities
E. + Maintenance and Repairs
F. + Miscellaneous
G. = Average Housing Expenses

Explanation

A. Loan Payments—Based on the terms of the loan(s) anticipated

B. Insurance—Premiums are based on the type and amount of coverage you expect to obtain

C. Property Taxes—Estimate 1 percent to $1\frac{1}{2}$ percent of market value per year

D. Utilities—Depends on how prudent you are in consuming these valuable resources

E. Maintenance and Repairs—Usually 1 percent of value of improvements per year. Exact figure depends on age and condition of house

F. Miscellaneous—Any other housing expenses not listed above

G. Average Housing Expense—The total of A through F

To make a rough estimate of your total housing expenses per month, take $1\frac{1}{4}$ percent of the price of the house you plan to buy. $1\frac{1}{4}$ percent is a ballpark figure for all housing, new and used, and should cover all housing expenses. For example, for a $100,000 house, $1250 should cover loan principal and interest, insurance, taxes, utilities, maintenance, and repairs. Incidentally, two of these items, taxes and insurance, might be included in your regular monthly payment through a so-called impound or escrow account.

As can be seen from Step 1, the income available for housing expenses would just barely make the monthly outlay for the average housing expenses. Of the $1250 outlay, $771.46 would be attributable to trust deed payments (item A) based upon a 12-percent interest rate and a 30-year repayment schedule. The rest would be for items labeled B through E. If the bottom line in Step 1 were less than $1250, you could not afford the $100,000 house unless you negotiated a lower price, better terms, or increased the down payment. Housing income above the $1250, on the other hand, would provide a cushion of security.

A rule of thumb used by lenders for over a half century is that you should not pay more than 25 percent of your income for housing expenses. In light of the escalating housing prices in California, many lenders have relaxed this rule to allow closer to one third of your salary for housing expenses. In feudal days serfs turned over to their landlords 25 percent of a year's crops to pay their rent, and this may be the origin of the so-called "25 percent" rule; i.e., that you pay about that percentage of your gross income for housing costs.

One reason for the obedience to the guideline is that lenders want to be able to sell their loans in the secondary market and replenish their supply of funds.

Many lenders now use a percentage rate of 28 percent instead of the previous 25 percent, setting up the following as guidelines:

1. You should pay no more than a maximum of 28 percent of your gross income on the principal, interest, taxes and insurance on your home.
2. The tax component refers to real estate taxes; the insurance component includes homeowner insurance and private mortgage insurance as well.
3. The formula assumes you are making a 20-percent down payment on your home.
4. Your layer of debt, coupled with your housing costs, should not exceed 36 percent of your gross income.

These are no more than guidelines. They represent the maxium amount most lenders like to use in the current state of the market. Some lenders prefer costs plus debt at no more than 33 percent. In a fluctuating market, of course, these formulas may change, but they probably will not change too drastically.

Some additional tips: If you have a large family with many expenses; or if you spend quite a bit for cars, vacations, and entertaining, then you may have to pare your housing budget. On the other hand, if you make full use of a home for your recreation, then perhaps you are justified in paying more for a house than a family that is "never at home."

Another consideration is how you feel about upkeep—painting and other maintenance. If you are willing to do most of this work yourself, your costs will be less, and you may therefore be justified in paying more for a house.

WHAT TO LOOK FOR IN A HOUSE

Before being concerned with choosing exactly the right house, the prospective buyer should first consider the choice of a neighborhood.

What should one look for in judging a neighborhood? The *location* of schools, employment centers, churches, shopping facilities, parks and playgrounds, recreation and entertainment facilities, and hospitals is important, as well as the availability of transportation. What is the general condition and appearance of the neighborhood? Condition of adjoining housing? How are traffic conditions? Street surfacing and drainage? Are there excessive smoke, odors, or fumes? How is the fire and police protection? Is there adequate garbage and rubbish removal? How are the public utility services, including utility rates in the community? Indeed, this last point, utility rates, is becoming a vital consideration, sometimes exceeding the payments on the trust deed.

Once you've decided on a community and neighborhood, then consider the house itself. What choices do you have when in the market for a house?

1. Purchase an already built new house
2. Purchase a used house
3. Build a house
4. Rent a house

Assuming you want to *buy* a house, should you buy an existing house or a new one? How do you know what to look for in selecting a house?

New Houses

New houses are generally built as part of a development forming a new community or neighborhood, except for those custom built on vacant lots. While most new housing offers the benefits of modern construction methods, there are a number of items that the prospective buyer should examine carefully:

1. Don't be dazzled by the appearance of a glittering model home. All that glitters isn't gold. Pin down exactly which features come with the house, and those designed only for display, for which you'd pay extra. Don't assume any item is included. If you think those fancy shutters in the kitchen come with the house, get it in the contract!
2. If the community is to have new street paving, gutters, water and sewer lines, lighting, sidewalks, make sure you know who is to assume the costs—you or the builder. You might also want to check out the charges for water and trash collection at this stage.
3. If you're selecting a lot before building, is the size and setting right for you? After the bulldozer has arrived it may be too late to get the

kind of shape and slope that you expected to get.
4. Be sure your contract with the builder definitely stipulates the completion date of your new house. And don't be afraid to check construction progress regularly while the house is being built. Incidentally, if a house is purchased before completion, the builder may allow minor changes in design.
5. If you're considering a home in a subdivision, check the reputation of the builder. Talk with people who are living in houses constructed by the builder you are considering.
6. Before taking title to the property—that is, before close of escrow—make a thorough inspection trip. Check all equipment, doors, windows, cabinets, mechanical parts, plumbing, and so on. This may be your last chance to request changes.
7. What about the contract itself? Obviously it should be in writing, and should set forth the total sales price, completion date, any warranties, and extra features that are to be included. If possible, try to locate a lender who will allow you to take advantage of lower interest rates that may apply at the time of closing. In any event, avoid an arrangement which would allow the lender to increase the rate if market conditions change between the date of loan commitment and the close of escrow.
8. Finally, before you take possession, insist on these papers: (a) warranties from all manufacturers for equipment in the house, (b) certificate of occupancy, (c) certificates from the Health Department clearing plumbing and sewer installations, and (d) any other certificates of code compliance which your city or community requires, and (e) policy of title insurance.

Used Houses

What should you look for if you're in the market for a used house? Some of the legal considerations mentioned in the discussion of new houses also apply here, but the purchase of a used house often involves placing a greater emphasis on the condition of the structure itself. Buying a house in need of extensive repair can have the effect of adding thousands of dollars to the purchase price. The following are important aspects of a house to consider. Figure 14.2 may be consulted to help understand some of the terms used.

1. Subsidence (settling). Do the walls and floors show cracks—even hairline cracks—that indicate a sagging structure? Look carefully at the squareness of exterior walls.

2. Termites and dry rot. Perhaps part of the sagging is caused by infestation of termites and dry rot, also called wood rot. California is one part of the country that is vulnerable to termites, so a clearance by a licensed termite inspector is a must.

3. Wiring. Be sure that there is sufficient amperage and enough electric outlets. You can request inspection by the local building department for code compliance to make sure the wiring is not dilapidated, exposed, or dangerous.

4. Insulation. In these times of energy scarcity, anything that will help to conserve fuel consumption is especially important. Have the attic and the space between interior and exterior walls checked to see what kind of insulation material was used, the quantity, and how it was installed.

5. Heating. Check to see that the heating system is in working condition and adequate for your family's needs. Installing a new heating system is a costly project.

6. Water Heating. Check the type and capacity of the water heater tank to determine if there will be sufficient hot water for your family needs. Look for signs of rust or leaks. If there is still any guarantee in effect on the water heater, be sure to ask the owner for the contract.

7. Roof and gutters. What is the condition of the roof, and how old is it? Even if in good condition, if it is more than ten years old, you would need to set aside reserve funds for replacement. Also check inside the attic for water stains and discolorations. Again, if there is a guarantee on the roof, ask the owner for it. Types of roofs are shown in Figure 14.3.

8. Basement. Relatively few basements exist in southern California, but in northern California this can be a critical area. A basement that looks dry in summer may be three inches under water in the spring. Look for signs of water penetrating around the foundation walls.

9. Plumbing. Choose a home that is connected to a public sewer system in preference to one served by a septic tank or a cesspool. Have a plumber determine the condition of the plumbing and test for water pressure.

Finally, it should be noted that there is no perfect house. Just be sure you know in advance the shortcomings of the house you are buying. Don't wait to be shocked after you move in. We've covered the major areas of concern. But even minor items can be a great source of irritation—things like the paint and wallpaper, tight or loose doors and windows, a fireplace damper that doesn't operate, and on and on.

OTHER HOUSING CHOICES

A prospective buyer has several other choices of housing besides new and used single-family dwellings.

Condominiums

The condominium was discussed in Chapter 3 as a form of subdivision. Here we discuss it as a housing structure. A condominium is a legal form of home ownership in which the individual owner is entitled to a divided interest in a cubicle of space—a sort of "space lot," in contrast to the land lot in the traditional detached house. The condominium purchase also includes an undivided interest in the common area.

Divided interest means separate ownership of the unit occupied by the owner, just as in a single dwelling and characterized by a separate deed, separate title policy, tax bill, hazard insurance policy, utility bills, and separate trust deeds.

Undivided interest means joint ownership. Each of the joint owners shares in the ownership of the common facilities. No land is individually owned, but is held in common, as are recreational facilities, parking structures and spaces, building roofs and exterior walls, water mains and sewer laterals.

Each owner is a member of a homeowners association, or HOA, and entitled to vote according to its bylaws. An HOA is usually a nonprofit corporation, chartered by the state, formed by all of the individual owners within a particular condominium for the purpose of providing common facilities and sharing common expenses. The following characteristics are common to all California HOAs.

1. Board of directors, elected by the general membership

2. Covenants, conditions, and restrictions (CC&Rs) and bylaws

Figure 14.2
Residential Construction Nomenclature

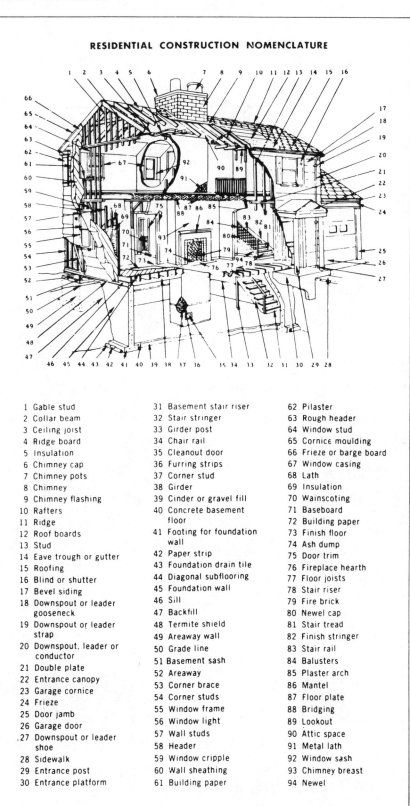

RESIDENTIAL CONSTRUCTION NOMENCLATURE

1 Gable stud	31 Basement stair riser	62 Pilaster
2 Collar beam	32 Stair stringer	63 Rough header
3 Ceiling joist	33 Girder post	64 Window stud
4 Ridge board	34 Chair rail	65 Cornice moulding
5 Insulation	35 Cleanout door	66 Frieze or barge board
6 Chimney cap	36 Furring strips	67 Window casing
7 Chimney pots	37 Corner stud	68 Lath
8 Chimney	38 Girder	69 Insulation
9 Chimney flashing	39 Cinder or gravel fill	70 Wainscoting
10 Rafters	40 Concrete basement	71 Baseboard
11 Ridge	floor	72 Building paper
12 Roof boards	41 Footing for foundation	73 Finish floor
13 Stud	wall	74 Ash dump
14 Eave trough or gutter	42 Paper strip	75 Door trim
15 Roofing	43 Foundation drain tile	76 Fireplace hearth
16 Blind or shutter	44 Diagonal subflooring	77 Floor joists
17 Bevel siding	45 Foundation wall	78 Stair riser
18 Downspout or leader	46 Sill	79 Fire brick
gooseneck	47 Backfill	80 Newel cap
19 Downspout or leader	48 Termite shield	81 Stair tread
strap	49 Areaway wall	82 Finish stringer
20 Downspout, leader or	50 Grade line	83 Stair rail
conductor	51 Basement sash	84 Balusters
21 Double plate	52 Areaway	85 Plaster arch
22 Entrance canopy	53 Corner brace	86 Mantel
23 Garage cornice	54 Corner studs	87 Floor plate
24 Frieze	55 Window frame	88 Bridging
25 Door jamb	56 Window light	89 Lookout
26 Garage door	57 Wall studs	90 Attic space
27 Downspout or leader	58 Header	91 Metal lath
shoe	59 Window cripple	92 Window sash
28 Sidewalk	60 Wall sheathing	93 Chimney breast
29 Entrance post	61 Building paper	94 Newel
30 Entrance platform		

Figure 14.3.
Types of Roofs

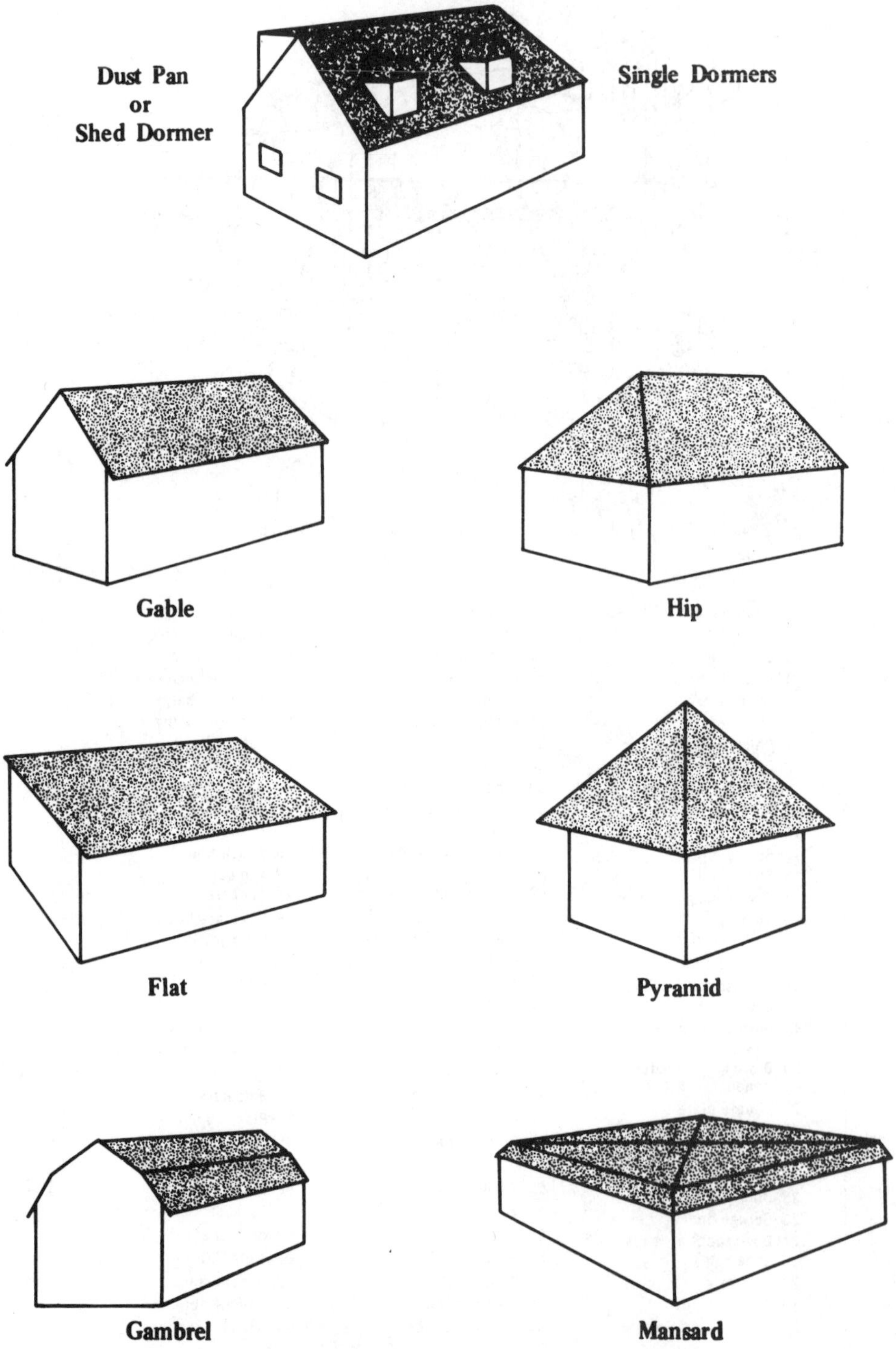

Dust Pan
or
Shed Dormer

Single Dormers

Gable

Hip

Flat

Pyramid

Gambrel

Mansard

3. Annual budget with provisions for reserves for replacement
4. Monthly (or annual) dues or assessments to be paid to the HOA by its members. In essence, an HOA is a sort of mini-government.

Because condominium owners own their individual units, they are responsible for their own maintenance expenses, property taxes, insurance, and loan payments. They are also responsible for the common facilities, and are assessed periodically, usually monthly, for the upkeep. However, "condo" owners are not responsible for the units owned by others. Since a fee interest is conveyed on each unit, one would not be liable for the default of his or her neighbors.

Why do people buy condominiums instead of the traditional detached house? Some claimed benefits include freedom from maintenance, lower original down payment and costs, greater security, and recreational facilities offered at shared costs.

Townhouses

The term *townhouse* originated to describe the city residence of one whose main house was in the country. Today, a typical townhouse is a two-story structure containing multiple units joined together physically as an apartment, but for which an owner holds title to the land under his unit (see Chapter 3).

Whether part of a two-unit building or a two-hundred-unit building, the term *townhouse* is basically used to describe a type of structure. A townhouse is characterized by the fact that residents have no one living above or below them. The unit and the land upon which it rests are conveyed together to an owner. Depending upon the provisions in the deed, a townhouse may take on the form of a "townhouse condominium" or be part of a PUD (see chapter 3). Where the townhouses are connected to each other by common walls, forming one continuous building—such as those found in San Francisco—the term *rowhouse* may be used.

Sometimes the word *plex* is used. If two units are connected to each other, the structure is a duplex; if three, a triplex; if four, a four-plex or quadraplex. A person may own an entire "plex," in which he occupies one unit, and rents out the others.

Cooperative

A cooperative is a housing project that is owned by a corporation which issues certificates of stock to each occupant of an individual unit. Instead of rent, each stockholder pays a proportionate monthly assessment to cover trust deed payments, taxes, and operating costs. The tenant does not own a unit, but as stockholder is entitled to exclusive possession of the unit. Such tenants are said to be given a "propriety lease," under which they agree to abide by its terms just as with any lease, except that they have a propriety or ownership interest in the premises by virtue of their stock certificate. Such owners are sometimes referred to as "tenant stockholders."

As was discussed in Chapter 3, the chief distinction between a co-op and a condominium is that in a co-op the tenant shareholder does not receive a separate deed, title insurance policy, trust deed, tax bill, or fire and hazard insurance policy. These items are instead attached to the corporate ownership of the entire property. Thus, there exists the possibility of liability for the default of neighboring stockholder-occupants.

This liability may apply to other types of cooperatively owned properties as well, but in this chapter we are confining ourselves to residential cooperatives. Thus, for example, one would not apply the term HOA to a commercial or industrial cooperative complex.

It should also be made clear that in some areas of both condominium and co-op ownership, there may be a "duality" of interest. For instance, while both forms of ownership will require contributions for fire and insurance premiums to cover common areas, each member of the complex will naturally want to purchase additional but separate coverage for his or her personal property within the unit. The condominium owner would most economically accomplish this by purchasing a homeowner package that insures both the unit and its contents.

Finally, another difference between the co-op and a condominium is in the area of transfer of interest. Many cooperative agreements contain a "right of first refusal." Hence, if you wished to sell your unit, the corporation's bylaws would specify that an option be granted for some specified time—usually thirty days—in which the corporation may buy the stock for a price that is determined according to a formula set out in the bylaws. By contrast, such right of first refusal

THE THREE STAGES OF HOMEOWNERS ASSOCIATIONS

Much has been said about homeowners associations (HOAs), both good and bad. The U.S. Department of Housing and Urban Development has conducted studies that have resulted in the identification of three stages that seem to be experienced by HOAs in their growth process:

1. The *Honeymoon* stage, when purchases of condos, townhouses, and PUDs (planned unit developments) are preoccupied with selecting, occupying, and improving units. No substantial repairs or replacements are needed. Monthly fees are low.

2. The *Awakening* stage, when the owners come to realize that *they are* the HOA. Turnover takes place; dues collection begins to falter; replacement reserves and methods for calculating and predicting costs are found to be inadequate. Construction defects begin to surface, but by then the builder's one-year warranty has expired. Inadequately designed community facility equipment begins to fail, particularly swimming pools and irrigation systems. Monthly fees are found to be inadequate to meet current expenses and reserve obligations. HOA directors feel frustrated and overworked, and resign or refuse to run for additional terms. Residents begin to violate architectural, parking, and pet restrictions.

3. *Coming of Age*, when the directors come to realize that whining and avoiding are no substitutes for action. Budgets are refined; collection methods are tightened; violations of CC&Rs are controlled; and improved working relationships are established.

options are accorded to condominiums only where an apartment house is being converted to condominiums. In such cases, the tenants are given the first right to purchase their apartment unit.

Mobile Homes

As defined by the Health and Safety Code, a mobile home is "a vehicle designed and equipped to contain not more than two dwelling units to be used without a permanent foundation."

A mobile home is transported to a homesite where it is connected to the necessary utilities. It is designed and built for use as a permanent residence. It cannot ordinarily be pulled by an automobile.

Advantages to and characteristics of mobile home ownership include relatively low cost; low lien taxes, except if delinquent in payment for over 120 days, or if purchased prior to July 1, 1980; low real property tax if on permanent foundation; and transportability to a new site in the event the owners decide to relocate.

Disadvantages include rapid depreciation, resulting in lower resale value; severe restriction in many communities (in some places mobile homes may be prohibited altogether); and the fact that the typical mobile home is not suitable for large families.

QUESTIONS FOR CHAPTER 14

Chapters 14 and 15 contain 50 multiple choice questions, many of which are included for review purposes and are based on the material in the preceding chapters of the book.

1. In today's market a percentage of income used as a guideline in determining whether or not a person should buy a home is
   a. 20 percent of gross income
   b. 28 percent of gross income
   c. 36 percent of gross income
   d. 40 percent of gross income
2. When investing in land, the investor will be concerned with the
   a. condition of the title
   b. location of the boundaries
   c. deed restrictions
   d. all of the above
3. Investment properties include
   a. multiresidential
   b. commercial and industrial
   c. recreational
   d. all of the above
4. The sketch to the right illustrates what type of roof?
   a. hip

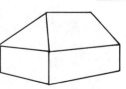

ADOPTION OF UNIFORM MANUFACTURED HOUSING CODE URGED BY FANNIE MAE

Adoption of a uniform manufactured housing code as a practical way of ensuring a supply of affordable homes for American families was suggested by the president of the Federal National Mortgage Association in a speech before the World Congress on Mobile Home Financing.

Since building codes, zoning laws and other practices, as well as problems of inflation, make it difficult to build low-cost conventional houses, many families have turned to mobile homes as a solution to their housing problems.

Mobile homes accounted for about 80% of all under-$60,000 housing produced in the U.S. in 1986.

"The overall challenge is to adapt house design, building, land use, and marketing and financing laws, regulations and practices to the production of housing that more people can afford to buy," the president stated. "One giant step forward would be a uniform manufactured housing code. A mobile home code is not enough. We should go all the way. That is the only way that manufactured housing can be produced and sold throughout the United States with maximum efficiency and economy at minimum prices."

---

    b. pyramid
    c. mansard
    d. gable

5. An owner of a mobile home would pay what kind of annual tax once installed on a foundation?
    a. real estate
    b. personal property
    c. trailer
    d. none of the foregoing

6. The amount of money available for housing expenses is
    a. income less payroll deductions
    b. income less payroll deductions and non-housing expenses
    c. income less all cash expenditures
    d. income less payroll deductions and cash reserves

7. Two-story houses attached side by side, where no one lives above or below any other person, are popularly referred to as
    a. mobile homes
    b. townhouses
    c. condominiums
    d. apartment houses

8. Available Funds less Cash Reserves equals Adjusted Available Funds. For the prospective home buyer Adjusted Available Funds less Cash Expenses equals
    a. down payment you can afford for a house
    b. amount available for housing expenses
    c. amount of financing you would need for the purchase of a house
    d. average housing expenses

9. Which of the following types of taxes can apply to real property?
    a. ad valorem tax
    b. transfer tax
    c. income tax
    d. all of the above

10. Some of the advantages of owning a home include
    a. possible depreciation and equity buildup
    b. immobility and ad valorem taxes
    c. tax benefits, depreciation, and equity buildup
    d. home improvements, tax benefits, possible appreciation and equity buildup

11. A disadvantage of owning a home is generally considered to be
    a. high property taxes
    b. high sales taxes
    c. increased income taxes
    d. greater inheritance taxes

12. An advantage to the condominium owner over that of the cooperative appartment owner is that the condominium owner
    a. is technically a renter
    b. has one vote in the management of the condominium project, regardless of the size of the unit
    c. becomes an owner in fee
    d. pays a prorata share of all carrying charges on the project

13. Under the corporate form of cooperative apartment house, each individual owner
    a. may sell his or her interest at will

b. purchases share of stock
c. receives a separate deed to his or her cubicle of space
d. ordinarily makes payments on mortgages which attach to his or her unit of space only

14. A disadvantage of mobile home ownership is
a. taxation at higher personal property rates
b. its high cost when compared to single-family dwellings
c. rapid depreciation
d. nontransportability of the unit

15. A type of subdivision where the residential unit and the land upon which it rests are conveyed together to the individual owner is customarily referred to as a
a. townhouse
b. planned unit development
c. rowhouse
d. cooperative apartment house

16. Which of the following is a part of the condominium "unit"?
a. exterior walls
b. central heating installation
c. elevator
d. interior walls

17. Select the correct statement.
a. It is substantially cheaper to own a house than to rent.
b. The basic price of a mobile home usually includes skirting and foundation piers.
c. Raw land includes acreage not now in use.
d. An apartment complex converted to condominiums does not constitute a subdivision.

18. Older homes offer the buyer certain advantages over recently constructed ones because of
a. less risk involved for lenders, thereby increasing the loan-to-value ratios
b. better construction in older dwellings
c. accelerated depreciation benefits accorded older properties
d. the security of buying in a proven residential area

19. A disadvantage of the older, or used, home includes one of the following:
a. larger home for comparable price
b. lower assessment for tax purposes
c. proven construction
d. deferred maintenance

20. The highest point of construction in a conventionally constructed house is the
a. gutter
b. ridge board
c. rafter
d. collar beam

21. The way in which a structure is placed on a lot in relation to other structures in the same area is called
a. topography
b. orientation
c. elevation
d. conformity

22. Included in the conveyance of a condominium unit is
a. fee simple title
b. separate property tax liability
c. undivided interest in the common areas
d. all of the above

23. The principal difference between a cooperative and a condominium is in the area of
a. occupancy
b. ownership
c. use
d. the homeowner association

24. A "right of first refusal" would most likely be associated with a
a. condominium
b. rental of a house
c. cooperative
d. mobile home

25. Purchase price less down payment equals
a. financing required
b. equity at time of purchase
c. unearned increment
d. amount available for housing

26. An owner of property that is sold for nonpayment of taxes has a statutory right to redeem for a specified period of time after the first tax sale. This period of time consists of
a. five years
b. seven years
c. ten years
d. one year

27. A subordinate lien on real property is one which is
a. inferior
b. superior
c. equal
d. on a parity

28. Assume that the assessed value of property was $25,000. The tax rate for the year was $3.75 per $100 of assessed value, which resulted in a total tax of $937.50. If in the following year, the tax rate were increased to $4 per $100 and the total tax were $1000, the assessed value for the year would be
a. lower
b. higher

c. the same

d. variable

29. The instrument used to remove the lien of a deed of trust from the records is called a
    a. satisfaction
    b. deed of reconveyance
    c. release
    d. redemption

30. The type of mortgage loan which permits the borrower to obtain additional funds at a later date is called
    a. a package mortgage
    b. an open-end mortgage
    c. an expendable mortgage
    d. an equitable mortgage

31. Equity in real property is basically the
    a. total of all mortgage payments made to date
    b. assessed value
    c. cash flow the property will generate
    d. difference between mortgage indebtedness and market value

32. Private restrictions on the use of land may be imposed by
    a. deed
    b. agreement
    c. subdivision general plan
    d. any of the above

33. A loan to be repaid in equal installments over a period of time is known as a
    a. partially amortized loan
    b. fully amortized loan
    c. balloon payment loan
    d. graduated payment mortgage loan

34. The instrument used to secure a loan on personal property is called
    a. a bill of sale
    b. a security agreement
    c. an assignment
    d. a bill of exchange

35. A person holding fee title to real property in severalty would most likely have
    a. a life estate with power of sale
    b. sole ownership
    c. ownership in common with others
    d. any of the above

36. Appraisals of single-family dwellings are usually based on
    a. capitalization of rental value
    b. assessed valuation
    c. asking price of comparable houses
    d. selling price of comparable houses

37. Governmental land use planning and zoning are important examples of
    a. eminent domain
    b. police power
    c. deed restrictions
    d. condemnation

38. A "loss in value from any cause" is a common definition of
    a. depreciation
    b. obsolescence
    c. reverse leverage
    d. all of the above are true

39. A CLTA standard average policy of title insurance insures against loss occasioned by
    a. false personation
    b. forgery
    c. invalid trust
    d. all of the above

40. A township contains 36 sections, uniformly numbered. Section 31 of a theoretical section is located at the
    a. NW corner
    b. NE corner
    c. SE corner
    d. SW corner

41. A acceleration clause in an installment note secured by trust deed is one that provides for
    a. increasing interest rates
    b. decreasing interest rates
    c. money becoming immediately due upon a specified event
    d. extension of due date

42. Upon execution and delivery of a land sales contract buyer obtains the
    a. equitable title
    b. legal title
    c. entire title
    d. none of the above

43. A co-owner of real property may bring an action against the other owners requesting a severance of their respective interests. Such an action is called
    a. an execution sale
    b. a partition
    c. a dissolution
    d. a foreclosure

44. When value of an income property is computed by using as factors the net earnings and a fair percentage of return on the investment, the appraisal process is termed
    a. the accrual method
    b. the comparative method
    c. capitalizing the income
    d. the reproduction cost method

45. Mortgages which are not insured or guaranteed by the government are generally referred to as
    a. conventional loans

b. amortized loans
c. discount loans
d. straight loan mortgages

46. The recording of a "Request for Notice of Default" is ordinarily done by the
a. trustee on the prior trust deed
b. trustor on the prior trust deed
c. beneficiary on the junior trust deed
d. trustee on the junior trust deed

47. The main purpose of regulating the sale of subdivisions by the Real Estate Commissioner is to
a. prevent fraud
b. regulate the physical aspects of subdivision
c. control sales commissions
d. all of the above

48. The same word in the real estate field can have different meanings, depending on the way it is used. The word "patent" when used as an adjective and not as a noun, has a meaning *opposite* to

a. apparent
b. obvious
c. latent
d. lateral

49. *Escheat* is a legal word meaning
a. an owner has been the victim of fraud and deceit
b. title to property has reverted to the state
c. an agent's license has been revoked
d. property under a deed of trust has been reconveyed

50. If the balance on a loan is $12,000 and the interest rate is 6½ percent per annum, what would be the monthly interest on the next payment?
a. $65
b. $72
c. $120
d. $150

15

CAREERS IN REAL ESTATE

In this chapter, we consider the many and varied roles, responsibilities, and activities which offer an opportunity for a career in real estate. Undoubtedly, you already realize that the real estate field can be exciting, stimulating, and rewarding. The opportunities for economic rewards are considerable—usually the primary concern in selecting a career. But the field of real estate is not only rewarding from an economic point of view, it offers much more; it is actually instrumental in the realization of a way of life.

It is a recognized fact that real estate underlies all phases of human endeavor and growth. Real estate is a basic necessity, and is tangible and meaningful to everyone. The home is at the center of the American concept of freedom and opportunity. If, through knowledge and training, people in the real estate field can help make this center more sound, the branching out into all other activities of life has a better chance to succeed. Because real estate plays such a tremendous role in the lives of all citizens, present and future, it can be one of the most satisfying activities in which to plan a career.

Real estate as a career offers opportunities for both indoor and outdoor activities, depending upon one's inclination. A person may choose to go into one or more of the many areas of sales, including such specialties as residential, commercial, industrial, raw land, or recreational properties, exchanging, or syndication. Besides the challenge of selling all types of property, there are a number of special fields within real estate such as financing, appraising, property management, couseling, planning, development and research, to name a few. These various areas of activity are reviewed in the material that follows. Some involve working mainly with people instead of things; some involve a knowledge of figures and how to measure and calculate. All involve the use of a specialized vocabulary and the ability to communicate; all involve a need for a continuing study of real estate; and all involve continuous contact with highly skilled, capable, and professional people.

The colleges in California offer a variety of courses designed to provide professional educational opportunities for real estate practitioners and for students who want to make a career in real estate. These programs are especially designed to raise the standards of the profession. They are also designed to meet the increasing requirements of the Calfornia Department of Real Estate.

MASTER PLAN FOR PROFESSIONALISM

Anyone choosing a career in real estate should be familiar with the *master plan* for the professional development of the real estate industry in California, designed some time ago by a special committee composed of representatives of the CAR and the Department of Real Estate. The committee felt that a professional plan would give meaning and direction to the efforts of the thousands of real estate people already attempting to raise their standards of education, accountability, and training. The committee also believed that the plan would be the catalyst for similarly oriented efforts elsewhere in the United States. It represents a giant step forward.

History

In 1966, the real estate commissioner's office drafted and distributed a "Blueprint for Professionalization of the Real Estate Business in California." The blueprint was designed to provide a frame of reference for discussion which might lead to a consensus on the part of all those interested in developing a general plan to raise the standards of real estate practitioners in the years ahead.

The initial blueprint was revised several times, based upon the development of greater educational opportunities in the interim. Its "starting point" was a proposal for departmental legislation to require that certain real estate courses be passed before a real estate broker's license is issued. These courses can be taken at universities, state colleges, community colleges, or at private real estate schools under prescribed conditions. The Blueprint and the master plan developed from it are part of a continuing effort over the years to raise the professional standards of the real estate field. The following shows the step-by-step progress in the professional development of licensees:

1919 Real estate brokers required to register with the Department of Real Estate.

1923 Salesman license required to be in possession of employing broker; broker required to maintain sign; definition of broker expanded.

1931 Written examination mandatory—criteria to pass examination different for Real Estate Brokers and Real Estate Salesmen.

1949 Applicants for R.E.B. license require two years full time experience as a real estate salesperson or equivalent experience or education.

1955 "Original" and "renewal" licenses distinguished; REER (Real Estate Education and Research) Fund; Mortgage Loan Brokerage Law enacted.

1959 Real property loan brokers required to be registered.

1961 Real Property Securities Dealers Law enacted.

1963 Additional examination in legal aspects and real estate practice; REER fund changed to REER&R Fund (Real Estate Education, Research and Recovery Fund. Shortened to Real Estate Fund in 1978.)

1968 Passage of educational bill requiring college level courses in Real Estate Practice and Legal Aspects of Real Estate.

1969 Increase broker responsibility requirements: Phase I.

1970 Two formerly supplemental courses made mandatory; two optional supplemental courses added, Finance and Appraisal, in lieu of additional exams.

1971 Increase broker responsibility requirements: Phase II. Written employment agreement between broker and salesperson made mandatory.

1972 Four college courses mandated for R.E. broker: Practice, Legal Aspects, Appraisal, and Finance.

1974 Six college-level courses required for R.E. broker.

1975 Multi-state exam implemented. (Discontinued in 1978.)

1976 Redefine *broker* and *salesperson:* increase broker responsibility requirements: Phase III.

1977 Continued study of licensing renewal requirements.

1978 Forty-five clock hours of study made optional for renewal of salesperson license. Salesman changed to *"Salesperson."*

1981 Forty-five clock hours of continuing education (CE) for renewal of any real estate license.

1983 Three clock hours of continuing education in ethics required.

1986 Three college level courses required for sales persons, starting with Real Estate Principles. Broker course requirement increased from six to eight.

1987 Two additional courses required for renewal of salesperson's license.

Following a basic concept of the master plan, a portion of the real estate licensees' fees has been used to help lay the groundwork to make available throughout California courses which cover the real estate field. At least one hundred community colleges have participated in the program by giving one or more real estate courses each semester. Many of the state colleges also offer these courses, as well as the University of California and several private institutions of higher learning. Private real estate schools have also offered the required courses.

The special committee drafted the master plan after many alternatives were advanced, debated, and recommended. This approved plan was agreed to as the method that would best achieve professional recognition for those engaged in the real estate business in California. As can be seen from the preceding summary, the original plan that had envisioned a college degree (four years) has been deleted in favor of designated courses and continuing education requirements.

Basic Concepts of the Plan

Studies of the real estate business's image formally undertaken in the 1950s and 1960s by academic institutions, the Department of Real Estate, and by the organized real estate industry showed that many real estate licensees were inadequately prepared for the complex field in which they operated. A "good image" is, of course, desirable for all licensees. The public is not likely to recognize a group of workers as professionals unless all the ingredients of the professional are required in the

prequalification process. In general, these ingredients include an in-depth test of competence, a substantial amount of experience, a broad academic base, and the acceptance of a full measure of responsibility.

If professional recognition is to be attained through a statutory licensing framework it will be necessary, as each new requirement is advanced, to establish that the public interest will be better served by the additional requirement. Further, a realistic approach suggests that the industry itself must generate and sustain enthusiasm for the concept if real estate industry support is to be gained and retained. The legislature and the administration must also be convinced that the statutory changes are needed. The educational program now moves ahead in the atmosphere of a wide availability of college-level courses in real estate and related fields, a growing acceptance by real estate brokers of their responsibilities, and the dedication of thousands of licensees to furthering the work that has been accomplished in the Blueprint.

The master plan is a program unique to the real estate industry. There are no exact parallels of activity in any other arena of the business or professional scene. The committee, when it developed and approved the plan, recognized that events could cause the timetable to change—that experience and new techniques could lead to revisions of the plan at any step along the way.

THE MANY FIELDS OF REAL ESTATE ACTIVITY

The range of real estate activities is broad, and calls for the use of many talents. The related subject matter seems to be as wide as the list of subjects offered at the average school or college. The many careers available in real estate extend from the ABC (Alcoholic Beverage Control) board to zoning administration. In the material that follows, we highlight the various possible careers, some of which have already been discussed in previous chapters.

The federal government, the state, and numerous local governmental agencies offer a wide variety of opportunities for persons interested in a career in real estate. Ownership, regulation, and taxing are three aspects of governmental activity that call for real estate expertise. Community and land use planning are becoming increasingly important. And the Department of Real Estate offers career opportunities that are extremely diversified for appraisers, analysts, and enforcement officers, among others. There are over one hundred different agencies at all three levels of government dealing with real estate. These include county assessors, city community development departments, HUD, etc.

Brokerage

We encountered this subject when we discussed the role of the broker (Chapter 5). The term *brokerage* signifies an activity which involves the sale of a commodity through an intermediary, the broker who most often acts on behalf of a seller, although not infrequently a broker's services are utilized by a buyer. The broker ordinarily receives for his or her services a previously agreed-upon compensation based upon a percentage of the gross selling price. Real estate brokerage varies little from this general definition except that the real estate broker has greater need for a specific written authorization or an agency employment agreement with the seller. In addition to the agency relationship, the fiduciary and trust relationship is implicit in the activities of a real estate broker.

The operations of a broker include the following:

1. Securing listings, i.e., developing an inventory through leads and direct canvassing
2. Finding buyers by means of various advertising media
3. Negotiating or bringing together a meeting of the minds of the buyer and seller
4. Closing the transaction or assisting in the closing.

While selling is the chief objective in real estate brokerage, there is considerable administrative and paper work involved, ranging from setting up listing cards, filling out forms such as deposit receipts and loan applications, ordering special reports, to preparing closing statements and writing general correspondence. In the small office, these duties are performed by the broker, perhaps with some secretarial or bookkeeping aid. In the large offices, the functions may be detached and delegated to specialized departments.

The medium-sized firm is ordinarily manned by a "sales manager broker." In the large offices the broker usually has only executive and administrative duties.

Currently the trend among real estate brokers is toward specialization, either selling a certain type of property, or concentrating in a specified area or locale. However, the duties are quite diverse: the broker is called upon not only to sell property, but also to lease property or space in a building, to place mortgages, to collect rents, and to perform many other services for a percentage of the money value of the transaction. The broker's activity cuts across all lines of the real estate industry, for he or she may be called upon for appraisal work, selling, trading, renting, or advising on planning and development of real property. The broker is probably the most versatile of those working in the real estate field. In a sense the broker is the jack-of-all-trades in the industry.

Reviewing the broker's duties, it becomes obvious that the field of real estate involves much more than just selling houses. It offers many possibilities of financial success if a person is willing to think creatively and work hard. Nor is it a physically confining profession. The sale of lots, tracts, farms, houses, apartment and office buildings, hotels, motels, and industrial complexes as well as real estate financing, making leases, exchanges, and appraisals, all give the salesperson or broker a wide variety of interests and the opportunity—and necessity—of spending much time out-of-doors.

A well-rounded education is a prime necessity for a broker. Universities and colleges offer courses in real estate and related subjects which will help an applicant for a real estate license to pass the state examination. As listed in Chapter 5, broker prerequisite courses are: real estate practice, legal aspects of real estate, real estate finance, and appraisal, plus one course in either real estate economics or accounting, plus three of the following: real estate principles, advanced real estate legal aspects, advanced real estate finance, advanced real estate appraisal, business law, escrows, property management, or real estate office administration. An applicant should take a business law course in addition to the course in real estate law required by statute. The combination of the two courses gives the student a good business sense as well as an orientation in the legal concepts involved in real estate transactions. A course in accounting is also recommended by the Department of Real Estate; in fact, an accounting course may be taken instead of the course in real estate economics required of broker candidates. Much brokerage experience involves accounting for clients' funds (deposits, down payments, etc.—otherwise known as trust funds). This accounting requires a considerable amount of time and business acumen. In addition to various basic courses, there is an increased need for advanced courses and courses designed to keep the licensee and others informed of the latest changes and trends in real estate law and related fields. These courses can also apply toward a degree in business administration.

All fifty states and the District of Columbia require a broker to be licensed. And in most states, including California, as a general rule he or she must start as a licensed salesperson and serve a minimum period before being allowed to apply for a broker's license. During this period, the licensee can earn while learning: He or she can take advanced courses and eventually obtain a college or university degree. A licensee can learn much, too, from the conferences, training programs, and seminars presented by the California Association of Realtors and other associations. Experience has shown that a good real estate salesperson is not necessarily a "born salesman." But with the right training, imagination, and perseverance, plus a willingness to be of service, one can succeed in this vital field and eventually become a leading figure in the growth of the community.

Some successful brokers own their own offices and have several salespeople working under them. Like any other form of free enterprise, this operation requires some investment of capital. Brokers may serve as salespeople for a period until they have both the experience and the capital to open their own offices. The opportunities as a broker are normally limited only by the desire of the individual to have a going concern of his or her own.

In a career in real estate brokerage, passing the real estate license examination is only the beginning. Many more things must be learned about the actual practice of real estate brokerage. Selling experience in other lines is valuable, but selling real estate is different in many respects, including the following:

1. The product is more complex and individualized; there are ordinarily no standard units.
2. The sales period is longer and often more tedious, requiring a vast amount of patience on the part of the broker.
3. The transfer is frequently beset with legal requirements which must be understood and met.
4. The product often represents the largest single purchase the buyer will ever make, and it is only natural that he or she will want to proceed with caution.
5. The broker's role is primarily as a negotiator; he or she is acting as an intermediary between two parties.
6. The psychology or predicted behavior of the parties involved is more complicated in home selling than in selling less personalized consumer goods.
7. The requirement of a license imposes upon the holder certain definite legal and ethical restrictions in the conduct of his or her business.

The real estate broker must have much more than a layman's knowledge of the city and district in which he or she lives or seeks to operate. The broker's knowledge should be of the past, present, and future of the area. He or she needs to know what is going on in the local real estate market, in the city hall, and in the county courthouse. All should be included in his or her storehouse of facts. Above all, the real estate broker must know the product; i.e., the specific product he or she is marketing. A broker should know its value, its construction, its neighborhood, and the type of buyer who will be attracted.

People identify the business of real estate with the person running it. To be established in the community, particularly in civil and social activities, and to gain a well-accepted reputation is highly important for a broker's ultimate success.

In short, there is more to selling real estate than being a good salesperson. Indeed, some of the "good" salespeople have been known to oversell, which creates both legal and practical difficulties. Others have failed to qualify buyers properly, that is, to find the person who needs *and can afford* the property that is on the market.

Real Estate Financing

Another challenging career opportunity is in the field of real estate finance. It has been said that financing is the oil that keeps the wheels of the industry turning. Very few real estate transactions today are made on a cash basis, and thus lenders of mortgage money play a significant role in the industry and, indeed, in the total economy.

In Chapters 7 and 8, we touched upon many important aspects of real property financing. The largest flow of loan funds comes through banks, savings and loan associations, and insurance companies. New sources will be coming of age as we approach the 1990s and beyond.

Mortgage Banking. The primary business of mortgage banking is to originate and service mortgage loans for insurance companies, banks, and pension funds, and to make it possible for lending institutions to invest in real estate loans throughout the United States. Obviously mortgage bankers are not bankers in the usual meaning of the word. A mortgage banking company is a "mortgage correspondent"—a middleman—which provides a medium for placing funds from lenders' surplus savings accounts to various geographic areas of the United States and Canada where demand for real estate loan money exceeds the supply. Thus, mortgage banking performs a basic function in the national economy. Capital from eastern investors, brought in by means of the mortgage banking correspondent system, contributed considerably to the growth of the western sector of the nation.

Mortgage bankers make conventional loans, FHA-insured loans, and VA-guaranteed loans secured by trust deeds or mortgages on real property. In a typical transaction the mortgage company makes the original loan to a borrower, then sells it to a bank or insurance company through a commitment arrangement. The bank or insurance company is rarely interested in the mortgage or trust deed except as an investment; the investor doesn't want the problems of collecting monthly installment payments, paying property taxes, etc. Therefore, for a small fee the mortgage company performs this additional service on behalf of the lender-investor. Lenders' portfolios of loans have a wide range in dollar amounts, with several over a billion dollars.

The real estate finance man or woman is called upon to manage the real estate mortgage section of commercial and savings banks, along with savings and loan associations and insurance companies (and their agents). This management effort is aimed at producing the highest profit for the firm by extending credit on the security of sound real estate mortgages. These mortgages may be on such types of property as single-family residences, multiple dwellings, unimproved land, and commercial or industrial properties.

Persons active in real estate finance must have specialized knowledge of the mortgage and money markets, of appraisal, and of the local and national economy; they must understand the complex relationships of interest rates, risk, and yields; they should have training in accounting, appraisal, mathematics, real estate law, finance, and especially economics, for they are in effect applied economists specializing in the real estate market.

Those specializing in real estate finance must also keep abreast with ever-changing financing instruments. For example, since 1980 we have seen the introduction of such new financing techniques as the so-called FLIP mortgage, graduated payment mortgage (GPM), flexi-loans, rollover mortgage, dual rate variable mortgage, deferred interest plans, and other alternative mortgage instruments.

Opportunities for employment, in addition to those with the government, exist primarily with financial institutions, although many positions exist in large industrial firms with sizeable real estate investments.

A prospective real estate finance expert will probably begin his or her employment by specializing in appraising, loan processing, interviewing loan applicants, or servicing loans. Later he or she may negotiate lending agreements with other lenders. A finance expert may also specialize in a certain type of loan; e.g., construction loans, government-underwritten loans, etc.

Real Property Securities. Another career opportunity for a person holding a real estate broker's license is that of a real property securities dealer. The Business and Professions Code contains registration and regulatory requirements for such dealers and their operations. The activities of such dealers relate to bulk transactions in trust deeds, real property sales contracts, and investment plans dealing with such transactions.

BUSINESS AND PROFESSIONAL ASSOCIATIONS

As is true in other businesses and professions, numerous professional associations also exist in the real estate finance field. These associations have an important impact upon the entire real estate industry and include such organizations as the American Bankers Association, the U.S. Savings and Loan League, the American Savings and Loan Institute, the Society of Real Estate Appraisers, the National Savings and Loan League, and the Mortgage Banking Association.

The many mortgage bankers' associations are very active. Membership consists of dedicated professional representatives from the mortgage banking companies, banks, insurance companies, and title companies. The MBA (Mortgage Bankers Association) is the national group. Organized in 1914 as the Farm Mortgage Bankers Association with forty-five members, today's Mortgage Bankers Association of America is the only nationwide organization devoted exclusively to the field of mortgage banking. Having changed its name in 1926 to reflect the increased accent on urban lending, the MBA has served the industry for over half a century, supplying its two thousand members with technical information, education, and assistance, in an effort to assure a healthy and progressive industry.

The MBA sponsors a School of Mortgage Banking at Northwestern University in Chicago, and at Stanford University in Palo Alto. The MBA headquarters in Washington, D.C. represents its members at the national level, maintaining a close liaison with government agencies and congressional committees.

The CMBA (California Mortgage Bankers Association) is the statewide organization in California. It was organized in 1955 and maintains a full-time legislative advocate in Sacramento. Headquartered in Los Angeles, CMBA holds two regularly scheduled meetings each year, at which time members throughout the state are invited to participate in programs dealing with matters of serious interest to a mortgage banker.

The SCMBA (Southern California Mortgage Bankers Association) was organized locally in 1930. The members meet on a monthly basis for workshops and other kinds of meetings. Counterparts of the SCMBA in other parts of the state are: Northern California Mortgage Bankers Association (NCMBA), San Diego MBA, and Inland Empire MBA, representing Riverside, San Bernardino, and Imperial counties. These groups may be staffed by professionals in the field of real estate finance.

The mortgage banking field offers considerable opportunities for qualified people. The secondary mortgage market also heavily involves mortgage bankers.

ESCROW SERVICES

In Chapter 6 we considered the role of the escrow in real estate transactions and described the activities of the California Escrow Association. To introduce the student to career opportunities in the escrow field, the association has produced a filmstrip entitled *Where the Action Is*. Many colleges in California offer courses leading to a California Escrow Association Certificate. The holder of such a certificate may be well on his or her way to a successful future in an essential phase of real estate.

A skilled escrow officer is usually one of the most sophisticated persons in a real estate transaction. He or she performs functions ranging from clerical to those requiring the exercise of the highest degree of tact and diplomacy. The escrow officer is at the center of every type of transaction, whether it's the sale of a large shopping center, the sale of an undeveloped parcel of land, a loan for the construction of a large hotel or multiple housing development, or the sale, exchange, or refinancing of a residence.

The escrow industry is dynamic and offers many challenges and rewards. The duties of an escrow officer are varied. Among many functions, the escrow officer computes the cash settlement in a sales transaction; adjusts taxes, rents, interest, insurance premiums, and other matters as required; completes various types of documents to implement the instructions; applies knowledge of regulatory laws affecting his or her business and the particular transaction; and is called upon to use an abundance of patience, diplomacy, and common sense.

Among the organizations needing the services of escrow personnel are banks, savings and loan associations, mortgage companies, private escrow companies, title insurance companies, and governmental agencies.

INSURANCE SERVICES

The subject of title insurance and the many services afforded by a title insurance company were discussed in Chapter 6. Other types of insurance offer some, but not as much opportunity for those who are real estate oriented.

Insurance is often a part of a real estate broker's day-to-day functions. We frequently see signs such as R. F. JONES, REAL ESTATE AND INSURANCE. We are then apt to believe that the two activities are in the same category of business. Actually, the bulk of property or hazard insurance is sold through specialized agencies. Nonetheless, it is common for the larger real estate brokerage offices to represent insurance companies in placing policies.

Insurance is a natural feeder business and extra source of income for the real estate broker who is able to tap the lead at its source, from sales transactions originating in his or her office. The insurance department of a realty firm is like a loan or property management agency in that both are natural adjuncts of the regular brokerage practice. Insurance companies offer in-house training, and community colleges and business colleges have a variety of courses for those choosing to enter this facet of real estate activity.

REAL ESTATE COUNSELING

Because the business of real estate development has become incredibly complex over the years, few projects can be built without the help of a great many experts in a variety of fields. Gathering the information required to determine the need for a particular kind and quantity of structures, in a particular location, at a reasonable price, plus obtaining cost estimates and all documents needed to procure zone changes, environmental approvals, and other required permits; and, finally, securing financing; can only be accomplished by people who have experience and training in the fields of finance, marketing, construction, land use, government regulations, and economics. Thus, the field of real estate consulting has expanded markedly. Government departments at all levels must have staff able to weigh research, changing regulations, changing demographics, public tastes, and population increases. Large firms in the business of lending or investing, construction, construction material processing, designing, and marketing, will have departments able to provide information to the decision makers so that well-considered decisions can be made for the firm. Small firms must be able to seek the needed information from independent consulting firms. Since nearly every phase of life can be construed as relating in some way or another to real estate, you can see that the career opportunities in nearly every aspect of business abound for those interested in real estate.

A discussion on housing consulting follows, but much of the information relates also to commercial building, industrial siting and construction, and planned community development consulting. Because in-depth information is required for both the present situation and the projected future situation, consultants are necessary for those agencies or firms that deal with a small project having little impact on the greater community.

HOUSING CONSULTING

Housing is no longer just a matter of basic shelter, with a builder or developer putting up homes in response to demand. Instead, housing involves questions of community and social planning, legislation, market analysis, financing, and tax shelter. The increase in the number of government programs has complicated the picture, as has the entry of nonprofessional groups such as churches and neighborhood organizations into the role of sponsor-developer. It has been said that the modern housing expert has to be a community relations expert, sociologist, financial wizard, political scientist, and legal expert all rolled into one.

Consultants with various specialties are not new in the housing field. For instance, architects and engineers, real estate research firms, and marketing firms have been around for some time. They are of great value to a housing sponsor who knows what he or she is doing, such as the professional developer, but even here some developers are operating under rules that are no longer applicable. The professional developer sometimes can be led astray by the various types of legislation and financing programs, and by the changing effects of the market, which can restrain his or her activities on the one hand or open up new opportunities on the other.

The growing need for expertise in the housing field has been made all the more acute by the country's mounting backlog of unfilled housing requirements. Community groups, individuals, and public officials in cities of every size are faced with a growing housing problem but often lack the skills to deal with it.

As housing needs grow, it is anticipated that more and more firms will enter the housing consultant field. Such firms may become involved with many of the auxiliary areas, such as social services, education, economic development, and new legislation. The work of a comprehensive consulting firm involves several major areas, including the following:

1. Market potential analysis. This amounts to gathering data about a proposed project on a specific date and determining whether the project will succeed or fail. Conversely, it

means finding the best use for a particular site under existing financing.

2. Developing complete housing packages for nonprofit groups. For instance, some housing consultants set up the mechanics for obtaining housing, find a sponsor and the necessary financing, help arrange for the land, and train personnel in the techniques of development.

3. Putting together housing packages for groups that are profit oriented. These packages are tailored to the investment objectives of the sponsor, either cash flow, tax shelter, or long-term capital gains.

4. Legislative and administrative analysis, including aid to governmental bodies in assessing housing needs and interpreting economic and demographic trends.

5. Community analysis, involving studies of community needs other than housing, including health, welfare and educational services, and the evaluation of administrative procedures.

6. Assessing economic trends, future supplies and costs of materials, changing household size and makeup, and changing consumer tastes.

APPRAISAL

As we have seen in Chapter 9, the appraisal process is one of estimating past, present, or anticipated value. As appraisal relates to real estate, it may be the estimation of the value of any one of the estates or interests in real property, e.g., fee simple, leasehold, life estates, reversions and remainders, easements, and mineral and air-space rights.

The appraiser is called upon to render his or her estimation of value not only in the sale or purchase of realty, but also in such matters as leases; options to buy; trust deeds; foreclosures; insurance; property-tax assessments; estate and income taxes; urban-renewal projects; condemnations; corporate transactions including merger, consolidation, and liquidation.

A qualified appraiser should have training in mathematics, including algebra, geometry, and statistics; geology; accounting; economics; including urban land economics; city planning; investment principles; building methods and materials and their cost; and marketing research.

Employment opportunities for appraisers are available in institutions such as banks, insurance companies, saving and loan associations, and mortgage and investment companies. These firms invest millions of dollars each year in real property. Appraisers are retained by many industrial firms and large retailers to help them arrive at sound decisions when renting, buying, or selling their vast holdings of real property.

An appraiser usually has several years' experience in real estate before he or she is considered an expert. Usually an appraiser will specialize in a particular class of realty such as residential, industrial, commercial, or agricultural. In addition he or she will usually be an expert in a given geographical area. However, a good appraiser will also be able to change his or her location of operations without too much difficulty; the principles employed are substantially the same in any area.

A large proportion of the professional appraisers are employed by government agencies at local, county, state, and federal levels. As an example, the assessor in Los Angeles County has over 400 appraisers to cover in excess of 4,000 square miles of land in that county. Over $2\frac{1}{2}$ million dwelling units alone are reviewed periodically.

A study of the appraisers in the assessor's office in Los Angeles County revealed the following information regarding the average appraiser: He or she is a college graduate with one full year of intensive training in the appraisal field. The quality of training is so high that UCLA Extension gives course credit to students who participate in this program. They receive not only classroom instruction by qualified teachers, but practical field work as well under the supervision of experienced appraisers. They must pass a state-approved examination and complete in-service training each year to maintain their professional status.

In the field, appraisers are armed with slide rule· and a field book containing maps showing the boundary lines of property, zoning, and other pertinent data. You may encounter some of these people driving around in your neighborhood; they are there to review the area, and they sometimes stop to fill out reports.

Occasionally the appraiser finds himself under the scrutiny of the local police who have answered a call reporting a "suspicious-looking character" in the neighborhood. One appraiser, while reviewing a neighborhood that had recently been subjected to numerous burglaries, was questioned by the police. He explained that his knocking at a few doors was only to verify recent sales in the area.

Los Angeles County's rugged mountain terrain is reviewed by appraisers on horseback. These people will spend eight to ten hours riding through thick brush and up steep cliffs to cover terrain even a jeep cannot penetrate.

For those who meet the experience, educational, age, and test requirements, the professional designation MAI—Member, Appraisal Institute—may be awarded.

REAL PROPERTY MANAGEMENT

As we have seen from the discussion in Chapter 11, a real property manager is one who operates a particular parcel of real estate for the owner. In essence, his or her job is to see that the property produces a profit for the client. A property manager may supervise single-family units, multiple dwellings (including condominium projects), commercial properties (including stores and office buildings), or industrial property. In all of these, he or she is concerned with the renting, maintaining, and supervising of the property.

A qualified manager should be able to sell, negotiate, prepare quality advertising, and should possess much information on the fundamentals of construction. He or she should have training in real estate law, insurance, economics, accounting, including cost accounting, finance, and marketing. His or her main objective is to operate each supervised property in the most efficient and profitable manner possible. To do this he or she must keep abreast of the changing real estate market conditions both locally and nationally.

Opportunities for the prospective real property manager exist wherever there is property for rent. He or she may get a first start and gain valuable experience with a sales firm dealing in commercial property. Many sales firms have separate management divisions, and of course there are companies that deal strictly with the management function. Banks, insurance companies, and private real estate corporations or syndicates all have a need for qualified property managers.

For those who meet the Institute of Real Estate Management's (IREM) experience, educational, and test requirements, the professional designation CPM—Certified Property Manager—may be awarded.

PLANNING AND DEVELOPMENT

The subject of planning and development was considered in Chapter 12. Briefly stated, a person engaged in this field of real estate would be concerned with the concept of the highest and best use of property. He or she may be developing raw acreage or involved in vast urban renewal projects, or any number of other types of development. One of his or her major assignments could be to take a given parcel of real property and determine its most profitable use. Or he or she might be working for a large chain retailer with the task of locating, acquiring, and developing a parcel for a new outlet for the company.

To qualify for such a position a person should be well versed in economics, especially on the local and state levels. He needs a wealth of knowledge with respect to zoning and building regulations. A general business education should also be a requisite, with emphasis in real estate finance, financial analysis, taxation, appraisal, and law.

Opportunities for employment range from local planning boards to firms that specialize in real estate consulting and development and industrial or commercial firms that plan new locations. Government at all levels has a great need for qualified planners in the wake of recent interest in urban renewal and redevelopment projects.

A planner and developer obviously needs to have extensive experience in real estate, especially in appraisal and construction. He or she should be able to prepare economic base studies and long-range market projections.

SUBDIVIDING, BUILDING, AND ARCHITECTURAL SERVICES

As noted in Chapter 12, there is a need for a considerable number of qualified experts in the development of land and buildings. Some experts have already been utilized before the raw land is subdivided and construction of improvements commenced. Others will be needed as the development progresses, including the architect and building contractor.

At the initial level of actual development, the owner will be engaged in the process of converting raw land into lots for building purposes. This involves a knowledge of the subdivision laws and other state and local government regulations. Also, a survey will ordinarily be needed; the owner may employ either a licensed surveyor or a registered civil engineer.

The owner may then go a step further and build houses or other structures for sale and thus become an operative builder. Ultimately, he or she can plan, develop, and sell a planned community that includes not only single-family houses, but multiple units, apartments, store buildings, and even shopping centers.

With respect to architects, a recent survey disclosed that the public often has little knowledge of what an architect actually does. Services provided by architectural firms vary, of course; some of the larger firms offer such comprehensive services as space programming and planning, site selection, economic analysis, engineering, interior design and decoration, graphic design, and construction management. However, every architectural firm does offer basic architectural services.

The architect begins by studying the client's building project, whether it is a single-family home or a multibuilding high-rise complex. He or she studies present and future needs and desires, and from his or her background of training and experience, suggests needs and reveals desires the owner may not have considered.

After guiding the owner in obtaining a survey of the site and tests of subsurface soil conditions, the architect begins to solve the problem on paper, developing space sizes and relationships while creating schematic plans and sketches showing the general design approach, method of construction, and the basic material that he or she proposes to use. When the schematic drawings are completed, these—together with a cost estimate—are presented and explained to the owner for consideration and review.

Following approval of the schematic plans, more detailed preliminary plans are developed. During this period, the architect researches specific materials, consults building codes, begins working with a structural engineer if he or she has not already done so, and brings an electrical and a mechanical engineer into the project. The architect may suggest specialized consultants for such subjects as acoustics and traffic, depending on the requirements of the particular project.

Preliminary plans are more detailed than the schematics, and the architect might consult periodically with the owner during their preparation. Preliminary plans are submitted for the owner's approval together with a set of outline specifications and another cost estimate.

The next step for the architect is preparation of working drawings and detailed specifications called the "contract documents." These are the documents on which the building contractor's price is set and which guide the contractor in every detail of construction. The resulting job and the final cost depend heavily on how well these documents are prepared.

After the architect has obtained building and other permits from the municipality, he or she helps the owner place the contract documents out to bid. He or she then helps evaluate contractors' bids, and aids in arranging the contracts between the owner and the contractor.

But the architect does not leave the job when it enters construction. Services during construction include regular on-site inspections to assure that the plans and specifications are being followed, a job which includes the checking of shop drawings developed by subcontractors. Most projects in most communities require completion of environmental impact assessment forms and mitigation plans for possible negative impacts.

In large communities with complex requirements for land use, building and safety requirements, and a variety of fees, permits, and approvals, expediters are frequently hired expressly to process project plans through the maze of paperwork. Such a person or firm must generally be registered as a paid consultant or advocate in order to legally act on behalf of a client. Generally, training and experience in real estate, planning and civil engineering are helpful in entering this field.

RESEARCH AND ANALYSIS

A person choosing this phase of real estate activity can enter either the pure or applied research sectors. An applied research analyst is mainly concerned with market and feasibility studies, while a pure research analyst is more concerned with basic land-use studies, such as the reason urban areas develop as they do.

In either case a formal education in economics, business administration, public administration, urban studies, sociology, or psychology is considered to be essential. Mathematics, statistics, political science, appraisal, finance, and related areas are also required. Appraisal experience along with market research and feasibility study experience would be quite helpful.

The growing awareness of the complexity of real estate activity plus the realization that real property offers many advantages over other investments has led to an increased number of real estate research firms. These companies are a source of employment for the applied researcher. Also, many planning and development firms have large research staffs, as do commercial retail chains, industrial firms, trust departments of large lenders, insurance companies, pension funds, and credit unions.

The pure research analyst will find many opportunities in the academic world of colleges and universities. All levels of government are also becoming more aware of the need for such individuals so that adequate, sound, and timely planning can be undertaken.

REAL ESTATE LAW

The services of an attorney are frequently quite essential in real estate transactions, and the role of the attorney is an important one. Many times brokers, escrow officers, and others are requested by a customer to prepare documents that go beyond their customary duties and that may constitute the unlawful practice of law. Performing such duties should firmly be declined and the party should be requested to consult his own attorney when there is a need for legal advice. However, attorneys are not necessarily versed in real estate law. Again, because real estate activity has become increasingly complex, attorneys who wish to specialize should study real estate law and familiarize themselves with the major laws and interpretations affecting real estate transactions.

Relationships between lawyers and brokers and others in the real estate field have not always been harmonious, but organized communication in the form of educational seminars, liaison committees, and conferences has helped to solve the problem in many areas. Understanding the role and function of the attorney is of primary concern.

Many times persons in the real estate field, particularly those employed by large corporations or by governmental agencies, will decide to make law their career. They often attend law school at night. When they eventually complete their course of study and are admitted to practice law, it is a very rewarding experience.

Only persons who are active members of the State Bar of California are entitled to practice law in this state. The right to practice law is actually a statutory privilege. The adequate protection of public interests and the inherent complexities pertaining to the practice of law require supervision by the state, through the courts, over the conduct of the members of the legal profession.

The members of the State Bar are persons who have been admitted and licensed to practice law in the state. Most lawyers are also members of bar associations. These associations are private organizations among lawyers, usually combining social, educational, and professional purposes. They may be national, local, or sectional.

The conditions under which a person may be admitted to the practice of law in this state are prescribed by statute (State Bar Act) and by the Rules Regulating Admission to Practice Law in California which are issued by the State Bar in implementation of the statutory provisions.

The requirements for admission to the State Bar include the following:

1. Bona fide residence in the state
2. Good moral character
3. Satisfactory compliance with examination requirements.

The profession of attorney at law is essentially a learned profession which requires not alone a basic honesty, but also an intellectual capacity. Most attorneys now have the equivalent of six or more years of college education. The attorney's relation to his or her client is both *fiduciary*, committing the attorney to the most scrupulous good faith, and *confidential*, committing him or her to professional secrecy.

Attorneys are bound to comply with certain ethical standards, based on general principles of morality. Attorneys are also held to a requisite degree of skill and care. An attorney can be sued by his or her client for a want of ordinary skill and care. By accepting employment to give legal advice or to render other legal services, an attorney impliedly agrees to use ordinary judgment, care, skill, and diligence in the performance of the task he or she undertakes; this agreement is breached by failure to use such care and skill. The care and skill required is that which lawyers of ordinary skill and capacity commonly possess and exercise.

Many people who need legal help are reluctant to see an attorney because they have heard that legal services are expensive. Actually, fees are usually small in comparison with the benefits gained or losses avoided. Often no specific fee can be fixed in advance because the facts of various cases are different, require different amounts of time and skills, involve different amounts of property or money, etc. In any event, an attorney is prepared to answer questions on fees at any time, and a person does not have to proceed with a case or other matter unless he or she thinks it advisable.

ESTATE PLANNING

Estate planning may be included among the services provided by an attorney specializing in real estate law. However, accountants, insurance underwriters, large bank trust departments, and tax experts also provide estate planning. The past has shown that real estate holdings can be the cornerstone on which an individual successfully builds an accumulation of wealth. However, such holdings can cause tremendous problems of liquidity and taxes to the individual's heirs unless the proper planning has been done. In order to maximize the after-tax wealth that an individual may leave to his or her heirs, there must be an effective plan which has taken into account the effects of estate, gift, and income taxes. An estate planner can assist a client in deciding whether to dispose of property by gift during life or by will at death. The interplay of tax laws with legal and economic considerations becomes very important; such decisions nearly always require the assistance of competent legal counsel.

REAL ESTATE EDUCATION

The need for competent real estate instructors is constantly increasing. The real estate curriculum at the colleges and universities continues to expand. A survey disclosed that a real estate curriculum is available in over one hundred of California's community colleges. Most of these colleges offer an associate of arts degree with a specialization in real estate. Most of the nineteen state colleges offer B.A. degrees with a real estate major, and many offer master's degrees. The University of California has Ph.D. programs in urban land economics. Consequently, there is an increased need for more teachers, text material, visual and audiovisual aids. These needs offer a challenge to the ingenuity and creativity of potential instructors.

The many licensed private real estate schools also provide opportunities for instructors in a variety of real estate courses.

The State Department of Real Estate has information on schools offering courses in real estate.

Internship programs are also available at some colleges which will increase the opportunities in real estate through education. The objective of these programs is to furnish an opportunity for college students to participate in a full-time paid-work experience in the real estate environment during vacation periods.

SUMMARY OF MAJOR CAREER AREAS

Opportunities in the principal areas of real estate are summarized in outline form below.

I. **Real Estate Brokerage**
   A. Means aiding persons to buy and sell, to rent and lease property, exchange property
      1. Homes
      2. Apartments
      3. Condominiums and cooperatives
      4. Commercial buildings
      5. Industrial developments
      6. Municipal buildings
   B. Largest branch of real estate industry
      1. Tendency on part of average person to feel selling of residential property is major part of real estate business
      2. Residential sales only part of it
   C. Who should enter real estate brokerage?
      1. Those who like salesmanship
      2. Those who are individualistic, outgoing, enthusiastic, healthy
         a. Importance of having experience in this field, with eye to future livelihood
      3. Those who like to be their own boss, who can organize their own days
      4. Those who enjoy people
      5. Those who can adjust to changing conditions, to unscheduled changes
      6. Those who are community oriented
      7. Those who prefer to work close to home surroundings
      8. Those who enjoy giving service
      9. Those who enjoy developing their own initiative
   D. Educational requirements
      1. Becoming more and more important for salesperson to be educated

    a. On formal level
    b. On practical and technical level
  2. Desirable to have education at formal level
    a. Degree in business administration
    b. Degree in land economics
  3. Necessity to be educated on practical level
    a. Community college courses
    b. Seminars, institutes, correspondence courses (CAR and NAR)
    c. Selling experience
    d. Office procedure
  4. Specific college courses required for brokers

E. Compensation—commission basis
  1. The more a salesperson lists and sells, the more he or she makes as commission
  2. Five-figure income not uncommon, even for beginner
  3. Many offices expect salesperson to earn between $15,000 to $20,000 for privilege of a desk
  4. Depends principally on initiative
  5. Must be able to cope with fluctuating income

F. Security benefits—increasing lately in order to compete with industry
  1. Offices interested in helping new salesperson get good start
  2. Many offices offer drawing accounts for beginners
  3. Some offices offer salaries for a certain length of time
  4. Many offices offer group insurance (medical and life) plans
  5. More lenient restrictions on part of government for self-employed retirement funds

G. Advancement
  1. May become part of existing business
    a. As partner
    b. As stockholder
  2. May become cooperative owner of inner-office investment group
  3. May become broker-owner of own firm
  4. May enter specialized brokerage
    a. Commercial real estate
    b. Industrial real estate
    c. Farm brokerage
  5. Constant demand for enterprising salesperson

II. Property Management
A. Property manager handles every aspect of income-producing property for owner of property
  1. Leasing
  2. Tenant relations
  3. Collections
  4. Advertising
  5. Maintenance
  6. Accounting

B. Importance of management in real estate equal to importance of management in any other business
  1. Residential management (apartments)
  2. Commercial management
  3. Shopping centers
  4. Industrial centers

C. Who should enter this field?
  1. Those with a mind for detail
    a. Accountants
    b. Those trained in managing income
  2. Those who like construction and mechanics
    a. With ability to understand building equipment
    b. With ability to oversee proper repairs
  3. Those who enjoy supervisory work
    a. Need for tact
    b. Ability to make sound judgments
    c. Ability to manage property on income-producing basis
    d. Ability to hire and supervise maintenance personnel

D. Educational requirements
  1. College trained preferred
    a. Degree in business administration
    b. Degree in accounting
    c. Degree in engineering
  2. Specialized training necessary
    a. Technical schools
    b. Property management courses
    c. Designation as Certified Property Manager (CPM) earned through Institute of Real Estate Management

E. Compensation
  1. Salary paid by owners of property
  2. Salary paid by management firm, with bonuses paid by some
  3. Regular income, steady employment

F. Security benefits
  1. Medical, insurance, retirement, according to firm

2. Individual or group policy
G. Advancement
 1. Commensurate with ability and experience
 2. Great demand for qualified property managers
    a. Trained
    b. Experienced
    c. Competent
 3. Demand will increase in future
    a. Increasing number of investors in real property
    b. Investors want their return, not the details of management
    c. Investors willing to pay for these services
 4. Opportunity of operating own firm
 5. Opportunity of procuring prime investments on individual basis

III. Mortgage Risk Financing
A. All or part of business of many real estate firms
B. Generally speaking, means finding mortgages for investors
 1. Aids investors in gaining a return on their money
 2. Aids purchasers in purchasing and financing real property
C. Who should enter?
 1. Those who are interested in the field of finance and banking
 2. Those who have an administrative mind
    a. With ability to understand mortgage market
    b. With ability to appraise property
    c. With managerial ability
 3. Those with initiative and patience
D. Educational requirements—formal education preferred
 1. Degree in business administration
 2. Degree in banking and finance
E. Compensation
 1. Commission
 2. Salary
 3. Combination
F. Security benefits
 1. Depend upon firm
 2. Medical insurance, individual or group
 3. Individual or firm retirement plans
G. Advancement
 1. Opportunities never at a standstill

2. Opportunity to become a member of firm
3. Opportunity to own individual business
4. As reputation grows, so does advancement

IV. Appraisal
A. Means evaluation of property
B. Closest to scientific process in field of real estate
 1. Appraiser must be able to give estimate of value
 2. Appraiser must be able to give written report, using established methods
    a. Market data approach
    b. Cost approach
    c. Income approach
 3. Today's qualified appraiser is recognized as a professional
C. Who should enter?
 1. Those with an analytical mind
 2. Those with a technical mind
 3. Those who are methodical and enjoy an orderly process
 4. Those with a flair for mathematics and accounting
D. Educational requirements
 1. College education preferable
    a. Degree in business administration
    b. Degree in mathematics
    c. Degree in accounting
 2. Technical education essential
    a. Principles of appraisal must be learned
    b. AIREA-sponsored courses
    c. Designation received for appraiser qualification
    d. Constant self-education on up-to-date appraisal methods
    e. Special courses and latest knowledge found in publications and journals
E. Compensation
 1. Fee (never commission)
 2. Salary if employed by a firm
F. Security benefits
 1. Individual, if self-employed
 2. According to firm, if employed
G. Advancement
 1. Constant need for qualified appraisers
 2. Many fields of employment
    a. Real estate firms of all types
    b. Financial institutions
    c. Branches of government

      d. Insurance companies

    3. Opportunities unlimited, according to individual performance and excellence

      a. As individual appraiser

      b. As member of firm

      c. As owner of firm

V. Real Estate Research and Education

  A. Research

    1. Big new field in real estate

    2. Becoming vital to the real estate industry

    3. Precise information needed in all categories of real estate

      a. Planning

      b. Production

      c. Marketing

      d. Financing

      e. Methods

      f. Computers

      g. Physical research—efficiency and production of construction materials

  B. Education

    1. Qualified faculty needed in colleges and universities

    2. Qualified faculty needed at community college level

    3. Qualified faculty needed at institute and seminar level

  C. Who should enter?

    1. Those of scientific mind

    2. Research-oriented persons

      a. Research in real estate equivalent to research in medicine—for benefit of profession

      b. Those who prefer to work individually, often introverts

    3. Those with a love of teaching and the academic life

    4. Academicians

      a. Schools of business administration

      b. School of economics

      c. Schools of sociology

      d. Schools of law

  D. Compensation

    1. Salary

    2. Return from publications

    3. Educational grants

  E. Educational requirements

    1. Degree through formal academic education

      a. Business administration

      b. Law

      c. Engineering

      d. Sociology

      e. Land economics

    2. Advanced degrees at university level

    3. Teaching experience

  F. Security benefits

    1. According to firm

    2. According to university or college

  G. Advancement

    1. Unlimited opportunities for those interested in research

      a. Universities

      b. Real estate industry

      c. Institutions of all types

    2. Academic advancement at university level

VI. Land Development

  A. Challenge of the immediate future—of vital importance to our nation

  B. Means actual planning and developing

    1. Home neighborhoods

    2. Shopping areas

    3. Multifamily projects

    4. Commercial centers

    5. Industrial centers

    6. Planned communities

  C. Includes knowledge of many facets of real estate

    1. Site securement

    2. Cost analysis

    3. Financing

    4. Installation of improvements

    5. Construction

    6. Merchandising

    7. Management

    8. Economic feasibility

  D. Who should enter?

    1. Those who are willing to work and learn

    2. Those who have executive ability

    3. Those who can accept responsibilities under pressure

    4. Those with a knowledge of construction

    5. Those with keen judgment

    6. Those willing and able to take risks for large gains

  E. Educational requirements

    1. Formal education preferable

      a. Degree in business administration

      b. Degree in financing

      c. Degree in engineering

      d. Degree in architecture

2. Experience in some phases of land development
F. Compensation
   1. Salary, if employed
   2. Commission, if self-employed
   3. Often, both salary and commission
G. Security benefits
   1. According to development firm
   2. Individual
H. Advancement
   1. Member of firm
   2. Own firm
   3. Financial success has no limits for successful developer

VII. **Summation**
A. Six major fields of specialization
   1. Brokerage (including residential, commercial, industrial, farm)
   2. Property management
   3. Mortgage risk financing
   4. Appraisal
   5. Research and education
   6. Land development
B. Compensation
   1. Commission basis general method of remuneration in all brokerage and land development
   2. Salaries and fees general method of remuneration in all other fields of specialization
   3. Sometimes both salaries and commissions
C. Educational requirements
   1. As in all industry, formal education advisable
      a. Choice employer will pick up the better educated person
      b. Necessity in research and education
   2. Technical courses, with earned designation
      a. Necessity in appraisal
      b. Preferred in property management
   3. Training for all major fields of specialization
      a. Semiformal education at community college level
      b. Courses by professional groups of NAR
      c. Institutes at the state level
      d. Seminars and lectures
      e. Correspondence courses
      f. Schools of real estate, private

g. Training and experience in the real estate firm
h. Indoctrination courses at the local board level
D. Advancement
   1. Literally unlimited possibilities
   2. As in all fields of endeavor, measured by individual enterprise and successful application of knowledge
E. Real estate field has everything to offer
   1. Complex industry
   2. Opportunities for various types of persons
   3. Opportunities for unlimited income
   4. Is, and will remain, constant source of livelihood
      a. "Under All Is the Land" not simply a phrase
      b. Land in the United States has resulted in the development and economy of our nation
         (1) Our greatest source of wealth
         (2) As long as private ownership of land exists, there will be a need for the real estate industry.

QUESTIONS FOR CHAPTER 15

Select the correct answer to each of the following:

1. Career opportunities in real estate are
   a. limited
   b. restrictive
   c. confining
   d. unlimited
2. The activities of a real estate broker may include
   a. managing
   b. leasing
   c. appraising
   d. any of the above
3. Effective January 1, 1986, the number of college courses required to obtain a broker's license is
   a. four
   b. six
   c. eight
   d. none of these
4. Subjects of considerable value for those studying real estate finance include
   a. mathematics
   b. accounting
   c. appraisal
   d. all of the above

REAL ESTATE, 1990: THE SHAPE OF THINGS TO COME . . . IN A NUTSHELL

1.	House Prices	Average new house, $200,000. Resale, $225,000.
2.	Condominiums	One in four housing starts will be condos or some variation of "own your own."
3.	Mobile Homes	One in four houses will be "mobiles"; their permanency and "immobility" will render them as real property, subject to realty taxes as is now the case in California.
4.	Air space	Multiple use of this valuable resource will be widely leased or sold, particularly along freeway routes.
5.	Marketing	A uniform land transaction law to protect buyers and borrowers against unreasonable risks and losses.
6.	Licensing	Harder to obtain and maintain. Stringent competency requirements. Full-time salespersons constitute the real estate field. Greater specialization.
7.	Organized Exchange	Computers widely used to match buyers, sellers, investors, and builders to level out the kinks in housing and development.
8.	Franchising	Small real estate firms united under one of many franchise banners in order to compete with the giants.
9.	Financing	Many variations to fit almost every borrower. Greatly expanded use of secondary markets to assure smoother flow of funds into housing. Alternative mortgage instruments will be the order of the day, especially the adjustable rate mortgage or variation.
10.	Mortgage Insurance	The state will provide insurance for the purchase and rehabilitation of existing homes in mortgage-deficient areas.

5. Teaching offers a career in the real estate field. Which of the following serve the greatest number of real estate students?
   a. community colleges
   b. state colleges
   c. universities
   d. private schools

6. The real estate commissioner is appointed by the
   a. secetary of state
   b. state legislature
   c. governor
   d. real estate commission

7. A real estate license is required of agents for which of the following activities:
   a. purchasing real property
   b. exchanging real property
   c. negotiating real property loans
   d. all of the above

8. Doing business under a fictitious name in Calfornia is
   a. illegal
   b. a fraud on creditors
   c. regulated by statute
   d. none of the above apply

9. To be entitled to a commission, a broker must
   a. be duly licensed
   b. have an oral agreement with his or her principal
   c. be a member of a multiple listing service
   d. all of the above

10. Which state was first to require licensing of real estate salespersons?
    a. New York
    b. Pennsylvania
    c. California
    d. Washington

11. A member of the National Association of Realtors is authorized to use the title
    a. Realator
    b. Realtor

11. Warranties	Express and implied warranties to insure inhabitability, fitness for use, quality, sound construction, and against defective materials. "Caveat emptor" replaced by "caveat venditor." Home protection plans standard practice.
12. Apartments	Low rise, two- to four-story row dwellings replacing highrise apartments for low-income families. HUD jointly involved with municipalities in rehabilitation and modernization of existing stock to improve living conditions in public housing projects.
13. Rent Control	Statewide controls instituted for most apartment projects over four units.
14. Environment	Coastal land use subjected to ever-tightening rules and regulations. "No growth" patterns changed to limited or "controlled growth."
15. Energy	Solar collectors mounted on practically every rooftop. Increased use of nuclear energy.
16. New Towns	Both the private entrepreneur and HUD involved in creating new towns in areas where natural resources can be relocated.
17. Institutional and Foreign Ownership	Banks, insurance companies, pension funds heavily buying income-producing properties for their own accounts and their clients, both domestic and foreign. Principal foreign investors: Europe, Great Britain, Middle Eastern nations, Canada.
18. Industrial Real Estate	Industrial development returning to the inner city, replacing blighted sections with industrial parks and providing jobs for residents of inner city.
19. Metrication	House dimensions are quoted in metric scale, with more stabilization in the building industry. Land measured in square meters and hectares. Buildings leased and sold by measures of square meters.
20. Households	One-person households forming at increasing rates. California's population: 32,000,000.

    c. Realatist
    d. Realtist
12. A member of the National Association of Real Estate Brokers is authorized to use the title
    a. Realator
    b. Realtor
    c. Realatist
    d. Realtist
13. The real estate business is considered to be
    a. a very lucrative one for anyone who can get a license
    b. extremely competitive
    c. rapidly losing ground to the "for sale by owner" trends
    d. relatively noncompetitive
14. Which of the following statements concerning real estate specialists is true?

    a. The majority of real estate transactions in California are handled by attorneys.
    b. All brokers are Realtors, but not all Realtors are brokers.
    c. An architect's job continues long after construction of a project begins.
    d. An MAI is a professional designation found in the mortgage industry.
15. To obtain an active real estate salesperson license, the applicant must be
    a. a resident of California for one year
    b. sponsored by a broker
    c. a citizen of the United States
    d. twenty-one years of age
16. "C.M.B.A." is identified with the field of
    a. financing
    b. appraising
    c. management

    d. escrow

17. A consumer who has obtained a judgment against a real estate licensee because of a fraudulent act may be able to collect through the
    a. California Association of Real Estate Brokers
    b. California Association of Realtors
    c. California Real Estate Fund
    d. the affected local Board of Realtors

18. Of the following, which is *not* an objective of organized real estate?
    a. promote high standards
    b. cooperate in economic growth and development
    c. establish commission rate schedules
    d. unite members for their common good

19. Real estate brokers must have what type of written agreement with their salespersons?
    a. employment
    b. withholding tax
    c. independent contractors
    d. agency

20. The Real Estate Fund primarily protects
    a. real estate agents
    b. private lenders
    c. the Department of Real Estate
    d. the buying public

21. MAI is a professional designation awarded to a qualified
    a. appraiser
    b. lender
    c. real estate salesperson
    d. property manager

22. CPM is a professional designation awarded to a qualified
    a. appraiser
    b. lender
    c. real estate salesperson
    d. property manager

23. All real estate brokers are
    a. independent contractors
    b. employees of their principals
    c. agents for their principals
    d. subagents for other agents

24. A real estate agent may offer advice on
    a. method of taking title
    b. how to evade taxes
    c. ethnic preferences among buyers
    d. none of the above

25. An escrow holder is ordinarily responsible for
    a. ordering title report
    b. prorating taxes
    c. obtaining beneficiary statements
    d. all of the above

26. An escrow holder should have a basic understanding of
    a. law of contracts
    b. law of agency
    c. rules of conveyancing
    d. all of the above

27. The amount of simple interest on a real property improvement loan of $30,000 for 4 years at a rate of 16 percent, computed on an annual basis, is
    a. $30,000
    b. $24,000
    c. $19,200
    d. $14,400

28. The numbers 17, 23, 37, and 43 are examples of
    a. decimals
    b. mixed numbers
    c. fractions
    d. prime numbers

29. Multiplication serves a purpose similar to
    a. subtraction
    b. addition
    c. proration
    d. division

30. An extended coverage policy of title insurance excludes from coverage
    a. the validity of an easement deed
    b. the validity of a court decree affecting title
    c. the priority of a deed of trust
    d. compliance with consumer protection laws

31. Off-record risks not insured by a standard coverage policy of title insurance include
    a. right of a tenant under an unrecorded lease
    b. exact location of improvements on the property
    c. location of boundaries on the ground
    d. all of the above

32. A physical inspection of the property is ordinarily not required by a title insurer in case of
    a. an ALTA owner's policy
    b. an extended coverage policy
    c. a CLTA standard coverage policy
    d. mechanic's lien insurance

33. The choice of a title insurer basically should be the responsibility of the
    a. insured
    b. real estate broker
    c. escrow holder
    d. real estate salesperson

34. A standard coverage policy of title insurance does not insure
    a. adequacy of consideration
    b. marketability of title

c. validity of a joint tenancy

d. authority of an attorney-in-fact

35. The sum of 482 plus 517 plus 633 plus 95 is

   a. 1517

   b. 1627

   c. 1727

   d. 1747

36. To subtract fractions, the common denominator is used

   a. the same way as in addition

   b. the opposite way from addition

   c. to multiply the numerator

   d. to cancel the numerator

37. A broker has a home listed for sale at a price of $106,000. An offer is submitted that is 12 percent less than the listed price. The sellers inform the broker that they will accept the offer if the broker will reduce his 6 percent commission by 16 2/3 percent. If the broker agrees to reduce his commission, he will earn

   a. $6664

   b. $5300

   c. $5620

   d. $4664

38. A property produced an 8 percent gross return on a $100,000 purchase for a one-year period. The owner's only expense resulted from a 9 percent annual interest charge on an $80,000 trust deed loan on the property. What is the percentage of return the owner will realize on his equity?

   a. 4 percent

   b. 6 percent

   c. 8 percent

   d. 10 percent

39. The net income of a property is $12,000, which is an 8 percent return on the total investment in land and improvements. The improvements are valued at $100,000. The land represents what portion of the value of the land and improvements?

   a. 25 percent

   b. 33 1/3 percent

   c. 66 2/3 percent

   d. 75 percent

40. An apartment building has a net income of $20,000. If 10 percent is considered a fair rate of return, the capitalized value of the property is

   a. $100,000

   b. $120,000

   c. $120,200

   d. $200,000

41. An individual borrowed $7500 on a straight note at an interest rate of 14.4 percent. If his total interest payment was $1350, the term of the loan was

   a. 12 months

   b. 15 months

   c. 18 months

   d. 24 months

42. The owners of a house list it with a broker under a "net" listing. After deducting 6 percent commission and paying $2000 for other sales expenses, the sellers received $125,850. The gross selling price was

   a. $125,840

   b. $133,448

   c. $136,000

   d. $144,000

43. A $10,000 loan has payment of $100 per month, including interest at 8 percent. After the first monthly payment has been made, the balance due will be

   a. $9975.00

   b. $9966.67

   c. $9950.00

   d. $9933.34

44. Referring to question 43, after the first and second monthly payments have been made, the balance due will amount to

   a. $9950.09

   b. $9933.34

   c. $9933.11

   d. $9925.00

45. You sell your house for $120,000 subject to an existing $80,000 first trust deed loan, and carry back a second trust deed loan for $16,000 after a down payment of $24,000. The amount of documentary transfer tax is

   a. $44.00

   b. $105.60

   c. $114.40

   d. $132.00

46. A rectangular lot with a 90-foot frontage, containing 1080 square yards, would have a depth of (see Figure 2.11 for hint)

   a. 12 feet

   b. 36 feet

   c. 72 feet

   d. 108 feet

47. Escrow instruction for the sale of a residence and any amendment thereto

   a. must be in writing to be enforceable

   b. must have a definite termination date

   c. can be modified orally

   d. are subject to modification by seller's broker

48. Until final payment is made, a deed of a trust is ordinarily retained by the

a. trustor
b. trustee
c. beneficiary
d. land owner

49. The word *constructive* applies in which of the following areas?
    a. recording
    b. trusts
    c. landlord/tenant relationship
    d. all of the above

50. A person who is engaged solely in the appraisal of real estate is required to hold a
    a. California real estate broker's license
    b. California real estate appraiser's license
    c. membership card in the M.A.I.
    d. none of the above apply

CALIFORNIA DEPARTMENT OF REAL ESTATE
CODE OF ETHICS AND PROFESSIONAL CONDUCT

Regulations of the Real Estate Commissioner as contained in Title 10 of the California Administrative Code.

Article 11, Ethics and Professional Conduct Code

In order to enhance the professionalism of the California real estate industry, and maximize protection for members of the public dealing with real estate licensees, the followingt standards of professional conduct and business practices are adopted:

(a) **Unlawful Conduct.** Licensees shall not engage in "fraud" or "dishonest dealing" or "conduct which would have warranted the denial of an application for a real estate license" within the meaning of Business and Professions Code Sections 10176 and 10177 including, but not limited to, the following acts and omissions:

(1) Knowingly making a substantial misrepresentation of the likely market value of real property to its owner either for the purpose of securing a listing or for the purpose of acquiring an interest in the property for the licensee's own account.

(2) The statement or implication by a licensee to an owner of real property during listing negotiations that the licensee is precluded by law, regulation or by the rules of any organization, other than the broker firm seeking the listing, from charging less than the commission or fee quoted to the owner by the licensee.

(3) The failure by a licensee acting in the capacity of an agent in a transaction for the sale, lease or exchange of real property to disclose to a prospective purchaser or lessee facts known to the licensee materially affecting the value or desirability of the property, when the licensee has reason to believe that such facts are not known to, nor readily observable by a prospective purchaser or lessee.

(4) When seeking a listing, representation to an owner of the real property that the soliciting licensee has obtained a bona fide written offer to purchase the property, unless at the time of the representation the licensee has possession of a bona fide written offer to purchase.

(5) The willful failure by a listing broker to present or cause to be presented to the owner of the property any offer to purchase received prior to the closing of a sale, unless expressly instructed by the owner not to present such an offer, or unless the offer is patently frivolous.

(6) Presenting competing offers to purchase real property to the owner by the listing broker in such a manner as to induce the owner to accept the offer which will provide the greatest compensation to the listing broker, without regard to the benefits, advantages, and/or disadvantages to the owner.

(7) Knowingly underestimating the probable closing costs in a transaction in a communication to the prospective buyer or seller of real property in order to induce that person to make or to accept an offer to purchase the property.

(8) Failing to explain to the parties or prospective parties to a real estate transaction the meaning and probable significance of a contingency in an offer or contract that the licensee knows or reasonably believes may affect the closing date of the transaction, or the timing of the vacating of the property by the seller or its occupancy by the buyer.

(9) Knowingly making a false or misleading representation to the seller of real property as to the form, amount and/or treatment of a deposit toward purchase of the property made by an offeror.

(10) The refunding by a licensee, when acting as an agent or sub-agent for seller, of all or part of an offeror's purchase money deposit in a real estate sales transaction after the seller has accepted the offer to purchase, unless the licensee has the express permission of the seller to make the refund.

(11) Failing to disclose to the seller of real property in a transaction in which the licensee is acting in the capacity of an agent, the nature and extent of any direct or indirect interest that the licensee expects to acquire as a result of the sale. The prospective purchase of the property by a person related to the licensee by blood or marriage, purchase by an entity in which the licensee has an ownership interest, or purchase by any other per-

son with whom the licensee occupies a special relationship where there is a reasonable probability that the licensee could be indirectly acquiring an interest in the property, shall be disclosed.

(12) A representation made as principal or agent to a prospective purchaser of a promissory note secured by real property with respect to the fair market value of the securing property without a reasonable basis for believing the truth and accuracy of the estimate of fair market value.

(13) Making an addition to or modification of the terms of an instrument previously signed or initialed by a party to a transaction without the knowledge and consent of the party.

(b) Unethical Conduct. In order to maintain a high level of ethics in business practice, real estate licensees should avoid engaging in any of the following activities:

(1) Representing, without a reasonable basis, the nature and/or condition of the interior or exterior features of a property when soliciting an offer.

(2) Failing to respond to reasonable inquiries of a principal as to the status or extent of efforts to market property listed exclusively with the licensee.

(3) Representing as an agent that any specific service is free when, in fact, it is covered by a fee to be charged as part of the transaction.

(4) Failing to disclose to a person when first discussing the purchase of real property, the existence of any direct or indirect ownership interest of the licensee in the property.

(5) Recommending by a salesperson to a party to a real estate transaction that a particular lender or escrow service be used when the salesperson believes his or her broker has a significant beneficial interest in such entity without disclosing this information at the time the recommendation is made.

(6) Claiming to be an expert in an area of specialization in real estate brokerage, e.g., appraisal, property management, industrial siting, etc., if, in fact, the licensee has had no special training, preparation or experience in such area.

(7) Using the term "appraisal" in any advertising of offering for promoting real estate brokerage business to describe a real property evaluation service to be provided by the licensee unless the evaluation process will involve a written estimate of value based upon the assembling, analyzing and reconciling of facts and value indicators for the real property in question.

(8) Failing to disclose to the appropriate regulatory agency any conduct on the part of a financial institution which reasonably could be construed as a violation of the Housing Financial Discrimination Act of 1977 (anti-redlining)—Part 6 commencing with Section 35800) of Division 24 of the Health and Safety Code.

(9) Representing to a customer or prospective customer that because the licensee or his or her broker is a member of, or affiliated with, a franchised real estate brokerage entity, that such entity shares substantial responsibility, with the licensee, or his or her broker, for the proper handling of transactions if such is not the case.

(10) Demanding a commission or discount by a licensee purchasing real property for one's own account after an agreement in principle has been reached with the owner as to the terms and conditions of purchase without any reference to price reduction because of the agent's licensed status.

(c) Beneficial Conduct. In the best interests of all licensees and the public they serve, brokers and salespersons are encouraged to pursue the following beneficial business practices:

(1) Measuring success by the quality and benefits rendered to the buyers and sellers in real estate transactions rather than by the amount of compensation realized as a broker or salesperson.

(2) Treating all parties to a transaction honestly.

(3) Promptly reporting to the California Department of Real Estate any apparent violations of the Real Estate Law.

(4) Using care in the preparation of any advertisement to present an accurate picture or message to the reader, viewer, or listener.

(5) Submitting all written offers as a matter of top priority.

(6) Maintaining adequate and complete records of all one's real estate dealings.

(7) Keeping oneself current on factors affecting the real estate market in which the licensee operates as an agent.

(8) Making a full, open, and sincere effort to cooperate with other licensees, unless the principal has instructed the licensee to the contrary.

(9) Attempting to settle disputes with other licensees through mediation or arbitration.

(10) Complying with these standards of professional conduct, and the Code of Ethics of any organized real estate industry group of which the licensee is a member.

Nothing in this regulation is intended to limit, add to or supersede any provision of law relating to the duties and obligations of real estate licensees or the consequences of violations of law. Subdivision (a) lists specific acts and omissions which do violate existing law and are grounds for disciplinary action against real estate licensee. The conduct guidelines set forth in subdivisions (b) and (c) are not intended as statements of duties imposed by law nor as grounds for disciplinary action by the Department of Real Estate but as guidelines for elevating the professionalism of real estate licensees.

CODE OF ETHICS OF THE NATIONAL ASSOCIATION OF REALTORS®

Preamble . . .

Under all is the land. Upon its wise utilization and widely allocated ownership depend the survival and growth of free institutions and of our civilization. The REALTOR® should recognize that the interests of the nation and its citizens require the highest and best use of the land and the widest distribution of land ownership. They require the creation of adequate housing, the building of functioning cities, the developoment of productive industries and farms, and the preservation of a healthful environment.

Such interests impose obligations beyond those of ordinary commerce. They impose grave social responsibility and a patriotic duty to which the REALTOR® should dedicate himself, and for which he should be diligent in preparing himself. The REALTOR®, therefore, is zealous to maintain and improve the standards of his calling and shares with his fellow REALTORS® a common responsibility for its integrity and honor. The term REALTOR® has come to·connote competency, fairness, and high integrity resulting from adherence to a lofty ideal of moral conduct in business relations. No inducement of profit and no instruction from clients ever can justify departure from this ideal.

In the interpretation of this obligation, a REALTOR® can take no safer guide than that which has been handed down through the .centuries, embodied in the Golden Rule, "Whatsoever ye would that men should do to you, do ye even so to them."

Accepting this standard as his own, every REALTOR® pledges himself to observe its spirit in all of his activities and to conduct his business in accordance with the tenets set forth below.

Article 1

The REALTOR® should keep himself informed on matters affecting real estate in his community, the state, and nation so that he may be able to contribute responsibly to public thinking on such matters.

Article 2

In justice to those who place their interests in his care, the REALTOR® should endeavor always to be informed regarding laws, proposed legislation, governmental regulations, public policies, and current market conditions in order to be in a position to advise his clients properly.

Article 3

It is the duty of the REALTOR® to protect the public against fraud, misrepresentation, and unethical practices in real estate transactions. He should endeavor to eliminate in his community any practices which could be damaging to the public or bring discredit to the real estate profession. The REALTOR® should assist the governmental agency charged with regulating the practices of brokers and salesmen in his state.

Article 4

The REALTOR® should seek no unfair advantage over other REALTORS® and should conduct his business so as to avoid controversies with other REALTORS®.

Article 5

In the best interests of society, of his associates, and his own business, the REALTOR® should willingly share with other REALTORS® the lessons of his experience and study for the benefit of the public, and should be loyal to the Board of REALTORS® of his community and active in its work.

Article 6

To prevent dissension and misunderstanding and to assure better service to the owner, the REALTOR® should urge the exclusive listing of property unless contrary to the best interest of the owner.

Article 7

In accepting employment as an agent, the REALTOR® pledges himself to protect and promote the interests of the client. This obligation of absolute fidelity to the client's interests is primary, but it does not relieve the REALTOR® of the obligation to treat fairly all parties to the transaction.

Article 8

The REALTOR® shall not accept compensation from more than one party, even if permitted by law, without the full knowledge of all parties to the transaction.

Article 9

The REALTOR® shall avoid exaggeration, misrepresentation, or concealment of pertinent facts. He has an affirmative obligation to discover adverse factors that a reasonably competent and diligent investigation would disclose.

Article 10

THE REALTOR® shall not deny equal professional services to any person for reasons of race, creed, sex, or country of national origin. The REALTOR® shall not be party to any plan or agreement to discriminate against a person or persons on the basis of race, creed, sex, or country of national origin.

Article 11

A REALTOR® is expected to provide a level of competent service in keeping with the standards of practice in those fields in which the REALTOR® customarily engages.

The REALTOR® shall not undertake to provide specialized professional services concerning a type of property or service that is outside his field of competence unless he engages the assistance of one who is competent on such types of property or service, or unless the facts are fully disclosed to the client. Any person engaged to provide such assistance shall be so identified to the client and his contribution to the assignment should be set forth.

The REALTOR® shall refer to the Standards of Practice of the National Association as to the degree of competence that a client has a right to expect the REALTOR® to possess, taking into consideration the complexity of the problem, the availability of expert assistance, and the opportunities for experience available to the REALTOR®.

Article 12

The REALTOR® shall not undertake to provide professional services concerning a property or its value where he has a present or contemplated interest unless such interest is specifically disclosed to all affected parties.

Article 13

The REALTOR® shall not acquire an interest in or buy for himself, any member of his immediate family, his firm or any member thereof, or any entity in which he has a substantial ownership interest, property listed with him, without making the true position known to the listing owner. In selling property owned by himself, or in which he has any interest, the REALTOR® shall reveal the facts of his ownership or interest to the purchaser.

Article 14

In the event of a controversy between REALTORS® associated with different firms, arising out of their relationship as REALTORS®, the REALTORS® shall submit the dispute to arbitration in accordance with the regulations of their Board or Boards rather than litigate the matter.

Article 15

If a REALTOR® is charged with unethical practice or is asked to present evidence in any disciplinary proceeding or investigation, he shall place all pertinent facts before the proper tribunal of the member board or affiliated institute, society, or council of which he is a member.

Article 16

When acting as agent, the REALTOR® shall not accept any commission, rebate, or profit on expenditures made for his principal-owner, without the principal's knowledge and consent.

Article 17

The REALTOR® shall not engage in activities that constitute the unauthorized practice of law and shall recommend that legal counsel be obtained when the interest of any party to the transaction requires it.

Article 18

The REALTOR® shall keep in a special account in an appropriate financial institution, separated from his own funds, monies coming into his possession in trust for other persons, such as escrows, trust funds, clients' monies, and other like items.

Article 19

The REALTOR® shall be careful at all times to present a true picture in his advertising and representations to the public. He shall neither advertise without disclosing his name nor permit any person associated with him to use individual names or telephone numbers, unless such person's connection with the REALTOR® is obvious in the advertisement.

Article 20

The REALTOR®, for the protection of all parties, shall see that financial obligations and commitments regarding real estate transactions are in writing, expressing the exact agreement of the parties. A copy of each agreement shall be furnished to each party upon his signing such agreement.

Article 21

The REALTOR® shall not engage in any practice or take any action inconsistent with the agency of another REALTOR®.

Article 22

In the sale of property which is exclusively listed with a REALTOR®, the REALTOR® shall utilize the services of other brokers upon mutually agreed upon terms when it is in the best interests of the client.

Negotiations concerning property which is listed exclusively shall be carried on with the listing broker, not with the owner, except with the consent of the listing broker.

Article 23

The REALTOR® shall not publicly disparage the business practice of a competitor nor volunteer an opinion of a competitor's transaction. If his opinion is sought and if the REALTOR® deems it appropriate to respond, such opinion shall be rendered with strict professional integrity and courtesy.

The Code of Ethics was adopted in 1913. Amended at the Annual Convention in 1924, 1928, 1950, 1951, 1952, 1955, 1956, 1961, 1962, 1974 and 1982.

CODE OF ETHICS OF THE NATIONAL ASSOCIATION OF REAL ESTATE BROKERS, INCORPORATED

PART I. RELATIONS TO THE PUBLIC

1. A Realtist is never relieved of the responsibility to observe fully this Code of Ethics.
2. A Realtist should never be instrumental in establishing, reenforcing or extending leased or deed restrictions that limit the use and/or occupancy of real property to any racial, religious or national origin groups.
3. The Realtist realizes that it is his duty to protect the public against any misrepresentations, unethical practices or fraud in his real estate practices, and that he offer all properties on his listing solely on merit and without exaggeration, concealment, deception or misleading information.
4. A Realtist should always avoid offering a property without (a) written authorization of the owner or a person acting in his behalf by power of attorney, (b) fully informing himself of the pertinent facts concerning the property, and (c) advising his client to secure advice of counsel as to the legality of instruments before receiving or conveying title or possession of real property, laws, proposed legislation and public policy relative to the use and/or occupancy of the property.
5. The Realtist should always offer the property at the price the owner has agreed to accept, but never greater.
6. The Realtist should always inform all parties of his own position in the transaction and should not demand or accept a commission from both parties, except with the knowledge and consent in writing and signed by all parties.
7. The Realtist should be diligent in preventing property under his management from being used for immoral or illegal purposes.
8. The Realtist realizes that all contracts and agreements for the ownership, use and/or occupancy of real properties should be in writing and signed by all parties, or their lawfully authorized agents.
9. The Realtist should disclose the fact, if he is purchasing a property to the account of his client and if he has a personal interest in the ownership.

Professional Relations

1. The Realtist should always be loyal to his local Board of Real Estate Brokers and active in its work. The fellowship of his associates and the mutual sharing of experiences are always assets to his own business.
2. The Realtist should so conduct his business as to avoid controversies with his fellow Realtists. Controversies between Realtists, who are members of the same local Board of Real Estate Brokers, should be submitted in writing for arbitration in accordance with the regulations of his or her Real Estate Board and not in an action at law. The decision in such arbitration should be accepted as final and binding.
3. Controversies between Realtists who are not members of the same local board should be submitted for arbitration to an Arbitration Board consisting of one arbitrator chosen by each Realtist from the Board of Real Estate Brokers to which he belongs and one other member, or a sufficient number of members to make an odd number, selected by the arbitrators thus chosen.
4. All employment arrangements between broker and salesmen should be reduced to writing and signed by both parties. It is particularly important to specify rights of parties, in the event of termination of employment. All listings acquired by a salesman during his tenure of employment with the Broker shall be the exclusive property or right of the employing Broker after such termination.
5. A Realtist should never publicly criticize a fellow Realtist; he should never express an opinion of a transaction unless requested to do so by one of the principals and his opinion then should be rendered in accordance with strict professional courtesy and integrity.
6. A Realtist should never seek information about fellow Realtists' transactions to use for

the purpose of closing the transaction himself or diverting the client to another property.

7. When a cooperating Realtist accepts a listing from another Broker, the agency of the Broker who offers the listing should be respected until it has expired and the property has come to the attention of the cooperating Realtist from a different source, or until the owner, without solicitation, offers to list with the cooperating Realtist; furthermore, such a listing should not be passed on to a third Broker without the consent of the listing Broker.

8. Negotiations concerning property which is listed with one Realtist exclusively should be carried on with the listing Broker, not with the owner.

9. The Realtist is free to negotiate fees in the lease, sale or exchange of Real Estate. Fees should be based on reasonable compensation for services to be rendered to the client. The Realtist should refrain from making any vestage of unfair competition or making fee structures and/or the advertising thereof in such a manner as to be demeaning to the real estate profession.

10. A Realtist should not solicit the services of any employee in the organization of a fellow Realtist without the written consent of the employer.

11. Signs should never be placed on any property by a Realtist without the written consent of the owner.

APPENDIX D

CALIFORNIA ESCROW ASSOCIATION CODE OF ETHICS

The Escrow Holder is the instrumentality through which, ideally, most real estate transactions are carried on, the responsibility and obligations undertaken in escrow being of the utmost importance. The Escrow Officer, therefore, is zealous to maintain and improve the standards of his calling and shares with his fellow escrow officers a common responsibility for its integrity and honor. Wherever the word Escrow Officer is used within the context hereof and hereinafter, such designation shall be deemed to refer to all persons who are practicing any type of escrow activity who are members of the California Escrow Association.

Every person engaged in the processing of escrow work who holds such membership in the California Escrow Association pledges himself to observe the spirit of and conduct his business in accordance with the following Code of Ethics:

Article I–An Escrow Officer shall keep himself informed as to legislation and laws affecting the escrow profession in order to contribute to the public thinking on matters relating to escrows, real estate, financing and other matters and questions relative to the escrow profession.

Article II–Protection of public against fraud, misrepresentation and unethical practices in the escrow profession shall be uppermost in the mind of the Escrow Officer and he shall, at all times, be ready to expose such offenses.

Article III–An Escrow Officer should expose, without fear or favor, before the proper tribunal, corrupt or dishonest conduct in the profession.

Article IV–It is the duty of an Escrow Officer to preserve his clients' confidence, including all matters surrounding an escrow, either opened or closed; he should never reveal the contents of any file to any person not entitled to such contents except where a subpoena has been issued, or to expose corrupt or dishonest practice.

Article V–An Escrow Officer shall not be a party to the naming of a false consideration in an escrow.

Article VI–An Escrow Officer shall not engage in activities that constitute the practice of law and should never hesitate recommending that a party seek legal counsel in connection with an escrow.

Article VII–An Escrow Officer shall accept escrow instructions only in writing; acceptance of instructions verbally does a disservice to the public.

Article VIII–An Escrow Officer shall deliver copies of all instructions to all parties who are affected by such instructions.

Article IX–An Escrow Officer must maintain strict neutrality as an "Unbiased Third Party" to each transaction.

Article X–An Escrow Officer should not accept an escrow which he knows is outside of his scope of knowledge unless he makes such fact first known to his principals.

Article XI–An Escrow Officer should not seek unfair advantage over his fellow Escrow Officers and should willingly share with them lessons of his study and experiences.

Article XII–An Escrow Officer shall conduct his profession so as to avoid controversies with fellow Escrow Officers. In the event of a controversy between Escrow Officers, such controversy shall be arbitrated at the level of the Regional Association.

Article XIII–In the event of controversy between Escrow Officers of different Regional Associations, such controversy should be arbitrated by a board comprised of two members from each Association of members so involved.

Article XIV–An Escrow Officer shall cooperate with his fellow Escrow Officers in escrow matters which affect each mutually.

Article XV–When an Escrow Officer is charged with unethical practices, he should place all pertinent facts before the proper tribunal of the Regional Association to which he belongs, for investigation and judgment.

Article XVI–An Escrow Officer shall never disparage the professional practice of a competitor, nor volunteer an opinon of a competitor's transaction. If his opinion is sought, it should be rendered with strict professional integrity and courtesy.

Article XVII–An Escrow Officer should not solicit the service of an employee in the organization of a fellow Escrow Officer without the knowledge of the employer.

Article XVIII–It is the duty of an Escrow Officer, at the outset of an escrow, to disclose to the clients all circumstances, if any, of his relationship to the parties, and any interest in or connection with the escrow which might influence one or both clients in the selection of an escrow holder.

Article XIX–It is the duty of an Escrow Officer to his clients and the public in general to be punctual and direct in the closing of his escrows.

Article XX–In the best interests of society, his associates and his own profession, an Escrow Officer shall be loyal to the California Escrow Association and the Escrow Association of his local vicinity and be active in its work, and conform to this Code of Ethics and the By-Laws of this Association.

Adopted August 2, 1969

APPENDIX E

SOCIETY OF REAL ESTATE APPRAISERS STANDARDS OF PROFESSIONAL PRACTICE AND CONDUCT

As Amended February 27, 1986 by the Board of Governors

PREAMBLE

The purposes of the Society of Real Estate Appraisers are to elevate the standards in real estate appraising and analysis, to aid in the solution of the many problems of the profession in appraising and analyzing real estate, and to designate certain members as having attained certain skills and knowledge. The members are pledged to maintain a high level of trust and integrity in their practice. It is the responsibility of the members to keep up to date with techniques, tools and market practices; to know and exploit data sources, and to be aware of environmental influences in which client decisions must be made.

CODE OF ETHICS

This code of Ethics is a set of dynamic principles guiding the member's conduct and professional practice. It is the member's duty to practice his/her profession according to this Code of Ethics.

Each member agrees that he/she shall:

COE 1.0000 Conduct activities in a manner that will reflect credit upon himself/herself, real estate appraisers and analysts, and the Society of Real Estate Appraisers.

COE 2.0000 Cooperate with the Society of Real Estate Appraisers and its officers in all matters, including, but not limited to the investigation, discipline, or dismissal of members who, by their conduct, prejudice their professional status or the reputation of the Society of Real Estate Appraisers.

COE 3.0000 Obtain appraisal and analysis assignments, and accept compensation only in a professional manner in accordance with the provisions of the Standards of Professional Practice and Conduct of the Society of Real Estate Appraisers.

COE 4.0000 Accept only those appraisal and analysis assignments for which he/she has adequate time, facilities and technical ability to complete in a competent professional manner, and in which he/she has no unrevealed present or contemplated future interest.

COE 5.0000 Render properly developed, unbiased and objective value opinions, and render properly developed, unbiased and objective analyses.

COE 6.0000 Prepare an adequate written appraisal for each real estate appraisal assignment accepted, and prepare an adequate written analysis for each real estate analysis assignment accepted.

COE 7.0000 Reveal value and analysis conclusions and opinions to no one other than the client, except with the permission of the client or by due process of law, and except when required to do so to comply with the rules of the Society of Real Estate Appraisers.

COE 8.0000 Conform in all respects to this Code of Ethics, the Standards of Professional Practice and Conduct, and the Bylaws of the Society of Real Estate Appraisers as the same may be amended from time to time.

STANDARDS OF PROFESSIONAL PRACTICE

The following constitute what the Society considers to be the minimum required of the appraiser and analyst in their valuation practices, analysis practices, and reporting practices. The appraiser and analyst should, however, utilize all of the recognized appraisal and analysis methods and techniques that will materially contribute to a proper valuation or analysis.

Members properly utilizing these procedures will be deemed to be acting competently in carrying out real estate appraisal and analysis assignments. However, because of the varied nature of assignments, the Society recognizes that occasionally there is justification for departing from carrying out some aspect of these procedures. In this event, the member must have a valid basis for such a departure, and the reasons for the departure must be explained and supported in the written appraisal or written analysis.

SPP 1.0000   Real Estate Valuation Practice

SPP 1.1000 Prudent and professional real estate appraisal practice suggests these recommended steps in reaching a supportable conclusion of value:

SPP 1.1100 An adequate and definite description of the property being appraised.

SPP 1.1110 The appraiser should include a description of the subject property, and identify it by including a legal description, street address or other means of specifically and adequately locating the property.

SPP 1.1120 The appraiser should consider matters relating to title that may affect the final value conclusions, such as:

SPP 1.1121 The nature of the ownership, i.e., fee simple, or an explanation of other division of ownership interest.

SPP 1.1122 Easements, restrictions, encumbrances, leases, reservations, covenants, contracts, declarations, special assessments, ordinances, or other items of a similar nature.

SPP 1.1130 Each appraisal should be predicated upon a valuation of the property for its highest and best use. The highest and best use of the property as presently improved may or may not result in a value conclusion exceeding the value of the site alone. The appraiser should support estimates of highest and best use.

SPP 1.1140 The appraiser should include an accurate and adequate description of the political, social and economic factors affecting the property including the effect on both the site and the physical improvement to the site.

SPP 1.1150 The appraiser should consider all physical, functional and external market factors as they may affect the value conclusion.

SPP 1.1200 Purpose of the appraisal and a definition of the value estimated:

SPP 1.1210 The appraiser should state the type of value being sought, and clearly define the value estimated.

SPP 1.1300 The effective date of the appraisal:

SPP 1.1310 The date of the value estimate ordinarily should be the date of the last property inspection except when the appraisal requires a prior date.

SPP 1.1400 The data and reasoning supporting the value conclusion which may include the direct sales comparison approach. The exclusion of any of the usual three approaches must be explained and supported.

SPP 1.1410 The appraiser should recognize that each of the approaches to value is a function of market phenomena.

SPP 1.1420 The appraiser should consider appropriate units of comparison. Whenever possible, practical and appropriate adjustments should be made for all factors of dissimilarity deemed to affect value.

SPP 1.1430 The direct sales comparison approach (when applicable):

SPP 1.1431 The appraiser should collect, inspect, verify, analyze and reconcile such comparable sales as are available to indicate a value conclusion. The pertinent comparable sales would be identified and adequately described. No pertinent information shall be withheld. When pertinent, a recent sales history of the subject should be included.

SPP 1.1440 The income approach (when applicable):

SPP 1.1441 The appraiser should, when applicable, collect, inspect, verify, analyze and reconcile such comparable rentals as are available to indicate an appropriate estimate of the market rental of the property being appraised. No pertinent information shall be withheld.

SPP 1.1442 The appraiser should, when applicable, collect, verify, analyze and reconcile such data on comparable operating expenses as are available to support an appropriate estimate of all operating expenses of the property being appraised. No pertinent information shall be withheld.

SPP 1.1443 The appraiser should, when applicable, collect, verify, analyze and reconcile such comparable data relating to appropriate rates of capitalization and/or rates of discount. No pertinent information shall be withheld.

SPP 1.1444 Any method, process or technique of capitalization used should be appropriate to the type and characteristics of the property being appraised.

SPP 1.1445 In the case of single-family dwellings, the appraiser should collect, inspect, verify, analyze and reconcile such data on comparable sales and rentals as are available to indicate a value conclusion by use of the gross rent multiplier technique. No pertinent information shall be withheld.

SPP 1.1450 The cost approach (when applicable):

SPP 1.1451 The appraiser should collect, verify, analyze and reconcile such comparable cost data as are available to estimate the cost new of the subject improvements (if any).

SPP 1.1452 The appraiser should estimate and include the site value.

SPP 1.1453 The appraiser should collect, verify, analyze and reconcile such comparable data as are available to support and explain the difference between cost new and the present worth of the improvements reflecting items of deterioration and obsolescence (accrued depreciation). No pertinent information shall be withheld. The appraiser should qualify the data sources and cost methodology used in the cost estimate.

SPP 1.1460 Land or site value:

SPP 1.1461 The appraiser should value the land or site by a direct sales comparison method, land residual, or other appropriate valuation technique.

SPP 1.1500 The final reconciliation and value estimate:

SPP 1.1510 In the final value estimate, the appraiser should consider the purpose which the appraisal serves, the type of property being appraised, the emphasis which typical users or investors would accord to the quality and quantity of data available and analyzed within the approaches used, and the applicability or suitability of the approaches used.

SPP 1.1600 The assumptions and limiting conditions:

SPP 1.1610 The appraiser should set forth all the assumptions and limiting conditions under which the value estimate is made, and support their validity and feasibility. The acceptance of any other assumptions and limiting conditions imposed by the client requires that the appraiser must clearly set forth this fact in the purpose of the appraisal, identify these assumptions and limiting conditions, and indicate their impact on the value conclusion.

SPP 1.1700 The appraiser's certification and signature:

SPP 1.1710 The appraiser should certify, except as otherwise noted in the appraisal report:

SPP 1.1711 That he/she has personally inspected the subject property.

SPP 1.1712 That he/she has no present or contemplated future interest in the real estate that is the subject of this appraisal report.

SPP 1.1713 That he/she has no personal interest or bias with respect to the subject matter of this appraisal report or the parties involved.

SPP 1.1714 That the amount of the fee is not contingent upon reporting a predetermined value or upon the amount of the value estimate.

SPP 1.1715 That to the best of his/her knowledge and belief the statements of fact contained in this appraisal report, upon which the analyses, opinions and conclusions expressed herein are based, are true and correct.

SPP 1.1716 That this appraisal report sets forth all of the assumptions and limiting conditions (imposed by the terms of the assignment or by the undersigned) affecting the analyses, opinions and conclusions contained in this report.

SPP 1.1717 That this appraisal report has been made in conformity with and is subject to the requirements of the Code of Ethics and Standards of Professional Practice and Conduct of the Society of Real Estate Appraisers.

SPP 1.1720 While the appraiser is ultimately responsible for any report which he/she has signed, he/she should acknowledge those phases of the appraisal process performed by others, and when appropriate they should become signatories to the report.

SPP 1.1800 It is unethical for a member to omit, without good cause, any of the foregoing minimum requirements from any appraisal report transmitted to the client. If, with good cause, any of the foregoing minimum requirements are not included in the appraisal report transmitted to the client, the appraiser should clearly set forth within the appraisal report transmitted to the client a statement to the effect that the portions excluded (named specifically) are included in the appraiser's written appraisal which has been prepared and retained in the appraiser's file for this assignment, and that said written appraisal is incorporated into the appraisal report by reference and is an integral part of the report.

SPP 1.2000 It is unethical for an appraiser:

SPP 1.2100 To appraise fractional parts of a property and to report as market value the sum of fractional parts if the reported value exceeds the market value that would be derived if the property were considered separately as a whole.

SPP 1.2200 To estimate the market value of the fractional legal or financial ownership interest of a property without giving consideration to the possibility that it may be more or less than the market value of the unencumbered fee simple ownership interest of the entire property.

SPP 1.3000 It is unethical for an appraiser to base the value conclusion upon the assumed completion of public or private improvements unless he/she clearly defines the conditions, extent and effects of such assumption. Any such assumption must be predicated upon sound valuation principles.

SPP 2.0000 Real Estate Analysis Practice

SPP 2.1000 Prudent and professional real estate analysis and counseling practice suggests these recommended steps:

SPP 2.1100 Identification of objective and definition of the problem:

SPP 2.1110 The analyst should ascertain and clearly identify the client's objective, which may not necessarily be explicit in the client's statement of the assignment.

SPP 2.1120 The analyst should clearly and precisely define the nature of the problem the client faces.

SPP 2.1130 The analyst should identify alternative routes to achievement of the objective, and state their implications.

SPP 2.1140 The analyst should identify both known and anticipated constraints or obstacles present in each alternative route, and measure their impact.

SPP 2.1150 The analyst should identify those productive resources actually or expected to be available to achieve the client's objective, and measure their impact.

SPP 2.1200 The identification of the property or properties involved, if any:

SPP 2.1210 If the analysis involves a specific property or properties, the analyst should include a legal description, street address or other means of specifically and adequately locating the property or properties being analyzed.

SPP 2.1300 The effective date of the analysis:

SPP 2.1310 The analysis should include its effective date.

SPP 2.1400 The data and the analysis of the data:

SPP 2.1410 The analyst should collect, verify and reconcile such pertinent data as may be required to complete the assignment.

SPP 2.1411 If the market value of a specific property is pertinent to the analysis assignment, a written appraisal should be included in the data collected.

SPP 2.1420 The analyst should apply the appropriate tools and techniques of analysis to the data collected.

SPP 2.1430 In a market analysis: (A market analysis is defined as a study of general real estate market conditions that bear upon the competitive supply, demand and prices for particular types of facilities or properties.)

SPP 2.1431 The analyst should carefully define and delineate the pertinent market area for the analysis, and justify that delineation.

SPP 2.1432 The analyst should identify, investigate and analyze the forces that make up the pertinent real estate market, as well as measure and forecast demand.

SPP 2.1433 The analyst should identify, measure, and forecast economic changes in the pertinent market area.

SPP 2.1434 The analyst should identify what the present market is, and forecast how future supply may affect the subject property based on competition in its market.

SPP 2.1440 In a cash flow and/or investment analysis: (A cash flow analysis is defined as a study of any flow of cash, in or out, of an investment. An investment analysis is defined as a process by which the relative attractiveness of an investment opportunity is determined by analyzing a number of measures which reflect the relationship between acquisition price and anticipated future benefits from the investment.)

SPP 2.1441 The analyst should investigate and evaluate the quantity and the quality of the income stream.

SPP 2.1442 The analyst should evaluate and analyze the history of expenses and reserves, and analyze their stability.

SPP 2.1443 The analyst should investigate and analyze financing availability and terms, and analyze their effect on the subject property or properties.

SPP 2.1444 The analyst should select and support the appropriate method of processing the income stream.

SPP 2.1445 In an investment analysis, the analyst should consider the cash flow returns plus reversions to the specific investment position over a projected time period.

SPP 2.1450 In a feasibility analysis: (A feasibility analysis is defined as an analysis of whether the cost-benefit ratio of an economic endeavor meets the client's objective.)

SPP 2.1451 The analyst should first prepare a complete market analysis.

SPP 2.1452 The analyst should apply the results of the market analysis to the alternative courses of action as they relate to the client's objective.

SPP 2.1453 The analyst should identify the probable outcome of each course of action.

SPP 2.1454 The analyst should identify the probable costs of achieving each outcome, and identify probability and costs of altering any constraints or obstacles.

SPP 2.1500 Final conclusions or recommendation, if any:

SPP 2.1510 When a conclusion or recommendation is required by the nature of the assignment, the analyst should identify the optimum course of action in terms of the client's objective.

SPP 2.1600 Assumptions and limiting conditions:

SPP 2.1610 The analyst should set forth all of the assumptions and limiting conditions under which the analysis is made, and support their validity and feasibility. The acceptance of any other assumptions and limiting conditions imposed by the client requires that the analyst must clearly set forth this fact in the identification of the objective, identify these assumptions and limiting conditions and indicate their impact on the final conclusion(s).

SPP 2.1700 The analyst's certification and signature:

SPP 2.1710 The analyst should certify, except as otherwise noted in the analysis report:

SPP 2.1711 That he/she has personally inspected the subject property (if applicable).

SPP 2.1712 That he/she has no present or contemplated future interest in the real

estate that is the subject of this analysis report.

SPP 2.1713 That he/she has no personal interest or bias with respect to the subject matter of this analysis report or the parties involved.

SPP 2.1714 That the amount of the fee is not contingent upon reporting a predetermined opinion, conclusion, or recommendation, or upon any result, value, or subsequent transaction.

SPP 2.1715 That to the best of his/her knowledge and belief the statements of fact contained in this analysis report, upon which the analyses, opinions and conclusions expressed herein are based, are true and correct.

SPP 2.1716 That this analysis report sets forth all of the assumptions and limiting conditions (imposed by the terms of the assignment or by the undersigned) affecting the analyses, opinions and conclusions contained in this report.

SPP 2.1717 That this analysis report has been made in conformity with and is subject to the requirements of the Code of Ethics and Standards of Professional Practice and Conduct of the Society of Real Estate Appraisers.

SPP 2.1720 While the analyst is ultimately responsible for any report which he/she has signed, he/she should acknowledge those phases of the analysis process performed by others, and when appropriate they should become signatories to the report.

SPP 2.1800 It is unethical for a member to omit, without good cause, any of the foregoing minimum requirements from any written analysis.

SPP 3.0000 Reporting Practice

SPP 3.1000 An adequate written appraisal containing a supported value shall be prepared for each appraisal assignment accepted, and shall include the following as minimum requirements:

SPP 3.1100 An adequate and definite description of the property being appraised.

SPP 3.1200 The purpose of the appraisal and a definition of the value estimated.

SPP 3.1300 The effective date of the appraisal.

SPP 3.1400 The data and reasoning supporting the value conclusion which may include the direct sales comparison approach, the income approach and the cost approach. The exclusion of any of the usual three approaches must be explained and supported.

SPP 3.1500 The final reconciliation and value estimate.

SPP 3.1600 The assumptions and limiting conditions.

SPP 3.1700 The appraiser's certification and signature.

SPP 3.1800 It is unethical for a member to omit any of the above minimum requirements from his/her appraisal report transmitted to the client without good cause. If, with good cause, any of the above minimum requirements are not included in the appraisal report transmitted to the client, the appraiser shall clearly set forth within the appraisal report transmitted to the client a statement to the effect that the portions excluded (named specifically) are included in the appraiser's written appraisal which has been prepared and retained in the appraiser's file for this assignment, and that said written appraisal is incorporated herein by reference and is an integral part hereof.

SPP 3.2000 An adequate written analysis shall be prepared for each analysis assignment accepted, and shall include the following as minimum requirements:

SPP 3.2100 The identification of objective, and definition of the problem.

SPP 3.2200 The identification of the property or properties involved, if any.

SPP 3.2300 The effective date of the analysis.

SPP 3.2400 The data and the analysis of the data.

SPP 3.2500 Final conclusions or recommendation, if any.

SPP 3.2600 Assumptions and limiting conditions.

SPP 3.2700 The analyst's certification and signature.

SPP 3.2800 It is unethical for a member to omit any of the above minimum requirements from the analysis report transmitted to the client without good cause. If, with good cause, any of the above minumum requirements are not included in the analysis report transmitted

to the client, the analyst shall clearly set forth within the analysis report transmitted to the client a statement to the effect that the portions excluded (named specifically) are included in the analyst's written analysis which has been prepared and retained in the analyst's file for this assignment, and that said written analysis is incorporated herein by reference and is an integral part hereof.

SPP 3.3000 A true copy of each written appraisal and written analysis shall be prepared and retained by the member for a period of five years and after preparation or following final disposition of any court or other judicial proceeding (including all appeals) or after having been informed that a professional practice complaint has been filed against said member, and it shall be sent on request to a duly constituted Professional Practice Committee of the local chapter or of the International Society of Real Estate Appraisers.

SPP 3.4000 It is unethical to issue a separate appraisal report on only a part of a whole property without stating that it is a fractional appraisal and as such subject to use in a manner consistent with such limitation.

SPP 3.5000 It is unethical to issue a separate appraisal report or analysis report when another appraiser or analyst assigned to appraise or analyze the same property has had a part in the formation of the value opinion or the analysis conclusion and/or recommendation.

SPP 3.6000 It is unethical for an appraiser or analyst to reveal in any way the substance of any appraisal or analysis without permission of the client except under due process of law, or when required to do so in compliance with the rules and regulations of the Society of Real Estate Appraisers.

STANDARDS OF PROFESSIONAL CONDUCT

SPC 1.0000 It is unethical for an appraiser or analyst to become an advocate of any other than his/her own unbiased and objective opinions.

SPC 2.0000 It is unethical for an appraiser or analyst to engage in conduct which will in any manner prejudice his/her professional status or the reputation of any appraisal organization or any other appraiser or analyst.

SPC 3.0000 It is unethical to accept an appraisal or analysis assignment of a type with which he/she has had no previous experience unless, in making the appraisal or analysis, he/she associates with an appraiser or analyst who has had experience with that type of assignment, or makes full disclosure of the degree of his/her experience, background, and training to the client.

SPC 4.0000 It is unethical for an appraiser or analyst to:

SPC 4.1000 Contract for or accept compensation for appraisal or analysis services in the form of a commission, rebate, division of brokerage commissions, or any similar forms.

SPC 4.2000 Receive or pay finder's or referral fees.

SPC 4.3000 Accept an assignment to appraise or analyze a property for which employment or fee is contingent upon reporting a predetermined value or upon the amount of the value estimate; or upon reporting a predetermined opinion, conclusion, or recommendation; or upon any result, value or subsequent transaction.

SPC 4.4000 Make the compensation on any basis other than a fair professional fee for the responsibility entailed and the work and expense involved.

SPC 5.0000 It is unethical for an appraiser or analyst to advertise or solicit appraisal or analysis assignments in any manner which is false, misleading, or exaggerated; or which compromises the impartiality required in appraising; or which is in a form not consistent with currently accepted standards in professions generally at the time. Recognizing the public's need for information and professional practice of the highest standards, the Society has established the following provisions as the standards of professional advertising practices for all classifications of membership:

SPC   5.1000 Candidate   and   Associate Members
It is unethical for Candidate and Associate members to refer to membership in the Society of Real Estate Appraisers in any kind of advertising or solicitation of the general public.

SPC 5.2000 All Members
It is unethical for a member of any classification of membership to advertise in the following ways:

SPC 5.2100 *Deceptive Advertising.* No member may engage in false, misleading, or exaggerated advertising relating to skills, qualifications, or the services being offered. Advertising shall be regarded as false or misleading where it is likely to confuse the members of the public to whom it is directed.

SPC 5.2200 *Appraiser's Competency and Impartiality.* The member's fundamental responsibility is to arrive at properly developed, unbiased and objective value opinions or analyses. No member may advertise or solicit in a way that compromises this professional competence and impartiality. Any advertising or solicitation which suggests or implies predetermined results or value opinions or fees based on value determinations is included within this prohibition.

SPC 5.2300 *Currently Accepted Standards of the Professions.* No member may advertise in a manner or form which is inconsistent with currently accepted standards in professions generally at the time. However, nothing in this rule shall prevent a member or member's firm from advertising in a lawful manner accurate information on fees, fee schedules, or methods of calculating fees for professional services offered to the public.

SPC 5.2400 *Designations and Society's Emblems (logos).* The member's designation, the Society's designation emblems (logos) and/or reference to membership in the Society of Real Estate Appraisers shall not be used by a member in advertising or material in such a way as to create any misleading impressions that the membership refers to the member's company or anyone other than that individual member. The Society's corporate emblem (logo) shall not be used by members. The Society's corporate emblem (logo) is intended for use by the International Society and its chapters in institutional advertising, such as the Yellow Pages telephone directory listings, official publications, etc.

SPC 6.0000 It is unethical for an appraiser or analyst to claim professional qualifications which may be subject to erroneous interpretation, or to state professional qualifications not possessed. Professionally designated members may refer to their membership in the Society and to their designations. When a member uses the designation, it must be used accurately. A member holding the SRA designation may indicate the designation as "SRA" or "Senior Residential Appraiser." A member holding the SRPA designation may indicate the designation as "SRPA" or "Senior Real Property Appraiser." A member holding the SREA designation may indicate the designation as "SREA" or "Senior Real Estate Analyst."

SPC 7.0000 It is unethical to fail to report to the Society the actions of any member who, in the opinion of the reporting member, has violated these Standards of Professional Practice and Conduct.

GLOSSARY

In the field of real estate; as in other fields, the student encounters many new words and phrases. He or she also finds new or different meanings for familiar words; as well as different pronunciations for such words.

Words and their meaning are important since, among other things, an applicant for a real estate license must have an appropriate knowledge of the English language including reading, writing, and spelling and of arithmetical computations common to real estate practice. Words and figures are frequently our principal stock in trade. Rights are often dependent upon the particular choice of language. And a precise word, properly selected, will in many cases do the job of several less meaningful words.

Many of our real estate rules had their origins in the feudal period in England and many words have Latin or French sources. There is also the Spanish and Mexican source, as reflected in the historical background of the development of Califorina.

The following list includes substantially all of the words and phrases in common use in the field of real estate in California with the exception of detailed construction terminology. The latter is included in the glossary of the Real Estate Reference Book.

Abandonment. Giving up any further interest in a thing or a right.

Abatement of Nuisance. The extinction or termination of an offensive activity; such as pollution of the atmosphere.

ABC Law. Alcoholic Beverage Control Law. Regulates the sale of alcoholic beverages. Encountered in connection with escrows handling the sale of a liquor license.

Absolute Ownership. See **Fee Simple Estate**.

Abstract. A brief summary; an abridgment.

Abstract of Judgment. A summary or condensation of the essential provisions of a money judgment in a civil action. When recorded, it creates a general lien on real property of the judgment debtor in the county where the abstract is recorded.

Abstract of Title. A summary of the condition of title to real property based on an examination of public records. Includes a digest of the deeds or other transfers, encumbrances, and other instruments reflecting ownership of title or matters which may impair the title.

Abstraction. A method of valuing land. The indicated value of the improvement is deducted from the sale price.

Abutting Owner. Owner whose land touches a road or highway or other public place.

Accelerated Cost Recovery System (ACRS). The system for figuring depreciation (cost recovery for depreciable real property acquired and placed into service after January 1, 1981 under the former federal income tax law).

Accelerated Depreciation. Allowing for a greater amount of depreciation of property in the earlier years of the life of the investment. Distinguished from **Straight-line Depreciation** (also see), which allows for equal amounts of depreciation each year.

Acceleration Clause. A provision in a note or deed of trust permitting the owner of the note to declare the entire unpaid balance due and payable earlier than the stated due date in the event of a default, such as failure to pay taxes or an installment when due, or in the event of the sale of the property.

Acceptance. Act indicating that the terms and provisions of a proposed contract are satisfactory and are agreed to; usually preceded by an *offer* by one contracting party, which is *accepted* by the other party. Evidences a "meeting of the minds" that is an essential element of a contract.

Access Right. The right of an owner to have ingress and egress (a means of entry and exit) to and from his or her property to a public street or way.

Accession. Acquisition of property by its incorporation or union (uniting) with other property. It may occur by the processes of **Accretion, Reliction,** or **Annexation.**

Accommodation Party. A person who *accommodates* another party by signing a note without receiving value him-or herself, but for the purpose of permitting the other party to obtain credit.

Accounts Payable. An aggregate or total of amounts *owed to* creditors; a liability.

Accounts Receivable. An aggregate or total of amounts *due* a creditor *from* his debtors; an asset.

Accretion. Increase of land on shore or bank of a river by the gradual deposit of sand or soil by natural action of the water.

Accrual Basis. Method of recording income and expenses in which each item is reported as earned or incurred without regard to when actual payments are received or made. Distinguished from **Cash Basis.**

Accrued. To be added or accumulated as a matter of periodic gain or advantage, as interest on money. Used variously, such as accrued dividends, accrued interest, or accrued depreciation.

Accrued Depreciation. The difference between the cost of replacement of a building new as of the date of a previous appraisal and the present appraised value.

Accrued Items of Expense. Those incurred expenses which are not yet payable. The seller's accrued expenses are credited to the purchaser in an escrow closing statement.

Acknowledgment. A form for authenticating instruments conveying property or otherwise conferring rights. A declaration before a notary public or other official by the party executing an instrument that it is his or her act and deed. Many instruments must be acknowledged before they are entitled to be recorded.

Acquisition. Act or process of acquiring or gaining title to or possession of property.

Acre. A measure of land equaling 160 square rods, or 4840 square yards, or 43,560 square feet. A football playing field (300 × 160 feet) contains a little more than an acre of land.

Acre Foot. A unit volume of water in irrigation; the amount covering one acre to a depth of 1 foot, equal to 43,560 cubic feet.

Action. A court proceeding to enforce a right or redress (obtain satisfaction for) a wrong.

Action in Personam. A court action which seeks a judgment against an individual or person, as distinguished from a judgment against property. An action for damages for injury to the person is an *action in personam.*

Action in Rem. A court action which seeks a judgment against property, such as a **Quiet Title** action.

Act of God. Any unavoidable disaster which is a the result of natural causes, rather then man-made, such as earthquakes, violent storms (cyclones or tornadoes), lightning, or flooding.

Actual Notice. Having actual knowledge of a fact, as compared with implied or inferred notice.

Adjudication. Judicial determination of a case, controversy, or conflict.

Adjusted Cost Basis. The cost basis of property with certain additions, such as the cost of improvements, and certain subtractions, such as depreciation in value.

Adjustments. In appraising, a means by which characteristics of a residential property are reflected by dollar amount or percentage to conform to similar but not identical characteristics of another residential property.

Administrator. A person appointed by a probate court as the representative of a deceased person's estate where the decedent left no will. A woman appointed as the representative is called the *administratrix.*

Administrator c.t.a. Administrator with the will annexed. This person is the representative of a decedent's estate where the decedent left a will, but no one is named as executor, or if the named executor is unable or unwilling to act. The letters *c.t.a.* stand for the Latin phrase *cum testamentum annexo* (with will annexed).

Ad Valorem. According to the value. Encountered in taxation of real property. An ad valorem tax assesses real property in relation to its value.

Advance Fee. A fee charged in advance for advertising or for preliminary expenses in connection with the sale of real estate or a business opportunity. Advance fees are regulated by statute.

Advances. Money advanced by the beneficiary under a trust deed to pay real estate taxes, hazard insurance premiums, or other items needed to protect the beneficiary's interest under the trust deed. Also refers to additional funds loaned under an open-end mortgage or trust deed.

Adverse Possession. A method of acquisition of title to property based on hostile use and occupation of another person's property for a continuous period of five years and payment of taxes.

Affiant. A person who makes an affidavit.

Affidavit. A statement or declaration reduced to writing and sworn to or affirmed before some officer or official, such as a notary public, who has authority to administer an oath or affirmation.

Affirm. To state or assert that a statement made is true, but without oath. Also, to confirm or ratify a judgment of a lower court by an appellate court. Also, to ratify and accept an otherwise voidable transaction.

Affirmation. The statement or assertion that something is true; similar to an affidavit, except that the person making the statement, due to religious beliefs, does not take an oath but merely affirms. Many affirmations are specificallly made under penalty of perjury.

Agency. The relationship between principal and agent whereby the agent represents the principal in dealings with a third party.

Agenda. Things to be done; matters to be attended to, particularly at a business meeting.

Agent. A person who acts for another, who is called a principal.

Agreement. An expression of assent by two or more parties to the same object. The word actually ranges in meaning from a simple mutual understanding to a binding obligation, such as a formal contract.

Agreement of Sale. A written agreement or contract between a seller and purchaser of property in which they have reached a meeting of the minds on the terms and provisions of the sale.

Air Rights. The rights in real property to the reasonable use of the air space above the surface of the land.

Alcalde. Chief magistrate or mayor (Spanish).

Alias. Also known as. Shortened from *alias dictus,* meaning otherwise called. Frequently encountered in litigation.

Alien. An unnaturalized foreign resident; a foreigner; distinguished from citizen.

Alienate. To transfer or convey property to another.

Alienation. The voluntary parting with the ownership of real property; the transferring of property by the owner to another person; opposite of acquisition.

Alienation Clause. A clause in a note or trust deed permitting the payee or beneficiary to declare the entire unpaid balance immediately due and payable upon a subsequent transfer of the property. Also referred to as a *due-on-sale* clause.

Allegation. An assertion made by a party in a legal proceeding which he expects to prove in order to establish his or her case. A complaint in a lawsuit contains numerous allegations and statements of facts.

All-Inclusive Deed of Trust. A trust deed that includes the amount due under another or other trust deed on the same property; also called a *wraparound,* or *overriding* deed of trust.

Alluvion. Soil or sand added by the process of accretion; i.e.; the gradual increase of land on the shore of a lake, sea, or ocean or on the bank of a river; also known as *alluvium.*

ALTA. American Land Title Association, the trade association of title insurance companies in the United States.

ALTA Policy of Title Insurance. An extended coverage form of title insurance policy which extends the coverage of a standard coverage policy to include various off-record risks, such as matters disclosed by a survey, or by an inspection of the land, or by inquiry of persons in possession of the land.

Amenities. Intangible benefits in real property ownership arising from such factors as pride of ownership, desirable social or cultural environment, architectural excellence, etc.; conditions of agreeable living.

Amortization. The liquidation or payment of a principal debt or financial obligation either on an installment basis or by creating a sinking fund; also, recovery over a period of time of cost or value.

Amortized Loan. A loan to be repaid by a series of regular payments, which are equal or nearly equal, over the life of the loan.

Ancillary. Auxiliary or supplemental or secondary, such as an ancillary administration of a decedent's estate in a place other than the decedent's domicile. The person appointed as the representative of the decedent's estate at such place would be called the *ancillary administrator.*

Annexation. The addition to property by adding or attaching other property to it, such as a fixture. Also, the addition of unincorporated territory in a county to a city or town.

Annual Percentage Rate. The actual cost of credit as determined under the Federal Truth in Lending Act.

Annuity. An amount of money payable yearly or at other regular intervals for a specified period of time.

Annul. To cancel or to make void and of no legal effect.

Antenuptial Agreement. A contract between a man and a woman made in contemplation of marriage regarding their property.

Anticipation, Principle of. Affirms that value is created by anticipated benefits to be derived in the future.

Antideficiency Legislation. Legislation, originally enacted in the early thirties, which prohibits a seller from obtaining a judgment for money against a defaulting buyer in proceedings to regain the property. The seller's only remedy is to get back the property in cases where the buyer is unable or unwilling to pay for the purchase.

Appearance. As used in the law, an appearance is the coming into court of a party to a lawsuit.

Appellant. The party appealing a court decision or ruling.

Appraisal. An opinion or estimate as to the fair market value of property; may be made for various purposes, such as sale, condemnation, assessment, taxation, etc.

Appraise. To estimate or render an opinion as to the value of property.

Appraiser. A person qualified by education, training, and experience to estimate the value or real or personal property.

Appropriation of Water. The taking of water flowing on the public domain from its natural course and the application of the water to some beneficial use to the appropriator.

Appurtenance. Something annexed to or made a part of another thing and transferred as an incident to it. This may be a dwelling or a garage or a barn or an orchard or other thing that becomes part of the land.

Appurtenant. Belonging to.

Arbitrary Map. A phrase encountered in the title industry. It refers to a map made by a title insurance company for its own convenience in locating property in an area in which the recorded descriptions are by metes and bounds. The term is shortened to *arb* for ready reference.

Architectural Style. Generally, the appearance and character of a building's design and construction.

ARM. Adjustable rate mortgage.

Articles of Incorporation. An instrument setting forth the basic rules and purposes under which a private corporation is formed.

Assess. To estimate officially the value of property as a basis for taxation.

Assessed Value. The value placed on property for the purpose of taxation.

Assessment. The valuation of property for the purpose of levying a tax; also, the amount of the tax levied. Assessments can also be imposed specially and locally upon property particularly benefited by a local work of improvement, such as sidewalks, curbs, lighting, sewers, etc.

Assessor. The official who has the responsibility for determining the assessed value of property. County tax assessors do not fix the amount of

the property tax, nor do they collect the tax; these are responsibilities of other officials.

Assets. Items of ownership convertible into cash; things of value (opposed to liabilities).

Assign. To transfer one's interest in personal property, such as a contract or a leasehold estate.

Assignee. The person to whom property is assigned.

Assignment. A transfer by writing of a person's right, title, or interest in intangible property, usually of a chose in action (see **Choses**) such as a contract right.

Assignment of Rents. A usual provision in a mortgage or deed of trust that permits the lender, upon default, to collect the rents and apply them to the amount due.

Assignor. One who assigns or transfers his or her interest in property.

Assumption Agreement. Undertaking or adopting a debt or obligation primarily resting upon another person, such as the assumption by the purchaser of real property of a mortgage executed by the seller in favor of a third party lender. If the purchaser merely took *subject to* the mortgage, he would have no personal liability for the debt. By assuming the debt, he may become personally liable for payment.

Assumption Fee. A lender's charge for changing over and processing new records for a new owner who is assuming an existing loan.

Attachment. A seizure of property by judicial process while a court action is pending.

Attachment Lien. A lien on real property obtained prior to judgment in an action for money; obtained by levy of a writ of attachment.

Attest. To affirm or certify that a statement or document is true or genuine.

Attestation Clause. A clause in an instrument or writing stating that the persons therein named have affixed their names as witness.

Attorn. To accept and acknowledge a new landlord, following foreclosure of a trust deed on the fee title, for instance.

Attorney-in-fact. An agent authorized to act for another person under a power of attorney.

Attractive Nuisance. A potentially dangerous object or condition on an owner's property that is likely to attract young children who may become injured. Even though the children are trespassers, the owner is ordinarily liable in damages for their injury.

Authorization to Sell. Formal name for a listing agreement under which a real estate broker is authorized to obtain a buyer for the owner's property.

Avulsion. The sudden removal of soil from an owner's property and its deposit on the property of another, as by a sudden change in the course of a river or other watercourse.

Axial Growth. City growth which occurs along main transportation routes. Usually takes the form of star-shaped extension outward from the center.

Backfill. The replacement of excavated earth into a hole or against a structure.

Bailment. The delivery of personal property to another party as security for a debt or other obligation and returnable when the debt or other obligation is discharged. The thing deposited is referred to as a **Pledge**.

Balance. Used as a verb, this means to reconcile an account. Used as a noun, this represents the amount of loan still owed.

Balance Sheet. Statement showing assets, liabilities, and net worth as of a certain date.

Balloon Payment. The final installment payable on an installment note; it pays the note in full but is ordinarily considerably greater than the periodic installment payments called for by the note.

Bank. An institution for receiving, lending, exchanging, and safeguarding money and other things of value, and transacting other financial business. May be incorporated under state law or under federal law such as a national banking association.

Bankruptcy. A proceeding initiated under federal law whereby an insolvent debtor may obtain relief from payment of certain of his or her debts.

Bargain and Sale Deed. Any deed that recites a consideration and purports to convey the real estate.

Base and Meridian Lines. Imaginary lines used by surveyors to find and describe the location of land. A *base line* runs east and west, whereas a *meridian* runs north and south. Their intersection forms a starting point for the measurement of land. There are three principal base and meridian lines in California, located on Mt. San Bernardino in San Bernardino County, Mt. Diablo in Contra Costa County, and Mt. Pierce in Humboldt County.

Base Price. See **Cost Basis**.

Basis. See **Cost Basis** and **Adjusted Cost Basis**.

Bench Marks. A ground location indicated on a durable marker by surveyors and used to locate or describe real property.

Beneficiary. As used in a trust deed, the lender is designated as the beneficiary, i.e., the lender obtains the benefit of the security.

Beneficiary's Statement. Statement from a secured lender setting forth the unpaid principal balance and other information concerning the debt. Frequently obtained by an escrow agent during an escrow for the sale of real estate. Commonly referred to as a "Benny" statement.

Benevolent Association. Voluntary groups which are formed not for profit, but to render financial or other aid to their members. May acquire title to real property in the name of the association.

Bequeath. To make a gift of personal property by will.

Bequest. A gift of personal property by will.

Betterment. An improvement upon property which increases the property's value; considered a capital asset, as distinguished from repairs or replacements where the original character or cost are unchanged.

Bid. An offer.

Bilateral Contract. A contract in which a promise is given by both parties; distinguished from a unilateral contract which calls for an act by one party in exchange for a promise by the other.

Bill of Sale. A written instrument evidencing the transfer of title to tangible personal property, such as furniture and furnishings, as distinguished from a chose in action (see **Choses**), such as contract right. The latter is transferred by an **Assignment**.

Binder. An agreement to consider a downpayment for the purchase of real estate as evidence of good faith on the part of the purchaser and binds the parties. Also, a notation of coverage on an insurance policy, issued by an agent, and given to the insured prior to the issuance of the policy.

Blacktop. Asphalt paving used in streets and driveways or other areas such as playgrounds.

Blanket Mortgage. A single mortgage or other encumbrance which covers more than one piece of real property; may describe "all real property" owned by the mortgagor in a designated county.

Blighted Area. A declining area in which real property values are seriously affected by destructive economic forces. May be caused by the infiltration of people from lower social and economic classes, by the rapid depreciation of the buildings, or by the inharmonious use of the property.

Block. A small section of a city or town enclosed by neighboring and intersecting streets, often used as dividing lines in zoning; also, a part of a scheme for subdividing a large parcel of land by the creation of blocks and lots in a tract, such as "Lot 3 in Block A of the Smith Tract."

Blockbusting. The practice on the part of unscrupulous speculators or real estate agents of inducing panic selling of homes below market value, especially by exploiting the prejudices of property owners in neighborhoods in which the racial make-up is changing or appears to be on the verge of changing. It is an actionable wrong.

Board Foot. A unit of measurement of lumber; one foot wide, one foot long, and one inch thick, consisting of 144 cubic inches.

Board of Equalization. A state or county board with the power and authority to adjust inequalities in tax assessments.

Bobtail Escrow. An escrow transaction where one escrow agent handles one side of a transaction, and the other side is handled by another escrow agent. Rarely encountered today.

Bona Fide. In good faith; without fraud.

Bona Fide Purchaser. A person who buys property in good faith, for a fair value, and without notice of any adverse claims or rights of third parties.

Bond. A written promise of a surety, i.e., one who makes himself responsible for the faithful performance of an act by another person. Also, evidence of a debt or obligation owned by a governmental agency or other entity, such as a private corporation.

Bonus. Something given or paid over and above what is actually due.

Book Value. Total cost of property minus total depreciation; the value of property as stated in a book of accounts (distinguished from market value).

Boot. In real estate exchange language, this represents cash or something else of value that is unlike the property in exchange. Applicable where the parcels being exchanged are not of the same value.

Boundary. Anything that indicates bounds or limits in the area or location of property.

Bounds. Boundaries. The word *bounds* is used with the word *metes* as **Metes and Bounds,** one of the principal methods for describing real property.

Breach. The violation of an obligation, or failure of duty, or the breaking of a law.

Broker. An agent who finds a buyer or seller of property for a principal on a commission basis; also may act as a loan broker in arranging loans on real property, or in other capacities.

Building Code. A regulation of construction of buildings within a municipality established by ordinance or statute.

Building Line. Lines established by ordinance or statute limiting how close an owner can build to the street; also referred to as *setback* lines (see **Setback Ordinance**).

Building Restrictions. Zoning regulations or deed provisions limiting type, size and use of a building.

Built-In. Cabinets or similar features built as part of the house.

Bulk Sales Law. State law regulating the sale of business establishments, including stock in trade; enacted for the purpose of protecting the interest of creditors of the business.

Bundle of Rights. The various interests or rights that owners have in their property.

Bureau of Land Management. A federal bureau within the Department of the Interior which manages and controls certain lands owned by the United States.

Business Opportunity. As used in the Real Estate Law, refers to the sale or lease of the business and goodwill of an existing business enterprise or opportunity separate and apart from the real property.

Buyer's Market. The conditions which exist when a buyer is in a more commanding position as to the price and terms of sale, primarily because real property offered for sale is in plentiful supply compared to demand.

By-laws. Rules governing the operation of the business and affairs of a corporation in addition to the rules set forth in its charter or articles of incorporation.

Cal-Vet Loan. A loan made under the California Veterans Farm and Home Purchase Program as an aid to veterans in purchasing a home or farm at low financing costs.

CC & Rs. Covenants, conditions, and restrictions.

Capacity. Legal qualification for entering into a contract; being capable.

Capital. Any form of wealth, whether money or other property, employed or capable of being employed in the production of more wealth.

Capital Assets. Assets of a permanent nature used in the production of income, such as land, buildings, machinery, and equipment. Under income tax law, it is usually distinguishable from *inventory*, which comprises assets held for sale to customers in the ordinary course of trade or business.

Capital Gains. Gains on the sale of property; under the income tax law there are tax advantages in *long-term* capital gains, i.e., gains on the sale of certain property held longer than a prescribed period of time.

Capitalization. In appraising, to determine the value of property by considering net income and the percentage of reasonable return on the investment.

Capitalization Rate. The rate of interest which is considered a reasonable return on the investment, and used in the process of determining value based upon net income.

Capitol. The building in Sacramento where the state legislature meets in annual sessions.

Caprice. A value, not economic, created by a special circumstance, such as a particular location.

Caption. The heading or title of a document.

CAR. California Association of Realtors.

CARET. California Association of Real Estate Teachers.

Cash Basis. Method of recording income and expenses in which each item is entered as received or paid. Distinguished from **Accrual Basis**.

Cash Flow. The measure of cash generated from income and depreciation after debt-servicing expenses.

Cause of Action. The basis for bringing a lawsuit; a ground for legal action; the matter over which a person goes to court. The party filing an action is the **Plaintiff**, who sets forth his or her cause of action in a pleading called a complaint.

Caveat Emptor. "Let the buyer beware." Usually, when a buyer examines the goods or property sold, he buys at his or her own risk, in the absence of misrepresentations.

Certificate of Eligibility. Certificate issued by the government evidencing an individual's eligibility to obtain a Veterans Administration (GI) loan.

Certificate of Reasonable Value. Certificate which informs a veteran under GI loan of the appraised value of the property and the maximum VA guaranteed loan a private lender may make.

Certificate of Sale. A certificate issued to the purchaser at a judicial sale, such as an execution sale. After the time for redemption has expired, the holder of the certificate is entitled to a deed.

Certificate of Taxes Due. A written statement in the form of a guaranty of the condition of the taxes on a particular property made by the County Treasurer of the County where the property is located.

Certificate of Title. A certification as to the ownership of land and the condition of title, based on an examination of the public records.

Chain. A unit of measurement used by surveyors. A chain consists of 100 links equal to 66 feet.

Chain of Title. A chronological list of recorded instruments affecting the title to land, commencing with the document under which title was transferred from the government to private ownership, and ending with the latest document transferring title. In order to have marketable title, there must be an unbroken chain of title.

Change, Principle of. Holds that it is the future, not the past, which is of prime importance in estimating value. Change is largely the result of cause and effect.

Characteristics. Distinguishing features of a residential property.

Chattel. Personal property.

Chattel Mortgage. A mortgage of personal property to secure payment of a debt. Since the adoption of the Uniform Commercial Code, chattel mortgages are referred to as Personal Property Security Agreements.

Chattel Real. An interest in real estate less than a freehold, such as an estate for years.

Choses in Action. A thing in action, i.e., a personal right not reduced to possession, but giving the owner the right to bring a court action for its possession or for damages.

Civil Action. A court action involving the civil law and private rights of parties, rather than the criminal law.

Civil Law. A body of law that is derived from the Roman system of law, rather than the common law of England. Often called statutory law in this country.

Civil Rights. Basic rights of freedom and liberty guaranteed to United States citizens by the 13th and 14th Amendments to the Federal Constitution and by later federal laws.

Closing Costs. The numerous expenses buyers and sellers normally incur in the transfer of ownership of real property.

Closing Statement. Statement furnished by an escrow holder to the principals at the time of closing an escrow, setting forth the charges and costs.

Cloud on Title. Any conditions revealed by a search of title, such as an ancient pipeline easement, which affect the marketability of title to property. Although sometimes seemingly unimportant, there may be a need to remove them by either a quitclaim deed or a court decree.

CLTA. California Land Title Association, the trade association of title insurance companies in California.

Code. A system of law. In California most of the statutes have been codified in a series of codes, such as the Civil Code and the Business and Professions Code.

Code of Ethics. A set of rules and principles expressing a standard of accepted conduct for members of a professional group.

Collateral. Something additional, such as *collateral security*, i.e., a separate obligation attached to a contract to guarantee its performance. Also, the property subject to the security interest. Also, in estate matters, collateral means descended from the same stock but in different line, i.e., not lineal. For example, a cousin is a collateral relative.

Collateral Assignment. An assignment of an interest in property, such as a note secured by a trust deed, to secure performance of an obligation. It is distinguishable from an absolute assignment.

Collateral Loan. A loan secured by collateral, i.e., something of value to give greater assurance of payment.

Collateral Security. A separate obligation attached to a contract to guarantee its performance; the transfer of something of value to insure the performance of a principal agreement.

Collusion. An agreement between two or more persons to defraud another of his or her rights by going through the forms of the law, or to obtain an object that is forbidden by law, such as obtaining the property of a client by devious means.

Color of Title. That which gives the appearance of good title but is not title in fact because of some defect, such as an erroneous or insufficient legal description.

Commercial Acre. A term applied to the remainder of an acre of subdivided land after the area devoted to streets, sidewalks, curbs, etc., has been deducted from the acre.

Commercial Loan. A personal loan from a commercial bank, usually unsecured and for a short term, for other than mortgage purposes.

Commercial Paper. Drafts, notes, and bills of exchange used in commercial transactions.

Commingling. Unauthorized mixing of funds of a customer or client with one's own personal funds.

Commission. An agent's compensation for performing the duties of his agency. In real estate practice, commission represents a percentage of the selling price of the property, such as 6 percent, or a percentage of rentals collected, etc.

Commissioner. The legislature has created various commissioners, such as the real estate commissioner and the corporations commissioner, to carry out the responsibilities of various state agencies, including the enforcement of the law.

Commitment. A pledge or a promise or firm agreement to perform an act, such as commitment to make a loan.

Common Law. Body of unwritten law, founded upon general custom, usage, or common consent, that developed in England "since the memory of man runneth not to the contrary." Prevails in England and most of the United States. Sometimes referred to as case law in this country.

Common Stock. That class of corporate stock to which there is ordinarily attached no preference with respect to the receipt of dividends or the distribution of assets upon corporate dissolution.

Community Property. Property acquired by husband or wife or both during marriage when not acquired as separate property. Basically, property of a married person in California is either separate property or community property.

Compaction. Whenever extra soil is added to a lot to fill in low places or to raise the level of the lot, the added soil is often too loose and soft to sustain the weight of improvements.

Accordingly, it is necessary to *compact* the added soil by pounding it with appropriate tools so that it will carry the added weight of buildings without the danger of their tilting, settling or cracking.

Comparable Sales. Sales which have similar characteristics as the subject property and are used for analysis in the appraisal process. Commonly called *comparables*, they are recent selling prices of properties similarly situated in a similar market.

Comparison Approach. A real estate comparison method which compares a given property with similar or comparable surrounding properties to determine value.

Competent. Legally qualified.

Competition, Principle of. Holds that profits tend to breed competition, and excess profits tend to breed ruinous competition.

Component. One of the features making up the whole property.

Compound Interest. Interest paid on original principal and also on the accrued and unpaid interest which has accumulated.

Con. In opposition to; against.

Conclusive Presumption. An inference the law makes that cannot be contradicted.

Condemnation. The exercise of the power of eminent domain, i.e., the taking of property for a public use upon payment of just compensation; also refers to condemnation of unsafe structures under the government's police power.

Condition. A qualification annexed to an estate upon the happening of which the estate is enlarged or defeated. It may be a *condition precedent*, which is a condition which must be fulfilled before an estate can vest. Or it may be a *condition subsequent*, which is a condition by the failure or nonperformance of which an estate already vested may be defeated.

Conditional. Not absolute, depending on a condition; made or allowed on certain terms.

Conditional Commitment. A commitment by an FHA lender of a definite loan amount on a specified property for some unknown purchaser of satisfactory credit standing.

Conditional Sales Contract. A contract for the sale of property where title remains in the seller until the conditions of the contract have been performed by the buyer.

Conditional Use Permit. Permitting a use of a parcel of property in contravention of zoning upon a finding that the permitted use is essen-

tial or desirable to the public convenience or welfare and is in harmony with the objectives of the master plan. Various conditions are imposed in granting such use permit.

Condominium. Ownership of a divided interest; i.e., an individually owned unit, in a multifamily or other structure, combined with joint ownership of the structure and the land. Sometimes referred to as a "horizontal" subdivision; involves both a vertical and a horizontal division.

Confirmation of Sale. Court approval of the sale of property by an executor, administrator, guardian, or conservator.

Conformity, Principle of. Holds that the maximum of value is realized when a reasonable degree of homogeneity of improvement is present.

Consent. To permit, approve, or agree.

Conservation. The process of utilizing resources in such a manner which minimizes their depletion.

Conservator. A person appointed by the probate court to take care of the person or property of an adult person needing such care. Similar to a guardian.

Consideration. The inducement for entering into a contract; it consists of either a benefit to the promisor, or a loss or detriment to the promisee. Anything of value given to induce entering into a contract. It may be money, personal services, or in some cases even love and affection.

Construction Loans. Loans, usually short term, made by a lender for the purpose of constructing homes or commercial buildings; funds are disbursed by the lender in stages after periodic inspections.

Constructive. Deduced by *inference* (see **Constructive Notice**).

Constructive Notice. Notice given by the public records of a claim of ownership or interest in property. Generally, the law presumes that a person has the same knowledge of instruments properly recorded as if he or she were actually acquainted with them. The word constructive is frequently encountered in real estate. For instance, *constructive eviction* is applicable in the landlord-tenant relationship. *Constructive possession* may be involved in a claim of title based on adverse possession. And in the field of trusts, the courts may establish a *constructive trust* in property. **Fraud** also may be constructive or actual.

Consumer Goods. Goods used or bought for use primarily for personal, family, or household purposes. The term is used in the Commercial Code in connection with personal-property security agreements.

Contiguous. Adjoining or touching upon, such as contiguous parcels of land.

Contingent. Dependent upon an uncertain future event.

Contour. The surface configuration or shape of land.

Contract. An agreement by which a person undertakes or promises to do or not to do a certain thing. Must be supported by **consideration** to be enforceable.

Contribution, Principle of. A component part of a property is valued in proportion to its contribution to the value of the whole. Holds that maximum values are achieved when the improvements on a site produce the highest (net) return, commensurate with the investment.

Conventional Loan. A mortgage loan which is not insured or guaranteed by a governmental agency, such as the FHA or VA.

Conversion. Change from one character or use to another. Also, the unauthorized appropriation by a person of property belonging to another.

Conveyance. A written instrument transferring the title to land or an interest therein from one person to another.

Co-op. Community apartment projects owned as "stock cooperatives," where individual owners each acquire a share of stock in the corporation which owns the title, with each person owning the exclusive right to occupy a particular apartment.

Corner Influence. The increase in value of a corner lot due to its location.

Corporation. An artificial being, created by law, and possessing certain rights, privileges, and duties of natural persons. A corporation may acquire title to real property in its corporate name.

Corporation Sole. A corporation consisting of one person only and his successors in office, and incorporated by law in order to give some legal capacity not otherwise owned, such as ownership of property in perpetuity. An example is the Roman Catholic Archbishop of Los Angeles, who may acquire title to real property on behalf of the church in his name as a corporation sole.

Corporeal Rights. Possessory rights in real property.

Correction Lines. A system for compensating inaccuracies in the Government Rectangular Survey System due to the curvature of the earth.

Correlation. A step in the appraisal process involving the interpretation of data derived from the three approaches to value, leading to a single determination of value. Also referred to as "reconciliation."

Correspondent. An abbreviated term meaning mortgage loan correspondent. A mortgage banker who services mortgage loans as agent for the owner of the mortgage or investor. Also applied to the mortgage banker in his or her role as originator of mortgage loans for the investor.

Co-signer. A second party who signs a promissory note together with the promissory obligor (borrower).

Cost Basis. A property value determined at the time of acquisition. The amount is dependent upon the method of acquisition, and subsequently serves as a base figure in determining profit or loss for income tax purposes.

Cost New. Represents the present construction costs of a new building, including labor, material, and other expenditures.

Counter Part. A copy of a lease executed by one party in a group of many lessors. Ordinarily encountered in oil and gas leases.

County. A political division of the state. There are 58 counties in California, each with a county recorder, tax collector, courthouse, and many other offices.

Covenants. Agreements contained in deeds and other instruments for the performance or non-performance of certain acts, or the use or non-use of property in a certain manner. Basically, a covenant is a promise to do or not do a certain thing.

CPM. Certified property manager. A member of the Institute of Real Property Management of the NAR.

Crawl Hole. Exterior or interior opening permitting access underneath a building, ordinarily required by building codes.

Creditor. A person to whom a debt is owed. Any person extending credit to another person.

CREEA. California Real Estate Educators Association.

CRV. Certificate of reasonable value, used in connection with GI loans.

Cul-de-sac. A street, lane, or road closed at one end; a blind alley.

Curable Depreciation. Items of physical deterioration and functional obsolescence which are customarily repaired or replaced by a prudent property owner.

Curtail Schedule. A listing of the amounts by which the principal sum of an obligation is to be reduced by partial payments, and of the dates when each amount will become payable.

Curtesy. The life estate or the tenure that (in some states, but not in California) the husband has in the lands of his deceased wife. Takes effect by the common law, when he has had issue by her capable of inheriting her lands.

Custodial Accounts. Bank accounts used for deposits of funds belonging to others.

Cyclical Movement. The sequential and recurring changes in economic activity of a business cycle, moving from prosperity through recession, depression, recovery, and back again to prosperity.

Damages. The amount recoverable by a victim of the wrongful or negligent act of another.

DBA. "Doing business as." Applicable where a person engages in business under a fictitious name, such as "John Smith, doing business as the Acme Building Company."

Debit. A bookkeeping entry on the left side of an account; opposite of credit.

Debt. That which is due from one person to another; obligation; liability.

Debtor. A party owing money to another. Under the Uniform Commercial Code the debtor is the party who "owns" the property subject to a security agreement, where previously this person was referred to as the mortgagor or pledgor.

Declaration of Homestead. The document which is recorded in order to obtain an exemption from forced sale of a person's home in satisfaction of certain types of creditors' claims

Decree. A type of court order in a judicial proceeding. Courts are empowered to make various types of judgments, orders, and decrees.

Decree of Distribution. An order of the probate court by which property of a decedent is distributed to his heirs or devisees.

Decree of Foreclosure. Decree by a court ordering the sale of mortgaged property and the payment of the debt owing to the lender out of the proceeds.

Dedication. A setting apart or donation of land by its owner for a public use. The dedication may be of the fee, perhaps for a park, or of an easement, such as a roadway.

Deed. Writen instrument by which the ownership of real property is transferred from one person to another.

Deed Restrictions. See Restriction.

Deed of Trust. Written instrument by which title to real property is transferred to a third party trustee as security for a debt or other obligation owed to another person. Used in place of mortgages in many states, including California. Also called *trust deed.*

Default. Failure to fulfill a duty or promise or to discharge an obligation; the omission or failure to perform any act.

Default Judgment. A judgment entered against a party who fails to make an appearance in the action.

Defendant. The party against whom a court action is brought.

Deferred Maintenance. Existing but unfulfilled requirements for repairs and rehabilitation of property.

Deficiency Judgment. A personal judgment in a lien foreclosure action for the amount of the debt still remaining due after a sale of the security.

Defunct. No longer operating or functioning, such as a defunct corporation.

Delivery. Giving possession of a document, such as a deed, by one party (the grantor) to the other (the grantee) with the intent to convey title.

Demise. A transfer made by the owner of land to another person of an estate for years, for life, or at will.

Deponent. A person who makes a statement or gives testimony under oath or affirmation.

Deposit Receipt. Document used when accepting "earnest money" to bind an offer for property by a prospective purchaser; when properly filled out and executed by both parties, it may result in a binding contract.

Depreciation. Loss of value in real property brought about by age, physical deterioration, functional or economic obsolescence, or any other cause.

Depth Table. A statistical table that may be used to estimate the value of the added depth of a lot.

Deraign. To trace or prove ownership, such as title to land.

Descendant. One who is descended from a specific ancestor; an offspring.

Descent. Succession to property by an heir of a decedent.

Desist and Refrain Order. An order, which the real estate commissioner is empowered by law to issue, directing a person to desist and refrain from committing acts in violation of the Real Estate Law.

Deterioration. Impairment of the condition or utility of property, brought about by wear and tear, disintegration, use in service, or the action of the elements. One of the causes of depreciation and reflecting loss in value.

Determinable Fee. An estate which will end on the happening of an event which may or may not occur.

Devise. A gift of real property by will.

Devisee. One who receives real property by will.

Dictum. An opinion by a judge on a point of law not essential to the decision on the main question. Often mistakenly relied upon by persons appearing in pro per (in propria persona) as stating a rule of law of general application. (Plural of dictum is *dicta*.)

Directional Growth. The location or direction toward which the residental sections of a city are destined or determined to go.

Disclosure Statement. Statement required under the federal Truth in Lending Act which sets forth the details of a loan transaction, including all finance charges.

Discount. To sell at a reduced price; to purchase or sell a note before maturity at a reduction based on the interest for the time it still has to run, or for market reasons.

Divest. To deprive of a right or title.

Divided Interest. Ownership of a particular piece or portion of a larger parcel of real property, such as a condominium; distinguished from an *undivided* interest.

Dividend. A sum of money paid to shareholders of a corporation out of earnings; also, anything received as a bonus or reward. In mathematics, the number divided by the divisor.

Document. An original or official paper relied upon as the basis, proof, or support of anything else. A more comprehensive word than *instrument*.

Documentary Transfer Tax. Counties are authorized to impose a documentary transfer tax to apply on transfers of real property located in the county; collected at the time of recording the document.

Domicile. A person's legal residence.

Domiciliary Administrator. An administrator of a decedent's estate appointed in the place of residence of the decedent; distinguished from *ancillary administrator*.

Dominant Tenement. The tenement (property) obtaining the benefit of an appurtenant easement.

Donee. A person to whom a gift is made.

Donor. A person who makes a gift to another.

Dower. The legal right or interest which the wife acquires by marriage (in some states, but not in California) in the real estate of her husband.

Dual Agency. An agency relationship in which one agent acts concurrently for both of the principals in a transaction.

Due-on-sale Clause. An acceleration clause granting the lender the right to demand full payment of the mortgage or trust deed upon a sale of the property, also called an **Alienation Clause**.

Duress. Unlawful constraint or coercion, such as a threat of bodily harm, exercised upon a person whereby he or she is persuaded to do some act against his or her will. Renders invalid a contract or other act entered into or performed under its influence.

DVA. Department of Veterans Affairs. The state agency that administers the California Veterans Farm and Home Purchase Program (Cal-Vet loans).

Earnest Money. Something given as a part of the purchase price to bind a bargain.

Easement. A right, privilege or interest in the land of another existing apart from the ownership of the land, such as a right of way (a right to cross over another person's property). (See **Prescriptive Easement**.)

Easement by Implication. An easement that is implied or inferred from conduct or circumstances rather than being expressed.

Ecology. The relationship between organisms and their environment.

Economic Life. The period during which a property will yield a sufficient return on the investment to justify maintaining it.

Economic Obsolescence. A loss in value due to factors not part of the subject property but adversely affecting the value of the subject property.

Egress. A means, or place, of going out.

Eleemosynary. Charitable.

Emblements. Crops produced annually by labor and industry as distinguished from crops that grow naturally on the land.

Eminent Domain. The power of the government to take property for a public purpose upon payment of just compensation.

Encroachment. The extension of an improvement or branch of a tree or other vegetation onto the property of another person.

Encumbrance. A lien or charge or burden on land (also spelled *incumbrance*).

Endorsement. A writing on a negotiable instrument, such as a note, by which the instrument is transferred. Also, a provision or rider added to an insurance policy to alter or enlarge the terms of the insurance contract. (Sometimes spelled *indorsement*.)

Enjoin. To prohibit or restrain by an injunction.

Equitable Lien. A lien recognized only in a court of equity.

Equitable Title. Title of the purchaser under a contract of sale.

Equity. Value of an owner's interest in property in excess of mortgages and other liens. Also, a system of jurisprudence or a body of doctrines and rules developed in England and followed in the United States which serves to supplement and remedy the limitations or inflexibility of the common law.

Equity Buildup. The increase of an owner's equity in property due to mortgage principal reduction and to value appreciation.

Equity of Redemption. The right which the mortgagor has of redeeming his or her property for a limited period of time after a foreclosure sale.

Erosion. The gradual wearing away of land by the action of the elements, such as tidal water or winds.

Escalation. The right reserved by the lender to increase the amount of the payments and/or interest upon the happening of a specified event.

Escalator Clause. A clause in a contract providing for the upward or downward adjustment of specified items, such as interest or rent, to cover certain contingencies, such as higher or lower costs of living.

Escheat. Reverting of property to the state of California when an owner dies without a will and without heirs.

Ecrow. The deposit of a deed or other instrument with a third party for delivery upon performance of a condition. Also, the transaction in which a third party acts as the agent for the buyer and seller or borrower and lender in carrying out the instructions of the parties and handling and disbursing the papers and funds.

Sales escrow is one relating to the sale of a parcel of property, as distinguished from a loan or an exchange escrow.

Escrow Holder. The party who acts as the agent for the principals in an escrow transaction.

Estate. The degree, quantity, nature, and extent of the interest a person has in real estate, such as a fee or a life estate or lesser estate. Also refers to the property left by a decedent that is subject to probate administration, or the property of a bankrupt.

Estate at Sufferance. An estate arising when a tenant wrongfully holds over after the expiration of the term. The landlord has the choice of evicting the tenant (through court action) or accepting the tenant on the same terms and conditions of the previous occupancy.

Estate at Will. Occupation of lands and tenements by a tenant for an indefinite period of time; terminable by either party at any time on proper notice.

Estate for Life. An estate that continues for the duration of a person's natural life.

Estate for Years. An estate that continues for a specified period of time; usually created by a lease.

Estate from Period to Period. An interest in land where there is no definite termination date but the rental period is fixed at a certain sum per week, month, or year. Also called a periodic tenancy.

Estate of Inheritance. An estate which may descend to heirs, such as a fee estate.

Estimated Remaining Life. The period of time (usually years) it takes for the improvements to become valueless.

Estoppel. A doctrine which bars a person from asserting rights inconsistent with a previous position or representation.

Ethics. That branch of moral science, idealism, justness, and fairness concerned with the duties which a member of a profession or craft owes to the public, to his or her clients or patrons, and to fellow members of his or her profession or craft.

Eviction. Dispossession of a defaulting tenant or other person wrongfully in possession of property by bringing a court action.

Exception. In a deed, some part of a thing granted which is excluded from the conveyance and remains with the grantor. In zoning, it refers to an instance or case not conforming to the general rule.

Exchange. To transfer property for other property of equivalent value; to trade one parcel of property for another.

Exclusive Agency Listing. A written instrument giving one agent the right to sell property for a specified period of time but reserving the right of the owner to sell the property without payment of a commission.

Exclusive Right to Sell Listing. A written agreement between owner and agent giving the agent the right to collect a commission if the property is sold by anyone, including the owner, during the term of the agreement.

Exculpatory Clause. A clause in a contract which attempts to relieve a party from liability for his wrongful or negligent act or omission.

Execute. To sign a deed, or to perform or carry out a contract; to give effect or force to a law or decree of a court.

Executed. As used in contract law, this relates to a contract that has been fully performed.

Execution Sale. A sale of a judgment debtor's property by the sheriff to satisfy the judgment.

Executor. A person who is designated in a will as the representative of the decedent's estate.

Executory. As used in contract law, this relates to a contract that is yet to be performed.

Executrix. Feminine of executor.

Exemption. An immunity from some burden or obligation.

Expediente. Early California (Spanish and Mexican) land grant file. A complete statement of every step taken in the proceedings to acquire a Spanish or Mexican land grant.

Expenses. Certain items which appear on a closing statement in connection with a real estate sale, chargeable to either buyer or seller.

Expressed. Something definitely stated rather than implied.

Extension Agreement. A grant of further time within which to pay an obligation.

Facade. Front of a building.

Facsimile. An exact copy.

Fair Market Value. The highest price estimated in terms of money which a parcel of property will bring on the open market where neither buyer nor seller is under any compulsion to act.

False Pretenses. A deliberate misrepresentation of facts as a means of obtaining money or title to property.

Fannie Mae. See **Federal National Mortgage Association (FNMA)**.

Farmers Home Administration (FmHA). An agency of the Department of Agriculture. Primary responsibility is to provide financial assistance for farmers and others living in rural areas where financing is not available on reasonable terms from private sources.

Federal Deposit Insurance Corporation (FDIC). Agency of the federal government which insures deposits at commercial banks and savings banks.

Federal Home Loan Bank (FHLB). A district bank of the Federal Home Loan Bank System that lends to member savings and loan associations.

Federal Home Loan Bank Board (FHLBB). Federal agency which regulates federally chartered savings and loan associations.

Federal Housing Administration. See **FHA**.

Federal Land Bank System. Federal government agency making long-term loans to farmers.

Federal National Mortgage Association (FNMA). Known as "Fannie Mae," a quasi-public agency converted into a private corporation whose primary function is to buy and sell FHA and VA mortgages in the secondary market.

Federal Reserve System. The federal banking system of the United States under the control of a central board of governors (Federal Reserve Board) involving a central bank in each of twelve geographical districts with broad powers in controlling credit and the amount of money in circulation.

Federal Savings and Loan Association. An association chartered by the FHLBB in contrast to a state-chartered savings and loan association.

Federal Savings and Loan Insurance Corporation (FSLIC). An agency of the federal government that insures savers' accounts at savings and loan associations.

Fee. A charge for services, such as attorney's fees. See also **Fee Estate**.

Fee Estate. An estate of inheritance in real property, often referred to as a *fee simple*.

Fee Simple Absolute. The highest type of estate or interest a person may have in property. In modern usage, it expressly establishes the title to real property in the owner, without limitation or end. The owner may dispose of it by sale or trade or will as he or she chooses.

Fee Simple Defeasible. A fee estate that is subject to a qualification, condition, or limitation.

Fee Title. Ownership of a fee estate.

Feudal Tenure. A real property ownership system where ownership rests with a sovereign who, in turn, may grant lesser interests in return for service or loyalty.

FHA. Federal Housing Administration. A federal agency, created by the National Housing Act of 1934, for the purpose of expanding and strengthening home ownership by making private mortgage financing possible on a long-term, low-down-payment basis. The vehicle is a mortgage insurance program, with premiums paid by the homeowner to protect lenders against loss of these higher-risk loans. Since 1965, FHA has been part of the Department of Housing and Urban Development (HUD).

FHA Insurance. An undertaking by FHA to insure the lender against loss arising from a default by borrower.

Fictitious Name. An assumed name; a name used for business which does not include the actual name of the owner, such as "Ace Lumber Company."

Fidelity Bond. A security posted for the discharge of an obligation of personal responsibility.

Fiduciary. One who holds a thing in trust for another person, or who acts in a trust capacity, such as an escrow holder.

Fiduciary Duty. That duty owed by an agent to act in the highest good faith toward the principal and not to obtain any advantage over the latter by the slightest misrepresentation, concealment, duress or pressure.

Fill. To build up the level of a lot with earth, rock, gravel, etc.

Financing Process. The systematic five-step procedure followed by major institutional lenders in analyzing a proposed loan, which includes filing of application by a borrower, lender's analysis of borrower and property, processing of loan documentation, making the loan, and servicing (collection and record keeping).

Financing Statement. Evidence of a personal property security agreement that is filed or recorded to give public notice. Has replaced the term *chattel mortgage* (see **Security Agreement**).

Firm Commitment. The amount an FHA lender will loan on a specified property with a specified borrower.

First Mortgage. A legal document pledging collateral for a loan (See **Mortgage**) that has first priority over all other claims against the property except taxes and bonded indebtedness. A mortgage superior to any other.

First Trust Deed. A legal document pledging collateral for a loan (See **Trust Deed**) that has first priority over all other claims against the property except taxes and bonded indebtedness. A trust deed superior to any other.

Fiscal Controls. Federal tax revenue and expenditure policies used to control the level of economic activity.

Fiscal Year. A business or accounting year as distinguished from a calandar year.

Fixity of Location. The physical characteristic of real estate that subjects it to the influence of its surroundings.

Fixture. A thing that was originally personal property but that has become attached to and is considered as part of the real property.

FNMA. Federal National Mortgage Association (see). Popularly known (for its initials) as Fannie Mae (or Fanny May).

Forbearance. The act of restraining from doing something. A creditor's giving an additional time after the date originally designated for payment.

Foreclosure. A proceeding to enforce a lien by a sale of the property in order to satisfy the debt.

Forfeiture. A loss of some right, title, estate, or interest in consequence of a default or failure to perform. Not readily enforceable, since the courts abhor a forfeiture. Liquidated damage clauses frequently have replaced forfeiture clauses in contracts of sale.

Forgery. The false making or alteration of a writing or signature by which the legal rights or obligations of another person are apparently affected. A forged document, such as a deed, conveys no title.

Foundation. The supporting portion of a structure below the first floor construction, or below grade, including the footings.

Franchise. A right or privilege conferred by law to carry on a business activity in a specified area, such as a franchise for a street railway; also, the permission granted by a manufacturer to a distributor or retailer to sell or service the manufacturer's product in a particular area or locale.

Fraud. The intentional and successful employment of any cunning, deception, collusion, or artifice, used to circumvent, cheat or deceive another person whereby that person acts upon it to the loss of property and to legal injury. (**Actual Fraud:** A deliberate misrepresentation or representation made in reckless disregard of its truth or its falsity, the suppression of truth, a promise made without the intention to perform it, or any other act intended to deceive.)

Fraudulent. Characterized by fraud, such as a fraudulent transfer of property.

Freehold. An estate of inheritance or for life.

Frontage. A term used to describe or identify that part of a parcel of land or an improvement on the land which faces a street. The term is also used to refer to the lineal extent of the land or improvement that is parallel to and facing the street, e.g., a 75-foot frontage.

Front Foot. A method of property measurement for purposes of sale or valuation, usually of commercial property. The property is measured by the front foot on its street line or boundary and valued at so much a front foot.

Front Money. The minimum amount of money necessary to initiate a real estate venture, to get the transaction underway.

FSLIC. Federal Savings and Loan Insurance Corporation (see).

Full Reconveyance. A release of all the property covered by a deed of trust.

Full Release. A complete release of liability under a contract or other obligation.

Functional Obsolescence. Loss of value of a structure due to adverse factors from within it which affect its utility, such as old age, poor design, or faulty equipment.

Future Benefits. The anticipated benefits the present owner will receive from the property in the future.

Gain. A profit, benefit, or value increase.

Garnishment. A statutory proceeding whereby property, money, or credits of a debtor in possession of another are seized and applied to payment of the debt.

General Lien. A lien on all the property of a debtor.

General Plan Restrictions. Restrictions on the use of property imposed for the benefit of more than one parcel of property, usually a tract containing many lots.

GI Loan. Loans available to veterans of the armed services under a federal government program administered by the Veterans Administration.

Gift Deed. A deed where there is no material consideration; often given in consideration of "love and affection," especially between relatives.

GNMA. Government National Mortgage Association. Popularly known (for its initials) as Ginny Mae (or Ginny May). An agency of HUD, which functions in the secondary mortgage market, primarily in special housing programs.

Good Will. An intangible, salable asset arising from the reputation of a business and its relations with its customers, distinct from the value of its stock in trade and other tangibles.

Gore. A small, rectangular piece of land. There is a saying, "A court abhors bits and gores."

Government Survey. A method of specifying the location of parcels of land using prime meridians, base lines, standard parallels, guide meridians, townships and sections.

Grade. Ground level at the foundation of a building.

Graduated Lease. A lease which provides for a varying rental rate, often based upon future determination, such as periodical appraisals; used mostly in long-term leases.

Graduated Payment Mortgage. Provides for partially deferred payments of principal at start of loan. There are a variety of plans; usually after the first five years of the loan term the principal and interest payments are substantially higher, to make up the principal portion of payments lost at the beginning of the loan. (See **Variable Interest Rate**).

Grandfather Clause. A clause creating an exemption based on previously existing circumstances.

Grant. A transfer of real property by deed.

Grant Deed. A form of deed used in the transfer of real property; distinguished from a quitclaim deed.

Grantee. The person to whom a grant is made.

Grantor. The person who makes a grant.

Gratuitous Agent. A person not paid by the principal for services on behalf of the principal, who cannot be forced to act as an agent, but who becomes bound to act in good faith and obey a principal's instructions once he or she undertakes to act as an agent.

Grazing Rights. A right to pasture cattle or other livestock on the property of another person.

GRI. Graduate, Realtors Institute.

Groin. Any structure offering or intended to offer substantial resistance to the coastwise movements of littoral sands (sands along the shore).

Gross Income. Total income from property before any expenses are deducted.

Gross National Product (GNP). The total value of all goods and services produced in an economy during a given period of time.

Gross Profit. What is left after a business pays all its bills excluding taxes. See **Net Profit**.

Gross Rate. A method of collecting interest by adding total interest to the principal of the loan at the outset of the term.

Gross Rent Multiplier. A number which, times the gross income of a property, produces an estimate of value of the property. Example: The gross income from an unfurnished apartment building is $200,000 per annum. If an appraiser uses a gross multiplier of seven percent, then it is said that based on the gross multiplier the value of the building is $1,400,000.

Ground Lease. An agreement for the rental of the land only; sometimes secured by improvements placed on the land by the tenant.

Ground Rent. Earnings of improved property credited to earnings of the ground itself after allowance is made for earnings of the improvements; often termed *economic rent.*

Guarantee. An assurance or undertaking as to the performance or quality or accuracy of a product.

Guaranty. A promise to answer for the payment of another person's debt or obligation.

Guardian. A person appointed by the probate court to care for the person or estate of a minor or incompetent person.

Habendum. That clause in a deed which states, "to have and to hold to said grantee, his heirs, successors and assigns, forever." Not required in California.

Hand. A linear measure equal to 4 inches.

Hard Money Loan. Loan from a private lender through an intermediary; actual money loaned, secured by a trust deed, as distinguished from a purchase money trust deed in favor of a seller.

Hazard Insurance. Insurance of property against such risks as fire, wind, floods, etc.

HBM. Humboldt base and meridian, one of the three principal bases and meridians in California.

Heirs. The persons designated by law to succeed to the estate of a decedent who leaves no will.

Hereditaments. Anything capable of being inherited.

Highest and Best Use. An appraisal term meaning that type of use which will produce the greatest return to the land and improvements over a given period of time.

Holder in Due Course. A phrase encountered under the Negotiable Instrument Law. Refers to a person who has taken a promissory note, check, or bill of exchange in due course before the due date, in good faith and for value, and without knowledge of any defects.

Holdover Tenant. Tenant who remains in possession of leased property after the expiration of the lease term.

Holographic Will. A will entirely written, dated, and signed by the testator in his own handwriting.

Homestead. A home upon which the owner has recorded a Declaration of Homestead under California law which affords protection from creditors' claims up to a specified amount. Exemption may also be claimed in an action for money without recording a Declaration of Homestead under prescribed conditions. Also, under federal law, the limited right to claim a small tract of the public domain by establishing residence or making improvement on the land. The latter is sometimes referred to as a *jackrabbit homestead.*

Horizontal. Measured or contained in a plane parallel to the horizon and to level ground; at right angles to the vertical.

Hostile. A claim to possession of land in denial of the validity of claims of another person, including the record owner.

Housing Financial Discrimination Act of 1977. California Health and Safety Code Section 35800, et seq., designed primarily to eliminate discrimination in lending practices based upon the character of the neighborhood in which real property is located. (See **Redlining**).

HUD. Housing and Urban Development, an agency of the federal government.

Hundred Percent Location. A city retail business location which is considered the best available for attracting business.

Hypothecate. To give a thing as security without parting with possession.

I.e., That is to say (abbreviation of the Latin *id est*).

Implied. Presumed or inferred, rather than expressed.

Impound Accounts. Funds retained in a special account by a secured lender to cover such items as taxes and hazard insurance on the property.

Improvement(s). Buildings and other structures on real property; a valuable addition made to the land.

Inchoate. Incomplete; not perfected (such as an attachment lien which is dependent upon a later judgment being entered before the property can be sold to satisfy the claim).

Income Approach (Capitalization). One of the three methods of the appraisal process generally applied to income producing property. It involves a three-step process: (1) find net annual income, (2) set an appropriate capitalization rate or "present worth" factor, and (3) capitalize the income dividing the net income by the capitalization rate.

Income Participation Loan. A mortgage loan whose terms give the mortgagee the right to share in a portion of the mortgaged property's future income.

Income Tax. A tax imposed on gross income from a business or enterprise. Income tax laws (both federal and state) also apply to gains on real estate sales, and deductions are allowed for losses on such sales.

Incompetent. Unable to manage or incapable of managing one's own affairs, based on such factors as minority, illness, old age, insanity, etc.

Incorporeal. Intangible; without physical existence but existing as a legal right, such as a cause of action.

Increment. An increase; most frequently used to refer to the increased value of land based on population growth and increasing wealth in the community. The term *unearned increment* is used in this connection, since values supposedly increase without effort on the part of the owner.

Incumbrance. See **Encumbrance**.

Indenture. Deeds or other instruments that are executed by both parties.

Independent Contractor. A person who acts for another but who sells final results and whose methods of achieving those results are not subject to the control of another.

Indorsement. See **Endorsement**.

Ingress. A means or way of entering onto property.

Inheritance. Property passing at the owner's death to his or her heirs; i.e., those entitled by law to succeed to the owner's estate.

Injunction. An order of a court of equity prohibiting some act, or compelling an act to be done.

In Personam. "Against the person," such as an action against a person for money damages. Distinguished from an action *in rem* (against property).

In Propria Persona. "In his own person"; by himself, as in an action where the party acts as his or her own attorney (abbreviated as *pro per*).

Input. Data, information, etc., that is fed into a computer or other system.

In Re. In the matter of.

In Rem. Against a thing or property and not against a person. For instance, an action to quiet title to real property is an action *in rem*.

Installment Note. A promissory note providing for payment of the principal in two or more certain amounts at stated or periodic times.

Installment Sales Contract. Commonly called contract of sale or **Land Contract**. Purchase of real estate wherein the purchase price is paid in installments over a long period of time, title is retained by seller, and upon default by buyer (vendee) the payments may be forfeited.

Institutional Lenders. A financial intermediary or depository, such as a savings and loan association, commercial bank, or life insurance company, which pools money of its depositors and then invests funds in various ways, including trust deed and mortgage loans.

Instrument. A writing, such as a deed, made and executed as the expression of some act, contract, or proceeding.

Insurable Interest. An interest in property of such a nature that the occurrence of the event insured against would cause financial loss to the insured. Such interests may be that of an owner, a mortgagee, a lessee, a trustee, etc.

Insurance. Coverage by contract in which one party (the insurer) agrees to indemnify or reimburse another (the insured) for any loss or damage that may occur under the terms of the contract.

Intangible. Incapable of being perceived by the senses, as incorporeal or immaterial things; also, existing only in connection with something else, such as an intangible asset in the form of the good will of a business.

Inter. Among or between, such as interstate commerce, i.e., commerce between the states.

Interest. A share, right, or title in the ownership of land or the degree thereof; also, a sum paid or charged for the use of money.

Interest Rate. The percentage of a sum of money charged for its use.

Interim Loan. A short-term, temporary loan used until permanent financing is available, e.g., a construction loan.

Interlocutory Decree. A court decree that does not finally dispose of an action but requires that some further steps be taken, e.g., an interlocutory decree in a condemnation action.

Intermediation. The process of pooling and supplying funds for investment by financial institutions called intermediaries. The process is dependent on individual savers placing their funds with these institutions and foregoing opportunities to directly invest in the investments selected.

Interpleader. An action brought by a third party (such as an escrow holder) in order to determine conflicting rights between two or more other parties (such as the principals to the escrow).

Intervene. To interpose and become a party to an action between two or more other parties in order to protect some interest or right in the subject matter of the action.

Inter Vivos. Between living persons, such as an inter vivos trust, as distinguished from a **Testamentary Trust**.

Intestate. Without a will; a person who died without leaving a will.

Intra. Within, such as *intrastate*, i.e., a transaction comsummated entirely within the state.

Inure. To accrue to the benefit of a person.

Inventory. The amount of stock in trade or goods of a business.

Involuntary Lien. A lien not voluntarily created by the debtor, such as a judgment lien.

Ipso Facto. Of itself; by the very fact.

Irrevocable. Incapable of being recalled, revoked, or withdrawn; unchangeable.

Irrigation Districts. Quasi-political districts of the state created under special laws to provide for water services to property owners in the district.

Jarvis-Gann Initiative. See **Proposition 13**.

Joinder. Acting jointly with one or more other persons; joining, such as joinder of causes of action.

Joint Note. A note signed by two or more persons who have equal liability for payment.

Joint Tenancy. Title held by two or more persons in equal shares with right of survivorship, i.e., when one joint tenant dies, his interest vests in the surviving joint tenant or tenants.

Joint Venture. Two or more individuals or firms joining together on a single project as partners.

Judgment. The final determination by a court having jurisdiction over the parties and subject matter of the action, of a matter presented to it for decision.

Judgment Lien. A statutory lien created by recording an abstract or certified copy of a judgment for money in the county recorder's office.

Junior Lien. A subordinate or inferior lien; behind another lien.

Junior Mortgage. A mortgage recorded subsequently to another mortgage on the same property or made subordinate by agreement to a later-recorded mortgage.

Jurat. A certificate or statement evidencing the fact that an affidavit was properly made before an authorized officer.

Jurisdiction. The power of a court to hear and determine a matter.

Key. The solution to a problem.

Key Lot. A lot so located that one side adjoins the rear of another lot; usually near a corner and considered less desirable.

Laches. Inexcusable delay in asserting a right; failure to do a thing at the proper time.

Land. The solid material of the earth and anything affixed permanently to it, including buildings, trees, minerals, water flowing on the land or beneath it, and air space above it.

Land Contract. A contract often used when property is sold on a small down payment where the seller does not choose to convey legal title until all or a certain portion of the purchase price has been paid by the buyer. Also referred to as a *land sales contract*.

Landlocked. Shut in completely by adjoining land without a means of access to or from a public highway or road.

Landlord. An owner of real property who leases it to a third party, called the *lessee* or *tenant*.

Landowner's Royalty. That interest in unsevered oil and gas which is retained or reserved by the landowner on the occasion of the transfer of an interest in the real property involved.

Lands, Tenements, and Hereditaments. Inheritable lands or interests therein.

Late Charge. A charge assessed by a lender against a borrower failing to make loan installment payments when due.

Latent. Hidden from view; concealed, such as a latent ambiguity in a document; distinguished from **Patent**.

Lateral Support. The support which the soil of an adjoining owner gives to a neighbor's land.

Lawful Object. Allowed or permitted by law; one of the requisites of a valid contract.

Lease. A contract for the possession of land for a designated period of time in consideration of payment of rent.

Leasehold Estate. A tenant's right to occupy real estate during the term of the lease. This is a personal property interest.

Legacy. A gift of money or other personal property by will.

Legal. Lawful; not contrary to law.

Legal Description. A description satisfactory in law, i.e., one by which property can be definitely located on the ground by reference to a recorded map or government survey.

Legatee. One to whom personal property is given by will.

Lessee. The tenant under a lease.

Lessor. The landlord under a lease, i.e., the person who transfers the right to occupy property to another person by a lease.

Level-Payment Mortgage. A loan on real estate that is paid off by making a series of equal (or nearly equal) regular payments. Part of the payment is usually interest on the loan and part of it reduces the amount of the unpaid principal balance of the loan. Also sometimes called an *amortized mortgage* or *installment mortgage*.

Leverage. Use of borrowed funds to purchase property in anticipation of substantial increase in value of the property; may produce a high return on a low down payment.

Levy. A seizure of property by judicial process, such as a levy under a writ of execution; a property tax is also a levy (collection of an assessment) under authority of law for governmental purposes.

Liability Insurance. Insurance covering the insured person against loss arising from injury or damage to another person or to property.

License. A personal privilege to enter upon or do some act on the land of another; also, authorization to engage in a business, an activity, or profession.

Licensee. A person to whom a license is issued or granted. In real estate, a person who has completed the requirements (including passing the examination) for a broker's or salesperson's license.

Lien. A charge upon property for the payment of a debt or performance of an obligation; a form of encumbrance. Liens include taxes, special assessments, and judgments, as well as mortgages. Additionally, there are mechanics' and material-men's liens for furnishing labor or materials to a work of improvement.

Life Estate. An estate in real property measured by the life of a natural person.

Limitations, Statute of. The commonly used identifying term for various statutes which require that a legal action be commenced within a prescribed time after the accrual of the right to seek legal relief.

Limited Partnership. A partnership composed of one or more general partners and one or more limited partners. The contribution and liability of the latter are limited.

Line. The outline or boundary of a piece of real estate.

Lineal. In a direct line, such as a lineal descendant.

Linear. Involving measurement in one dimension only; pertaining to length, such as a *linear measure*, i.e., a foot, a yard, a meter, etc.

Liquidated Damages. Damages in an ascertained amount that may be recovered in a lawsuit.

Liquidity. Holdings in or the ability to convert assets to cash or its equivalent. The ease with which a person is able to pay maturing obligations.

Lis Pendens. A recorded notice of the filing of an action affecting real property.

Listing. An employment contract between a real estate broker (as agent) and a principal authorizing the broker to perform services in connection with the sale, purchase, exchange, or leasing of real property. There are various types of listing agreements, such as open, exclusive agency, option, etc.

Littoral. Pertaining to the shore.

Livery of Seisen (Seizin). The appropriate ceremony at common law for transferring the possession of lands by a grantor to a grantee.

Loan Administration. A general term encompassing those aspects of a mortgage lending operation that deal with the administration or servicing of loans after they have been put on the books, e.g., collection of monthly payments, accounting for payments, handling of real estate taxes and hazard insurance.

Loan Application. The loan application is a source of information on which the lender bases a decision to make the loan; defines the terms of the loan contract, gives the name of the borrower, place of employment, salary, bank accounts, and credit references, and describes the real estate that is to be mortgaged. It also stipulates the amount of loan being applied for and repayment terms.

Loan Closing. When all conditions have been met, the loan officer authorizes the recording of the trust deed or mortgage. The disbursal procedure of funds is similar to the closing of a real estate sales escrow. The borrower can expect to receive less than the amount of the loan, as title, recording, service, and other fees may be withheld, or can expect to deposit the cost of these items into the loan escrow. This process is sometimes called "funding" the loan.

Loan Commitment. Lender's contractual commitment to make a loan on the appraisal and underwriting.

Loan Correspondent. One who acts as agent for lenders. Most often a large, incorporated mortgage banker representing institutional lenders such as eastern life insurance companies.

Loan Value. Value set on property to aid in determining the amount of a mortgage or trust deed loan to be made. Loan to value ratio is the percentage of a property's value that a lender can or may loan to a borrower. For example, if the ratio is 80 percent this means that a lender may loan 80 percent of the property's appraised value to a borrower.

Lot. A plot of ground.

LS. From the Latin *locus sigilli*, "the place of a seal." Often appears in an instrument instead of an actual seal.

MAI. Designates a person who is a member of the American Institute of Real Estate Appraisers of the National Association of Realtors (NAR).

Margin of Security. The difference between the amount of the mortgage loan or loans and the appraised value of the property.

Marginal Land. Land which barely pays the cost of working or using it.

Marketable Title. The status of a title when viewed in the light of whether or not it is in such a condition as to attract a purchaser; a title that is free from reasonable doubt in law and in fact.

Market Data Approach. One of the three methods in the appraisal process. A means of comparing similar type properties, which have recently sold, to the subject property. Commonly used in comparing residential properties.

Market Price. The price actually paid for property on the open market.

Market Value. The highest price estimated in terms of money which a property will bring if exposed for sale in the open market, allowing a reasonable time to find a purchaser with knowledge of the property's use and capabilities for use.

Marketable Title. Title which a reasonable purchaser, informed as to the facts and their legal importance and acting with reasonable care, would be willing and ought to accept.

Material Fact. Significant fact; a fact which, for instance, an agent realizes is likely to affect the judgment of the principal in giving his or her consent to the agent to enter into a particular transaction of the specified terms. For example, the amount of income from rental property is a material fact.

MDBM. Mt. Diablo base and meridian (in Contra Costa County).

Mean. Intermediate, such as mean high tide.

Meander. To follow a winding course; not fixed.

Meander Line. A zigzag traverse (series of distances and angles or bearings), to define the approximate margin of a natural body of water.

Mechanic's Lien. A statutory lien in favor of laborers and material men who have contributed to a work of improvement.

Memory Bank. Data and information held in storage in a computer.

Merger of Title. The absorption of one estate in another, such as the acquisition of land benefited by an easement by the owner of land burdened by the easement.

Meridians. Imaginary north-south lines which intersect base (east-west) lines to form a starting point for the measurement of land.

Mesne. Intermediate; intervening, such as previous conveyances in a chain of title.

Mesne Profits. Profits from land use accruing between two periods; e.g., money owed to the owner of land by a person who has illegally occupied the land after the owner takes title but before taking possession.

Metes. Measurements.

Metes and Bounds. Measurements and boundaries; a term used in describing the boundary lines of land, setting forth all the boundary lines together with their terminal points and angles.

Mile. 5,280 feet.

Minor. All persons under eighteen years of age. Prior to March 4, 1972, minors were persons under twenty-one years of age.

Misplaced Improvements. Improvements on land which do not conform to the most profitable use of the site.

Misrepresentation. A false or misleading statement or assertion.

Mobilehome. As defined in Business and Professions Code Section 10131.6(c), "mobilehome" means a structure transportable in one or more sections, designed and equipped to contain not more than two dwelling units to be used with or without a foundation system. "Mobilehome" does not include a recreational vehicle, as defined in Section 18010.5 of the Health and Safety Code; a commercial coach, as defined in Section 18012 of the Health and Safety Code; or factory-built housing, as defined in Section 19971 of the Health and Safety Code.

Modular. A system for the construction of dwellings and other improvements to real property through the on-site assembly of component parts (modules) that have been mass produced away from the building site.

Monetary Controls. Federal Reserve tools for regulating the availability of money and credit to influence the level of economic activity, e.g., adjusting discount rates, reserve requirements, etc.

Monument. A fixed object or point designated by surveyors to establish land locations.

Moratorium. The temporary suspension, usually by statute, of the enforcement of liability for debts.

Mortgage. A written document executed by the owner of land by which the land is given as security for the payment of a debt or performance of an obligation.

Mortgage Banker. A company or individual engaged in the business of originating mortgage loans with its own funds, selling those loans to long-term investors, and servicing the loans for the investor until they are paid in full.

Mortgage Guaranty Insurance. Insurance against financial loss available to mortgage lenders; in effect, guarantees payment of the debt; commonly referred to as *Private Mortgage Insurance (PMI)*.

Mortgage Investment Company. A company or group of private investors that buys mortgages for investment purposes.

Mortgage Loan Disclosure Statement. The statement on a form approved by the Real Estate Commissioner which is required by law to be furnished by a mortgage loan broker to the prospective borrower of loans of a statutorily prescribed amount before the borrower becomes obligated to complete the loan.

Mortgagee. The party who obtains the benefit of a mortgage; the lender.

Mortgagor. The party who executes a mortgage; the borrower.

Multiple Dwelling. A dwelling that is designed for occupancy by two or more families.

Multiple Listing. A listing, usually an exclusive right to sell, taken by a member of an organization composed of real estate brokers, with the provision that all members will have the opportunity to find an interested client, and the commission will be shared by the listing broker and the selling broker; a form of cooperative listing.

Muniments of Title. Deeds and other original documents showing a chain of title to a parcel of property.

Mutual. Reciprocal; possessed, experienced, understood, or performed by each of two or more persons. One of the requisites of a valid contract is *mutual consent*. Also, *mutual mistake*, either of a fact or law, may be grounds for avoiding a contract.

Mutual Savings Banks. Financial institutions owned by depositors, each of whom has rights to net earnings of the bank in proportion to his or her deposits.

Mutual Water Company. A water company organized by or for water users in a given district or area with the object of securing an ample water supply at a reasonable rate for its members who are issued shares of water stock.

NAR. National Association of Realtors.

NAREB. National Association of Real Estate Brokers.

Narrative Appraisal. A summary of all factual materials, techniques, and appraisal methods used by the appraiser in setting forth his or her value conclusion.

Natural Person. A person who is born and will die someday; distinguished from an artificial person, such as a corporation.

Naturalization. The conferring of the rights of citizenship upon a person who was an alien.

Navigable Water. A waterway deep and wide enough to afford passage to ships.

Neap Tides. Those tides which happen between the full moon and change of the moon twice in every twenty-four hours.

Negotiable. Capable of being negotiated; transferable in the ordinary course of business, usually by endorsement.

Negotiable Instrument. A promissory note or check or certificate of deposit or draft (bill of exchange) which under the Negotiable Instruments Law (now contained in the Commercial Code), entitles an endorsee to greater rights than an assignee, under certain prescribed conditions.

Net. Amount remaining after deduction of charges and expenses.

Net Income. Gross annual income less allowable expenses.

Net Lease. A lease requiring a lessee to pay certain charges against the property such as taxes, insurance and maintenance costs in addition to rental payments.

Net Listing. A listing agreement which provides that the broker may retain as compensation for his or her services all sums received over and above a net price to the owner.

Net Net. A term commonly used in connection with leases which means that all monies received by the lessor as rent are over and above all expenses of ownership, including taxes.

Net Profit. What is left after all bills and taxes are paid.

Net Worth. The difference between assets and liabilities.

Nil. Nothing; naught; zero.

Notary Public. A public officer or other person authorized to authenticate contracts, acknowledge deeds, take affidavits, etc.

Note. A signed written instrument acknowledging a debt and promising payment.

Notice. Being made aware. There are three types of notice: (1) *Actual Notice.* Express knowledge of a fact. (2) *Constructive Notice.* A fact, imputed to a person by law, which should have been discovered because of the person's actual notice of circumstances and the inquiry that a prudent person would have been expected to make, or implied or inferred from the public records. (3) *Legal Notice.* Information required to be given by law.

Notice of Cessation. A notice recorded under the mechanic's lien law after work has ceased for a period of time. Shortens the time for filing mechanics' liens.

Notice of Completion. A notice recorded under the mechanic's lien law after completion of the work of improvement. Shortens the time for filing mechanics' liens.

Notice of Default. Recorded notice that a default has occurred under a deed of trust and that the beneficiary intends to proceed with a trustee's sale.

Notice of Nonresponsibility. Notice recorded by an owner of real property to relieve the land from mechanics' liens which may result from an improvement on the property by a tenant or by a purchaser under a land sales contract.

Notice to Pay Rent or Quit. Notice to a tenant to either pay rent that is due or vacate the premises. Also known as a three-day notice to quit.

Novation. The substitution of a new obligation in place of an existing one.

Nuisance. Anything that is offensive and works an injury or harm to a person or property.

Null. Without legal force and effect; not valid.

Nuncupative Will. An oral will; has limited application (applies only to personal property not exceeding $1000 in value).

Obiter Dictum. That which is said in passing (plural, *obiter dicta*). Remarks in a court's decision that are not strictly essential but which contain meaningful observations.

Obligatory. Mandatory, such as obligatory advances under a deed of trust; compared with *optional.*

Obligor. One who places himself or herself under a legal obligation, e.g., a mortgagor or trustor under a deed of trust.

Obsolescence. Impairment of desirability and usefulness of property; one of the causes of depreciation in value of property. Economic obsolescence is due to changes in the character of the neighborhood. Functional obsolescence relates to the declining usefulness of the structure itself.

Offer to Purchase. The proposal made to an owner of property by a potential buyer to purchase the property under stated terms.

Offset Statement. Statement furnished to an escrow from a tenant regarding his or her right of possession (payment of rent, security deposits, etc.); also, by an owner of land subject to an encumbrance as to the unpaid balance.

Omnibus Clause. A clause in a decree of distribution by which property owned by the decedent but not described in the proceeding will pass to the distributees without specific mention; also, as used in a mortgage, refers to all property owned by the mortgagor without specific description.

Open End Mortgage. A mortgage which secures additional advances which the lender may make to the mortgagor; permits the mortgagor to borrow additional money without rewriting the mortgage.

Open Housing Law. Congress passed a law in April, 1968 which prohibits descrimination in the sale of real estate because of race, color, or religion of buyers. California has enacted comparable laws.

Open Listing. A nonexclusive listing; provides that the broker is to receive a commission if he or she is the first one to obtain a buyer ready, willing, and able to purchase the property on the seller's terms. Open listings may be given to any number of agents.

Operating Expenses. Expenses incurred in the operation of a business.

Operative Words. Words in a deed or lease that effect a transfer of title to or an interest in property; a requisite of any conveyance.

Option. A right given for a consideration to acquire property upon specified terms within a specified period of time.

Optional. Not obligatory; discretionary.

Optionee. The person who is given an option by the owner of property.

Option Listing. A type of listing which gives the broker the option to buy the property for a specified price.

Optionor. The person (owner) who gives an option to another person.

Oral. Spoken; verbal.

Oral Contract. A contract not in writing.

Ordinance. A legislative enactment of a city or county.

Orientation. Placing a house on its lot with regard to its exposure to the rays of the sun, prevailing winds, privacy from the street, and protection from outside noises.

Original Contractor. Under the mechanic's lien law, a contractor who contracts directly with the owner of real property; others are designated as subcontractors.

Outlawed Claim. A claim that can no longer be prosecuted because barred by the statute of limitations.

Overimprovement. An improvement which is not the highest and best use for the site on which it is placed by reason of excess size or cost.

Overriding Royalty. That interest in unsevered oil and gas which the lessee under an oil and gas lease may retain when executing a sublease or an assignment.

Overt. Open; not concealed.

Ownership. The right to the use and enjoyment of property to the exclusion of others.

Own-Your-Own Apartment. Joint ownership of an apartment building as tenants in common, with the exclusive right of each individual owner to occupy a specified unit.

Package Mortgage. A type of mortgage used in home financing covering real property, improvements, and movable equipment/appliances.

Par. An equality in value; the state of a loan which is purchasable at face value.

Paramount Title. Title which is superior or foremost to all others.

Partial. Affecting a part only.

Partial Payments. Parts of payments which are collected on a note and usually held until the total collections amount to a full payment.

Partial Reconveyance. A release of a part only of the property described in a deed of trust.

Partial Release Clause. A clause in a deed of trust that requires the beneficiary, under prescribed conditions, to cause a designated portion of the property to be released prior to payment in full of the obligation.

Participation. Sharing of an interest in a property by a lender. In addition to base interest on mortgage loans on income properties, a percentage of gross income is required, sometimes predicated on certain conditions being fulfilled, such as a minimum occupancy or a percentage of net income after expenses, debt service and taxes. Also called *equity participation* or *revenue sharing*.

Parties. Persons who are involved in a lawsuit, designated as plaintiffs and defendants; also, those entities taking part in a transaction as a principal, e.g., seller, buyer, or lender in a real estate transaction.

Partition. An action which seeks to have property owned by two or more persons sold and the proceeds divided, or the property itself divided between the parties if physical division of the property is practical.

Partnership. A voluntary association of two or more persons to carry on as co-owners of a business for profit.

Party Wall. A wall for the common benefit and use of adjoining owners of property, their property being separated by the wall.

Par Value. Face value.

Patent. A conveyance of the title to public lands by the federal government. Also, when used as an adjective, it means something that is evident or obvious, such as a *patent* ambiguity in a document, and as such is distinguished from **latent** or hidden.

Penalty. A loss or forfeiture resulting from non-fulfillment of a contractual obligation, such as payment of an additional amount, called a late charge, if a note becomes delinquent.

Per Autre Vie. During the life of another. A life estate, for instance, may be measured by the life of a person other than the one who has the life estate, and would be referred to as a life estate *per autre vie*.

Per Capita. By the head. In the distribution of an estate, persons are said to take per capita when each one claims in his or her own right, based on an equal degree of kinship, an equal share of the estate. It is compared with the term *per stirpes*, which means by right of representation (according to the roots). In the latter situation the children of a deceased heir would all take but one share and would not share equally with the other heirs in their own right.

Percentage Lease. A lease under which the rent is computed as a percentage of the gross receipts from the business of the tenant, with provision (usually) for a minimum rental.

Periodic Tenancy. Tenancy for specified periods, such as month to month, which can be terminated at any time by either party on proper notice.

Per Se. By itself; as such.

Personal Property. Movable property; all property consisting of chattels as contrasted with real estate, e.g., furniture, car, clothing, etc.

Per Stirpes. According to the roots; by right of representation (see **Per Capita**).

Physical Deterioration. Impairment of condition. Loss in value brought about by wear and tear, disintegration, use, and actions of the elements; termed *curable* and *incurable*.

PIQ. Property in question; i.e., the property that is the subject of a title search.

Plaintiff. The party who brings a court action.

Planned Unit Development (PUD). A land-use design which provides intensive utilization of the land through a combination of private and common areas with prearranged sharing of responsibilities for the common areas. Individual lots are owned in fee with joint ownership of the open areas.

Planning Commission. The city or county agency that administers zoning regulations.

Plans and Specifications. Building plans with a detailed description of the requirements, dimensions, materials, etc., of the proposed structure.

Pleadings. The successive statements filed in an action by which the plaintiff sets forth his or her cause and claim, and the defendant sets forth his or her defense.

Pledge. The depositing of personal property by a debtor with a creditor as security for a debt or other obligation.

Pledgee. One who is given a pledge as security.

Pledgor. One who gives a pledge as security.

Plottage Increment. The appreciation in unit value created by joining smaller ownerships into one large single ownership.

POB. Point of beginning; the commencement point in a good and sufficient legal description of land.

Points. Additional charges for obtaining a loan computed like interest; i.e., one point is comparable to one percent interest.

Police Power. The power to enact laws and regulations deemed necessary for the common welfare.

Power of Attorney. A written authorization to an agent to perform specified acts on behalf of his or her principal. May be a *general* power or a *limited* power. Also, may be a *durable* power or a *springing* power.

Power of Sale. As used in a will, authorizes the executor to sell estate property without the necessity of publishing a notice of sale.

PRD. Planned residential development. Used interchangeably with PUD, planned unit development.

Preamble. An introductory statement; preface; the introductory part of a statute, deed, or other document.

Precedent. Used as an adjective, means going before, such as a *condition precedent*, i.e., a condition or event which must first occur before an estate can be terminated.

Pre-emption. Right to purchase before or in preference to others, such as a right of first refusal.

Prefabricated House. A house manufactured and sometimes partly assembled before delivery to a building site.

Preferred Stock. A class of corporate stock entitled to preferential treatment such as priority in distribution of dividends.

Prepaid Items of Expense. Prorations of prepaid items of expense which are credited to the seller in the closing escrow statement.

Prepayment. Provision made for loan payments to be larger than those specified in the note.

Prepayment Penalty. Penalty by way of an additional payment for the privilege of paying in full a mortgage or trust deed note prior to the due date.

Prescribe. To set forth in writing, such as a statute, a rule, or a course to be followed.

Prescription. The obtaining of title to or a right in property by adverse possession, i.e., by occupying it openly, notoriously, and hostilely for a five-year period. By paying the real property taxes, the fee title can be claimed.

Prescriptive Easement. An easement obtained by prescription (adverse possession); payment of taxes is not required to obtain an easement by prescription.

Present Value. The lump sum value today of an annuity. A $100 bill to be paid to someone in one year is worth less than if it were a $100 bill to be paid to someone today. This is due to several things, one of which is that the money has time value. How much the $100 bill to be paid in one year is worth today will depend on the interest rate that seems proper for the particular circumstances. For example, if 6% is the appropriate rate, the $100 to be paid one year from now would be worth $94.34 today.

Presumption. That which may be assumed as true without further proof. May be either a conclusive presumption or a rebuttable presumption.

Pretermitted Heir. A forgotten child; a child not mentioned in a will.

Prima Facie. Presumptive on its face; assumed correct unless overcome by further proof.

Primary Money Market. A market where loans are made directly to borrowers by a lender who retains the loan in his portfolio rather than sell it to an investor.

Prime. Of the greatest commercial value, such as a prime building lot.

Principal. This term is used to mean the employer of an agent; or the amount of money borrowed, or the amount of the loan. Also, one of the main parties in a real estate transaction, such as a buyer, borrower, seller, lessor.

Principle. An accepted or professed rule of action or conduct.

Prior. Earlier in point of time or right.

Priority. The state or quality of being earlier in point of time or right, as the priority of a first mortgage over a second mortgage.

Private Mortgage Insurance. Mortgage guaranty insurance available to conventional lenders on the first, high risk portion of a loan (PMI).

Privity. Closeness or mutuality of relationship.

Privity of Contract. The relationship which exists between the persons who are parties to a contract; the original contracting parties.

Pro. In favor of a proposition (opposite of *con*).

Probate Court. Department of the Superior Court which has authority over the estates of decedents, minors, incompetents, and missing persons.

Procuring Cause. The cause of originating a series of events that leads to the consummation of a real estate sale and normally entitles a broker to a commission.

Profit. Pecuniary gain resulting from the employment of capital in any transaction.

Profit à Prendre. The right to take part of the soil or produce of land.

Progress Payments. Scheduled, periodic, and partial payment of construction loan funds to a builder as each construction stage is completed.

Progression, Principle of. The worth of a lesser valued residence tends to be enhanced by association with higher valued residences in the same area.

Promissory Note. A written obligation containing a promise to pay a definite amount of money at or prior to a specified time.

Property. Anything of which there may be ownership; classified as either *real* property or *personal* property.

Property Management. A branch of the real estate business involving the marketing, operation, maintenance and day-to-day financing of rental properties.

Pro Per. See **In Propria Persona.**

Proposition 13. A 1978 initiative limiting amount of property taxes that may be assessed to one percent of market value.

Pro Rata. In proportion; according to a certain rate.

Proration. A proportionate division or splitting of taxes and other expenses and income from real estate between buyer and seller in a sales escrow transaction; usually computed as of date escrow closes.

Proscribe. Prohibit.

Prospective. Applicable in the future, as opposed to retroactive.

Proximate Cause. That cause of an event which, in a natural and continuous sequence unbroken by any new cause, produced that event, and without which the event would not have happened. Also, the **Procuring Cause.**

Public Records. As used in a title policy, those records which impart constructive notice of matters relating to the land described in the policy.

Public Report. Report of the real estate commissioner containing information about subdivided property.

PUD. Planned unit development (see).

Purchase and Installment Saleback. Involves purchase of the property upon completion of construction and immediate saleback on a long-term installment contract.

Purchase of Land, Leaseback, and Leasehold Mortgages. An arrangement whereby land is purchased by the lender and leased back to the developer with a mortgage negotiated on the resulting leasehold of the income property constructed. The lender receives an annual ground rent, plus a percentage of income from the property.

Purchase and Leaseback. Involves the purchase of property by buyer and immediate leaseback to seller.

Purchase Money Mortgage. A mortgage (or trust deed) given as part or all of the purchase price of real estate.

Pyramid. To build an estate by multiple acquisitions of property.

Quantity Survey. A highly technical process in arriving at cost estimate of new construction and sometimes referred to in the building trade as the *price take-off* method. It involves a detailed estimate of the quantities of raw material (lumber, plaster, brick, cement, etc.) used as well as the current price of the material and installation costs. These factors are all added together to arrive at the cost of a structure. It is usually used by contractors and experienced estimators.

Quasi. Of similar nature; seemingly but not actually.

Quasi Contract. A contract implied by law to prevent unjust enrichment.

Quiet Enjoyment. Right of an owner to the use of property without interference of possession.

Quiet Title. A court action to establish title to real property; similar in effect to an action to remove a cloud on title.

Quitclaim Deed. A deed which conveys whatever present right, title, or interest the party executing the deed may have.

Rancho. A large parcel of land used primarily for grazing purposes.

Range. Part of a government survey; one of a series or divisions numbered east or west from the principal meridian of the survey and consisting of a row or tier of townships, each six miles square, which in turn are numbered north or south from a base line, e.g., Township 1 North, Range 3 East, SBBM (San Bernardino base and meridian).

Ratable. Proportionate, such as ratable distribution of wealth.

Rate. The amount of a charge or payment, such as interest rate.

Ratification. The adoption or approval of an act performed on behalf of a person without previous authorization.

Ratify. To confirm or approve.

Raw Land. Land on which there are no improvements, such as buildings or other structures; undeveloped land.

Re. With reference to; in the case of; regarding.

Ready, Willing, and Able Buyer. One who is fully prepared to enter into the contract, really wants to buy, and unquestionably meets the financing requirements of purchase.

Real Estate. Real property; land and things affixed to land or appurtenant to land.

Real Estate Board. A local organization whose members consist primarily of real estate brokers and salespersons; affiliated with both the state association (CAR) and national board (NAR).

Real Estate Investment Trust (REIT). An association recognized under federal and state laws whereby investors may pool funds for investments in real estate and mortgages and avoid taxation as a corporation.

Real Estate Law. As codified in California, relates to the provisions of the Business and Professions Code creating the Department of Real Estate. Under this law the real estate commissioner has regulatory and disciplinary authority over real estate licenses, land sale transactions such as the sale of subdivided lands in or outside the state, and other related transactions.

Real Estate Settlement Procedures Act (RESPA). A federal law requiring the disclosure to borrowers of settlement (closing) procedures and costs by means of a pamphlet and forms prescribed by the United States Department of Housing and Urban Development.

Real Estate Syndicate. An organization of investors, usually in the form of a limited partnership, who have joined together for the purpose of pooling capital for the acquisition of real property interests.

Real Estate Trust. A special arrangement under Federal and State law whereby investors may pool funds for investments in real estate and mortgages and yet escape corporation taxes, profits being passed to investors who are taxed as individuals.

Real Property. Land and things attached to land or appurtenant to land; distinguished from personal property or chattels.

Real Property Loan Law. Article 7 of Chapter 3 of the Real Estate Law under which a real estate licensee negotiating loans secured by real property within a specified range is required to give the borrower a statement disclosing the costs and terms of the loan and which also limits the amount of expenses and charges that a borrower may pay with respect to the loan.

Real Property Sales Contract. An agreement to convey title to real property upon satisfaction of specified conditions which does not require conveyance within one year of formation of the contract.

Realtist. A member of the National Association of Real Estate Brokers.

Realtor. A real estate broker holding active membership in a real estate board affiliated with the National Association of Realtors (NAR).

Rebuttable Presumption. A presumption that is not conclusive; it may be contradicted by evidence.

Recapture. The rate of interest necessary to provide for the return *of* an investment (i.e., return of capital); distinguished from interest rate, which is the rate of interest *on* an investment (i.e., rate of return). May be more or less than the recapture amount.

Receipt. Written acknowledgment that money or other thing of value was received; as used in real estate practice, a deposit receipt when duly executed is also evidence of a contract between a buyer and seller.

Receiver. A person appointed by a court, such as a bankruptcy court, to take charge of a business or property of other persons, pending litigation.

Reconciliation. The act of bringing into harmony or agreement, such as reconciling an account, i.e., making it compatible or consistent.

Reconveyance. A conveyance to the landowner of the title held by a trustee under a deed of trust.

Record. An official writing or other document to be preserved; used as a verb, it means to make a public record of a document.

Recordation. Filing for record in the office of the county recorder.

Record of Survey. A recorded survey made in conformity with the practice of land surveying by a licensed land surveyor or registered civil engineer.

Recovery Fund. A fund established by the Department of Real Estate from license fees to underwrite uncollectable court judgments against licensees based on fraud.

Redemption. Buying back one's property after a judicial sale, such as an execution or foreclosure sale.

Redemption Period. The time allowed by law during which the owner may redeem his or her property by paying, for instance, the amount of the sale on a foreclosed mortgage.

Redlining. A lending policy, illegal in California, of denying real estate loans on properties in older, changing urban areas, usually with large minority populations, because of alleged higher lending risks without due consideration being given by the lending institution to the creditworthiness of the individual loan applicant.

Refinancing. The paying-off of an existing obligation and assuming a new obligation in its place. To finance anew, or extend or renew existing financing.

Reformation. An action to correct a mistake in a deed or other document.

Regulate. To control or direct by a rule or law.

Regulation. A rule or direction prescribed under the authority of a statute, such as regulations of the real estate commissioner.

Rehabilitation. The restoration of a property to satisfactory condition without drastically changing the plan, form or style of architecture.

Reinstate. To cure a default under a note secured by deed of trust.

Release Clause. A clause in a deed of trust providing for release of specified portions of the property upon compliance with certain conditions.

Reliction. Gradual recession of water from the usual water line or mark.

Remainder. A right to future possession after the expiration of a life estate.

Rent. Consideration paid for the use and possession of property under a rental agreement.

Rents, Issues, and Profits. The yield or proceeds from land or other property.

REO. Real estate owned by a lender which was acquired on foreclosure of a loan.

Replacement Cost. The cost to replace a structure with one having utility equivalent to that being appraised, but constructed with modern materials and according to current standards, design and layout.

Reproduction Cost. The cost of replacing the subject improvement with one that is the exact replica, having the same quality of workmanship, design and layout, or cost to duplicate an asset.

Res. An object or thing or matter.

Rescission. An action to cancel or annul the effect of executing a contract or other document, based on fraud, mistake, etc.

Rescission of Contract. The abrogation or annulling of contract; the revocation or repealing of contract by mutual consent by parties to the contract, or for cause by either party to the contract.

Reservation. The creation on behalf of the grantor (in a deed) of a new right issuing out of the property granted, such as the reservation of a mineral interest.

Residual Cost. Accounting term for *book value*; the cost of a fixed asset, less any portion of the cost that has been treated as an expense, such as depreciation.

Residue. That portion of a decedent's estate that has not been specifically devised.

RESPA. (See **Real Estate Settlement Procedures Act**.)

Restriction. An encumbrance created by deed or agreement which limits the use and enjoyment of property; often created by a recorded Declaration of Covenants, Conditions and Restrictions (CC&R).

Resulting Trust. A trust which is implied in law from the acts or relationship of parties, such as a situation where one party furnishes the consideration for a deed but title is taken in the name of another person for convenience.

Retroactive. Operative with respect to past transactions or occurrences.

Return. A yield or profit from land or other property.

Return Premium. The refund of unearned advance premium resulting from cancellation of a hazard insurance policy prior to its expiration date or the date to which the premium has been paid.

Reversion. The residue of an estate remaining with a grantor after the expiration or termination of a lesser estate, such as an estate for years.

Reversionary Interest. The interest a person has in lands or other property upon the expiration or termination of a preceding estate.

Revocation. Nullification or cancellation or withdrawal, such as revocation of an offer to sell or an offer to buy a parcel of property.

Right of Redemption. The statutory right to buy back one's property after a judicial sale during a prescribed period of time, usually one year.

Right of Suvivorship. The distinguishing feature of joint tenancy, i.e., when one joint tenant dies, title vests automatically in the survivor without probate.

Right of Way. A right to cross or pass over, across, or under another person's land, for such purposes as ingress and egress, utility lines, sewer pipes, etc.

Right, Title and Interest. A term used in deeds to denote that the grantor is conveying all of that to which the grantor held claim.

Riparian. Pertaining to the bank of a river.

Riparian Rights. The right of a landowner to water located on, under, or adjacent to his or her land.

Risk Analysis. A study made, usually by a lender, of the various factors that might affect the repayment of a loan.

Risk Rating. A process used by the lender to decide on the soundness of making a loan and to reduce all the various factors affecting the repayment of the loan to a qualified rating of some kind.

Royalty. Compensation or portion of the proceeds payable to an owner as rent under an oil and gas lease.

Rural. Pertaining to the country, as distinguished from the city.

Sale. Transfer of property for money or credit.

Sale-Leaseback. A transaction where the owner of a parcel of property sells it to another person (buyer) and retains physical possession by leasing it from the buyer.

Sales Contract. A contract by which a buyer and a seller of property agree to the terms of a sale.

Sales Escrow. See **Escrow.**

Sales Tax. Tax on the sale of tangible personal property.

Salvage Value. In computing depreciation for tax purposes, the reasonably anticipated fair market value of the property at the end of its useful life, which must be considered with all but the declining balance methods of depreciation.

Sandwich Lease. A leasehold interest which lies between the primary lease and the operating lease; an in-between lease.

Sans. Without.

Satisfaction. Performance of the terms of an obligation.

Satisfied. Paid in full; fully performed.

Saving and Loan Associations. Either federally chartered or state licensed lending institutions that account for the greatest share of the home loan market.

SBBM. San Bernardino base and meridian.

Seal. An impression upon a document that lends authenticity to its execution.

Secondary Financing. A loan secured by a second mortgage or trust deed on real property.

Secondary Money Market. A market in which existing mortgages are bought, sold or borrowed against, as distinguished from a *primary market*. The latter is made up of lenders who supply funds directly to borrowers and hold the mortgage until the debt is paid.

Section. One of the divisions employed in a government survey; measures one mile on each side and contains 640 acres of land.

Secured Party. The party having a security interest, such as a mortgagee, conditional seller, pledgee, etc.

Security. Something of value given or deposited to secure payment of a debt or performance of an obligation.

Security Agreement. Document now used in place of a chattel mortgage as evidence of a lien on personal property. A *financing statement* may be filed or recorded to give constructive notice of the security agreement.

Security Deposit. A deposit of money or other thing of value made to assure performance of an obligation; frequently required of lessees or tenants.

Security Interest. The interest of the creditor in the property of the debtor in all types of secured transactions.

Seisen. The possession of land under a claim of a freehold estate (also spelled *seizen*).

Seller's Market. The market condition which exists when a seller is in a more commanding position as to price and terms because demand exceeds supply.

Senior Lien. A lien that is ahead of or prior to or superior to another lien on the same property. Distinguished from *junior* lien.

Separate Property. Property of a married person acquired before marriage, and property acquired during marriage by gift, devise, descent, or bequest. Distinguished from *community* property.

Servicing Loans. Supervising and administering a loan after it has been made. This involves such things as: collecting the payments, keeping accounting records, computing the interest and principal, foreclosure of defaulted loans, and so on.

Servient Tenement. An estate burdened by an easement.

Servitude. A right in the nature of an easement in another person's property.

Setback Ordinance. An ordinance prohibiting the erection of a building or structure between the curb and the setback line.

Severalty Ownership. Sole ownership; owned by one person only, as compared with co-ownership, or ownership by two or more persons.

Sheriff's Deed. Deed given pursuant to an execution sale of real property to satisfy a judgment.

Shopping Center, Regional. A large shopping center with 250,000 to 1,000,000 square feet of store area, serving 200,000 or more people.

Sill. The lowest part of the frame of a house, resting on the foundation and supporting the uprights of the frame. The board or metal forming the lower side of an opening, as a door sill, window sill, etc.

Simple Interest. Interest computed on the principal amount of a loan only, as distinguished from compound interest.

Single Person. A person who has never been married. See **Unmarried Person.**

Sinking Fund. A fund created for the purpose of extinguishing an indebtedness, usually a bond issue; also, fund set aside from the income from property which, with accrued interest, will eventually pay for replacement of the improvements.

Situs. Location.

Slander of Title. False and malicious statements disparaging an owner's title to property and resulting in actual pecuniary damage to the owner.

Social and Economic Obsolescence. Reduction in value of property due to factors outside of the property; compared with **functional obsolescence**.

Special Assessments. Charges against real property imposed by a public authority to pay for the cost of local improvements, such as street lights, sidewalks, curbs, etc., as distinguished from taxes levied for the general support of the government (police and fire protection, etc.).

Specifications. See **Plans and Specifications**.

Specific Performance. An action to compel performance of an agreement such as an agreement for the sale of purchase of land.

Spouse. A husband or wife.

SRA. Designates a person who is a member of the Society of Real Estate Appraisers.

Standby Commitment. The mortgage banker frequently protects a builder by a *standby* agreement, under which banker agrees to make mortgage loans at an agreed price for many months into the future. The builder deposits a *standby fee* with the mortgage banker for this service. Frequently, the mortgage broker protects himself or herself by securing a standby from a long-term investor for the same period of time, paying a fee for this privilege.

Stare Decisis. The doctrine that the decisions of the court should stand as a precedent for future guidance.

State Contractors License Law. Law designed to protect the public against unqualified building contractors; establishes standards and requirements that must be met by contractors.

State Housing Law. State law which prescribes minimum building standards.

Status. The standing of a person before the law, i.e., whether an adult, a married person, etc.

Statute. Federal laws enacted by Congress, and state laws enacted by the state legislature.

Statute of Frauds. State law which provides that certain contracts must be in writing to be enforceable, such as a contract for the sale of land, or a contract to pay a real estate broker a commission.

Statute of Limitations. Law which limits the time within which court action may be brought to enforce rights or claims.

Statutory Law. See Civil Law.

Stock in Trade. Merchandise held by a business for sale to customers.

Straight-Line Depreciation. Definite sum of money set aside annually from income to pay cost of replacing improvements on property, without regard to interest it earns.

Straight Note. A promissory note that provides for repayment in a lump sum, as distinguished from installments.

Subagent. A person upon whom the powers of an agent have been conferred, not by the principal, but by an agent as authorized by the agent's principal.

Subcontractor. As used in the mechanic's lien law, a contractor hired by the general contractor rather than by the owner.

Subdivision. A parcel of property divided into lots for real estate development.

Subject to. The taking of real property *subject to* an encumbrance, such as a mortgage or deed of trust, is done without being personally liable to the holder of the note for payment of the debt; distinguished from *assuming*.

Sublease. A lease given by a lessee to another person for a term less than his or her own. The lessee retains a reversion. Distinguished from an *assignment*.

Subordinate. To make subject to, or junior to, another encumbrance.

Subordination Agreement. An agreement under which a prior lien is made inferior to an otherwise junior lien; changes the order of priority.

Subpoena. Court process for the summoning of witnesses.

Subpoena Duces Tecum. Subpoena that directs a witness to produce documents or other papers.

Subrogate. To substitute one person in the place of another with reference to a right or an obligation.

Subrogation. Replacing one person with another in regard to a legal right or obligation. The substitution of another person in place of the creditor, to whose rights he or she succeeds in relation to the debt. The doctrine is used very often where one person agrees to stand surety for the performance of a contract by another person; also, an insurer is subrogated to the rights of the insured against a third party causing a loss.

Subsequent. Occurring or coming later in time.

Suburb. An area lying immediately outside a city or town.

Substitution, Principle of. Affirms that the maximum value of a property tends to be set by the cost of acquiring an equally desirable and valuable substitute property, assuming no costly delay is encountered in making the substitution.

Succession. The taking of property by inheritance.

Successor. One who acquires or succeeds to the interest of another person.

Summons. Court process which directs a defendant to make an appearance in an action filed against him or her.

Supply and Demand, Principle of. In appraising, a valuation principle stating that market value is affected by interaction of supply and demand forces in the market as of the appraisal date.

Surety. A person who binds himself or herself with another, called the principal, for the performance of an obligation; a guarantor.

Surplus Funds. Money obtained at a foreclosure sale in excess of the amount to satisfy or pay the obligation in full.

Surplus Productivity, Principle of. The net income that remains after the proper costs of labor, organization and capital have been paid, which surplus is imputable to the land and tends to fix the value thereof.

Survey. A map or plat containing a statement of courses, distances, and quantity of land, and showing lines of possession.

Syndicate. A pooling arrangement or association of persons who invest in real property by buying shares in an organization in the form of a partnership, joint venture, corporation, or other entity.

Take-out Loan. The loan arranged by the owner or builder developer for a buyer. The construction loan made for construction of the improvements is usually paid in full from the proceeds of this more permanent mortgage loan.

Tangible. Having actual physical existence; capable of being touched.

Tangible Assets. Anything of value having form or substance, such as real estate, chattels, etc.

Tax. A levy, under authority of law, for governmental purposes.

Tax Base. The value of property for determining the tax. For property taxes, it is the assessed value; for income taxes, it is the net taxable income.

Tax Deed. A deed issued to the purchaser at a tax sale of real property.

Tax-Free Exchange. The trade or exchange of one real property for another without the need to pay income taxes on the gain at the time of trade.

Tax Sale. Sale of property by the tax collector for nonpayment of taxes.

Tax Shelter. Under income tax law, a situation where cost and depreciation equal income from property, hence no income tax is payable.

Tenancy by the Entireties. A modification of a joint tenancy between husband and wife. Has the quality of survivorship, but neither spouse can convey his or her interest so as to break the joint tenancy. Recognized in some states, but not in California.

Tenancy in Common. Ownership of property by any two or more persons in undivided interests (not necessarily equal), without right of survivorship.

Tenant. One who occupies property of another person under an agreement to pay rent.

Tender. An unconditional offer to pay a debt.

Tenements. All rights in land which pass with a conveyance of the land.

Tentative Map. Under the Subdivision Map Act, a subdivider initially submits this map to the local planning commission for approval.

Tenure. The manner in which title to land is held.

Term. Used variously in the real estate field; denotes any provision of a contract, or the period or provisions of a loan, or the period of a lease.

Termites. Antlike insects that feed on wood.

Testament. The written declaration of one's last will.

Testamentary Trust. A trust created by will, effective when the testator dies, as distinguished from a living or inter vivos trust, effective during the lifetime of the trustor or donor.

Testate. Having made a will (as an adjective, "a person died testate").

Testator. A man who makes a will.

Testatrix. Feminine of testator.

Third Party. Persons who are not parties to a contract which affects an interest they have in the object of the contract, such as a third-party beneficiary.

Thirty-day Notice. Notice to tenant to vacate the premises within a thirty-day period. No reason required.

Tidelands. Lands that are covered and uncovered by the ebb and flow of the tide.

Tight Money Market. A market in which demand for the use of money exceeds the available supply.

Time is of the Essence. A clause in a contract that requires *strict compliance* with the stated time limitations (within which a contracting party may perform).

Time-Share Estate. A right of occupancy in a time-share project (subdivision) which is coupled with an estate in the real property.

Time-Share Project. A form of subdivision of real property into rights to the recurrent, exclusive use or occupancy of a lot, parcel, unit, or segment of real property, on an annual or some other periodic basis, for a specified period of time. (see **Subdivision**.)

Time-Share Use. A license or contractual or membership right of occupancy in a time-share project which is not coupled with an estate in the real property.

Title. Evidence of a person's right or the extent of his or her interest in property.

Title Insurance. Assurances as to the condition of title; protects owner or other insured, such as a lender, against loss or impairment of title.

Title Plant. A physical collection of documents, maps, and other data which may be pertinent to future title searches. Maintained by title companies.

Title Report. A report which discloses condition of the title, made by a title company preliminary to issurance of title insurance policy; usually called a preliminary report of title.

Toll. To bar; defeat.

Topography. Nature of the surface of land, e.g., the topography may be level, rolling, mountainous, etc.

Torrens System. A method of registration of land titles based on court proceedings; not applicable in California, although authorized at one time.

Tort. A wrongful act; violation of a person's legal right; a civil wrong not arising out of contract.

Tort-feasor. A wrongdoer; one who commits or is guilty of a tort.

Townhouse. One of a row of houses usually of the same or similar design with common side walls or with a very narrow space between adjacent side walls.

Township. A part of a subdivision of the public lands of the United States; each township contains 36 sections.

Tract. A real estate development; an expanse or area of land.

Trade Fixtures. Articles of personal property, annexed to real property by a tenant, that are necessary to the carrying on of a trade and are removable by the owner of the fixtures upon termination of the tenancy.

Trade-in. A method of guaranteeing property owners a minimum amount of cash on sale of their present property to permit them to purchase other property. If the property is not sold within a specified time at the listed price, the broker agrees to arrange financing to purchase the property at an agreed-upon discount.

Trade Name. The name under which a firm does business.

Transaction. That which is conducted or processed as a business deal.

Transfer Fee. A charge made by a lending institution holding or collecting on a real estate mortgage to change its records to reflect a different ownership.

Transfer Tax. A tax payable upon the conveyance of property, measured by the consideration paid.

Trespass. An invasion of an owner's rights in his or her property; a wrongful entry upon the land of another person.

Trust. A fiduciary relationship in which one party (trustee) holds the title to property for the benefit of another party (beneficiary).

Trust Account. An account of property which is held in trust for another person; distinguished from personal account.

Trust Deed. See **Deed of Trust**.

Trustee. The person to whom property is conveyed in trust.

Trustee's Deed. Deed given by the trustee under a deed of trust when the property is sold under the power of sale.

Trustee's Sale. A foreclosure sale conducted by the trustee under a deed of trust after a default occurs.

Trust Funds. Money or other things of value received by a broker or salesperson to be held for the benefit of others.

Trustor. The person who conveys property in trust.

Truth in Lending. The name given to the federal statutes and regulations (Regulation Z) which are designed primarily to insure that prospective borrowers and purchasers on credit receive credit cost information before entering into a transaction.

Turnover. The number of times per year a given amount of inventory sells; change or movement of people, such as tenants, customers, etc.

UCC. Uniform Commercial Code, which establishes a unified and comprehensive scheme or plan for regulation of security transactions in personal property.

Ultra Vires. Beyond their powers. A corporation, for instance, is said to act *ultra vires* when it acts beyond the authority granted to it.

Underimprovement. An improvement which, because of its deficiency in size or cost, is not the highest and best use of the site.

Underwriting. Insuring something against loss; guaranteeing financially.

Undivided Interests. Nature of each owner's interest in property when owned as tenants in common or in joint tenancy.

Undue Influence. Taking fraudulent or unfair advantage of another person's weakness of mind or distress to induce him or her to do something he or she otherwise would not have done, such as disinheriting a close relative.

Unearned Increment. Increase in value of real estate due to no effort on the part of the owner; often due to increase in population.

Unenforceable. A claim or demand or agreement that cannot be sustained in court.

Uniform Commercial Code. Establishes a unified and comprehensive method for regulation of security transactions in personal property, superseding the existing statutes on chattel mortgages, conditional sales, trust receipts, assignment of accounts receivable and others in the field.

Unilateral Contract. A contract where one party makes a promise in exchange for an action on the part of the other contracting party; distinguished from a *bilateral* contract.

Unit-In-Place Method. The cost of erecting a building by estimating the cost of each component part, i.e., foundations, floors, walls, windows, ceilings, roofs, etc., (including labor and overhead).

Unities. As related to joint tenancy, there are four *unities* necessary to create a valid joint tenancy, namely, *time, title, interest,* and *possession.*

Unlawful Detainer. An action to recover possession of real property.

Unmarried Person. A person who was once married, and whose marriage was dissolved by court action.

Unruh Act. A California act which, among other things, precludes discriminatory practices based on race, color, religion, national origin, or ancestry.

Unsecured. A loan that is not secured by a mortgage, pledge, or other security instrument.

Urban Property. City property; closely settled property.

Usury. Taking more interest than the law allows on a loan.

Utilities. Refers to services rendered by public utility companies, such as light, gas, water power, telephone, etc.

Utility. The ability to give satisfaction and/or excite desire for possession. An element of value.

VA. Veterans Administration; federal agency which administers GI loans. See **Veterans Administration**.

VA Guaranty. An undertaking by the federal government to guarantee the lender, subject to limitations, against loss arising from a default by the borrower under a GI loan.

Vacancy Factor. The percentage of a building's space that is unrented over a given period.

Valid. Sufficient in law; effective.

Valuation. The act or process of estimating value.

Value. The amount a property will command from a reasonable buyer in the open market.

Variable Interest Rate. (VIRs or VMRs, Variable Mortgage Rates). An interest rate in a real estate loan which by the terms of the note varies upward and downward over the term of the loan depending on money market conditions.

Variance. A departure from the general rule; an exception.

Vendee. The buyer or purchaser under a contract of sale.

Vendor. The seller under a contract of sale.

Venue. Place where an acknowledgment is taken, or county where a court action is brought or tried.

Verification. An affidavit attached to a pleading or other document which states that the matters set forth are true.

Versus. Against (abbreviated vs. or v.).

Vertical. Upright; being in a plane perpendicular to the horizon.

Vest. To give an immediate, fixed right, title, or interest in property, with either present or future enjoyment of possession; also denotes the manner in which title is held.

Vested Interest. An interest in property that is fixed or determined.

Veterans Administration. An independent agency of the federal government created by the Servicemen's Readjustment Act of 1944 to administer a variety of benefit programs designed to facilitate the adjustment of returning veterans to civilian life. Among the benefit programs is the Home Loan Guaranty program designed to encourage mortgage lenders to offer long-term low-down-payment financing to eligible veterans by guaranteeing the lender against loss on these higher-risk loans.

Viz. Namely (abbreviation for *videlicet*).

Void. Having no legal effect; null.

Voidable. An instrument that appears to be valid, but is in fact lacking in some essential requirement.

Voluntary Lien. A lien voluntarily created by the debtor, such as a mortgage or deed of trust as contrasted with a judgment lien.

Waive. To relinquish or abandon; to forego a right to enforce or require something.

Waiver. A relinquishment or abandonment of a right.

Warranty. An assurance or understanding that certain defects do not exist.

Warranty Deed. A deed containing express warranties of title and quiet possession. Commonly used in other states, but not in California, since assurances are given by way of title insurance.

Warrenty of Authority. A representation by an agent to third persons that the agent has and is acting within the scope of authority conferred by the principal.

Waste. The destruction or material alteration of or injury to premises by a tenant.

Water Right. The right to make use of the water bordering on or underneath an owner's land.

Water Table. Distance from surface of ground to a depth at which natural groundwater is found.

Wear and Tear. Depreciation of an asset due to ordinary usage.

Will. A disposition of property effective upon the owner's death; often referred to as "my last will and testament."

Witness. Used as a verb, means to see or know by personal presence and perception. As a noun, the person who sees or knows.

Wraparound Mortgage or Trust Deed. See **All-Inclusive Deed of Trust**.

Writ. A process of the court under which property may be seized or sold by the sheriff. A writ of execution is an example.

Yield. The interest earned by an investor on an investment (or by a bank on the money it has loaned). Also, called *return* or *profit*.

Yield Rate. The yield expressed as a percentage of the total investment. Also, called *rate of return*.

Zone. Area in a community set off by a zoning authority for specified uses, such as single-family residence.

Zoning. Governmental regulations by a city or county relating to the use of real property; imposes limitations regarding use.

INDEX